Women in Russia

Women in Russia

Edited by Dorothy Atkinson, Alexander Dallin,
and Gail Warshofsky Lapidus

Stanford University Press, Stanford, California   1977

Stanford University Press
Stanford, California
© 1977 by the Board of Trustees of the
Leland Stanford Junior University
Printed in the United States of America
ISBN 0-8047-0910-6
LC 75-39333

Preface

THIS VOLUME grew out of a conference, held on the Stanford University campus May 29–June 1, 1975, under the title, "Women in Russia: Changing Realities and Changing Perceptions." The three editors constituted the organizing committee of the conference. The interest which it aroused, the wide participation, and the scholarly discussions which preceded and followed, all underscore the importance—and heretofore, the relative neglect—of the subject.

The status of women in the Soviet Union may be considered a topic in its own right (or rather, a complex of topics related to society, politics, history, culture, and economy). It may also be viewed as one more approach to an understanding and assessment of the Soviet experience. And it may be treated as a case—a major and important case—in the comparative study of women in modern and modernizing societies.

An examination of sex roles and attitudes over time highlights both change and continuity in Russian society and culture. A review of past and promise, expectation and achievement, and of the varying priorities and strategies of Soviet development as they have affected the position of women, bears on the elusive balance of successes and failures since 1917, on the gap between rhetoric and reality, on doctrine, adaptation, and the unintended consequences of official behavior. To any reader of the issues raised by feminists in the West a study of the Soviet record is bound to suggest both striking similarities and elements of distinctiveness.

We would not pretend that this book offers definitive answers. It presents the results of recent research and reflection by a number of scholars— historians, political scientists, sociologists, anthropologists, and economists. Many of them expect to pursue their work on these and related topics further in the future. We hope that this book, and the conference on which it is based, will help stimulate wider and more active interest in and research on the problems here raised. Nor (as the careful reader will discover) do all the contributors agree among themselves: this is how it should be, and as editors we have not sought to impose any single viewpoint on our group of contributors. The particular interpretations offered here are those of the several authors.

Much to our regret, not all the papers presented at our conference could be included in this volume. Difficult choices were made largely on the basis of topical coherence. We have encouraged other participants to publish their contributions in the form of articles or as parts of their own larger monographs and wherever possible we have cited their work.

One can readily think of various topics of investigation which have been entirely by-passed. In particular, the cultural and literary aspects, from folklore and church to contemporary belles-lettres, deserve further systematic study; fortunately, work on some of these questions has been and continues to be done. The study of Russian social history invites innumerable further investigations beyond the survey offered here. Demographic trends, as they affect the status of women, are receiving the attention of specialists, both in the Soviet Union and abroad. Inevitably the most elusive target is that of private attitudes and informal behavior, especially in an area as veiled in myths, stereotypes, and prejudices as that of women and sex: we have not done justice to this dimension.

It is only natural that scholars often pursue topics on which sources are relatively more accessible and plentiful. In our case this has meant the urban and more modern sectors of Soviet life rather than the more traditional strata and especially rural society, which remains less thoroughly surveyed. Even more important—given the complexities, varieties, and multiplicities of conditions attaching to the ethnic diversity of the USSR, and the difficulties in dealing with the cultural, social, and linguistic backgrounds of the Soviet nationalities—we have limited ourselves to the ethnically (Great) Russian population, except for occasional references intended to round out or amplify the coverage. Studies of women in other parts of the Soviet Union remain to be done.

In addition to the authors represented in this collection, whose cooperation we gratefully acknowledge, we wish to express our sincere thanks to all who took part in the conference and particularly to the following participants:

Jeremy R. Azrael, University of Chicago
Reinhard Bendix, University of California, Berkeley
Judith Blake, University of California, Berkeley
Barbara Evans Clements, University of Akron
Vera Broido Cohn, London, England
Walter D. Connor, University of Michigan

Carl N. Degler, Stanford University
Helen Desfosses, Harvard University
Vera S. Dunham, City University of New York
Warren W. Eason, Ohio State University
Terence L. Emmons, Stanford University
Sheila Fitzpatrick, Columbia University
Patricia Albjerg Graham, Radcliffe Institute
Joan Delaney Grossman, University of California, Berkeley
Charles J. Halperin, Indiana University
Carol Eubanks Hayden, University of California, Berkeley
Gayle Durham Hollander, Radcliffe Institute
Paul Hollander, University of Massachusetts, Amherst
Barbara Wolfe Jancar, Union College
Jane S. Jaquette, Occidental College
Joyce K. Kallgren, University of California, Berkeley and Davis
Simon Karlinsky, University of California, Berkeley
Nannerl O. Keohane, Stanford University
Victor H. Li, Stanford University
Martin Malia, University of California, Berkeley
William Mandel, Highgate Road Station, Berkeley
Gregory L. Massell, City University of New York
Klaus Mehnert, Aachen, Germany
Rochelle Goldberg Ruthchild, Goddard College
Myra H. Strober, Stanford University
Reginald E. Zelnik, University of California, Berkeley.

Although it was not possible to reproduce the valuable comments of the discussants, their observations contributed greatly to the final version of the papers here presented.

We are most grateful to those colleagues who chaired the sessions of our conference, notably Richard A. Brody, Stanford University; Rita Ricardo Campbell, Hoover Institution; Jing Lyman, Stanford University; Eleanor M. Maccoby, Stanford University; Wayne S. Vucinich, Stanford University; and Karl-Eugen Wädekin, University of Giessen.

An expression of enduring gratitude is due those organizations, foundations, and agencies whose financial support made possible the conference and the preparation of the papers. The conference was sponsored by the Center for Russian and East European Studies, Stanford University, and the Committee on Research and Development of the American Association for the Advancement of Slavic Studies. It was supported also by the Center for Research in International Studies, the Center for Research on Women, and the Hoover Institution on War, Revolution and Peace, all at Stanford University; and by the Johnson Foundation, of Racine, Wisconsin; the National Science Foundation; and the Office of External Research, U.S. Department of State. The assistance of all the above and the helpful attitude of their responsible officers were as gratifying as they were essential for the success of the enterprise.

We also wish to acknowledge the willingness of the International Research and Exchanges Board, New York, to provide the funds to make possible the participation of six Soviet scholars and specialists to whom invitations were extended but who, much to our regret, were unable to attend.

Finally, mention must be made of the unsung helpers whose assistance with a variety of matters, large and small, was essential in making possible, first, the conference and then, this book: Paul Carpenter, Constantine Galskoy, Betty J. Herring, Elise Johnson, and above all, the conference coordinator, George A. McMillan. Finally the editors would like to thank *their* editor, Peter J. Kahn, for his conscientious efforts, good sense, and good spirits throughout the long process of manuscript preparation. It has been a pleasure for all of us to work through him with the Stanford University Press, whose first consideration at all times has been the standard of scholarly excellence.

D.A.

A.D.

G.W.L.

Contents

Contributors

DOROTHY ATKINSON is Assistant Professor of History at Stanford University, where she earned her Ph.D. in 1971. Her special interests are socioeconomic and comparative history, and she is currently involved in a collaborative study of the social sciences in Russia at the turn of the century. Her publications include *Revolution and Social Change: The End of the Russian Land Commune* and several articles on the societal roles of women.

JANET G. CHAPMAN is Professor of Economics and Director of Russian and East European Studies at the University of Pittsburgh. She received her Ph.D. from Columbia University in 1963. Her publications include *Real Wages in Soviet Russia Since 1928* (1963), *Wage Variations in Soviet Industry: The Impact of the 1956–60 Wage Reform* (1970), and articles on various other aspects of Soviet wages and consumption.

ALEXANDER DALLIN is Professor of History and Political Science at Stanford University and Senior Research Fellow at the Hoover Institution. He was formerly Director of the Russian Institute and Adlai E. Stevenson Professor of International Relations at Columbia University. Among his many publications on Soviet affairs are *The Soviet Union at the United Nations* (1962), *The Soviet Union and Disarmament* (1964), and *Political Terror in Communist Systems* (Stanford, 1970).

RICHARD B. DOBSON received his Ph.D. in 1977 from Harvard University, where he was associated with the Russian Research Center. He is Assistant Professor of Sociology at the University of Colorado in Colorado Springs. He has published papers on education and social mobility in the Soviet Union in J. Karabel and A. H. Halsey, eds., *Power and Ideology in Education* (1977) and in the *Annual Review of Sociology*, Vol. 3 (1977).

NORTON T. DODGE is an economist specializing in the Soviet Union. He is a graduate of Harvard's Russian Regional Studies Program, and was a Graduate Fellow at the Russian Research Center at Harvard before becoming Associate Professor of Economics at the University of Maryland. He is the author of the pioneering study *Women in the Soviet Economy* (1966) and of numerous other articles and books.

ETHEL DUNN is the Executive Secretary of the Highgate Road Social Science Research Station in Berkeley, California. A graduate of Rollins College, she earned a Master's degree in history and a Certificate from the Russian Institute at Columbia University in 1956. She has collaborated with her husband, Stephen P. Dunn, on many articles, books, and translations, including a study of Molokans in America.

BEATRICE BRODSKY FARNSWORTH is Associate Professor of History at Wells College, Aurora, New York. She received her Ph.D. from Yale University in 1959, and is the author of *William C. Bullitt and the Soviet Union* (1967). She is currently working on a full-length study of Aleksandra Kollontai, who figures in her paper in this volume and was the subject of an article she wrote for *The American Historical Review* (April 1976).

ROSE L. GLICKMAN received her Ph.D. from the University of Chicago in 1967, and has taught European and Russian history and women's history at the University of California, Riverside, and at Mills College, Oakland. She is currently writing a monograph on women workers in Russia.

JERRY F. HOUGH is Professor of Political Science at Duke University. He is the author of numerous studies on Soviet politics and the Soviet elite.

PETER H. JUVILER received his Ph.D. in Public Law and Government in 1960 from Columbia University, where he is Professor of Political Science at Barnard College and an Associate of the Russian Institute. He has written various articles on Soviet law, policy, and society, and has been coeditor of *Soviet Policy-Making: Studies of Communism in Transition* (1967) and *Revolutionary Law and Order: Politics and Social Change in the USSR* (1976).

GAIL WARSHOFSKY LAPIDUS is Assistant Professor of Political Science and Sociology at the University of California, Berkeley. She received her Ph.D. from Harvard University, and is the author of *Women in Soviet Society* (1977) and of several articles on Soviet politics.

BERNICE MADISON was born in Central Asiatic Russia, received her Ph.D. from the University of Chicago in 1952, and has been a member of the faculty at San Francisco State University since 1954. She is the author of *Social Welfare in the Soviet Union* (Stanford, 1968) and of numerous articles on aspects of social work and social welfare education in this country and abroad.

ALFRED G. MEYER was born in Germany and received his Ph.D. from Harvard University. He is Professor of Political Science at the University of Michigan, and the author of several books and numerous articles on Soviet domestic and foreign policy and on communist ideologies and movements. He is currently working on a biography of Friedrich Engels.

JOEL C. MOSES received his Ph.D. from the University of Wisconsin in 1972, and is now Associate Professor of Political Science at Iowa State University. In addition to having written articles on political leadership in the Soviet Union, he is the author of *Regional Party Leadership and Policy-Making in the USSR* (1974). His current research interest is the problems of women workers in the Soviet economy.

MOLLIE SCHWARTZ ROSENHAN has taught history at Hunter College, Douglass College, and Cheyney State College. Most recently she was instrumental in developing and teaching in the interdisciplinary Women's Studies program at San Jose State University. Her research interests include women in the Soviet Union and problems in the theory and organization of Women's Studies.

MICHAEL PAUL SACKS received his Ph.D. from the University of Michigan in 1974, and is Assistant Professor of Sociology at Trinity College, Hartford, Connecticut. He is the author of *Women's Work in Soviet Russia: Continuity in the Midst of Change* (1976), and he is currently working on a comparative study of the occupations of men and women in the fifteen republics of the USSR.

COLETTE SHULMAN is a free-lance writer and a research associate of the School of International Affairs, Columbia University. She has published articles and book reviews on Soviet youth and women and on current Soviet affairs. Her present research interests focus on education and upbringing in the Soviet Union.

RICHARD STITES received his Ph.D. from Harvard University and is now Assistant Professor of Russian History at Georgetown University. He is the author of *The Women's Liberation Movement in Russia: Feminism, Nihilism, and Bolshevism, 1860–1930* (1977), and is currently working on a book on utopianism and experimentalism in the Russian Revolution.

PART ONE

The Historical Heritage

Dorothy Atkinson

Society and the Sexes in the Russian Past

THE EARLIEST historical references to women in Russia are not to Russian women. They deal with the Amazons, a legendary society of women thought to be located in the region of present-day southern Russia between the Don (the Tanais River of the ancients) and the Caucasus Mountains. Ancient accounts link the Amazons with the Scythians and the Sarmatians, who successively dominated the south of Russia for a millennium extending back to the seventh century B.C. The descendents of these peoples were absorbed by the Slavs who came to be known as Russians.[1]

The Amazons depicted in early Greek texts were an independent community of women at war with the masculine world. Except for seasonal sexual consort, they lived apart from men; and they reared only their female children. Described as skilled horsewomen and fighters, they were credited also with a lively intelligence. Herodotus reports that they easily learned the language of the Scythians, although the Scythian men were unable to master the Amazon tongue. Their law, he relates, required an Amazon to kill a man before she could mate, which led the Scythians to call them the "man-slayers" (*oiorpata*; *oior* = Greek *aner*, "man").[2] The word "Amazon" is of uncertain origin, but it has been claimed that this name—used historically to describe societies of or dominated by females—is a later Greek corruption ɔf the old Slavic name for the Amazons, *Omuzhony*, "masculine women."[3]

[1] The Amazons are discussed by Homer, Pindar, Herodotus, Lysias, Plato, Isocrates, Plutarch, and Arrian; Strabo alone of early writers is said to have questioned their historical existence. For an exhaustive review of the literature on the Amazons to the twentieth century, see M. O. Kosven, "Amazonki: istoriia legendy," *Sovetskaia etnografiia*, 1947, nos. 2 and 3.

[2] Herodotus, *The Persian Wars*, Book IV, chaps. 110–17.

[3] V. K. Tred'iakovskii, *Sochineniia* (SPb, 1849), vol. 3, p. 351. Some of Tred'iakovskii's derivations appear to be the product of a venturesome imagination.

The reports about Amazons have some claim to the attention of those tracing sex roles and attitudes toward the sexes in societies: as social fantasy, Amazon lore may reveal something of the anxieties, aspirations, or aggressions of the sexes. There is also the possibility that something akin to what was described by the earliest historians actually existed. Modern ethnographers have found sexually segregated communities among the Circassians in the Causasus where men and women lived apart from one another by long-standing tradition. This custom may have been influenced by a pastoral economy that kept the herdsmen away from home much of the time.[4]

None of the early accounts about Amazons offers an explanation of how or why such a social system might have arisen. Some modern writers, however, have suggested that the legend represents traces of a folk memory of an earlier matriarchal structure of society. The existence of matrilineal social bonding in some primitive societies is well established, and the explanation for it is fairly obvious: the tie between mother and child is apparent at birth whereas the relationship of father to child must be learned. Yet evidence for the historical existence of matriarchy is scant in general, and this holds true in the Slavic/Russian record.[5]

Various early accounts describe Slavic women as warriors and hunters. Byzantine historians claimed that women among the Slavs dressed in masculine attire and fought alongside their men, and a smatter of archeological findings adds some substance to these reports. A number of excavations have revealed weapons in ancient female graves in southern Russia. Some modern historians have contended that women enjoyed high status in ancient Slavic society; but this conjecture is based on inferential and controversial evidence. For example, the old Slavic custom of marrying bachelors posthumously has been taken to indicate a belief that men needed female companions to gain entry to paradise.[6] But the assignment of relative status on such grounds might well be debated, since Western, Byzantine, and

[4]Still another possibility is suggested by modern discoveries about sex chromosomes. Females lacking one of the two typical X chromosomes have been described in recent scientific literature as "masculine women." Although this "XO condition" renders most women sterile, the possibility that genetic aberrations could be related to unsuccessful mutations in the evolution of society remains to be explored along with other questions in the expanding field of sociobiology. See Christopher Ounsted and David Taylor, eds., *Gender Differences: Their Ontogeny and Significance* (London, 1972), esp. pp. 27–28, 41.

[5]Joan Bamberger, "The Myth of Matriarchy: Why Men Rule in Primitive Societies," in Michelle Z. Rosaldo and Louise Lamphere, eds., *Women, Culture, and Society* (Stanford, Calif., 1974), pp. 263–80. M. F. Vladimirskii-Budanov, *Obzor istorii russkogo prava* (Kiev, 1886), pp. 87–88, denies historical evidence of matriarchy among the Slavs; however, the eminent prehistorian Tadeusz Sulimirski states (in *The Sarmatians* [New York, 1970], p. 34) that Sarmatian graves are considered evidence of a matriarchal social order in southern Russia; and George Vernadsky accepts the Amazon legend as evidence of matriarchy in the area (*Ancient Russia* [New Haven, Conn., 1943], pp. 54, 113; *Kievan Russia* [New Haven, Conn., 1948], p. 155).

[6]Sergei Solov'ev, *Istoriia Rossii s drevneishikh vremen* (M, 1962), vol. 1, p. 288, n. 68.

Arab writers reported that wives (and slaves) in some Slavic tribes were consigned to the funeral pyre along with deceased males.[7]

Further discoveries in Soviet archeology and in prehistory may help to resolve many questions about the social relations of the sexes in the distant Russian past. Yet the few and fragmentary shadows of real women and men reaching from the past, even in distorted form, take on particular interest because of the relatively late appearance of a written form of Slavic and thus of Russian historical records. The social attitudes and values of the previous era, transmitted through custom and oral tradition, are unlikely to have disappeared without leaving cultural traces. But whatever the matrix from which Russian society evolved, by the time its autobiographical record begins in the ninth century it was solidly patriarchal—a society organized along tribal/clan lines with social units under the authority of males.

The sections that follow will survey aspects of the relations between the sexes—particularly with respect to marriage, legal status, and social attitudes—in successive stages of the Russian past: the Kievan, medieval, and Imperial eras.

KIEVAN RUSSIA

Sources that provide information about the society of Kievan Russia (ninth to thirteenth centuries) are limited, yet certain features emerge from them with reasonable clarity. One of the first things to become evident about the sexes is the social significance of the words identifying them. In ancient Russia the words for "woman" and "man" were the same as those used then and now for "wife" and "husband" (*zhena* and *muzh*). Sexual identity was derived not just from biological differentiation, but from social relationship as well. The modern words for "woman" (*zhenshchina*) and "man" (*muzhchina*) are simply extended forms of the older terms. The word for "wife" was used until fairly recently to designate any woman regardless of her actual marital status.[8] But although the term for "husband" once similarly described any adult male, this form of homonymic confusion was neither as extensive nor as enduring as the conceptual fusion of "woman" with "wife."

Women make their first appearance in the earliest Russian annals—the *Primary Chronicle*—in a discussion of marriage customs. The reputed practices of various societies, including the Amazons, are described along with the mating habits of the different Slavic tribes. Among the latter, the

[7]A. A. Kotliarevskii, *O pogrebal'nykh obychaiakh iazycheskikh slavian* (M, 1868), pp. 46–62.

[8]I. Zabelin, *Opyty izucheniia russkikh drevnostei i istorii* (M, 1872), vol. 1, p. 147. *Zhena* is linked etymologically with a group of words having to do with marriage; there is no such association with *muzh*. See F. Miklosich, *Radices linguae Slovenicae* (The Hague, 1970), pp. 28, 55. The linguistic fusion of "woman" with "wife" and of "man" with "husband" is not peculiar to premodern Russia but occurs also in other early Indo-European-speaking societies.

Christian chronicler reports the existence of such "pagan" customs as polygyny and interclan raiding to capture women for brides. With evident disapproval, he describes festivals among the villages where men and women gathered for games, dancing, and other "devilish amusements." "On these occasions," complained the monk, "the men carried off wives for themselves and each took any woman with whom he had arrived at an understanding." [9]

According to modern Russian legal historians, such arrangements, and prearranged "abductions," amounted to contractual marriage despite the chronicler's refusal to recognize them as such. The contract was sealed (and interclan hostilities averted) by the man's payment of a bride-price, the *veno*, to the woman's family or clan. Though the custom of paying bride-prices has often been said to show that women were considered chattels,[10] it may have affected social evaluation of females positively: an Arab writer reported that, among the Russians, "whoever has two or three daughters is made rich, while two or three sons make a man poor." [11]

In time, the practice of raiding for brides faded away, leaving only symbolic rites retained in folk weddings; but the bride-price remained a part of the marriage agreement. The contract imposed obligations on the woman's family as well as on the man's. Because a woman left her own clan on marriage, she was provided with a dowry (*pridanoe*), in the form of movable or immovable property, to help improve her position in the alien clan.[12] The dowry remained her personal property throughout the marriage, and she was free to dispose of it or to bequeath it at will.

Both the bride-price and the dowry are subject to dual interpretation. They can be cited as evidence of the value placed on women and of the family's concern for the welfare of its daughters. Yet if bride-price meant that women were treated as property, the dowry may indicate that the property was not well maintained. The numerous Russian folk songs of all periods lamenting the unhappy fate of the bride in the household of her in-laws suggest that the dowry may have filled psychic as well as economic needs. It linked a woman palpably with her own childhood and with the future of her children and heirs, and it shielded her from total dependency on her husband's family.

According to an eleventh-century church charter, the consent of the woman was required for marriage. Parents were fined if they prevented daughters from marrying at all and were ordered not to force them into unwelcome unions. If suicide resulted from such coercion, they were warned that they would "answer to the Metropolitan for this." [13] The *Pri-*

[9] Samuel H. Cross and O. P. Sherbowitz-Wetzor, trans. and eds., *The Russian Primary Chronicle. Laurentian Text* (Cambridge, Mass., 1953), p. 56.
[10] The term *veno* derives from the verb *veniti* (Latin *vendere*), "to sell" (Miklosich, p. 14).
[11] Kazvini, cited by Vladimirskii-Budanov, p. 90.
[12] Solov'ev, vol. 1, pp. 106–7.
[13] Ia. N. Shchapov, "Brak i sem'ia v drevnei Rusi," *Voprosy istorii*, 1970, no. 10, p. 218.

mary Chronicle relates the tale of the Prince of Polotsk's daughter, Rogneda, who rejected a marriage proposal from Prince Vladimir (later Vladimir I, Grand Prince of Kiev, r. ca. 980–1015). Although Vladimir's rank was high, his mother had been a slave and Rogneda declined to "take off the boots of a slave's son." Her reply referred to a part of the marriage ceremony that called for the bride to remove the groom's footwear in token of her submission to him. The account of Rogneda's rejection of Vladimir is often cited as evidence that at least some women had a say in the choice of their marriage partner.[14] But the boot ceremony (a form of which was still retained in some areas in the nineteenth century) shows clearly that a wife was expected to play a subservient role in marriage.[15]

Another revealing ceremonial custom involved the transfer of a whip from the bride's father to her husband. One legal historian, emphasizing the positive aspects of the position of women in ancient Russia, contrasted this symbol of authority with the sword used in German weddings: the sword symbolized the German husband's power of life and death over his wife, whereas the whip showed that the Russian husband had only the right to punish.[16]

The case of Vladimir and Rogneda was exceptional, but it raises the question of parental transmission of social status. The earliest surviving Russian legal code, the *Pravda Russkaia*, stated that children of a free man by his slave were to be freed (along with their mother) after his death, though they did not share the inheritance rights of his other children.[17] In defining slave status in Russia, there was no recognition of the Roman principle of *partus sequitur ventrem*, whereby the child of a free man and a female slave inherited the mother's status.[18] In this strongly patriarchal society, paternal lineage was ordinarily all-important.

Since a woman's identity was a functional derivative of her role as wife, and since wives were subject to husbands, it follows that women were hardly equal to men in Kievan society. Thanks to the *Pravda*, the degree of inequality can be established with some precision. The first article of the

[14] It may clarify the historical picture without necessarily weakening that argument to point out that Rogneda's refusal led to an attack by the rejected suitor, to the devastation of Polotsk, to the death of her father and brothers, and to her marriage by force to Vladimir—who was, incidentally, said to have six wives and 800 concubines. Cross, p. 91.

[15] V. I. Sergeevich, *Lektsii po istorii russkogo prava* (SPb, 1890), p. 564. Sergeevich states that the ceremony symbolized the status of the wife as a slave of her husband.

[16] Vladimirskii-Budanov, p. 91. The transfer of a whip from the bride's father to the groom was still a part of the wedding customs observed in Kostroma at the end of the nineteenth century. Sergeevich, p. 564.

[17] Variant texts, commentaries, and facsimiles of the *Pravda* are available in B. D. Grekov, ed., *Pravda Russkaia v trekh tomakh* (M-L, 1940–63). In different texts, article 98 refers either to the freeing of the children after their father's death or to their emancipation with their mother. E. I. Kolycheva, in *Kholopstvo i krepostnichestvo (konets XV–XVI vv.)* (M, 1971), pp. 235–36, concludes that both variants reflect actual practice still observed in Russia in the sixteenth century.

[18] *Expanded Pravda*, article 98. For a comparative perspective on the transmission of slavery through maternal lines, see David Brion Davis, *The Problem of Slavery in Western Culture* (New York, 1966), pp. 38, 40, 277–80.

earliest *Pravda*, which dates from the eleventh century, authorized males to avenge the murder of their brothers, fathers, sons, and uncles. Where there was no capable avenger, the law stipulated that the murderer must pay a fine, which remained the same whoever the victim. Provisions that were added later in the century outlawed personal vengeance and established a system of fines scaled to the social status of the man killed: for example, the murder of one of the prince's officials was fourteen times more costly than that of a peasant. Not until the twelfth century was the value of female life considered in the law. "If anyone kills a woman," stated article 88 of the *Expanded Pravda*, "he is tried in the same way as if he killed a man. If he is found guilty, [he shall pay] one half of the fine."

The rate applied to all social categories. A woman shared her husband's social position but was valued in the law at only half his social worth. Yet in a few places at the very bottom of the social scale the system of fines placed a higher value on women than on men: in several instances the loss of a female slave elicited a slightly higher fine than the loss of a male slave. This apparently reflected the greater economic value of the women as potential producers of more slaves. In addition, female slaves were often trained in handicrafts and may have been more valuable as skilled workers.

Marriage to female slaves was a cause of enslavement in the Kievan era. When a man married another man's slave, he became a slave of her owner unless a specific agreement to the contrary was concluded in advance. This was a major consequence of a refusal to abandon, even in part, the principle of paternally derived social status. Reconciliation of this principle with that of property rights in slavery was achieved legally by depriving of his free-dom any man marrying another's slave. Since children assumed their fa-ther's status, slave owners would otherwise have lost their rights to the offspring of female slaves. Yet though men were enslaved through mar-riage, the law said nothing about free women marrying slaves and there is said to be no case recorded in Kievan legal or literary records of a woman losing her freedom through such a marriage.[19] Although marriages be-tween members of different social strata were not prohibited, the corporate character of society appears to have made them rare.

Vladimir Monomakh (1053–1125), the ruler who was responsible for the first legal recognition of the value of female life, left a widely quoted testa-ment in which he urged his sons to love their wives but also warned them to "grant them no power over you."[20] The advice would seem to imply that some women had power, or perhaps that all women had some potential power.

Anthropologists have described at length a "fear of women" that is appar-

---

[19] B. A. Romanov, *Liudi i nravy drevnei Rusi* (M-L, 1966), p. 64. Kolycheva argues (p. 29) that the absence of a statement in the *Pravda* on the enslavement of women through marriage was not accidental and reflected social practice.
[20] "The Testament of Vladimir Monomakh," in Cross, pp. 210–11.

ent in primitive societies.[21] There is evidence to suggest that this may have been present in early Russia. The Scythians had a nameless sun goddess, and the pagan Slavs worshiped another—Lada, the source of the female power of sexual attraction. Just as the sun could make men grow warm, so women, drawing on Lada's heat, could generate ardor in them. One of the pagan games, a game of chase, was a playful form of bride capture. The name of the game (which survives in a modern Russian game of "tag," *gorelki*) was derived from the word "to burn."[22] Fire, symbolizing the un-comprehended forces of nature, was considered a gift of the goddess to women. This, along with the mysterious cyclical functioning of the female body and its role in the creation and sustenance of human life, may have given rise in early Russia, as it has in other societies, to a feeling that women had powers that made them at least potentially dangerous. The fact that the attraction of a woman could lead to literal enslavement would have made the female menace a social reality in Kievan Russia.[23]

If "fear of women" in early Russia must remain conjectural, the existence of another (and possibly related) attitude is easier to document. This con-cerns admiration for strong women. Folk literature preserves a whole rank of warrior heroines, the *polianitsy*, who might have been modeled on the Amazons. Some of these vigorous females, early Russian prototypes of women in "black leather jackets," are shown as possessing great physical strength. These are clearly positive heroines, but there are times when ad-miration of them seems tinged with masculine uneasiness.[24]

[21] Wolfgang Lederer, *The Fear of Women* (New York, 1968); H. R. Hays, *The Dangerous Sex: The Myth of Feminine Evil* (New York, 1972). Boris Porshnev notes, in *Social Psychology and History* (M, 1970), pp. 87–88, that it is the sense of "otherness" which leads primitives to impute magical powers and evil intent. Thus the failure to develop an independent social identity for females may indicate that such an identity would have appeared threatening to both sexes.

[22] A. P. Shchapov, *Sochineniia* (SPb, 1906), vol. 2, p. 74. This article, "Vliianie ob-shchestvennogo mirosozertsaniia na sotsial'noe polozhenie zhenshchiny v Rossii" (*Sochineniia*, vol. 2, pp. 55–104), was published originally in *Delo*, 1871, nos. 7 and 8. The two parts are printed together in the *Sochineniia* without any textual division, but their order has been reversed. Part 1 starts with the paragraph on p. 80 beginning "V otdalennye drevnie vremena. . . ." Many other cultures have linked women with the moon owing to the menstrual cycle. See Helen Diner, *Mothers and Amazons: The First Feminist History of Culture* (New York, 1965). The cosmogony of northern peoples who feminize the life-giving sun suggests the influence of environmental factors. A legend from Greenland, for example, describes a female sun pursued by a male moon; J. G. Herder, *Reflections on the Philosophy of the His-tory of Mankind* (Chicago, 1968), p. 43.

[23] It is of interest here that the Russian word for "passion" (*strast'*) also means "horror" in colloquial usage. Vitalii Shul'gin. *O sostoianii zhenshchin v Rossii do Petra Velikogo; Is-toricheskoe issledovanie* (Kiev, 1850), pp. iii–iv, lists two sources of female "power over men"—sexual attraction, and influence over the young. A. P. Shchapov, in many of his writ-ings, elaborates on the force of fear throughout Russian history. Tracing this to environmen-tal, cultural, and political factors. A legend from his deliberate manipulation of the masses by church and state through the use of fear, he articulates a view that strikingly anticipates modern political theory on terrorism. See his article "Vliianie . . ." cited in n. 22, and "Estestvenno-psikhologicheskie usloviia umstvennogo i sotsial'nogo razvitiia russkogo naroda," in *Sochineniia*, vol. 3, pp. 1–120.

[24] One example is noted by S. S. Shashkov, *Istoriia russkoi zhenshchiny* (2d ed.; SPb,

The most important historical female of Kievan Russia is a strong woman of a different sort—Olga. According to the *Primary Chronicle*, Olga was the resourceful widow of Prince Igor (d. 945), son of Riurik, the semilegendary founder of the Kievan dynasty. Ruling as regent for her son Sviatoslav, she managed through deception and trickery to avenge her husband. Enemy leaders were lured to their doom through her offer to wed. The cleverness of this *femme fatale* is described by the chronicler with enthusiasm. Olga's emergence as a major figure in the early annals recorded by the monks appears to be connected with her role in the introduction of Christianity.[25] Late in life she became a convert and tried to persuade Sviatoslav to accept Christianity. Although he demurred, his son Vladimir (Rogneda's suitor) officially adopted the faith of his grandmother, and of his powerful Byzantine neighbors, near the end of the tenth century.

The influence of Christianity on the position of women in Russia has been a matter of extended discussion. On the one hand, canon law governed domestic relations, and the opposition of the church to the abduction of girls, to polygyny, and to the abandonment of wives is said to have improved the social condition of women. However, marriage in the church spread very slowly and was adopted only by the upper class in the Kievan period.[26] Yet the church safeguarded the interests of widows, providing economic support in cases of need, and in at least one instance it became a supporter of female education when an eleventh-century princess established a school for girls at a monastery in Kiev.[27] On the other hand, the Christian concept of woman as source of temptation and reason for the Fall of Man was ultimately to have dismal consequences for Russian women.[28] Though the church permitted divorce, the grounds stipulated in a document dating from the late twelfth or early thirteenth century refer to the failings only of wives, not of husbands. If a married woman went off with another man, then he was fined by the church. But the woman was permitted neither to remain with him nor to return to her husband; she was sent to a church house. Both men, apparently, were free to (re)marry. Unmarried mothers also were sent to such institutions. Though the church disapproved, women seem to have tried to control births to some extent, for a twelfth-century bishop gave reassurance that a miscarriage resulting from a woman's working was not sinful as long as she had not taken a "potion" to induce abortion.[29]

1879), p. 7. A translation of the semihistorical legend of Dobrynia, mentioned by Shashkov, is available in Isabel Hapgood, *The Epic Songs of Russia* (New York, 1916), pp. 140–51. In these old folk tales the word for "hero" (*bogatyr*) suggests the divine in its echo of the word for God (*Bog*), whereas the word for "heroine" (*polianitsa* or *polenitsa*) is unmistakably mundane—deriving from the word for field (*pole*).

[25]Cross, pp. 78–87. Olga is among the very few women canonized by the Russian Orthodox Church.

[26]Shashkov, p. 116; Vladimirskii-Budanov, p. 109; Romanov, p. 192.

[27]"Zhenskoe obrazovanie," *Entsiklopedicheskii slovar'* (SPb-M, 1894), vol. 11, p. 866.

[28]For the view of women introduced to Kievan Russia with Christianity, see Cross, p. 109.

[29]Ia. N. Shchapov, pp. 218–19.

Contradictions concerning the status of women existed outside of as well as within the church in Kievan Russia. Although women had the right to own property, that property consisted mainly of what was given to them in the form of a dowry or as gifts. A woman had no inheritance rights to her husband's estate beyond what was specifically willed to her, or a share provided in usufruct. Yet her property was subject to confiscation along with her husband's in punishment of his crime; and she could be exiled along with him even though uninvolved in his criminal act. A wife could also be held responsible for the debts of her husband.[30] Daughters did not inherit unless there were no sons, and even then only the daughters of boyars could do so.[31] In the absence of a will, a boyar estate was divided equally among the sons, who were instructed by law to provide "such dowry as they can" for unmarried sisters. The lands of peasants who died without sons were taken over by the prince, whose responsibility it became to provide unmarried daughters with a maintenance portion of the land. A married daughter had no claim to inheritance. However, a woman was free to bequeath her personal property to, or among, any of her children. If she died intestate, her property went to the child with whom she had been living.

An analysis of Kievan social history focused on the sexes leads to an interesting general observation. All the major categories in Kievan society are identified by the names for the males in the group. At the top were the boyars (originally "warriors") and the "prince's men"; the middle classes were known simply as "the men" or "the people"; below them were the peasants, the *smerdy* (a term applied only to males). The lowest social rank was filled by slaves, the *kholopy*. The term *kholop*, introduced in the tenth century, was used only for males yet provides the name most often assigned to the entire institution of slavery (*kholopstvo*); women in the group were described in the law by the old name for a female slave, *roba* (*raba*).[32] Yet for all the annalistic, legal, and linguistic evidence of male dominance, women were clearly not without influence and rights in Kievan society. *Ecce* Olga.[33]

There is little direct testimony on the roles assumed by women in the Kievan economy. Both the information available and the logic of a sexual

---

[30] Sergeevich, pp. 570–71. *Expanded Pravda*, article 7; however, article 121 stipulated that the wives and children of slaves were not to be turned over to an injured party along with the offending slave unless they had participated in the crime. This exception to joint responsibility was in the property interests of the slaveholders.

[31] There is some difference of opinion on this point. See the commentary of A. Riasanovskii on article 90 of the *Pravda* as well as the discussion of article 92 in Grekov, vol. 2, pp. 618, 634–39. Cf. A. Dobriakov, *Russkaia zhenshchina v do-mongol'skii period* (SPb, 1864), p. 23.

[32] M. D'iakonov, *Ocherki obshchestvennogo i gosudarstvennogo stroia drevnei Rusi* (3d ed.; SPb, 1910), pp. 99, 111. According to A. A. Zimin (*Kholopy na Rusi* [M, 1973], p. 20), *roba* originally meant a "plow-woman" and later came to designate an unfree woman. Recent Soviet scholarship indicates that in the post-Kievan period the status of the *kholop* varied as different forms of servitude developed; this makes a blanket translation of *kholopstvo* as "slavery" inadequate for the later period.

[33] It remains the case, however, that Olga gained prominence only through a path opened to her as the widow of her husband, and the mother of a son.

division of labor suggest that men carried out the heavy work in the fields, though women were probably involved in some agricultural work in addition to their responsibilities for child care and domestic tasks. In economies close to a subsistence level, where survival is dependent on physical strength, male dominance may be socially functional to some degree and its legitimacy may be seen as axiomatic. In the Kievan economy the assignment of land rights primarily to males amounted simply to giving the right to make decisions about the land to those who were most responsible for making it produce. Limitation of the inheritance rights of wives and daughters would not be viewed as discriminatory since every woman was expected to have a husband; moreover, the division of a household's lands among daughters, who would move away upon marriage, would only disrupt the household economy. This was particularly the case where peasants shared the use of certain communal lands with other households. Among the upper classes, however, the situation was somewhat different. Where the level of wealth relieved the proprietor from personal physical labor on the land, ownership involved management only and females could be accepted as landowners. This may explain the apparent difference in the inheritance rights of boyar and peasant daughters. It suggests that the affluent society, or at least the more affluent elements in society, can afford to be more egalitarian.[34]

Kievan Russia was an economically advanced society for its time, and a relatively wealthy society. Contacts with the West were active, and there was considerable intermarriage between the Russian ruling house and the Western dynasties. Though basically agrarian, Russia enjoyed a high level of trade and was comparatively highly urbanized. Urbanization is a reflection of the specialization of labor, and as this develops, physical strength loses some of its social significance. Decreasing emphasis on muscle power reduces the premium placed on male children and enhances the value of females in society. Such factors may help to account for the positive aspects of the position of women in Kievan Russia, however limited these may seem from a modern perspective. Russians have always looked back on the Kievan period as an era of past glory. Judged by contemporary standards of egalitarianism, the golden age of Kiev may emerge somewhat tarnished. Yet it retains a patina, burnished perhaps by distance and dearth of documentation, when compared with the period that followed.

MEDIEVAL RUSSIA

From the thirteenth century to the end of the seventeenth, Russian women for the most part appear to have held an unenviable status. The medieval period began with the Mongol conquest, which completed the disintegration of the Kievan state and fractured Russia into separate seg-

---

[34] David Potter argues that it is precisely economic "abundance" that is responsible for the release of modern women from subordination to male authority. See his *People of Plenty* (Chicago, 1954), p. 206.

ments. During these centuries the population center of Russia shifted from the southwest toward the northeast. Moscow emerged as the new geographic and demographic center, and its autocratic rulers, with the support of the Orthodox church, gradually reconsolidated the country.

The earlier centuries of the period saw extensive economic dislocation: trade declined, ties with the West were broken, many urban centers disappeared. This regression may have had a negative effect on the social position of women for reasons indicated above. Yet those who view this period as one of active deterioration generally explain developments by reference to other factors. It has been suggested by different writers that the decline is related to (1) the change in the physical environment, (2) the influence of the Mongols, or (3) the role of the church.

The first argument is made most explicitly by the great nineteenth-century Russian historian Solov'ev. The movement of the population from the milder southern climate of Kiev to the harsher, less fertile northern regions, he wrote, made the struggle for survival more intense. Under such conditions, society became coarsened. It became more difficult to find time for the arts and for the gentler refinements of life (women included). As a result, both culture in general and the position of women in particular suffered.[35]

Solov'ev was not the first to connect the position of women in a society with the nature of its physical environment.[36] Whatever the limitations of this view (or of his version of it), the argument cannot be disregarded. It is certainly possible, indeed probable, that the heightened economic struggle increased the relative importance of physical strength—with negative consequences for the status of women.

The argument for Mongol influence stresses the importation of "Asiatic" attitudes denigrating women, and the practice of separating the sexes socially. It was in this period that separate quarters for women—the *terem*—appeared in the houses of the upper classes.[37] Though there have been strong objections raised against claims for Mongol influence in general,[38] it is possible that the shattering invasions of the Hordes had something to do with the growing practice of sequestering women in the home. Part of the explanation for this development may be connected with the attitude of the descendants of Genghis Khan toward the women of their enemies.[39] The

---

[35] Solov'ev, vol. 1, pp. 78.   [36] See, for example, Herder, pp. 61–62.

[37] The word *terem* was used in Kievan Russia to signify a palatial residence (Solov'ev, vol. 1, p. 248). Later it designated a tower room reserved for women, or, more generally, the female part (frequently an elevated section) of residences large enough to provide separate quarters for women.

[38] Those cited in this article who argue against Mongol influence in Russia included Solov'ev, Zabelin, Vladimirskii-Budanov, D'iakonov, and V. A. Riasanovsky. The argument for Mongol influence is supported by Sergeevich, Vernadsky, Chudinov, Dubakin, and Shashkov.

[39] V. A. Riasanovsky points out that the seclusion of women ascribed to Mongol influence was a custom totally unknown to the Mongols. Yet his quotation from Maxim 30 of Genghis Khan on the delightful uses of enemies' wives suggests a motive for the initial adoption of the custom. While warning against exaggeration of Mongol influence, Riasanovsky acknowledges

seclusion of women could have been simply an outgrowth of the general insecurity of the times. Although there was no extended occupation of the country, there were frequent raids and constant internal strife. The brutalization of life was reflected in the legal codes of the period: flogging, torture, and capital punishment appeared now as penalties for the first time in Russian law. Mongol overlordship was cast off in the course of the late fourteenth and fifteenth centuries, but devastating attacks occurred even on Moscow itself far into the sixteenth century.

The influence of the church on the role of women in Russia appears to be even more controversial than that of the Mongols. As Muscovy expanded, the authority of the church spread with it. As noted above, Christianity had two counterposed attitudes toward women. The church venerated the mother of God and projected a positive view of woman as mother. Russian ikons are a supreme artistic expression of maternal love and compassionate tenderness. Yet alongside Mary the Mother was the image of Eve the Temptress. In this politically troubled era, when many sought refuge in monastic life, views on women that have been described as "Byzantine" were set adrift by the church. A new ethic of asceticism diabolized sex. Similar attitudes are discernible in late Kievan literature, but only with the social extension of the church do they appear to have gained popular currency.

Women were associated with sin. The warmth of sexual attraction was no longer associated with sunshine; it was connected now with hellfire. The only good woman was the desexualized female: the elderly saint, or the virgin. Mothers and wives gained approbation to the extent that they were self-effacing and dedicated to their husbands and children, if not directly to the divine. The ascetic outlook condemned sex as sinful but was forced to accept it within marriage as a necessary evil. Nevertheless, even conjugal relations were forbidden on the eve of holidays, on feast days, and on the numerous fast days (including the entire season of ·Lent). Not only were couples threatened with punishment in case of disobedience, but they were warned that any resultant offspring would turn out badly. Women who had given birth were considered temporarily unclean, as were menstruating women. Significantly, only elderly women were permitted to bake the bread used in church for the sacrament. Though Russian priests married, a priest could not offer the sacrament or hold mass if he had had sexual relations with his wife the previous night. Moreover, a layman was expected to divest himself of his cross before sleeping with his wife.[40] By the sixteenth and

that the conquest brought about a "general crudening of moral standards" and exposure to habits of "unconditional obedience." "The Influence of Mongol Culture and Law on Russian Culture and Law," *The Chinese Social and Political Science Review*, 20, no. 4 (1936–37), pp. 499–530.

[40] Similar restrictions were prescribed by the church earlier, but sexual constraint became more rigorous in Muscovite Russia. See G. P. Fedotov, *The Russian Religious Mind* (New York, 1965), pp. 189–92; Shashkov, p. 76.

seventeenth centuries, the reports of foreign observers persistently commented on the prevalence of male homosexuality among all classes of Muscovite society.[41]

Ecclesiastical influence had been strongest initially among the upper classes, but as the church became increasingly wealthy and powerful, its moral authority was extended over a broader social range. The church came to have considerable landholdings, and with them came substantial control over numerous peasants. As serfdom grew from the late fifteenth century on, that control was strengthened, with the result that the attitudes of the church about women, reflected in such sources as the sixteenth-century *Domostroi*, were widely dispersed. In the *Domostroi*, a treatise on household management aimed at the better-off strata of urban society, the proper role of women was delineated in detail. A woman was to devote herself entirely to domestic duties and the supervision of servants, and was to follow the instructions of her husband in all matters. She was to avoid social contacts outside the home and was even to go to church only when her husband deemed it appropriate. Her conversation with guests was to be restricted to discussion of household routine. Should a wife disregard her husband's orders or wishes, it was his responsibility to discipline her physically. If the problem was serious, she was to be lashed, blouse removed; but this was to be done privately, "politely," and without anger.

The maternal aspect of woman, so warmly portrayed in the ikons that reached an artistic crest in these medieval centuries, takes on a different dimension in the *Domostroi*. The mother's essential relationship with her children, as presented there, is not emotional or spiritual but material; her function is to provide the comforts of a well-run home and to accumulate a dowry for her daughters.[42]

Church literature on women from earlier centuries obtained broad circulation in the medieval period. Especially popular was the "Parable of Feminine Evil," written by the revered church father John Chrysostom,[43] in which moral instruction was presented in the form of a conversation between a man and his son. The dialogue firmly insists upon the depravity of women. Although the youth rises at first to the defense of females, in the end he is completely won over by the paternal indictment. The language used to describe the female sex constitutes an impressive lexicon of invective. Women are "insinuating, cunning, stealthy; slanderers, ensnarers,

[41]Samuel N. Baron, trans. and ed., *The Travels of Olearius in Seventeenth-Century Russia* (Stanford, Calif., 1967), p. 142; George Turberville, "To Dancie," in L. E. Berry and R. O. Crummey, eds., *Rude and Barbarous Kingdom* (Madison, Wisc., 1968), p. 76; S. Herberstein, *Description of Moscow and Muscovy, 1557* (New York, 1969), p. 40.

[42]A. Orlov, ed., *Domostroi po kosinskomu spisku* (M, 1908), text in the original Old Slavonic. For discussion of the work, see Solov'ev, vol. 4, esp. pp. 180–81.

[43]The writings of John Chrysostom (Ioann Zlatoust) gave rise to the ninth-century *Zlatostrui*, the oldest literary work in ancient Russia. It provided material for the sixteenth-century *Domostroi* as well as for the misogynic *Slovo* of Daniil Zatochnik, which dates from the twelfth century. There is one variant of the latter from the thirteenth century, and a number of editions appeared in the seventeenth century.

heretics, wolverines, serpents, scorpions, vipers. . . ." In short, "the most evil of all evils is an evil woman."[44]

Another popular tale of the times expatiated on "The Wisdom of Solomon." It ended with the sage concluding that "an intelligent man is found only once in a thousand, but an intelligent woman is not to be found in all the world." The general opinion of female intelligence was summed up in a popular aphorism attributed to the seventeenth-century religious leader Avvakum: "Woman's hair is long, but her wit is short." Women in this period appear no longer to be admired, as Olga had been, for qualities of mind. Not only physically weaker, they were considered mental inferiors—a view that may have been encouraged by the cramped intellectual horizons of upper-class women cloistered within their homes.

Yet if women were no longer credited with "cleverness," they were still held to be capable of slyness and craftiness. The same word (*khitrost'*) that had been used earlier in a complimentary sense now assumed a pejorative connotation—just as the English word "craft" takes on quite different connotations in different contexts. Women, considered devoid of natural intelligence, were suspected of resorting to supernatural intelligence—witchcraft.

Early Russian folklore is full of women who had magical powers that could be used for good or evil.[45] In the medieval period, however, magic in the hands of women became "black magic," with an inherently evil portent. Men's use of the occult was another matter, as we see from a seventeenth-century "medical" manual that recommended the practice of magic for soldiers desiring prowess on the battlefield.[46] Some women, constrained in their social roles and confronted with social pressures they were powerless to resist, may well have sought efficacy through witchcraft, just as others appear to have sought escape through alcoholism. At any rate, reports of witches and of brutal punishment of those suspected of witchcraft are common from the fifteenth through the seventeenth centuries.[47]

During this period there appears to have been a brisk demand in the magic market for love potions, as women struggled to retain or enhance

[44]Zabelin, vol. 1, pp. 159–88; A. P. Shchapov, vol. 2, pp. 108–9; Shashkov, pp. 79–82.

[45]A striking example is the folktale about Fevronia and Peter of Murom. Fevronia (d. 1228) is credited with magical powers clearly not of divine origin, yet she was canonized by the church. The story is one of many revealing cultural paradigms analyzed by Joan Delaney Grossman in an insightful survey "Feminine Models in Russian Culture: Literature, Art, Religion," forthcoming in *California Slavic Studies*.

[46]A. P. Shchapov, vol. 2, p. 96. The ratio of witches to wizards punished by law in medieval Russia has been estimated at 10,000 to 1. "Zhenshchina," *Entsiklopedicheskii slovar'* (SPb-M, 1894), vol. 11, p. 886.

[47]The practice of blaming and punishing women for all sorts of natural catastrophes can be traced from the Kievan period through the nineteenth century. According to the *Primary Chronicle* (Cross, p. 153), "Particularly through the agency of woman are infernal enchantments brought to pass, for in the beginning the devil deceived woman, and she in turn deceived man." See P. Efimenko, "Sud nad ved'mami," *Kievskaia starina* (Nov. 1883), p. 396; N. Aristov, "Sud'ba russkoi zhenshchiny v do-petrovskoe vremia," *Zaria*, 1871, no. 3, pp. 191–92; Shashkov, pp. 85, 89.

their "power" over men.[48] Many of the reports of foreign observers mention a point of some interest in this connection. They indicate that if women were being painted in gloomy colors by churchmen, they compensated to some extent by painting themselves, literally, in livelier hues. It became fashionable for women to use makeup, and it was applied with a heavy hand. To Europeans the effect was overdone; the church condemned the practice; but Russian men apparently found some charm in it since (according to one observer) no man ever refused his wife money for cosmetics.[49]

By the seventeenth century, the position of women in Muscovite Russia appears to have reached its nadir. This was the time when editions of the "evil woman" literature proliferated most. It is notable that throughout the long span of time that extends from the Kievan to the imperial period in Russian history, there were no women in roles of political authority in Muscovy. A vigorous widow managed for a time to succeed her husband in office in Novgorod (see below, p. 22), and a few other women played minor public roles in some of the larger towns. But there were no Olgas in this period. Sex ratios recorded in slavery documents suggest the possibility of widespread female infanticide at the lowest social level; and seventeenth-century writers provide a dismal description of the life of upper-class women at the other end of the social scale.[50] The room at the top (for women) was the prisonlike *terem*. Women spent their entire lives there, eating apart from men and rarely going out except to church (where they had a special entrance and were separated from male worshippers). Occasionally they were allowed out to visit close relatives. The higher the social position of a family, the more rigorously were its women shielded from public view. Women of the tsar's family were particularly restricted. A popular saying proclaimed that "A maiden seen is copper, but the unseen girl is gold."[51] In seventeenth-century Russia, copper was debased currency.

The seclusion of women was no longer just a question of their security, but was a matter of family honor. The custom was similar to the Oriental

---

[48]In 1497, Ivan III had some women thrown into the Moscow River because they had supplied magic potions to his second wife (at her request); she was engaged at the time in a struggle to establish the succession rights of her son. Aristov, pp. 191–92.

[49]Turberville, p. 76; see also Baron, pp. 127, 169; and Giles Fletcher, *Of the Russe Commonwealth* (Cambridge, Mass., 1966), pp. 113–14. Clerical disapproval of the custom is noted by V. O. Kliuchevskii, *Kurs russkoi istorii*, in *Sochineniia* (M, 1956–59), vol. 3, p. 308. The feminine ideal called for a chalk-white face with bright red cheeks. Eyes were often painted blue and outlined in black.

[50]Documents (primarily from Novgorod) analyzed by Richard Hellie show 62 male slaves recorded for every 38 female slaves. Female infanticide is only one possible explanation of the discrepancy. Among the better-off category of "elite" registered slaves (2 percent of the sample), the sex ratio was a normal fifty-fifty. "Slavery and Law in Muscovy" (paper presented at the Third International Conference on Muscovite History, Oxford, September 1975), pp. 2a–4a. On upper-class life in the seventeenth century, see Grigorii Kotoshikhin, *O Rossii, v tsarstvovanie Alekseia Mikhailovicha* (2d ed.; SPb, 1859), pp. 12, 122–23; and Baron, pp. 158, 168–69.

[51]Zabelin, vol. 1, p. 155.

practice of foot-binding insofar as it incapacitated upper-class women for reasons of status. Only the wealthiest class, the leisure class, could afford the luxury of squandering human resources in this way. A code of conspicuous consumption dictated eating and sleeping habits that were designed to produce women of substance as incarnations of the social weight of the family. By the prevailing standards, "a thin body was considered as bad a flaw as small feet."[52]

Wives of merchants, lesser boyars, and minor officials were likely to be caught between conflicting social codes—the cultivated indolence practiced in high society, and the protobourgeois industriousness advocated by the *Domostroi*. But economic necessity automatically excluded the lower-class women from the unproductive world of the *terem*. Most Russian women were directly involved in the basic economic activities sustaining the household, and this precluded the degree of segregation of the sexes that developed among the wealthy elite. In this period, then, affluence would appear to be inversely related to sexual egalitarianism, although an argument might be made for a "separate but more equal" status of upper-class women: one foreign observer claimed that women were respected more and treated better in the higher social strata than in the lower. Yet others in the sixteenth and seventeenth centuries noted a general lack of affection between spouses in Russia and found this especially true among the upper classes.[53] The problem was attributed to a lack of acquaintance before marriage. Marriages were arranged by parents or matchmakers, and partners frequently had not set eyes on one another before the ceremony. Such practices as secretly substituting a less favored daughter or son at the last minute, or concealing mental or physical defects, were common.[54]

A woman's place in the social hierarchy continued to be defined by her husband's position. As previously, a free man marrying a woman who was not free lost his freedom, but now women, too, lost freedom through "mixed marriages." Moreover, a woman was automatically enslaved if her husband became a slave.[55] However, if a free woman married a man of a higher

[52] Shashkov, p. 98.
[53] Herberstein, p. 40. Fletcher, however, felt that upper-class women were better treated (p. 103).
[54] Kotoshikhin, pp. 129–30; Baron, pp. 164–65. The groom got to see the bride only at, or after, the wedding ceremony.
[55] Article 66 of the 1497 *Sudebnik* (law code) and article 76 of the 1550 *Sudebnik*. See Horace W. Dewey, trans. and ed., *Muscovite Judicial Texts, 1488–1556* (Ann Arbor, Mich., 1966), pp. 21, 67. Documents from the fourteenth to the sixteenth centuries cited by Kolycheva (p. 30) and Zimin (p. 283) suggest the existence of a convention whereby daughters produced by the marriage of a free woman and a slave remained free, but sons were considered the slaves of their father's owner. After 1497 it became far more difficult (and technically illegal) for a man marrying a slave to escape enslavement through prior agreement with the woman's owner. However, a free woman who married a slave without knowledge of his true status (e.g., a fugitive) could have the marriage dissolved on discovery, as could a woman married to a free man who sold himself into slavery without her knowledge. In the 1589 *Sudebnik* the provision on the enslavement of women through marriage was repealed, but by this time the institutionalization of serfdom was depriving the bulk of the peasant population of freedom.

social level, she assumed his status and it was passed on to their children; a man was not similarly elevated when he married above his own social category. In other words, association with a man could lead in some cases to an improvement in status, but association with a woman could lead only to lower status.

The double standard led to some remarkable legal differences in the treatment of the sexes in the *Ulozhenie*, the code of laws that formalized serfdom in the mid-seventeenth century. Although there was no penalty stipulated for the murder of a wife by her husband, the law (subsequently repealed) was quite explicit about the fate of a woman who, for whatever cause, killed her husband: she was to be buried alive up to her neck and left to perish. Local authorities were warned that pleas for mercy from children or other relatives were to be disregarded.

The legal picture was not all dark, however. Throughout the medieval period women were recognized as legal personalities with the right to initiate suits. In such instances, though, a woman was usually represented by a male relative. Under the provisions of a fifteenth-century Novgorod Charter, an upper- or middle-class husband kissed the cross in court (the equivalent of oath-taking) for his wife, and a son did the same for his widowed mother. When a woman brought suit against a man in Pskov at this time, she kissed the cross herself but was granted the privilege of hiring a substitute to represent her if the case was to be decided by combat.[56] Under such circumstances, the man had the option of hiring a substitute also. If a woman brought suit against another woman, however, the two of them might be subjected to trial by combat.

Women in medieval Russia retained the right to own property as individuals. Such property could include the dowry, an inheritance from a mother, gifts from a husband, and any purchases made in a woman's own name. As earlier, a woman was legally free to sell or bequeath her property independently, although it appears that husbands on occasion disposed of their wives' property without their consent. A wife was still held responsible for the debts of her husband, and her property could be taken in payment of them. At times even the wife herself could be taken, since debtors could be forced to sell their wives and children. A woman's property remained subject to confiscation along with that of her husband in case of a criminal judgment against him.

When a man was sent into exile, his wife and children were obliged to follow him. A husband, however, not only was not required to follow his banished wife, but could dissolve their marriage if she were forced into exile.[57]

During the reign of Ivan the Terrible in the sixteenth century, wives and

[56] Novgorod Charter, articles 16 and 17 and the Pskov City Charter, articles 36 and 119, in George Vernadsky, trans. and ed., *Medieval Russian Laws* (New York, 1947). The latter provisions are repeated in article 52 of the Muscovite *Sudebnik* of 1497.

[57] Sergeevich, p. 587; Shashkov, p. 67.

children were executed along with many a male victim. Even earlier, boyars had been required to sign contracts with the Grand Princes of Moscow in which they pledged their wives and their wives' property as guarantees of their promise not to defect.[58] In the juridical language of Muscovy, the word *sem'ia* ("family") meant an agreement to conspire, a band of conspirators. A family was a close association whose interests might be inimical to those of the State, and hence it was forbidden to "familiarize" against the State.[59]

As previously, a widow did not automatically inherit her husband's estates. Moreover, with the appearance of the service estate system in this period, it became difficult or impossible for her to inherit even through an explicit bequest, since the possession of landed estates now entailed an obligation to perform military service. Accordingly, a portion of the estate (generally one-fourteenth) was set aside now for widows.[60] They no longer became wards of the church routinely, but only when unable to provide for themselves. Daughters continued to be excluded generally from inheritance of a father's estate, but the Law Code of Ivan III in 1497 (article 60) repeated the earlier rule that permitted them to inherit an intestate estate in the absence of sons. Where military service was a condition of possession, an inheriting daughter had to provide a husband capable of fulfilling the service obligation.

The evolution of the "service state," in which everyone had his place and function, resulted in a crystallization of the social structure under pressures imposed by absolutism. Increasing rigidity was reflected even in the formalization of social manners. For example, there was a proper way to eat—with the right hand only. And those who deviated were roundly criticized. The use of the right hand has been associated traditionally with the masculine sex, possibly as a result of conventions involving the use of weapons by men in military formations. Those "masculine women," the Amazons, were said to have seared the right side of the chest of infant girls to prevent the development of the breast and to strengthen the right arm.[61]

Recent studies of the brain indicate left-hemisphere dominance in verbal conceptualization and right-hemisphere dominance in visual-spatial modes

---

[58] A. P. Shchapov, vol. 2, p. 110.   [59] Vladimirskii-Budanov, p. 86.

[60] D. N. Dubakin suggests that this became necessary because the seclusion of women cut them off from their sons and reduced the natural filial bond of concern for widowed mothers. Thus he views the provision as a sign of status deterioration. *Vliianie Khristianstva na semeinyi byt russkogo obshchestva v period do vremeni poiavleniia 'Domostroia'* (SPb, 1880), pp. 177–83. The fifteenth-century *Pskov Charter* (articles 88, 89) stipulated that widowers and widows had life usufruct (until remarriage) of the property of a spouse who died intestate.

[61] Adams, vol. 1, p. 174. Cf. Donald J. Sobel, *The Amazons of Greek Mythology* (New York, 1972), pp. 110–12. A tenth-century Arab writer, Ibn Fotslan (Fadhlan), described the garb of Russian men as covering the left shoulder but loosely fastened on the right side "so that the right arm was completely free" (cited in Kotliarevskii, Appendix, "Slaviane i Rus' drevneishikh arabskikh pisatelei," Kotliarevskii, [Appendix], p. 020 [*sic*]). The implications of sex-sidedness could be pursued in connection with the moral connotations of "sinister" (from the Latin for "left") and "Right" (one of the meanings of *Pravda*). Recent studies indicate that there is a

of apprehension. Interestingly enough, the superiority of women (including Herodotus' Amazons) in verbal ability, and of men in visual-spatial skills, is among the few widely accepted beliefs about psychological differences between the sexes to have been substantiated by scientific investigation.[62] The relationship between handedness and hemispheric dominance is not yet clear, but a widespread cultural lateralization of the sexes is historically evident. Traditionally, the left side has been the feminine side, or, in political usage, the orientation of the nondominant as opposed to that of the dominant. Russian women stood (and stand) on the left side in church. The question might be raised, then, whether the emphatic use of the right hand at this time could have had some connection with the low status of women and a rejection of femininity. But such fanciful speculation invites a host of additional unanswerable questions.

Another social custom that became more rigid in this period involved the reluctance of men to shave. The church opposed shaving on the grounds that man had been created in the image of his maker and that it was therefore blasphemous to alter that image. It was also the case that shaving made a man look more like a woman, and beardless women obviously were not created in the divine image. In view of the social condition of women at this time, any loss of masculinity would have been considered especially debilitating. Whereas men prided themselves on their beards, married women were required, in the interests of modesty, to keep their hair covered. Publicly and privately a wife was expected to behave with decorum.[63]

Adultery was grounds for divorce, but here again a double standard prevailed. Gradually, through the efforts of the church, the principle was established that both partners in a marriage had an exclusive right of sexual consort with each other. Nonetheless, an adulterous wife was confined to a monastery though a philandering husband remained at liberty.[64] Unless a husband elected to take back his erring wife within two years, she remained in her cell permanently. An unwanted wife could thus be disposed of quite simply since "witnesses" were easily purchased. A woman who could disprove a charge of adultery was permitted to divorce the husband who had falsely accused her, but in general it was almost impossible for women to escape unhappy marriages.

This description of women's position in the medieval period has focused

---

general contralateral relationship between handedness and cerebral hemispheric dominance. Although 93 percent of the adult population is right-handed, left-handedness is more common among men than women. See R. C. Oldfield, "The Assessment and Analysis of Handedness: The Edinburgh Inventory," *Neuropsychologia*, 9 (1971) pp. 97–113; Anthony W. Buffery and Jeffrey A. Gray, "Sex Differences in the Development of Spatial and Linguistic Skills," in Ounsted and Taylor, pp. 123–57.

[62] See Eleanor E. Maccoby and Carol N. Jacklin, *The Psychology of Sex Differences* (Stanford, Calif., 1974).

[63] Travelers' accounts suggest that this was not always the case. See, e.g., Herberstein, p. 40; Baron, p. 170.

[64] Vladimirskii-Budanov, pp. 113–14.

largely on Muscovite Russia. The situation may have been somewhat more favorable outside the central territory that gradually nucleated around Moscow. Novgorod to the north had been largely spared the devastation of Mongol attack by agreeing to pay tribute and, unlike the rest of the country, had managed to retain and continue an active commercial life. Trade with the Hanseatic cities of northern Europe kept Western ties alive here for several centuries after the fall of Kiev. Not only was the oligarchic political system of Novgorod distinct from the autocratic system emerging in medieval Muscovy, but Novgorod's commercially oriented economy gave rise to social roles different from those of Muscovy. The recently discovered Novgorod birchbark documents provide evidence of some female literacy and show women engaging in various economic activities connected with commerce.[65] And it is Novgorod that provides the only case in medieval Russia of a woman in a prominent political role. A boyar magnate's wife, Marfa Boretskaia, succeeded her deceased husband as mayor there for a time; but in a move that may have presaged a deterioration of female status in the north, she disappeared from the political scene when Novgorod's independence was ended by the expansion of Muscovy in the late fifteenth century.

The position of women in the western and southwestern Russian territories that escaped Mongol domination appears to have remained relatively favorable for a long period. In these regions, separated from northeastern Russia for centuries, some of the earlier traditions of Kievan Russia persisted, and Western influences were introduced through Lithuanian and Polish rule. Women were in a more advantageous position here than in Muscovy, with extensive property rights, and with civil rights close to those held by men. The main exception in the latter area was their exclusion from positions of public responsibility. Girls of the upper classes were often educated along with their brothers. The dowry here could amount to a quarter of the paternal estate along with gifts from maternal property. In accordance with an old custom preserved in the Lithuanian Statute of 1569, the bridegroom presented his bride with a *veno* list that made over to her one third of his immovable property in exchange for her dowry. The wife had independent control over this property both during and after her husband's lifetime.[66]

Divorce was not common owing to social disapproval, but among those recorded in the southwest, many appear to have been concluded amicably on grounds of mutual incompatibility. In effect, it was possible to obtain a

[65] See A. V. Artsikhovskii, ed., *Novgorodskie gramoty na bereste* (5 vols; M, 1953–63), vol. 2, docs. 43, 49, 53; vol. 3, doc. 125; vol. 5, docs. 227, 229. I am indebted to Professor Charles Halperin for these references.

[66] Orest Levitskii, "Semeinye otnosheniia v iugo-zapadnoi Rusi v XVI–XVII vv.," *Russkaia starina* (Nov. 1880), pp. 551–54. Shashkov, p. 93, observes that women in western Russia were as "enslaved" as those in the rest of Europe, but far better off than women in Muscovite Russia.

"no-fault" divorce here in the sixteenth and seventeenth centuries. Though contrary to civil and canon law, such arrangements were recorded—usually by civil authorities, but occasionally even with the participation of the church.

One of the most celebrated divorce cases of the times was that of Andrei Kurbskii, a nobleman whose correspondence with Ivan the Terrible after his defection to Lithuania has recently been the subject of scholarly controversy. Kurbskii had left his hapless wife and child behind in Muscovy, where they soon came to a sorry end. He then remarried and ended up embroiled in a tangled divorce case, which was later reopened after a third marriage.[67] The case record is of interest here mainly because it attests to the ability of women in this region to initiate and pursue legal action. Typically, charges of witchcraft, adultery, and bought witnesses entered into the proceedings.[68]

The southwest area was reabsorbed into the Russian state under Muscovite rule in the course of the seventeenth century. After this time, divorce became more difficult to obtain; the church refused to recognize incompatibility as a ground, and as Orthodoxy gained in authority, divorce became rarer. It is notable that as it disappeared from legal records, the incidence of recorded crimes of violence between marriage partners rose.[69]

If the reunion of the western lands with the rest of Russia had negative consequences for some women, there were also other, more positive consequences. A renewal of contacts with the West introduced new ideas about social relations into Russia. One historian, looking back over the dismal portraits of woman depicted in the ecclesiastical and popular literature of seventeenth-century Russia, suggested that when ideological models deviate from reality, conflicting perceptions give rise to a tension that leads inevitably to a search for "another view of life, another way of thinking."[70]

There is no question about the existence of social stress in seventeenth-century Russia. The century was punctuated with popular disturbances culminating in a major uprising in the 1660's. Historians have linked the upwelling of discontent with the coincident process of enserfment. It may be that the social disequilibrium engendered by the treatment of women

[67]The church ordinarily limited marriages to two; a third marriage was permitted only in special cases.

[68]Kurbskii's domestic travail is discussed by D. L. Mordovtsev, *Zamechatel'nye istoricheskie zhenshchiny na Rusi, Vol. I. Russkie zhenshchiny do Petra* (4th ed.; SPb, 1911), pp. 189–93. See also Levitskii, pp. 568, 570–71.

[69]Levitskii, who analyzed these legal records, notes (p. 573) that the elimination of divorce was not the only cause of the deterioration of family relations, but adds that it was "not the least important reason." Statistics show that in late-nineteenth-century France women initiated divorce proceedings two to three times as often as men but were responsible for only 20 percent of murders between spouses. In Russia at this time, when divorce was difficult to obtain (and virtually impossible for peasants), women were responsible for up to 45 percent of spouse murders, though for only about 10 percent of all other crimes brought to court. "Zhenshchina," *Entsiklopedicheskii slovar'* (SPb-M, 1894), vol. 11, p. 887.

[70]Zabelin, vol. 1, pp. 177–78.

also contributed to the general unrest.[71] The same decade of the 1660's witnessed the great religious crisis of the Schism, in which women played a prominent role. The dissident Old Believers, who were prepared to accept women on terms of greater equality, had many female adherents and patronesses.[72]

It is hardly accidental that the period that represents the low point in the history of Russian women—the time of their greatest social degradation—is precisely the period in which serfdom took hold in Russia. The coincidence of these two major social developments suggests that no single causal factor—nature, Mongols, or church—can account for the decline in women's status, although all of those mentioned are likely to have contributed to it.

These two simultaneous developments can be viewed as parallel by-products of the same set of causes: the results of physical insecurity, economic struggle, and the evolution of absolutism. Alternatively, it could be argued that one development gave rise to (or contributed to) the other. It could be posited, for example, that in a society with a tradition of male dominance, men threatened with a loss of status by the spread of serfdom reacted by depressing the status of women to still lower levels. In any social hierarchy, insecurity of status invites the oppression of inferiors. There were trade-offs in the patterns of political and social dominance: men compelled to surrender to the authority of tsar and/or boyar were given greater authority in domestic relations. The formula ran, "As the tsar answers to God, so a boyar answers to the tsar, a peasant to his lord, a woman to her husband."[73] On the other hand, a decline in the position of women can be viewed as having originated independently of, but as having contributed to, the process of enserfment by lowering social standards. Social recognition of human dignity is a moral value not subject to distinctions of sex.

By the end of the seventeenth century, it would seem that many Russians were searching for "another view of life." And with the gradual extension of the western frontier—then more abruptly with the Westernizing policies of Peter the Great—new perspectives were opening up.

IMPERIAL RUSSIA

The role of Peter in Russian history has been the subject of diverse interpretations. Critics point out that many developments attributed to his

[71] Little attention has been devoted to the role of women in Russian popular uprisings of the period, although the participation of women in social unrest elsewhere in the seventeenth century has been noted by Soviet historians, e.g., B. Porchnev, *Les Soulèvements populaires en France de 1623 à 1648* (Paris, 1963), p. 274.

[72] The most publicized seventeenth-century figure in this connection was the boyarina Morozova, dramatically portrayed in 1887 on Surikov's huge canvas. Russian women were persistently involved in religious dissidence. A mid-nineteenth-century group of female sectarians traced their origins to Marfa Boretskaia of fifteenth-century Novgorod. D. D'Istria (pseud. of E. Kol'tsova-Masal'skaia), *La Russie*, vol. 1 of *Les femmes en orient* (Zurich, 1859), p. 161.

[73] The pattern noted is not unique. A broad correlation has been established between au-

reign trace their origins to earlier days. Yet few deny that under Peter preexisting tendencies were accelerated. It has been said that, as far as the question of women is concerned, Peter's policies affected only the upper classes. And indeed, if we look at some of his innovations in manners and morals, it is undoubtedly the case that the immediate effect was confined to the higher social strata; but eventually the ideas and forces behind his notorious social tinkering had a major impact on all levels of society.

From about the beginning of the eighteenth century there was a perceptible improvement in the social status of women in Russia that persisted throughout the Imperial era. The reign of Peter the Great marked a turning point in several ways. Peter began his reign in 1682 as co-ruler with his half brother Ivan V under the regency of their older sister, Sophia. This was the first time a woman had held such power in Russia since the regency of Olga in the tenth century. As the result of an unsuccessful bid for independent political power, Sophia was stripped of her regency in 1689 and confined to a convent. Yet female influence in dynastic politics was to continue. Peter proclaimed the right of the Russian ruler to designate any successor and by crowning his second wife Catherine as tsarina (an unprecedented move) he made way for her to be declared ruler in her own right after his death in 1725. Catherine I died in 1727, and when her successor Peter II died unexpectedly in 1730, boyar magnates decided to recognize the unprepossessing daughter of Ivan V as tsarina in the confident expectation that they could control her and rule through her. But Anna (r. 1730–40) confounded them and asserted her prerogatives as autocrat. She was followed in turn by her infant great-nephew, Ivan VI, whose mother was named regent. The regency was short-lived, however; Elizabeth, daughter of Peter the Great and Catherine, overthrew Ivan and his mother and established herself as ruler (r. 1741–62). Her nephew and successor, Peter III, was in turn deposed by his wife, whose long and eventful reign as Catherine the Great (1762–96) firmly consolidated the power of Russia in European affairs. Thus in the eighteenth century, a period recognized by modern scholarship as one of dynamic development in Russian cultural and economic life,[74] the Russian state was headed by a woman ruling in her own name in four different reigns that covered in all close to 70 years. At the end of the century Catherine's son Paul, who had narrowly missed being bypassed in the line of succession himself, was quick to establish a law of male primogeniture. Women were never again to rule in Russia.

It is obvious that the status of women in any society cannot be derived solely from a study of female rulers; these are a special group whose per-

thoritarian relationships within families and autocratic political systems in agrarian societies. See W. N. Stephens, *The Family in Cross-Cultural Perspective* (New York, 1963), p. 335.

[74] Heightened interest in eighteenth-century developments is evident in recent Soviet economic history and in such Western studies as Gilbert Rozman, *Urban Networks in Russia, 1750–1800, and Premodern Periodization* (Princeton, N.J., 1976).

sonal position may be due to a variety of accidents. But social images of Russian women in general were undergoing transformation in this period, and the appearance of the many tsarinas would seem to be related to the attitudinal changes taking place. Clearly, something happened to modify the attitudes that had prevailed previously. And at least some of the changes can be traced directly to the social leavening of Peter the Great. The energetic, self-made emperor had traveled in the West (the first Russian ruler to do so since the Kievan era) and had witnessed mixed social gatherings there. As part of his determination to modernize and secularize Russia, he decreed an end to the seclusion of women and commanded the sexes to mix socially. Women were to take part in evening "assemblies" with men, to socialize, to converse, even to dance. This was the "coming-out party" of the feminine elite. Western dress was prescribed, and men were ordered to shave. These regulations affected mainly the upper classes and the urban areas, both of which were extremely limited social sectors. Yet these were sectors of prime cultural significance. Peter's roughshod social remodeling has given rise to many an anecdote, but it effectively brought the sexes together in new modes of social intercourse. These were sustained and extended by the model of the court under the subsequent succession of tsarinas.

Western literature, which had filtered into the country even earlier, gained increasing influence as Russia's borders continued to move westward. From these literary sources came a new notion of women as partners in love relationships that extended beyond the physiological bond between the sexes. This was far from the medieval Western concept of chivalric love, which had no counterpart at any time in Russia; but the idea of an intense mutual devotion between a man and a woman suggested that women were subject to the same feelings and thoughts as men. The recognition of common characteristics and shared experience laid the groundwork for a reappraisal of the relations between the sexes. These new perceptions were refined and idealized, along with images of women, in the expanding world of eighteenth-century Russian literature.[75]

By the turn of the century the "genteelization" of upper-class attitudes on women had given rise to a sentimentalized literature that bemoaned the fate of a steady stream of unfortunate heroines: "Poor Liza," "Poor Masha," "Unhappy Margarita," and so forth. This literary chorus reached its climax in the nineteenth century with the poet Nekrasov's popular lines on the hard fate of women in Russia, and with his tribute to the wives of the revolutionary Decembrists of 1825 who had voluntarily followed their husbands into exile. These women, though members of the nobility, were presented

[75] See A. N. Chudinov, *Istoriia russkoi zhenshchiny v posledovatel'nom razvitii ee literaturnykh tipov* (Voronezh, 1872). Some women participated in the literary development of the period, though without notable achievement for the most part. A *Dictionary of Russian Authoresses (1759–1859)* listed some 60 entries according to V. Mikhnevich, *Russkaia zhenshchina XVIII stoletii* (Kiev, 1895), p. 261. On changing attitudes about courtship in the eighteenth century, see chap. 8 of this work.

as models of "Russian Women"—qualifying by their exemplary traditionalism (they were completely apolitical) and by their long-suffering dedication to their men.[76] Literature of this sort was the *Uncle Tom's Cabin* of the emancipation of women in Russia, as sentimentalism and romanticism agitated further the social conscience whose stirrings they reflected. The "repentant noble" was sorely discomfited by the treatment of both women and serfs in Russian history.[77]

But alongside the weeping women, and against a background of "superfluous men," there emerged a new strain of "positive" and even "formidable" heroines in nineteenth-century Russian literature.[78] Even Nekrasov's Russian ladies were notable for the strength of their dedication and for their endurance. Literary models cannot be pursued here, but they merit mention because of their close relationship to shifts in social attitudes. Interestingly enough, as strong women surfaced in literature there was a marked revival of interest in the Amazon legend. This is discernible within both the scholarly community and high society as early as the eighteenth century. Philologists and ethnographers joined historians in sympathetic analyses of the legend of strong women in the Russian past. When Catherine the Great visited the Crimea in 1787 on a carefully staged tour, she was greeted by a group of local upper-class women who had been formed into an "Amazon company" by the set designer, Prince Potemkin. The locals were appropriately outfitted and armed for the occasion.[79] Scholarly researchers who investigated the evidence about the Amazons generally accepted the essential historical validity of the legend in this period.

From the beginning of the nineteenth century, men in Russia began to take active roles in promoting greater equality between the sexes. As a proper starting place, fresh attention was devoted to the education of females. The eminent statesman Speranskii wrote his daughter in 1820 that there was no reason to believe that women had weaker wills or less character than men. Yet he felt that most women *were* weak and indecisive because they had been kept on "leading strings" and made to depend on men, a state of affairs that "has advantages for men, but is completely disadvantageous for women." His advice was to study science, which "stands

---

[76] N. A. Nekrasov, *Polnoe sobranie stikhotvorenii, v trekh tomakh* (L, 1967). In vol. 2 we find the lines "Three heavy lots were cast by fate:/First—to have a slave as mate/Next—to mother the son of a slave/Third—to be enslaved to a slave to the grave./And all these frightful fortunes fell/on women in Russia" (from "Frost, the Red Nose" [1862–63]), p. 109. "Russian Women" (1872) is also in vol. 2, pp. 309–74. For a recent study of the Decembrist women, see Anatole G. Mazour, *Women in Exile: Wives of the Decembrists* (Tallahassee, Florida, 1975). Ironically, these consummately traditional women became model heroines for later revolutionaries.

[77] It may be more appropriate to speak of a distinct, though related, category of the "repentant male" as suggested by Joan Grossman in her paper "Feminine Models."

[78] Vera S. Dunham, "The Strong-Woman Motif," in Cyril E. Black, ed., *The Transformation of Russian Society* (Cambridge, Mass., 1960), pp. 459–83; Antonia Glasse, "The Formidable Woman: Portrait and Original," *Russian Literature Triquarterly*, 9 (Spring 1974), pp. 433–53.

[79] "Amazonskaia rota," *Entsiklopedicheskii slovar'* (SPb-M, 1894), vol. 1, p. 601.

on its own feet" and would help women to do the same.[80] The prospect of educated women raised some concern, however. An 1811 article in *Vestnik Evropy* conceded that female intelligence was equal to that of males but inquired uneasily whether teaching women to love learning might not divert their love from marriage.

Despite such hesitation, female education made headway. Modest efforts to provide schooling for girls had been initiated by Catherine and were intensified by her successors. The gains were irregular and were interrupted by setbacks, but substantial progress was made in the later nineteenth and twentieth centuries. Special advanced "women's courses" were made available to females, although women were kept from regular university enrollment.[81] Exceptional women, such as the mathematician Sophia Kovalevskaia (educated abroad, like many of her more fortunate female contemporaries), were denied academic employment in Russia and forced to work abroad. A few others, including Aleksandra Efimenko—the first woman to receive a doctoral degree in Russian history (in 1910)—found it possible to teach other women in the special courses.

As women became better educated, resignation to the social limitation of female roles became increasingly difficult for many. The resultant "sexual frustration" led some to develop sympathies with revolutionary programs, and female revolutionaries were promptly labeled "Amazons" by their contemporaries. Politicization was all the more easy since radicals such as Chernyshevskii were focusing on the social position and problems of women and taking an active role in pressing for women's rights. Chernyshevskii's *What Is to Be Done?* (1863) addressed itself specifically to the "woman question"—a question that surfaced as a social issue, in tandem with the question of serf emancipation, only after Russia's defeat in the Crimean War in 1856.[82] It is striking, and significant, that an acute sensitizing of attitudes about the social condition of women coincided historically with the liberation of the serfs in 1861; as shown above, the deterioration of women's social position had similarly paralleled the extension of serfdom in Russia. Chernyshevskii's work was widely influential among the radical intelligentsia: Lenin read it more than once and borrowed the title for one of his own works on a different theme. As the revolutionary movement pulsed erratically through the latter half of the century, the "woman question"

[80] A. P. Shchapov, vol. 3, p. 592. Another letter to his daughter, reporting a conversation with the wife of an English diplomat (1822), noted Speranskii's agreement with the woman's statement that the "gauge of social life and of the progress of civilization is the manner that men have with women." *V pamiat' grafa Mikhaila Mikhailovicha Speranskogo, 1772–1872* (SPb, 1872), p. 566. Cf. Herder, pp. 62–63: "The manner in which women are treated must be the first point of distinction in the history of our species. [Nothing] so decisively shows the character of a man, or a nation, as the treatment of women."

[81] The most important of these courses were offered in the capital, and are described in S. N. Valk, ed., *Sankt-Peterburgskie vysshie zhenskie (Bestuzhevskie) kursy, 1878–1918* (2d ed.; L, 1973).

[82] For an excellent discussion of the crystallization of social consciousness on the topic at this time, see Richard Stites, "M. L. Mikhailov and the Emergence of the Woman Question in Russia," *Canadian Slavic Studies*, 3, no. 2 (Summer 1969), pp. 178–99.

helped to sustain it.[83] And it is notable that as the modern "Amazons" enlisted in its ranks, scholars seemingly remote from the contemporary political scene developed the novel theory that an Amazon society might have arisen in antiquity from a revolt of women against male oppression.[84]

If the status of women was improved in several ways in the Imperial period, in one area it suffered a relative setback. This had to do with the civil status of women in the light of the new concept of citizenship. Until the appearance of the modern Russian state and the development of a social conception of statehood, there was little notion of citizenship (as distinct from a sense of folk community) or of the rights and responsibilities attendant on that role. It has often been observed in the historical literature that the difference between slaves and serfs disappeared with Peter the Great's tax reforms in the early eighteenth century, which, by taxing both groups alike, dissolved the only legal distinction remaining between them.[85] Peter shifted the direct tax base from the household to the individual, i.e., to the individual *male*, "from the very oldest to the very latest born." Slaves and serfs may have been equalized, but the reform had negative, if largely theoretical, implications for the equality of men and women. Citizenship in Peter's "service state" was earned in one of two ways: through direct government service (in a military, bureaucratic, or court office), or, for the lower classes, through the payment of taxes or military service. But both state service (including army duty) and the payment of taxes were essentially *male* responsibilities. Under this scheme women would have to be considered second-class citizens at best.

Peter's attempts to create a meritocracy with official careers "open to talents" simply bypassed feminine talents. Though an increasing number of women obtained court appointments under the tsarinas, and though a woman was named head of the Academy of Sciences by Catherine, women on the whole continued to be excluded from public and civic roles. The only significant exceptions were widows who might be accepted locally as heads of households at meetings of peasant communes. Following Peter's fiscal reforms, the communes periodically redistributed members' lands in an attempt to equalize the peasants' ability to pay their taxes. The male "soul" taken as the assessment unit for tax purposes became also a common unit of reckoning in the readjustment of the size of household land allotments. This system made females an economic liability to a peasant household. Daughters would go off upon marriage, but sons improved the household's chances of obtaining more land and remained to work on the land and to

[83] On the number of female revolutionaries, see Robert H. McNeal, "Women in the Russian Radical Movement," *Journal of Social History*, vol. 5 (Winter 1971–72), p. 144. For personal profiles of some of the leading women in the Russian revolutionary movement see Barbara Engel and Clifford Rosenthal, *Five Sisters: Women Against the Tsar* (New York, 1975).

[84] This hypothesis was advanced first by the Swiss scholar J. J. Bachofen, who developed the theory of matriarchy. See Kosven's article cited in note 1 above, no. 3, p. 30.

[85] The change had actually been effected by tax legislation in 1679 except for household serfs, but Peter's reform extended it to include all categories by 1723. D'iakonov, pp. 406–7.

provide ultimately for elderly parents. The "soul tax," as the per capita levy on males was called, was collected until the 1870's. Since the nobility had been released from its service obligations to the state a century earlier without any loss of civil status, it could be argued that the whole concept of contributory citizenship had lost any practical significance from that point on. Yet the argument would apply best to the upper classes, where the most marked improvement in women's position actually occurred.

The idea of individual responsibilities and rights promoted by Peter did have beneficial repercussions on the status of women in other areas. Greater legal emphasis was placed on the consent of partners to marriage: serf owners were ordered not to force marriages on their serfs;[86] a betrothal period of six weeks was required by law to give the contracting parties time to become acquainted; and parents were warned not to pressure their children to agree to a marriage against their own wishes. The Law Code later stipulated prison terms of from four to sixteen months for forcing an unwanted marriage on a child of either sex.[87]

Property arrangements had always been a part of marriage contracts in earlier periods; in fact, the term for "matchmaker" (svat) had been used for anyone who concluded a business contract.[88] The reform of family law at the beginning of the eighteenth century put an end to the obligation to include property provisions in a marital contract. There was no longer any legal need for a dowry. In 1720 the requirement that a wife follow her husband into exile was abolished. If either partner in a marriage were exiled, the marriage could be dissolved legally. Later in the eighteenth century it became possible for a noblewoman to marry a commoner without forfeiting her noble status. It remained impossible, however, for such a woman to extend her status to her spouse or to pass it on to their children—although a nobleman could do both.

Earlier, marriages between the free and the unfree had generally led, as noted, to a loss of freedom. But from the late eighteenth century, enserfment through marriage was restricted. Toward the end of the century, legal modifications permitted a special group of serf women who had married free men to gain their freedom. This was regularized and became standard practice. In such cases the permission of the serf owner was required before

[86] Recorded instructions of estate owners to their managers make it clear that the law was disregarded in many cases; and the peasant commune even into the late nineteenth century continued to interfere in the marriages of its members and to arrange those of orphans. See V. A. Aleksandrov, Sel'skaia obshchina v Rossii (M, 1976), pp. 303–309; G. Vernadsky, ed., A Source Book for Russian History from Earliest Times to 1917 (New Haven, Conn., 1972), vol. 2, pp. 441–49.

[87] On the other hand, parental consent to marriage was required and punishment was stipulated for violation, though this was enforced only for minors. The ages at which marriage was permitted by the church were 12 (female) and 14 (male) in the Kievan era, 12 and 15 in the mid-sixteenth century, and 13 and 15 in the eighteenth century. Earlier marriage was not uncommon. In 1830 the state issued a law setting the minimum ages at 16 and 18. The age of full civil adulthood was 21 for both sexes. Vladimirskii-Budanov, pp. 94–97. Legislation on marriage is in the Civil Law Code in Vol. X, Part 1, Svod zakonov Rossiiskoi Imperii, 1914 ed.

[88] Vladimirskii-Budanov, p. 86.

the woman could marry; and since few serf owners were likely to consent to the loss of their "baptized property," these provisions of the law had limited social impact. They are significant, though, as indicators of shifting norms; for at least in principle it was recognized that serf women might gain freedom through marriage with free men. As previously, however, the sex roles were irreversible: a male serf marrying a free woman could not ordinarily achieve freedom through the marriage.[89] Ultimately, a legal ruling early in the nineteenth century put an end to the enserfment of free women through marriage to serfs.[90] Thus the general relationship of the sexes to the institution of marriage showed certain continuities: a woman could improve her social position by marrying upward; a man could not. But a woman could lose social rights through marriage with social inferiors, whereas a man faced less difficulty here. The emancipation of the serfs in 1861 brought to a close the problem of marriages between the free and the unfree, yet the legal status and social prerogatives of the nobility survived to 1917 as constraining factors in the selection of marital partners.

The growth of property rights, including those of women, was accelerated from the beginning of the eighteenth century. Peter reiterated the long-standing legal principle that a wife's movable or immovable property was to be considered her personal property, separate from that of her husband. (Despite earlier legislation, there had been some confusion on this point and local variation in practice, with instances of legal recognition of joint or common property of spouses.) The law specified that a wife could sell, mortgage, or bequeath her property independently of her husband. The fact that it was necessary in 1769 to repeat the legal prohibition against husbands' disposing of their wives' property indicates that the practice continued either in defiance or in ignorance of the law.[91]

Under Catherine the Great confiscation of the property of individuals condemned for capital offenses was limited in the interests of wives and children. State confiscation of the property of criminals was later partially restored by Nicholas I in punishment of the Decembrists, but was finally abolished in 1846.

Throughout the Imperial period the individual property rights of spouses were upheld by the law. Russian law did not ordinarily recognize common ownership by a husband and wife of family property.[92] Peasant land was

[89] A. S. Lappo-Danilevskii, "Ekaterina II i krest'ianskii vopros," in A. K. Dzhivelegov, ed., *Velikaia reforma* (M, 1911), vol. 1, pp. 174–75.

[90] Sergeevich, p. 567.

[91] In a case that came up during Catherine's reign, the sale of property by a wife to her husband was forbidden owing to evidence of pressure on his part to compel her to sell. (This will sound familiar to readers of Aksakov's *Family Chronicle*.) The case established a legal precedent, though there was inconsistency in practice until an early-nineteenth-century ruling authorized sales of property by women to their husbands. Sergeevich, p. 574.

[92] Chernigov and Poltava provinces constituted a partial exception to this general rule. Family estates were treated as a special type of inalienable property and relatives had preemptive rights in case of the sale of such property. Property rights of spouses are stipulated in articles 109–18 of the *Svod zakonov*, vol. X, part 1.

generally held by and allotted to households. For practical purposes the "household" amounted to the male head of the family, although basic decisions about land use might involve consultation with other adult (primarily male) members of the household. When the Revolution of 1905 precipitated a reform that permitted household allotments to be taken out of communes, the appropriated land became the individual property of the head of the household. Daughters were customarily excluded from the inheritance of peasant land. Outside the peasantry, daughters had received only one-fourteenth of the immovable property if there were sons to inherit an intestate estate. A major reform of the inheritance law in 1912 increased the share of daughters to one-seventh of nonurban landed property and provided that all other property was to be divided equally among sons and daughters. The 1912 law also stipulated that widows and widowers alike were entitled to one-fourth of the immovable, and one-seventh of the movable, property of their deceased spouse.

The property rights of Russian women had a significance that extended beyond the economic and social spheres, for property rights were linked with political rights. When voting procedures were set up in connection with the reform of local government from the 1860's on, and when a representative national assembly (the Duma) was established after the Revolution of 1905, electoral rights were based on property qualifications. Women with sufficient property had the right to vote in elections, but they had to cast their votes through male relatives. In the absence of such relatives, they were disfranchised.[93]

For the great majority of Russian women, the extension of voting rights to considerable numbers of the male population, like the earlier articulation of civil status, perversely constituted a regressive movement. Male enfranchisement placed females at a relative disadvantage. Peasant women petitioning the Duma for the vote after 1905 pointed out that previously they had been equal to men at least in their common lack of political rights.[94] However, concern for political rights was outweighed for most women in early-twentieth-century Russia by concern for the rights of women in marriage.

The civil code at this time retained a statement dating from the late eighteenth century that defined the obligations of husbands and wives. In language suggestive of a feudal contract, where protection is exchanged for vassal servitude in a context of institutionalized devotion, the law proclaimed: "A husband is obliged to love his wife as his own body, to live with her in concord, to esteem and protect her, to excuse her deficiencies, and to assist her in her infirmities. He is required to provide his wife with food and maintenance according to his status and ability." A wife, on the other hand,

[93] V. I. Sergeevich, "Vseobshchee izbiratel'noe pravo" (reprinted from the *Zhurnal Ministerstva Iustitsii* [May 1906]; SPb, 1906), p. 34.
[94] Vera Bil'shai [-Pilipenko], *The Status of Women in the Soviet Union* (M, 1957), p. 13.

was "obliged to obey her husband as the head of the family; to abide with him in love, honor, and unconditional obedience; to render him all satisfaction and affection as the master of the house."[95]

The law stipulated that husbands and wives must live together. A married woman did not have a separate passport but was listed on her husband's. She had no legal right to reside separately or to go out to work without his permission. An unmarried daughter could establish a separate residence at age 21. A son could do so at seventeen. In the first half of the nineteenth century the authority of husbands over their wives was limited by the law. Husbands were forbidden now—for the first time—to beat or mutilate their wives. However, these provisions did not directly affect the peasantry or the peasant practice of wife-beating, which was sanctioned by customary law.

As the norms governing social relationships received fuller expression in eighteenth- and nineteenth-century legislation, law itself became a reflection of the prevailing cultural and social bifurcation. Formal law encompassed only the upper strata of a polarized society. The rural masses that still constituted the vast majority (about 85 percent) of the Russian populace at the beginning of the twentieth century remained under customary law and had resort to a separate system of courts. As a result, some of the improvements introduced by law in this period affected only a narrow segment of the female population. Although legal dualism presents a special difficulty in the modern period, it is related to a more general problem that can arise from any attempt to trace the social position of women through a study of law. Law typically reflects horizontal stratification (e.g., class, caste, estate), but societies are bisected vertically along sex lines. Because the situation of women in different strata varies, global assessment of female status is problematic. Yet when the law reveals consistent variations at all levels between the "left" and "right" sides of society, or when it reveals changes over time, it permits a degree of generalization about the status of women.

If law tended to segregate social blocks, religion was a unifying factor in Russian society. The steady movement of the state into the sphere of domestic relations was accompanied by a seemingly paradoxical growth of church influence in this area. The explanation lies in the fact that secularization in Russia did not imply a separation of church and state so much as an ingestion of church by state. From the time of Peter, and even earlier, the authority and property of the church came increasingly under the direct control of the government. By the eighteenth century, most marriages took place in the church. This created a problem for the large group of priestless Old Believers. In 1874, after several alternative policies had been tried, the government authorized civil marriages for them. By this time some of their female members, either succumbing to a persistent ascetic strain among

---

[95] *Svod zakonov,* vol. X, part I, articles 106–7.

the dissidents or rebelling against the female lot in general, had organized a minor social protest movement whose members used their own blood as ink to record their opposition to marriage.[96]

The widespread conviction that marriage and the domestic circle circumscribed the only roles appropriate for women had all the weight of Russian tradition behind it. But as the "woman question" emerged, tradition came in for closer scrutiny. Only in the second half of the nineteenth century did social analysts in Russia begin to turn their attention to the study of women in the Russian historical past. One of the earliest books on this subject, by V. Shul'gin (see n. 23), dates from 1850, and a handful of pioneering writings appeared in the next few decades. The first scholarly work to survey the position of women throughout Russian history was published in 1871.[97] The writers of these works, and others who pursued the topic later, generally portrayed women in the Russian past as objects of social oppression, as victims of tradition; yet they themselves often displayed a striking commitment to traditional values and attitudes.

The author of the 1850 study, for example, paints a stereotypical contrast between the masculine and the feminine personality. Women are characterized by such traits as sensitivity, love, and modesty; men, by intellect, honor, and sense of duty. Women *feel* the good, the true, the beautiful; men try to *understand* them. Women show their strength in suffering; men, in deeds. He concludes that men predominate naturally in civic life as do women in the domestic sphere: "The family is the kingdom [*sic*] of woman—her life."[98] In a story entitled "The Ideal," a nineteenth-century woman writer discussed sex roles in Russia with less complacency. Men, she conceded, placed women on a throne, but one on a shaky foundation. Women were chained to it by social expectations. "Sometimes it seems that God created the world for men only. . . . For them there is fame and art and learning; for them there is freedom and all the joy of life. . . . But if a woman does not achieve happiness in family life, what is left for her?"[99]

In 1906 an eminent historian who supported extension of the voting rights of Russian women nevertheless argued against the inclusion of women in government. Acknowledging that women had been subjected to male domination "from the very beginning of historical time," he insisted that the situation had greatly changed. In his view, the change had occurred despite the nonparticipation of women in the legislative process because men were the "devoted protectors" of women. After all, he asked

[96]A. P. Shchapov, vol. 2, p. 132. There are interesting parallels here to a limited antimarriage movement that appeared among Chinese women in the nineteenth century. See Marjorie Topley, "Marriage Resistance in Rural Kwantung," in Margery Wolf and Roxane Witke, eds., *Women in Chinese Society* (Stanford, Calif., 1975), pp. 67–88.

[97]This was the first edition of S. S. Shashkov's work cited in n. 24.

[98]Shul'gin, pp. iv–viii.

[99]A. P. Shchapov, vol. 3, p. 605. Mikhnevich points out (p. 243) that a well-known *Dictionary of Memorable Russians* listing some 500 prominent people throughout Russian history into the nineteenth century included only twelve women.

rhetorically, "What is a woman?" His answer: "a daughter, a wife, a mother."[100]

CONCLUSION

Family life, marriage. These were the critical parameters of female identity, the determinants of the Russian woman's world at the beginning of the tenth century. They remained such, for the most part, at the beginning of the twentieth century. This is hardly a peculiarity of Russian social history, but analysis of the Russian situation may shed some interesting light on a pattern that transcends national or cultural boundaries.

The usual explanation of the limitation of female roles in traditional societies stresses biological factors and the resultant specialization of labor, which together establish a pattern perpetuated by cultural traditions. This obviously accounts for a large part of the story, but it fails to explain why women in some societies assume a wider range of roles and achieve greater sexual equality than do women in other societies. Differences among societies clearly involve a long list of variables, but there are two sets of factors affecting sex roles that appear critical in many cases: social stratification, and economic development. The first may be less apparent than the second, but its importance has been suggested by this survey.

In the Russian case, sex roles were determined not just by biology and by cultural conditioning to male dominance, but also by class structure and its implementation through the law. As a vehicle for upward social mobility, marriage consistently offered more to women than to men. The reason for this seems clear: social elevation of men through marriage would have expanded, and thus depreciated, upper-class ranks. But a woman entering a higher class through marriage was socially negligible as long as she remained under her husband's authority. To the extent that women assumed independent roles outside the domestic sphere, they potentially weakened the authority of husbands (and fathers) and constituted a threat to the entire system of social stratification. Therefore, as long as the hierarchical structure was supported by the law, the subjection of wives (women) and the limitation of feminine roles were essential elements in social relations. The only alternative would have been a caste system forbidding marriage between ranks.[101] This suggests the hypothesis that in legally stratified societies recognizing interclass marriages, equality between the sexes may be precluded. Progression toward sexual equality would become possible only as class barriers dissolved and social mobility increased. Equality

[100] Sergeevich opposed the entry of women into government service because of anticipated effects on society: "The social structure would change, but hardly for the better. I see no progress in a situation where women sit in offices, conduct investigations, serve as judges, etc., while men [deprived thus of jobs] stay home as housewives" ("Izbiratel'noe pravo," pp. 35–37).

[101] If the dominant role in a legally stratified society were assumed by females, the implications for the possibility of sex equality would be the same, of course. The actual extent of interclass movement is not important as long as the principle is accepted.

among men, then, would seem to be a precondition of equality between the sexes.

The place of marriage and the family in defining the social universe of women in Russia suggests a continuity persisting over ten centuries of Russian history. Yet this survey has revealed a variety of important changes—legal, institutional, and attitudinal. The historical outline indicates that the status of women in Russia changed significantly at least twice. A decline is evident following the Kievan period, and an upswing arcs from the early eighteenth century into the twentieth century. What is of greatest interest in reviewing the pattern is the fact that this curve follows the same general contours as that of the position of the masses of men in Russian society. Two distinct questions—that of the status of the sexes relative to one another, and that of the general condition of men and women in society—turn out to be closely connected historically, since factors that affected the position of women vis-à-vis men similarly affected the social relations of men. The relative deterioration in women's status in the medieval era was paralleled by an absolute deterioration in the quality of life for the masses in Russia, just as the improvement of female status in the Imperial period was part of a major and progressive social development.

Modernization has meant different things to different societies, but changes in sex roles have been a universal aspect of the process. The modification of women's roles inevitably generates a need for changes in the roles of men because of the interdependency of the sexes in traditional social structures. Societies resist change; they harbor an innate conservatism that helps to ensure their cohesiveness and to preserve them. A major driving force is required to propel a society out of traditional molds. Modernization is generally associated with economic development; and it is no mere coincidence that the beginning of the eighteenth century, the period of the initial phases of social transformation, witnessed the introduction of industrialization into Russia. Economic growth was accelerated in the late nineteenth century and has surged dramatically in the Soviet era. Industrialization involves the adoption of new techniques and resources to permit more effective utilization of the natural environment. It has been described as the process of unbinding Prometheus;[102] as the papers that follow make clear, the process has also involved Promethean woman.

Models of "strong women" are particularly useful in Soviet society, where military, economic, and demographic considerations have at various stages called for the mobilization of all human resources. In the fighting that accompanied and followed the fall of Imperial Russia in 1917, and again during the Second World War, Russian women became active military combatants.[103] Dressed in masculine attire and bearing arms, they revived the ancient role of female warriors. Though the hoary legends about the past are treated with skepticism by Soviet scholars, the Amazon continues to

---

[102] David Landes, *The Unbound Prometheus* (Cambridge, Mass., 1969).
[103] Women fought on both sides in the Revolutions and in the Civil War.

captivate the popular imagination and is alive and well in the Soviet press today.[104] Some aspects of the model, however, would appear to be problematic, since the independence of Amazon women is associated with conflict between the sexes. Yet the problem disappears if social evolution is approached as a dialectical process. Sex is the ultimate dialectic. The sexual division of mankind may be the source of the very concept of the dialectic: achievement of a higher stage of being through the integration of opposites. Beginning with the fact (thesis) of sexual division, history might be said to record a movement through the antagonism (antithesis) of dominance, toward the sexually synthesized egalitarian society. It has been a long and lively passage, and only recently has the route been marked out for study as a result of the maturation of social self-consciousness. History may or may not have predictive value, but societies must know where they have been in order to know where they are.

The uses of the past were evident to the first scholar who attempted to trace the history of women in Russia. "The present," he observed in his introduction, "is the result of the past and comes constantly under the influence of traditional authority. . . . So many outmoded principles act on contemporary life that it is impossible to speak of the past without coming up against the vital problems of today."[105] The observation remains valid. But in the course of the century that has passed since it was recorded, many problems and principles have changed for Russian women. Nonetheless, the study of women in the Russian past continues to be a largely neglected subject. Work in this area had only begun at the time of the October Revolution of 1917 but, perhaps in part because the "woman question" was considered essentially resolved by new policies introduced then, Soviet historians have not returned to the topic. Thus, the exploratory survey ventured in these pages represents a preliminary attempt to identify some major issues in Russian social history that invite more intensive scholarly investigation.

The abrupt nature of the social transformation that took place after the Revolution of 1917 propelled Soviet women and men almost overnight into a radically modified institutional and legal framework. The transformation of social attitudes has been a more time-consuming and difficult process. The changes that have taken place have not been an unmixed blessing to

---

[104] See the discussion of M. Ganina's recent book, *Povest' o zhenshchine*, in *Literaturnaia gazeta*, June 24, 1974.

[105] Shashkov, preface. Serafim Serafimovich Shashkov (1841–82) was in many ways a typical representative of the Russian intelligentsia of the period. The son of a priest, he was a talented writer who met with repeated career disappointments in the course of a life cut short by illness. He published a vast number of articles and was known especially for his conscientiously researched analyses relating events of the past to contemporary problems. History for Shashkov not only shed light on the present but provided opportunity in autocratic Russia for discreet social commentary. His work was popular with Russian youth, and the persistence of his influence is indicated by the publication in 1898 of a two-volume collection of his historical writings, including his pioneer work on the history of women in Russia.

women in Russia; accidents of history have created unanticipated new problems; and some old problems have turned out to be unexpectedly resistant to solution. But the Soviet experience in this aspect of social engineering provides a unique model that warrants study by social scientists and by the architects, the common laborers, and the sidewalk superintendents of modern social reconstruction.

Richard Stites

Women and the Russian Intelligentsia:
Three Perspectives

B EGINNINGS ARE often illuminated by ends. In a typically caustic comment on the weaknesses of the Bolshevik women's movement and on
the neglect of it by the male supremacists in the Party, the Marxist scholar
David Riazanov in 1927 voiced the view that there were some comrades
who aspired to a permanent division of labor between men and women—
women's affairs to be handled by the *Zhenotdel*, the women's section of the
Party, and all the rest (that is, the important matters) by the "*muzhotdel*."[1]
Aside from being a gloomy adumbration of the demise of a relatively autonomous effort among Bolshevik women to liberate their backward sisters, the
remark and the implied sympathies of its author sharply underline a basic
aspect of the history of Russian radicalism's attitude toward women's equality: the acceptance of it by some radicals as a principle; the willingness of
others to make it a reality. In the following pages I will address myself to
three separable, if closely related, aspects of the question: the reaction of
antifeminists to the progress of women's emancipation, and the articulation
of that reaction; the motives and ideas of the male members of the intelligentsia, mostly radical, who helped shape the image of the liberated Russian woman; and the various and often conflicting self-images and responses of women themselves.

   Examining antifeminist positions of the nineteenth (or any) century—
though often personally unnerving because it arouses both anger and

---

[1]*Letopisi Marksizma*, vol. 3 (1927), p. 26. I wish to express here my gratitude to the Russian Research Center at Harvard University for the opportunity to conduct research on this
and other subjects. I also wish to thank Professor Abbott Gleason of Brown University for his
innumerable kindnesses. For the purposes of this volume I have cited where possible recent
scholarship, published or about to be published.

guilt—has its rewards. At the most obvious level, it helps substantiate the tie one always feels exists between antifeminism on a principled plane and conventional self-interested conservatism. It has been pointed out repeatedly since the time of the Mills that conservative arguments about women, however systematic and universal in form, are tightly moored to social reality. I shall essay a general comment on this at the end of this section.

The first authentic voice of modern conservatism in Russia, Prince Shcherbatov, lamented in the eighteenth century that the artificial and superficial process of cultural Westernization, in corroding so many of the cherished traditions of the Russian way of life, was unraveling the fabric of traditional sexual relations as well. The fashionable practice of "feminine intrigue," imported from the salons and ballrooms of France, had transformed certain upper-class ladies from relatively passive and silent creatures into aggressive and cunning devotees of *liaisons dangereuses*. What critics such as Shcherbatov deplored was not that woman was a sex object, but rather that she was a conscious participant in the erotic game. In the course of time, the Gallic fashion of salon intrigue gave way to the Germanic and romantic exaltation of woman, either in the classical mode of the citizen-mother or in the more vaporous mood of the beautiful soul; and in the early nineteenth century, Russian literature and philosophy shimmered with the image of woman as pure spirit and immaculate vessel of metaphysical love. Nestor Kotliarevskii, a perceptive observer of the link between literature and life, offered this composite sketch of the woman of the 1840's. "She spoke little or not at all, but rather whispered or sang. The meaning of her words in song and speech was unclear, but in them one could feel much sadness. Why? Who can say? In any case, it was not her lack of equal rights which saddened her. Her grief was not of this world, and she seemed to yearn after some distant, mountainous clime. To earthly concerns, except for love, she was indifferent. Ready for sacrifice, she never initiated any, but went where she was led in humble submission. In the end she preferred to perish early, exchanging terrestrial life for heaven; and in the full flower of her strength, she already hinted at the imminent parting."[2]

When tastes in the realm of spirit and flesh began to change at the end of the 1840's the sensuous woman made her appearance again in a guise that seemed to subsume and transcend both the carnal triviality of the eighteenth century and the austere purity of the early nineteenth. On the banner of woman's moral liberation was now inscribed the motto "emancipation of the heart." The European source of the new ethos was George Sand, and the emulators of her literary heroines acted out their impulses to freedom in bold exploits of infidelity known to contemporaries as the *zhorzh-*

[2]Kotliarevskii, in A. Tyrkova, ed., *Sbornik pamiati Anny Pavlovny Filosofovoi* (Petrograd, 1915), vol. 2, p. 77. For some of the literature on changing images of women from the eighteenth to the nineteenth centuries, see my dissertation, "The Question of the Emancipation of Women in Nineteenth Century Russia" (Harvard, 1967), chap. 2.

zandshchina. This phenomenon, an interesting, short-lived, and little-studied episode in Russian upper-class family history, evoked a storm of invective from the praetors and censors of Russian ways, who launched an assault both upon George Sand's "emancipation of the heart" and upon Enfantin's far more radical and sweeping "rehabilitation of the flesh"; these critics frequently made no distinction between the two—though it was precisely their differences that ultimately were to divide Russian radicals at the end of the long quest for sexual and moral freedom.[3] But in the meantime the Russian gentry had settled on a sexual ethic that tolerantly, if reluctantly, accepted infidelity—provided it was either practiced exclusively by gentlemen or indulged in discreetly by ladies, unaccompanied by the flourish of a belletristic apologia.

All of this preceded the debate on the "woman question" and the accompanying outward and conscious manifestations of freedom by Russian women—both of which began only in the late 1850's and early 1860's. The occasion for the first outburst of genuinely antifeminist (as opposed to mere moral) indignation was the open movement for sexual and personal freedom and equality among the young women who came to be called *nigilistki* (female nihilists). In some cases prefiguring, in others imitating, the goings on in Chernyshevskii's *What Is to Be Done?*, women by the score bade farewell to parents, husbands, and even children and fled their gentry nests to seek the free air of Russian cities to work, to study, or to join a circle, cooperative, or commune. Catching the spirit of Enfantin's celebrated commune of men and women in the Ménilmontant district of Paris (1831), gentry girls, lower-middle-class women, and priests' daughters joined similar enterprises in St. Petersburg and other cities, pooling their possessions and sharing the work. Though most of this activity seems to have been conducted in the most properly celibate of circumstances, it became the target of vitriolic attacks leveled against "dirty nihilists" and "free-love communes" by anti-Western journalists, moralizing professors, and not a few major literary figures—Leskov, Pisemskii, and Goncharov among them. A major theme of these invectives was that the sexual seduction of genuine Russians by "un-Russian" people (i.e., radicals, nihilists, and Poles—Jews were added later) was the analogue of political seduction—again of decent Russians by alienated émigrés and Polish conspirators. A minor theme is suggested by the fact that many of the remarks about women's desertion of their husbands and families were couched in language usually used to describe crimes against the state such as military desertion, illegal emigration, and treason. Indeed, the portions of the Russian Code dealing with the family sound like the fundamental laws of a miniature autocracy. In any case, "free love," in the eyes of the antinihilist writers,

[3] On the *zhorzhzandshchina*, see the references in n. 6 of my article "M. L. Mikhailov and the Emergence of the Woman Question in Russia," *Canadian Slavic Studies*, 3, no. 2 (Summer 1969), p. 180; *Novyi zhurnal inostrannoi literatury. . .* , 2, no. 4 (Apr. 1899), pp. 2–11; and articles in *Russkii arkhiv* between 1885 and 1895.

was intimately connected with general civic immorality, political unreliabil-
ity, and—in some cases—hopeless degeneracy.[4]

The linkup of political deviance and sexual naughtiness appears again
and again in antifeminist responses to the appearance of radical women.
Gendarmes, when taking "nihilist" women into custody during the so-
called White Terror of 1866, were wont to ask them if they lived in sin with
their male comrades and if they emulated the heroines of *What Is to Be
Done?* Shocked observers such as Prince Odoevskii wondered if they copu-
lated without bathing. A year or so later, a rumor was afloat about a reputed
"beautiful nihilist" who sold her body in order to finance the radical activities of a tiny circle known as the Smorgon Academy. When the government
decided to force the Russian student community at Zurich to disperse in
1874, its decree made sweeping imputations of radicalism and immorality
against the women students and implied that they were studying medicine
in order to perform abortions on one another. For all its efforts, the regime
was never able to build a convincing case that Russian revolutionary
women were, by the nature of things, depraved. On the contrary, once they
began appearing in court as political offenders, the public was struck by the
impressive honesty and the exalted purity of female defendants such as
Sofia Bardina. The last effort before 1917 to identify "advanced" women—
in this case students—with political radicalism and immorality was a series
of remarks made in the Duma by the right-wing deputies Purishkevich and
Obradtsev, who labeled female students "street girls" and depraved Jewess-
es who defiled "our youth" and who "by the hundreds gave themselves to
drunken sailors."[5]

This kind of thinking died hard. The final and most bitterly ironic episode
of the sort was the slander campaign against Aleksandra Kollontai in the
early 1920's. Kollontai's trouble had begun at the very peak of her career as
tribune of the Revolution and first woman commissar in the Soviet government. Her stormy love affair with Dybenko (a younger man), his own irresponsible actions, and her vigorous defense of him evoked caustic comments from Bolshevik leaders—including Lenin, who once remarked to
Klara Zetkin that he did not trust women who intertwined love affairs with
politics. When Kollontai championed the cause of the Workers' Opposition
in the early 1920's—thus recreating the traditional figure of the radical
woman in league with male comrades against the established order—she
was attacked in language reminiscent of the mudslinging of the old regime.
A press campaign was launched against her allegedly immoral sexual

---

[4] A brief description of the literary side of the antinihilist campaign may be found in Charles
Moser, *Antinihilism in the Russian Novel of the 1860s* (The Hague, 1964).

[5] Episodes of the 1860's: *Kolokol*, Jan. 1, 1867, pp. 1889–95; Odoevskii's diary in *Literatur-
noe nasledstvo*, no. 22–24 (1935), p. 211; Franco Venturi, *Roots of Revolution*, trans. F. Has-
kell (New York, 1960), p. 351. The Zurich decree: V. Bogucharskii, *Aktivnoe narodnichestvo
semidesiatykh godov* (M, 1912), pp. 213–15. The Duma deputies: V. Purishkevich, *Materialy
po voprosu o razlozhenii sovremennogo russkogo universiteta* (SPb, 1914), pp. 35–36, 190,
261–64; *Zhenskoe delo* (Mar. 15, 1911), p. 2.

teachings—a campaign that, though far from being wholly cynical or insincere, provided a convenient opportunity for discrediting Kollontai's oppositional activity. To be fair, we should note that Lenin had no hand in this campaign (although he opposed both her politics and her sexual ideas) and that anti-Bolshevik opinion about Kollontai was vastly more vicious and distorted.[6]

One more comment about sex. In the last generation of prerevolutionary Russia, official sexual morality, as described in the marriage manual *Family Life in Its Joys and Sorrows* (1888) and in the sweetly pious effusions of Orthodox priests, was set against the imputed fantasies of "the socialists," who were accused of promoting a sex life resembling that of cattle and pigs, of aspiring to turn all women into prostitutes, and of generally advancing "the moral equality of the gutter." The actual sexual behavior of "privileged" Russia is too well known to require detailed comment here; and it has received encyclopedic treatment in the remarkable *Running Sores of St. Petersburg* (1886) by V. Mikhnevich—a marvelous moral supplement to the better-known *Petersburg Slums* by V. Krestovskii—and in the vast literature on prostitutes and their clients.[7]

Hostility to women's education on the part of antifeminists was couched in the simplest of arguments—one embedded in the question "For what?" The debate over new girls' high schools in the 1860's showed the mixed feelings of local school officials and parents: one local school administrator was concerned for small girls who might have to pass along the muddy streets of Odessa on their way to school, whereas a bureaucrat plainly stated that "nowadays girls are learning too much."[8] The university and ministry officials who voted in 1863 against allowing women to remain in the universities (which they had spontaneously begun to attend in the late 1850's) did not elaborate on their motives—though it seems reasonable to assume that inertia and the fear of novelty and distraction played as great a role in the decision as the uncovering of a few radical female students. The same was true of the bureaucracy's foot-dragging in opening preparatory courses in the late 1860's. That university courses and a medical school finally were opened to women in the 1870's was primarily the result of fear that the

[6]The documentation on this is from chap. 11, sec. 2 ("The New Morality") of my forthcoming book *Women's Liberation in Russia: Nihilism, Feminism, and Communism* (Princeton, N.J., 1977).
[7]*Semeinaia zhizn' v eia radostiakh i pechaliakh: pravila zhiteiskoi mudrosti dlia muzhei i zhën* (SPb, 1888); *Pravoslavnoe obozrenie*, 3, no. 11, Nov. 1882), pp. 578–93; V. Silov, *Zhenshchina zamuzhem* (2d ed.; M, 1897); M. G. Bolkvadze, *Ne razvrashchaite zhenshchin!* (SPb, 1908); and the titles listed in n. 9 of my article on "Women's Liberation Movements in Russia: 1900–1930," *Canadian-American Slavic Studies*, 7, no. 4 (Winter 1973), p. 464. V. Mikhnevich, *Yazvy Peterburga: opyt istoriko-statisticheskago isledovaniia nravstvennosti stolichnago naseleniia* (SPb, 1886). Some of the literature on prostitution is reviewed in my article on "The Prostitute" to appear in Rose L. Glickman and Richard Stites, eds., *Women in Nineteenth Century Russia* (forthcoming).
[8]E. Likhacheva, *Materialy dlia istorii zhenskago obrazovaniia v Rossii* (SPb, 1890–93), vol. 2, pp. 7–14. Parents' fears of education for their daughters at a later period are nimbly described in Mikhail Chekhov's story *Sinii chulok* (SPb, 1904).

scores of young women who had gone to Zurich to study were fast becoming infected in the poisonously radical miasma that hung over the city. Later, when these institutions appeared to be doing nothing to stem the influx
of women into the revolutionary populist movement (though in fact their
existence probably did so), and after a woman had been hanged for the
murder of the tsar in 1881, the dynasty, reactionary bureaucrats and journalists (e.g., Prince Meshcherskii), and the police—who called the courses
for women "a veritable sewer of anarchist disease"—combined in the 1880's
to close them down temporarily.[9]

Though modern social scientists seem to agree that education in and of
itself does not necessarily generate radical thought and behavior, and
though most of the women students counted themselves among the
"academics" and not the "politicals," the government, unversed in the ways
of modern sociology and hard put to make nuanced assessments, often
came to the conclusion that a *kursistka* (coed) was automatically a
revoliutsionerka. During the erratic and stormy history of the revived
women's courses in the years between the self-immolation of Mariia Ve-
trova in 1897 and the First World War, the central dilemma of education
ministers with regard to women's higher education was this: if we give
them more, the courses will only train more radicals; if we do not, the
women will explode in active opposition. It was a dilemma by no means
confined to women's education, to that time, or to that place. To relate this
to another matter: Minister of Justice Shcheglovitov, in voicing his opinion
that Russian women, if drawn too closely into political life (i.e., given the
vote), would be tempted by the seductions of revolutionary ideas, might
have been recalling also that a female student had almost succeeded in
assassinating him a few years back. And so some female revolutionary students were hanged; but their courses, despite all battering, remained
open.[10]

The last chapter in the life of conservative antifeminism—its opposition
to women's suffrage—holds no surprises for students of either the Russian
Right or Western antisuffrage thought. There were some strident voices:
one writer equated the extension of suffrage with the spread of vice; and
Purishkevich once described a very proper congress of feminists as an as-
semblage of prostitutes. But most bureaucrats and leaders of Duma parties
from the Octobrists on over to the extreme right contented themselves with
responses such as "not natural," "no need for it," and "unprecedented." The
left—Social Democrats (SDs), Social Revolutionaries (SRs), Trudoviks, and

[9] See P. Zaionchkovskii, *Rossiiskoe samoderzhavie v kontse XIX stoletiia* (M, 1970), pp.
340–42.
[10] Government correspondence, including Shcheglovitov's, on the 1912 suffrage bill is to be
found in full in the Central State Historical Archives in Leningrad (TsGIAL), f. 1405 (1912),
op. 452, d. 321. For radical women students, see the brief sketch in S. N. Valk et al., eds.,
Sankt-Peterburgskie vysshie zhenskie (Bestuzhevskie) kursy, 1878–1918, (2d ed.; L, 1973),
pp. 22–70. The literature on women students in tsarist Russia is very large; the best treatment
in English is Ruth Dudgeon's chapter in Glickman and Stites.

others—provided the necessary symmetry by proclaiming the principle of complete political equality of the sexes. Of greater interest was the center—for the dividing line on the issue ran right through the middle of the Kadet party, and indeed through the family of its leader, Miliukov, who opposed his feminist wife on the matter. In reply to various pre-Duma queries about their position of female suffrage, prominent figures from the "unions," the Zemstvos, and the liberal parties tended to offer such evasive answers as "They don't have it even in Europe yet," or "Of course we favor it, but the time is not ripe." The Kadets, at least, finally moved to a pro-feminist position and supported women's suffrage bills in the Duma—but of course to no avail.[11]

Antifeminists generally stuck to opposing particular aspects of women's emancipation, usually on practical or expedient grounds. When they did venture to construct systematic philosophical arguments, the results were not particularly distinguished. Even the most talented of the antifeminists, Nikolai Strakhov, could offer no more than a negative argument against the excessive rationalism and "Western"-style optimism of J. S. Mill's emancipatory rhetoric. No Russian produced anything like the lush and frenetic antifeminism of a Michelet or a Proudhon, or even a Von Sybel or a Frederic Harrison—although the opinions of these men, as well as those of the near-pathological Otto Weininger, found their echoes and adherents in Russian journalism. In the end, the most influential of antifeminist writers, Tolstoi, was also the bluntest and the crudest, drawing as he did upon the church and upon the peasant ethos. In an interview with a feminist, he summed it all up by saying that if the husband wanted his wife to wash his shirts, she had to do it—for thus it had been for a thousand years.[12]

To the question "What kind of people opposed women's emancipation in tsarist Russia?" I have nothing more original or surprising to answer than this: though antifeminism could be found in all walks of life, those sectors of more or less educated society that were conservative in most other matters were also the most resistant to changes in the status of women. This includes the dynasty, the bureaucracy, the police, most landlords, the merchant class, and the clergy. To these must also be added the vast majority of the unenlightened classes—especially the peasants, though for different and somewhat simpler reasons. In general, the social elements that nurtured such aspects of conservatism as antimodernism, anti-Westernism, and even anti-Semitism usually opposed the extension of women's rights. Konstantin Pobedonostsev, in admonishing the Russian people "to choose a work and a field according to our measure," added antifeminism to a long array of revulsions against the apparent tendencies of the modern world.[13]

---

[11] For background and sources, see Stites, "Women's Liberation Movements."

[12] N. Strakhov, *Zhenskii vopros* (SPb, 1871), a reprint of his *Zaria* article of 1870. On Tolstoi, see *Zhenskoe delo* (June 25, 1910), pp. 21–22.

[13] Konstantin Pobedonostsev, *Reflections of a Russian Statesman*, trans. R. C. Crozier (Ann Arbor, Mich., 1965), p. 121.

We may leave this unpleasant but not wholly valueless subject of inquiry with an inversion of Fourier's well-known remark about measuring the progress of a society by the status of its women: it may be that the relative backwardness of a society can be measured, in a preliminary way at least, by gauging the numbers, power, and influence of the antifeminists in it.

There was little outward evidence before the late 1850's that the Russian left would be any more sympathetic to the emancipation of women than was most of the European left in the early nineteenth century. The Decembrist secret societies, for example, banned women from membership, as did their Tugendbund and Carbonari contemporaries, and gave them no more than a traditional citizen-mother role in their visions of the future society. The "men of the forties," though privately echoing many of the feminist sentiments of some of their French socialist inspirers, said very little about it—and did less. And yet it was they—particularly Belinskii and Herzen—who first included women in the sweeping notion of all-human liberation that was to be such a characteristic feature of the intelligentsia. The notion itself arose from the life circumstances and social perspectives of the early *intelligenty* rather than from the "metaphysical pogroms" inflicted upon them by the Germans. As Malia has amply and eloquently demonstrated, the idea world of the Russian intelligentsia was born out of the frustration of being sensitive and cultivated flowers in the barren fields of official autocracy and ignorant peasant masses.[14] It took shape in a mood of perceived oppression and degradation, a mood that produced a countermystique of exaltation of the human spirit and total social liberation. This countermystique rejected not only the crude societal primitivity of the tsarist value system but also the hypocritical *juste milieu* of the bourgeois West. *All* the underprivileged and *all* the oppressed were to be freed—or none at all could be genuinely free. The piecemeal, selective techniques of Western liberalism could find no moral sustenance in this atmosphere: the intelligentsia demanded the liberation of all human beings—including women.

But it was the "men of the sixties"—and I shall comment on my use of the word "men" in a moment—who translated the philosophical formulations of the early intelligentsia into a specific program for women's emancipation and who then tried to put it into practice. The most interesting and difficult question, it seems to me, is why this occurred precisely in the late 1850's and early 1860's. Nowadays historians (including this one) would tend to seek part of the answer, at least, in the social origins of the new generation of publicists and activists who supported women's equality. This included Mikhailov, Shelgunov, Chernyshevskii, Dobroliubov, Pisarev, Sleptsov, Pomialovskii, and Lavrov, as well as a host of young people who did not reach print (the Petersburg youth circles, for example, so eloquently

[14] Martin Malia, *Alexander Herzen and the Birth of Russian Socialism* (Cambridge, Mass., 1961).

described in the memoirs of Elizaveta Vodovozova).[15] There surely was something in the home life and early environment of some of these men that may have impelled them (or made it easier for them) to establish natural, open, and egalitarian relations with their female peers. But the class and family backgrounds of these writers and their silent disciples are simply too varied to be of much help in talking about the group as a whole; they constituted a blend of *raznochintsy* (people of mixed ranks) and gentry about as balanced as the more frequently mentioned (but as little studied) social coalition of gentry and professionals who fashioned and nurtured twentieth-century Russian liberalism.

Until more research has been done on the "people of the sixties" as people and not merely as carriers of ideas, we must, I believe, seek explanations arising out of general mood, social style, and density of relationships. The mood was clearly one of great intensity and towering optimism. "Even the temperature of the blood went up among the people of those years," Vodovozova recalled.[16] Their style, social as well as intellectual, was dominated by the compulsion to live a life that was fully consistent with their ideas—a repudiation of "the Fathers" as well as of their own fathers. The consistency could now be sustained by a sense of community. Partly for political reasons (the regime's policy of broadening the university student body) and partly for more directly economic ones (the influx to the cities before and after the serf emancipation), there was greater "sociological density" in the new generation of the intelligentsia than there had been in the old—that is, greater numbers, more continuous interaction (and consequent reinforcement of behavior patterns), and much greater contact between men and women in the cities than ever before.

As we shall note in the following section, the presence of women played an important role in all of this. But there is no question that the articulators and popularizers of women's equality in these critical years were almost exclusively men, ranging from liberal reformers and pedagogues to radical and semiradical publicists. Dr. N. Pirogov, keeping within a rather traditionalist framework, spoke of educating women to take their places in the unfolding progressive society. M. L. Mikhailov, the first to apply the broad categories of the intelligentsia to the "woman question" as a whole, also believed that education was the central problem; but to this he added the suggestive notion of transforming marriage into an equal partnership of comrades. Chernyshevskii, in *What Is to Be Done?*, outlined the techniques and the attitudes by which men could liberate women and by which women could liberate their sisters: fictitious marriages to rescue socially incarcerated women; total equality in relations and living habits; rational solutions to love triangles; work, study, and collective enterprise. Out of these themes, and their elaboration in numerous circles and evening parties of

---

[15] Elizaveta Vodovozova, *Na zare zhizni*, ed. E.S. Vilenskaia and L. I. Roitberg (2 vols.; M, 1964), see esp. vol. 2.
[16] *Ibid.*, vol. 2, p. 34.

the period, emerged a widely accepted position of the intelligentsia on women which included a full, positive, ungrudging affirmation of the equality of the sexes and a belief that the two sexes ought to march together in some common struggle (itself in the process of being defined). But it also betrayed a sharp, if not yet crucial, division over the future of sex relations and the family.[17]

Equality of the sexes was put into practice in a variety of ways. A few men, best typified by V. A. Sleptsov, established cooperative ventures of all sorts—ranging from journals run along artel principles to residential communes—largely for the purpose of providing work, housing, and a suitable environment for the young women who were fleeing from their rural nests. Similar techniques were employed by outright radicals such as Ishutin and Khudiakov a few years later to draw women, artisans, students, and poor people into their circles. It was, in a way, an urban prelude to the "Movement of the People" of the 1870's. Behind this handful of organizers stood an army of tutors and teachers, seminarians, medical students, and officers on leave who acted as the vehicles for the distillation and transmittal of the "new" ideas of St. Petersburg into the consciousness of their women friends, sisters, cousins, neighbors, or casual acquaintances. The sources attest eloquently to the prevalence of this social communication. The men developed a kind of egalitarian chivalry toward women that was helpful, supportive, and respectful rather than patronizing. Kropotkin's description of the young males who refused to rise when "ladies" entered the room but who walked across town to give lessons to aspiring female students is firmly based in reality. It is also depicted in *What Is to Be Done?*, whose major characters were based on real people.[18] Eventually women tried to act as their own consciousness-raisers (as in the Kornilova-Perovskaia and the Fritschi circles, among others);[19] and they even managed to reverse roles by teaching factory workers in Sunday schools and propaganda circles (Bardina and Krupskaia come to mind) or by educating politically unversed husbands (Kollontai and Dybenko). But the pattern of male teacher and female student remained a persistent one.

The device of fictitious marriage arose from the same impulse. Widely used in the 1860's and 1870's, it provided ample testimony to the aspirations for mobility of many young women of the time. Scores, and perhaps hundreds, of them felt trapped at home by their parents and the passport system, and yearned to go to a big city to work, study, taste life, and meet

[17] Stites, "M. L. Mikhailov"; N. G. Chernyshevskii, *Chto delat'?* (M, 1963).

[18] Among the myriad sources for these attitudes, see P. Kropotkin, *Memoirs of a Revolutionist*, J. A. Rogers, ed. (New York, 1962); Sofia Kovalevskaia, *Vospominaniia detstva i avtobiograficheskii ocherk* (M, 1945); Vodovozova, vol. 2; Solomon Reiser, *Artur Benni* (M, 1933); Kornei Chukovskii, *Liudi i knigi shestidesiatykh godov* (L, 1934).

[19] B. S. Itenberg, *Dvizhenie revoliutsionnogo narodnichestva* (M, 1965), pp. 142–44; Elena Segal, *Sofia Perovskaia* (M, 1962), pp. 62–124; Amy Knight, "The Fritschi: A Study of Female Radicals in the Russian Populist Movement," *Canadian-American Slavic Studies*, 9, no. 1 (Spring, 1975).

people. Hearing of their plight, young men offered themselves as fictitious husbands who would marry them in order for the women to acquire permission and the transfer of documents. Having settled his "wife" in a city somewhere in Russia or abroad, the young man was then expected to bow out. Though many of these arrangements blossomed into genuine marriages (Sinegub's is the best-known example), others turned out badly because of the problems of divorce, remarriage, illegitimate children, or because all too often the fictitious husband betrayed the code and demanded his conjugal rights after the ceremony.[20] All these patterns of behavior were echoed (or anticipated) in the fiction of the day, with familiar scenes of the bright young man from the town dazzling the manor house *baryshnia* (Turgenev, Krestovskii-Pseudonym), or of the poor student intriguing the isolated young townswoman (Pomialovskii, Chernyshevskii). Skabichevskii, in exaggerated but essentially accurate terms, described it this way: "The novels of the time could not begin in any other way than with the sudden appearance of 'him' who struck 'her' with the breadth of his knowledge and erudition, the depth of his ideas, and the dizzying novelty of his daring views."[21] The fact that these women were frequently disappointed, not to say repelled, by their original spellbinders—in life as well as in literature—did not prevent large numbers of them from continuing to succumb to the intellectual blandishments of radical or "nihilist" males.

The second point in the intelligentsia's unwritten platform on women had to do with their expected role in the revolutionary movement. With the growing presence of women in radical circles in the 1860's, a kind of doctrine emerged that might be called that of "the common cause." Its first explicit expression was in the illegal manifesto of 1869–70 addressed to women. Answering its own question about the correct path for women, it proclaimed the following: "Your cause is intimately tied to that of the entire mass of oppressed working people. Join them. Destroy the empire of the landowners. Destroy it and its legal framework which binds the people in oppression. Only then will a free field of women's work be opened; only then will your rights be equal to those of men."[22] Though vibrant and direct, the message was simply a summing up of what had been assumed in the day-to-day relations of male and female radicals. It meant that the intelligentsia ought to stop concerning itself about the "woman question" as such and concentrate on what N. K. Mikhailovskii called the "human question." It also implied that women were to be equals in the revolutionary movement. This principle was challenged in a number of ways: in the 1860's by the cynical and manipulative attitude toward women radicals dis-

[20] See Kropotkin; Kovalevskaia; Reiser; Chukovskii; and Vodovozova, vol. 2, pp. 255–57.

[21] A. M. Skabichevskii, *Literaturnye vospominaniia* (M, 1928), pp. 124–25. I am indebted to Abbott Gleason for drawing my attention to this passage.

[22] The manifesto is cited in Stites, "Women's Liberation Movements," p. 460, n. 2.

played in the Ishutin-Khudiakov and the Nechaev circles; and in the 1870's by well-meaning men who feared that the presence of women in "To the People" or in the factories might endanger conspiratorial work—as indeed it did. Symbolically, the psychological and numerical apex of female participation in the prerevolutionary radical movement was the Executive Committee of the "People's Will," a third of whose members were women, including one who directed the final assault on Tsar Alexander II. But even then, women were outnumbered two to one at the top and by a far greater ratio farther down the pyramid; and men still dominated the decision-making process and accounted for the formulation of theory—what little there was of it. In the next generation, roughly from 1890 to 1917, the Social Revolutionary heirs of the populist tradition retained the general spirit of the "common cause"; but the SRs and related parties (e.g., the Anarchists and the Left SRs) remained essentially men's parties, even though the last mentioned was titularly headed by a woman, Mariia Spiridonova.[23]

In terms of relations between men and women in the leadership, the Marxist parties made no improvement on the established norms. And yet it seems senseless and even anachronistic to carp at any of these radical movements for not having an even ratio in the ranks or in the leadership, particularly since no other radical movement in the West showed anything remotely close to the level of women's participation in the Russian revolutionary movement. What might be noted, however, is that the peasant-oriented parties never made any serious effort to reach their female constituents-to-be—village women. Here Marxist men made a somewhat better showing. Faced with the growth of feminist groups that were organizing working women, the Marxists were constrained to make a suitable theoretical response, the nature of which I will describe in the final segment of the paper. Male response to the imported Marxian formulas was ambivalent. The theoretical edifice was accepted whole, as were programmatic positions on such subjects as maternity benefits and equal voting rights. But the active side of things, a special "proletarian women's movement," was not so warmly welcomed. From the beginning (1905), a number of Bolsheviks, Mensheviks, and old-time Liberation of Labor figures (of both sexes) balked at the idea of an auxiliary effort for working women because it seemed to smack of bourgeois feminism. Neither Bolsheviks nor Mensheviks gave it much attention or support until around 1913–14, when both apparently realized that a large potential constituency was being neglected. They then launched journals and celebrated International Women's Day. The movement all but collapsed during the war but was revived in 1917 and later refashioned by the Bolsheviks as the *Zhen-*

[23] For recent treatments of the subject, see the chapters by Barbara Engel (for 1860–81) and Amy Knight (for 1890–1917) in Glickman and Stites; Robert McNeal, "Women in the Russian Radical Movement," *Journal of Social History*, no. 2 (Winter 1971–72), pp. 143–61.

otdel. But grumblings among male Bolsheviks about "feminist tendencies" hovered around this agency until it was abolished in 1930.[24]

We have been speaking thus far about the radical wing of the intelligentsia. But we must not ignore the extremely influential group that, for want of a more precise and broadly accepted term, we may call the "liberal intelligentsia." Though still operating from older bases—the academy, the professions, the Zemstvos, the press—this section of "society" had expanded steadily with the growth of the professional classes and, furthermore, had acquired dozens of organizational outlets for its opinions and activities (political parties, private associations, unions, professional congresses). These bodies gave structure to liberal opinion almost for the first time; lamentably, though, they have not yet captured the attention of many scholars in the West, despite the fact that the older generation of those very scholars was, and remains, very much in the debt of the Russian liberals of the prerevolutionary decade for their general views of Russian society and of its potential for development. I stress this both because of its larger importance for Russian historiography and because much of the sustenance for the legal side of the women's movement was provided precisely by these elements and their structures. A few examples will suffice. The Russian medical profession was not only far more generous than those in the West in allowing women into its midst, but was also active in such feminist-inspired efforts as the struggle against legalized prostitution. Professors, though occasionally capable of uttering silly opinions on women (e.g., that they could never be engineers because their long skirts would prevent them from mounting ladders), were for the most part exceptionally willing to give higher education to women as well as to write scientific or philosophical apologies for women's equality. The work of the Kadets on behalf of the suffrage movement, however grudgingly it emerged and however marginal some might think the suffrage movement was, was characteristic of the moderate liberal approach to the problem. Professor Petrazhitskii, an eminent jurist and a Kadet deputy, personified the entire liberal outlook when he made the first full-scale parliamentary speech on behalf of the economic, educational, civil, and political equality of women.[25]

The final legacy of the generation of the 1860's was a certain ambivalence (reinforced by reticence) about sex, marriage, and the family. The radical position was enunciated by Peter Zaichnevskii in the underground proclamation *Young Russia* (1862), which described marriage as immoral and which called for its abolition and for the public upbringing of children. Later comments in the Nechaev-Bakunin press were merely programmatic and unelaborated repetitions of this. Though it crops up again, the idea as

[24] For sharply contrasting appraisals of Bolshevik feminism, see Ann Bobroff, "Bolsheviks and Working Women," *Soviet Studies* (Oct. 1974), pp. 340–67, and Richard Stites, "Zhenotdel: 1917–1930," to appear in *Russian History*.

[25] *Rech' Petrazhitskago* (SPb, 1907); *Zhenskii vopros v Gosudarstvennoi Dume* (SPb, 1906).

stated never really had the solid endorsement of the intelligentsia. There is evidence that even the "Young Russia" circle did not take it seriously, though undoubtedly Bakunin and later anarchists did. It was repudiated by an important contemporary radical, Putiata, in his *Answer to "Young Russia."* Circles of young people debated the issue in all-night sessions over cups of tea. Proponents of abolition (reacting mainly against their own families) argued that the selfish and petty-bourgeois atmosphere of the family mutilated the social spirit of children, who, they believed, ought to be raised by the state. Their opponents stressed natural impulses of maternal love and the child's need for parental tenderness in the early years.[26] The two components of the radical program—abolition of marriage and the public rearing of children—were not seen to be separable, though modern society, Soviet and otherwise, has shown that the possibility of separating them has been one of major means of preserving marriage, though in a modified form. And though the human sanctity of marriage has been affirmed as part of the Soviet resolution of the "woman question," debates on the relative role of the parents and the state in child-rearing continue to this day to be staple items in the press and in sociological journals.

Those who accepted marriage—stripped, of course, of all its juridical and ecclesiastical impediments—then divided over the nature of that relationship. Some voiced scornful hostility to the notion of choosing a mate on the basis of "love," preferring to see the relation between man and woman as a partnership, a union of comrades in the struggle for progress rooted not in personal, erotic, or emotional attraction but rather in ideological compatibility. This idea made its way down through the years in various guises, reappearing in a rather virulent form as one of the notorious "Twelve Commandments" of that voice in the sexual wilderness, Doctor Aron Zalkind, who announced in 1925 that sexual attraction to a class enemy was as much a perversion as mating an ape with an alligator.[27] In practice, "mixed marriages" (even of different kinds of socialists, e.g., Sukhanov and Flaxerman) were exceptional among revolutionaries, though most of them seemed to have interpreted Mikhailov's idea of a comradely union as one that required mutual affection as well as political and moral unanimity.

Regarding the physical side of sexual life, there was also some divergence of opinion and difference in emphasis. The Chernyshevskii novel reflected this. In it one may find acutely sensitive descriptions of sexual ecstasy and of the positive role of sexuality in a Fourieristic cycle of work-pleasure-rest.[28] These are rarely mentioned in the endless commentaries on the

[26] For "Young Russia," see V. Burtsev, ed., *Za sto let (1880–1896)* (London, 1897), p. 40. Putiata's unpublished "Otvet 'Molodoi Rossii,'" is in the Central State Archives of the October Revolution (TsGAOR), f. 95, op. 1, d. 214, 11, 67-a/2 ob.-3 and is cited and described by the editors of Vodovozova, vol. 2, p. 539 (n. 2 to chap. 18). See also Vodovozova, p. 121.

[27] Vodovozova, vol. 2, chap. 15. Aron Zalkind, *Revoliutsiia i molodezh* (M, 1925), pp. 77–90 (the "Twelve Commandments").

[28] Chernyshevskii, pp. 186, 239, 338, 390, 410. Most of these passages cannot be found in the abridged English translation, *What Is to Be Done?* (New York, 1961).

book, even though the author's accompanying remarks about tasting wine and about "abnormal thirst" lend themselves nicely to any comparative discussion of Lenin's diatribe against the "drink of water" attitudes toward sex in the early Soviet years. The other aspect was the one-sided asceticism of Rakhmetov. Though it is true that real-life revolutionaries had little to say about the erotic joys of the future and tended to live according to an early version of "revolutionary sublimation," it is also true that most of them married or cohabited and thus saw Rakhmetov more as an ideal to be admired than as a model to be emulated. Throughout the nineteenth century, the radical intelligentsia neither exalted carnal pleasure as an end in itself, nor degraded it to a mere physiological function. They accepted it, in conjunction with emotional attachment; they doubtless enjoyed it; but they seldom reflected on it in public.

The "people of the sixties," though disagreeing on important aspects of the sexual question, did agree in rejecting the traditional family code and in affirming freedom and equality in sexual relations; and their notion of "free love" became part of the ethos of the broad intelligentsia. By the twentieth century, as one of the early historians of pornography put it, preaching free love in Russian society was like knocking on an open door. But this interpretation of free love laid heavy stress upon a more or less permanent civil or *de facto* marriage—and *not* on compulsive promiscuity. Among Russian Marxists, this tradition was reinforced by German Social Democratic doctrine on the subject, which, though somewhat reluctantly allowing for divorce, also stressed seriousness and permanence of sexual unions. The controversy over Artsybashev's novel *Sanin* (1907) revealed in a flash the moral solidarity on this issue among all segments of the intelligentsia, from the Bolsheviks and neo-populists to the liberals. They were all repelled—and they voiced their revulsion in remarkably similar terms—by the antisocial moral behavior of Artsybashev's vulgar and meretricious hedonists and their imitators among Russian youth.[29]

The widespread "social" revulsion against the individualistic decadence of the *saninshchina* so dominated the discussions of sex in the years before the First World War that nuances tended to be blurred. This is perhaps one of the reasons why Kollontai's early ruminations about a new proletarian morality passed unnoticed. Kollontai, though incorporating the old ethos of freedom and equality and repudiating the physiological crudities of the Saninists, also advanced a positive view of erotic pleasure (the "love game" and the "erotic friendship") that was clearly in the tradition of Fourier, Enfantin, and Chernyshevskii, though it was directly inspired by contemporary socialist interpretations of Freud. Published in the émigré press, her

[29]G. S. Novopolin, *Pornograficheskii element v russkoi literature* (SPb, 1909), p. 239. Contemporary reactions to Saninism are too numerous to cite here. For a sampling, see *Rech'*, May 27, 1907, and May 13, 1907; Ia. Abramovich, *Zhenshchina i mir muzhskoi kul'tury* (M, 1913), p. 92; B. P. Gorodetskii, *Istoriia russkoi kritiki* (M, 1958), vol. 2, pp. 575–76, 595, 686; Archimandrite Michael, *Zakonnyi brak* (SPb, 1908), pp. 1–11; *Russkoe bogatstvo* (June 1908), pp. 159–68; *Russkaia mysl'*, 29, no. 2 (Feb. 1908), p. 155–73.

writings created no stir in Russian society at the time (1911–13), though they were destined to do so in Soviet circles after their republication in 1918 as *The New Morality*.[30] Another reason why socialists did not launch a full-scale debate on sex was that most of them seemed to agree that the abolition of private property and all that went with it would bring the solution of the sexual problem in its wake. Few recognized, as did some anarchist writers at the very end of the tsarist period, that the enemy of woman's dignity was not only capital- and wage-slavery but also the masculine sexual authoritarianism of "bandits, rapists, bastards, cads, and literary seducers" who strove to conquer and dominate (*vlastvovat'*) her.[31] Fewer still could foresee that, in the aftermath of the Revolution, the banner of a new Saninism—however much embellished by slogans of proletarian morality—would be borne mainly by workers, students, and Young Communists.

Before turning to the major responses of active Russian women themselves, a few preliminary observations are in order. First let me say another word about the relative roles of men and women in the emergence of the woman's movement in Russia. Writings about it by Mikhailov and others did not create the "woman question." Had there been no large contingent of women in gentry and urban Russia to respond to these writings, the issue would have died of social undernourishment (as it did in Britain after the brief flurry over Mary Wollstonecraft's seminal but premature treatise of 1792). One need not embrace the cruder formulations of the relationship between economic crises and intellectual movements to recognize that ideas do not spring, fully armed, from the heads of publicists. There was a clear relationship between the existing or anticipated impoverishment of many landowners (with the inevitable dislocation of female dependents) and the alacrity with which notions of women's emancipation were received—and voiced—in the late 1850's. Dreams of independence, of migration to the city and a life of one's own, of work and action—in short, the whole range of social daydreaming so prominent in the fiction of the time—arose not only from the intellectual pull of the capitals and the spectacle of other people's emancipation, but also from the real or perceived economic squeeze at home, though the relationship between these forces was complex and interacting. It should be remembered also that the most influential writings by a woman, those of Mariia Vernadskaia (in 1858–60), were aimed specifically at preparing upper- and middle-class women for a role in the work force.[32]

[30] For the dating of these writings and their significance, see Richard Stites, "Kollontai, Inessa, Krupskaia," *Canadian-American Slavic Studies*, 9, no. 1 (Spring 1975), pp. 84–92.
[31] A. L. and V. L. Gordin, *Rechi anarkhista* (M, 1919), p. 106. The Gordin brothers viewed women as one of the five "oppressed" categories, along with workers, youths, minorities, and personalities. The sexual question in the Revolution is the subject of my paper "Eros and Intelligentsia in Three Generations" (unpublished).
[32] For documentation of Vernadskaia's writings, see Stites, "M. L. Mikhailov," p. 181, n. 11.

Second, it may be worth musing a bit over the kinds of educated women who rejected the women's movements altogether (probably the vast majority). Some were actively antifeminist (as well as antiradical)—for instance, the women who joined the conservative, racist, and antisuffrage Union of Russian Women; or the anonymous author of *Voice of a Russian Woman* (1906), who envisioned a monarchist, purely Russian and Orthodox utopia in whose National Duma propertied women over thirty would constitute 10 percent of the deputies and would discuss only laws relating to health, education, social welfare, and the amenities of life. There were also the self-made women who were rendered indifferent or hostile to feminism (or any cause) by the nature of their careers: we can cite the dancer Anna Pavlova, whose humble origins followed by a brilliantly successful life contributed nothing to her social consciousness; or the poet Zinaida Gippius, who recovered from her brief flirtation with social reality and then, from the aesthetic heights of her tower, poured scorn upon the feminists and vitriol upon the Revolution. Even a few socialist women—Sofia Dubnova-Erlikh, for one—felt the conflict between the attractions of Silver Age culture and the moral imperatives of a socialist sensibility, though all too few have told us much about these tensions and their modes of resolving them.[33]

If aloofness and hostility among women were the most obvious foes of the women's movement, a kind of female Oblomovism—apathy, impotence, and moral immobility—may have been the most insidious. There is hardly a better way to illustrate this mood than to offer a quotation from the diary of an educated, unmarried, twenty-five-year-old "superfluous woman" who looks bleakly ahead into the void:

I do not have the preparation, the zeal, or the perseverance for serious study. And now I am old. It is too late. You do not begin studying at twenty-five. I have neither the talent nor the calling for independent artistic creation. I am unmusical and understand nothing about it. As for painting, I have done no more than study for a few years as a schoolgirl. And literature? I have never written a thing except this diary. So only civic activity remains. But what kind? Fashionable philanthropy which is held up to ridicule in all the satirical journals? Establishing cheap dining rooms? That's like trying to patch up a piece of crumbling, rotting flesh. Opening literacy schools

For evidence of economic pressures, see S. S. Shashkov, *Sobranie sochinenii* (SPb, 1898), vol. 1, p. 858; S. S. Shashkov, *Istoricheskiia sud'by zhenshchiny* (SPb, 1871), pp. 312–13; Vodovozova, vol 2, p. 326; V. N. Shchegolov, *Zhenshchina-telegrafist v Rossii i za granitseiu* (SPb, 1894), p. 8; *Zhenskii vestnik* (Apr. 1867), p. 76; V. V. Stasov, *Nadezhda Vasil'evna Stasova* (SPb, 1899), p. 215; and Kovalevskaia's useful novella *Nigilistka*.

[33] The mission of the Union of Russian Women was to unify *Russian* women of all classes for the purpose of "elevating the well-being of the Russian people and preserving its peculiar creative character by practicing, studying, and upholding the Russian past, Russian art, and in general the immemorial creative foundations and national customs of the Russian people" (*Ves' Petrograd na 1917* [P, 1917], p. 1118). E. M., *Golos russkoi zhenshchiny* (SPb, 1906). See Temira Pachmuss, *Zinaida Hippius* (Carbondale, Ill., 1971) and Gippius' comments on the feminists in her *Siniaia kniga: Peterburgskii dnevnik, 1914–1918* (Belgrade, 1929), pp. 125–26. S. Dubnova-Erlikh, *Obshchestvennyi oblik zhurnala "Letopis"* (New York, 1963), pp. 2–3.

when it is universities that we need? I myself have jeered at these attempts to empty the sea with a teaspoon. Or perhaps I should turn to revolution? But to do that, one has to believe. But I have no faith, no direction, no spiritual energy. What then is left for me to do?[34]

As for the main components of the women's movements, the first to emerge, organizationally if not psychologically, were the feminists—a tiny group of educated and usually well situated women whose determination to focus on women and on "smaller deeds" than those that attracted the radicals led them to concerns that were more philanthropic than philosophic. Charity, education, self-help, and assistance to other women—mostly of their own class—claimed most of their energies. The charity, as usual, brought only modest results; but the feminist agitation for educational opportunities for their sex was eventually helpful, if not decisive, in opening university courses and a medical school for women.[35] In spite of some early friction between nihilist women and upper-class feminists in the 1860's, there was little contact and less hostility between feminists and radical women in the first generation (c. 1860–1880). Nihilists and radicals, having "solved" the "woman question" to their satisfaction, gladly enrolled in the courses that the feminists helped open and generally allowed their more cautious sisters to go about their legal business. The feminists, though eschewing radical behavior themselves, tended to look with sympathy upon the women who were bold enough to move into the forefront of the violent struggle against the autocracy. Even the later feminists, who were far more hostile to radical women, often looked back upon such women as Vera Figner and Sofia Perovskaia as predecessors and pioneers of women's independence.[36]

These later, political feminists were active in the women's suffrage movement that spanned the years 1905–17. In Western Europe and America at the turn of the century there took place a shift in emphasis from the older "organizational" feminism, crowned in 1892 by the formation of the International Women's Council, to the new "political" feminism, whose growth was spurred after 1904 by the International Women's Suffrage Association. The shift was reflected in Russia. During the Revolution of 1905, a new generation of women—impressed by the spectacle of political ferment in Russia and by the vigorous activity of their Finnish sisters, who won the vote within a year, and doubtless impatient with the slow and patient style of the older feminist pioneers—founded a number of women's suffrage organizations. The largest and most active by far was the Union of

[34] The diary is quoted in Iu. Elets, *Poval'noe bezumie* (SPb, 1914), pp. 33–38.
[35] For some documentation on the early feminists, see Stites, "Women's Liberation Movements," p. 462, n. 5.
[36] Kropotkin, p. 174; A. F. Koni, *Na zhiznennom puti*, vol. 4, pp. 326–29; I. S. Knizhnik-Vetrov, *Russkie deiatel'nitsy Pervogo Internatsionala i Parizhskoi Kommuny* (M, 1964), pp. 211–12; Valk, pp. 173–74. For the interesting attempt to relate the suffrage movement to the tradition of Russian female radicalism, see *Pervyi zhenskii kalendar'*, 8, (1906), pp. 335–43 and the cartoon.

Women's Equality (1905–8), which demanded a democratic constitution with universal suffrage, and which at its peak boasted thousands of members. Like the Kadet party with which it was associated by personal ties and mutual sympathies, it cast its net wide and sought to enlist under its banner women of varied social backgrounds—including workers. The Women's Progressive party, headed by Dr. Mariia Pokrovskaia, was smaller, more cautious, and less willing to work for women's goals in league with men. The Suffrage Section of the older Women's Mutual Philanthropic Society chose to operate almost exclusively by lobbying influential government officials and was quite willing to accept privileged suffrage for propertied men and women on an equal basis. The Union of Women's Equality disappeared in the years of reaction (1908–9) and was succeeded by the League for Women's Equality, which, with the Women's Progressive party and the Philanthropic Society, lasted until 1917.[37]

Cutting through these self-defined organizational lines, and at the risk of oversimplifying some very complex material, we may record the following main categories of the movement in terms of attitude toward two potential allies or enemies: males and socialists. The first category was composed of individual women who were male-oriented and liberal, notably Anna Miliukova, Ariadna Tyrkova, and Ekaterina Kuskova, all three of whom worked for women's suffrage but only incidentally and through male-led organizations—the Kadet party and the cooperative movement. The second and largest category was the liberal feminists, whose outlook was shared by the vast majority of women in the Union and its successor the League. It sought liberal—not socialist—goals, but preferred to maintain women-operated organizations that lobbied among and cooperated with sympathetic male groups without being absorbed by them; the Philanthropic Society simply adopted a more conservative version of this approach. A third category included women with more "feminist" tendencies, who were often members of the Women's Progressive party. Their thinking was given voice by the journalist Praskoviia Arian, who recoiled from joining a general liberation movement and advanced the notion of the "private struggle of small groups with their own demands, aspirations, and ideals" (i.e., an exclusively feminist struggle for and by women). Even within the Union such a woman as Anna Kalmanovich aspired to a more sexually militant movement, one wholly independent of untrustworthy men—socialist or liberal. The "social feminists," our final category, were too committed to an independent struggle for women's rights to join the "proletarian women's movement"—to be discussed presently—and were too sympathetic to working women to repudiate the socialists altogether, as did some of their comrades in the feminist movement.

The history of the suffrage movement and related feminist activities fol-

---

[37]The best treatment of Russian feminism in English is Rochelle Ruthchild-Goldberg's "The Russian Feminists, 1905–1917" (paper presented at the Conference on Women in Russia, Stanford University, May 1975).

lowed the general curve of Russia's social and political history between the two revolutions. Its heroic period was the years 1905–7, when the suffragists held huge meetings, secured thousands of signatures on petitions, lobbied among the parties and in the new legislative body, and waited with rapt attention as their well-wishers and their enemies debated the issue of votes for women on the floor of the Duma. A women's suffrage bill was in preparation when the First Duma was dissolved; the episode was repeated the following year in the Second Duma (1907). Suffrage activity declined precipitously in the following years, and most local groups either withered away or were restricted by the authorities. Ironically, during the very nadir of Russian feminism, the first All-Russia Women's Congress was held in St. Petersburg in 1908 with over a thousand women in attendance. But though the congress was important in many ways (particularly as a source of our knowledge of the feminists and their outlook in those days), it did nothing to halt the decay of feminist political work.[38] With the emergence of the League there was a revival of activity, and suffrage bills were presented to the last two Dumas—but again to no avail. During the First World War, Russian feminists—like those almost everywhere—lent their wholehearted support to the war effort in the hopes of being rewarded with the vote at the victorious conclusion of hostilities. We women, said the president of the League, must "devote all our energy, intellect, and knowledge to our country. This is our obligation to the fatherland, and this will give us the right to participate as the equals of men in the new life of a victorious Russia."[39] When the Revolution intervened, the sixty-year-old history of Russian feminism came to an end, to be replaced by a wholly new kind of women's movement.

It would be unwise to make too many generalizations about a group of people as complex and varied as the Russian feminists, but a few observations may help to put them in perspective. Their organizations, as in the West, tended to follow a standard pattern: there was a framework of general meeting, executive committee, and specialized committees; and there was a dynamic of self-perpetuated leaders, co-optations of friends, and infrequent internal democratic ferment. All the standard methods of agitation and propaganda (except that of the deed) were also employed—lobbying, petitioning, personal contact, and the printed word. In social composition—again as in the West—Russian feminism was urban and roughly "middle class" with an "upper-class" frosting. Whereas the older feminists came mostly from gentry-officer families, the suffragists of 1905 and after included large numbers of daughters of priests, junior officers, businessmen, professionals, and Jews. They were highly educated; in fact, trained professional women, especially doctors, dominated the movement as a whole. This was in contrast to the situation in America and England, where

---

[38] A detailed analysis of this congress can be found in Linda Edmondson, "Russian Feminists and the First All-Russian Congress of Women" (forthcoming in *Russian History*).
[39] *Zhenskoe delo* (Aug. 15, 1915), pp. 1–2.

the later feminist leaders tended to be wives of professionals rather than self-employed professionals themselves. Keeping in mind the problems involved in such comparisons, it might even be said that the Russian suffragists had more democratic social values than had the suffragists of the Anglo-Saxon countries. The outlook of the feminist intelligentsia, though ranging politically from an ultrademocratic liberalism to a vague and sentimental populism, was generally "social" (*obshchestvennyi*), outward-looking, public-spirited, and nonviolent. In many ways the Russian feminists were as much the spiritual disciples of the people of the 1860's as were the radical women who opposed or ignored them.

The women radicals, in life-style, appearance, and views of sexual and personal autonomy, drew much from what was loosely called nihilism in the 1860's. But they were not coterminous with *nigilistki*, because many of the latter hankered only after personal identity, not service to a "common cause." Most radical women ended by abandoning personal and professional fulfillment as well as feminist aspirations. But this was not always accomplished without tension and a phase of transition from women's consciousness to radical consciousness. Sofia Perovskaia, for example, was reluctant to merge her reading circle of young women with the Natanson group for fear of becoming intellectually dependent on males. Elizaveta Koval'skaia, who had taught women's rights and socialism in her Pink House in Kharkov, abandoned this operation and feminism to join the Chaikovskii group. Rozaliia Idelsohn's Women's Club in Zurich was founded so that its female members could polish their rhetoric and test their convictions without the threatening presence of men. But there were also women who had never felt the tensions of this transition, and their attitude toward feminism is tersely summarized in a quotation from Vera Figner describing Russian students abroad, many of whom became revolutionaries. "As a whole [they] were not proponents of the woman question and reacted with a smile to any sort of recollection of it. We had arrived, not worrying about being pioneers or about realizing the actual solution to this question; to us the woman question did not seem to need a solution. It was passé: equality of men and women, in principle, already existed in the 1860's and left to the next generation a precious heritage of democratic ideas." [40]

The new generation of radical women—SRs, Anarchists, Bolsheviks, and Mensheviks—carried over the tradition of fighting "shoulder to shoulder"

[40] Segal, p. 63; Itenberg, p. 157; J. M. Meijer, *Knowledge and Revolution* (Assen, The Netherlands, 1955), p. 69; V. N. Figner, *Zapechatlënnyi trud* (M, 1964), vol. 1, pp. 116–19. The quotation is from V. N. Figner, "Studencheskie gody (1872–1873)," *Golos minuvshego* (Oct. 1922), p. 181. For more particulars on the years 1860–81 and for some illuminating personal observations, see Vera Broido-Cohn, "Women in the Russian Revolutionary Movement" (paper presented at the Conference on Women in Russia, Stanford University, May 1975). The best work in English on the mood of women radicals of the 1870's is Barbara Engel and Clifford Rosenthal, eds. and trans., *Five Sisters: Women Against the Tsar* (New York, 1975).

with radical men. But now vast differences in style and ideology divided them among themselves as well as from the feminists. Older figures tended to become more conservative. Vera Figner, after 22 years of confinement in a fortress, held aloof from all parties for some time and then found herself amidst the feminists in 1917. Ekaterina Breshkovskaia, originally a self-styled "flame-seeker" who preached mutiny and agrarian terror, became a hypernationalist, pro-Entente, right-wing SR in 1917. And Vera Zasulich, who had helped launch the era of political assassinations in the 1870's, abjured terror altogether and became an adherent of Plekhanov's Unity Group. Most of the women of the SR party worked as teachers or Third Element technicians in the villages, spreading propaganda when suitable occasions arose. But others revived the violent traditions of the 1870's. In October 1907 the twenty-one-year-old Tolia Ragozinikova, ignoring Zasulich's 1901 pronouncement against terror, emulated her by entering Okhrana Headquarters in St. Petersburg with thirteen pounds of explosives strapped to her bodice and shooting the prison superintendent. A host of others, including the most famous, Mariia Spiridonova, committed themselves to individual terror and combat activities in which they took no back seat to men. "Experience shows," said a St. Petersburg prison official, "that women, in terms of criminality, ability, and possession of the urge to escape, are hardly distinguishable from men." [41]

Among the Marxist professional revolutionary women, there was a notable contrast in style between Bolsheviks and Mensheviks. Typical of the former was Elena Stasova, "the girl with the briefcase," whose precision, iron reliability, attention to detail, and worship of punctuality earned her the nickname "Comrade Absolute." Eva Broido, "the girl with strivings," was a striking example of a Menshevik woman, for they tended to be softer, more cerebral, and often Jewish. From modest conspiratorial beginnings as *Iskra* smugglers and distributors, many SD women developed into full-time, professional revolutionaries who could with equal facility deploy armed trolley cars in the Moscow Uprising of 1905, purge a local section of the party, or serve as commissar to an entire front in the Civil War (such were some of the activities of Roza Zemliachka). We can say that these young women with their strange underground code names (e.g., "Bunny," "Falcon," "Gangster," and "Beast"), were as important to this stage of the revolutionary movement as women had been a generation earlier—no more so. Apart from the psychological advantages their presence lent to the movement, the female cadres provided it with a significant reserve of talent, but always at secondary or lower levels of leadership. This pattern would be repeated with the Bolsheviks in the Civil War, when the female commissar stood beside, but slightly behind, the male commander; and it would be repeated in Soviet society at large after the war, when the trained Communist woman

[41] On Ragozinikova and Spiridonova, see I. Steinberg, *Maria Spiridonova* (London, 1935), esp. p. 89. The quotation is from *Zhenshchiny goroda Lenina* (L, 1963), p. 33.

acted out the role of deputy, assistant, or vice-director in almost every walk of life.[42]

Between the all-woman tendency of the feminists and the all-masses tendency of the "pure radicals" grew up a third response—Marxism. Since its theoretical dimensions have been ably explored in Professor Meyer's chapter, I shall focus my attention on its practical elaborations by German and Russian Social Democrats. Building upon, and partly opposing, Bebel's formulation of the "woman question," Klara Zetkin, a self-reliant former schoolteacher from Saxony who had married a Russian revolutionary, worked out in the years 1889–1907 a formula that may be summarized as follows: (1) class struggle supersedes sexual struggle, and thus the "woman question" cannot be solved by bourgeois feminists; (2) women must join the general proletarian struggle; (3) however, since women workers have particular problems related to their sex and are also politically backward, there must be a special effort within the socialist parties—but never separate from them—to organize and educate working women and to immunize them from the seductions of the feminists. This was the programmatic basis of the *Arbeiterinnen-Bewegung*, which was counterposed to the *Frauenbewegung* in Germany and elsewhere in continental Europe. By the eve of the First World War, Zetkin had institutionalized her program in a separate journal for working women, *Die Gleichheit*; in a network of women's sections in the German Social Democratic Party; and in a series of conferences of socialist women. But much of this had to be accomplished in the face of indifference and even hostility on the part of male socialists, who thought Zetkin's efforts smacked of bourgeois feminism.[43]

Zetkin's ideas were transplanted to Russia by Lenin's wife, Krupskaia, on the theoretical plane, and by Aleksandra Kollontai in the practical arena. The latter's independent awareness of the problem arose both out of her own background and out of the political temper of the times, though the immediate impulse to her activity was the effort of the Russian feminists to capture the allegiance of the factory women of St. Petersburg for their suffrage campaigns. Kollontai's response was encapsulated in Marxist ideology only afterwards in conversations with Zetkin. The Zetkin-Kollontai formula of radical devotion to the larger cause (which had indigenous roots in Russia) plus attention to the special needs of working women (which did not) was indeed a combination of socialism and feminism. As such, it was a distinct modification of the firmly grounded tradition of putting off the

[42]On Stasova, see her *Vospominaniia*, ed. V. N. Stepanov (M, 1969); and S. M. Levidova and E. G. Salita, *Elena Dmitrievna Stasova* (L, 1969). On Broido, see Eva Broido, *Memoirs of a Revolutionary*, ed. Vera Broido (London, 1967). Two complementary treatments in English of the revolutionary women of this period are the Knight article in Glickman and Stites (statistical and analytical) and Stites, *Women's Liberation in Russia*, chap. 8, sec. 4 (personal and biographical).

[43]Ganna Ilberg, *Klara Tsetkin*, trans. A. Shtekli (M, 1968); C. Zetkin, *Arbeiterinnen- und Frauenfrage an Gegenwart* (Berlin, 1889); C. Zetkin, *Woman Suffrage*, trans. J. B. Askew (London, 1906).

"woman question" until the day after the revolution. Because of this, it was opposed not only by those male "antifeminists" of Russian Social Democracy alluded to in the previous pages, but also by a large number of professional women revolutionaries who preferred to take their places in what Riazanov would call the "*muzhotdel*" of the party. For these and other reasons a coalition of *intelligentki* and working women—somewhat inflatedly called the "proletarian women's movement"—had to pass through two false starts (in 1905–7 and in 1914) before achieving either institutional status or operational success.[44]

A final comment—again about sex. From the 1860's on, women radicals had less to say about sexual ethics than did men—who said little enough. When women did voice an opinion or make a gesture, it was not in the direction of erotic self-expression. Some, like Mariia Kolenkina, who exclaimed "I love the movement," paraded their indifference to men; others were said to have sported "extreme ideas on sexual relations," though this almost certainly meant simply the code of the 1860's. More often we hear of women such as Perovskaia and Olga Liubatovich, who resisted men initially and then succumbed to love in a properly revolutionary liaison: technically illegal, but emphatically monogamous. Their marriages were, as far as we know, perfectly normal—or as normal as they could be in the conditions of underground life. If we look at another group of *intelligentki*, women students in the period 1900–1914, we get a similar picture: a few who despised marriage, a few more who contracted Platonic or "Tolstoian" marriages, and the great majority who married in the more familiar fashion. If we can judge by student questionnaires and other snippets of evidence, "decadent" literature and behavior had little or no attraction for most of these women, who seem to have been as serious (i.e., conventional) about sex as they were about their studies.[45] But there were also advanced women, Inessa Armand and Kollontai among them, who wished to explore the outer limits of sexual freedom instead of merely parroting the mellow radicalism of the 1860's. What was to be seen as excessive (and obsessive) curiosity on their part by influential Bolsheviks would eventually result in a mild reprimand for Armand (by Lenin) and a much sharper one for Kollontai (by the Party); and in the campaigns against the "new morality" of the 1920's, one could hear more than overtones of the austere revolutionary morality of bygone days.

[44] N. K. Krupskaia, *Zhenshchina-rabotnitsa* (n.p., 1901); A. M. Kollontai, "Avtobiograficheskii ocherk," *Proletarskaia revoliutsiia*, 3 (1921), pp. 261–302; A. M. Kollontai, *Izbrannye stat'i i rechi* (M, 1972), pp. 283–94; *Kommunistka*, no. 8–9 (Jan.–Feb. 1921), pp. 12–15.

[45] For the 1860's, see Lev Deich, "Iuzhnye buntari," *Golos minuvshego*, 9 (1920–21), pp. 50–51, 56–58; *Byloe* (May 1906), pp. 208–48, and (June 1906) pp. 108–54 (on Olga Liubatovich). On students, see *Slushatel'nitsy S-Peterburgskikh vysshikh zhenskikh (bestuzhevskikh) kursov* (SPb, 1912), p. 122; Elizaveta Diakonova, *Dnevnik* (2d ed.; SPb, 1905), pp. 122, 283; P. Ivanov, *Studenty v Moskve: byt, nravy, tipy* (2d ed.; M, 1903), pp. 99–102; G. Gordon, "Brak i prostitutsiia va suzhdeniiakh sovremennoi molodezhi," *Novaia zhizn'* (Feb. 1913), pp. 190–205.

Rose L. Glickman

The Russian Factory Woman, 1880-1914

THE FACTORY WOMAN in tsarist Russia shared with her male co-workers the travails, dislocations, poverty, and exploitation of early industrialization. Yet until the mid-1880's she was all but invisible to the public eye. To the extent that educated, moneyed, or official society noted her existence in the labor force, it was with the unquestioned assumption that she would work in the factory just as her peasant predecessor, or she herself, had worked in the village—the factory was simply a change of venue. The peasant economy had always been dependent on women's labor in the field. Though denied certain jobs by tradition (notably sowing and beekeeping[1]), peasant women participated in mowing, reaping, and threshing, as well as in tending the vegetable garden. And women had full responsibility for certain agricultural tasks—for example, turning, raking, and baling the hay[2]—and for all the household tasks, including childraising. Yet a woman's reward was hardly commensurate with her contribution to the peasant family's survival. The rigidly patriarchal structure of the peasant world denied her full humanity; as a proverb put it, *kuritsa ne ptitsa i zhenshchina ne chelovek,* "a hen is not a bird and a woman is not a person." Ordinarily, she was forbidden to sit in the village councils that determined the economic and civic life of the commune. Within the family she had no voice in the allocation of economic resources, for these decisions were made by the male head of the household in consultation with other male family members.[3] Married or unmarried, she had no rights of inher-

The author wishes to acknowledge a grant from the American Philosophical Society in 1973 that made some of the research for this paper possible. The present paper is part of a larger work in progress on the woman worker in Russian industry.

[1] V. A. Aleksandrov, ed., *Narody evropeiskoi chasti SSSR* (M, 1964), vol. 1, pp. 174, 465.
[2] *Ibid.*, pp. 174–82. [3] *Ibid.*, p. 465.

itance aside from her dowry and certain domestic utensils as long as a male relative lived. (The rare exceptions were widows, and even here attitudes varied considerably from one region to another.[4]) Thus the fact that women were doing hard physical labor as factory workers, or indeed, as any kind of wage earners, rural or urban, was not considered especially noteworthy.

The burgeoning proportions of the labor problem from the 1880's and the growing number of women in the industrial labor force elicited some slow and selective cognizance of the Russian factory woman, although her importance in the labor force and the magnitude of her problems were never properly recognized.

In this essay I propose to review the position of women in industry between the 1880's and 1914, the conditions under which they lived and worked, the responses of various groups to their problems, and, to a lesser extent, women's own attitudes toward their lives.

WOMEN IN THE INDUSTRIAL LABOR FORCE

Women had participated in nonagricultural market production from the very origins of Russian industrialization. An ukase issued by Peter the Great in his desperation to provide a labor pool for existing or planned factories prescribed that women in Moscow and the provinces who had been convicted of various crimes were to serve out their sentences in factories. Subsequent decrees ordered that the streets be swept clean of vagrants, paupers, and prostitutes, and that they, too, be assigned to factory labor. In March 1762, the police were empowered to distribute to factories in St. Petersburg and its environs the idle, able-bodied wives of soldiers, sailors, and other service people.[5] Later in the eighteenth century, however, women were increasingly recruited from "freely hired labor."[6]

Statistical data on factory workers for this period are sparse, and what figures exist are not broken down by sex. But we can be reasonably certain that within the textile industry—where the greatest numbers of women workers were to be found—about 18 percent of the labor force in the second half of the eighteenth century were women.[7] Nor was it exceptional to find women in other areas of production—for example, in mining and metallurgy, which drew indiscriminately from the serf population, so that women came to dig ore and do heavy labor alongside men.[8] By the middle of the nineteenth century, women worked only rarely and in insignificant numbers in heavy industry, but increasingly in textiles and other light industries. On the basis of official information gathered in 1859, we find that in

---

[4] Teodor Shanin, *The Awkward Class* (Oxford, 1962), p. 222.

[5] M. I. Tugan-Baranovsky, *The Russian Factory in the 19th Century*, trans. Arthur and Claora Levin (Homewood, Ill., 1970), p. 17.

[6] "Freely hired labor" refers to workers who were employed in factories on the basis of contracts concluded between the factories and individual workers, even though the workers might have been serfs.

[7] K. A. Pazhitnov, *Ocherki istorii tekstil'noi promyshlennosti dorevoliutsionnoi Rossii* (M, 1955), pp. 56–57.

[8] A. G. Rashin, *Formirovanie promyshlennogo proletariata v Rossii* (M, 1940), p. 51.

the city and *uezd* (county) of St. Petersburg women constituted 20 percent of the total labor force; but they constituted 44.3 percent of workers in the cotton-spinning industry and 34.2 percent of workers in the tobacco industry, the two industries in which they were most highly represented.[9]

Labor statistics, as students of Russian labor history are painfully aware, are flawed in many ways throughout the prerevolutionary period. For example, no one in the nineteenth century—or in the early twentieth century for that matter—could decide on the definition of a factory, so from one set of data to another the "factory" may vary from a small unmechanized workshop to an enterprise employing thousands of workers and utilizing sophisticated machines. Often the data do not address the same questions, so comparisons from one year to the next or between regions are impossible. The questions one might ask about women workers specifically are subject to further complications—it is often not clear, for example, whether the information pertains to all female workers, including children and adolescents, or only to adults. Nonetheless, from the mid-1880's there is sufficient qualitative and quantitative improvement in the data to construct a reasonably accurate and reliable picture for some areas of Russia and to discern unmistakable overall trends.

Of course, as the picture becomes fuller, it also becomes more complicated. What is true of urban factories is not always true of rural ones. What can be said of one rural area with some concentration of industry often cannot be said of another, owing in part to differences in agricultural productivity, in the types of industries, and in the division between local and migrant labor in the two areas. These variables and others influence the numbers, age, and marital status of women workers, and help explain why and how women were drawn into the factories.

The first serious attempt to compile information about the factory population as a whole came with the establishment of a factory inspectorate in 1882. The 48 European Russian *gubernii* (provinces) were arranged into nine factory *okrugi* (districts), each one under the supervision of an inspector and a small staff of technical assistants; the results of the efforts of the first group of dedicated and quite extraordinary factory inspectors were published in 1886. I have given the percentages of women employed in factories in 1885 in Table 1. In European Russia (exclusive of the Kingdom of Poland), women constituted 22.1 percent of all factory workers. However, it is noteworthy that in the three most heavily industrialized *okrugi*, namely Moscow, Vladimir, and St. Petersburg, their percentage in the total industrial labor force was substantially greater than 22 percent. This was partly owing to the fact that Russia's major industry—textiles—was concentrated in these three areas and made great use of women workers.[10] A

---

[9] *Proekt pravil dlia fabrik i zavodov v St. Petersburge i uezde* (SPb, 1860), in S. N. Valk, ed., *Istoriia rabochikh Leningrada* (L, 1972), vol. 1, p. 93.

[10] In Moscow *guberniia*, one of the six provinces in Moscow *okrug*, for example, 86 percent of all workers were employed in textiles. See F. F. Erisman, *Sbornik statisticheskikh svedenei po Moskovskoi gubernii. Otdel sanitarnoi statistiki* (M, 1890), vol. 4, pt. 1, p. 99.

TABLE 1

Percentages of Women Employed in Factories in European Russia
in 1885, by Industry

Okrug (with component gubernii)[a]	Pct. of women employed in selected industries			Total pct. of women employed in all industries
	Textile	Paper	Tobacco	
Moscow (Moscow, Tver, Smolensk, Tula, Riazan, Kaluga)	31.2%	47.2%	47.5%	31.7%
Vladimir (Vladimir, Vologda, Kostroma, Nizhnii Novgorod, Iaroslavl)	25.0	41.5	10.2	36.3
St. Petersburg (St. Petersburg, Olonets, Arkhangelsk, Estliand, Lifliand, Pskov, Novgorod)	45.6	28.8	84.3	36.5
Kiev (Kiev, Volynia, Podolia, Kherson)	32.2	27.4	22.7	10.1
Kharkov (Kharkov, Poltava, Ekaterinoslav, Chernigov, Oblast Voiska Donskogo)	54.7	27.3	56.9	22.6
Kazan (Kazan, Perm, Viatka, Simbirsk, Ufa, Orenburg)	40.0	—	—	5.2
Voronezh (Voronezh, Penza, Samara, Saratov, Astrakhan, Kursk, Tambov, Orel)	25.6	48.9	47.3	18.2
Vilna (Vilna, Kovno, Grodno, Minsk, Mogilev, Kurliand, Vitebsk)	39.0	30.0	59.4	16.3
TOTAL	36.7%	35.9%	46.9%	22.1%

SOURCE: Factory inspectors' reports for each okrug (all published in St. Petersburg, 1886). The form of the title in each case is Otchet za 1885 g. fabrichnogo inspektora ... okruga. The authors are I. I. Ianzhul (Moscow), P. A. Peskov (Vladimir), K. V. Davydov (SPb), I. O. Novitskii (Kiev), V. V. Sviatlovskii (Kharkov), A. V. Shidlovskii (Kazan), V. I. Miropol'skii (Voronezh), and G. I. Gorodkov (Vilna).

[a] I have not included the Warsaw okrug, which contained the ten gubernii of the Kingdom of Poland, because factory conditions in Poland were substantially different from those in the rest of European Russia and require separate analysis.

glance at the first column in Table 1 shows that anywhere from a quarter to over half of all textile workers in Russia were women. Yet these averages do not reflect the considerable variations in female employment from factory to factory. In Kazan okrug, for example, where women were 40 percent of the textile workers, the Stepanov cloth factory employed 590 men and not one woman. Similar examples can be cited from Kiev okrug, where the percentage of women workers overall was relatively small: the records show some tobacco factories where women were more than half the work force and others where no women were employed.[11]

[11] The Kazan example is from A. V. Shidlovskii, Otchet za 1885 g. fabrichnogo inspektora Kazanskogo okruga (SPb, 1886), p. 12; the Kiev one is from I. O. Novitskii, Otchet za 1885 g. ... Kievskogo okruga (SPb, 1886), pp. 42–44. Subsequent references to these and other factory inspectors' reports will not list the authors' names or the place and date of publication (all

Women were scarcely present at all in the metalworking industries, although again there are some interesting local variations, especially in areas with relatively little industry. In Vilna *okrug*, where metalworking was the third-largest industry after textiles and tobacco, no women were employed in the iron foundries; but in the manufacture of metal buttons and needles, women were as much as 89 percent of the work force.[12] Another area of high female concentration in some factory districts was the manufacture of matches: in Moscow *okrug*, women were 42.6 percent of the work force in this industry; and the figures were higher for Kharkov and Vilna.[13] In most other industries the fluctuations in the numbers of female workers were considerable; an analysis would require an intensive discussion of local conditions beyond the scope of this paper.

The government found the factory inspectors' reports of 1885 so critical of the conditions under which workers lived and labored that subsequent reports were not published until 1900. From 1900 to 1914 the reports were published again, but only as a *Svod*, or *Summary*, for all European Russia. The 1897 census, however, showed that the percentages of women working in textiles in the three major industrial *okrugi* had increased significantly since 1885. In Moscow *okrug* women went from 31.2 percent of the work force in textiles to 40.8 percent; in Vladimir *okrug* the increase was from 25.0 percent to a startling 42.9 percent; in St. Petersburg *okrug* the increase was from 45.6 percent to 46.2 percent.[14] The *Svod* for 1901 calculated that women workers were 26.8 percent of the total factory work force, pointing out that in the highly industrialized *okrugi* (and therefore in textiles) they were considerably more.[15] By 1909 the estimate was up to 30.9 percent.[16] It was noted that there was a slow but consistent increase in the number of women working in industries where they previously had not been employed—for example, in the sugar, glass, rope, cement, and brick-making industries.

The factory inspectors from 1900 to 1914 responded to this trend with some alarm, for it appeared that the number of women workers was increasing at the expense of the male work force. From 1900 to 1901, the number of male workers decreased by 13,000 whereas the number of female workers increased by 12,000.[17] In 1905 the senior factory inspector remarked hopefully that some of this increase might represent women replacing children and adolescents in the work force.[18] But by 1909 the trend was unmis-

---

are SPb, 1886). The titles will be shortened as in the Novitskii citation above. For a complete listing of these reports and their authors, see the source note to Table 1.

[12]*Otchet za 1885 g. . . . Vilenskogo okruga*, p. 23.

[13]*Otchet za 1885 g. . . . Khar'kovskogo okruga*, p. 23; *Otchet za 1885 g. . . . Vilenskogo okruga*, p. 21.

[14]N. A. Troinitskii, ed., *Chislennost' i sostav rabochikh v Rossii na osnovanii dannykh Pervoi Vseobshchei Perepisi Naseleniia Rossiiskoi Imperii 1897 g.* (SPb, 1906).

[15]*Svod otchetov fabrichnykh inspektorov za 1901 g.* (SPb, 1903), p. xiv.

[16]*Svod otchetov fabrichnykh inspektorov za 1909 g.* (SPb, 1910), p. xiv.

[17]*Svod . . . za 1901 g.*, p. iv.

[18]*Svod otchetov fabrichnykh inspektorov za 1905 g.* (SPb, 1908), p. viii.

takable: since 1900 the labor force had shrunk in absolute numbers as a result of economic crisis, the Russo-Japanese War, and the political disturbances of 1905; child labor had remained roughly the same; and employment of adolescent boys had increased slightly though with considerable variations from year to year. But the absolute numbers of women workers and their percentage in the labor force had steadily grown.[19]

Throughout the nineteenth century, it was assumed both in Russia and in Western Europe that women and children worked in the factory because mechanization eliminated the sheer brawn previously necessary in many industrial processes; and as mechanization overtook handwork, it was expected that women would be ever more employed. To be sure, the generalization holds true for some industries. In textiles, even in 1885, women were employed in consistently greater numbers than men in weaving factories using mechanized looms. The greater the number of mechanized looms in a factory, the greater the number of women; and, conversely, the greater the number of handlooms, the more men. In Vilna *okrug*, for example, handloom weaving was done exclusively by men; but in factories with mechanized looms, women made up more than half the work force. In silk and velvet factories, all mechanized weaving was done by women.[20] In Vladimir *okrug* women were 30 percent of the handloom weavers and 44.9 percent of the mechanized-loom weavers.[21] However, once we look beyond weaving the generalization breaks down. Even within the textile industry we find women heavily represented in some of the preparatory processes— like wool cleaning—that required physical strength and endurance but little skill.[22] The 1885 factory inspector's report for Kiev *okrug* noted that women accounted for 90 percent of the wool cleaners in the district (p. 44); the report for Kharkov *okrug* cited a figure of 89 percent (p. 19).

Nor does the generalization hold up outside the textile industry. The tobacco industry, for example, did not begin widespread conversion from hand to machine production until the 1890's (in 1890 only 13.2 percent of tobacco factories used machines). And factories relying entirely on hand production were still being built in the early years of the twentieth century. Yet this was an industry dominated by women workers throughout the period under consideration.[23] Moreover, in every *okrug* some industries requiring no physical strength at all, such as wine distilleries, glove and perfume factories, and mineral water enterprises, employed few or no women

---

[19] *Svod . . . 1909 g.*, p. xv.

[20] *Otchet za 1885 g. . . . Vilenskogo okruga*, p. 22.

[21] *Otchet za 1885 g. . . . Vladimirskogo okruga*, p. 19.

[22] "Wool trampling in wet clay (a primitive method of washing wool) is also done by women. This harmful operation consists of the following: scores of barefooted women, skirts raised high, trample in large containers full of filthy wool mixed with water and clay. This work becomes especially harmful as the weather grows colder in the autumn. The result is considerable muscular pressure on the legs, often leading to inflammation of the vaginal tendons characterized by cracking, pain, and inflammation of the skin." V. V. Sviatlovskii, *Fabrichnyi rabochii. Iz nabliudeniia fabrichnogo inspektora* (Warsaw, 1889).

[23] M. V. Dzhervis, *Russkaia tabachnaia fabrika v XVIII i XIX vekakh* (L, 1933), pp. 17–19.

workers. Thus although mechanization was without question a very important factor in the increasing employment of women in the factory, it was everywhere tempered by many other factors—by local economic conditions, by custom, and primarily by wages.

Throughout Russia, women's nominal wages were from one-half to two-thirds of men's in every industry and for every job—even where men and women did identical work, and even in industries or specialties where women predominated. Moreover, the de facto earnings of women workers could be, and often were, lower than these ratios suggest. After the prohibition of night work for women (see pp. 73–76), factory owners justified decreased daily wages for women on the grounds that night work was more demanding. Women were also highly susceptible to the system of fines by which employers were able to reduce a worker's nominal wage for numerous real or alleged errors in production. Women with children were particularly hard hit, for fines were levied against them—or bonuses were withheld—for various types of absenteeism over which they had little control, such as caring for sick children or taking time off to nurse infants. Where wages were based on piecework, the female worker was doubly penalized in these cases: she was fined for taking time off, and she was therefore less likely to make as many pieces.[24]

The increasing employment of women followed from the fact that women were cheap labor, but the relationship was not clear to early observers—not even to the most lucid and sympathetic. In 1884, I. I. Ianzhul, factory inspector for the Moscow *okrug*, predicted that "the more men's wages rise in the future as the techniques of industry improve and hand labor is replaced by mechanical devices, the greater will be the demand in our factories for female and child labor. The demand for men's labor will drop correspondingly."[25] However, it was not the case that the wages of men rose with mechanization; rather, mechanization made it possible to employ women in jobs that previously had been too difficult for them physically or that had demanded skills they had not acquired. The demand for cheap labor was nothing new, but as the tempo of industrialization quickened and as mechanization increased, it simply became increasingly possible to replace male with female labor. Moreover, women were hired with growing frequency to do unskilled, arduous hand labor. By the early years of the twentieth century, though, the factory inspectors were beginning to understand the importance of wages as a factor and were reporting that "substitution of women for men where possible is a positive preference on the part of

[24] There is no deviation on the question of women's lower wages and earnings in the vast literature that makes reference to it. See, for example, Ia. Mikhalovskii, "Zarabotnaia plata i prodolzhitel'nost' rabochego vremia na russkikh fabrikakh i zavodakh," in Ministerstvo Finansov, Departament torgovli i manufaktur, *Fabrichno-zavodskaia promyshlennost' i torgovlia Rossii* (SPb, 1896), pp. 465–492; V. V. Sviatlovskii, *Fabrichnyi rabochii*, p. 51; S. I. Antonova, *Vliianie stolypinskoi reformy na izmenenie v sostave rabochego klassa* (M, 1951), p. 170.

[25] I. I. Ianzhul, "Zhenskii fabrichnyi trud," *Drug Zhenshchin*, 5 (1884), p. 94.

factory administrations."[26] Thus in 1908 the senior factory inspector of
Moscow *guberniia* noted that "wallpaper factories that previously employed
only men are now hiring women. The Azibera factory, which manufactures
tin boxes, began hiring women in the soldering department, and now they
are employed in other departments and even work at mechanized lathes.
The substitution of female for male labor allows the factory to economize on
wages."[27]

The increasing prevalence of women workers stemmed not only from the
fact that they would accept lower wages than men but also from the fact
that since the promulgation of the factory legislation of 1882–83 the employment of children—like women another source of cheap labor—was
subject to strict regulation. Although the Factory Law of June 1, 1882,
made no mention of women workers, its effects on them were considerable.
It was designed to prohibit employment of children under the age of ten and
to establish an eight-hour day for children aged ten to fifteen.[28] Despite
confusion and misunderstanding on the part of factory owners—not to
mention deliberate evasions—the law soon produced perceptible results.
Child workers were replaced by adolescents and women, who, as one factory inspector pointed out, received the wages of children.[29] By 1885 in
Moscow *okrug*, the number of children in factories was 32.5 percent of
what it had been in 1882. Some of these child workers were not replaced at
all, owing to the economic crisis of the first half of the 1880's; some were
replaced by adolescent boys; but most were replaced by women. In cotton
manufacture women went from 35.4 percent of the total work force in 1882
to 39.1 percent in 1885; in wool they went from 28.6 percent to 32.5 percent; and in tobacco they replaced child labor almost entirely.[30] Since even
by 1885 the news of the law had barely penetrated beyond Moscow *guberniia*, the rate of increase of women workers was greatest there. In the other
guberniia of Moscow *okrug*, the rate of increase was in proportion to the
level of comprehension of the law on the part of factory management.[31]
Subsequent child labor legislation further encouraged employment of
female workers. As it became illegal—or at least more complicated (and
therefore less profitable)—to hire children and adolescents, the employer's
quest for the other cheap source of labor—women—quickened.

Closely related to the fact that women were cheaper to hire than men was
the conviction on the part of factory owners that women were the "calmer,
steadier element."[32] Women workers were definitely less demanding than
men, although, as we shall see, they were not entirely without initiative.
Relevant here is that the demands of most concern to factory administra-

[26] *Svod . . . za 1905 g.*, p. ix.
[27] *Svod otchetov fabrichnykh inspektorov za 1908 g.* (SPb, 1910), p. 12.
[28] M. Balabanov, *Ocherki po istorii rabochego klassa* (Kiev, 1924), pp. 267–74.
[29] *Otchet za 1885 g. . . . . Vladimirskogo okruga*, p. 30.
[30] *Otchet za 1885 g. . . . . Moskovskogo okruga*, p. 51.
[31] *Ibid.*, p. 52.   [32] *Svod. . . . za 1905 g.*, p. ix.

tions were obviously demands for higher wages; and to the extent that factory owners had less to fear from women, women were more desirable as workers. As the *Svod* for 1907 noted, "The increase in female labor is especially marked in the cotton-weaving industry, where the woman weaver is forcing men out. The reasons are the same as before. They are more industrious, attentive, and restrained (they do not drink or smoke), as well as more submissive and less demanding regarding wages."[33] These specific reasons for preferring women workers are not apparent before the 1890's, but with the great strikes of that decade and the events of 1905, factory administrations clearly perceived that their economic interests were best served by seeking out labor that promised to remain relatively docile, especially in demands for increased wages.

CONDITIONS OF WORK AND LIFE

The conditions under which factory workers labored and lived in Russia are well known: they were deplorable not only in retrospect but even in comparison with conditions in other countries at comparable stages of industrialization. The absence of safety measures; the disregard for ventilation; the primitive sanitary conditions; the long hours of arduous labor; the almost complete absence of regular procedures for hiring, firing, and paying wages; the wretched living quarters; and the humiliating treatment were shared equally by men and women workers. But women workers suffered in ways specific to their sex. Women working in the most deleterious industrial processes were forced by economic necessity to work through pregnancy to the very last moment with neither hygienic nor sanitary safeguards, and without physical respite. All observers remarked on the tremendous pressure felt by the woman to continue working through pregnancy and to return to work almost immediately after childbirth. Obviously there was no question of payment of wages during her absence; rather, the issue was whether she would be rehired if she left her position for too long a time.

Once factory women had children, new domestic responsibilities and burdens were simply added to their already long hours and exhausting toil. There were basically three alternatives for factory women who could not stay at home with their children. The first was to send infants to relatives in the country, if possible, or to leave them in the care of an elderly female relative or an older child who lived with the family.[34] The second, which was permitted only in exceptional cases, was to bring infants to the factory. This enabled the mother to breast-feed her child, although she was docked for the time she spent doing it. The last alternative, a practice that was observed in 1884 and that increased over the decades, was baby farming. This was an arrangement whereby elderly women near the factory or fami-

---

[33] *Svod otchetov fabrichnykh inspektorov za 1907* (SPb, 1908), pp. vii–viii.
[34] This practice has persisted in the Soviet period.

lies in the country earned income by caring for as many children of factory workers as possible. The system usually had unfortunate consequences for the children farmed out since profits could be increased by economizing on the youngsters' food.

The single woman worker had her specific problems, too. Though the disparity in wages—both nominal and actual—between men and women was unjust for all women, it was hardest on the self-supporting factory woman. She had to survive on one-half to two-thirds the income of her male counterpart, and even men's wages barely sustained any but the highly skilled workman. When a single woman had children to support, the burden became tremendous. The undeviating consensus from various budget studies, as well as from more impressionistic observations, was that female workers consistently ate far less than male workers and that their food was of much poorer quality. From a study done by the sanitary section of the Moscow *zemstvo* in the early 1880's, it would appear that the male cotton-spinner spent one-third of his income on food and the female spinner two-thirds; yet she consumed only 71 percent of the protein and 65 percent of the fat that he did.[35] There was no change in this situation over the years.

Single women working in urban industry, where housing was rarely provided by the factory, had the same problem with housing as with food. Because of their lower incomes, they spent a higher proportion of their earnings on housing than men did. More often than not, shelter for a single woman worker meant a corner in a room occupied by another family. Frequently, it was shared with a male lodger. In factories that provided housing (usually barracks), women shared with men cramped quarters, lack of privacy, poor ventilation, and primitive sanitary conditions. Many factories arranged for one bunk to be shared by several people, who slept in it by turns according to the shift they worked. The sensitivities of women were of little concern to the factory owner, who often installed single men and women in the same barracks room.[36]

Another disadvantage that all factory women experienced was lack of access to literacy. The problem of literacy in this context is an extremely complex one that is beyond the scope of this study, but the rates of literacy of men and women factory workers are an interesting gauge of the relative deprivation of women workers.[37] To be sure, more women workers than women in the total population of the Russian Empire were literate, just as

[35] Mikhailova, "Polozhenie fabrichnykh rabotnits na moskovskikh fabrikakh i uezdakh," *Drug Zhenshchin*, 5 (1885), p. 122. Though we would have to correct for the greater amounts of nutriment required by the average male, it is clear that a higher percentage of the woman worker's income went for food and that it was of poorer quality.

[36] M. I. Pokrovskaia, "Peterburgskaia rabotnitsa," *Mir Bozhii*, 12 (1900), p. 37.

[37] In order to deal adequately with this complex issue, one would have to break down the factory population into hereditary workers and newcomers to the factory (to take one example), since there is evidence that the latter tended to be drawn from among the most literate strata in their areas of origin—i.e., they came to the factory already literate. See V. A. Anderson, "Internal Migration in a Modernizing Society. The Case of Late Nineteenth-Century European Russia" (Ph.D. dissertation, Princeton University, 1973).

more men workers than men in the total population were literate. In 1897, only 13.1 percent of all women in Russia were literate, whereas 21.3 percent of factory women were.[38] The comparable figures for men in 1897 were 29.3 percent for the total population and 56.5 percent for the factory population, respectively. And despite the fact that the literacy rate for women in textiles rose to 37.5 percent by 1918, the level of literacy of women workers consistently lagged behind that of men workers to a very considerable extent. Consider, for example, the literacy rates for the cotton industry in 1908: 72.5 percent of the men in the industry were literate as compared to 25.3 percent of the women.[39]

OFFICIAL POLICY TOWARD THE FACTORY WOMAN

Official interest in the position of factory women was sporadic and inconsistent. Women and children were usually placed in the same category—useful but expendable—with the weight of sympathy, such as it was, on the side of children rather than women. The law of 1885 that prohibited night work for women (and adolescents) in the textile industry was enacted as much to ameliorate the severe economic crisis of the 1880's as to correct the inhumane conditions under which women worked. The negotiations preceding passage of the law illuminate the mentality of both industrialists and the government. In response to a government initiative, a group of St. Petersburg textile manufacturers gathered to discuss ways of easing the economic crisis. As the lesser of several evils, they opted for abolition of night work for women and adolescents; this, they claimed, would mitigate the crisis by equalizing supply with demand. The current economic difficulties were blamed on the widespread use of night work in the central industrial region and resultant overproduction. Behind this argument, however, was the long-standing competition between St. Petersburg and the central industrial region. St. Petersburg manufacturers stood to gain by prohibiting night work because cheaper access to raw materials, greater mechanization, and higher work productivity had already made it nearly obsolete in St. Petersburg. The Moscow industrialists, on the other hand, felt dependent on women's night work in order to compete with St. Petersburg and were vehemently against the proposed law. The ensuing debate reflected this ongoing battle, each side mustering morality and compassion for women to prove its point. To St. Petersburg's claim that night work was "physically excessive" and "morally harmful" to women and adolescents,[40] Moscow retorted that night work was no worse for workers than "the barracks and drinking establishments which existed for debauchery . . . and from which it is impossible to avert the working people."[41] In the end, a few of the big

---

[38] A. G. Rashin, *Formirovanie rabochego klassa Rossii* (M, 1958), pp. 579, 593, 602.
[39] *Ibid.*, pp. 579, 593, 598.
[40] F. C. Giffen, "Prohibition of Night Work for Women and Young Persons. The Russian Factory Law of June 3, 1885," *Canadian Slavic Studies*, 2, no. 2 (1968), p. 211.
[41] Balabanov, p. 278.

Moscow industrialists who could afford to dispense with night work de-
fected from the Moscow position and the law was approved. In its final
form, the law prohibited night work (defined as work from 9 P.M. to 5
A.M.[42]) for adolescents to age 17 and women in three industries—cotton,
linen, and wool. The law might have had very positive effects for women
workers, since the great majority of them worked precisely in those industries. However, evasions were difficult to uncover and punish, since the
factory inspectorate entrusted with enforcement of the law was far too limited in numbers and financial resources to do an effective job. Subsequent
legislation took away with one hand what it had given with the other: factory owners were permitted to hire women for night work in busy seasons
and to fill rush orders; certain industries were exempted entirely from the
night work prohibition; and night work was redefined to mean work from
10 P.M. to 4 A.M.

Between 1890 and 1899 a few *gubernii* attempted to regulate medical aid
for pregnant women. In 1892, St. Petersburg *guberniia* required that a
midwife be employed by factories where the number of women workers
exceeded 100. Similar laws went into effect in several other *guberniia*. But,
as a member of the medical profession pointed out, these laws were poorly
defined; moreover, in the majority of cases, supervision for their execution
was almost entirely lacking.[43]

Until the late 1890's the people most concerned about the wretched lives
of Russian women workers were the early factory inspectors, *zemstvo*
sanitary officials, and doctors. These were highly trained, well-educated
specialists who knew the conditions of Russian factories from years of study
and first-hand observation and who were well acquainted with the literature on factories, labor legislation, and workers' living conditions in Western Europe as well. Though at one time or another most of them held official positions, it would be a distortion to characterize their views on labor
problems as "official," for between the early 1870's (in some cases even
earlier) and the late 1890's they carried on a losing battle against both government agencies and industrialists.

Their attitude toward women in the factory was a fascinating blend of
pragmatism, sincere compassion, and traditional prejudices. This combination inspired them to suggest some very advanced solutions to the problems
of the factory woman and to ignore other obvious ones.[44] "If industry has
such a ruinous effect on male workers, as we can see from the data, . . .
then obviously the pernicious influence on women is far greater. In general
women have more delicate, sensitive constitutions and are more weakly

[42] A. N. Bykov, *Fabrichnoe zakonodatel'stvo i razvitie ego v Rossii* (SPb, 1909), p. 155.

[43] "Odin iz voprosov professional'noi gigieny v sektsii akusherstva i zhenskikh boleznei na
predstoiashchem IX Pirogovskom s"ezde vrachei," *Promyshlennost' i zdorov'e*, 8 (1903), pp.
147–48.

[44] The following general discussion does not consider nuances of attitudes among these
specialists, which deserve analysis not possible within the constraints of this essay.

defended against illness than men. Therefore all the harmful conditions of factory life reflect more harshly on women workers than men."[45]

Whether or not women are more delicate than men is a question that need not detain us here. What is important is that the people who knew the conditions of factory life from their own studies and observations perceived that these conditions—terrible for all workers—exacted a greater price from the woman worker than from the man because of her dual role as worker and mother. But the factory inspectors and other experts, unlike their Western counterparts, never proposed sending the factory woman back to some utopian rural bliss; they understood perfectly that women of the peasantry did hard physical labor and that this was appropriate to peasant conditions.[46] They accepted the fact that women were indispensable participants in industrial labor, and felt that female factory labor was necessary for women, for industrialists, and for the well-being of the entire nation. What they sought was to ameliorate and humanize the working woman's life. As they hoped for nothing from industrialists, they looked to the government to pass appropriate legislation to safeguard the health and well-being of working women. They envisioned laws to end night work for all women, to regulate factory women's hours, to prohibit women from working in especially arduous and dangerous industries, and to make medical facilities available to all women, especially mothers. For mothers, too, they envisioned facilities for the care and education of young children. It should be noted that they were often in advance of their Western counterparts in these demands. And they were optimistic. As the Moscow *zemstvo* doctor F. F. Erisman wrote in 1890: "Between the factory owners' following their own personal interests [cheap labor] and the government which is morally obligated to protect the weak and defenseless, there will be a new struggle which will have the same character as the contemporary struggle over child labor; but it will be played out on other no less important grounds—on the soil of the protection of women's labor."[47]

Unfortunately, such optimism was based on their own sense of justice, not on a realistic estimate of the forces ranged against the promulgation of such legislation. The anticipated battle for the protection of women in the factory never came to pass.

These dedicated, knowledgeable, and compassionate men were bound by the universal belief that primary to women was "the fulfillment of her maternal functions dictated by nature";[48] and though they had the facts and figures at their disposal to prove otherwise, they based all their analyses, predictions, and solutions on the assumption that all women were or would be married and would have children. In fact, one of the main reasons they felt it was important to protect the health of the factory woman was that

[45] I. I. Ianzhul, *Ocherki i izsledovaniia* (M, 1884), p. 381.
[46] Sviatlovskii, *Fabrichnyi rabochii*, p. 12.
[47] Erisman, p. 209.   [48] Ianzhul, *Ocherki*, pp. 392–93.

"the sacrifice of women's strength and health affects the future generations of the working classes."[49] Yet, in Moscow *guberniia* in 1885–87, 59.4 percent of the 35,890 women workers were unmarried. To be sure, between the ages of 20 and 50 only 28.8 percent were unmarried.[50] However, the statistics do not indicate how many women, married or unmarried, were the sole support of themselves and their children. And, the fact remains that most factory women were self-supporting at some time in their lives, and many were all of their lives. But nowhere in the proposals of the factory inspectors, medical experts, and *zemstvo* officials do we find a discussion of or a solution to the hardships of the single factory woman. Aside from the barbarous working and living conditions, the main obstacle to a decent life for the self-supporting factory woman was her indecently low wage. Nowhere is there the recognition that equal wages for equal work might be a just and tenable demand to make of either industrialists or government.

FEMINISM AND THE FACTORY

Educated and articulate women of the upper classes, conscious of the oppression of women in general, had very little to say about women in the factory before the mid-1880's. The *zhenskii vopros* ("woman question") debates were carried on solely by, and to suit the needs of, the intelligentsia. The factory woman's experience was so distant from their own that they barely noted her existence. Moreover, the major goal in the early stages of concern with the "woman question" was to find ways to release upper-class women from enforced idleness and economic dependence. To the extent that the intelligentsia was even aware of the woman in the factory, it seemed to them that she was already a step ahead—she, after all, already worked for her daily bread. One of the earliest journals devoted to women's problems, *Zhenskii Vestnik* (1866–67), carried only one article on factory women.[51]

Drug Zhenshchin, a journal published in the mid-1880's with the active collaboration of educated upper-class women, contained several serious articles on factory women, some of which were based on the most exhaustive data available. Typical was one that queried "Why does our peasant woman leave her deprived, laborious, but free peasant life in exchange for crowded, gloomy factories?"[52] The answer was the growing number of mouths that could no longer be nourished from the meager peasant allotment. What were the consequences of this exchange? The factory woman's low wages, poor diet, wretched living conditions, and long hours of hard work were all

---

[49] Ianzhul, "Zhenskii fabrichnyi trud," p. 101.

[50] Erisman, p. 71.

[51] P. N. Tkachev, "Vliianie ekonomicheskogo progressa na polozhenie zhenshchiny i sem'i," *Zhenskii Vestnik*, 1–2 (1886). This article, by the radical Tkachev, is long, complex, confused, and fascinating. His main point is that industrialization, which theoretically should have provided the working woman with the possibility of economic independence from men, was in fact a disaster for her.

[52] Mikhailova, p. 180.

carefully noted and lamented. But the most deleterious effect of the factory, in the author's opinion, was that it took the peasant woman away from her natural place by the domestic hearth, and was thus an "expression of the economic disintegration of the peasant family."[53] It followed that the woman worker was doomed to moral degeneration: "The constant combination of both sexes [in the factory] in the absence of a moral regimen which provides people with a settled domestic life with mutual, shared economic and family concerns cannot help but contribute to the degeneration of [women's] morals."[54]

The practical results of this concern were minimal and were merely extensions of the episodic philanthropic activities that had been aimed at the urban poor since the 1860's. In 1897 the Society for the Care of Young Girls was formed in St. Petersburg to "protect young girls, primarily of the working class . . . from the influence of morally damaging conditions of life."[55] The Society sponsored Sunday gatherings for women workers at which they were taught to sew and to read and write. They heard lectures on hygiene and religion, listened to concerts, and danced. About 200 young women came each week, mostly tobacco and textile workers, but some seamstresses from small workshops and a few domestic servants. The members of the Society wrung their hands in despair over the wretched lot of the St. Petersburg factory woman, but class condescension prevented them from seeing beyond the alleged immorality into which factory life led her. The goal of the Society was limited to providing a "bright and joyful moment" in the life of the factory woman in the hopes that it would contribute to her "spiritual well-being" and keep her from sin.[56]

But alongside this philanthropic outlook, a broad and increasingly sophisticated feminism was emerging as a generation of professionally educated women perceived another dimension to women's problems. The most articulate representative of this generation was Mariia Ivanovna Pokrovskaia, a doctor who had a profound knowledge of and compassion for factory workers in general and women workers in particular. For many years she practiced among St. Petersburg's workers, making her own independent studies and expending vast amounts of energy to bring the realities of the factory woman's life to the attention of anyone who would listen—women of her own station, the medical profession, the government. She had too much experience practicing medicine in the countryside to have illusions about the life of the rural woman and fully accepted the inevitability of women in industry.[57] She was a major influence in keeping alive some interest in working women within the feminist movement, which from its

[53] *Ibid.*   [54] *Ibid.*, p. 123.
[55] M. I. Pokrovskaia, "Peterburgskie voskresnye sobraniia dlia rabotnits," *Mir Bozhii*, 3 (1889), p. 4.
[56] *Ibid.*
[57] M. I. Pokrovskaia, *Kak ia byla gorodskim vrachem dlia bednykh. Iz vospominanii* (SPb, 1903).

inception in the early years of the twentieth century to its demise in 1917 was mainly concerned with the problems of middle- and upper-class women. But as the feminist movement grew in size and sophistication, as it began to attract women who were touched by Pokrovskaia's broad perspective and especially as it became politicized after 1905, the woman in the factory became a consistent, if minor, concern. The journals representing the various women's political groups from 1904 to 1917—*Zhenskii Vestnik*, *Soiuz Zhenshchin*, and *Zhenskoe Delo*—included many notes and articles, more informative than analytical, on women workers in Russia and abroad. The most conservative of the journals, *Soiuz Zhenshchin*, was "dedicated to questions connected with the struggle for feminine equality, mainly [women's] right to vote as the first necessary step on the road to emancipation," and was only minimally interested in factory women. *Zhenskii Vestnik*, on the other hand, edited by Pokrovskaia, reflected her approach and was more assiduous in the collection, publication, and analysis of information on the working woman. In varying degrees, all foresaw a women's political movement including women of all classes and felt that the vote would be the ultimate panacea for the oppression of women. In 1905 the feminists made their first concrete attempt to draw factory women into the struggle for political rights with the formation of four women's political clubs in St. Petersburg. The clubs functioned for almost two months before they were closed down by the police in 1906 after the dismissal of the First Duma.[58]

Until the last decade of the nineteenth century the radical tradition offered little more than the feminist movement did to the Russian factory woman. To be sure, in the early 1870's as part of a broad effort to reach the people, the *narod*, a few populist women assumed the identities of factory women and actually worked in the factories of Moscow and other cities. The exposure was terrifying. "I remember the Sunday night preceding Monday at 4 A.M., 1874, when Gravchevskii and I surrendered Betia Kaminskaia to the Moiseev factory. . . . It seemed to me as if we were leading this girl to some kind of terrible execution and that Subbotina wept as if foreseeing this execution."[59] A week later, "We greeted Kaminskaia as if we had literally not seen her for years. And, in fact, she had changed markedly, as if years had passed. Before she was rosy-cheeked and fresh. Now she looked pale, thin, and exhausted."[60]

The effort to contact factory women was fleeting, for the mass arrests of 1874 put an end to this phase of radical activity. Even before the arrests, however, there was dissension within the movement over the wisdom of subjecting populist women to the horrors of the factory.[61] Though the histo-

---

[58]A. Kollontai, *Sotsial'nye osnovy zhenskogo voprosa* (SPb, 1909), pp. 23–24.

[59]I. S. Dzhabadari, "Protsess piatidesiati (Vserossiiskaia Revoliutsionnaia Organizatsiia 1874–1877)," *Byloe*, 10, no. 22 (1907), p. 170.

[60]*Ibid.*, p. 171.

[61]*Ibid.*, pp. 174–75.

ry of radical attempts to work with women in the factory after these modest beginnings remains to be thoroughly explored, there is nothing to suggest that interest in awakening women workers to the possibility of radical or revolutionary action was programmatic. On the contrary, a common tactic of radical circles was to make initial and exploratory approaches to workers not in the factories but in the taverns—not a very likely place to run into women workers.[62]

CLASS AND GENDER

Most of these groups in the 1870's and 1880's fell somewhere on a blurred continuum between populist and proto-Marxist. As Marxist thinking penetrated Russia's radical oppositional movement, the importance of addressing propaganda and organizational efforts to factory women received a theoretical basis. The emancipation of women was an integral part of Marxist ideology. It clearly recognized the double oppression of working-class women—by virtue of their sex (which affected women of all classes) and by virtue of their exploited position as workers within a capitalist system. Moreover, it insisted on the absolute necessity of including working women in the revolutionary struggle, not only for their own emancipation, but for the success of the proletarian revolution as a whole. Thus, some Marxist circles of the 1890's made special efforts to reach factory women, usually with considerable success.[63] Sometimes this was done by male organizers and sometimes by female social-democratic intellectuals. The method followed the traditional pattern for underground activity in the factory. An *intelligent* made contact with a promising woman worker and exposed her to books, usually on a wide variety of topics. When she was considered sufficiently "developed," she was encouraged to assume a leading role in other groups. A number of women workers educated in this manner remained very active through the revolutionary ferment of the early twentieth century.[64]

Like every European country with a Marxist movement of any significance, Russia before 1917 had Marxist women leaders fiercely dedicated to the emancipation of women workers. And in Russia, as elsewhere, these women had to struggle on two fronts—the ideological one, against what were considered the conceptual errors of the bourgeois feminist movement; and the practical one, against the indifference or even hostility toward women workers within the Marxist camp. For though there was no lack of rhetoric about, and no absence of compassion for, the plight of the

[62] R. A. Kazakevich, *Sotsial-demokraticheskie organizatsii Peterburga* (L, 1960), p. 44; V. M. Sablin, *Protsess 193* (M, 1906), p. 21.

[63] V. M. Karelina, "Na zare rabochego dvizheniia v S-Peterburge," *Krasnaia Letopis'*, 4 (1922), pp. 12–20; O. A. Varentsova, *Severnyi Rabochii Soiuz i Severnyi Komitet RSDRP* (Ivanovo, 1948), p. 5; S. I. Muralova, "Iz proshlogo," in S. I. Mitskevich, ed., *Na zare rabochego dvizheniia v Moskve. Vospominaniia uchastnikov moskovskogo rabochego soiuza. 1893–1895* (M, 1932), pp. 153–55.

[64] Karelina, pp. 12–20.

woman worker, in practice women workers were always very low on the list of Marxist priorities.

The main reason for this was the pervasive and profoundly ingrained attitude toward women in general that the social-democratic leadership, worker or intelligentsia, shared with male workers. The experience of Vera Karelina, a woman worker active in the underground from the 1890's on and one of the social-democratic members of the Gapon organization, is typical. When she attempted to bring women workers to the attention of the organization (with Gapon's backing), she met with the following obstacles: "Then the masses of workers held the opinion that any social activity was not a woman's business. She has her own business—at the factory, the machine; at home, the children, the diapers and the pots. I recall what I had to put up with when the question of female membership in the *Obshchestvo* was discussed. There was not a single mention of the woman worker, as if she were entirely nonexistent, as if she were some kind of appendage— despite the fact that there were industries in which the workers were exclusively women."[65] Nonetheless, Karelina managed to form women's sections within the Gapon organization, to which women workers flocked. But she shouldered the burden alone: "A few times the attempt was made to attract women of the intelligentsia to this activity. But the same general alienation and hostility to working with women that existed in intelligentsia sections . . . was an obstacle."[66]

The stormy events of 1905, the strike movement, and the tremendous outburst of union organization provide further evidence of how revolutionary parties and the industrial proletariat regarded women workers in practice. In principle, most unions—with a few exceptions—were not against including women workers, but very little energy was directed at organizing or educating them.[67] The leaders of the Bolshevik-dominated textile unions of the Moscow region, for example, at their first regional conference in February 1906, noted that "in the textile industry women are a very significant part, at times the overwhelming majority of workers, and that women's labor increases day by day." They further considered that "the only solution to the problems of improving the position of the working class in general, and of women in particular, is organization of the proletariat." Given that "women, because of their economic and domestic situation, are much less capable of defending themselves against the bondage and exploitation of capital," the conference proposed that "all measures be taken to attract women on an equal basis with men into unions and all other workers' organizations."[68] What these measures should be and how the proposal

[65] V. M. Karelina, "Rabotnitsa v Gaponovskikh obshchestvakh," in P. F. Kudelli, ed., *Rabotnitsa v 1905 g. v S-Peterburge* (L, 1926), p. 14.

[66] V. Sviatlovskii, *Professional'noe dvizhenie v Rossii* (SPb, 1907), p. 83.

[67] K. Dmitriev (P. N. Kolokol'nikov), *Professional'noe dvizhenie i soiuzy v Rossii* (SPb, 1909), pp. 61–62.

[68] M. Zaiats, *Tekstily v gody pervoi revoliutsii, 1905–1907* (M, 1925), p. 186.

might be implemented were not discussed. Nor is it likely that the leaders of the unions, social-democratic or otherwise, had much more than a rhetorical interest in the problem. The strike literature of the 1905–7 period clearly shows that—whatever lip service was paid to the importance of including women in strike and union activities—the exhortations to *action* were addressed to the "true *sons* of the army of labor whose name is proletariat."[69] In a call to "*all* textile workers" of the Moscow region in 1907, the workers were asked to "Stop and look at your endless tortured labor, . . . at your constant unfulfilled needs, at your *wives'* tears"[70] (emphases mine). In short, in real situations as opposed to paper ones, the workers called to action were envisaged as exclusively male. The examples are legion.

To be sure, actual strike demands throughout 1905–7 more often than not reflected women workers' needs. There is scarcely a strike document—in industries employing women—that does not mention, in some form, demands for paid maternity leave (usually four weeks before and six weeks after childbirth), for time off for feeding infants, and for construction of nurseries at the factory.

But these kinds of demands, of course, were strictly related to the woman worker's maternal or domestic functions. In a 1907 textile strike in Ivanovo-Voznesensk, strikers even demanded that women be released for half a day to launder clothes.[71] The demand for equal wages for men and women workers, though now heard with some frequency, was by no means universal. And there were cases where an explicit minimum wage was requested with lower rates for women than for men.[72]

It is not surprising, then, that the number of women workers in unions was far less than the number of men; moreover, it was considerably less than the proportion of women in the industrial work force would lead us to expect. In Moscow in 1907, for example, women were only 4.4 percent of union members.[73] They were somewhat better represented in the rest of the central industrial region and especially in St. Petersburg, but the percentages never reached impressive proportions.[74]

It should be noted, however, that women workers were not always passive, that they did not invariably conform to the employers' stereotype of a "calmer, steadier element." In 1878 some 300 women tobacco workers from two St. Petersburg factories marched en masse to negotiate with the management over arbitrarily lowered piecework rates. When the management responded with curses and threats, the women returned to the factories to throw everything—tools and furniture—out the windows. The manage-

---

[69] Iu. Milonov, *Moskovskoe professional'noe dvizhenie v gody pervoi revoliutsii* (M, 1925), p. 408.
[70] Zaiats, p. 235.
[71] *Ibid.*, p. 256.
[72] A. Pankratova, *1905. Stachechnoe dvizhenie* (M-L, 1925), pp. 269–70.
[73] Milonov, pp. 383–87.
[74] P. Kolokol'nikov, "Otryvki iz vospominaniia," in *Materialy po istorii professional'nogo dvizheniia v Rossii*, Sbornik 4 (M, 1925), pp. 269–70.

ment acceded to their demands.[75] From that time on there is ample evidence of women's participation in every type of workers' protest. Examples range from a rowdy strike initiated by women workers in the St. Petersburg tobacco factory of Laferm in 1895 to a massive strike, also in 1895, at a weaving factory in Ivanovo-Voznesensk where several women were among the 25 workers who negotiated with the factory management.[76]

What this and other evidence suggests is that as long as protest was spontaneous, as long as it remained in a relatively unideological, unorganized stage and was therefore not "bureaucratized," women workers were capable of manifesting their discontent in concrete ways. But as soon as protests began to assume more organized forms, from the time of the formation of the Gapon organization through the rest of the prerevolutionary period, women workers seemed unable to sustain consistent participation. This cannot simply be put down to the insensitivity of male-dominated unions and political groups toward working women, and to the unwillingness of male activists to solicit female support. To understand this development we must recognize the complex relationship between men's attitudes toward women workers and women's own image of themselves; and we must recall the low levels of female literacy, the low incomes of women vis-à-vis those of men, the double role of laboring women as both workers and mothers, and the general psychological makeup of women. Vera Karelina expressed the feelings of women workers toward participation in workers' groups: "Well, I do want to express myself, but then I think it over—so many people, they will all be looking at me and what if someone laughs at what I say. . . . I grow cold with these thoughts, I'm filled with terror. So—you sit silently, but your heart is enflamed." [77]

From the mid-1880's the factory woman's existence began to penetrate public awareness and the hardships unique to her situation assumed the dimensions of a social problem. Yet, as a social problem she was treated as a minor appurtenance to some related issue. She was the occasional recipient of philanthropic sympathy directed at the urban poor in general. She was an appendage to a broader labor problem; amelioration of the conditions of her life was sometimes seen as a partial solution to the problems of labor unrest or as a way to insure future generations of healthy workers. From time to time populist activists caught a glimpse of her within the factory walls and made desultory efforts to include her in their tactical calculations. Concern for the factory woman grew somewhat more intense at the beginning of the twentieth century. First, official Russia, with some astonishment, began to

[75] *Zemlia i Volia*, 3 (Jan. 15, 1879), p. 2, cited in V. Iakovlev, *Revoliutsionnaia zhurnalistika 70kh godov* (Paris, 1905), pp. 296–98.

[76] A. Katz, "Khronika professional'nogo dvizheniia rabochikh v Rossii (1890–1903)," in *Materialy*, Sbornik 1 (1924), p. 174. "Stachka tkachei Ivanovo-Voznesenskoi manufaktury v 1895," *Krasnyi arkhiv*, 5, no. 72 (1935). p. 117.

[77] Karelina, "Rabotnitsa," p. 15.

take serious note of the growing numbers of women in the factory, partly because the increase was at the expense of male labor. Second, feminism evolved into a cohesive movement that maintained a peripheral but consistent solicitude for women workers. Third, the Marxist opponents of tsarist Russia, armed with an ideology that included women among the victims of capitalist exploitation, perceived women workers as important allies and attempted, at least sporadically, to draw them into revolutionary struggle. But throughout the period under consideration the woman worker remained a bas-relief rather than a freestanding figure. Her full historical dimensions remain to be further investigated and revealed.

Alfred G. Meyer

Marxism and the Women's Movement

THE RELATIONSHIP between Marxism and the women's movement has been like many a bourgeois marriage: an initial strong mutual attraction has been followed by lingering disillusionment; and persistent claims to superiority made by the male proletarian movement have evoked responses from the women ranging from total submission through bewilderment to rebellion and separation, although often the two have stayed together for decency's (or appearances') sake.

In this paper I shall explore the theoretical and practical considerations underlying the relationship between Marxism and feminism before the First World War. I shall also cast a casual glance at the tactical and organizational conclusions the Marxist movement has drawn from these considerations. What generalizations I make will refer to the founders of the movement and to the first generation of their followers in Europe and North America.

My limited familiarity with the women's movement in nineteenth-century Russia has led me to believe that its relationship with the Russian revolutionary movement was somewhat different from the troubled interaction between feminism and revolutionary movements in the Western countries. Yet the difference appears to be most pronounced with reference to Russian revolutionary populism and "nihilism," and least important in the case of the Marxist movement.[1] Of course, the question of whether Marxism is relevant for an understanding of the Russian Revolution and the subsequent development of Soviet society has remained controversial. Readers of this volume will be able to judge for themselves the relevance of that aspect of Marxism discussed here to Soviet social experience.

[1] This is made clear in an excellent article by Aileen Kelly, "Revolutionary Women," in *New York Review of Books*, 22, no. 12 (July 17, 1975), pp. 20–22.

When Marx and Engels began to formulate their ideas in the mid-1840's, they clearly and repeatedly expressed their concern with the oppression of women in contemporary society. Both obviously were deeply impressed by the writings of Charles Fourier—particularly Engels, who throughout his life continued to express his admiration for this early socialist. In their first joint work, Marx and Engels cited with approval Fourier's statement that "the change in a historical era can always be determined by the progress of women toward freedom, for the victory of human nature is most evident in the relation of women to men, of the weak to the strong. The degree of the emancipation of women is the natural measure of general emancipation."[2] Marx urged his readers to recognize that the general position of women in contemporary society was inhuman, quoted Fourier's denunciation of bourgeois marriage as intensified prostitution, and then once more cited Fourier at length:

The transformation of a historical era can always be determined by the condition of progress of women toward liberty, because it is here, in the relation of women to men, of the weak to the strong, that the victory of human nature over brutality appears most evident. The degree of female emancipation is the natural measure of general emancipation.

The humiliation of the female sex is an essential characteristic of civilization as well as barbarism, only with the difference that civilized order raises every vice, which barbarism practices in a simple manner, to a form of existence that is composite, ambiguous, deceptive, and hypocritical. Nobody is hit more profoundly than the man by being condemned to keep women in slavery.[3]

Such abstract recognition of the humiliation of women in modern society was matched in some of the early works of Marx and Engels by concern specifically with the sufferings of proletarian women, with the disintegration of the proletarian family, and with the problem of prostitution. In his *The Condition of the Working Class in England*, Engels goes into these

[2]This seems to be Marx's paraphrasing of the following passage from Charles Fourier's *Théorie des quatre mouvements et des destinées générales*, quoted in Jonathan Beecher and Richard Bienvenu, eds., *The Utopian Vision of Charles Fourier* (Boston, 1971), pp. 195–96: "*Social progress and changes of period are brought about by virtue of the progress of women toward liberty, and social retrogression occurs as a result of a diminution in the liberty of women.* Other events influence these political changes; but there is no cause which produces social progress or decline as rapidly as a change in the condition of women. . . . In summary, *the extension of the privileges of women is the fundamental cause of all social progress.*" I am grateful to Nannerl O. Keohane for pointing out the significance of the liberties Marx took in translating this passage: what Fourier asserts to be a *cause* of progress Marx turns into a *measure*, an indicator, of progress, which shows that his notion of progress was markedly different from that of Fourier. Moreover, the importance of women's liberation differed in the two men's overall schemes. (Compare these statements by Marx and Fourier with those of Speranskii and Herder cited in fn. 80, p. 28 above.—Ed.)

[3]Marx and Engels, *Die heilige Familie*, in Marx and Engels, *Werke* (Berlin, 1968–71; hereinafter cited as MEW), vol. 2, pp. 205–8. All translations in this paper are my own. For other expressions of their general appreciation of Fourier's work, see Marx and Engels, *Die deutsche Ideologie* (MEW, vol. 3), pp. 498–503; and Engels, *Die Entwicklung des Sozialismus von der Utopie zur Wissenschaft* (MEW, vol. 19), pp. 188–97.

matters at length; and Marx, in his "Economic-Philosophic Manuscripts of 1844," has obviously drawn on Engels's accounts as well as on French economists in order to make some remarks about proletarian women.[4] In later years Marx also incorporated material on the condition of women in *Capital*.

Prostitution in particular is a theme that Engels returned to on various occasions, never treating it at great length, but always regarding prostitutes with sympathy, as victims of capitalist society. Prostitution, he wrote in 1847, is "the most corporeal exploitation of the proletariat by the bourgeoisie." It is that aspect of exploitation where all pious sentiments are revealed to be bankrupt and the most vengeful class hatred comes in.[5] Indeed, for both Engels and Marx the prostitute was, in a sense, the paradigmatic victim of capitalism. For them, after all, capitalism was a system kept in motion by the overwhelming drive to accumulate; it transformed all human relations into marketable commodities. Human labor was seen as a means of production, and human beings were seen as instruments. Women in this system become instruments of production, reproduction, and gratification, as Engels pointed out in his *Principles of Communism*,[6] a passage that reappeared, slightly altered, in the *Communist Manifesto*. Love, like all other human emotions, has been turned into a marketable commodity, and capitalist society thus has become a giant whorehouse. Money, wrote Marx in the "Economic-Philosophic Manuscripts of 1844," "is the universal whore, the universal pimp of human beings and nations"; and in subsequent passages he continued to use language suggestive of erotic imagery to describe this all-pervasive prostitution:

Whoever can buy bravery is brave even though he is a coward. Since money is exchangeable, not for a specific quality, a specific thing, or [specific] forces of the human essence, but for the entire human and natural world of things, therefore, seen from the point of view of its possessors, it exchanges every quality for every other quality, even though it be a contradictory quality or thing; money means the fraternization of impossibilities, it coerces the diametrically opposed into intimacy [*es zwingt das sich Widersprechende zum Kuss*].

Posit the *human being* as *human being*, and his/her relationship to the world as human; then love can be exchanged only for love, confidence only for confidence, etc. . . . Every one of your relationships to human beings—and to nature—must be a *determined expression* of your *actual individual* life corresponding to the object of your will. If you love without evoking reciprocating love—i.e., if your loving, as loving, does not produce reciprocating love, if you through your *expressing your life* as a loving human being do not make yourself into a *loved human being*—then your love is powerless and a misfortune.[7]

---

[4] See, for instance, MEW *Ergänzungsband* (Supplementary Volume) 1, p. 481.
[5] Engels, "Die wahren Socialisten" (MEW, vol. 4), p. 267.
[6] *Ibid.*, p. 377.
[7] Marx, "Economic-Philosophic Manuscripts of 1844" (MEW, *Ergänzungsband* 1), pp. 565–67. Other translations I have seen somehow obscure the erotic overtones of Marx's words.

The sympathy Marx and Engels express for women in their degradation, and for the universal degradation and corrosion of all human relationships in capitalist society, is thus an expression of their general humanism. The oppression of women is perhaps no more than an example of the oppression of all—though Marx, again echoing Fourier, suggests that it might be regarded as the most blatant or most significant of all the oppressive relationships:

The infinite degradation in which the human being exists for him/herself is expressed in the relationship between man and *woman*. . . .

The immediate, natural, necessary relationship of one human being to another is the relationship between *man* and *woman*. In this *natural* special relationship, the human being's relation to nature is immediately his/her relationship to the human being, just as the relationship to human beings is immediately his/her relationship to nature, his/her *natural* determination. Thus the measure in which the human essence has become nature for the human being *manifests* itself *sensually*, i.e., reduced to an observable *fact*, in this relationship. Hence on the basis of this relationship one can judge the entire stage of development [*Bildungsstufe*] of the human being. From the character of this relationship one can conclude how far the human being as a *species being*, and a *human being*, has become him/herself and grasped him/herself; the relationship of male to female is the *most natural* relationship of human to human. It therefore reveals the degree to which a person's *natural* behavior has become *human* or to which the human essence has become *natural* essence for him or her, to which human nature has become *nature* for this person. The relationship also reveals the extent to which a human being's need has turned into *human* need, to which therefore the *other* human being, as human being, has become his/her need, to which he/she in his/her most individual existence is at the same time a social being.[8]

In all its opaqueness, this passage in effect restates the sentiments of Fourier, quoted earlier in this paper, and incorporates them in the Marxist theory of alienation. Let this be stated baldly here, because it would require much too much space to explain it.[9]

Everything Marx and Engels wrote about prostitution could easily be integrated with what Marx said about hucksterism in such works as *The Poverty of Philosophy* or the essay *On the Jewish Question*, so that his remarks concerning the emancipation of the Jews could be applied, by analogy, to the emancipation of women. Hence one could conclude, by analogy, that all attempts at emancipation *into politics* are false as long as politics remains the communal life of alienated and selfish human beings. Genuine emancipation can only be a universal human emancipation that includes the emancipation from selfishness, acquisitiveness, religion, ideology, class interest, and other aspects of alienation.

[8]*Ibid.*, p. 533.
[9]With only slight reservations, I accept the interpretation of Marx's theory of alienation offered by Bertell Ollman in *Alienation: Marx's Conception of Man in Capitalist Society* (Cambridge, Eng., 1971).

Further, just as the demand for emancipation within the system hides the facts that, first, the system already is thoroughly Jewish, if Jewishness is identified with acquisitiveness, and, second, that the Jews in fact already are emancipated, since all Christians have become "Jews," so, again by analogy, one could imagine Marx arguing that all human beings in capitalism have become pimps and prostitutes. Indeed, he and Engels can be interpreted as implying that capitalism has turned most men into women, just as it has turned many women into men, in both cases robbing them of their humanity.

However convoluted some of their prose, it is obvious that Marx and Engels were advanced and libertarian in their concern with the oppression of women—at least when compared to established opinion in the middle of the last century, which took women's inferiority to men for granted. Nor is there any evidence that they ever repudiated this general position. Yet from the point of view of anyone sympathizing with the women's movement, their stand is not very satisfactory, since it is too abstract and, at least in the form in which I have presented it so far, totally unrelated to any action program. It has this in common, of course, with the general liberational philosophy elaborated by Marx and Engels in the first few years of their collaboration.

As the two young men developed their theory, they concentrated their attention more and more on what they considered to be the principal key to the understanding of capitalist society—its class structure. Everything they examined, including the oppression of women and the relationship between the sexes within and outside the family, was to be understood in its functional relationship to the class structure and the class struggle. The first step Marx and Engels took in this direction—in *The German Ideology*—was the attempt to interpret sexual differences as an instance, perhaps the primal one, of the division of labor.[10] Thus the reproductive coupling of men and women is the beginning of the division of labor, and the fall from grace is linked accordingly to sexual activity. Similarly, Marx and Engels asserted in the same work that property, and with it inequality in the allocation of work and enjoyments, has its germ, or its first form, in the family, where wives and children are the slaves of men: "The latent slavery—however crude—in the family is the first property [; and this definition,] incidentally, corresponds fully to that offered by modern economists, according to which [property] is the power to dispose of the labor power of others."[11]

This, too, is abstract and unrelated to an action program. Written in 1846, it was virtually the last pronouncement either Engels or Marx made about male-female relationships for four decades, except for the brief statements

[10] Marx and Engels, *Die deutsche Ideologie* (MEW, vol. 3), p. 31. But see Marx's *Misère de la philosophie*, where he asserts that the first significant division of labor was the differentiation between city and country (MEW, vol. 4, p. 145).

[11] Marx and Engels, *Die deutsche Ideologie* (MEW, vol. 3), p. 32.

made in the *Principles of Communism* and the *Communist Manifesto*, both written in 1847, and the occasional references to the plight of female workers in *Capital*. In general, Marx and Engels concentrated on the analysis of capitalism as a socioeconomic system. They were interested in the development and workings of the capitalist economy and in the complications of its politics. They sought to promote the struggle of the working class, and thus were interested in questions concerning strategy, organization, and leadership. The role of the family and the oppression of women—not to mention the problem of dealing with this oppression—did not seem to be of concern to them even though they clearly recognized that proletarian women were among the most exploited and oppressed in contemporary society.

Toward the end of his life, Marx became acquainted with the work of the American anthropologist Lewis Morgan and discussed Morgan's ideas with Engels. After Marx's death, Engels was stimulated by Marx's copious notes on Morgan to integrate the anthropologist's ideas into their own theories. The result was Engels's *The Origin of the Family, Private Property, and the State*, which is relevant here because it deals more directly with the liberation of women than any of the joint writings of Marx and Engels did. On the first page of the preface, Engels asserts that according to the materialist interpretation (meaning Marxism) the ultimate determinants of all history are the production and reproduction of life. And as though this were not clear enough, he spells out that this assertion refers, on the one hand, to the production of means of subsistence as well as of tools, and, on the other hand, to the production of new human beings. One must marvel at the nonchalance with which he makes this statement. For all their lives, he and Marx had argued, with considerable heat, that society must be understood as a mechanism for production, and that the determinant driving force of all historic change was to be found in the development of the means of production. Suddenly, now, the production of means for survival and the production of children are mentioned as equally basic activities. Suddenly the sexual act is on a par with productive work, and the relations between male and female are as significant as those between capitalists and proletarians. Indeed, Engels goes beyond this by asserting that the farther back we go into history or prehistory, the more important kinship becomes as the organizing matrix of society. It is only in civilized societies that production relations and class structure become primary.[12]

In the book itself, Engels seeks to link this changing balance between productive and reproductive activities and the subjection of women by asserting that the earliest human societies were matriarchies, in which

[12] Engels, *Der Ursprung der Familie, des Privateigentums und des Staats* (MEW, vol. 21), pp. 27–28. In studying the development of social institutions Marx and Engels became interested in the work of the young Russian scholar (sociologist, historian, ethnographer) Maxim M. Kovalevskii, whose *Tableau des origines et de l'évolution de la famille et de la propriété* was published (in Stockholm, 1890) and was cited by Engels in later editions of his own work.

women were highly respected and carried out important tasks. Here Engels leaned heavily on the work of the Swiss legal historian and anthropologist, J. J. Bachofen. It is not clear whether he meant to convey that prior to their defeat women ruled over men or that there was a reciprocal division of labor not entailing rule of one sex over another. In my opinion, Charnie Guettel is correct in asserting that Engels had in mind a relationship without domination and oppression since, after all, the divisive institution of property did not yet exist; and the ascent of men over women was, in Engels's judgment, related to the development of property.[13] Throughout the book, Engels conveys the impression that matriarchy was preferable to male domination and that it corresponded to a nobler and more humane way of life. Matriarchy reigned in a communistic, propertyless community blessed with equality, sexual freedom, general self-respect, and respect for others.[14]

Just as Engels regarded matriarchy as a male-female relationship functional to early communism, so he posited the oppression of women as linked to class oppression. The first class antagonism, he wrote, coincided with the development of the antagonism between men and women; and in this antagonism it was the men who established their supremacy. Class antagonism arises simultaneously with the defeat of the female sex. Slavery and monogamy appear at the same time.[15]

This close association of slavery and exploitation with the monogamous family is central to the thinking of Engels and has become an essential element of Marxist thinking on the family. Yet I have tried to show that it was not at all central to the writings of the two founders and that indeed the very mention of reproduction and of the family was very much an afterthought. In its broad outlines, Marxist theory did not seem to require a systematic treatment of the family. Indeed, within the body of Marxist doctrine developed by the two founders and their successors in the Second International, the provocative theses advanced by Engels in 1884 were not followed up, certainly not systematically. Neither the roots and functions of sexual (and sexist) oppression nor the structure of the capitalist or proletarian family was explored with any thoroughness.

This is not to say that these themes were totally neglected. Engels, for one, repeatedly expressed his totally negative appraisal of the bourgeois family, which he regarded as a microcosm of capitalist class relations and as organized prostitution. Because the husband in the bourgeois family is the sole wage earner, he dominates his family totally; he is the bourgeois, and

[13] Charnie Guettel, *Marxism and Feminism* (Toronto, 1974), p. 11.

[14] I am not aware that anyone has ever pointed out the striking similarity between the image of the noble savage presented by Engels and that proffered by Montaigne in his essay "Of Cannibals," written 1578–80. See Donald M. Frame, trans., *The Complete Works of Montaigne* (Stanford, Calif., 1957), pp. 150–59.

[15] Engels is careful to add that both monogamy and slavery were, from the historical point of view, advances. But all historical advances, he points out, have at the same time been regressions. All advances so far have meant that the well-being and development of one group were obtained at the cost of misery and oppression for the others.

his wife and children are the proletariat.[16] Healthy sexual relations are per-
verted as long as economic ties rather than love and affection bind the
family together.[17] In fact, in its very origins the monogamous family is not
based on love but is a business deal. Hence every bourgeois wife is a prostitute, different from the streetwalker only because she is hired for life rather
than for a few hours.[18]

As a young gymnasium student, Engels undoubtedly learned to recite
Schiller's famous "Ode to the Bell," with its glorious description of the
bourgeois family as an affectionate partnership of two people brought together by the fleeting madness of sexual attraction, a romantic illusion that
is shattered as soon as the virginal bride is deflowered. Engels thoroughly
disliked Schiller and would have sneered at the idea that the frantic acquisi-
tive life portrayed in this poem was fulfilling human purposes. And for the
chaste housewife he would only have had pity. But at least Schiller's
idealized bourgeois woman performed useful work and must have had a
sense of accomplishment; the bourgeois woman Engels found predominant
two generations later was the woman of refinement and leisure, who had
her housework done for her by domestic servants.

The comments Engels made, on many occasions, about the bourgeois
lady of leisure were scathing and contemptuous, even though he was well
aware that she was a victim of the system. In some of his remarks it is
difficult to disentangle his contempt from his compassion.[19] His compassion is much more obvious when he discusses divorcées and actual prostitutes. In both cases, he was aware that the double standard of sexual morality, which condemned divorce as well as prostitution, was applied only
against women and stigmatized them grievously.[20]

One can find in the writings of Engels occasional beginnings, or
suggested beginnings, of a Marxist sociology of the family—for instance, in
his witty comparison of bourgeois family life in Catholic and Protestant
countries.[21] But here, too, he did not elaborate; and his clever observations
do not constitute a theory.

When we turn from the analysis of the status of women to the proposals
Marx and Engels made for their liberation, we encounter a similar mixture
of vague sympathy and unwillingness to deal with the problem intensively.

---

[16] Engels, *Der Ursprung* (MEW, vol. 21), p. 74.
[17] *Ibid.*, p. 68. See also Engels, *Die Lage der arbeitenden Klasse* (MEW, vol. 2), p. 371.
[18] Engels, *Der Ursprung* (MEW, vol. 21), p. 73.
[19] A striking example is Engels's account of the plight of English ladies during the siege of
Lucknow, "Der Entsatz Lakhnaus," which appeared in the *New York Daily Tribune* on February 1, 1858. (MEW, vol. 12, pp. 370–71.) For a straightforward condemnation of the lady of
leisure, see Engels, *Der Ursprung* (MEW, vol. 21), p. 54.
[20] On divorcées and their plight, see Engels's letters to Karl Kautsky of Oct. 11, 1888, Oct.
17, 1888, and June 25, 1892. All references to letters by Engels or Marx are to MEW, where
vols. 27–39 contain their correspondence in chronological order. On the double standard in
condemning prostitution, see Engels, *Der Ursprung* (MEW, vol. 21), p. 69; and his letter to
Bebel of Dec. 22, 1892.
[21] Engels, *Der Ursprung* (MEW, vol. 21), pp. 72–73.

Moreover, it becomes apparent that the incorporation of Morgan's and Bachofen's findings did not have any effect whatever on Engels's practical proposals. The prescriptions he offered for the liberation of women in the 1890's were not substantially different from what he and Marx had suggested in the 1840's.

Let me begin with the obvious, their support for equal rights before the law and equal participation in politics. To the wife of a friend Engels wrote that under socialism these would be guaranteed: "When we come to power, women shall not only vote but also run for office and make speeches; this latter thing happens here [in London] already at the school board, and last November I gave all my seven votes to a lady who indeed received more votes than any of the other seven candidates running. Incidentally, the ladies on the school boards have distinguished themselves by talking little and working very hard, every one as hard on the average as three men."[22]

I said above that this position was obvious. And in fact the socialist parties were, at first, the only parties that placed into their programs the demands for women's suffrage and for the full legal equality of women. They did this fairly late, however; the German party did it in the form of a resolution presented to the Reichstag in February of 1895. Not until 1907 did the Second International adopt a resolution obliging all its constituent parties to agitate for legal and political equality between men and women.

A resolution concerning women's suffrage passed by the International Socialist Women's Conference meeting in 1907 makes clear why the Marxist movement approached even this obvious agitational issue with a certain amount of reluctance and indeed with strong ambivalence: the fight for women's suffrage was, in the final analysis, a bourgeois problem, even though the working class did have a stake in it. Let me quote at some length from the resolution.[23]

The demand for women's right to vote is the result of economic and social transformations engendered by the capitalist mode of production, but especially the revolutionary change in the nature of work as well as in the position and the consciousness of women. Essentially it is a derivative of the bourgeois-democratic principle demanding the abolition of all social distinctions not based on property and proclaiming the full legal equality of all adults in private and public life to be the right of every individual. Hence individual thinkers have demanded women's suffrage in connection with all struggles in which the bourgeoisie fought for the democratization of political rights as a precondition of its political emancipation and domination as a class. However, it has acquired driving and compelling power as a mass demand only through the rising wage labor of the female sex, and especially through the inclusion of proletarian women into modern industry. Women's suffrage is the correlate of the economic emancipation of women from the household and of their economic independence from family owing to their professional work. . . .

[22] Engels's letter to Ida Pauli, Feb. 14, 1877. Perhaps one should be grateful that, for all his condescension, Engels did not write that the lady he voted for "worked like a man."

[23] *Dokumente und Materialien zur Geschichte der deutschen Arbeiterbewegung* (Berlin, 1967), vol. 4, pp. 206–7.

The class differences that are effective for women as much as for men cause the value and chief purpose of the franchise to be different for women of the different classes. The value of the franchise as means of social struggle is inversely proportional to the amount of property and the social power it imparts. Depending on the class situation, its chief purpose is either the full legal equality of the female sex or the social emancipation of the proletariat through the conquest of political power with the aim of abolishing class rule and bringing about a socialist society which alone guarantees the full human emancipation of women.

Because of the class contradictions within the female sex the bourgeois women's movement does not fight for the general female suffrage in total unity and with maximal possible force. Hence in fighting for their full citizen's rights the female proletarians have to rely on their own resources and on the resources of their class. The practical requirements of its fight for emancipation as well as its historical insight and that sense of justice which springs from its class position—all these make the proletariat into the most consistent fighter for complete equality of political rights for the female sex. Hence in principle as well as in practice, the socialist parties, the political fighting organizations of the class-conscious proletariat, fight for women's suffrage.

With the sharpening of the class struggle, the question of women's suffrage rises in importance. In the ruling reactionary classes, there is a growing tendency to strengthen the political power of property by introducing a limited franchise for women. One must, today, understand the limited women's suffrage less as a first step toward the equality of political rights for the female sex than, rather, the last step in the social emancipation of property. It emancipates the women not as an individual but as the carrier of property and income; hence it functions as the plural franchise of the possessing classes, leaves broad masses of proletarian women without political rights, and consequently does not, in fact, signify the equality of political rights for the entire female sex. For the proletariat there is an increasing necessity to revolutionize the minds and to place its adult members into the battlefront well armed, without regard to sex differences. The fight for universal female suffrage is the most suitable means to use this situation in the interest of the proletarian struggle for liberation.

Engels, too, even though he was in favor of pressing for legal and political equality for women, had pointed out that the attainment of juridical and political equality would not liberate women from their proletarian status within the family. On the contrary, he predicted it would become all the more obvious, just as the exploitation of the working class is intensified when the workers have acquired political rights and legal equality. True liberation, he argued, could be won only when women participated fully, and equally, in production processes. In the past, women have been kept in servant roles because of their relative weakness; and with the development of private property, the men they served foremost were the male heads of households. Full participation in productive work is possible now because work in the future will be less arduous, and household duties will be less demanding; much of household work would become a public enterprise (though Engels obviously took it for granted that whatever household chores were not carried out by public industry would be done by women). But for all this to be accomplished, the monogamous family would have to cease functioning as an economic unit.[24]

In the first draft of the *Communist Manifesto* Engels already had made similar demands. Among the immediate measures to be taken by a communist regime he had included the establishment of public child-rearing institutions for all children no longer requiring care by their own mother, the merging of all education with productive work, and the recognition of equal rights of inheritance for illegitimate as well as legitimate children.[25] In the long run, he foresaw the abolition of all property, and argued that this, together with public child-rearing institutions, would destroy the basis of contemporary marriage, the dependence of women on men and of children on parents.[26]

What kinds of sexual relations might develop, or on what principles they might be based, once the monogamous family was abolished becomes apparent in a passage stricken from the manuscript of *The German Ideology*. Here the authors distinguish between natural needs and needs artificially engendered by different social systems. They state that the natural needs will have to be developed naturally and will have to be satisfied. The false needs will then simply disappear. The communists, the passage concludes, do not seek to abolish natural needs, but wish to create a system that makes their satisfaction possible.[27]

Marx and Engels did not add much to this formulation in the next fifty years, although they stated repeatedly that in the communist society of the future the relations between the sexes would become a purely private matter, of no concern to church, state, or neighbors. Engels took it for granted that men and women would form binary unions for extended periods. These unions would be based solely on mutual affection and would be dissolved if that affection cooled. He refused to speculate further, arguing that the precise relations would not become apparent until there was a generation of men who had no experience at all of what it was to buy a woman with money or power, or until there was a generation of women who had no experience of sexual intercourse for any reason except love, and who had never refused intercourse out of fear of the economic consequences. All children in this future world would be extramarital.[28]

Charnie Guettel summed up the total contribution Marx and Engels made to the "woman question" as follows: "Just as Marx and Engels had no theoretical work on racism, a phenomenon that has become a central brake

[24]Engels, *Der Ursprung* (MEW, vol. 21), pp. 75–76, 158. See also *Die deutsche Ideologie* (MEW, vol. 3), p. 29.

[25]Engels, *Grundsätze des Kommunismus* (MEW, vol. 4), pp. 373–74.

[26]*Ibid.*, p. 377.

[27]*Ibid.*, pp. 238–39.

[28]Engels, *Der Ursprung* (MEW, vol. 21), pp. 77–83; see also Engels, *Anti-Dühring* (MEW, vol. 20), p. 296; and Marx, *Das Kapital*, vol. 1 (MEW, vol. 23), p. 514.

on progress in the working-class movement in the stage of imperialism, so did they lack a developed critique of sexism under capitalism. Their class analysis of society still provides us with the best tools for analyzing both forms of oppression, although concerning women it is very underdeveloped."[29] This criticism is a bit harsh. For their time, Marx and Engels were advanced; and though most of their ideas about the oppression of women were much too abstract, they did provide at least some elaboration. Perhaps the comment is unfair also because it does not recognize that Marx and Engels could have advanced one very simple but compelling reason *not* to write about the "woman question." This was their belief that the matter had been treated adequately, and in their own spirit, so that any ideas they might elaborate would be redundant. Marx and Engels were very busy people. They did not wish to waste time on a matter that had been taken care of to their satisfaction. The satisfactory treatment of the "woman question" I am referring to is the work of their close friend and associate, August Bebel, whose book *Woman and Socialism* they considered entirely compatible with their own views, and which was similarly regarded in the working-class movement before World War I.[30] Because the book has been unduly neglected, and Bebel's relationship with Engels and Marx has at times been misunderstood—Firestone lists him, repeatedly, as one of precursors of Marx and Engels—I shall discuss it at some length.

August Bebel, twenty years younger than Engels, was born in 1840 in southwestern Germany. A woodturner by trade, he later became an independent manufacturer of metal door handles. He joined the budding working-class movement as a youth, quickly became one of its leading spokesmen, and was one of the very first socialists who enjoyed the full confidence of Marx and Engels. Bebel was instrumental in bringing about the eventual victory of the Marxian faction over Lassalle and other German socialist rivals, and he ended as the acknowledged leader of the German Social Democratic Party until his death in 1913.

Bebel's book on the "woman question" was first published in 1879 (about the same time that Engels published his philippics against Eugen Dühring). For several decades it remained the most authoritative statement made by the Marxist movement on the subject of the oppression and liberation of women. (Incidentally, it also contains an elaboration of the Marxist view of the future that is of great interest. Edward Bellamy's *Looking Backward*, which appeared a few years after the first English translation of *Woman and Socialism*, so closely parallels Bebel that at the time some people accused Bellamy of plagiarism.) The outline of the book is simple. It begins with a survey history of the subjection of women, in which much of what Engels wrote five years later in *The Origin of the Family* is anticipated. There follows a lengthy analysis of women's present condition, in-

---

[29]Guettel, p. 15.
[30]I have used the 24th edition: August Bebel, *Die Frau und der Sozialismus* (*Die Frau in der Vergangenheit, Gegenwart und Zukunft*) (Stuttgart, 1894).

cluding chapters on the sexual urge and marriage, on prostitution, and on women in the professions, law, politics, and society. Then there is that elaborate look into the future of relations between women and men, which is followed by brief chapters on the international movement and on population problems.

Many of Bebel's propositions echo those of Marx and Engels. Like them, he denounces bourgeois marriage as prostitution: "The German Penal Code (paragraphs 180 and 181) punishes pimping with many years in the penitentiary; but when parents, guardians, or relatives prostitute their children, their wards, their own kin, for life to an unloved man or an unloved woman, merely for the sake of money, gain or status—in short, for the sake of external advantages—then there is no public prosecutor who can interfere; and yet a crime has been committed."[31]

Bebel acknowledges, too, that divorce is an insidious system in which, more often than not, the fault is with the man but the punishment is meted out to the woman.[32] Like Marx and Engels, he condemns the hypocrisies of the double standard in sexual morality and predicts a mating arrangement for socialist society based on natural sexual attraction, on intellectual and spiritual compatibility, and on a measure of rationality to balance blind passion. All these things, he argues, usually are absent in capitalist marriages.[33] "Our bourgeois society is like a great carnival costume party where each seeks to deceive the other and to make a fool of him; where each wears his official mask with dignity, only to give in to his unofficial likes and passions with all the less restraint. And all the time in appearance everything drips with virtue, religion, and morality."[34]

Like Engels, Bebel believes that women's true liberation from oppression by men can come only through the abolition of private property and the liberation of both sexes from the monogamous family. But unlike Engels, Bebel stresses the importance of liberating women from legal and political discrimination.[35] Nonetheless, genuine equality presupposes not only equal rights but also the public ownership of all means of production; the fullest use of modern technology; productive work carried out by everyone; and a resultant substantial decrease in the individual work load and increase in individual leisure. "Only in this way can the woman become a member of society as productively useful as the man, and having equal rights. Only then can she develop all her physical and intellectual abilities fully, and carry out her sexual duties and rights. Facing the man free and his equal, she is protected against any demeaning proposition."[36]

In his speculations about the liberation of women from household chores and about their increasing participation in political and cultural life, and in his arguments about the increasingly nonfunctional nature of the family, Bebel often goes a bit further than Engels, if only by providing more detail.

[31]*Ibid.*, p. 89.
[33]*Ibid.*, p. 82.
[35]*Ibid.*, pp. 105–7.
[32]*Ibid.*, p. 94
[34]*Ibid.*, p. 150.
[36]*Ibid.*, p. 174.

He also goes further in his attempt to mobilize women for their self-liberation. After pointing out that men have systematically kept women in subordinate positions, he writes, "Women must not wait for men to help them out of this condition, just as workers do not wait for help from the bourgeoisie."[37] In short, he argues that women's liberation must be the work of women themselves; and although this is nothing but an application of Marxist truisms, it draws conclusions that Engels himself fails to draw. Moreover, in urging women to participate fully in the socialist movement, which alone guarantees their liberation, Bebel also admonishes the men in the movement to rid themselves of their prejudices and to support the women in their political activities.

Bebel goes beyond Marx and Engels and back to the ideas of Fourier (whether he knew it or not) in his scattered suggestions for a psychology of female oppression. He seeks to show that in all societies the social structure and the natural needs of human beings are in contradiction. We are all of us dual beings, and our natural-sexual identity is in conflict with our social identity. This contradiction is sharpest in capitalist society, Bebel writes; and what makes his argument interesting is that he derives not only vice and degenerate practices from this conflict, but also physical and psychic illness. It is interesting also that he once again sees women as the principal victim of this dualism. Why? Because he believes that in women the sex urge may, at least periodically, be stronger than in men, hence that they need sexual satisfaction more urgently to promote their physical and mental health. Puritan morals conceal whoredom; "loose" morals, i.e., a free sex life, is more natural. Yet though women have stronger urges and a natural right to their satisfaction, it is usually men alone who have enjoyed such freedom. Hence the numerical predominance of women in insane asylums is a function of the extraordinary sexual repression to which they are subjected.[38] Though Phyllis Chesler's thesis is far more sophisticated, one can nonetheless recognize that Bebel anticipated some of her ideas a hundred years ago.[39]

Bebel's book is not without its inconsistencies. Though he recognized the sexual urge as a natural human need, he nonetheless was horrified by promiscuity; though he hated prudery and argued that one ought to be honest about one's natural needs, he also talked about the natural feeling of shame and morality.[40] In short, despite the fact that he took pride in his advanced and libertarian views concerning sexual matters, he was filled nonetheless with a Victorian loathing of sensualism. Like Engels, he detested homosexual practices as unnatural.[41]

Again like Engels, he believed that matriarchy made women beautiful, proud, dignified, and independent. He also argued that light, natural cloth-

[37] Ibid., p. 117.
[38] Ibid., p. 75. See also pp. 59–61, 71–73.
[39] Phyllis Chesler, Women and Madness (New York, 1972).
[40] Bebel, pp. 99–100.   [41] Ibid., p. 29.

ing went with a freer life and a more liberated personality. Moreover, he could talk about sexual practices of other cultures with tolerance and sympathy (though underneath that relativism we sense his revulsion; and at times, when it suits his polemic purposes, his loathing comes through with full force).[42] Still, for a product of the Victorian age, it is a remarkably advanced book.

However advanced and enlightened all these ideas may have been, it is obvious that the liberation of women was a matter of relatively low priority for Engels and Marx. There is no record that they ever discussed the problem among themselves; and it is curious to note the lack of excitement with which Engels commented on Bebel's book, which its author had sent him around Christmas of 1883—four years after its first publication. He read it with great interest, he wrote to Bebel: "There are lots of very good things in it. I found particularly clear and nice what you say about the development of industry in Germany. . . ." Hm![43]

I have already suggested the principal reason for this obvious lack of interest: the preoccupation of Engels and Marx with class relations and class structure, which caused them to relate all forms of oppression to the economic base, so that implicitly they distinguished primary and secondary, basic and derivative, forms of oppression. Since the basic oppression is that of one class by another, all other forms of oppression—racial, sexual, national, religious, and so on—are to be understood only as functions of class relationships, either derived from class conflict or devised to perpetuate the class structure.

Now if sexism, racism, nationalism, and so on are recognized as functions of the class struggle, then a Marxist strategy to achieve liberation from class oppression might be to remove these props from under the system. But such an approach was systematically played down by Marx and Engels, as we shall see. Instead of incorporating the movements for women's liberation into their political program and organization, Marx, Engels, and most of their followers tended to regard the "woman question" as an unwanted side issue of distinctly marginal importance that took attention from the key struggle. In short, the relative neglect of the "woman question" was built into Marxist theory.

This is not to say that we could not extend Marxist methods to an analysis of women's problems. For instance, we could build on the observation Marx made in *Capital* that the family, which used to be a production unit in precapitalist societies, has under capitalism yielded its production functions to factories. Moreover, as Guettel suggests, we could develop a psychology of male chauvinism by examining the anxieties attendant on the man's responsibilities as breadwinner. Indeed, Marx's own very pronounced male

[42]*Ibid.*, pp. 30, 37–39.
[43]Engels to Bebel, Jan. 18, 1884, MEW, vol. 36, p. 87.

chauvinism, which I will discuss below, can be explained nicely in this fashion. I personally believe that the most fruitful and imaginative extensions of Marxist methods have been in works dealing with the political economy of domestic work.[44] Finally, we could argue that a Marxist analysis of the oppression of women is most potent in the writings of Wilhelm Reich and others who merge Marxian assumptions with Freudian ones and see class domination and sexual oppression as reinforcing each other.

Why did Marx and Engels themselves not show much interest in pursuing these possibilities for extending their method into an analysis of the "woman question"? The reason is not only the work done by Bebel, but also their own personal lack of involvement in this problem. This is obvious in the case of Marx, though far less so in that of Engels.

In referring to these personal matters, I am entering dangerous ground. It has always been tempting for critics of Marxism to adduce the personal lives of these two men as proof of the unworthiness of their ideas. Certainly Marx and Engels were as human as the rest of us: they had their foibles and their spleens; got along well with some and badly with others; said many foolish things; and, in the course of their stormy lives, made friends with some unworthy people and antagonized some very worthy ones. A knowledge of their troubles with alcohol, money, or their own bodies may help us to understand the circumstances under which their works were produced, but neither adds to nor detracts from their accomplishments. Nonetheless, such knowledge may at times explain inclusions or omissions, emphases, and preoccupations or neglects in their treatment of some particular problem. Hence a brief glimpse into the relationships Engels and Marx had with women and the experiences they had with family life may be relevant here.

In private life, Marx was a Victorian patriarch who admired his father, doted on his daughters (even though he wished they were sons), adored his wife, and slept with her domestic servant. Though he often chafed under the restrictions of family life, in his declining years he longed for the comfort to be found in this microcosm. His family seemed to him then to be the last refuge of humanness, the only place where a man could simply be himself.[45] If the *Communist Manifesto* ridiculed this idyll, the sentiments probably had been those of Engels.

Marx had wooed the most eligible young lady in his hometown for many years, and throughout his life he treated her in conformity with bourgeois traditions. This included either his failure to understand her strong need for

---

[44] See Margaret Benston, *The Political Economy of Women's Liberation* (Toronto, 1973); Wally Secombe, "The Housewife and Her Labor Under Capitalism," *New Left Review*, 83 (Jan.–Feb. 1974), pp. 3–24; several articles in Richard C. Edwards et al., *The Capitalist System* (Englewood Cliffs, N.J., 1972); Marilyn Power Goldberg, "The Economic Exploitation of Women," in David M. Gordon, ed., *Problems in Political Economy: An Urban Perspective* (Lexington, Mass., 1971).

[45] See Marx's letter to his daughter Jenny Longuet, June 4, 1882; see also Sheila Rowbotham, *Women, Resistance and Revolution* (New York, 1972), pp. 70–71.

active and equal participation in his political and intellectual life or, if he understood it, his failure to afford her sufficient opportunity to satisfy it; and she herself was too much committed to the role of a middle-class lady— however bitterly she resented that role—to put herself forward.[46] Family life in Marx's house could get rough and bitter, and arguments over money often led to a hell of mutual recriminations, so that Marx sometimes cursed his marriage, saying that a revolutionary could not afford to be burdened with such a responsibility. In good bourgeois fashion, Marx treated the son he sired by his wife's domestic servant as though he did not exist and brutally interfered in his daughters' choices of husbands. Surrounded by women in his home, he does not appear to have sought their company outside it. Perhaps he gladly left them to Engels, who treated them more as equal partners. The depth of Marx's patriarchal views is best gauged, perhaps, by his responses to a questionnaire one of his daughters once submitted to him. Asked his favorite virtue, Marx replied "simplicity." His favorite virtue in men, he said, was "strength"; in women, "weakness." His idea of happiness was "to fight"; of misery, "to submit." His favorite heroes were Spartacus and Kepler, and Gretchen was his favorite heroine. "Servility" he called his most detested vice.[47]

Marx thus conveys a strong sense that men and women are fundamental opposites, and that women are distinctly inferior. As Nannerl O. Keohane put it in commenting on this paper: "The identification of weakness with women in such a basic sense, by someone whose whole life was posited on strength, struggle, and fighting, is a poor basis for any theory of women's liberation."

In many respects, Engels was the exact opposite of Marx. Deeply devoted to his mother, he had a very tense relationship with his father; and his scathing comments on bourgeois marriages are obviously generalizations based on observations he had made in his parental home. A self-styled bohemian, he frankly enjoyed the company and the favors of beautiful women, though during the long years of his common-law marriage with Mary and Lizzy Burns he appears to have refrained from intercourse with anyone else.

In many of his pronouncements, Engels made it clear that he regarded women as partners rather than as sex objects. Unlike Marx, he rejected the stereotype of the "soft," dependent, childlike woman, arguing instead that women should join as equals in the revolutionary struggle, where he was confident they would demonstrate that the sentimental female was no more than a bourgeois affliction.[48] Nonetheless, until his very old age, Engels apparently had no intimate relations at all with women of his own, bourgeois class. His numerous partners were always women from the work-

---

[46] See Jenny Marx, letter to Marx of March 1843, and letter to Wilhelm Liebknecht, May 26, 1872.

[47] Replies to his daughter's questionnaire, MEW, vol. 31, p. 597.

[48] See Engels's letter to Natalie Liebknecht, July 31, 1877.

ing class or the peasantry, i.e., women who were beneath him in status and educational level, and who therefore could not easily share his many intellectual interests or linguistic accomplishments and thus were almost inevitably relegated to servant roles. In this Engels seems to have been like Lenin, who theoretically recognized the subjection of women and the petty tyranny of household duties, but who in practice surrounded himself with serving women. At least neither Engels nor Marx, nor indeed Lenin, was like Ferdinand Lassalle, who summarized his life's aim as knowledge, action, and the enjoyment of women's bodies, who obviously did not know the meaning of the word "love" and was interested only in sex, and who stated that "for the woman, fulfillment means submission to the man."[49]

Altogether, Engels was far more liberated than most of his friends and associates were in sexual matters, which he believed were natural human concerns that should be discussed freely. He was disturbed by the prudish reticence of his fellow socialists, and by their readiness to treat women as a dirty joke. This did not, however, prevent him from exchanging pornographic jokes with Marx. Despite his generally advanced views and practices, Engels repudiated the ideas of Fourier and others who preached freedom from all restraints in sexual matters, arguing that such views were an irrational extravagance typical of early, utopian phases of every revolutionary movement, and that they must yield to more restrained views when the movement ripens. Engels cited Christianity, too, as a revolutionary movement that had gone through its phase of radical sexual liberation.[50] Moreover, his occasionally enlightened views on sexual matters were balanced by many of the prejudices of the Victorian age, including a deep revulsion against homosexuality and the conviction that masturbation leads to madness. He was, in short, a man of the Victorian age, with all the intellectual handicaps this implies for dealing with the "woman question."

In the remainder of this paper I shall provide some glimpses into the actual relations between the women's movement and the workers' movement in the period of the First and Second Internationals, with emphasis on a few case studies of radical women who, coming from the women's movement, sought to merge the two causes by concentrating on the problems of female proletarians.

The women workers' movement goes back at least to the late 1840's. In France at that time, Flora Tristan sought to create a workers' association in which women would participate on equal terms with men. An American feminist, Margaret Fuller, participated actively in the Revolution of 1848 in Italy and was clearly drifting toward the socialist movement at the time of her premature death. In Germany in 1849, Luise Otto-Peters, who had also been active in the Revolution of 1848, founded a women's newspaper, *Die*

---

[49]Shlomo Na'aman, *Lassalle* (Hannover, 1970), pp. 18, 27, 53–54.
[50]See Engels, "Das Buch der Offenbarung" (MEW, vol. 21), p. 10; and *idem*, "Zur Geschichte des Urchristentums" (MEW, vol. 22), p. 462.

Deutsche Frauenzeitung, which demanded equal treatment for women in general. In the revolutionary commune in Paris in 1848, a woman ran for election as workers' representative in the Commission du Travail. She received fifteen votes—"amid general derision."[51] The derision this woman suffered, like that Margaret Fuller met at the hands of Ralph Waldo Emerson and his circle, shows that even advanced or revolutionary men were not yet ready to accept women as partners in their political and economic struggles or in their intellectual pursuits. The exception to this rule, as indicated in the beginning of this paper, was the revolutionary movement in Russia, where, beginning certainly by the 1860's, women participated in significant numbers and often assumed positions of leadership and notoriety.

Feminism as a movement does appear to have come into vogue in the 1860's, as can be shown by the spate of books published about the "woman question" between 1860 and 1880.[52] And the end of the 1860's saw the creation of several organizations specifically for women workers. In Germany, Gertrud Countess von Guillaume-Schack founded her *Verein zur Vertretung der Interessen der Arbeiterinnen* (Association for Representation of the Interests of Working Women); and at about that time in New York, Victoria Woodhull and her sister, Tennessee Claflin, created a similar association and began to publish a journal, *Woodhull & Claflin's Weekly*. Woodhull's organization applied for admission to the International Workingmen's Association (First International) and was accepted.

The efforts of women such as these to associate their radical feminist organizations with the workers' movement indicate that, around 1870, the opportunity existed for a merger of the two movements. Yet a good deal of this opportunity was squandered, for several reasons. First, male workers often regarded women not as allies but as competitors—and unfair competitors at that. As Marx and Engels repeatedly pointed out, capitalism had mobilized women for industrial work in ever increasing numbers. Because these women usually were paid less than men for similar work, their employment tended to depress wages. Thus from the point of view of the male workers, women were scabs. Hence the demand for equal rights for men and women was not readily accepted by militant proletarians. "Indeed, some of the men . . . fought against it. Just as earlier they had smashed the machines because they saw in them the greatest obstacles to their earning opportunities, so later they turned against the women who had come in large numbers to serve the machines, and who were threatening to turn into scab competitors as unskilled working hands."[53]

Sentiments of this kind were expressed clearly and loudly at various con-

[51] Jörg Ueltzhöffer, "Women," in *Marxism, Communism and Western Society: A Comparative Encyclopedia* (New York, 1973), vol. 8, p. 341.
[52] An impressive bibliography is listed in Anna Blos, ed., *Die Frauenfrage* (Dresden, 1930), p. 22. See also Lily Braun, *Die Frauenfrage, ihre geschichtliche Entwicklung und ihre wirtschaftliche Seite* (Leipzig, 1901), part 2, chap. 7, pp., 431–62.
[53] Braun, p. 14.

gresses of German workers' associations in the 1860's—at Stuttgart in 1865 and at Eisenach in 1869, for example. Such congresses repeatedly debated moves to press for the abolition of all female work. Nor did this agitation abate quickly. Twenty years after the Stuttgart congress, von Guillaume-Schack complained in a letter to Engels that German socialists persisted in their demand for restrictions on female labor. In her opinion, the French socialists were preferable to the Germans, for the French socialist platform demanded equal wages for women and men. (She apparently did not know that a French workers' congress in 1877 had debated the issue with considerable heat before voting down a resolution to have women barred from work.) Engels's reply is interesting. He wrote that if the French workers were less insistent in demanding restrictions on female labor, the reason was that factory work played less of a role in France than in Germany; in short, France was economically less advanced. As for equal pay, Engels argues that all socialist parties demanded equal pay *for equal production*, regardless of sex—his implication clearly being that women can be expected to produce less efficiently.

That the working woman because of her particular physiological functions needs special protection against capitalist exploitation seems clear to me. The English women who fight for the formal rights of women to be exploited by the capitalists as thoroughly as the men are, most of them, interested directly or indirectly in the capitalist exploitation of both sexes. I must admit that I am more interested in the health of the coming generation than in the absolute equality of formal rights for the sexes during the last years of the capitalist mode of production. Real equality of rights for women and men can, in my opinion, become a fact only when the exploitation of both of them by capital has been abolished and private house work has been transformed into public industry.[54]

It is interesting to note that in the last sentence Engels at first added a phrase indicating that capitalism had been developed on the basis of male domination. In the letter he finally sent off to von Guillaume-Schack this was omitted.

Bebel, partly because of his more direct day-to-day involvement in the socialist movement, was far more active than Engels in the fight against barring women from gainful employment. Yet he also sympathized with the workers' view of women as scabs and argued that the right to work was primarily the aim of bourgeois career women. Without doubt, he wrote, women should have equal political, social, economic, and professional rights. Yet all these rights could be attained within the framework of capitalism and would not ameliorate the basic inequities of the system. Moreover, opening all professions to women would in fact stiffen competition and depress wages; hence opening work opportunities for *proletarian*

[54] Gertrud von Guillaume-Schack to Engels, July 1, 1875; Engels to von Guillaume-Schack, July 5, 1875. See also explanatory note no. 453 in MEW, vol. 36, pp. 798–99.

women would in fact be in the interests of the capitalists. All that the bourgeois men wished to prevent was women's competition for elite jobs. And though proletarian men did not need to be concerned about that, they should also know that equality of career patterns for a few successful and privileged women would never end the vast majority's misery, dependency, sexual domination, and prostitution.[55]

Whatever his sympathies for women in their oppression, Bebel here came close to dismissing all women's struggles for equality as essentially bourgeois. And if this was not what he meant, then at least we can recognize in him, as in Engels and most of the men who expressed sympathy with women, a deep suspicion of all feminist organizations and movements that were not strictly proletarian. Within the socialist movement the conviction was general that bourgeois feminism expressed the special needs of educated and wealthy women—expressed their desire to participate in the exploitative system, to partake of the privileges of the ruling class. Their struggle for sexual liberation was dismissed as frivolous.

The abstract formulation that even bourgeois women were "proletarians" within the bourgeois family did not imply that sympathy would be shown them when abstract ideas were translated into practice. That this prejudice against bourgeois feminists is still very much alive, and has been accepted even by some women, is shown in the recent work of Juliet Mitchell. Early in her book *Woman's Estate*, Mitchell concedes that the educated bourgeois woman may be in a better position to ask questions about the system than the Appalachian mother of fifteen children who experiences her situation as natural and inescapable. Within a few pages, however, Mitchell laments that the early middle-class feminists misdirected their struggle by focusing largely on bourgeois issues. In making this statement, she does the early feminist movement an injustice.[56]

The resistance and occasional brusque treatment Bebel, Engels, and other leaders of the Marxist movement accorded feminist leaders within their own ranks may have been occasioned, to some extent, by their ever-present fear of rivals; indeed, any leaders who showed inclinations toward independence or eccentricity were viewed with suspicion. Though Marx and Engels manifested such suspicions toward many a male rival—Lassalle comes to mind most readily—they expressed themselves most sharply in the case of some feminist leaders within the movement. Neither Victoria Woodhull nor Gertrud von Guillaume-Schack stayed with the workers' movement for very long: both were welcomed by Engels at first but were soon criticized and denounced by him for having big egos and wanting to assume leadership. Though in both cases there were other reasons for his being dissatisfied with them, one gets the feeling that from female leaders Engels expected a bit more discipline, not to say submissiveness. His final

[55] Bebel, Introduction.
[56] Juliet Mitchell, *Woman's Estate* (New York, 1973), pp. 22, 36.

comment on von Guillaume-Schack was typical: "This person is determined, cost what it may, to play a big role."[57]

If this remark makes Engels appear to be something of a male chauvinist,
we must recognize that in the rank and file of the workers' movement sentiments and prejudices infinitely more patriarchal tended to prevail, and
that both Engels and Bebel protested against them.[58] This culture of male
domination and prudery goes far toward explaining the troubled relations
between the socialist movement and Victoria Woodhull.

Woodhull and her sister, Tennessee Claflin (sometimes referred to as
Tenney C. Claflin), had worked themselves up from poverty in a fashion
that at the time was considered unsavory, but they had become rich.
The journal that they founded was ideologically committed to socialism,
spiritualism, and free love. In it they wrote about prostitution and venereal
disease, about abortion and female sexuality, and about the struggle of
working women. Meanwhile, their totally uninhibited sex lives soon became a source of embarrassment to the various movements with which
they were associated—including the women's suffrage movement and the
socialist International. In 1872, the year Woodhull ran for president of the
United States on the People's party ticket, Susan B. Anthony expelled her
from the Suffrage Convention.

The working women's association Woodhull had created in New York in
the late 1860's applied for admission to the International Workingmen's
Association, was accepted, and became Section 12 of the American units in
the First International. Almost at once, however, the section became embroiled in bitter controversy. Accusations reached the leadership of the
International (i.e., Engels and Marx) that Section 12 contained a strange
and undesirable group of rich ladies, playboys, homosexuals, free-love advocates, and spiritualism freaks who had invaded the socialist movement
and were threatening to subvert it. Before long Section 12 was expelled
from the International, primarily through the efforts of Engels.

Engels judged this case by long distance on scanty evidence, and I believe he judged hastily and without examining the issues carefully. One can
accuse him also of applying standards to Woodhull that he did not always
enforce in judging other socialists: he argued later that her most grievous
offense against the socialist movement (or at least the final straw proving
her unsuitability) had been her decision to run for president. Yet what he
condemned in 1872—the use of the electoral process of the bourgeois
state—Engels not many years later would advocate as the surest road to
socialism.

The explanation for this arbitrary condemnation of Victoria Woodhull

[57]Engels to Natalie Liebknecht, Nov. 29, 1887. See also his letter to Eduard Bernstein, May
5, 1887, in which he criticizes von Guillaume-Schack for excess zeal to do something.
[58]For one of Engels's protests against the Victorian prudishness of the workers, see MEW,
vol. 21, p. 8. For Bebel's admission that the average worker regarded women as inferior, see
Bebel, p. 7.

must be sought, I believe, in a virtue that Engels at times practiced to excess: loyalty to his friends. In this case he relied entirely too much on the reports of his old cronies in New York City and Hoboken, New Jersey—honest craftsmen, brave veterans of the 1848 revolutions, unyielding radicals and socialists, but also traditional patriarchal Germans who were much less ready than he to understand or tolerate women, nonconformists, and libertines. To these men of limited sophistication, Woodhull and her adherents were indeed a bunch of freaks about to wreck the movement; and Engels was too much devoted to them to question their judgment.

The tactical conclusions drawn from this general suspicion of bourgeois feminism often were foolish and self-defeating and led to the elimination from the movement of many courageous women who might have been valuable leaders. Consider the experience of von Guillaume-Schack: Engels at first seems to have been pleased that police harassment had impelled her to merge her feminist association with the workers' party. He found her personally pleasant, intelligent, and lots of fun; and although he was suspicious of her nonsocialist contacts from her feminist days, he could not disagree on principle with her agitating for the women's cause within the socialist movement. Nonetheless it did disturb him. He considered its effect divisive, especially at a time when the party in Germany was outlawed. Moreover, he assumed that women were unable to maintain party discipline. As soon as women started to disagree with each other, he wrote, they would tattle about party activities or even denounce their own comrades to the police. But what disturbed him most of all was that von Guillaume-Schack was still maintaining political relations with nonsocialists. Her agitation against the proposed law to regulate prostitution was fine, he wrote, "but in pursuing it she is in league with the religious bourgeois ladies of the Anti-Contagious-Disease Acts Agitation and with sundry anarchist elements in the Socialist League."[59]

Similarly, Lily Braun was eliminated from the German socialist movement around the turn of the century. Braun was the daughter of a general from the Prussian nobility. For the first 25 years of her life she pursued the mindless pleasures—dinners, dances, flirtations—then considered appropriate for young ladies. Adversity, however, brought about an abrupt conversion: Braun became a fighter for radical causes, notably social reform, women's liberation, and finally the struggle of the working class against capitalism. Her major book, *The Woman Question* (1901), linked these themes in a fashion that sought to stay within the narrow bounds of Marxist orthodoxy as it was then understood. Though Braun placed her treatment of women's history within the context of democratic historiography, her point of departure was the economic position of women—their world of work and leisure—and she showed the exploitation, domination, and stunting of human potential that economic position caused. Throughout the

[59] Engels to Friedrich Adolph Sorge, June 4, 1887.

book she sought to show that moral concepts and life-styles change with changes in economic relations. Despite her attempt to maintain orthodoxy, in some significant details the book went beyond the formulations that party leaders were then willing to accept. Hence while middle-class feminists denounced it as too socialist, Marxist reviewers criticized it as bourgeois; only Werner Sombart hailed it as the classical formulation of the "woman question" from the socialist point of view.

The Woman Question did become a highly influential book, saw many editions, and was generally considered the best socialist treatise on women's problems. Infinitely more erudite and detailed than the pertinent works by Engels and Bebel, it was based on an extensive study of history, the classics of political philosophy, eighteenth- and nineteenth-century novels, and contemporary statistics. The message of the book might be summarized as follows. Capitalism destroys women, children, and the family. It makes work into hell (especially for women, and most especially for mothers), even though it will be meaningful work alone that will liberate us from capitalism. Hence work will have to become a source of happiness, a path toward personal worth and independence, and a means of fostering the spirit of collectivism. Finally, the book implies that socialism cannot be the result merely of economic restructuring but must reconstitute human beings in their innermost selves: socialism can come only with a thorough change in our consciousness.

Planned to form the first volume of a two-volume work, *The Woman Question* begins with a history of male-female relations from matriarchy to monogamy. It contains a thoughtful discussion of what Christianity did to exalt women in theory and to degrade them in practice—and thus to disturb profoundly the relationship between the sexes. It contains vast amounts of detail about medieval marriage and work and a remarkable discussion of feminism from the Renaissance to the eighteenth century. Emphasizing the importance of women in the Revolution of 1789, Braun's account of the relationship between revolutionary feminists and Jacobins provides a remarkable foretaste of what was to happen to sensitive women in the Marxist movement and in the Russian Revolution.[60] Braun becomes most eloquent and offers the greatest wealth of detail in the main part of her book, which deals with women in the capitalist economy. She carefully distinguishes between the situations and interests of bourgeois and proletarian women, and paints a horrifying picture of exploitation, discrimination, and miseducation of women in general (and old maids in particular). But she becomes most eloquent when she describes the lot of female proletarians, peasants, and domestic servants. The book is a relentless guided tour from one branch of industry to another, in which the various worlds of work turn into different circles of hell.

---

[60] See especially Braun's account of Olympe de Gouges, pp. 80–86.

In this best of all worlds, poverty is a crime punished by life-long forced labor; and children's children still carry the Cain's mark of their ancestors. True, the rod and the whip have disappeared when the slaves were driven to work; but out of the gold which the poor have torn from the womb of the earth bourgeois society has forged a weapon more terrible than all instruments of torture. With it, it dominates and subjects those without possessions and forces them to dig further and further for gold, with bent backs and callous hands, for the rulers' benefits. . . .

Whereas the bourgeois woman seeks work as the great liberator, for the proletarian woman it has become a means of enslavement; and though the right to work is one of the noblest human rights, to be condemned to work is a source of demoralization. But a social order based on this, a social order built on dehumanization of labor and the enslavement of those who work, is condemned to death.[61]

Braun thus concentrates on the alienation of labor to explain the condition of women in contemporary society. In this she emphasized a theme no longer of great interest to Marxist theorists. Furthermore, Braun was the first Marxist to convey a fine sensitivity to the sexism that praises outstanding women for "arguing like men"; she was the first Marxist, also, to recognize a conflict between creative work and the sex role ascribed to women.[62]

She strayed from orthodoxy by emphasizing the contributions women, as women, could make to socialism. She believed that socialist agitation tended to drive bourgeois women, too, to the left because socialism had a particularly strong appeal for women.

Socialism, angrily resisted by bourgeois society, nonetheless penetrated like the air we breathe through locked and barricaded doors and windows. In many of its traits it was virtually predestined to win the women over; just as, long ago, Christianity attracted countless female disciples because it appealed to sentiment, because it promised to help those "who are weak and heavily laden," so it is the sentimental side of socialism which today has such a strong effect on women, often without their knowledge, and most of the time without their wishing to admit it.[63]

At the end of her book, she condemns capitalism because it destroys motherhood.

Without women's work the capitalist economic order cannot continue to exist and will be less and less able to continue in existence. But women's work undermines the old form of the family, shakes the ethical conceptions on which the moral code of bourgeois society is built, and endangers the existence of the human race, for which healthy mothers are an essential precondition. If the human species does not, in the end, give up on itself, it will have to give up the capitalist economic order.[64]

Most students of Marxism today would see little in these statements in conflict with the ideas of Marx. Indeed, the emphasis on what work conditions do to human relations is well within the spirit of the writings of Marx and Engels. Yet around the turn of the century their orthodox epigones

[61] Braun, p. 431.
[63] *Ibid.*, p. 469.

[62] *Ibid.*, pp. 56–57.
[64] *Ibid.*, p. 556.

regarded Braun's views as heretical. The stress on changes in consciousness was criticized as a concession to idealism; and the emphasis she laid
on the happiness and fulfillment of the individual must have sounded much
too hedonistic to the stern and arid theologians of the movement.

In subsequent writings and pronouncements, Braun laid increasing
stress on these allegedly un-Marxian themes. Where orthodox Marxism
had regarded the mobilization of women for full professional life as the solution, had sought liberation in socially useful work and in the women's liberation from household chores, Braun now moved more and more toward a
more general humanism, in which intellectual development as well as sen-
sual enjoyment became as important as productive labor. In short, earlier
than many she rebelled against the dreary economic determinism that
Marxist dogma had imposed on the socialist movement.

Her doctrinal disagreements with the party leadership intermingled with
personality conflicts, especially in her relations with Klara Zetkin (whom I
will discuss in a moment). I am tempted to argue that Zetkin was the more
radical Marxist of the two, whereas Braun was more radical in her feminist
program. But Braun's entire life-style did not fit into the party. Her outlook
was not sufficiently sober for the exceedingly Prussian, bureaucratic, and
dogmatic party; and soon everything she proposed was criticized. Her
interests in the immediate improvement of the condition of proletarian
women, as well as her practical proposals to that end, were denounced as
reformism and as activities that would splinter the energies of the movement. Her efforts to find new adherents either among intellectuals or even
among domestic servants were regarded with suspicion and were seen as
threats to the solidarity of the workers' movement. Her admonitions that
proletarian women should school or educate themselves were taken as
slander of the proletariat. Her suggestion that the party as a whole strive for
a higher level of education, self-discipline, responsibility, and mutual respect was regarded as arrogant. In short, the German Marxist movement
was led by narrow-minded, arrogant, dogmatic prigs who could not tolerate
anyone with a larger view or with élan and imagination. This pattern again
and again led to confrontation between Marxists and radical feminists; and
again and again the radical feminists, like Lily Braun, left the party.[65]

This did not happen inevitably. Those women recruited into the socialist
movement who defined auxiliary roles for themselves often became lifelong
functionaries in its sprawling bureaucracy. Such auxiliary roles could be
found in organizational work, in journalism, and also in the various kinds of
mutual-aid work undertaken by the party. Of these activities, journalism
was the first to be promoted actively by the movement; indeed, Engels him-

[65] Blos, pp. 37–41. See also Julie Vogelstein, "Lily Braun: Ein Lebensbild," introduction to
Lily Braun, *Gesammelte Werke* (Berlin, 1923), vol. 1, pp. lxiii-lxv. For some generalizations
about the relationship between feminism and left-wing parties that seem to fit these cases, see
Shulamith Firestone, *The Dialectic of Sex* (New York, 1970), pp. 33–34.

self, in the last years of his life, assisted and encouraged the two surviving daughters of Marx, his companion Louise Kautsky-Freyberger, and the Austrian working-class woman Adelheid Dwořák Popp to found a journal for women workers that would draw them into the movement by addressing itself to their problems. On the whole, this journal refrained from theoretical discussions.

Yet a theoretical line had to be developed sooner or later to define the place of women's liberation within the workers' movement. This line was elaborated primarily by the editor of the women's journal for the German party, Klara Zetkin. Zetkin later joined the communist wing of the movement, and because she discussed the "woman question" with Lenin she is recognized as one of the chief feminists in the communist movement. The position Zetkin developed is summarized neatly in a book by Anna Blos, another women who stayed in the socialist movement, though in the social-democratic wing. For Zetkin, says Blos, the difference between proletarian and bourgeois feminism is decisive. The female workers' movement is an integral part of the total workers' movement. It is not a fight of women against men, because proletarian women work side by side with their men and share their goal—to improve the lot of the workers.[66]

One important implication of this position, as should be clear by now, was the complete rejection of any women not affiliated with the party organization; this was reflected in the total ban on any contact with such women. Soon after joining the Marxist movement, Lily Braun wanted to honor a commitment she had made to lecture to a congress of bourgeois women about the problems of proletarian women. Her undisputed oratorical gifts might have made converts to the socialist movement; or she might have been able to work out areas of cooperation with nonproletarian feminists. Nonetheless, the party leadership forbade her appearance—and in terms so brusque that Braun had her first doubts about having joined the socialist party. Subsequently, the party incorporated these strictures into its by-laws.[67]

My impression is that the work of mobilizing women for active participation in the socialist party was done slowly, that it was given low priority, that the demands made by women so mobilized tended to be modest, and that relevant resolutions passed by socialist congresses were equally modest.[68] To be sure, we have seen that Engels actively promoted the creation of a journal for working-class women, which came into being around 1890; and at the Zurich Congress of the Socialist International, which he attended, he rejoiced in the fact that the delegates included some women (young and

[66] Blos, pp. 10–11.
[67] See the agreement between the party leadership and the socialist women's organization made at the party congress in Nürnberg, Sept. 1908, in *Dokumente und Materialien zur Geschichte der deutschen Arbeiterbewegung*, vol. 4, p. 253.
[68] For resolutions passed by German socialist congresses in 1900, 1904, and 1906, see *ibid.*, pp. 48–51, 117–18, and 185–86.

pretty ones, at that). But we must realize that these women were a small handful: Klara Zetkin was the one woman among 97 men in the German delegation; Adelheid Dwořák (unmarried as yet) was the only woman among the Austrians. Only the Russian delegation, significantly, included several women. In the European movement as a whole, the acceptance of women was very grudging indeed.

Once women were accepted, they could adopt a variety of stances. Like Rosa Luxemburg, they could deny the very existence of a "woman question." In this Luxemburg was entirely consistent, for she also manifested total unconcern with the Jewish question, the Polish question, or the national question—all of which she regarded as a waste of effort and energy for the working class. Like Zetkin, they could acknowledge the existence of special women's concerns, but at the same time systematically subordinate them to the concerns of the proletariat in general. Again, like Eleanor Marx or Adelheid Dwořák (Popp), they could concentrate on the lot of proletarian women and recruit them into the movement. Finally, like von Guillaume-Schack, Woodhull, and Braun, they could express their concern over the oppression of women in general. As we have seen, the last category of women did not find the Marxist movement congenial, whereas the women in the first category became relatively prominent in it.

Most of the generalizations I have made in this paper appear to me to apply to the Marxist movement in Russia, despite the greater recognition that the Russian revolutionary movement as a whole tended to give to its female militants. But this is a topic I shall leave to other contributors to this volume.

PART TWO

Sex Roles and Social Change

Gail Warshofsky Lapidus

Sexual Equality in Soviet Policy:
A Developmental Perspective

THE REVOLUTIONARY leaders who proclaimed the establishment of the new Soviet state in October 1917 promised a radical social transformation to bring about the full equality of women in economic, political, and family life. Their efforts to draw women into new economic and political roles, to redefine the relationship between the family and the larger society, and, above all, to alter deeply rooted cultural values, attitudes, and behavior represent the earliest and perhaps most far-reaching attempt ever undertaken to transform the status and role of women.

In its very first months, the new government promulgated new legal and civil codes that extended full citizenship to women and proclaimed their equality in economic, political, and family life. It launched a major campaign for the political mobilization of women—a campaign intended to communicate new values to women and to draw them more extensively into public roles. But new economic relationships were seen as the real key to any durable alteration of women's position. Only when women were drawn out of the narrow confines of private households and had entered social production on a large scale would they achieve the economic independence essential to full equality.

If the formal commitment of the Soviet regime to sexual equality is not in doubt, the nature and extent of its achievements over the past 60 years have been a subject of considerable controversy. Soviet official sources, as well as a number of Western accounts, point with pride to Soviet efforts and cite a long list of accomplishments: the full political and legal equality of women; the extensive role of women in the labor force and professions;

I should like to express my appreciation to the National Fellows Program of the Hoover Institution, Stanford University, for supporting the research that made this study possible.

and the protective legislation and social services that sustain women in their dual roles as workers and mothers.[1] The observance of International Women's Year in 1975 gave new impetus to Soviet efforts to present these achievements as a model for other societies.[2] If no feminist movement exists today in the USSR, it is because the "woman question" is viewed as having been solved.

Other writers, including some Soviet commentators, have offered a less sanguine portrait of Soviet achievements.[3] They have pointed out that though women participate widely in the labor force and in public affairs they do not hold positions of responsibility and status in proportion to their numbers. In political as in economic life, the higher the level of authority, the fewer the women one finds. Moreover, the inadequate development of the service sector—despite the regime's extensive investment in public child-care facilities—and the limited production of consumer durables have meant that the heavy burden of domestic chores continues, and falls disproportionately upon the shoulders of women. New economic and political roles have been superimposed upon traditional family responsibilities to create a palpable "double burden" that is detrimental to women's health, welfare, and opportunities for self-realization.

These contradictory evaluations of Soviet achievements reflect the different priorities, standards of judgment, and goals of the different observers. But whether they applaud or deplore what they see, they approach the problem in essentially ahistorical and atheoretical terms. Accounts which emphasize the dramatic changes in the position of women resulting from the October Revolution ignore the persistence of traditional norms and behaviors in new economic and social conditions. Revolutionary change in the USSR has brought not a total rupture with the past but a partial assimilation and even reintegration of prerevolutionary attitudes and patterns of behavior that are not merely "bourgeois remnants" destined to evaporate in

[1] For three examples of the official Soviet position, see Tsentral'noe Statisticheskoe Upravlenie, *Zhenshchiny i deti v SSSR* (M, 1969), pp. 1–28; E. I. Bochkareva and S. T. Liubimova, *Women of a New World* (M, 1969); and Valentina Nikolaeva-Tereshkova, "Zhenskii vopros v sovremennoi obshchestvennoi zhizne," *Pravda*, Mar. 4, 1975, pp. 2–3. For a recent Western account expressing similar views, see William Mandel, *Soviet Women* (New York, 1975).

[2] For the Central Committee directive outlining such measures, see *Izvestiia*, Jan. 25, 1975, p. 3. The appointment of a special commission to lead the observance of International Women's Year, headed by a member of the Party Politburo, K. T. Mazurov, gave additional prominence to these efforts, as did the numerous public appearances of cosmonaut Valentina Nikolaeva-Tereshkova, head of the Soviet Women's Committee.

[3] See, for example, Barbara Jancar, "Women and Soviet Politics," in H. Morton and R. Tökes, eds., *Soviet Politics and Society in the 1970's* (New York, 1974); Gail Warshofsky Lapidus, "Soviet Women at Work: Changing Patterns," *Journal of Industrial Relations*, May 1975; *idem*, "Political Mobilization, Participation, and Leadership: Women in Soviet Politics," *Comparative Politics*, Oct. 1975; *idem*, *Women in Soviet Society: Equality, Development, and Social Change* (Berkeley, Calif., 1977); and Lotte Lennon, "Women in the USSR," *Problems of Communism*, July-Aug. 1971. Recent Soviet treatments include V. B. Mikhailiuk, *Izpol'zovanie zhenskogo truda v narodnom khoziaistve* (M, 1970); G. V. Osipov and Jan Szczepanski, eds., *Sotsial'nye problemy truda i proizvodstva* (M, 1969); and Z. M. Iuk, *Trud zhenshchiny i sem'ia* (Minsk, 1975).

the course of further development but defining features of a distinctive political culture.[4]

Moreover, in recent years students of Soviet politics and society have increasingly questioned models of the Soviet system that assume the omnipotence of the state and treat the process of social transformation as a simple revolution from above. The pervasive influence of deeply rooted cultural traditions and the role of diverse social forces and institutions have received increasing attention, and their impact on political structures, processes, and outcomes has become a central theme of current scholarship.[5] An excessive emphasis on "revolution from above" obscures this reciprocal relationship between regime and society and inhibits our understanding of the process of social change in the USSR.

A narrow focus upon elite orientations and power poses still further difficulties by assigning an intentional character to outcomes that were the secondary or even unintended consequences of other choices. Soviet efforts to alter the position of women have lacked the centrality, coherence, and deliberateness that are often assumed by admirers. Particularly since the 1930's, the position of women in Soviet society has been shaped in fundamental ways by economic and political choices in which a concern for sexual equality has been negligible.

Finally, to distinguish the specific impact of Soviet priorities and policies from the consequences of broader patterns of economic and social change is enormously difficult. In some respects, changes in the role of women in the USSR parallel such changes elsewhere associated with industrialization and urbanization generally, although in others the distinctive orientations and priorities of the Soviet regime leave their imprint.

Though the use of more systematic definitions and criteria of evaluation would clearly aid the effort at cross-national comparison, it is the purpose of this paper to shift the terms of the discussion itself. For the continuing controversy over the "successes" and "failures" of female liberation fails to appreciate their interdependence in the broader context of Leninist politics. The transformation of women's roles was but one dimension of a larger pattern of economic and political modernization that depended on the mobilization of a whole range of previously disadvantaged socioeconomic and ethnic groups. Soviet efforts to alter women's roles, therefore, owe far less to the libertarian individualism of either nineteenth-century feminism

[4]As Kenneth Jowitt has pointed out in more general terms, "Marxist-Leninist regimes simultaneously achieve basic, far-reaching, and decisive changes in certain areas, allow for the maintenance of prerevolutionary behavioral and attitudinal political postures in others, and unintentionally strengthen many traditional postures in what for the regime are often priority areas." "An Organizational Approach to the Study of Political Culture in Marxist-Leninist Systems," *American Political Science Review*, Sept. 1974, p. 1176.

[5]See Roger Pethybridge, *The Social Prelude to Stalinism* (London, 1974); Moshe Lewin, "Class, State and Society in the Piatiletka," in Sheila Fitzpatrick, ed., *Cultural Revolution in Russia, 1928–1933* (Bloomington, Ind., 1977); and Vera Dunham, *In Stalin's Time* (New York, 1976).

or Marxism than to a more instrumental, and in some respects traditionally Russian, awareness of the ways in which role change might be utilized as an important political and economic resource.

The Soviet commitment to sexual equality had deep roots in the intellectual and political history of prerevolutionary Russia. But the transmission of Western egalitarian values to the inhospitable environment of nineteenth-century Russia was accompanied by a subtle process of transformation and selective assimilation that ultimately altered the framework of discussion of women's roles. Though Western feminism did indeed have its Russian counterpart, the "woman question" in Russia was ultimately joined to the quest for a total social reconstruction by a radical intelligentsia which came to view the liberation of women not as a goal in itself but as both an instrument and a consequence of a broader transformation of social, economic, and political institutions. Thus a unique conjunction of feminism and revolutionary socialism occurred in Russia that eventually engulfed the moderate feminist movement, reshaped the terms of discussion of the "woman question," and proposed a new framework for its solution.

Placing the transformation of women's roles in the larger context of Soviet economic and political development contributes a new dimension to studies of both modernization and the Soviet system. The literature on modernization, whether or not it deals with the process of modernization in Marxist-Leninist systems, is essentially concerned with the "modernization of man," to borrow a current title.[6] The implications of different patterns of development for the role of women, and the role of women in the development process, have been largely neglected in both empirical and conceptual treatments until recently. Yet Soviet concern with the "woman question" reflects an explicit and unique recognition of the pivotal importance not only of family structures but specifically of women's roles in the process of modernization. Deliberate and long-term efforts to draw women into political and economic life in large numbers, to alter family roles and demographic patterns, and to inculcate new cultural values and norms in support of new roles—all reflect a unique and innovative attempt to incorporate the mobilization of women into a larger strategy of development.

Consequently, an examination of Soviet efforts to alter women's roles not only sheds light on the position of women in Soviet society today but also illuminates a distinctive approach to the problems of economic and political modernization that has served as a model for other Leninist regimes and that could usefully be incorporated into Western treatments of Leninist revolutionary and developmental strategies. By exploring Soviet approaches to women's roles at three successive stages of Soviet development, I hope to demonstrate the importance of role change in Soviet modernization, and to draw attention to its consequences both for the economic and political

[6] The term is used by Alex Inkeles in his contribution to Myron Weiner, ed., *Modernization* (New York, 1966).

capacity of the Soviet system and for the scope and limits of participation within it.

POLITICAL MOBILIZATION AND THE ROLE OF THE ZHENOTDEL

On the second anniversary of the Bolshevik Revolution, Lenin proudly announced: "In the course of two years of Soviet power in one of the most backward countries in Europe, more had been done to emancipate woman, to make her the equal of the 'strong sex,' than has been done during the past 130 years by all the advanced, enlightened, 'democratic' republics of the world taken together."[7] The extension of full citizenship to women and the elimination of their remaining legal, civil, and political disabilities in early Soviet legislation expressed a larger attempt to create a new political community defined in egalitarian, if not universal, terms.[8] The criterion for inclusion in this community was no longer sex but social class; women would henceforth share equally with men whatever rights and responsibilities their social background conferred.

If in some respects the Soviet conception of citizenship was more limited than that of other prerevolutionary opposition parties, in others it was more inclusive. The definition of rights and responsibilities was not confined solely to political life but extended to economic and social activities as well. Work, for example, was both a right and an obligation, a condition of citizenship that in principle extended to women as well as to men; and in theory, if not for the most part in practice, women were subject to labor conscription.[9] Indeed, motherhood itself was treated as a social obligation in early legislation, for the contribution that procreation made to social welfare justified the special measures taken by the state to safeguard it.

Early Soviet attempts to define a new political community involved an effort to create a direct relationship between citizen and state, unencumbered and uncontaminated by commitments to intermediary associations. A variety of measures intended to provide the juridical foundations for the independence of women had as their larger goal the destruction of the network of economic, religious, and family ties binding women to traditional social structures and inhibiting their direct and unmediated participation in the larger economic and political arena. Changes in property relationships

[7] V. I. Lenin, "Soviet Power and the Status of Women," *Collected Works* (M, 1960–70), 4th edition, vol. 30, p. 40.

[8] The Provisional Government had introduced universal direct suffrage in elections to the Constituent Assembly. The new Soviet government established an indirect form of suffrage with weighted voting and explicitly excluded certain social categories from political participation.

[9] The Labor Code of 1918 treated work as a form of service to society. Capitalist conceptions of contractual relationships were repudiated. In practice, the insistence on the obligation of women to work has been an effort to alter attitudes and expectations. Coercive sanctions have not been invoked. See E. H. Carr, *The Bolshevik Revolution, 1917–1923* (London, 1952), vol. 2, pp. 199–200.

and inheritance laws weakened the family as an economic unit and ended the dominance of the male household head, while new family codes undermined the legal and religious basis of marriage and removed restrictions on divorce. But it was a provision of the new marriage law that ended women's obligation to accompany a husband in a change of domicile that most dramatically underlined the larger implications of early Soviet legislation: its effort to sever the constraints of traditional social solidarities on individual freedom of movement.

The creation of a new political community depended ultimately on the political mobilization of hitherto untapped segments of the population and the formation of a new constituency under the tutelage of the Communist Party. As beneficiaries of new rights and opportunities, women might be expected to rally to the support of the new regime, but their mobilization would hinge on the Party's success in altering the subtle network of social pressures, sanctions, and rewards that shaped women's aspirations and behavior. To lead this particular revolution was the special task of the *Zhenotdel* (*zhenskii otdel*), a department of the Communist Party for work among women.

The problems it confronted were enormous. As late as 1922, only 8 percent of Party members were female. Even in the relatively urban and developed regions of European Russia, women played a minimal public role. In rural areas—and particularly in the Moslem regions of Soviet Central Asia where female seclusion was practiced—women were completely inaccessible to government and Party agencies. In order to reach such women and inform them of the new rights and responsibilities conferred upon them by the Soviet government, the Zhenotdel had to create new associational forms capable of penetrating traditional milieus.

The eradication of illiteracy was another requisite of effective political communication. Literacy, the Bolsheviks were aware, was a fundamental condition for participation in public affairs. "A person who can neither read nor write," Lenin insisted, "is outside politics; he must first learn the ABC's, without which there can be no such thing as politics, but merely rumors, gossip, fairy tales, and prejudices."[10] Increased female literacy would make it possible for the Zhenotdel to make contact with a widening circle of women through the network of Party journals. To this end, a growing array of periodicals designed specifically for a female audience and relying upon a network of worker and peasant correspondents emerged throughout the 1920's. *Kommunistka* was launched to serve as the Zhenotdel organ, and *Rabotnitsa*, a prewar journal for women workers, was revived to link the Zhenotdel leadership to its female constituency.

The ultimate objective of communication was to encourage women's entry into political affairs and to develop a growing pool of experienced

[10]V. I. Lenin, "Report to the Second All-Russia Congress of Political Education Departments," *Collected Works*, vol. 33, p. 78.

female cadres for Party and government work. Accordingly, the Confer- ences of Worker and Peasant Women, or Delegates' Assemblies, were de- vised to facilitate the political education, training, and recruitment of women. The effort to identify potential female cadres and train them to staff new social and political institutions was of particular importance in Soviet Central Asia, for it would gain for the new regime entry into a milieu hereto- fore closed to it. Moreover, the utilization of native women for social and political work would promote efforts at *korenizatsiia*, rooting the Soviet apparatus more deeply among ethnic minorities.

Finally, the Zhenotdel led an assault on patriarchal family structures and roles whose aim was to challenge traditional norms and authorities and destroy the kinship networks that obstructed the direct relationship be- tween women and the new regime. Insofar as traditional family patterns were a potential constraint on political mobilization and economic develop- ment, it was vital that the new values and behavior patterns communicated by the advanced sectors not be subverted by traditional attitudes per- petuated within the household. The challenge to traditional family struc- tures and values reached dramatic intensity in Central Asia, where Zhenot- del activists encouraged local women to initiate divorce actions, join in mass public unveilings, and enter new roles in direct competition with men. These campaigns, however, evoked a massive backlash by males and so endangered other regime priorities that they were abandoned in favor of more patient, incremental, and comprehensive strategies.[11]

The impact of the Zhenotdel is difficult to assess in quantitative terms. Certainly the obstacles to the political mobilization of women were fewer in urban areas than in rural ones. In rural areas, the Party's presence was still marginal by the end of the 1920's: three-fourths of all villages had experi- enced no Party activity at all; and although rural Party membership had increased from 200,000 to 300,000 between 1922 and 1927, there were still only 25 Party members for every 10,000 peasants.[12] But the widening circu- lation of Zhenotdel journals, the expanded activities of the Conferences of Worker and Peasant Women, the rising rates of female participation in elec- tions, and the increasing numbers of women elected as deputies to local soviets are evidence of the slow spread of new values and opportunities

[11] For an illuminating account of the evolution of revolutionary strategies designed to pene- trate the patriarchal Moslem communities of Central Asia, see Gregory Massell, *The Surrogate Proletariat: Moslem Women and Revolutionary Strategies in Soviet Central Asia: 1918–1929* (Princeton, N.J., 1974).

[12] Cited in Stephen F. Cohen, *Bukharin and the Bolshevik Revolution* (New York, 1973), p. 443. The correlation of census data and Party membership is based on figures compiled by Merle Fainsod, *How Russia Is Ruled* (Cambridge, Mass., 1963), p. 253. Accounts of the slow penetration of Party activity into rural milieus with references to the recruitment of women are found in Moshe Lewin, *Russian Peasants and Soviet Power* (London, 1968), p. 121; D. J. Male, *Russian Peasant Organisation Before Collectivisation* (Cambridge, Eng., 1971), pp. 67–70; Teodor Shanin, *The Awkward Class* (Oxford, 1972), p. 176; and Sula Benet, ed. and trans., *The Village of Viriatino* (New York, 1970), pp. 278–79.

during the 1920's. By 1928, according to a contemporary Soviet account, some 2,500,000 women were participating in the Delegates' Assemblies.[13] The proportion of women in the Party rose to 12 percent by 1927, and the new cadres were increasingly worker and peasant women of non-Russian nationalities—in contrast to the female membership of the Party at an earlier stage of its development. A small but growing number of women were also being appointed to responsible positions in the state and Party apparatus in response to the steady prodding of a stream of Party directives, although these women's functions and authority remained in many cases more nominal than real.[14]

The influence of the Zhenotdel was also evident in the more militant forms of self-assertion by women, whether in mass demonstrations and conferences or in the utilization of legal institutions to defend newly acquired rights. If its prominence in the literature of the 1920's is any indication, the impact of the Zhenotdel on public consciousness was even more dramatic. It had clearly contributed to a revolution in the status of women. Yet like all revolutions, this one provoked hostility as well as enthusiasm. Trotsky sketched one of the countless domestic tragedies that resulted from collisions between the old and the new consciousness: "An old family. The husband is a good worker, devoted to his family; the wife lives also for her home, giving it all her energy. But just by chance she comes in contact with a Communist women's organization. A new world opens before her eyes. The family is neglected. The husband is irritated. The wife is hurt in her newly awakened civic consciousness. The family is broken up."[15] The social dislocation resulting from war and civil war, revolution and nationalism, contributed far more to family instability than the sexual revolution or the activities of the Zhenotdel. But the very combination of visibility and vulnerability made the Zhenotdel a tempting target in the rising anxiety over social disintegration.

The vulnerability of the Zhenotdel had its roots in the structure of the Soviet political system, which established both the possibilities for and the limitations on women's political participation. Useful as a transmission belt for Party policy and as a mechanism for extending Party influence to an otherwise inaccessible female constituency, the Zhenotdel tended to function as a female auxiliary of the Party. Staffed by the wives and female relatives of Bolshevik leaders, as well as by recruits from factory circles, it was accorded organizational recognition but limited resources and mar-

[13]V. N. Tolkunova, *Pravo zhenshchin na trud i ego garantii* (M, 1967), p. 43.

[14]The major resolutions and decrees that guided recruitment efforts of the Zhenotdel, along with reports of progress made, are found in *Izvestiia Tsentral'nogo Komiteta* between 1919 and 1929, *Spravochnik partiinogo rabotnika, 1921–1929*, and *KPSS v rezoliutsiiakh i resheniiakh s"ezdov, konferentsii i plenumov TsK*, vols. 1 and 2. For a more detailed treatment, see Chap. 3 of my *Women in Soviet Society*; Richard Stites, "Zhenotdel 1917–1930: Bolshevism and Women's Liberation," *Russian History* (forthcoming); and Carol Eubank Hayden, "The Zhenotdel and the Bolshevik Party," *Russian History* (forthcoming).

[15]Leon Trotsky, "From the Old Family to the New," *Women and the Family* (New York, 1970), p. 24.

ginal status.[16] Yet this effort to limit its functions to those of a mere "transmission belt," which became increasingly pronounced in the course of the 1920's, conflicted with the commitments and goals of its original mission—the political mobilization of women as a new constituency of the Soviet regime. The creation of this new constituency involved treating women to some degree as a special social group—one with particular interests defined by sex and cutting across other identifications to family, region, nationality, religion, and even social class. Even as it sought to integrate women into the larger political community through its programs, the Zhenotdel tended to heighten the consciousness of women as women, to encourage them to take an active part in their own liberation, and to defend the distinctive needs of a female constituency.

The tension between these two orientations, which had its roots in the ambiguous relation of class to sex in Marxist theory, had manifested itself within the international socialist movement in controversy over the legitimacy in principle of separate women's organizations. (See the paper by Alfred Meyer in Part One of this volume for a treatment of the conflict between Klara Zetkin and Lily Braun over these issues.) Even Lenin's support for the creation of the Zhenotdel did not forestall continuing disagreement within the Party over the appropriate scope and limits of its activity. These conflicts became even more acute in the increasingly monolithic political climate of the 1920's. As early as the Twelfth Party Congress, in 1923, a resolution warned of the danger of feminist tendencies, which "under the banner of improving women's way of life actually could lead to the female contingent of labor breaking away from the common class struggle."[17] Resolutions at subsequent Congresses expressed similar fears of separatism and warned of the danger of viewing the "woman question" in isolation from the common tasks of the working class.[18]

Stalin's consolidation of power within the central Party apparatus and his inauguration of a crash program of industrialization and collectivization resulted in a redefinition of organizational and political needs. In 1930, as part of a general reorganization of the Central Committee Secretariat, the Zhenotdel was formally abolished. Its abolition was defended as an effort to intensify work among women by regular Party, state, and trade union organizations by holding them accountable for its success.[19] Yet from an organizational perspective, the very existence of a functionally distinct body with a specific mission and the authority of the Party behind it had compelled attention to the sphere of its activities. The abolition of the Zhenotdel

[16]The "abnormal" treatment of the Zhenotdel and the condescending treatment of its leaders by high Party officials were criticized by V. P. Nogin, reporter for the Auditing Commission, at the Eleventh Party Congress in 1922. See CPSU, *Odinnadtsatyi S"ezd RKP(b), 1922, Stenograficheskii otchet* (M, 1961), p. 67.

[17]*KPSS v rezoliutsiiakh i resheniiakh* (M, 1954), vol. 1, pp. 754–55.

[18]*Ibid.*, vol. 2, pp. 88–89.

[19]*Pravda*, Jan. 17, 1930. Women's Departments were preserved in the Central Asian Party organization until the mid-1950's.

ended preoccupation with the "woman question" as a distinct subject of ideological and political concern, submerging it in the broader current of social transformation launched by the First Five-Year Plan. A comprehensive index of Party resolutions and decrees lists 301 entries on the subject "women" for the period from 1917 to 1930 and only three for the next three decades.[20]

The rise and fall of the Zhenotdel had its counterpart in the stormy history of the *Evsektsiia*, or Jewish Section of the Communist Party, the only other group that in composition and goals similarly breached the sexual, ethnic, and organizational unity of the Party in an effort to reach and mobilize an otherwise inaccessible community.[21] Both were torn between two functions, acting as transmission belts of Party policy while simultaneously defending the distinctive identities and interests of their constituents within Party networks. Both flourished in the relative institutional fluidity and pluralism of the early 1920's, came under increasing pressure during the decade, and were abolished in 1930.

The fate of the Zhenotdel was thus a particular manifestation of broader trends in the evolution of the Soviet regime. Its creation reflected an awareness of the necessity of drawing women into the new political community, of basing claims to legitimacy on the democratization of political life, and of mobilizing women for new forms of political participation. The limited resources accorded this effort indicated its low priority and potentially disruptive implications. And the abolition of the Zhenotdel in 1930, like that of the Evsektsiia, confirmed that the libertarian implications of a fundamental transformation of sexual and social relationships were incompatible with the emerging organizational structure and political and economic priorities of the Stalin regime.

SOVIET INDUSTRIALIZATION AND THE ECONOMIC MOBILIZATION OF WOMEN

The abolition of the Zhenotdel completed a major shift in Soviet orientation toward the "woman question." Although the language of liberation continued in use, it had become a revolutionary myth, no longer informing policy but offering retroactive legitimation for measures that reflected very different concerns. The inauguration of the First Five-Year Plan in 1928, the collectivization of agriculture that accompanied it, and the transformation of political institutions and social values under Stalin drew new preoccupations to the forefront of Soviet political life and transformed the position of women in dramatic and unanticipated ways.

During the first decade of Soviet rule, efforts to alter women's roles had

[20] Robert H. McNeal, *Guide to the Decisions of the Communist Party of the Soviet Union, 1917–1967* (Toronto, 1972).
[21] For a detailed account, see Zvi Gitelman, *Jewish Nationality and Soviet Politics* (Princeton, N.J., 1972).

centered upon a combination of legal engineering and political mobilization. The entry of women into productive employment outside the household was viewed as essential to full emancipation, but the economic dislocation of the postrevolutionary years prevented any real progress there.
Indeed, widespread urban unemployment struck female workers with particular severity, and reports of their declining proportion in the labor force
alarmed Party leaders. A resolution at the Party Congress of 1924 insisted
that "the preservation of female labor power in industry is of political significance" and directed Party organs to take appropriate measures.[22]

The rapid expansion of the economy after 1928 transformed a politically
desired objective into a pressing economic need. But the massive entry of
women into social production in the 1930's was less a deliberate effort to
enhance their status and independence than a largely unplanned expression of a sustained economic and social crisis. Moreover, it was accompanied by new social values and family policies that expressed very different
concerns from those of the previous decade.

As late as 1929, the authors of the First Five-Year Plan still looked at
women's labor primarily as it affected women's economic and political situation and envisioned only a modest increase in female employment.[23] By
1930, however, an acute manpower shortage had developed, and Party and
government efforts to regulate the labor force were supplanted by measures
to assure its supply and proper allocation. A new perspective emerged in
official publications, one that viewed the employment of women not in
terms of its effect on women's status but in terms of its importance to the
fulfillment of the economic plan. Exhortations to draw more women into
production were followed by government decrees establishing quotas for
various industries and even listing occupations to be reserved exclusively,
or predominantly, for women—an extension of traditional conceptions of
"women's work" to a new context.[24]

The years between 1930 and 1937 saw a massive influx of women into
industry, with women constituting some 82 percent of all newly employed
workers between 1932 and 1937.[25] By 1937, over nine million women were
employed, and women were more than 40 percent of all industrial workers.
The trends set in motion during the first two Plans paved the way for the
even greater utilization of women workers during the Second World War
and for high rates of labor-force participation that continue to this day.

The entry of women into industrial production was interpreted by many
writers in the language of an earlier decade. The revival of utopian visions
during the First Five-Year Plan led many to seize upon the increased em-

[22]*KPSS v rezoliutsiakh*, vol. 2, p. 89.
[23]For the initial projections, see the *Five Year Plan of Economic Construction of the USSR*
(M, 1929), vol. 2, p. 180.
[24]Solomon Schwarz, *Labor in the Soviet Union* (New York, 1951), pp. 66–69.
[25]*Ibid.*

ployment of women as evidence of the imminence of full socialism, and a vast and vivid literature linked women's new economic roles to elaborate schemes for the communal reorganization of life.[26]

But other strains run through this literature as well, and they offer some insight into the ways in which women were increasingly seen as a major economic resource to be harnessed to developmental goals. Where Lenin had once stressed the human costs of household drudgery, it was now the social costs that received the greatest emphasis. S. G. Strumilin, one of the architects of the First Five-Year Plan, calculated that 30 million people devoted all their time to unproductive household labor, and that for every unit of population 700 hours a year were used in cooking, laundering, and caring for children.[27] The development of a wide network of communal institutions to replace household tasks was now urged not merely to free women from drudgery but to release a vast pool of labor for the expanding Soviet economy.

The architects and planners of the future socialist cities anticipated still other benefits from the increased employment of women. The substitution of urban women for rural migrants in the work force would limit the costs of new urban infrastructures. As one economist calculated: "During the third and fourth year of the Five-Year Plan we shall need at least one-and-a-half million new employees in industry alone, and about four million for the economic system as a whole. If we count even two members to a family, and if each family must have its own housewife engaged exclusively in unproductive labor, it would mean that we should have to bring in eight million people from the villages in order to get four million workers—and this in turn would mean a building program quite beyond our means."[28]

The employment of women would also reduce the ratio of dependents to wage earners. This expectation usually figured in defenses of the construction of communal housing; advocates claimed that such housing would be more economical than it appeared because it would facilitate the employment of women and thus reduce expenditures on dependents. But in the face of a precipitous decline in real wages, it was only the decreased ratio of dependents to wage earners that forestalled a decline in per capita urban consumption during the years of the first two Plans.[29]

---

[26] For a fascinating account of such utopian visions, see S. Frederick Starr, "The Anti-Urban Utopias of Early Stalinist Russia," in Sheila Fitzpatrick, ed., *Cultural Revolution in Russia, 1928–1933*. A collection of proposals is included in B. V. Lunin, ed., *Goroda sotsializma i sotsialisticheskaia rekonstruktsiia byta* (M, 1930). Proposals for communal housing and services, utopian in appearance, were plausible in the context of the First Five-Year Plan, Starr points out with a touch of irony. "Collectivization was a fact wherever factories were built without first constructing adequate housing"; and the shrinking allotment of space both in Moscow and in the newer cities meant that "communalization by necessity was already in practice."

[27] S. G. Strumilin, *Rabochii byt v tsifrakh* (M, 1926).

[28] Cited in Susan Kingsbury and Mildred Fairchild, *Factory, Family and Women in the Soviet Union* (New York, 1935), p. 202.

[29] The steady decline in the number of dependents per wage earner, from 2.46 in 1928 to 2.05 in 1930 to 1.59 in 1935 to 1.28 in 1940, reveals the simultaneous effect of declining urban

To what extent these were conscious objectives of the economic planners is difficult to say from the available evidence. Given the atmosphere in which the Plan was launched and the chaotic conditions that followed its introduction, it seems likely that the rising participation of women in the industrial labor force was a secondary consequence of the economic and social pressures created by Soviet policies, and that this rising participation was retroactively rationalized as a step toward liberation.

The rapid industrialization touched off by the First Five-Year Plan resulted in an increased demand for labor, which was met by an increased supply. The social upheaval of collectivization brought large numbers of rural women to the cities in search of work, while a sharp decline in real wages resulting from the inflationary effects of the Plan pushed increasing numbers of married women into the labor force as well. A deficit of males, already visible in the 1926 census, was intensified by collectivization, purges, and the Second World War. Political deportations and military service transformed wives and widows into heads of households, and the scarcity of men deprived a whole generation of women of the opportunity to marry. The deficit of males therefore obliged large numbers of women to become self-supporting. Almost 30 percent of Soviet households in 1959 were headed by women; and as one Soviet economist noted, "women could not but work, because their earnings were [often] the basic source of income for the family."[30] Thus, though we can be certain neither of the degree to which the rise in female employment was anticipated or intended by economic planners, nor of the degree to which it was part of a larger attempt to economize on urbanization,[31] we can state that female labor clearly became a major economic resource, facilitating a rapid expansion of the labor force at relatively low cost.

Whether the massive entry of women into the labor force would contribute to their independence, status, and welfare depended upon whether or not they would gain access to educational opportunities and to a broad network of social services. Though substantial educational investments made it possible for large numbers of women to acquire new skills, the development of services failed to keep pace with the transformation of roles. The whole pattern of Soviet industrialization, with its extreme concentration of investments in heavy industry, attached low priority to precisely those economic sectors and activities that might have lightened the burdens of working women. Rural underdevelopment and the continuing importance of private subsidiary agriculture, the inadequate provision of consumer dura-

---

birthrates and rising numbers of second wage earners in urban families. For a comprehensive discussion of the impact of Soviet policies on real wages, see Janet Chapman, *Real Wages in Soviet Russia* (Cambridge, Mass., 1963), p. 137.

[30] P. P. Litviakov, ed., *Demograficheskie problemy zaniatosti* (M, 1969), p. 103.

[31] The argument that socialist industrialization strategy involves an effort to economize on urbanization costs is developed in more comprehensive form, with supporting computations, by Gur Ofer, "Industrial Structure, Urbanization and Growth Strategy of Socialist Countries," Research Report No. 53, The Hebrew University of Jerusalem, 1974.

bles and housing, the limited development of the service sector and of retail trade, and restrictions on private economic activity—all had important economic and social consequences for the role of the household in Soviet economic development.

Briefly, Soviet patterns of growth required the household to continue to supply a wide range of services that in the development process are usually shifted to institutions outside it, or are performed by paid domestic labor. Except in the area of child care, and possibly communal dining, the Soviet household was obliged to provide for itself a large share of goods and services supplied by the market in other societies at comparable levels of development.[32] Thus, one of the consequences of the pattern of Soviet development has been the retention of significant economic activities by the household. This in turn makes heavy demands upon the time and energy of its members. Soviet studies of family time budgets, for example, reveal that adults spend an average of 21.2 hours per week on household chores—a figure not substantially below that recorded four decades earlier.[33]

The economic role of the household in Soviet development had direct consequences for the position of women. In the absence of a radical change in the sexual division of labor, the burden of household responsibilities fell largely on their shoulders. As a series of time budget studies have shown, although women devote roughly as much time as men to employment outside the home, the division of household chores remains highly unequal. Women devote almost two-and-one-half times as much time to domestic chores as do men, and have less than two-thirds as much time available for rest, recreation, or further education.[34] As two Soviet authors recognize, this not only limits women's educational and professional attainments directly, but also subsidizes indirectly the professional mobility of males:

From everything that we know about the structure of urban life, we can assert that [free time] is obtained by increasing the housework of working and non-working women—mothers, wives, and other relatives. This is the "contribution" they make to their children's and husbands' further education. And much evidence . . . shows that this is no "loan" repaid with interest, but a "free grant." Consequently, a cause that is on the whole progressive is "paid for" not just by society and not just by those of its members who obtain the fruits of a higher education. Combination of work and study has become so widespread in the USSR partly because it has been supported by the other part of society—people who often do not participate in study at all and even suffer a certain loss on education's account.[35]

[32] Gur Ofer, *The Service Sector in Soviet Economic Growth* (Cambridge, Mass., 1973).

[33] L. A. Gordon, E. A. Klopov, and T. B. Petrov, "K izucheniiu sotsialisticheskogo obraza zhizni: razvitie byta sovetskikh rabochikh," *Rabochii klass i sovremennyi mir*, 2, no. 32 (1976), p. 33.

[34] L. A. Gordon and E. A. Klopov, *Chelovek posle raboty* (M, 1972), Table 12. Their investigation of relative time expenditures by sex found that women spent an average of 27.2 hours on domestic chores, excluding the care of children, compared to an average of 11.4 hours for men. Comparable findings are reported in G. S. Petrosian, *Vnerabochee vremia trudiashchikhsiia v SSSR* (M, 1965), and B. Grushin, *Svobodnoe vremia: aktual'nye problemy* (M, 1967), to cite just two examples from a large body of such studies.

[35] Gordon and Klopov, *Chelovek posle raboty*, pp. 200–201.

Thus, the heavy burdens placed by Soviet priorities on the household itself, combined with the rising rates of female employment outside the domestic economy, meant that Soviet industrialization was partially financed by an intensification of female labor. The extraordinary demands placed upon women in turn adversely affected their opportunities for upward mobility in economic and political life, even while increasing their economic and political participation. A strategy of development that recognized the potential contribution of women to economic growth was also one that established sharp limits for their mobility relative to that of men and produced distinctive patterns of occupational segregation and sexual stratification that will be explored at greater length in other papers.

DEMOGRAPHIC PROBLEMS AND SOCIAL POLICY

In recent years, new problems and priorities have once again brought women's roles to the forefront of political discussion, this time with reproduction rather than production the focus of concern. A declining birthrate has provided the impetus for current controversies, calling into question the compatibility of women's employment with family responsibilities as they are now defined: But the Soviet family itself, as well as the role of women within it, has become the focus of anxious scrutiny. The relationship of changing women's roles to rising divorce rates, juvenile delinquency, widespread alcoholism, and general family instability has offered a tempting theme to a burgeoning number of demographers, sociologists, and journalists, all increasingly aware, as one writer put it, that contrary to earlier assumptions "improved conditions and equal rights for both sexes do not automatically strengthen the institution of marriage."[36]

Current controversies over women's roles reflect the problems and possibilities of a new stage in Soviet economic and political development. The partial repudiation of Stalinism has made it possible to question hitherto sacrosanct priorities and has encouraged new initiatives in economic and social life. A new emphasis on material abundance as the criterion of regime performance has focused attention on problems of *byt* (daily life) in which discussions of consumer goods and services and the use of nonworking time occupy a prominent place. The wider scope of political discussion and the growing reliance on professional expertise in decision-making have contributed to public controversy over policy issues affecting women and to the emergence, in still rudimentary form, of what might be identified as a "feminist tendency" in Soviet policy debates. Discussion of the obstacles to women's fulfillment in Soviet society and of the implications for sexual equality of institutional structures, policy choices, and popular attitudes reveals serious disagreements over the meaning of current social trends.[37]

[36] A. G. Kharchev, in *Zhurnalist*, 11 (Nov. 1972); trans. in *CDSP*, 25, no. 8.
[37] Discussions of these issues have received increased attention in official circles, and a number of articles have recently appeared in authoritative journals. For several examples among many, see L. A. Gordon, E. V. Klopov, and L. Onikov, "Sotsial'nye problemy byta," in

At the core of recent discussions is a preoccupation with the fate of the family in contemporary Soviet society. In the immediate postrevolutionary period, as we have seen, the family was viewed as the embodiment of tradition and the carrier of counterrevolutionary values.[38] It was, as Bukharin put it, "the most conservative stronghold of the old regime."[39] No matter whether the family as a social institution would "wither away" completely, as the Left Communists anticipated, or would simply undergo structural transformation; Soviet policy attempted to undermine it by weakening the religious, legal, economic, and sexual bonds that held it together and by encouraging the liberation of women from its confines.

The thrust of early Soviet policy involved the redefinition of women's roles through a shift of functions from the family to the wider community. Early Bolshevik ideology drew on the Marxian distinction between "productive" and "nonproductive" activities in devaluing family roles, and linked the liberation of women to their entry into public arenas. At the same time, it was strongly pronatalist in its assumptions, committed to procreation, if not to nurturance. Childbearing was emphasized as a uniquely feminine role; child-rearing, however, would be assumed by public institutions.

By the late 1920's, rising anxieties over social disintegration were expressed in a growing reaction against the excesses of liberation, and particularly sexual liberation. This reaction was ultimately codified in the social policies of the Stalin period. To a political regime increasingly dependent on social solidarity and stability, hierarchical relationships, and centralized authority, the family came to be seen as a bulwark of the social system, indeed as a microcosm of the new socialist order. Earlier measures designed to enhance the freedom and autonomy of women were whittled away by measures restricting divorce and abortion in a desperate effort to encourage family stability, to support the family's procreative and socializing functions, and to offer women greater protection in place of freedom.

Housework, once so harshly stigmatized by Lenin, was now considered socially useful labor, and Soviet wives were assured that creating a comfortable home life was an important and worthy goal. The status and identity of

---

Kommunist, 17 (Nov. 1974); "Sem'ia," the lead editorial in an organ of the Party Central Committee, *Sovetskaia kul'tura*, Feb. 4, 1974, p. 1; and the report of an *obkom* plenum specifically convened to discuss the role of women in the Ivanovo region in *Partiinaia zhizn'*, 16 (Aug. 1975), pp. 44–45. A vast array of books in the past few years have also been devoted to discussions of women's roles as workers and mothers, most recently in connection with the observance of International Women's Year. Among the most illuminating of these are V. B. Mikhailiuk, *Ispol'zovanie zhenskogo truda v narodnom khoziaistve* (M, 1970); N. A. Sakharova, *Optimal'nye vozmozhnosti ispol'zovaniia zhenskogo truda v sfere obshchestvennogo proizvodstva* (Kiev, 1973); *Problemy byta, braka i sem'i* (Vilnius, 1970); A. E. Kotliar and S. Ia. Turchaninova, *Zaniatost' zhenshchin v proizvodstve* (M, 1975); Z. M. Iuk, *Trud zhenshchiny i sem'ia* (Minsk, 1975); M. S. Rumiantseva and A. I. Pergament, *Spravochnik zhenshchiny-rabotnitsy* (M, 1975); V. N. Tolkunova, ed., *Zakonodatel'stvo o pravakh zhenshchin v SSSR* (M, 1975).

[38] For a more comprehensive treatment, see Kent Geiger, *The Family in Soviet Russia* (Cambridge, Mass., 1968); Alex Inkeles, "Family and Church in Postwar USSR," in his *Social Change in Soviet Russia* (Cambridge, Mass., 1968).

[39] Geiger, p. 52.

women were not exclusively functions of their independent role in social production but were redefined to include ascriptive elements deriving from marital and maternal roles. The new conception of femininity that emerged in the 1930's, in which a glorification of maternal and wifely virtues was joined to demands for economic productivity, is splendidly conveyed in the speech of a fictional heroine on a visit to the Kremlin in 1937: "Our feminine hearts are overflowing with emotions," she said, "and of these love is paramount. Yet a wife should also be a happy mother and create a serene home atmosphere, without, however, abandoning work for the common welfare. She should know how to combine all these things while also matching her husband's performance on the job." "Right!" said Stalin.[40] Soviet family policy, therefore, has involved an effort to superimpose new economic and civic responsibilities on the traditional housekeeping and childbearing functions of women, while lifting some of the burdens of the latter through the provision of public services. The overall goal has been to increase the size and productivity of the labor force without impairing the childbearing potential of women workers.

By the late 1960's there was increasing evidence that this effort to balance contradictory imperatives had not been altogether successful. A declining birthrate in the urban regions of European Russia, attributed at least in part to the excessive strains placed upon working mothers, has been a source of growing alarm to Soviet economists and demographers, who fear its adverse impact upon demographic structure, political and military power, economic development, and ethnic balance.[41]

Ambivalent Soviet reactions to these demographic trends are understandable, in view of the complex social patterns they reveal. Just as the economic independence and legal rights of Soviet women—a source of

---

[40] F. I. Panferov, *Bruski* (M, 1937), vol. 4, p. 132, cited in Xenia Gasiorowska, *Women in Soviet Fiction* (Madison, Wisc., 1968), p. 53.

[41] Although this decline has been continuous throughout the century, it was partially offset by declining mortality. In the 1960's, however, a leveling off of mortality rates resulted in a sharp drop in net population increase, from 18 per thousand in 1960 to 8.9 per thousand in 1973, a projected 7.5 per thousand in 1990, and a possible 5.8 per thousand in the year 2000. Although the latest fertility data indicate this decline has been temporarily reversed, the disparity between the present net reproduction ratio of 1.11 percent and the 1.21 percent that Soviet demographers consider optimal has created enormous anxiety. Moreover, regional variations create additional problems. The rate of population growth in the RSFSR, the Ukraine, and Belorussia was 1.8 percent between 1970 and 1973, whereas in Central Asia it was 7.6 percent. Contradictory analyses of the causes of population trends, and conflicting recommendations about how to deal with them, have been widely debated in the Soviet press as well as at many scholarly symposia. See, for example, the round-table discussion reported in *Voprosy filosofii*, 1974, no. 9, pp. 84–97; no. 11, pp. 82–96; and 1975, no. 1, pp. 57–78; and the report of an All-Union symposium on demographic problems of the family, in *Sotsiologicheskie issledovaniia*, 1976, no. 2, pp. 187–91. For useful surveys, see Helen Desfosses Cohn, "Population Policy in the USSR," *Problems of Communism*, 22, no. 4 (July-Aug. 1973), pp. 41–55; Murray Feshbach and Stephen Rapawy, "Soviet Population and Manpower Trends and Policies," U.S. Congress, Joint Economic Committee, *Soviet Economy in a New Perspective* (Washington, D.C., 1976), pp. 113–54; and Warren Eason, "Demographic Problems: Fertility," *Soviet Economy in a New Perspective*, pp. 155–61. For a more comprehensive analysis of these issues, see Lapidus, *Women in Soviet Society*, chap. 8.

great pride in many respects—are also associated with rising divorce rates, improved living standards appear to be correlated with declining birth-rates. The fact that fertility rates are highest among precisely those women who are least educated and whose labor-force participation is lowest creates delicate problems for public policy. Soviet economists and demographers are well aware that some of the patterns of family life emerging in the Soviet Union parallel those occurring in other developing societies and are at-tributable to such common factors as urbanization, industrialization, and rising educational levels. But the legacy of older expectations that socialism will encourage an expanding birthrate and the conviction that zero popula-tion growth will create enormous economic and political strains make it difficult to evaluate these developments without ambivalence.

A series of different, though not mutually exclusive, policy options pre-sent themselves for the consideration of Soviet planners. A first possible approach would rely on legal and administrative measures to alter demo-graphic behavior. Restricting divorces, and more importantly, restricting abortions, are obvious measures of this kind. Insofar as abortion remains a major method of birth control in the Soviet Union today, whose incidence exceeds in many cases the number of live births, limitations might have a small but desirable effect on present birthrates. It is therefore significant that although such a course of action has been adopted in Romania and Bulgaria, it has so far been resisted in the USSR. Indeed, opponents of such restrictions have been outspoken in warning that they are inadmissible in principle, ineffective in practice, and potentially harmful in their conse-quences. They urge that efforts be concentrated on altering attitudes rather than coercing behavior.

Advocates of a comprehensive population policy have therefore directed their recommendations to measures that would increase the incentives to higher fertility. Popular attitudes are the key to the birthrate in this second approach. It recognizes that changing assessments of the costs and benefits of children are responsible for smaller family size in all industrial societies. Following Lenin's famous dictum "better fewer, but better," families in-creasingly emphasize quality rather than quantity in raising children. As a leading demographer observed:

While the absolute majority of families want a first child, the thought of a second puts them off: Why deny themselves something they want? And it might crimp the style of the first child. Parents often misjudge the needs—and capabilities—of their first child, burdening him with a heavier load of music lessons, foreign-language classes, and athletics than they themselves could handle between the two of them. Five or eight years later they realize that in fact he is not another Mozart. But then his childhood is gone—if he ever had one. Wouldn't it be better to take the money, time, and energy that such parents put into turning their child into a Leonardo da Vinci and "give" him not a drawing teacher who bores him, or another expensive and hateful box of paints, but a little sister or brother instead?[42]

[42]G. Kiseleva, "Odin? Dva? Tri?," *Literaturnaia gazeta*, 27 (July 4, 1973).

Placing a share of the blame for low fertility on subjective factors, a number of demographers have called for a population policy specifically designed to reinforce pronatalist values. Advocates of this second approach favor a massive effort to persuade the public of the desirability of early marriages, high marriage rates, fewer divorces, and larger families. A veritable campaign has been launched to persuade young couples to have at least two, and preferably three, children. Western studies that point to the advantages enjoyed by only children notwithstanding, Soviet commentators deplore the "hothouse" atmosphere of small families, which nurtures an egotistical individualism at odds with a proper socialist upbringing.

Yet a third approach to population policy emphasizes material incentives rather than pronatalist values as the key to increasing fertility. Encouraged by opinion surveys that indicate a substantial discrepancy between ideal and actual family size, a number of writers have argued that economic constraints play a critical role in declining birthrates. Expanded child-care facilities, preferential housing for families with young children, better coordination of economic and social planning to prevent the development of cities with largely male or female populations, increased supplies of consumer durables and everyday services to lighten the burden of domestic responsibilities—all these have been urged as possible stimuli to higher urban birthrates. Attention has also been directed to the variety of family assistance programs developed in both Eastern and Western Europe. Such comparisons implicitly dramatize the inadequacies of current Soviet programs and indicate that serious consideration is now being given to new social policies which might have a more powerful pronatalist thrust.[43]

The most radical of such programs, which would require willingness to forego the short-term advantages of high female labor-force participation in the interests of long-term population increase, involves what one Soviet author has called "transforming maternity, in one degree or another, into professional, paid social labor."[44] Mothers of young children would be granted allowances to care for children at home, permitting them to withdraw from the labor force for extended periods of time and presumably encouraging them to have larger families. An elaborate economic rationale has been offered in support of such an approach. It argues that the high cost of employing mothers (particularly given high rates of absenteeism due to the illness of children), as well as the rising costs of public child-care facilities, make it more advantageous than it would otherwise appear to offer child-care grants to mothers to care for young children at home. Any additional expense would be more than offset by the contributions to future productivity of an additional increment of workers that such an approach might yield.[45]

---

[43] For a discussion of these programs, see Robert J. McIntyre, "Pronatalist Programmes in Eastern Europe," *Soviet Studies*, 27 (July 1975), pp. 367–80.

[44] Cited in Cohn, p. 55.

[45] K. Vermishev, "Stimulirovanie rosta naseleniia," *Planovoe khoziaistvo*, 12 (Dec. 1972). See also *Voprosy ekonomiki*, 1972, no. 3, p. 151. Similar concerns expressed in more ambigu-

Additional support has come from those who are persuaded that family-centered child care is more suitable for young children than present institutional arrangements.

Proposals such as these have provoked lively controversy in the Soviet press for they touch on fundamental questions of male and female roles. They clearly draw support from a residue of popular feeling that women have been "over-liberated" in the course of Soviet development. Complaints about the "masculinization of women" and the "feminization of men," anxiety that the trend toward female employment has eroded the incentives to domesticity, the view that the Soviet Union has now reached a point when it can afford the luxury of permitting a child to be raised by its own mother—all express a powerful undercurrent of support for a greater differentiation of male and female roles in contemporary Soviet life. Indeed, a recent proposal to encourage a reassertion of femininity by restoring separate education for boys and girls was greeted by a flood of approving letters, according to the editors of *Literaturnaia gazeta*. Typical of the many enthusiastic responses was a letter from one young woman who wrote:

Most men are sick of coarse, ultramodern women who behave like cowboys. I can't prove it statistically but can suggest that one reason there are so many divorces is women's loss of femininity. Many men do not enjoy playing the role of orderly to their wives, after all. Every man, so far as I know, dreams of a tender, affectionate, modest woman, and there are fewer and fewer such. The consequences are terrible: thousands of men avoid marriage, thousands of children are raised as orphans even though their fathers are alive, and the women themselves react indignantly and deluge the newspapers with letters about incompatibility, matchmaking services, and the like. No matter how far emancipation develops, women are primarily mothers, giving life to mankind. Bearing and raising children has always been and should continue to be the most important thing in a woman's life.[46]

Opponents of such measures have criticized the proposed withdrawal of mothers from the labor force as fundamentally regressive. By removing women from valuable and satisfying roles and interrupting their careers for long periods of time, these opponents claim, a division of roles on the basis of sex would be recreated with adverse effects upon the opportunities and status of women.[47] Greater support exists for measures that would shorten

---

ous form appeared to underlie a study which concluded that the proportion of women employed in the socialized sector of the economy actually exceeded the optimal level, and that societal interests would be advanced by a better balance between work in the public and the household-centered spheres among women: A. E. Kotliar and S. Ia. Turchaninova, *Zaniatost' zhenshchin v proizvodstve* (M, 1975), p. 16.

[46]*Literaturnaia gazeta*, Nov. 24, 1976, p. 11.

[47]The extent to which policies giving women greater freedom of choice might lead to massive withdrawals of women from the labor force is difficult to say given the available data. It is also hard to predict what social strata might be affected. The economic terms of such options would obviously have a major effect on the outcomes. Small-scale surveys to ascertain women's attitudes are reported in G. A. Slesarev and I. A. Iankova, "Zhenshchiny na promyshlennom predpriiatii i v sem'e," in Osipov and Szczepański, p. 422.

women's workday with no loss of salary, and indeed cautious steps are currently being taken in this direction.[48]

But commentators who have criticized this whole approach have focused instead on the allocation of roles within the family, and by implication within society, as the crux of the problem. They have suggested a different approach to current problems, one that would require a substantial redefinition of male as well as female roles. Pointing to the uneven distribution of household chores so vividly illuminated in studies of family time budgets, they have urged a redistribution of roles within the household as the only equitable solution to the "double burden" that women presently confront. Attacking the persistent notion that household chores and child-rearing are "women's work," one female scientist argued: "When, say, a new meat grinder is invented, the article is headed 'A Gift to Women'; or when a new grocery store is opened, you read 'Housewife Will Be Pleased.' That's an outdated philosophy and should be criticized in the press. Such confusion of relations and condescensions do a lot of harm; they prevent both men and women from learning the meaning of genuine equality. . . . The accent should be not on women's but on family work. The husband should do as much as his wife."[49] A redefinition of male roles within the family is perceived to be the condition of greater female opportunities outside it. But the further argument that men as well as women have dual roles, and that more flexible work schedules are needed to permit *parents* to combine work with family responsibilities, finds no expression in Soviet writings. The overriding concern with productivity, combined with the persistence of attitudes about "women's work," perpetuates a pervasive double standard and inhibits the reciprocal redefinition of male and female roles.

The emphasis on role-sharing as the key to sexual equality nevertheless has profound implications in the Soviet context. Rather than treating technological progress and consumer affluence as the solvents of social inequality, it directs attention to the structure of authority itself. In this respect it challenges conventional perspectives, for the dominant orientation of Soviet reformers, even those most committed to far-reaching improvements in the conditions of everyday life, emphasizes the allocation of resources rather than the distribution of power as the key to sexual equality. As one of its most eloquent advocates, Zoia Iankova, put it:

It would be wrong to think that the division of chores evenly between husband and wife will revolutionize daily life. Sharing chores may improve the woman's position

[48] A shortened working day for young mothers, and partial pay for a year's leave of absence at the time of childbirth, were promised at the 25th Party Congress. Proposals for establishing shorter workdays for women are currently under study by the USSR Council of Ministers; *Izvestiia*, July 23, 1976, p. 2. A discussion of how labor laws might be adapted for part-time work is found in *Sovetskoe gosudarstvo i pravo*, 10 (Oct. 1976), pp. 54–61. As a number of recent experiments have indicated, a shortened workday for women is also likely to reinforce a sex-based division of labor within the family, since husbands take advantage of the opportunity to shift a share of their household responsibilities to wives.

[49] Lidia Litvinenko, "More Than a Housewife," *Soviet Life*, Mar. 1972.

and establish a new type of relations within the family, but this is only a temporary measure that merely compensates for shortcomings in the service sector. Household chores impinge upon the social activity of men and women alike and cut into their free time. Thus, the main task is not to redistribute tasks that hinder personal development but to eliminate them by introducing fundamentally new ways to carry them out.[50]

All-purpose service centers, cooperative household and child-care arrangements, new shopping centers, mail-order facilities, a greater reliance on teen-aged and elderly volunteers—it is measures such as these, in her view, that will ultimately "revolutionize everyday life."

These conflicting approaches to questions of women's roles suggest both the scope and the limits of discussions of sexual equality in contemporary Soviet society. The insistence that economic independence is the prerequisite of sexual equality, and the rejection of marriage as a device for the economic support of women, remain the cornerstones of Soviet policy. At the same time, the continuing identification of femininity and maternity has been reinforced in recent years by rising concern with the demographic consequences of high female labor-force participation. Recent measures that emphasize the reproductive rather than the productive roles of women, and that attempt to elevate the status and rewards associated with childbearing, reflect wider pressures in the direction of a sharper differentiation of male and female roles. The advocates of role-sharing therefore face a difficult struggle, for they adopt an approach to sexual equality that has never been incorporated into official Soviet policy, an approach that emphasizes not the partial assimilation of women to male roles but the reciprocal redefinition of both.

SEXUAL EQUALITY AND SOVIET POLICY: AN ASSESSMENT

By placing the transformation of women's roles in the broader context of Soviet modernization, our discussion has pointed to the ways in which the changing problems and priorities of the Soviet system at successive stages of its development have provided the central impetus for shifting policies toward women. During the first decade of Soviet rule, the creation of a new political community made the political mobilization of women a major concern. The shift in priorities that accompanied Stalinization established new possibilities and limits for economic and political participation in subsequent decades. A strategy of industrialization that attempted to economize on urbanization encouraged the large-scale entry of women into the modern labor force, while limiting its impact on social structure and values by reinforcing the family as a fundamental social institution based on a sexual division of labor. At the present stage of Soviet development, when the optimal use of human resources has become a major political priority,

---

[50] Zoia Iankova, "Razvitie lichnosti zhenshchiny v sovetskom obshchestve," *Sotsiologicheskie issledovaniia*, 4 (Oct.-Dec. 1975), p. 50.

it is the role of women within the family that has come to the forefront of public concern. In each of these instances, the roles assigned to women have been a function of the larger requirements of political and economic modernization.

This subordination of woman's roles to larger regime priorities has in turn defined both the scope and limits of sexual equality in the Soviet system. For it is predominantly the mobilization of human resources, and the shift in boundary between private and public domains, that have brought about the distinctive patterning of women's participation in Soviet economic and political life rather than a deliberate effort to alter sex roles as such. Though Soviet ideology has been strongly committed to sexual equality, the definition of equality has emphasized women's participation in economic and political life but not their equal access to authority. Thus sexual equality in the USSR has meant an equal liability to mobilization rather than a redefinition of sex roles themselves.

Indeed, the very concentration of political and economic authority that facilitated Soviet efforts to alter women's roles and that made it possible to substitute social for private calculations in providing a broad network of supporting services also contributed to this result. Because Soviet political institutions have been designed to inhibit the aggregation and representation of group interests at the societal level, the responsiveness of the Soviet leadership to the special needs of women has not, on the whole, been the result of autonomous, organized action by women on their own behalf. The very structure of Soviet economic and political life, however much it has contributed to the creation of a new status and new opportunities for women, has perpetuated an essentially paternalistic and authoritarian style of political leadership. The pursuit of sexual equality, and indeed of social equality more broadly, was therefore both compelled and constrained by a distinctive set of imperatives that created new possibilities for women's participation in economic and social life while simultaneously establishing sharp limits.

Within this framework, nevertheless, there is clear evidence of an emerging feminist consciousness in recent years. This new awareness by women of their special identity and needs, however embryonic and fragmentary, has taken varied forms: a renewed interest in the history of female emancipation in the USSR (particularly in the 1920's), the cautious exploration of questions of sexual liberation that have been submerged for several decades, and the assertion of uniquely valuable, if not superior, feminine qualities. This new consciousness finds even more dramatic expression in the assertion of claims upon men—claims for recognition of talent, ambition, and needs, and for a redefinition of male roles in ways that would enhance the possibilities of self-realization for women. Finally, this consciousness has been articulated in the form of explicit claims upon the Soviet regime itself. Pressures for the remedy of discriminatory policies in education and in economic and political life, for greater concern with the behavior of officials who are insensitive and chauvinistic in their relations with women, and above all for the allocation of more resources to child care and consumer goods and services, with the fundamental reorientation of priorities such measures entail, express a new assertiveness by women that has its counterpart among ethnic minorities as well. These claims reflect a wider dissatisfaction with the present allocation of resources, status, and power, although they share no common program for reform.

The continuing tension between the opportunities generated by Soviet development, on the one hand, and the constraints upon full and equal participation that stem from the institutional structure and political priorities of the Soviet system, on the other, reveals the fundamental contradiction inherent in the Soviet commitment to sexual equality. The way this tension is resolved in the years ahead will provide an important measure of the internal transformation of the Soviet regime. For in the USSR, as in other places and times, changes in the scope and limits of sexual equality are an important measure of changes in social structures, values, and authority patterns, and therefore of changing opportunities for human self-realization.

Beatrice Brodsky Farnsworth

Bolshevik Alternatives and the Soviet Family: The 1926 Marriage Law Debate

AMONG STUDENTS OF Soviet history, a view prevails that in the 1930's family policy "changed from a radical to a conservative one," from an attack on the traditional family to support of it.[1] Such a theory encourages the notion that in the 1920's the regime held an advanced attitude toward women and a casual view of marriage, which suddenly gave way to a conservatism imposed by Stalin. Superficially this may seem to have been so; but as an interpretation of Bolshevik social policy during the first two decades of Soviet power, such a view is misleading.[2]

Stalinist social legislation in the 1930's represented not a reversal of policy but rather the triumph of certain traditionalist strains within Bolshevism that had been strong throughout the 1920's. Early Bolshevism was not monolithic, for radicals and conservatives within the Party opposed each other not only on political and economic issues but also on social ones. Thus those revolutionary principles that presumably underwent conservative change in the 1930's—women's genuine equality and independence from men, the noninterference of society in the relations between the sexes, collective responsibility for the upbringing of children, the absolute right of divorce, and the legalization of abortion—were in fact from the outset

Some of the material in this paper appeared in slightly different form in an article entitled "Bolshevism, the Woman Question, and Aleksandra Kollontai" in *The American Historical Review*, 81, no. 2 (April 1976), pp. 292–316.

[1] See, for example, H. Kent Geiger, *The Family in Soviet Russia* (Cambridge, Mass., 1968), p. 321. For other suggestions that the Communists launched an attack on the traditional family in the 1920's see Alex Inkeles, *Social Change in Soviet Russia* (New York, 1961), p. 5; J. D. Clarkson, *A History of Russia* (New York, 1969), p. 573; and Nicholas Riasanovsky, *A History of Russia* (New York, 1963), p. 621.

[2] Geiger, for example, refers to the "radical family legislation of the early years" (p. 321). Inkeles, Clarkson, and Riasanovsky present similar views.

sources of tension and conflict within the Party. Furthermore, the Soviet regime, however impeccable the socialism of its rhetoric, was never disdainful of the family in practice. Soviet society was too backward, the problems of economic reconstruction too vast, and the commitment of its leaders ultimately too ambivalent for serious innovation to occur in this intimate area.

If not a zeal for social experimentation, what did motivate the rush during the first revolutionary year to enact new marriage laws? In the area of marriage and divorce, the Communists saw an opportunity for legislation to overcome the backwardness of tsarist Russia. Determined to begin combating the influence of the church, the new Bolshevik government declared in the fall of 1918 that henceforth it would recognize only marriages registered with the civil authorities.[3] As for the absolute right to divorce granted in 1917, it was regarded as one of the great achievements of the October Revolution, intended to indicate at once that the Communists wanted freedom for women, traditionally subordinate and bound to their husbands. But the institution of marriage, far from being undermined, was to remain stable: instead, a new kind of union was to take the place of the traditional one. And by no means could the family, in accordance with the venerable socialist slogan, begin to wither away.[4] That remained for the distant communist future. For the time being, the Soviet family had responsibilities to fulfill.

The Bolshevik marriage laws of the first decade, far from being socialist, were no more than modern and Western, as Bolsheviks themselves acknowledged. A member of the Supreme Court of the USSR explained this when a new marriage law was being debated in 1926.

Our existing legislation on family and marriage relations was created by the methods of bourgeois law. This legislation has not and cannot have anything communist in it as some comrades are trying to prove. The new law that is being submitted to the present session of the All-Russian Executive Committee for approval likewise has nothing communist in it. . . . Under the prevailing conditions we are compelled to construct our law according to the methods of bourgeois law. The project for the Code of Laws on Marriage, Family, and Guardianship as drafted by the Council of People's Commissars contains nothing that would go against bourgeois law. . . . The State puts the matter thus: if two people propose to get married, these two must, first, undertake to help each other, and second, if they intend to have children, undertake to keep these children, feed them, rear them, and educate them. In a communist society this care is undertaken by the society itself, without making its individual

[3] See "Code of Laws Concerning the Civil Registration of Deaths, Births, and Marriages of October 17, 1918," in Rudolf Schlesinger, ed., *The Family in The USSR: Documents and Readings* (London, 1949), p. 33. Church marriages that predated the introduction of obligatory civil registration on December 20, 1917, had the validity of registered marriages.

[4] For the Communist belief that the traditional family would wither and disappear, see Friedrich Engels, *The Origin of the Family, Private Property, and the State* (New York, 1972), pp. 83, 89; and Marx and Engels, *The Communist Manifesto* (New York, 1955), pp. 27–28.

members bear these responsibilities. But during the period of transition we are forced to follow the methods of the bourgeois countries.[5]

Aleksandra Kollontai, who in 1917 had been People's Commissar of Public Welfare and who from 1920 to 1922 had been head of the *Zhenotdel* (the women's section of the Communist Party), made a similar observation in 1926, but as a criticism. "Our Soviet marriage law . . . is not essentially more progressive than the same laws that exist in other progressive democratic countries. . . . In the divorce question we are on a par with North America, whereas in the question of the illegitimate child we have not yet even progressed as far as the Norwegians."[6]

In this paper, then, I intend to illustrate my view that Bolshevik social policy in the 1920's was basically conservative—aimed at maintaining, not subverting, marital and family stability. By focusing on the marriage law debate in the Central Executive Committee and in the press—a debate that revealed widespread disagreement over the proper role of women—we will see clearly the internal conflicts within early Bolshevism in its interaction with Soviet society. For on the question of women's roles and the institution of marriage, traditionalism made itself felt in the villages, in the cities, and in the Party itself. Indeed, the very impetus for new legislation in 1926 was thoroughly conservative. Though the 1918 marriage code had included such "uncommunist" provisions as male responsibility for women, parental responsibility for children's upbringing, and the legal obligation of relatives for each other's economic well-being,[7] the regime thought it necessary midway through the 1920's to back away from its communist ideals still more. The reason for this was that the transition to the New Economic Policy (NEP) in 1921 had resulted in burgeoning female unemployment. The NEP meant not only a partial restoration of private enterprise but the end of labor conscription, a feature of "War Communism" that had provided work and rations for great numbers of people, especially women. Under the NEP, 70 percent of the initial job cutbacks resulting from the partial restoration of free market conditions involved women, the least skilled members of the labor force.[8] Simultaneously, as the government reduced its investment in protective arrangements—primarily child care—after 1922, the number of homes for mothers and children fell sharply.[9] For hundreds of thousands of unemployed women who had not registered their marriages with the civil authorities, the situation was potentially perilous: should their husbands leave them, they would be without means of support.

By 1925, after four years of widespread female unemployment, the strug-

[5] Statement of P. A. Krasikov, cited in Schlesinger, pp. 133–34.

[6] Aleksandra Kollontai, *The Autobiography of a Sexually Emancipated Communist Woman*, ed. Iring Fetscher, trans. Salvator Attanasio (New York, 1971), p. 43. This is a reprint of a work first published in Germany in 1926.

[7] For the 1918 marriage code, see Schlesinger, pp. 33–41.

[8] A. M. Kollontai, "Novaia ugroza," *Kommunistka*, 8–9 (1922), p. 6.

[9] Sofia Smidovich, "O novom kodekse zakonov o brake i sem'e," *Kommunistka*, 1 (1926), p.

gle against church weddings did not seem as urgent to the government as the need to protect women, the "weaker" party in marriage.[10] The Council of People's Commissars reacted by abandoning its policy of recognizing only marriages registered with the civil authorities. It proposed to the All-Russian Central Executive Committee in October 1925 a new family code that would make unregistered marriages legal.[11] The purpose, Commissar of Justice Dmitrii Kurskii explained, was to safeguard women by extending to nonregistered, de facto wives the right to receive alimony. Further, the government proposed to add to the 1918 law, under which a destitute spouse "unable to work" was entitled to her husband's support, the broader right to alimony simply "during unemployment." Though this right would apply to "either husband or wife," Kurskii explained, it was "primarily intended to safeguard the women. And it is right that this should be so."[12]

In the course of discussions of the new legislation, deeply rooted hostilities surfaced. One observer described as "passionate" the debate over the marriage law that swept the country. Another marveled at the intensity generated by an essentially "nonpolitical" matter. The framers of the new law themselves admitted that they had not expected such a reaction.[13] At a time when Party members were engrossed by the power struggle at the top, this surprise that the issues of marriage and the family should be considered significant enough to warrant excitement seems plausible.

Contemporary absorption with factionalism in the Central Committee in 1925 has been carried over into scholarly research: Western historians have generally ignored the controversy surrounding the development of the new marriage code, probably because of its distance from the male battleground. Support for or opposition to the proposed code did not break down along Left Bolshevik–Right Bolshevik lines, which is precisely why the controversy is important. For what it emphasized was the persistence of other, perhaps more fundamental schisms within Party and society: the traditional division between the sexes and, to a lesser extent, the friction between generations. These schisms transcended not only temporary political alignments but even, at times, the rural-urban cleavage. For the future of women and the family in Soviet Russia they were to be enormously significant.

47; S. Smidovich, "Nashi zadachi v oblasti pereustroistva byta," *Kommunistka*, 12 (1926), pp. 18–20.

[10] This was explained in a note to the 1926 draft of the "Code of Laws on Marriage, Family, and Guardianship of the RSFSR." Quoted in A. Godes, "The Conception of Legal and of *De Facto* Marriage According to Soviet Law," *Sovetskaia Iustitsia*, 19–20 (1939), reprinted in Schlesinger, p. 360.

[11] See projected marriage code of 1925 in *Brak i Sem'ia, Sbornik statei i materialov* (hereafter *Brak i Sem'ia*; M-L, 1926), pp. 25–35.

[12] Excerpt from a meeting, 2d Session of the All-Russian Central Executive Committee, RSFSR, as published in *Brak i Sem'ia*, p. 64.

[13] "Predislovie," *Brak i Sem'ia*, p. 3; F. Vol'fson, "K diskussii o proekte semeinogo kodeksa," *Brak i Sem'ia*, p. 5; N. V. Krylenko speaking to Zhenotdel, as quoted in J. Smith, *Woman in Soviet Russia* (New York, 1928), p. 109.

THE POSITION OF WOMEN IN 1925 AND THE PROPOSED
NEW MARRIAGE LAW

Before turning to examine the debates over the proposed new marriage law first in the Central Executive Committee and then, more broadly, among Party women as reflected in the press, let us see why the issues of marriage and the family should have generated such excitement. We have noted that the provisions of the 1918 marriage law concerning alimony and the distribution of property in the event of divorce were only applicable to couples who had registered their marriages with the proper authorities. Thus it was easy for men to protect themselves from the possibility of having to pay alimony or share property in a divorce simply by failing to register their marriages. As Kurskii's assistant in the Commissariat of Justice, Brandenburgskii, commented, it was impossible to deny that even after eight years "de facto [i.e., unregistered] marriages preponderate in our life." [14] Rural and urban men alike feared a new alimony law whose provisions could not be evaded simply by failing to register a marriage. To each the proposed law was a threat—even though rural and urban households were established on very different bases.

Urban men were unhappy about the proposed new marriage code because it included an article suggested by a delegation of women workers that provided for the equal division of property acquired by the spouses during marriage in the event of a divorce. For urban women, this was appealing: property acquired by one spouse or by mutual effort would become common property to be divided in a divorce. In the past, a nonworking wife who ran the household and took care of the children had not received any share of what her husband made—as the "provider," he kept everything. Under the new law this injustice would be remedied. [15]

The village family, on the other hand, did not consist of one economically isolated married couple, as the city family did. The rural couple was involved rather in an extended peasant household. The de facto marriages that the new law would recognize meant to the peasants not the unregistered church marriages they were accustomed to in the countryside but rather a "loose" living together associated with city life. Though there was rural objection to the recognition of de facto marriage on the grounds that it would increase the intrusion of "city ways" into the countryside, the peasant's primary objection stemmed from the possible economic threat of alimony to the *dvor*, the peasant household. The Land Code of 1922 had stipulated that the possessions of the *dvor* were common property belonging to all members of the extended household, including women and children. Did this mean an equal division of all holdings of the *dvor* for the wife in case of divorce? This was not clear. At least one commentator wondered

---

[14] Schlesinger, p. 104.
[15] The 1918 marriage code had not established community of property in the hope of further undermining marriages of economic calculation.

in 1925 whether peasant women were not better off under the Land Code of 1922 than they would be under the proposed marriage law: after all, he thought, the 1922 code did assure wives a share in the entire property of the *dvor*, whereas the proposed law would have her share only in her husband's property acquired after marriage. However, other clauses in the complex 1922 code had been designed to prevent the splitting up of farms and to permit the separation of movable goods only. Were these principles of the land code to be preserved in the new marriage code? The matter was confusing, and the peasants were not alone in wanting clarification.[16]

A common assumption held that alimony suits were numerous in the towns but uncommon in the countryside. Actually, there were quite a number in the villages: in some regions one-third of all the cases heard in the People's Court concerned alimony claims.[17] It was apparent, at least to the peasants, that those provisions of the new marriage code that would extend alimony to wives in unregistered marriages were going to add to the burdens of the entire peasant household. Much of the controversy in the Central Executive Committee focused on this issue.

It is striking that during the daily debates over the proposed new marriage law in the Central Executive Committee at the end of 1925 the factional issues being battled elsewhere in the Party's ruling circle never surfaced. If they were reflected at all, it was only in occasional elliptical remarks. So much were the participants absorbed in the unfolding conflict between the sexes that most of the delegates, whether rural or urban—including Mikhail Kalinin, the President of the Central Executive Committee, as well as jurists from the People's Commissariat of Justice—acted as though they were unaware of the Left Opposition's demand for rapid industrialization at the expense of the peasants. A delegate to whom the deeper nature of the dispute had become obvious expressed concern that alimony was leading to "nothing but a campaign of ill-feeling against women."[18] She spoke correctly.

As the debate continued, it became clear that members of the government did not always appreciate the nature or the scope of their own proposals. This failure of communication is illustrated by a series of exchanges between a peasant delegate and Public Prosecutor N. V. Krylenko. The peasant pointed out that since rural husbands and wives rarely lived by themselves but in most cases lived with the entire family, the relatives all suffered in the event of separation: "I divorce my wife. We have three children. My wife immediately appeals to the court and I am ordered to pay for the children. As there is a common household, the court decides that the entire household must contribute. Why should my brother be punished?"

[16] Vol'fson, pp. 8–9.
[17] Schlesinger, p. 151.
[18] The delegate was a Comrade Gnilova, speaking at the 3d Session of the Central Executive Committee, November 1926, as quoted in Schlesinger, p. 140; see also "Zakony-zhizn'-byt, iz sudebnoi khroniki," *Brak i Sem'ia*, pp. 43–44.

Krylenko objected: "The brother will not be called upon!" The peasant tried again: "If we live together the whole family suffers. If I am ordered to pay 100 rubles and the family owns two cows and one horse, we shall have to destroy the whole household." He used another example. "Two brothers live together; one of them has six children, the other is a bachelor but has fathered a baby. For a year he has not paid for it; then the court orders him to pay 60 or 70 rubles and the whole household has to be ruined." Again Krylenko insisted that the law would not make the family answer for the brother. Once more the peasant explained that the court makes the whole family pay since they live together. He urged the Central Executive Committee to see to it that payment be exacted only from the defendant's share in the *dvor*.[19]

Whereas to the peasant delegates nothing seemed more unfair than permitting the payment of alimony to interfere with peasant agriculture, to the sponsors of the projected law, notably Kurskii and Krylenko, a woman's right to support was basic. To them, the peasant in his endeavor to preserve intact the economic strength of the *dvor* would be forcing an unemployed woman onto the streets; he would be penalizing an innocent woman who had been divorced by her husband or forced to leave him because of the intolerable conditions in the still patriarchal *dvor*.[20] They reassured the peasants that the courts would take into account the duration of the marriage, the work contribution of the wife, and her actual need, and would seek to award alimony in a way least likely to hurt the economy of the *dvor*. In particular, they stressed that they would not force it to part with its chief asset, land; on this point the Land Code of 1922 would not be superseded.[21]

Now we must ask exactly how well the Land Code of 1922 had been protecting peasant women. After all, why should the peasant have resisted new alimony laws and the legal recognition of de facto marriage if he were already abiding by a theoretically more comprehensive land code that entitled a wife to an equal share of the land, the buildings, and the economic products of the *dvor*?[22] In fact, the 1922 code made the woman an equal member of the *dvor* only in the case of a legally recognized marriage and only as long as she remained married, and it did not guarantee that she could take from the *dvor* what she might consider her rightful share upon divorce. Because the code allowed only movable goods to be taken from the *dvor*, and because no demand for a sharing out of a *dvor* could be made where less than two years had elapsed since marriage, protection for women in divorce was less than effective. There were reports of women who had lived and worked in a family for over three years being ejected

---

[19] Excerpt from discussion of the marriage code in the 2d Session of the Central Executive Committee, October 1925, as quoted in Schlesinger, pp. 107–8.

[20] Schlesinger, p. 117.

[21] *Ibid.*, pp. 89–90.

[22] For this assumption, see I. Rostovskii, "Brak i sem'ia po teorii tov. Kollontai," *Brak i Sem'ia*, p. 140.

from the *dvor* with a few sacks of potatoes and a couple of pounds of flour. There was also the phenomenon one journalist called a "wife for a season," in which a peasant proprietor married a girl in the spring only to abandon her in autumn.[23]

Opposition to further expanding the number of women eligible for alimony by recognizing de facto unions emerged as a male-female issue. To peasant anxiety that alimony threatened the well-being of agriculture was added the general argument that giving alimony to women who had lived in unregistered marriages would increase sexual looseness and lead to debauchery. Nor was this feeling the result of purely peasant prejudice, as the historian E. H. Carr has suggested.[24] Aron Sol'ts of the Central Control Commission pleased many urban men when he insisted in a public debate with Krylenko in Moscow that only registered marriage should carry material consequences; but Sol'ts, alarmed that women might be encouraged by the proposed law to enter sexual relationships in order to get alimony, had in mind enforcing stricter morality, whereas the men sought protection against lawsuits.[25] In the Central Executive Committee, delegates spoke critically of the woman who lived with a man and tried to conceive a child so that she could receive one-third of his wages.[26] David Riazanov, founder and director of the Marx-Engels Institute, was prominent among those Bolsheviks who insisted with Sol'ts that in the interests of societal stability only registered marriage should be legal.[27] Riazanov also would have liked to see a decrease in divorce rates. Krylenko, on the other hand, was indignant at suggestions that a Soviet citizen's right to divorce be in any way infringed.[28]

There was suspicion that a desire to avoid work would create alimony-seekers. What if women, feigning illness, abused the institution? Admitting that the proposed law had a "danger spot" in the extension of alimony during unemployment, Kurskii thought that in practice there would have to be further clarification, such as registration at the labor exchange to establish the cause of unemployment.[29] Instead of exploring the fundamental issue, the lack of job opportunities for women under the NEP, additional questions suggested new areas for conflict. If a marriage were unregistered, how would the court know it existed when a woman, naming some man as her husband, sought alimony? What would distinguish a de facto marriage from a casual relationship? The lawyers began to argue. What is a wife? What are a "wife's rights"?[30] The definition of marriage elaborated by the

[23] Schlesinger, pp. 106, 89, 117.

[24] For the erroneous view that the moral objection to legalizing de facto marriage was limited to peasant prejudice, see E. H. Carr, *A History of Soviet Russia, Socialism in One Country, 1924–1926*, vol. 1 (Baltimore, Md., 1970), p. 47.

[25] For the Sol'ts-Krylenko debate, see report in *Izvestiia*, Nov. 17, 1925. Smidovich notes male applause for Sol'ts in *Brak i Sem'ia*, p. 93.

[26] Schlesinger, p. 96.

[27] *Ibid.*, pp. 150–51. See also David Riazanov, "Marks i Engels o brake i sem'e," *Letopisi Marksizma*, 3 (1927), p. 21, for more on his views on sex and marriage.

[28] Schlesinger, pp. 150–51, 106.

[29] *Ibid.*, p. 117.   [30] *Ibid.*, p. 111.

Council of People's Commissars—the fact of living together, a joint house-hold, and the announcement of such to a third party—produced its own confusion. What about the Communist couple whose Party work caused them to live for years in separate cities? Were they not married?[31]

There was another area of concern. Would recognition of de facto mar-riage lead to an increase in religious marriages and a general strengthening of the church? Millions, content with religious marriages, might not bother to register. Since the 1918 marriage law requiring registration had been promulgated, priests were obliged to ask couples if they had registered their marriages. If the new law were passed, the priest would no longer have to do this.[32] The peasant, in particular, would continue to be emotionally satisfied with a church ceremony.[33] Thus went the case against recogniz-ing the de facto marriage.

SUPPORTERS OF THE NEW MARRIAGE LAW

If alimony was seen as a threat to the peasant economy, and if a sig-nificant number of Party members believed that extending alimony to de facto marriages would on the one hand encourage "immorality" and on the other reinforce the church, why did the new marriage law propose to legalize unregistered marriages? The answer, as we have seen, was that so many marriages continued to go unregistered. Kurskii, citing Lenin, gave assurances that someday, under communism, there would be communal rearing of children.[34] But for now, in the transitional era, the family (i.e., the husbands) must be made responsible.

A woman delegate, referring to David Riazanov's moral scruples, added later: "If Comrade Riazanov intends to abolish de facto marriages, why has he not, in the sixty years of his life, arranged matters in such a fashion that we beget children only after registration; for now we beget them before registration, some before and some after. . . . We must recognize the de facto marriage. Who are the women bearing children? A widow, a young girl. . . . But we refuse to recognize the de facto marriage. We do wrong, comrades!"[35]

There is evidence that even in the countryside, where recognition of de facto marriage was generally opposed, younger people differed from their elders on this subject. At some of the meetings to discuss the proposed marriage law, young people, ambivalent toward the extended household, supported recognition of nonregistered marriages.[36] Party youth in particu-lar favored recognition, although the Komsomol (Communist youth league) did not necessarily endorse the government plan. According to Kurskii,

---

[31] *Ibid.*, pp. 93, 112.   [32] *Ibid.*, p. 95.
[33] Dem'ian Bednyi, " 'Vser'ez i . . . ne nadolgo' ili sovetskaia zhenit'ba," *Brak i Sem'ia*, p. 122, supported this point of view in a widely quoted poem. Bednyi also wondered why the Russian, loving festive song and ceremony, would want to register a marriage in a crowded, smoke-filled clerk's office.
[34] Schlesinger, p. 91.   [35] *Ibid.*, p. 141.
[36] *Ibid.*, pp. 125–26.

opinion in the towns, especially at discussions held in workers' quarters, was overwhelmingly in favor of the extension of legal protection to de facto marriage.[37] In fact, *Izvestiia* noted in reporting on the discussions throughout the provincial press that it was the women in the towns who favored the proposal to equate de facto with registered marriage, whereas the men were opposed for reasons of self-protection.[38] As the enthusiastic reaction of men to Sol'ts's arguments indicated, a good number of urban workers along with the peasant patriarchs would have preferred to see the status quo maintained. Still, the dichotomy between town and country seemed significant enough to cause Preobrazhenskii, a leading supporter of Trotsky's Left Opposition, to insist along with the government that "once we have, in the towns, taken a firm stand for the code . . . we cannot turn back from the code because some peasant *dvors* are behindhand with it."[39]

The government could simply have issued the new marriage law by decree in November 1925. But the Commissar of Justice, made uneasy by the widespread and quite unexpected opposition he met in the Central Executive Committee, wondered whether the project might not need further examination.[40] To an extent that seems astonishing today—in light of the rigidity that in less than a decade would overwhelm Soviet life—prominent Communists such as Kurskii, Riazanov, and Kalinin were scrupulously concerned that the new law be discussed widely since, as Kalinin said, it was one that would deeply affect the life and morals. Kalinin reminded Krylenko, who was irritated by the delay, that the Party had long ago decided to invite the masses to participate in legislation; he wondered if the peasants' sensibilities had perhaps been neglected, if the women's organizations had made known their final views.[41]

When the marriage law came up again in the Third Session of the Central Executive Committee, dissatisfaction was no less sharp despite a year of additional discussion. Although at least 6,000 village meetings had been held, according to calculations made by the Commissariat of Justice, attitudes remained the same. The peasants continued to oppose recognition of de facto marriage, the one feature of the law the government insisted on retaining.[42] To many delegates the law still seemed fair neither to peasants nor to workers but only to "NEPmen," profiteers of the partial restoration of capitalism, who alone had the money for alimony. As one delegate put it, "The law says the court will set alimony, but how do you collect it? You go to the peasant, he says he has nothing: 'This cannot be sold, that cannot be sold.' " A peasant woman, a delegate, objected, "We cannot wait until an extra lamb or an extra piglet is born on the defendant's farm. Even his cow

---

[37] *Ibid.*, p. 126.   [38] *Izvestiia*, Jan. 9, 1926.
[39] Schlesinger, pp. 145–46.
[40] *Ibid.*, pp. 118–19. Kurskii objected to Riazanov's contention that the marriage code had been insufficiently discussed locally. He had clippings to prove that the project had been widely argued in the press, if not in all *volost'* (rural district) and town meetings.
[41] Schlesinger, pp. 119–20.   [42] *Ibid.*, p. 121.

should be sold and the proceeds devoted to the child's upkeep."[43] Among workers, too, there was a lack of cash to pay alimony; but to enforce penalties for nonpayment in the countryside was even more difficult than it was in the towns.[44]

The concerns of the Russian peasant supported the socialist conviction that attitudes engendered by private property were a source of social backwardness. The experience with the proposed new marriage law seemed to validate Lenin's early view that, however pernicious, the factory system was "progressive" because by drawing women into production it led to their independence from the oppression of the rural, patriarchal family.[45] Still, there was pathos in the peasant situation. The anxiety over who would get the cow and the horse—or worse still, a part of the land—was sadly ludicrous. Within a few years, during forced collectivization, the peasants would lose everything. A main theme of the NEP in the mid-1920's was that peasant agriculture should be encouraged and that the "middle peasant" should not be alienated. How curious, then, that no attempt was made either in the Party or in the government to assuage peasant fears by finding an alternative to the hated institution of alimony. Was there no way to eliminate it, and in so doing ease peasant alarm and lessen the larger social conflicts between men and women, fathers and sons?

A SOCIALIST ALTERNATIVE: THE PROPOSALS OF ALEKSANDRA KOLLONTAI

The debate in the Central Executive Committee served not only to document dissatisfaction with the government's new marriage law but also to illuminate a more fundamental problem—the need to instill in Soviet society socialist concepts of collectivism. It would have been remarkable if among leading Bolsheviks there had been no voices in the mid-1920's to insist that the new marriage law be based not on the assumption of a man's increased economic responsibility toward a woman but on the socialist ideal of equality between the sexes, and if no one had pointed out that the concept of alimony was demeaning to women in its implication that husbands were obliged to provide for their former wives. Did no one argue that even in a transitional society there could be commitment to the revolutionary principle of collective responsibility toward members in need? In fact, only one prominent Bolshevik made these points—Aleksandra Kollontai.

In "exile" as a former leader of the Workers' Opposition, which in 1921 had opposed the regime's increasing centralization and had demanded workers' control of industry, Kollontai returned briefly to Moscow at the end of 1925 from her diplomatic post in Norway.[46] She immediately protested

---

[43]*Ibid.*, pp. 147–48.   [44]Vol'fson, pp. 20–21.

[45]V. I. Lenin, *Sochineniia*, Vol. 3, *Razvitie Kapitalizma v Rossii* (M, 1954), pp. 480–81.

[46]At its Eleventh Congress in 1922, the Party unsuccessfully tried to expel Kollontai and Alexander Shliapnikov from its ranks for having led the Workers' Opposition and for having protested Soviet Party policy to the Comintern. Instead of being expelled, Kollontai was sent

the Party's proposed marriage law. In retrospect it may seem all too obvious that Kollontai, a voice from the revolutionary heroic era, a former member of the Central Committee already cast aside by the regime, was bound to fail, that her ideological arguments in the era of the NEP would be treated as the fantasies of an impractical dreamer. To the Bolsheviks, their old comrade's theoretical views on communist morality in the area of marriage relations were already familiar.[47] The new communist woman should be a liberated individual, she had maintained, sexually active and living in a comradely marital union in which economic calculations should play no part. The private family should give way to the collective; jealousy, possessiveness, and narrow and exclusive concern for one's own child should be replaced by the higher value of collective love. Marriage would then lose its bourgeois stability, and a couple, now equal workers, would stay together only so long as their mutual love remained.[48] These were the views that Kollontai had developed before her "exile"; however, her specific proposals on her return in 1925 took a more pragmatic line. After all, had not Marx himself laid down that even during the transitional era communal forms should be developed?[49] Why Kollontai's proposals were so readily, even belligerently, rejected—particularly within the Party—involved reasons that went beyond the "go slow" spirit of the NEP and the economics of the transition period.

In the middle of the nineteenth century, John Stuart Mill, in a brilliant analysis of women's subjection, had pointed out that the question was not what marriage ought to be but what women ought to be. Once the latter issue was settled, the former would settle itself. But only Kollontai looked at the proposed new marriage law from that point of view, declaring at large public meetings, and repeating in the press, that the government was not dealing in a socialist way with the marriage question. Kollontai's analysis of the problem ran counter to the gloomy fears of certain workers in the Zhenotdel that adoption of the NEP had irrevocably doomed the possibility of a socialist solution to the perennial "woman question," and with it the questions of marriage and the family. Rather, Kollontai believed that continued expansion of the private sector of the economy under the NEP would mean an eventual increase in employment opportunities for women and that growing government resources would make possible further investment in public facilities to replace the individual household.

Before offering a counterproposal to the new marriage law, Kollontai

---

into effectively permanent "exile" as a diplomat first in Norway, then in Mexico, and finally in Sweden. From 1922 until her retirement in the 1940's she was in the Soviet Union only for short periods.

[47] See A. M. Kollontai, *Novaia moral' i rabochii klass* (M, 1919), which caused controversy in the Party when it appeared.

[48] A. M. Kollontai, "Tezisy o kommunisticheskoi morali v oblasti brachnykh otnoshenii," *Kommunistka*, 12–13 (1921), pp. 28–34.

[49] D. Riazanov, "Marks i Engels," *Letopisi Marksizma*, p. 24.

coolly explained why she believed it to be unacceptable in a society hoping to be socialist. Rather than being a progressive step, the proposal revealed the Party's failure, after eight years in power, to evolve an appropriate family policy. The government was creating categories of women—registered wives, unregistered wives, and casual lovers—and since the first two were now made equal in their rights, the third was necessarily deprived. Who were these "casual" women the new law refused to defend? They were peasant girls going to the city to work and living in factories and shops in conditions of frightful congestion. And what was the new law going to do for those registered and unregistered wives it was intended to defend? They were to be encouraged to abase themselves in court, to beg for their legal sop from unwilling men probably too poor to pay. Kollontai scoffed at the pointlessness of socialists defining marriage or seeking to strengthen it by legislation, as though abandoned, unemployed women could be aided by such means. Unlike those who agreed that alimony had failed but argued in the press and the Central Executive Committee that the courts must find ways to enforce payment, she insisted on the fundamental proposition that women who served society by providing it with future workers deserved society's support.[50]

How could Kollontai's theory be converted into practice? Writing in 1921 in *Kommunistka*, the journal of the Zhenotdel, Kollontai had anticipated the gradual but steady withering away of the isolated family and its replacement by communal living. In 1926, adapting herself to the less ideological mood of the NEP, she modified her radical enthusiasm. Where she had consistently proposed government protection for mothers in the form of state subsidies before,[51] now she discarded the idea of direct state aid from existing government resources and proposed instead to abolish alimony and create a General Insurance Fund. To it the entire adult working population would contribute on a graduated scale, the lowest contribution being two rubles a year. With 60 million adult contributors, the fund could count on an initial minimum of 120 million rubles, which would make possible the establishment of day nurseries and homes for children, and homes for mothers in need. Moreover, it would provide support for single mothers unable to work and for their children up to the age of one year. Later, as the fund grew, this child support could be extended until the age of three or four. Yes, Soviet society was poor, but Kollontai pointed out that its rate of economic growth in the mid-1920's was impressive. Within two or three years of its founding, the General Insurance Fund would no longer be a burden.[52]

Another important aspect of Kollontai's proposal was her plan for the crea-

[50] A. M. Kollontai, "Brak i byt," *Rabochii Sud*, 5 (1926), p. 371.

[51] A. M. Kollontai, *Sotsial'nye osnovy zhenskogo voprosa* (SPb, 1909).

[52] See *Komsomol'skaia Pravda*, 26(209) (Feb. 1926), p. 2; *Rabochii Sud*, 5 (1926), pp. 363, 378; and *Ekran*, 5 (1926), p. 1, for the substance of Kollontai's argument in 1926.

tion of marriage contracts that would safeguard the interests of housewives. By these contracts, a couple would voluntarily conclude an agreement upon marriage that would determine their economic responsibilities toward each other and their children. A rather weak idea that at first glance seems to have deserved the criticism it received, it was predicated on the assumption that Zhenotdel activists could manage the herculean task of organizing a network in the countryside to teach backward peasant women how to safeguard their economic interests. Though this part of her proposal was probably impractical, we should keep in mind that Kollontai was thinking in long-range socialist terms.[53]

A small group of followers and students responded warmly to Kollontai's optimistic proposals—which kept alive the hope that revolution still lived in NEP Russia—though the great majority of Party members rejected them. "For us young communist women," a Party worker recalled, "Kollontai was a lofty example of a revolutionary fighter, and we aspired to imitate her."[54] Another student, underscoring generational differences within the Party, wrote to *Komsomol'skaia Pravda* claiming that most students supported Kollontai and suggesting as a temporary means of strengthening her proposed General Insurance Fund a five-kopek tax on wine, theater tickets, and various amusements.[55] From reports on the debates in the Central Executive Committee, one senses that there were women delegates here and there who would have accepted Kollontai's plan had the government endorsed it. One, a peasant, declared that "above all we lack children's homes."[56] Another, echoing the same sentiment, wondered why the proposed code ignored the casual marriage.[57] A member of the Zhenotdel pointed out that according to the code many women would be left completely without aid, and she warned against cutting off the little channels of socialist public assistance that already existed to provide help to the destitute.[58] A woman member of the Presidium of the Central Council of Trade Unions wrote that if Kollontai's proposal for a general fund were to be discussed widely it would receive support.[59]

Some of Kollontai's critics were moderate, even mildly sympathetic. Iurii

---

[53] Kollontai's marriage contract idea was called unrealistic by Sofia Smidovich in "Otmenit' li registratsiiu braka i sistemu alimentov," *Komsomol'skaia Pravda*, 37 (220) (1926), p. 2. But Article 13 of the final text of the marriage code would affirm that married parties might enter into all kinds of agreements with regard to their property. A complementary section added that such agreements became legally void as soon as one of the parties considered his or her interests to have been violated. The People's Commissariat of Justice wrote only the first part, but Kurskii explained that the Council of People's Commissars introduced the addendum in an effort to safeguard the interests of the weaker party. Thus, the Zhenotdel would have had legal backing to aid women in cases of injustice in connection with marriage contracts (Schlesinger, p. 116).

[54] A. M. Itkina, *Revoliutsioner, tribun, diplomat* (M, 1970), p. 203.

[55] *Komsomol'skaia Pravda*, 65 (248) (Mar. 1926), p. 4.

[56] Schlesinger, p. 99.

[57] *Ibid.*, pp. 139–40.

[58] *Ibid.*, p. 136.

[59] "Za i protiv predlozheniia tov. Kollontai," *Brak i Sem'ia*, pp. 142–43.

Larin, whose articles on anti-Semitism and alcoholism had shown him to be, like Kollontai, a person concerned with social issues, observed that her idea for a General Insurance Fund accorded with the Party program for future state support for all children. In principle, of course, it was acceptable; but for now he considered it impracticable.[60] Others implied that replacing alimony with a general fund was unfair to the peasant majority, who would never willingly pay an extra tax to benefit mostly city women and children; and to compel payment would run counter to the NEP policy of lessening burdens on the peasantry.[61] Criticism of the fund on the grounds that the peasants would be opposed, however, tended to ignore the fact that the peasants vigorously objected to the government's own project. Kollontai's proposal for a general fund had the advantage of removing what to the peasants was the greatest threat—that the household might be forced to provide support for one member's abandoned wife.

Those who believed that the threat of alimony had the singular virtue of discouraging immorality and divorce in the countryside were particularly scornful of Kollontai's innovative marriage contract. Not only did it seem too ridiculous an idea to take seriously, its spirit was said to be capitalist not communist. Why, one critic asked, somewhat irrelevantly, should economic calculation be a part of marriage?[62] Those who accused Kollontai of inconsistency in presenting the public with, on the one hand, a "fantasy" in which the individual was liberated from the responsibilities of providing for a family and, on the other, a "*meshchanstvo*" (petty-bourgeois) proposal for marriage contracts missed her point.[63] Her critics completely failed to understand that Kollontai was attempting the difficult task of maintaining a sense of revolutionary purpose within the context of the NEP.

Urging increased taxation, Kollontai seemed to the Right to be thinking along the lines of Trotsky and Preobrazhenskii, who were arguing for systematic pressure on the peasants. But the Left Oppositionists sought increased taxation of the peasants to provide economic support for rapid industrialization, not social experiments. Indeed, Trotsky felt it was too soon for radical social experiments, by which the Party would run the risk of falling on its face and being embarrassed before the peasantry.[64] Thus Kollontai's plan was supported by neither the Left nor the Right factions within the Party. The Right's contention that Kollontai's plan for a two-ruble-per-year tax ran counter to government economic policy and resembled the pressures proposed by the Left was an exaggeration.

Among top-echelon Party leaders, only Trotsky, with his characteristic interest in social problems, took the time to discuss publicly the proposed new marriage code. The assumption on which Kollontai's proposals were based—collective responsibility for those in need—aimed at building an

[60] *Ibid.*, p. 141. [61] Smidovich, "Otmenit'," p. 2.
[62] Rostovskii, pp. 138–39. [63] *Ibid.*, p. 140.
[64] Trotsky, *Sochineniia* (M, 1927), vol. 21, p. 49. For Trotsky's view that the time was not yet ripe for social experiments, see Trotsky, *Voprosy byta* (M, 1923), p. 46.

increased socialist awareness among the people. Trotsky argued the other way around—that socialist awareness had to be developed first, that the state could not build new social institutions without cooperation from the masses.[65] But how was a socialist consciousness to be created if the Party did not slowly but steadily introduce socialist measures? The need for developing socialist attitudes was underscored by some of the reactions to Kollontai's plan. Here, for example, is how one working woman reacted: "Comrade Kollontai's tax is altogether unsatisfactory. . . . How can anyone speak of a general taxation of all men, when only one man is concerned in the begetting of a child? What affair is it of the community? The matter is far simpler: if you are the father, you must pay!"[66] Even Trotsky, curiously insensitive to the Thermidorian aspects of the government's new marriage code, was indignant about the grounds on which Sol'ts and Riazanov opposed it. To think that in Soviet society anyone could be so "thick-headed" as to deny a mother the right to help simply because she was not a registered wife; women needed all the protection they could get. Describing Soviet marriage legislation as socialist in spirit, Trotsky regretted that society lagged so dismally behind it.[67] Society did lag; so did Party leaders.

Trotsky shared with most of Soviet society a view of women that led him to praise as socialist legislation which Kollontai condemned as petty-bourgeois. Nor was Trotsky's perception necessarily "un-Marxist." As Alfred Meyer has pointed out in his contribution to this volume, Marx once filled out a "confession" for one of his daughters stating that the virtue he admired most in men was "strength"; in women, "weakness." Both Marx and Engels believed that the weak had to be protected from the strong, that men had to protect women. This notion ran through the debates over the new marriage code, countering the socialist assumption that the collective should provide social security for its members. Few Bolsheviks shared Kollontai's view that women were inherently strong and needed freedom from the debilitating protection of men which alimony represented. The new marriage code, in its assumption that women were weak, continued to project the image of woman as victim.

CONFLICTING IMAGES OF WOMEN IN BOLSHEVISM

Much of the reaction in the Party against Kollontai's plan for a General Insurance Fund to eliminate alimony stemmed from opposition to Kollontai herself and to the "new woman" she represented. Pointing to her allegedly

---

[65] Trotsky, *Sochineniia*, vol. 21, pp. 71–72.

[66] "Za i protiv predlozheniia tov. Kollontai," *Brak i Sem'ia*, pp. 143–44.

[67] Trotsky, *Sochineniia*, vol. 21, p. 434. Emel'ian Iaroslavskii, "Moral' i byt proletariata v perekhodnyi period," *Molodaia Gvardiia*, 3 (Mar. 1926), pp. 150–51, expressed identical views. Supporters of the marriage law liked to picture its opponents (in Krylenko's words) as philistines. Krylenko argued that Soviet policy was moving toward economic and political equality of the sexes despite opposition from philistines and peasants. A footnote in Trotsky, *Sochineniia*, vol. 21, p. 514, quotes with approval Krylenko's arguments in favor of the new marriage law.

dissolute sexual views, critics accused her of continuing to seek to corrupt Soviet youth by encouraging irresponsibility.[68] The leader of the Party's opposition to Kollontai in 1926 was Sofia Smidovich, who had replaced Kollontai as head of the Zhenotdel in 1922, holding that post until 1924, and who was now a member of the Party's powerful Control Commission; she was seconded by Kollontai's old friend Emel'ian Iaroslavskii, also a member of the Control Commission and now a Stalinist. Journals for which Kollontai used to write, *Molodaia Gvardiia* (the Komsomol journal) and *Kommunistka*, were now less open to her and her radical campaigns. Smidovich and Iaroslavskii, on the other hand, had free access to Komsomol youth publications, *Molodaia Gvardiia*, and the newspaper *Komsomol'skaia Pravda*. There they intimated that whereas the regime sought stability in marital relations, Kollontai advocated the opposite.[69] For although the Bolsheviks had provided women with the right to divorce, in 1926 they were not advising them to use that right.

Kollontai was saying "The collective will support the children, so why remain together once love is gone?" Without a doubt, she was unique among prominent Bolsheviks in seeking frankly to incorporate the concept of free sexuality into the revolutionary framework.[70] Other Party members spoke about "new people" but saw them inhabiting a distant, communist future. Iaroslavskii, though giving assurances that someday under communism there would be no need for moral laws, was in line with dominant Party attitudes when he warned that it was for bourgeois not proletarian youth to flit from flower to flower indulging in Kollontai's "love of the worker bees." In fact, Iaroslavskii recalled, for eight or nine years he had sat in prison and sexual abstinence had done him no harm.[71] Smidovich, though anticipating new forms in the future, conceived of herself as a member of an older, more staid generation that wanted to protect women from the "African" sexual passions and irresponsibility of young men.[72] To a visitor inquiring about sexual mores in the revolutionary society, Smidovich distinguished between generations: "Of course, we older communists believe that it is best to love one person and stick to him."[73] Meanwhile, Kollontai gazed boldly from the cover of the popular magazine *Ekran*, in whose pages she argued for the General Insurance Fund on behalf of "new women" who were strong and wanted to move forward to a trans-

[68] For the most slashing attack, see E. Lavrov, "Polovoi vopros i molodezh'," *Molodaia Gvardiia*, 3 (Mar. 1926), pp. 136–48.

[69] See, for example, Smidovich writing in *Komsomol'skaia Pravda*, 37 (220) (Feb. 1926), p. 2; Iaroslavskii writing in *Molodaia Gvardiia*, 3 (Mar. 1926), p. 150.

[70] See Kollontai, "Tezisy."

[71] Iaroslavskii writing in *Molodaia Gvardiia*, 3 (Mar. 1926), p. 150.

[72] Smidovich, "O liubvi," in I. Razin, ed., *Komsomol'skii byt* (M-L, 1927), pp. 268–73 (reprinted from *Pravda*). In the Razin volume, too, are articles by Aron B. Zalkind, a Professor at Sverdlov University who throughout the 1920's argued, based on a selective use of Freud, that sexual excess robbed the revolution of social energies. See his "Etika, byt i molodezh'," pp. 70–88, and "Otvet na anketu," pp. 166–68.

[73] Smith, *Women in Soviet Russia*, p. 102.

formed, freer life.[74] The two women, Smidovich and Kollontai, although both 54 years old, saw themselves as representing different constituencies. Smidovich acted on behalf of a Party leadership that was in this instance singularly united. She considered herself an orthodox militant defending the proletarian vanguard against the bourgeois intelligentsia, correcting the inadequate notions of the "great mass of our proletarian youth" on the question of sexual relations. In her widely published criticism of Kollontai's proposals, Smidovich took the line that the Soviet Union was still in the transitional era, moving painfully from capitalism to socialism; consequently, Kollontai's ideas were premature and would lead only to increased promiscuity.[75]

No doubt Smidovich believed she had no choice. Iaroslavskii and Smidovich, like Lenin before them, were hobbled not only by the Marxist paradigm that saw change in material conditions necessarily preceding changes in social relationships, but by a suspicion of sexuality as prejudicial to revolutionary performance. In his much-quoted conversation with Klara Zetkin in 1920, Lenin indicated his fear of "orgiastic" situations that endangered the revolution. Youth, he knew, was rebelling with all the impetuosity of its years, and nothing could therefore be "more false than to preach monkish asceticism." But he warned of the threat to the concentration of revolutionary forces if sex were to become youth's main mental concern.[76] Lenin would not have been interested in knowing that Freud, too, would analyze the cultural uses of repressed sexual energies.[77] As he told Zetkin, he distrusted Freudianism, scorning "eternal theories and discussions about sexual problems." Instead of the "present, widespread hypertrophy in sexual matters," Lenin advocated "healthy sport, swimming, racing, walking, bodily exercises of every kind, and many-sided intellectual interests."[78] Lenin's assumption that expending energy in athletic competition and intellectual activity was wholesome and not harmful to revolutionary concentration underscored his own rejection of free sexuality as inimical to political control.

The Old Bolsheviks—Lenin, Smidovich, and Iaroslavskii—thought it unwise for communists like Kollontai to push the revolution into areas of innovation beyond a definition of woman's liberty that meant freedom from the constraint of bourgeois marriage and the family laws of the bourgeois state.[79] Presumably these Old Bolsheviks did not share Kollontai's interest in a redefinition of sexual roles.

[74] Kollontai, "Brak, zhenshchiny i alimenty," *Ekran*, 5 (1926), p. 1.
[75] See Smidovich, "O liubvi," p. 268, and writing in *Komsomol'skaia Pravda*, 37 (220) (Feb. 1926), p. 2.
[76] Lenin to Zetkin, in Clara Zetkin, *Reminiscences of Lenin* (New York, 1934), p. 48.
[77] See Sigmund Freud, *Civilization and Its Discontents* (New York, 1962), pp. 50–51.
[78] Zetkin, pp. 45, 50.
[79] *Ibid.*, p. 48. This kind of liberty was defined in the marriage code of 1918 in provisions for legal and political equality for each marriage partner. Such equality was symbolized by the right to divorce, by the termination of the wife's obligation to follow her husband if he changed his residence, and by the right of the married couple to use the wife's surname.

Smidovich's use of the term "transitional" is curiously suggestive, for in reading her views on *byt* (daily life) one senses that Smidovich herself was transitional. She was one of the earliest Bolshevik leaders in the 1920's to espouse publicly the views on sex that were to become policy in the 1930's, one of the first frankly to break the nineteenth-century bond between socialism and female sexual liberty to which Bebel alluded.[80] Attacking the elegant Kollontai—in her aristocratic appearance and language so obviously outside the new Soviet culture, so clearly a holdover of the intelligentsia—Smidovich appealed to basic prejudices. Here was a preview of the assault on the intelligentsia that would take place a few years later. Paradoxically, in the case of sexual questions, it was Kollontai, the *intelligentka*, who spoke for the younger generation of Communists. The attitudes of Kollontai, Smidovich, and their followers by no means exhaust the range of controversies about *byt* that were raging in the Soviet Union in the 1920's. But the published views of these two women leaders define the coordinates by which nearly all the elements of the controversy can be located. For this reason, it will be useful to discuss an exchange of letters that appeared in *Komsomol'skii byt* between Smidovich and two young women, members of the Communist youth organization. This exchange brings into focus the image of women suggested by the debates on the new marriage code.

Of the young woman named Lida who wrote to Smidovich, we know only that she was a *komsomolka*, was nineteen years old, and lived far from Moscow. She wrote seeking guidance on sex and love, and wanted to know whether she should succumb to male desires and engage in transient love affairs that meant the possibility of crippling abortions or of raising a child alone. It was not material comforts Lida sought. She just wanted to live openly, not even necessarily in a registered marriage, but in a lasting union with the man she loved.[81] To Lida's fearful questions, which reflected the traditional attitudes in regions far from the center of revolutionary ferment, Smidovich gave answers that were on balance more conservative than avant-garde. She did not object to unregistered unions so long as they were serious and responsible. But advising Lida to trust her cautious, womanly instincts, Smidovich explained that for a woman love was not transient passion but an extended process of birth, nursing, and child-rearing. In fact, a woman's relationship to love was determined to a large degree by her role as mother. How much this seemed true Smidovich indicated in her revealing remark that she would not even discuss with Lida marriages without children: they were so rare as not to merit consideration.[82]

To discuss childless marriages would have involved mention of birth control, an awkward subject for Smidovich. Overpopulation did not trouble

---

[80] August Bebel, *Die Frau in der Vergangenheit, Gegenwart und Zukunft* (Zurich, 1883), trans. by Daniel De Leon as *Woman Under Socialism* (New York, 1971), pp. 82–85.

[81] "Pis'mo Komsomolki k tov. Smidovich," in Razin, ed., *Komsomol'skii byt*, pp. 172–73.

[82] Smidovich, "Otvet na pis'mo Komsomolki," in *Komsomol'skii byt*, pp. 174–75.

Russians: with their vast potential resources they could provide sustenance for many more people. And to many Marxists, who saw no lack of food and material resources but only their unequal distribution, birth control seemed a gesture of bourgeois defeatism. Smidovich's failure even to mention birth control to Lida, as well as her attitude toward sexual mores in her articles in *Komsomol'skii byt*, suggests a negative attitude stemming not only from Marxist unease but from a personal reluctance to condone Kollontai's interpretation of the free woman.[83] For Kollontai's vision of the life of socialism's new woman, although it might not please a feminist today, included a sexuality that offended Smidovich's image of woman as the responsible mother.[84]

Not Kollontai but one of the fledgling "new people" whose attitudes she had so often described replied to Smidovich. The *komsomolka* Lida, inexperienced and anxious, had written to Smidovich asking that the older comrade tell her how to live in the new society; now, however, another *komsomolka*, Nina Vel't, launched not a respectful inquiry but an angry attack. She challenged Smidovich's professed concern with the problems of women and marriage. Did Smidovich really care, or was she interested more in Soviet society's need for children? Nina considered Smidovich's advice to Lida "cheap moralizing" that neither she nor Lida needed. Rejecting Smidovich's admonition, in effect, to be continent or to be willing to assume the care of a family, Nina reminded Smidovich that the socialist does not bow to the laws of nature but seeks instead to alter them. Motherhood should result from choice, not inevitability. Nina ridiculed the Party's ambivalence about birth control as an attitude that led not to ointment being applied to a hurt finger, as she put it, but rather to amputation of the entire hand.[85] Yes, abortions could be crippling; Nina did not like them either. But in favoring larger families did Smidovich think that four sickly children whose parents were unable to support them properly were better for society than two healthy ones? And what of the mother's life? With two children there was still some chance for employment, but four children excluded the possibility. Did Smidovich even know the "new woman"? Surely she was not the married woman cut off from society and dependent for her living on a man because she had abandoned work and studies for motherhood. Nor could she be the pathetic person whom Smidovich suggested Lida emulate, a woman who defined herself in terms of her relationship to a man. A fear for the kind of future the Party had in mind caused Nina to press her attack, questioning Smidovich's larger image of Soviet

---

[83]See, for example, Smidovich, in *Komsomol'skii byt*, p. 268.

[84]See below, p. 161, for Kollontai's own objection to the "bourgeois" idea that women did not have to bear children. She believed that motherhood was a socialist woman's responsibility.

[85]Nina Vel't, "Otkrytoe pis'mo tovarishchu Smidovich," in Razin, ed., *Komsomol'skii byt*, pp. 181–83. See the report of a 1927 medical conference in Kiev where demands were made for development and production of adequate contraceptives as an alternative to abortion; reprinted in Schlesinger, pp. 183–87.

society. Why did Smidovich write approvingly of Lida's assertion that she did not seek a comfortable existence but wanted only to live with a man in an enduring relationship? Intuiting that Smidivoch was using asceticism as a defense against sensuality, Nina demanded: Why should a communist woman not want life's comforts? Did socialism have to be drab? Was a silk blouse a sign that one must be driven from the Party? [86]

Was the bold Nina a typical *komsomolka* or was the undemanding Lida more usual? The issues of morality and life-style were so widely debated that one might point to either young woman as representative. Certainly the Control Commission's concern with the issue of "debauchery" (*ras-pushchennost'*) and their fear that the institution of the family might be further weakened unless de facto marriage carried legal consequences suggest the existence of sizable numbers of "new women" like Nina who expressed "Kollontaish thinking." [87] The Party's concern over "sexual chaos," expressed through those provisions of the new marriage code that would widen the scope of male responsibility for women and children, and its attacks on Kollontai did not mean that Soviet youth was debauched. Sexual chaos and debauchery were subjective terms to which Kollontai refused to subscribe; where others saw chaos, she saw healthy sexuality. Would the Party, she wondered, prefer that its youth resort to old-fashioned bourgeois prostitution? [88]

The more Smidovich wrote, the more apparent it became that she rejected the idea of female sexual freedom and appealed instead to the idea of victimization. One article in particular typified her thinking. In it she analyzed the reasons for the suicide of a young Party member, a woman named Davidson. Smidovich blamed the girl's death on the cruel insensitivity of her husband Koren'kov, also a Party member, who flaunted his affairs with other women and forced Davidson to submit to three abortions. Although Smidovich must have known that a more self-confident, stable woman would not have remained in such a damaging marriage, she directed her anger at Party comrades who, despite their closeness to the dismal situation, had refrained from interfering, inhibited by a "misguided" belief that marital relations were not the business of the Party. Smidovich countered in anger that if Koren'kov had so much as uttered an "anti-Semitic abuse" his exclusion from the Party would have been certain. [89]

Smidovich, who was committed to the eradication of male chauvinism,

---

[86] Vel't, p. 184. For support of her position, see the speech by the Komsomol Secretary at the 7th All-Union Komsomol Congress in 1932: "For this reason we are not opposed to music, we are not opposed to love, we are not opposed to flowers or beautiful wearing apparel. We are not ascetics and do not preach asceticism. We are for a full, rich, beautiful life" (quoted in E. Winter, *Red Virtue* [New York, 1933], p. 36).

[87] See Lev S. Sosnovsky, *Bol'nye voprosy* (L, 1926).

[88] *Rabochii Sud*, p. 366. For a view of sexual morality among youth in the 1920's, see Klaus Mehnert, *Youth in Soviet Russia* (New York, 1933). Also see Sheila Fitzpatrick, "Sex and Revolution: The Sexual Mores of Soviet Students in the 1920's," unpublished paper.

[89] Smidovich, "O Koren'kovshchine," in Razin, ed., *Komsomol'skii byt*, pp. 132–33. This article also appeared in 1926 in *Molodaia Gvardiia*.

insisted on the political need to punish men like Koren'kov. What she ignored was the danger to individual privacy. The questions Smidovich raised about interference in the private lives of Party members were not new. The Party's approach to the issue had never been monolithic. Prior to the Revolution, Lenin had shocked the *Iskra* staff by insisting that the suicide of an abandoned, pregnant Party member was a private not a Party matter.[90] Smidovich had no doubts about the correct Communist approach, but Iaroslavskii would write in *Bol'shevik* in 1931, "I must emphatically condemn the Central Control Commission's rummaging into the private lives of Communists."[91] Kollontai's opinion was the exact opposite of Smidovich's: she believed that the proposal to classify women under the new marriage law as registered wives, unregistered wives, or casual lovers was a gross violation of privacy.[92]

THE QUESTION OF ABORTION

Perhaps the Bolsheviks came closest to agreement in matters of marriage and the family on the issue of abortion—and it is noteworthy that this was one area the Marriage Code of 1926 left unaltered. The legalization of abortion in 1920 had by no means been intended to launch a permanent social institution; rather, it had been a response to an emergency need arising from the misery of the Civil War. The operation was legalized amid Bolshevik agonizing over a move that went counter to Party belief about the need for socialist mothers to produce children for the future. Aversion to abortion was general, if not always for precisely the same reasons.[93]

Nadezhda Krupskaia, Lenin's wife, belying the puritanical, sexless, and humorless image presented by male historians,[94] boldly criticized Party members in 1920 who opposed legalized abortion. In the tones of a radical "new woman," Krupskaia poked fun at "our intellectuals," who, although generally free in their own sexual views, sounded like members of the bourgeoisie when they objected even to contraception on the grounds that it led to debauchery. Then, distinguishing very carefully between abortion and contraception as social remedies, Krupskaia spoke in favor of birth con-

[90] I. Getzler, *Martov* (Cambridge, Eng., 1967), p. 67.
[91] As quoted in Winter, p. 26. Even friendly observers would comment in the late 1920's on the degree of Party interference in private lives. See Mehnert, p. 216. By 1929, in a Party "cleansing," offenses against morality headed the list of causes for expulsion: 22.9 percent of those expelled from the Party were accused of "noncommunist conduct toward women," debauchery, and drunkenness.
[92] For indications that others shared her view, see the critical comments of V. Boshko, "The Registration of Marriage and Its Importance Under Soviet Law," *Sovetskaia Iustitsia*, 17–18 (1939), reprinted in Schlesinger, pp. 348–57.
[93] For Soviet society's agonizing over the question of legalizing abortion, see N. Semashko, "Eshche o bol'nom voprose," *Kommunistka*, 3–4 (1920), pp. 19–21. Iaroslavskii referred to abortion figures in Moscow and Leningrad as "horrifying" (quoted in Carr, p. 43).
[94] For a typically negative view of Krupskaia, see Adam Ulam, *The Bolsheviks* (New York, 1965).

trol, pleading the psychological needs of mothers who would be spared the emotional pain of abortion—as well as its physical risks—if the regime were to make contraceptives available as they were in Western Europe.[95] Aleksandra Kollontai agreed with Krupskaia that abortion was a necessary evil, permissible if dictated by harsh economic need and the lack of facilities for child care. The feminist idea that women had a right to control their own bodies seemed to her bourgeois selfishness, a failure on the part of women to understand their responsibility to provide the collective with future workers.[96]

Those who hold to the feminist belief that women have the right to control their own bodies might wonder how Kollontai's criticism of abortion as "bourgeois selfishness" differed substantially from Smidovich's own objections. Kollontai, Krupskaia, and women like them condoned abortion but disliked it, regarding the taking of a new life as an "offense" to the maternal instinct and, at the very least, selfish.[97] Smidovich, however, took a different view, linking abortion, like birth control, not with bourgeois selfishness but with promiscuity. Refusing to separate sex from procreation, Smidovich rejected all reasons for abortions other than to save a mother's life as the irresponsible rationalizations of young men eager to be rid of their problems. With her avidity for sentimentalizing women, she drew pathetic pictures of abortion waiting rooms where pale, haggard girls yearned hopelessly for maternity. If abortions were illegal, men would not feel justified in "forcing" them on their wives.[98]

We can not overlook the feelings of women on a subject so emotionally charged as abortion. Kollontai, Krupskaia, and Smidovich all believed in the maternal instinct.[99] Smidovich, however, seemed to doubt the vigor of female sexual desires, assuming that sexual activity was unfairly urged on young women by self-seeking men in the name of a new way of life. Unable to accept the concept of a sexually free "new woman," Smidovich bridged the gulf between the small group of radicals represented by Kollontai and the social conservatives who would eventually become dominant in the Party. There was no way to compel women to produce children and to make caring for them their primary role. What could be done was to put women in a situation where maternity and child care were the logical outcome. Smidovich urged stable marriages, ignored birth control, and condemned abortion. The culmination of this attitude came in 1936 when the Stalinists made divorce difficult to obtain and abortion a crime. But in 1926 this resolution of the questions of marriage, abortion, and the family was by no means predestined.

[95] N. Krupskaia, "Voina i detorozhdenie," *Kommunistka*, 1–2 (1920), pp. 19–20.
[96] Kollontai, *Polozhenie zhenshchiny v evoliutsii khoziaistva* (Petrograd, 1923), p. 178.
[97] Krupskaia, "Voina," p. 20.
[98] Smidovich in *Komsomol'skii byt*, pp. 268–73.
[99] Krupskaia, "Voina," p. 20.

THE 1926 MARRIAGE CODE AND ITS IMPLICATIONS

When the new marriage code was promulgated in 1926, it was mistakenly regarded in the West as so radical that it threatened the very institution of marriage. Did it not consider living together with neither legal nor clerical documents a marriage? Could divorce not be obtained by the simple application of one party? To these charges of the "bourgeois" press, Kurskii's aide Brandenburgskii indignantly replied that the law was not radical at all, that it encouraged marital stability and responsibility because it was promulgated out of concern for the potentially abandoned mother and child.[100] The Western bourgeoisie simply misunderstood the Soviet motivation in recognizing nonregistered marriage: rather than attacking the marital institution, it was formalizing the de facto relationship.[101] The code even defined a de facto marriage so that it would not be equated with a casual liaison. The fact of living together, a joint household, and the announcement of such to a third party—the concept of marriage arrived at during debates in the Central Executive Committee—appeared as Article 12 in the published version of the code.[102]

Far from attempting to undermine the family, the new marriage code expanded the obligation of relatives (even relatives by marriage and step-relatives) to support one another; to the responsibility of parents for children and of children for needy parents now was added responsibility for grandparents in need.[103] True, one could point to progressive new features. The absolute right to divorce granted in 1918 remained intact and was even simplified in 1926. Where the 1918 code required "verification that the petition for divorce actually issues from both parties," the 1926 legislation registered a divorce upon the petition of one party. Where the 1918 code granted maintenance to a needy ex-spouse unable to work until such time as a change in the spouse's condition took place, the 1926 legislation, in the interests of a second family, limited alimony to a former spouse to one year. (This change was added to the 1925 proposed code after the public discussions.) On the other hand, alimony under the new code covered not only the ex-wife who was unable to work but the wife who was simply unemployed;[104] upon divorce, the latter was now entitled to half the property

---

[100] *Izvestiia*, Jan. 14, 1926. In 1944 the law was changed and only registered marriage was given legal recognition.

[101] Essentially, de facto marriages were to be afforded protection only with respect to property rights and alimony. For other privileges arising from marriage, such as the right to join a communal dwelling, it was still necessary to register.

[102] In its first version in 1925 there was no definition of marriage. See the 1925 code in *Brak i Sem'ia*, pp. 25–35. For Article 12 see "Kodeks zakonov o brake, sem'e i opeke," *III Sessiia Vserossiiskogo Tsentral'nogo Ispolnitel'nogo Komiteta XII Sozyva (1926): Postanovleniia* (M, 1926), p. 126.

[103] Similarly, grandparents were responsible for needy grandchildren if the children were unable to obtain support from their parents and were under age or incapacitated ("Kodeks zakonov o brake, sem'e i opeke," p. 131).

[104] But in the final 1926 version, the stipulation "for six months only" was added ("Kodeks zakonov o brake, sem'e i opeke," p. 126).

acquired since marriage. On balance, the new code's progressive features did not outweigh its basically stabilizing functions, particularly in light of the fact that unregistered marriage (i.e., the prevailing form) would now carry legal consequences.

Some attempt was made in preparing the final version of the code to respond to and mollify objections that a year of discussion had brought out; but the fundamental opposition was simply not resolved. As we have seen, de facto marriage was painstakingly clarified so as to alleviate fears of alimony suits that might result from casual liaisons. But peasant objections persisted despite the new threefold definition of marriage and the reasonable time limit on payment of alimony to a former wife. Other efforts to ease anxiety were no more successful. A new section of the code explicitly stated that the rights of parents and children with regard to the property of a peasant *dvor* were to be "determined by the pertinent sections of the [1922] Land Code," whose rather muddled principles were now clarified and strengthened with a view to preserving the peasant's landholdings intact. Support payments of peasants were to be in the form of money or products of the household economy; land, inventory, and livestock were not to be disturbed.[105] One might conclude that the male peasant proprietor received preferential treatment compared to the urban worker, half of whose property acquired since marriage would go to his wife. Still, the peasants persisted in seeing a marriage code that legalized de facto marriage as antagonistic.

The Secretary of the Central Executive Committee, Aleksei Kiselev, agreed with Preobrazhenskii that the new code was necessary. But Kiselev, who as a member of the Workers' Opposition had objected to government neglect of the proletariat in 1921, was troubled now that the peasants felt ignored; that a hundred million peasants found their interests neglected by the code, he thought, could not go unchallenged.[106] He could not know that the 1926 code, coming two years before the onset of the First Five-Year Plan, would be among the last pieces of Soviet legislation to take into account any of the peasants' fundamental interests.

Did the peasants prefer Kollontai's plan for a General Insurance Fund? No, and they were unlikely to have accepted it without persuasion. But had it received strong government support, both peasants and proletarian workers probably could have been convinced of its merits. The cost to the individual would have been small, and a general fund would have removed what to the peasants was the most oppressive feature of alimony and the most divisive between the generations—the fact that one member's personal "mistake" could quite suddenly threaten the economy of the entire *dvor*.

Was there a larger significance to Kollontai's campaign against the new

[105] *Ibid.*, p. 131.
[106] Schlesinger, p. 148. For the view that the government in 1921 was ignoring basic interests of the proletariat, see A. M. Kollontai, *The Workers' Opposition* (Chicago, 1921).

marriage law? Virtually alone among leading Bolsheviks, she tried in 1926 to revive socialist promises in the area of marriage and the family. She spoke to women and to youth, both of whom she perceived as subordinate in the traditional family structure.[107] For them she tried to keep alive, in face of Party indifference, the heroic spirit of October. Yet there was in Kollontai's speeches no criticism of men; instead she explained how her plan would relieve husbands and fathers of support payments she knew they could ill afford.[108] Her general fund aimed not only at easing the hostilities between men and women by replacing alimony with a collectivist responsibility for children but at reducing the harmful distinctions between generations in both town and country and at bringing Soviet society, rather gently, toward a more humane socialism.

Party negativism toward Kollontai's proposal provides us with another perspective from which to analyze what Smidovich and others meant when they continued through the 1920's (sounding oddly like Kollontai) to refer to the "withering away of the family" and the advent of the "new woman." For Kollontai and her small group of followers, these twin concepts were myths in what Robert Tucker calls their truest meaning—a projection of one's own internal conflicts and needs onto society.[109] But for Smidovich, Iaroslavskii, Trotsky, and others, the "withering away of the family" and the "new woman" were communist myths in the looser sense of ritual slogans. The marriage code controversy of 1925–26 not only underscored peasant commitment to the status quo but crystallized the Communist Party's attachment to familiar images of women. It should come as no surprise, then, that the concepts of the "withering away of the family" and of the "new woman" moved within ten years from myth to heresy, with Kollontai's writings cited as their "undoubtedly harmful" source.[110]

[107] Kollontai appealed to youth on this basis in her speech to the Komsomol Congress in 1919. See A. M. Kollontai, *Izbrannye stat'i i rechi* (M, 1972), p. 298.

[108] *Rabochii Sud*, pp. 363–78. Smidovich was scornful of this sympathy for men whom she saw as abandoning women (*Brak i Sem'ia*, p. 93, and Smidovich in *Komsomol'skaia Pravda*, 37 [220] [Feb. 1926], p. 2).

[109] Robert Tucker, *Philosophy and Myth in Karl Marx* (Cambridge, Eng., 1971), pp. 218–32.

[110] V. Svetlov, "Socialist Society and the Family," translated and reprinted from *Pod Znamenem Marksizma*, 6 (1936), in Schlesinger, pp. 315–347. Whether Soviet society regarded revolutionary promises concerning the family with any enthusiasm is a matter of controversy. E. H. Carr contends that by the mid-1920's the Party had rejected Kollontai's position on the family, that it was already diverging in "practice and opinion" from Engels's doctrine of the liberation of women from domestic labor. Carr cites Trotsky's symposium for Party workers in 1923 to illustrate a desire for traditional life. More accurately, the symposium revealed the conflict between the conventional family attitudes of men and the desire for greater freedom on the part of women. Trotsky, *Voprosy byta*, pp. 84–88. For Carr's view, see *Socialism in One Country*, pp. 39–43. Many men no doubt preferred the traditional family, but many women eagerly awaited fulfillment of the promises of Party workers from the Zhenotdel, who, recognizing the growing response to their efforts, could do little about the lack of government support for social institutions except express distress and frustration in the pages of *Kommunistka*. Where "officially" but in the clubs, lamented a woman worker, could one even summon the collective spirit? *Kommunistka*, 12 (1926), pp. 32–36.

What then of the thesis that, historically, generational conflict has been a prime mechanism for social and attitudinal change? In questions involving women and the family the motor did not function appropriately in Soviet Russia because forces productive of change were not allowed to operate freely. In response to their own suspicions and traditionalist fears, the older generation in the Party decreed social transformation. Nor did supposed "changes" conform to observed reality. The Party, after a period of years, simply declared the advent of the "New Soviet Family"; but carefully as one might search, it was nowhere to be found.

Yet the thinking of Kollontai and her group of social radicals had an ironic legacy. Advances in communal child-care facilities and children's homes, and the provision of direct state aid to mothers—including those who were unmarried—came under Stalin, most notably in the marriage legislation of 1944, but from conservative motives quite different from Kollontai's.[111] Large, stable families were being encouraged, primarily to offset wartime losses. Marriage registration again became compulsory, and medals were given to the "heroine mothers" of ten children. Mothers, married and single, would continue in the work force, but they little resembled the "new people" whom Kollontai had glowingly depicted in the pages of *Kommunistka*. If for Party members there was little problem in 1944 in endorsing state subsidies to mothers instead of individual alimony, it was precisely because of this underlying difference in motive; for what had been unacceptable in 1926 was not Kollontai's general fund so much as her revolutionary concepts about sexually free, radical, "new women" who rejected the individual family.

The switch in Communist rhetoric signaling that the family would not wither away, and that the institution of marriage and the mother's role in it would remain essentially unchanged, coincided with the consolidation of the Stalin revolution of the 1930's. Should we conclude, as is customary, that Stalin determined the outcome? Not necessarily. His daughter Svetlana has asserted that her father, despite his public remarks about women's contribution to the economy, did not believe in their equality. His concept of home and family, and of woman's role in each, was conservative.[112] But Stalin needed only to welcome the strong forces in the Party that throughout the 1920's were moving in traditional directions, counter to the myths of the Revolution. He did not need to compel them.

---

[111] State aid now replaced alimony to unmarried mothers. Popular reasons given for limiting legal consequences, i.e., alimony, to registered marriages only included a desire to protect soldiers from responsibility for children they might have fathered and a need to increase the birthrate. See Schlesinger, p. 22. Maurice Hindus, a war correspondent in Moscow, reported that the law was popularly known as "a law for men.".M. Hindus, *House Without a Roof* (New York, 1961), p. 147.

[112] Svetlana Alliluyeva, *Only One Year* (New York, 1969), pp. 381–82.

Ethel Dunn

Russian Rural Women

I T S E E M S A P P R O P R I A T E to begin an inquiry into the present status of Russian rural women with some indication of their situation in the past. Accordingly, we shall consider briefly several aspects of the position of peasant women from the period before the Revolution through the Second World War. This will serve to introduce and illuminate the contemporary rural scene. It should be noted that this paper focuses on ethnically Russian rural women living in predominantly Russian areas of the RSFSR.

PEASANT WOMEN BEFORE THE REVOLUTION

Though the materials on this period available to the researcher are somewhat limited, there are a number of useful ethnographic studies covering different periods and regions of rural Russia. Among them are studies describing a village in Tambov *oblast*, several *kolkhozy* in Kalinin *oblast*, and Russian settlements in the Kuban region.[1] Sociologists have recently added information from Stavropol *krai* and Orel *oblast*, and we also have preliminary results of a restudy of Gadyshi, made famous by M. Ia. Fenomenov.[2] Nevertheless, establishing a baseline is more difficult than

---

[1] For the village in Tambov *oblast*, see P. I. Kushner, ed., *Selo Viriatino v proshlom i nastoiashchem: Opyt etnograficheskogo izucheniia russkoi kolkhoznoi derevni* (M, 1958), which appeared in English as *The Village of Viriatino*, trans. and ed. by Sula Benet (Garden City, N.Y., 1970). Benet appears to have edited out as "ideological" many of the details of *kolkhoz* economic life and family budgets that make Kushner's work valuable; a sketch of the deleted material can be found in Stephen P. Dunn and Ethel Dunn, *The Peasants of Central Russia* (New York, 1967). On the *kolkhozy* in Kalinin *oblast*, see L. A. Anokhina and M. N. Shmeleva, *Kul'tura i byt kolkhoznikov Kalininskoi oblasti* (M, 1964). On the Kuban region, see K. V. Chistov, ed., *Kubanskie stanitsy* (M, 1967).

[2] See P. I. Simush et al., *Kolkhoz—shkola kommunizma dlia krest'ianstva (Kompleksnoe sotsial'noe issledovanie kolkhoza "Rossiia")* (M, 1965); V. N. Kolbanovskii, ed., *Kollektiv kolkhoznikov: Sotsial'no-psikhologicheskoe issledovanie* (M, 1970); M. Ia. Fenomenov, *Sov-*

one might suppose, and cannot be done without considering the nature of the peasant family.[3]

Searching for the "typical" family, one is struck by the differences between regions. For example, in one village of Vladimir *uezd* early in the nineteenth century, small families and parents with unmarried children (and in some cases with married sons) made up about 70 percent of all families. Half of these households consisted of only two generations. Here, apparently, the necessity of earning a living by means other than farming inhibited the development of extended families. Yet elsewhere large families were typical of the prosperous peasantry.[4] According to some students of the problem, the size of the peasant family was directly related to the amount of land available and to the family's ability to rent or buy it.[5]

In most areas, particularly in the less fertile northern regions, some form of seasonal migrant labor (*otkhodnichestvo*) was a necessity. In Tver *guberniia* (Kalinin *oblast*) in the 1890's, of 240,000 peasant households some 350,000 people were engaged in nonagricultural labor, either locally or outside the region. Of these, 17 percent were women, almost half of whom were employed as servants.[6] Generally, a woman tried to save up enough money for a trousseau (*pridanoe*), although some money was sent back to help the family. In Viriatino (Tambov *guberniia*), where the chief nonagricultural work was in the mines, 156 men and two women were issued passports in 1881 as *otkhodniki*.[7] In the Kuban region, military obligations kept the men away from home for extended periods and wives were accustomed to managing the farms themselves. This won the women a certain measure of respect from men, but not an equal voice in village affairs. For example, women in the Kuban did not participate in the gathering of Cossacks, except to make requests.[8] Similarly, in Viriatino women had no

---

remennaia derevnia (M-L, 1925); L. V. Ostapenko, "The Village of Gadyshi Today," *Soviet Sociology*, 10, no. 1 (1971), pp. 46–63; and L. V. Ostapenko, "The Effect of Women's New Production Role on Her Position in the Family (Based on Data from a Study in Vyshnii Volochek *raion*, Kalinin *oblast*)," *Soviet Sociology*, 12, no. 4 (1974), pp. 85–99.

[3] Stephen P. Dunn, "Structure and Functions of the Soviet Rural Family," in James R. Millar, ed., *The Soviet Rural Community* (Urbana, Ill., 1971), pp. 325–45; Ethel Dunn, "The Importance of Religion in the Soviet Rural Community," in Millar, ed., pp. 346–75; Ethel Dunn and Stephen P. Dunn, "Religious Behavior and Socio-cultural Change in the Soviet Union," in B. R. Bociurkiw and J. W. Strong, eds., *Religion and Atheism in the U.S.S.R* (London, 1975), pp. 123–50; Stephen P. Dunn and Ethel Dunn, *The Study of the Family in the USSR and in the West* (AAASS special publication, in press); L. A. Anokhina, V. Iu. Krupianskaia, N. M. Shmeleva, Stephen P. Dunn, and Ethel Dunn, "On the Study of the Russian Peasantry," *Current Anthropology*, 14, no. 1–2 (Feb.–Apr. 1973), pp. 143–57.

[4] V. A. Aleksandrov et al., eds., *Narody evropeiskoi chasti SSSR* (M, 1964), vol. 1, p. 463.

[5] See Basile Kerblay, "Chayanov and the Theory of Peasantry as a Specific Type of Economy," in Teodor Shanin, ed., *Peasants and Peasant Societies* (Harmondsworth, Eng., 1971) pp. 150–60. Under the communal system of periodic land redistribution, a large family generally qualified for a bigger land allotment than a small family.

[6] Anokhina and Shmeleva, p. 21.

[7] Kushner, p. 35.

[8] Chistov, pp. 197, 234. Simush (p. 220) relates a popular saying: "What does the wife of a Cossack do when her husband is fighting? She works. And what does she do when he's not fighting? She works, and he talks of war."

voice in the *skhod* (village assembly), even when they were widows and heads of households.[9] In Tver *guberniia* in the 1890's, 70 communes allowed women to hold land on the same basis as men, but the extent to which they may have voiced their opinions in the *skhod* through older male relatives is unclear.[10] There is some evidence to indicate that peasant women were every bit as interested in land and property as peasant men were and that whenever they knew their rights they attempted to secure them, both through the courts and by other means.[11]

The First World War, with its huge demand for men—both for the army and for industry—left women to make up the bulk of the rural labor force. Women also formed the mobs that protested the surveys perliminary to land reorganization and vigorously opposed further division of communal lands—at least until the end of the war.[12] (A program to convert communal lands into individual farms had been under way since the introduction of the Stolypin Land Reform after the 1905 Revolution, but it encountered such opposition that a proposal was made in 1915 to suspend it temporarily.) Moreover, as might be expected, women were active in protesting against the high prices of manufactured goods.[13]

However, it is an open question whether any of these actions reveal a revolutionary consciousness in any area other than the problem of the land, monumental though the problem was. No systematic study of peasant women exists, although it is generally held that peasant women were mercilessly exploited, first by their fathers and husbands and then by the larger market-oriented society. Yet their position was partly eased by the fact that they possessed the only private property known to the peasant household, the trousseau, which they brought with them to their new families. Moreover, women were permitted to keep some portion of the money they received from the sale of the products of their own labor in order to provide clothes for themselves and their children.

In many areas where it was nearly impossible to live by farming alone, whole households and villages accepted assignments as part of a growing network of cottage industries. If women were paid less than men, it was because increasing specialization made it convenient to give women the unskilled part of the operation.[14] It is often said that the peasant did not see

[9] Kushner, p. 40.

[10] Anokhina and Shmeleva, p. 12.

[11] See Gleb Uspenskii, *Sobranie sochinenii* (M, 1957), vol. 8, pp. 52–522.

[12] Teodor Shanin, *The Awkward Class. Political Sociology of Peasantry in Developing Society: Russia 1910–1925* (Oxford, 1972), p. 176, n. 1, says women formed 71.9 percent of the total rural labor force during the war. On women's protests, see A. M. Anfimov, ed., *Krest'-ianskoe dvizhenie v Rossii v gody pervoi mirovoi voiny, iiul' 1914 g.–fevral' 1917 g. Sbornik dokumentov* (M-L, 1965), pp. 152–53, 232–34, 251–56.

[13] Anfimov, pp. 361–66.

[14] See chap. 6 of Lenin's *The Development of Capitalism in Russia (Collected Works*, vol. 3; M, 1964), pp. 385–453. It is interesting that Lenin opposed a combination of industry and agriculture, not because it provided nonagricultural employment for people who should have been producing food (for themselves and others), but because wages and working conditions in cottage industry were so miserable.

the necessity for educating females: "A girl will not go into military service, and she can weave and spin as she is [i.e., lacking formal education]."[15] However, in areas where literate women could be considered an asset to a peasant household, the rate of female literacy before the Revolution was higher than one might expect. Among the Cossacks of the Kuban region, where, as we saw, women managed the household economy, 47 percent of the population in 1913 was literate: 62.3 percent of the males and 32.1 percent of the females. The rate of female literacy was high here, especially when we compare the rates for selected provinces in Table 1.

Traditionally, women and young male members of the peasant household were subordinate to the male household head.[16] His wife commanded the female members of a large household, and she had considerable freedom and authority within her realm. Peasants considered it natural for young people to be subordinate, but it is probably a mistake to assume that subordination automatically meant oppression; moreover, it is unlikely that either sex saw the peasant division of labor into men's and women's tasks as crippling the personality. There was in village life a commonly accepted order that extended to leisure activities. Folk and church festivals were attended by all age groups and were designed to maintain group solidarity rather than to provide creative leisure for individuals.[17] The *posidelki*, or courting parties, which lasted in some areas until the late 1950's, were arranged by age groups,[18] and the traditional reluctance of married men and women to attend the *kolkhoz* club together in Viriatino began to break down only quite recently.[19]

EARLY SOVIET POLICIES

Among the noteworthy changes that followed the 1917 Revolution was an increase in the number of household partitions led by women and the returned servicemen eager to take advantage of their new rights and to establish their independence. The Bolsheviks were successful to some extent in organizing rural women by appealing to their underprivileged status. According to one scholar, "Heavy pressure from the Soviet government raised the proportion of female members of Rural Soviets from 1 per-

[15] Aleksandrov, p. 468.   [16] Shanin, *The Awkward Class*, p. 176.
[17] See L. A. Pushkareva and N. M. Shmeleva, "The Contemporary Russian Peasant Wedding," in Stephen P. Dunn and Ethel Dunn, eds., *Introduction to Soviet Ethnography* (Berkeley, Calif., 1974), vol 1, pp. 343–62; N. P. Alekseev, "Reasons for the Retention of Religiosity in the Psychology of the Kolkhoz Peasantry and Ways of Overcoming It," *Social Compass*, 21, no. 2 (1974), pp. 171–90; Z. A. Tazhurizina, "Les Superstitions, Mystification des Relations Quotidiennes," *Social Compass*, 21, no. 2 (1974), pp. 153–69; V. Ia. Propp, "The Historical Roots of Some Russian Religious Festivals," in Dunn and Dunn eds., *Introduction to Soviet Ethnography*, vol. 2, pp. 367–405; V. Ia. Propp, "The Russian Folk Lyric," in *Down Along the Mother Volga*, trans. and ed. Roberta Reeder (Philadelphia, 1975), pp. 1–73.
[18] Dunn and Dunn, *The Peasants of Central Russia*, p. 65.
[19] Present Soviet cultural work in both towns and villages appears to be hampered by the fact that the clubs are thought to be for unmarried people. This may be a survival of peasant attitudes.

TABLE 1

Literacy Rates Before the First World War, Selected Provinces

Years	Province	Rate of literacy		
		Total	Male	Female
1909–12	Moscow	41.7%	58.6%	25.9%
1911–13	Tver	34.1	51.0	18.5
1910–12	Tula	28.5	46.3	11.0
1908–11	Vologda	22.0	39.3	5.3
1911–13	Samara	19.5	31.1	8.1
1910–13	Penza	14.8	25.9	3.8
1910–11	Simbirsk	15.6	27.6	3.8

SOURCE: A. G. Rashin, *Naselenie Rossii za 100 let* (M, 1956), p. 294.

cent in 1922 to about 10 percent in 1925, but the more real [*sic*] positions of authority—chairmenship of Soviets and officership in the commune—remained in the hands of men."[20] In Viriatino in 1921 there was not a single woman among the 34 members of the rural soviet; in 1925, two women became members; at the end of the decade they were joined by two more.

It is interesting that almost all the politically active women mentioned in the Viriatino study were unmarried, divorced, or widowed. The single exception was a woman who moved to Viriatino from Kulevatovo, where her husband had been a hired laborer and she had worked as a servant.[21] For a peasant, the choice was often simple: Party or family. Even Komsomol work failed to attract many women, at least in Goritskaia *volost*, Tver *guberniia*, where only about one-tenth of the Komsomol members were female in the mid-1920's. One reason for the low participation of women may have been the reputation for immorality that the Komsomol had among the peasants.[22]

The divorced rural woman may have had greater opportunities for political activity, but she faced special economic difficulties. Women urged the partitioning of households as part of divorce settlements, but the courts generally awarded support only if the man had left the woman and not vice versa. This is at least part of the explanation for the decline in divorce cases brought before the courts during the 1920's: in Tver *guberniia*, from 18 percent of all cases in 1923 to 5.6 percent in 1926. A divorced woman denied support was forced to return to her parents, who were often not pleased to see her because she placed an additional strain on their own limited resources and was likely to return without the *pridanoe*.[23]

Education as an avenue for social mobility attracted rural dwellers stead-

[20]Shanin, *The Awkward Class*, p. 176.
[21]Kushner, p. 237. In Sosnovskaia *volost'* in 1924, 2,940 men and 51 women voted in elections to rural soviets. In 1925, of the 328 people elected, only seventeen were women.
[22]A. M. Bol'shakov, *Derevnia 1917–1927* (M, 1927), p. 331.
[23]*Ibid.*, p. 317.

ily. The proportion of peasants in day *rabfaks* (workers' factory schools) grew from 28 percent in 1923–24 to 37 percent in 1928–29. Perhaps it is not surprising that only 15.6 percent of the students in *rabfaks* were girls in 1928; but in the same year females constituted 28.1 percent of the students in *vuzy* (higher educational institutions). Their distribution by field was uneven: females were 52.0 percent of those studying in medical, 48.7 percent in pedagogical, 21.1 percent in social and economic, 17.4 percent in agricultural, and 13.4 percent in industrial, construction, and transportation *vuzy*.[24] The relative unpopularity of agricultural studies is noteworthy, as is the emphasis on nontechnical humanistic education for women.

Although educational opportunities for women may have been broadened by the Soviet regime, other benefits of early Soviet policy were less widespread in the countryside. For example, the medical care given peasants was clearly inferior to that available in towns. In 1926, only 10 percent of physicians were working in rural areas. Maternity leave and monetary subsidies for care of newborn were unavailable to the peasant woman.[25] In addition, in the mid-1920's villages received slightly less than half of all industrial goods produced, although more than 80 percent of the population was rural. It has been estimated that barely a third of peasant demand was satisfied by industry.[26] Some fraction of this demand must have been met through the revival of cottage industry and crafts during the NEP. In Nizhegorod *guberniia*, about 40,000 peasant women were involved in making lace, bast matting, and spoons, and in processing hides; in Elets *uezd*, 45,000 peasant women were involved in making lace. However, in 1925 a Komsomol inspector reported that in one village of Suvorov *volost*, Elets *uezd*, girls of six and seven earned only a ruble a week working thirteen- or fourteen-hour days; adult women earned more, but were mercilessly exploited—the choice being work or starvation.[27]

Because this was such a difficult time in rural areas, Western and Soviet researchers alike tend to picture peasant women as being largely concerned only with their private affairs and quickly roused to hysteria at the thought of losing their property. But this sort of generalization, accepted by Wesson, for example, needs careful qualification and much more research.[28]

[24] N. M. Blinov, "Sotsiologicheskie issledovaniia truda i vospitaniia sovetskoi molodezhi 20-kh godov," *Sotsiologicheskie issledovaniia*, 1975, no. 1, p. 152.

[25] Bol'shakov, pp. 293–95.

[26] V. P. Danilov et al., eds., *Sovetskoe krest'ianstvo. Kratkii ocherk istorii (1917–1970)* (2d ed.; M, 1973), p. 165.

[27] I. Ia. Trifonov, *Klassy i klassovaia bor'ba v SSSR v nachale NEPa (1921–1925 gg.)* (L, 1969), Part II, pp. 90, 93.

[28] Robert G. Wesson, *Soviet Communes* (New Brunswick, N.J., 1963), pp. 213–20; for another view, see Ethel Dunn and Stephen P. Dunn, "Religion as an Instrument of Culture Change: The Problem of the Sects in the Soviet Union," *Slavic Review*, 23 (1964), pp. 459–78. In the 1920's many sectarians were eager to join the property-sharing Soviet *kommuny* described by Wesson. Z. V. Kalinicheva (*Sotsial'naia sushchnost' baptizma 1917–1929 gg.* [L, 1972], pp. 105–22) describes the Baptist cooperative movement—a rather impressive effort for a sect which supposedly believes that inner change must precede social change.

THE COLLECTIVIZATION OF AGRICULTURE

Soviet researchers present agricultural collectivization as a necessity. Only in recent years have they begun to document the brutal haste with which prosperous peasants were "dekulakized" and whole families moved. Collectivization was launched only at the end of the 1920's, and it was virtually completed by the Second World War. Where the formation and operation of *kolkhozy* (collective farms) was somewhat below standard, families could be deprived of property and imprisoned for failing to fulfill obligations to the state, including the payment of agricultural taxes.[29] Kulaks were accused of distributing their cattle to distant relatives in other villages in order to avoid these taxes.[30] Undoubtedly this was a time for settling old scores, and political and social activists ran the risk of being murdered. Women, whose political participation was still widely resented in rural areas, were included among the victims.[31]

In Leningrad *oblast* by 1932, women made up 55 percent of the able-bodied *kolkhoz* population; and in some *raions* the figures were 75–85 percent.[32] Women's participation in elections to soviets rose from 36.3 percent of eligible women voters in 1927 to 60.1 in 1931. When short-term courses for training *kolkhoz* chairmen, account keepers, organizers, and tractor-drivers were set up in Gdov *raion*, 82 of the 644 persons enrolled were female. About one-fifth of the Party members and about one-third of the Komsomol members in this *raion* were women.[33]

Collectivization is said to have freed surplus farm labor for the cities and for the new program of industrialization. However, a survey made in November of 1929 of the settlement of Tosno, Kolpinskii *raion*, Leningrad *oblast*—i.e., before collectivization had had any noticeable effect—revealed that in the "Collective Work" artel of 122 households, only 30 were completely involved in agriculture. The rest had members who were involved in white-collar work or other outside employment. In Tosno itself, the 673 households drew an average of 517 rubles extra income from nonagricultural work.[34] Young peasants of both sexes were drawn to the cities in hopes of a better life. In January of 1929, 19,777 adolescents (51.4 percent female) registered with the Leningrad labor market. In April of 1930, the figure for unemployed adolescents in Leningrad was 13,000, and the proportion of females was 61.5 percent.[35]

---

[29] V. A. Seleznev and A. N. Gutarov, *Nachalo massovogo kolkhoznogo dvizheniia na Severo-Zapade RSFSR, 1930–1932. Leningradskaia oblast'. Kratkii istoricheskii ocherk* (L, 1972), p. 92, n.9.

[30] *Ibid.*, p. 95.　　　　　　　　　　　　　[31] *Ibid.*, p. 101.

[32] *Ibid.*, pp. 80, 82–83.　　　　　　　　　[33] Seleznev and Gutarov, p. 121.

[34] Blinov, p. 152, Table 4.

[35] Danilov, p. 372, n. 2. Iu. V. Arutiunian (*Sovetskoe krest'ianstvo v gody Velikoi Otechestvennoi voiny* [2d ed.; M, 1970]) writes that in 1944–45 many *kolkhoz* households even lacked able-bodied women (p. 328). In Arkhangel'sk *oblast*, about 20 percent of peasant households were so deprived, and in Velikie Luki, Kalinin, Kurgan, and Kursk *oblasti* and a number

THE SECOND WORLD WAR

The Second World War can be said to have tested both the gains made by Russian rural women since the Revolution and the loyalty of rural women to the regime. Women without families formed the basic labor force in agriculture and were subject to labor mobilization in construction, turf-cutting, lumbering, and industry during the war.[36] Between 1940 and 1944, the proportion of women *kolkhoz* chairmen for the entire USSR increased from 2.6 percent to 11.8 percent. The proportion of women book-keepers and account-keepers increased from 10.1 percent to 56.4 percent, of women brigadiers from 1.6 percent to 41.2 percent, and of women who were heads of livestock farms from 16.1 percent to 49.2 percent. Of the more than two million equipment operators trained during the war, about one million were women.[37] Yet these advances were accompanied by new problems. In the absence of machinery or fuel, and often of draft animals, women were obliged to hitch themselves to the plows and work the land under their own power.[38]

An account that discusses the number of women who served as *kolkhoz* leaders reveals wide variations in practice according to whether or not the *kolkhozy* were in the front lines. In Central Asia, for example, there were few women administrators and many more men on the *kolkhozy*. But in Smolensk *oblast*, 39.2 percent of *kolkhoz* chairmen in 1944 were women; in Leningrad *oblast*, the figure was 34.4 percent; and in Kalinin *oblast*, 34.9 percent. After the war these figures declined sharply. Just a year later, in 1945, the figures for the same three *oblasti* were down to 25.7 percent, 21.8 percent, and 25.9 percent, respectively. The figures for women *kolkhoz* chairmen for the entire RSFSR were significantly lower: 3.1 percent in 1940, 14.7 percent in 1944, and 10.4 percent in 1945.[39]

The end of the war and the return of the soldiers alleviated the shortage of males to some extent but did not restore the prewar labor supply or sex ratio. Even fifteen years later, women outnumbered men in the Soviet Union by almost 21 million. At the end of 1945, the *kolkhozy* of the USSR had 15 percent fewer people than they had had in 1940, and 32.5 percent fewer able-bodied people. Of an earlier 16.9 million men, only 6.5 million remained. Many *kolkhozniki*, especially men, lived on *kolkhozy* but worked in industry. On January 1, 1946, more than 1.2 million able-bodied persons were in that category. Much machinery and livestock had been lost during

---

of other regions, 10 percent. Therefore, in a number of *oblasti* such as Sverdlovsk and Chelia-binsk, mobilization of the agricultural population for industry was forbidden in 1944.

[36] Danilov, p. 372.

[37] *Ibid.*, pp. 373, 374–75.

[38] Arutiunian, pp. 408–10.

[39] I. M. Volkov, *Trudovoi podvig sovetskogo krest'ianstva v poslevoennye gody: kolkhozy SSSR v 1946–1950 godakh* (M, 1972), pp. 21–22.

the war, and many settlements had been razed.[40] That the general rural situation was not worse was clearly the result of the agricultural contributions of women. Throughout the war women spent about one-third of their working time on the household private plot, producing a critical supply of food that often saved the peasants from starvation. Whatever could be spared from the private plot was sold or bartered for manufactured goods.[41]

Despite the fact that the war seriously slowed down education among the rural population of the RSFSR, the total number of rural physicians in 1944 had increased by 13 percent over the number in 1940. And three-quarters of these physicians were women, 48 percent with less than five years' experience and 42 percent under 30. These young country doctors confronted special challenges since most medical supplies and transportation had been turned over to the army.[42] In what must rank as one of the wriest comments on the effects of the war, one Soviet scholar notes that the normal death rate for rural residents did not increase during the war, partly because the declining birthrate meant fewer infants, among whom mortality was often highest.[43]

One of the first tasks of the postwar period was to reestablish labor discipline. In 1950, 16.8 percent of the able-bodied *kolkhoz* population was not fulfilling the minimum norm in labor days, and 1.9 percent earned not a single *trudoden'* (labor day). In such agriculturally important regions as Penza, Tambov, and Riazan *oblasti* 20–25 percent of *kolkhozniki* failed to fulfill the norm.[44] One reason for this was that in many areas of the RSFSR payment for work in the public sector in agriculture was very low—lower than the average for the USSR. The punishment for noncompliance with *kolkhoz* labor input requirements was either to deprive the household of the right to a private plot (from which the *kolkhoz* family got most of its food and a considerable portion of its monetary income), or to expel the offender's household from the *kolkhoz* altogether. The latter occurred in some areas, primarily (it would seem) among the growing number of households in which a man lived on the *kolkhoz* but worked in industry.

Owing to the severe postwar demographic imbalance of the sexes, women still accounted for two-thirds of the *kolkhoz* labor force in 1949. Labor norms for women in the USSR were considerably lower than those for men, but women earned an average of only 197 *trudodni* (pl.) in 1940 and 211 in 1950. The corresponding figures for men were 326 and 324, respectively.[45] A partial explanation for the substantial difference between the two sets of figures lies in the fact that administrators and equipment operators earned more labor credits for each unit of time actually worked than field hands or livestock tenders did. In the postwar period, a clear division of labor emerged: the former were mostly male, the latter mostly female.

[40] Arutiunian, pp. 352–53, 355, 361.   [41] *Ibid.*   [42] *Ibid.*, pp. 365–66.
[43] *Ibid.*   [44] Volkov, pp. 109–10.   [45] *Ibid.*, pp. 116–18, 225.

WOMEN IN THE RURAL LABOR FORCE

By 1961 only 2 percent of collective farm chairmen and a mere 1 percent of state farm directors were women.[46] In 1966 there was not a single woman chairing a collective farm in Leningrad, Rostov, Sverdlovsk, Novosibirsk, or Omsk *oblasti*.[47] Though the initial postwar drop was clearly related to the return of servicemen, other factors such as specialized education and Party membership appear to have become increasingly important in the selection of collective farm chairman. In 1960, 95 percent of collective farm chairmen in the USSR were members of the Communist Party;[48] but in that same year women accounted for only about one-fifth of Party members. The postwar decline in the percent of women enrolled in higher agricultural schools (shown in Table 2) indicates that relatively fewer women today are receiving the advanced training increasingly necessary for leadership positions.

Limited access to higher specialized training remains a problem for women even within the larger category of equipment operators. In the USSR in 1959, only 17,000 tractor and combine drivers (1.5 percent of the total) and some 3,000 operators of other agricultural machinery (6.5 percent of the total) were women.[49] There are no comparable figures for the 1970 census. From 1961 to 1966 the number of equipment operators in the RSFSR increased by 268,000, but from 1966 to 1970 by only 78,000, although demand continued to grow.[50] A survey conducted in 1970–71 in Amur, Rostov, Moscow, and Leningrad *oblasti* found that 90.3 percent of the students in the rural professional-technical schools were male.[51]

In 1964, *Izvestiia* undertook a small-scale sociological study of the career plans of rural youth in Smolensk *oblast*.[52] A survey of 430 secondary-school graduates revealed that fewer than 20 percent planned to remain in the villages. A follow-up two years later gave some details on the problems encountered by young women. Not a single girl was accepted into the six agricultural mechanics schools in the *oblast* in 1965. Between 1961 and 1965, 11,179 persons had graduated from these schools, 667 of them women. Of these 667, only 65 were equipment operators (as contrasted to 9,000 men): fifteen went into industry; eleven went to the Virgin Lands (Kazakhstan); and 39 went home to their farms (where only 26 were actually working). Yet during this period, 60 percent of the agricultural labor force of Smolensk *oblast* was female.[53]

[46] Norton T. Dodge, "Recruitment and the Quality of the Soviet Agricultural Labor Force," in Millar, ed., p. 187.
[47] *Izvestiia*, Nov. 26, 1967, p. 2.
[48] See Robert C. Stuart, *The Collective Farm in Soviet Agriculture* (Lexington, Mass., 1972), pp. 161–87.
[49] Dodge, p. 183, Table 1.
[50] A. F. Tarasov, et al., *Professional'naia orientatsiia sel'skoi molodezhi* (M, 1973), p. 47.
[51] This survey is described in Dunn and Dunn, *The Peasants of Central Russia*, pp. 87–88.
[52] *Izvestiia*, Aug. 26, 1966, p. 3.   [53] *Ibid.*, Jul. 12, 1970, p. 3.

TABLE 2

Percent of Women in Secondary Specialized and Higher
Agricultural Educational Institutions, Selected Years

Years	Secondary specialized	Higher
1927–28	15%	17%
1945	66	79
1950–51	41	39
1960–61	38	27
1968	36	27
1970–71	37	30
1972	36	31
1972–73	36	32
1973–74	36	32

SOURCES: Norton T. Dodge, "Recruitment and the Quality of the Soviet Agricultural Labor Force," in Millar, ed., pp. 187–88 (see n. 3); Gail Warshofsky Lapidus, "USSR Women at Work: Changing Patterns," *Industrial Relations*, 14, no. 2 (1975), p. 188, Table 4; *Vestnik statistiki*, 1973, no. 1, p. 90; 1974, no. 1, p. 88; 1975, no. 1, p. 90.

By 1970, collective farmers in Smolensk *oblast* were earning on the average of 3.34 rubles per labor day (compared to 1.66 rubles in 1964), and the amount of money spent on consumer services per rural inhabitant had risen from 2.5 to 9 rubles. Perhaps for these reasons, 22 percent of the students interviewed in that year planned to remain in the villages. Yet in the six years that had elapsed since the initial survey, the *oblast* population had decreased by 14 percent overall, and by 40 percent among persons aged 20–29.[54] One of the major reasons for leaving was the low level of mechanization: only 1.5 percent of the major crop—flax—was harvested by machine. A far better reason for migrating was the low cultural level of the villages. A major problem in providing consumer services and schools was the great number of small settlements. And young people complained of poor roads, poor library and club facilities, the lack of cafés and sport facilities, and boredom because they had no contact with others their age.[55]

A survey conducted in 1970–71 in Amur, Rostov, Moscow, and Leningrad *oblasti* among a group of *kolkhozniki* and state farm workers [or *sovkhoz* workers], revealed that nearly a third of them were dissatisfied to some degree with the conditions of their jobs, with more women than men expressing dissatisfaction. For the women, a long working day and heavy labor were the chief complaints, although low wages undoubtedly played a role here also.[56] Only one-third of those who had chosen their profession accidentally had wages above 80 rubles a month, and these were mostly women. Dissatisfaction with various aspects of life in the villages was high,

[54]*Ibid.*, Aug. 14, 1970, p. 3.
[55]Tarasov, p. 69.
[56]*Ibid.*, p. 66. In 1970, the minimum wage had been raised to 70 rubles.

and four out of five included in the survey were described as harboring some discontent with rural life.

The problems indicated are fairly typical of the rural scene, yet it is true that they do not affect every village household in the RSFSR. It is true also that the educational level of rural women continues to rise, and that with every year more consumer goods are pumped into the countryside. Nevertheless, if one inquires not about quantity but about quality, it is evident that the emancipation of Russian rural women is encountering difficulties that cannot be expected to go away in a year or two. Let us look at the question of women's educational level in terms of what it allows them to do in rural areas.

The 1959 census revealed that of the 19.8 million women employed in agriculture, 15.8 million had no specific skills; about three million who had skills were working with livestock. Tables in a 1967–68 study of women in collective and state farms and at a lumber mill near Gadyshi show no skilled manual workers on the collective farm. The average level of education was 6.2 grades at the mill, 6.1 grades at the state farm, and 5.9 on the collective farm. When these figures are broken down by age and sex, it becomes clear that in the age groups 16–24 and 25–34, "the educational level of women surpasses that of men."[57]

According to data from the 1970 census, among the employed population with secondary and higher education in the RSFSR women outnumber men only in the category of those engaged in primarily mental labor, with the excess falling most clearly in rural areas in the category "white-collar workers."[58] Statistical estimates for 1974 indicate that women were 8.8 percent of the blue- and white-collar workers employed in agriculture and 8.3 percent of blue- and white-collar workers in *sovkhoz*, subsidiary, and other agricultural enterprises; in 1960, the corresponding figures had been 9.5 and 8.5 percent, respectively.[59] Ostapenko describes the employed women in her survey of Gadyshi as "already a majority among middle-rank executives and professional and semiprofessional people: 63 percent in Gadyshi, 68 percent in the state-farm villages, and 67 percent in the collective-farm villages. . . . Among nonmanual workers without specialized training, [women were] 70 percent, 77 percent, and 68 percent [respectively]. Between 1963 and 1968 the difference in the average monthly pay of an employed woman and an employed man diminished by nearly one-third. In nearly 20 percent of the families surveyed, the women earned more than the men."[60]

---

[57] Ostapenko, "The Effect," pp. 87–89, 97. Ostapenko, "The Village," p. 56. She adds that 40 percent of top-level executives under 34 in the *raion* are women.

[58] *Itogi Vsesoiuznoi perepisi naseleniia 1970 goda, Tom VI* (M, 1973), p. 610; *Itogi . . . Tom V* (M, 1973), p. 86. It is worth noting that among *kolkhozniki*, 178 per thousand employed women had higher and complete or incomplete secondary education in 1959; the 1970 figure was 321. Among men the corresponding figures were 227 and 391, respectively. There are marked differences by *oblast* and *krai*.

[59] *Vestnik statistiki*, 1975, no. 1, p. 86.   [60] Ostapenko, "The Village," p. 54.

One of the most difficult problems in Soviet agriculture today is the rational use of labor. On the collective farm "Rossiia," studied in the early 1960's, those who worked in the fields typically spent five hours a week getting to their job sites. In addition, many hours were spent each week in "nonworking time connected with work."[61] In three *kolkhozy* in Orel *oblast*, studied between 1963 and 1969, field hands worked an average of eighteen days a month.[62] The head of the USSR Central Statistical Bureau reported that in 1974 the *kolkhoznik* worked an average of twenty days a month, the *sovkhoz* worker, 23 days.[63] The three *kolkhozy* in Orel *oblast* may be a special case, but certain aspects of the situation there support the hypothesis that young women can acquire and maintain a skill only by leaving the village. A survey of 3,661 people revealed that 2,620 were employed in the public sector (1,114 men and 1,506 women); 39.7 percent of the men were employed as skilled laborers, whereas 95.7 percent of the women worked as field hands or stock tenders. Seventy percent of all workers under 30 were employed in the last two categories.[64] In the three *kolkhozy*, only 21 women had any degree of specialization: two were agronomists; one was a zootechnician; one was a veterinary assistant; threee were bookkeepers; four were engaged in culture and education; three were plasterers; two were painters; and three were tractor drivers.[65]

In our earlier work, Stephen P. Dunn and I assumed that women were considerably less mobile than men, as a result of both their relative lack of education and their family responsibilities.[66] Actually, women showed considerable mobility from one *kolkhoz* to another in Kalinin *oblast*, for example, in the late 1950's. One Soviet author found that "Women in the age group 16–19 are remarkable for high intensity of migration: in 1959, 1961, and 1962, the intensity of migration was equal to that of men; and in 1960, 1963, 1965, and 1966, it was higher than that of men in this age group." She also reported that women have limited choices for professions in agriculture and do not like being the majority of students in rural secondary schools.[67] Another writer, who conducted a survey of the relatives of migrants from villages in Leningrad *oblast* in 1969, cited family circumstances (31.6 percent), a desire to continue studying (19.9 percent), and dissatisfaction with housing (16.1 percent) as the three leading motives for migration, with people under 30 forming 52 percent of the migrants. How-

---

[61] Simush, p. 293. [62] Kolbanovskii, p. 105.

[63] V. Maniakin, "Po puti pod"ema," *Vestnik statistiki*, 1975, no. 3, p. 12.

[64] Kolbanovskii, p. 90, Table 18. Most field hands were said to be over 40; 11 percent had no schooling, and 22 percent had one to three grades. Ostapenko ("The Village," p. 57) puts the figure for "functional illiterates" in Gadyshi and the surrounding area at about 15 percent.

[65] Kolbanovskii, pp. 89–91. There is a discrepancy between tables and text; the three tractor drivers may have turned up after 1968, when a special effort was begun to train women equipment operators.

[66] Dunn and Dunn, *The Peasants of Central Russia*, pp. 86–87.

[67] M. T. Makhan'kova, "Nekotorye osobennosti migratsii molodezhi (po materialam RSFSR)," in D. I. Valentei et al., eds., *Problemy migratsii naseleniia i trudovykh resursov* (M, 1970), p. 59.

ever, as she admits, the rubric of "family circumstances" reveals little. This researcher found that men were somewhat more mobile than women. Among pensioners, however, the trend was reversed.[68] In 1970, only 11 percent of the tenth-graders in rural schools in Leningrad *oblast* went to work in agriculture; among eighth-graders, only 3.7 percent did. On the other hand, 3.1 percent of the tenth-graders and 7.9 percent of the eighth-graders entered the rural professional-technical schools.[69]

Soviet sources make it difficult to decide absolutely whether agriculture is an unpopular profession. A recent investigator duplicated a questionnaire used in the 1920's and administered it to 1,700 school children in the fourth to tenth grades in Rzhakskii *raion* of Tambov *oblast* between 1967 and 1974. Every fourth boy wanted to be a motor-vehicle driver, and nearly every fifth a pilot. Other professions boys named (presumably in order of popularity) were member of the military, engineer, sailor, mechanic, geologist, radio technician, doctor, builder, or tractor driver. Teacher ranked nineteenth, agronomist twenty-first, and technician thirty-sixth. Altogether 54 professions were named. Among the girls, 28.8 percent wanted to be doctors, 24.3 percent teachers, 8.2 percent educators (presumably of small children). These preferences were followed by actress, geologist, agronomist, salesperson, engineer, motor-vehicle driver, pilot, nurse, librarian, cook, etc. Forty-four professions were named. According to this report, of 8,408 tenth-graders who received diplomas in 1974, over half (61.7 percent) continued with either higher or secondary specialized study; one-third (33.6 percent) began to work. The latter group included 1,080 who went into industry and 1,204 who entered agricultural enterprises.[70]

Despite the fact that women were 45 percent of all workers in the agricultural labor force in 1974,[71] the migration of young women is cause for great concern throughout European Russia. This was highlighted by a series of letters and articles published in 1975 by the leading rural newspaper, *Sel'skaia zhizn'*, under the heading "Going to the Neighbors for Wives." The series noted that for every 100 men of marriageable age in Kirov *oblast* there are 89 girls; on smaller (less prosperous) farms, there are only 58 girls per 100 marriageable men. Among the reasons for the departure of young women were the facts that one-third of the milkmaids in the *oblast* did not yet have automatic milking machines, and that women were not being sent by their farms for professional training.[72] Letters from Smolensk, Donetsk, Lipetsk, Kharkov, Perm, and Arkhangelsk *oblasti* cited poor housing and lack of educational opportunities, as well as bad working conditions, as rea-

[68]G. M. Romanenkova, "K voprosu o migratsii trudovykh resursov v selakh Leningradskoi oblasti," in A. Z. Maikov, ed., *Migratsiia naseleniia RSFSR* (M, 1973), pp. 122–24.

[69]*Ibid.*, p. 125.

[70]*Literaturnaia gazeta*, Mar. 26, 1975, p. 12.

[71]*Vestnik statistiki*, 1975, no. 1, p. 86. Women were 52 percent of the work force in *kolkhozy* in 1974. *SSSR v tsifrakh v 1974 gody* (M, 1975), p. 37.

[72]*Sel'skaia zhizn'*, Jan. 14, 1975, p. 3.

sons for the migration of young women to the cities.[73] The discussion was summarized in a long article by Corresponding Member of the USSR Academy of Sciences T. I. Zaslavskaia, who stressed the need for improving the assortment of goods sold in rural areas; for building good roads and good schools; for improving technology; and, in the meantime, for increasing the wages for difficult or dangerous work.[74] The fact that the government is attempting to respond to these rural needs is suggested by a TASS report on the economic situation in the RSFSR for the first six months of 1975, which notes that wages for *kolkhozniki* were raised by 4 percent and that the volume of consumer services rose by 12 percent in rural areas, as compared to 8 percent in urban areas.[75]

DOMESTIC ROLES AND ATTITUDES

The flow of consumer goods and services, and the broadening of educational and professional opportunities for rural residents, can be and is being legislated. Women will certainly benefit from these policy changes. In 1974, 34 percent of all the women in the RSFSR lived in rural areas.[76] Legislating attitudes, however, is much more difficult. The material presented so far would seem to indicate that the occupational status of women in the Russian countryside is not as high in the 1970's as it was in the 1940's. Young women appear to be "rebelling" by leaving the countryside altogether. Yet demographic studies suggest that it is difficult for married women over 30 with children to migrate. Let us look briefly at their situation.

Ostapenko stated that many married women in Gadyshi would have liked to raise their educational level, and that 60 percent claimed that the burdens of housekeeping and the distance to educational institutions were the reasons they did not do so. In fact, only 2 percent of married women managed to continue their schooling after marriage. Twenty percent of the women questioned were prevented by housework from upgrading their skills. Given their economic responsibilities, rural women in Gadyshi were quite active in public affairs; nonetheless, 40 percent expressed a desire to be more active, stating that their daily routines prevented them from doing so.[77] Soviet scholars, Ostapenko included, assert that women's status is enhanced by their participation in public life.

The outside employment of women involves the men in their families in greater, though far from equal, assumption of domestic responsibilities. "In families in which women do not hold jobs outside the home, men's expenditure of time on housework is only 8.3 percent of women's"; but in families where the wife works, "men's contribution is 24 percent of women's. In families in which women enjoy a higher social status, this index is nearly

[73]*Ibid.*, Feb. 12, 1975, p. 3.   [74]*Ibid.*, Jul. 24, 1975, p. 3.
[75]*Ibid.*, Jul. 26, 1975, p. 2.   [76]*Vestnik statistiki*, 1975, no. 1, pp. 83, 88.
[77]Ostapenko, "The Effect," pp. 92, 95–96.

twice as high as in families in which the woman is engaged, for example, in unskilled physical work (30 percent and 18 percent, respectively)." In 60 percent of the families in which the wife did not work, husbands thought that women should only do housework and raise children; but where the woman was engaged in mental labor, only 9 percent of men gave this answer. "In Leningrad," Ostapenko wrote, "41 percent of the men favored having their wives drop their jobs if this were possible; in our study (at the lumber mill, and at the state and collective farm), 52 percent did."[78]

Iu. V. Arutiunian, reporting on a survey of three villages in Moscow *oblast*, stated that 72 percent of the wives of administrators and specialists carried out most of the housework, even though only 9 percent of the men thought that women should do only this. The highest percentage (42 percent) of those holding this view of "women's work" was found among those who were 41 to 50, and the lowest percentage (14 percent) was among those under 30. Arutiunian said that one reason men in this group failed to help with housework was sheer lack of time.[79] A survey of women's attitudes on the question of whether women should work, carried out in Moscow and Riazan *oblasti*, revealed that more than two-thirds of those questioned were against staying home and taking care of the children even if material conditions allowed them to. About one-quarter responded that they worked not only for wages and a pension but for respect. The type of work done by women and men strongly influenced their attitudes about whether women should work outside the home. Among workers engaged in qualified labor, 5 percent of women and 9 percent of men thought that women should be housewives; among white-collar workers, 17 percent of women and 31 percent of men thought that women should be housewives; and among manual laborers, 28 percent of women and 20 percent of men thought the same.[80]

WOMAN POWER AND THE RURAL HOUSEHOLD ECONOMY

The question of the working time expended at present by various categories of *kolkhozniki* is of considerable interest. As of 1971, able-bodied women *kolkhoz* members worked on the *kolkhoz* an average of 184 labor days per year in the USSR, 48 labor days fewer than men. Manual laborers, of both sexes, put in 185 labor days, and men and women of pension age contributed (on an average) 83 labor days per year.[81] This last figure is a cause for some concern among social scientists, who worry that the fate of

[78]*Ibid.*, p. 97.

[79]Iu. V. Arutiunian, *Sotsial'naia struktura sel'skogo naseleniia SSSR* (M, 1971), pp. 186–87, 216 (tables 55–56, 71).

[80]*Ibid.*, p. 214.

[81]I. F. Suslov, *Ekonomicheskie interesy i sotsial'noe razvitie kolkhoznogo krest'ianstvo* (M, 1973), p. 196. In 1971, 10,600,000 *kolkhozniki* received pensions because of old age. In 1974, 4,403,000 lived in the RSFSR (*Narodnoe khoziaistvo SSSR v 1973 g.*, p. 641). For changes over time, see S. L. Seniavskii, *Izmeneniia v sotsial'noi strukture sovetskogo obshchestva 1938–1970* (M, 1973), pp. 205, 279, 361, 425.

Russian agriculture is being left to people physically unable to cope with the work and educationally beyond training. In the RSFSR in 1971, men put in 250 labor days and women 195.

However, these figures are apt to be misleading. When the time put in on the private plot is counted as working time, men are occupied for about 268 days a year, and women for 292 days.[82] In 1970, men spent an eighth of their time on the private plot and women a little more than a third, according to Suslov. It is notable that the amount of time spent by women on private plots was greater in 1970 than it reportedly was in 1940.[83] Suslov points out that 80 percent of the meat products, 84 percent of the milk, 90 percent of the eggs and potatoes, and 75 percent of the melons and vegetables for the *kolkhoz* family's consumption came from the private plot.[84] For a number of reasons, a member of the rural intelligentsia ordinarily does not get as much from a plot as does a *kolkhoznik*. This has to do largely with the number of hours a specialist (for example, a teacher) has to put in on the job, with the size of family (the number of hands available to work the plot), and with the size of the plot itself. Information on *sovkhoz* workers has been more difficult to come by, but Karl-Eugen Wädekin indicated that in 1969, 21 percent of the *sovkhoz* worker's family income came from the private plot.[85] *Sel'skaia zhizn'* published an extensive account of the budget of a tractor driver on Kotel'skii *sovkhoz* in Kingisepp *raion* of Leningrad *oblast*, 120 kilometers from Leningrad. In 1969, money from the sale of produce from the private plot amounted to 892 rubles, or 20.2 percent of the family budget. The wife worked as a calf-tender, her wages being considered supplemental to the family's income; but in all probability it was she who made this 892 rubles available to the family, with the help of her fifteen-year-old grandson and seven-year-old daughter (three other daughters no longer lived at home). The family spent 23.6 percent of its income on food, less in percentage terms than in 1964, but more than double the ruble amount.[86]

The proportion of a rural family's budget spent on food has varied considerably over the years; if the percentages have decreased from year to year, it is not because food prices have dropped but sometimes because the family has more money to spend. *Kolkhozniki* and *sovkhoz* workers spend proportionally more on food than industrial workers do.[87] Soviet sources put the per capita norms for meat and meat product consumption per year at 70 kg., and for milk and milk products at 356 kg. They also stipulate a norm of 256 eggs per person a year. Table 3 shows that the USSR in 1973 was a considerable distance away from meeting those consumption standards. There-

[82] Seniavskii, p. 204.

[83] Suslov, p. 170; Arutiunian, *Sovetskoe krest'ianstvo v gody Velikoi Otechestvennoi voiny*, 2d ed. (M, 1970), p. 355.

[84] Suslov, p. 164.

[85] Karl-Eugen Wädekin, "Income Distribution in Soviet Agriculture," *Soviet Studies*, 27, no. 1 (Jan. 1975), p. 6.

[86] *Sel'skaia zhizn'*, May 24, 1970, p. 2.

[87] Arutiunian, *Sotsial'naia struktura*, p. 63.

TABLE 3
Consumption of Basic Food Products Per Capita, USSR, Selected Years

Food product, in kg.	Workers and white collar workers			Kolkhozniki			USSR 1970	USSR 1972	USSR 1973
	1960	1965	1968	1960	1965	1968			
Meat and meat products	44	43	51	30	33	37	48	51	53
Milk and milk products	245	257	290	228	234	268	307	296	307
Eggs (item)	117	124	143	122	123	146	159	185	195
Fish and fish products	12.0	14.4	15.9	5.4	7.1	9.0	15.4	15.1	16.1
Sugar	32.4	36.7	38.8	18.2	26.5	32.9	38.8	38.8	40.8
Vegetable oil	5.9	7.4	6.7	4.1	6.1	6.0	6.8	6.9	7.3
Potatoes	132	135	125	168	161	151	130	121	124
Vegetables & melons	74	78	83	59	56	65	82	80	85
Bread products[a]	153	149	142	188	177	172	149	145	143

SOURCES: I. F. Suslov, *Ekonomicheskie interesy i sotsial'noe razvitie kolkhoznogo krest'ianstvo* (M, 1973), p. 168; *Narodnoe khoziaistvo SSSR v 1972 g.*, p. 557; *Narodnoe khoziaistvo SSSR v 1973 g.*, p. 630.
[a] Bread, flour, groats, pasta, beans.

fore, it may be supposed that the efforts Russian rural women expend on their private plots will be of significant benefit to their families for some time to come, since those efforts contribute substantially to the nutritional well-being of rural households.

Some Soviet researchers have suggested that the time rural women put in on their private plots is, under the circumstances, a rational use of labor. They do not conclude, as I am tempted to, that the rural woman has in fact acceded to a traditional peasant division of labor. Soviet sources point out that rural specialists in particular are the most ready to give up the private plot. The difficulties involved in combining jobs and housework also put a strain on relations between the spouses, the more so because very little time is left for leisure and personal development, two things young women have been conditioned to expect. Motives for divorce in cases brought before the courts in three *raions* in Orel *oblast* suggest that maintaining a sense of equality within a family group is equally hard on men or women.[88]

THE STATUS OF RURAL WOMEN TODAY

The rural woman of the 1960's manifested little overt dissatisfaction with the conditions of her labor. Ostapenko's findings are typical: "Only 9 percent [of the women questioned] are displeased with their jobs; 19 percent are dissatisfied with their earnings; and only 1 percent of women are dissatisfied with both. It is typical that complaints about the content of their work are expressed chiefly by unmarried and young married women not

[88] Kolbanovskii, p. 216.

over 34 years of age, with more than 7 years of education (20 percent of all surveyed in this group)."[89] We should remember that it is precisely this age-group which is most mobile and which has the highest incidence of labor turnover. In addition to the personal problems rural women may have, they have a number of problems on the job which cannot be described simply as the result of discrimination. There is evidence to suggest that they are not participating fully in one of the major efforts to provide full employment and a better standard of living for the rural population: industrial subsidiary enterprises set up on *kolkhozy* have attracted mainly male workers, including some who have returned from cities. The result for women has been to send them to the cities in search of jobs and education. Women educated in cities who return to rural areas to take their places among the rural intelligentsia (primarily as teachers, cultural workers, medical workers, and administrative staff) cannot be induced to stay put without an adequate rural consumer network. *Sel'skaia zhizn'* quotes a letter from a young woman who completed a course in a forestry *tekhnikum* and was sent to work in a forestry enterprise in Leningrad *oblast*. She and her husband were promised an apartment as soon as possible. But even after the couple had had two children they still did not have an apartment. The woman is no longer working because she has no one with whom to leave the children. Now that her daughter is a year old, the family is moving to a place where there is a kindergarten and housing. "I may even have to change my specialty for this," she concludes.

In general, married women with children have great difficulty working. Often they must leave very young children alone unattended, or bring them to work with them. *Kolkhoz* administrators are frequently indifferent to the problems of working mothers: one woman who wanted a day off could not get one until *Sel'skaia zhizn'* intervened, and then she was told that she could have it as soon as the *kolkhoz* administration passed a resolution to that effect. A pig-tender in Kuibyshev *oblast* described difficulties in getting her old job back after taking a year's leave; the male Party secretary on the farm was no help, but the chairman of the *raiispolkom* subsequently reported that she was restored to her position. A woman working in a division of the Voronezh consumer's cooperative wrote that her problems began when she had her second child: "As a woman with a breast-fed child, I left work early. I felt that people didn't like this, but I tried not to pay attention. Then I realized that I was expecting a [third] child. I hid my condition for a long time, because I was very much afraid that it would reflect on the job situation." Then she bore a fourth child and took a year's leave. Because the family found it hard to live on one wage (six people lived in a one-room apartment), she decided to go back to work, sending two boys to kindergarten and leaving the daughter in the care of her fifth-grade son. Since her old job was taken, she was offered one that paid considerably less. After the

[89]Ostapenko, "The Effect," p. 93.

procurator intervened she was given her old job back, but she was soon transferred to another shop to wash wine bottles. "My hands are in water all day—at home, too, because of constant clothes washing. My hands are literally never dry. Why do they have this attitude toward me? I wasn't loafing—I was raising children." After the newspaper publicity, she, too, was restored to her former job.[90]

Revolutions and progress have a price, and it may be that in many ways, Russian rural women have been the victims of the emancipation of the non-Russian women (and men) of the Soviet Union. But the major question that arises from a survey of the Russian experience is whether the emancipation of rural women can be achieved in any way other than by modification of their biological roles. Russian rural women themselves appear to be answering the question negatively. The majority of Russian rural families are now two-generation, two-child families. The Soviet regime is far from content with this outcome but has great difficulty providing child-care facilities, housing, household appliances, and consumer services to rural areas. It would be nice if the data in this paper allowed us to conclude that Russian rural women either are or soon will be the equals of rural men, to say nothing of the urban proletariat. Unfortunately, conclusions about the status of Russian rural women can only be guarded. The regime knows it has a problem, but because of historically conditioned ideological attitudes toward peasants, it does not or cannot place women ahead of men or treat both equally.

This article has tried to discover whether another conclusion could be expected. It has tried to show that the rather striking regional variations encountered within the RSFSR itself have antecedents in the historical situation. Seasonal migrant labor was a permanent feature of the rural scene before the Revolution, and although the First World War accelerated the process of draining away men, women were a majority of the agricultural labor force in some areas even before the Revolution.

The Revolution was not entirely successful in liberating Russian women, despite concerted efforts to provide avenues of social mobility for them, because (1) Bolshevik power was competing with the family and was unable to provide a substitute for it; (2) very early in the Soviet period the type of education chosen by women was humanistic rather than technical, and women to a far greater degree than men (and with better reason)—desired to leave peasant status as quickly as possible; and (3) collectivization is usually thought to have freed surplus labor for industry. The data in this paper suggest that agricultural surplus labor was and remains female. Collectivization's main purpose was to gain control of the peasantry, not so much politically, although this happened, as culturally. The plan backfired in a curious way. The Bolsheviks thought it the height of humanism to offer men the chance to be industrial workers and women the chance to be

---

[90] *Sel'skaia zhizn'*, May 13, 1975, p. 4; Jul. 18, 1975, p. 2.

members of the intelligentsia—i.e., the group that educates and forms opinion. The policy left the peasantry a despised class, even among the men and women who were peasants. Men left for the cities as fast as possible. Women followed when they could. Agriculture suffered because women had been conditioned to reject rural life, or if they did not, to yield to men. Russian agriculture today needs technicians far more than it needs intelligentsia such as teachers, cultural workers, and physicians, even though there are not enough of these in rural areas. Women do not want to be technicians. Even when discontent with the content of their labor motivates them to change careers, they have great difficulty acquiring a technical education in rural areas.

The difficulties arise because the family is the primary social unit in Russian and Soviet society. Men and women really do have different but complementary functions. A family is not a family unless it contains, as the basic unit, at least one man and one woman. The Soviet and Russian countryside is neither healthy nor complete without two complementary types of workers—intelligentsia and technicians (female and male). Maintaining a balance on an individual family level, or on a national cultural level, has proven to be one of the most difficult problems faced by the Soviet regime. It is not a political problem, it is cultural and existential; and if the regime has to some degree failed, it has failed because it has tried to solve cultural problems with a policy that is not Russian but Soviet. It is still much too early to bring in a verdict on the elements of this Soviet policy, which is probably something entirely new in human history, as its admirers claim. We cannot yet bring in a verdict because there are a huge number of variables to be considered, only a few of which were suggested here.

Michael Paul Sacks

Women in the Industrial Labor Force

THE EXTENSIVE employment of women in industry has been a striking feature of Soviet economic life. Yet as Professor Glickman has shown in her paper in this volume, this phenomenon was by no means an innovation of the Soviet regime, but had in fact been evident before the 1917 Revolution. In European Russia in 1897, for example, women constituted about 15 percent of the workers in industry and in transportation and service enterprises.[1] As Glickman also notes, factory employment was not viewed very differently from the labor contribution women were obliged to make as members of the peasant household. Traditional expectations of women's role in collective economic survival simply came to be fulfilled in novel ways as economic opportunities arose in the course of early industrial growth.[2] Those opportunities also fostered greater diversity in the types of occupations women were entering, and thus reduced their overwhelming concentration in such industires as textiles and tobacco. This increasing diversity of women's work and an examination of those factors that led to the further movement of female workers from the agricultural to the industrial sector during the Soviet period forms the subject of this paper.[3]

DEMOGRAPHIC FACTORS

Around 1910, the population within the territory of what is now Soviet Russia (the RSFSR) was about equal to that of the United States. Sixty

[1] N. A. Troinitskii, *Chislennost' i sostav rabochikh v Rossii na osnovanii dannykh vseobshchei perepisi Rossiiskoi Imperii 1897 g.* (M, 1906), pp. 2–5.
[2] On women's traditional obligations, see Joan Scott and Louise Tilly, "Women's Work and the Family in Nineteenth-Century Europe," *Comparative Studies in Society and History,* 17 (Jan. 1975), pp. 36–64.
[3] For a comprehensive treatment of this subject, see my *Women's Work in Soviet Russia: Continuity in the Midst of Change* (New York: Praeger, 1976).

years later, the 205 million people of the United States were matched by only 130 million in the RSFSR.[4] The severe internal and international conflicts experienced by the USSR during the 30 years following the Revolution explain the difference in growth rates. In the USSR as a whole, an estimated 2.8 million more deaths than births occurred each year during the period of the Revolution and the Civil War (1917–21). The net population loss during collectivization (1929–35) was probably 5.5 million, and the estimated absolute decline in population during the Second World War was some 25 million. Periods of famine and the Great Purge (1936–39) also took a heavy toll.[5]

As we might expect, deaths of males far outnumbered those of females. As early as 1926, the deficit of men in the population over age sixteen was recognized as severe; it soon became far worse. On the eve of the Second World War, for example, there were only about 92 males for every 100 females in the population of the USSR.[6] Thus when the Soviet regime began its program of rapid industrialization, there were not enough men to meet the demand for industrial labor and women were recruited to fill the gap. The same lack of men that led to the need to employ women in the industrial labor force was one of the factors that led women to want to work there, for increasing numbers of Soviet women were now heads of families (and hence breadwinners) or unable to marry. About 69 percent of males sixteen and over were married in 1926, as compared to only 61 percent of females. This differential was to increase considerably, especially between 1939 and 1959 as a consequence of male losses during the Second World War. Research by Peter Mazur based on data from the 1959 Soviet census has shown that, by and large, for most of the Russian Republic one can predict the percentage of women who will be active in the labor force in a given region from the percentage of women who are married there: "The implication is that the limited opportunity for women to marry, often due to

[4]Donald J. Bogue, *Principles of Demography* (New York, 1969), p. 131; USSR, Tsentral'noe Statisticheskoe Upravlenie, *Itogi vsesoiuznoi perepisi naseleniia 1970 goda, tom 1* (hereafter *Itogi 1970 g., tom 1*; M, 1972), 7. The U.S. had a population of 92 million in 1910; the territory of the present-day RSFSR had a population of 90 million in 1913.
[5]The data for the USSR are very much representative of those for the RSFSR. This is apparent from a comparison of sex ratios and birthrates, for example, which show a marked similarity, although population losses in the RSFSR seem to have been greater than those in the USSR at least since the Second World War. The decline in birthrates in the RSFSR was also somewhat more extreme than that in the country as a whole, owing to the high birthrates sustained in the Central Asian republics. In several instances, my forced reliance of figures for the USSR as a whole in the absence of appropriate material for the RSFSR does not appear to have introduced any gross distortions. The estimated population decline during the Second World War comes from Norton T. Dodge, *Women in the Soviet Economy* (Baltimore, Md., 1966), p. 20. See also Mervyn Matthews, *Class and Society in Soviet Russia* (New York, 1972), chap. 1.
[6]By the end of the war there were only 74 males per 100 females in the USSR; the slowness of the demographic recovery can be seen in the figures for 1959 (82 males per 100 females) and 1975 (87 per 100). See Dodge, p. 6; and USSR, Tsentral'noe Statisticheskoe Upravlenie, *Narodnoe khoziaistvo SSSR v 1974 g.* (M, 1975), p. 8.

unfavorable age-specific sex ratios, determines their prerogative to remain in the labor force."[7]

For married women, the structure of the family can have a profound influence on their ability to enter the industrial labor force. If the care of young children can be left to older siblings or to a grandparent, and if the husband or a relative does a substantial share of the housework, women are more likely to be available for employment. Family structure takes on added importance in the absence of an extensive network of child-care centers and other service enterprises, and of modern appliances to facilitate time-consuming domestic chores. The deficiency of these aids has been acute during most of the Soviet period and only recently have there been signs of progress in meeting the needs of the population in this area.

Despite the substantial decline in the fertility of Soviet women during the past half century, the overall effect on family size was limited as a result of declining infant mortality.[8] In 1913 there were 273 infant deaths for every 1,000 live births within what is now Soviet Russia; by 1950 the figure had plummeted to 88; and today it is down to about 20.[9] Mazur notes that the increase in life expectancy at all ages has "enabled women by the age of 30 to have approximately the same number of children as their mothers and grandmothers managed to save in the course of higher reproduction by age 40."[10] This means that Soviet women today are free from child-care responsibilities for a substantial portion of their adult lives; however, it also means that the age spread of children is such that fewer women can leave young children in the care of older ones. Nor are grandparents readily available to take over child care and other household tasks, for despite increasing life expectancy, census data from 1959 show that grandparents now tend not to live in the families of their children. Indeed, data for workers' families for the entire Soviet period indicate that the extended family in any form has been uncommon.[11] Thus it is clear that for a married woman employment meant assuming a "double burden," for at the end of each workday she would have to return home and fulfill the onerous role of housewife and mother.

The massive shift of the population out of rural areas has been another

[7]Peter D. Mazur, "Fertility and Economic Dependency of Soviet Women," *Demography*, 10 (Feb. 1973), pp. 39–46. The published results of the 1939, 1959, and 1970 censuses do not show employment by marital status. The 1926 census does contain such data, which I hope to analyze.

[8]Peter D. Mazur, "Reconstruction of Fertility Trends for the Female Population of the USSR," *Population Studies*, 21, no. 1 (1973), p. 38, estimates that the total fertility rate of Soviet women had declined from 5,566 in 1926 to 2,905 in 1934. It rose to about 4,352 by 1938 and then steadily declined in the following years to a low of 1,762. The highest postwar level was 3,233. In 1966 the figure was 2,452.

[9]USSR, Tsentral'noe Statisticheskoe Upravlenie, *Itogi vsesoiuznoi perepisi naseleniia 1959 goda: RSFSR* (hereafter *Itogi 1959 g.*; M, 1963), p. 39; *Itogi 1970 g., tom 1*, p. 77.

[10]Mazur, "Reconstruction," p. 44.

[11]A. G. Kharchev, *Brak i sem'ia v SSSR* (M, 1964), p. 215.

demographic change of far-reaching significance for female employment. The movement of the population to the cities was partly a response to the collectivization of agriculture begun by Stalin in 1929. In addition to this "push" out of the countryside, people were "pulled" into the cities by the occupational opportunities they believed existed there as a result of industrial expansion. It is possible, too, that urban industrial expansion may have been a product in part of the increasing concentration of workers that could not be absorbed by the limited jobs available in agriculture in the cities; but at present we cannot determine how much of urbanization was a product of industrial growth or vice versa. By 1959 the urban population of the RSFSR was over four times as great as it had been in 1926; by 1970 it had grown an additional 31 percent. Currently about two-thirds of those in the RSFSR are urban residents, as compared to the 18 percent of urban residents in 1926.[12]

What makes the change all the more significant is the fact that the proportion of the urban population living in large cities (as opposed to small ones) has grown very rapidly. In large cities it is even less likely that agricultural employment can sufficiently occupy the labor pool. In 1926, about a third of the RSFSR's urban residents lived in cities with populations of 20,000 or less, whereas just under 40 percent lived in cities with populations exceeding 100,000. By 1939, only 22 percent lived in cities in the former category, whereas more than 50 percent lived in cities in the latter category. It is not surprising, then, that figures for the RSFSR show that the number of agricultural workers declined from about 46 million in 1926 to 20 million in 1939 and to 14 million in 1959.[13]

The inordinate increase in the educational attainments of the Soviet population has also had profound consequences for labor supply and demand. Naturally, the larger the labor pool with specialized training, the greater the demand for positions utilizing such training and providing desired status and monetary compensation. Yet the increase in supply can lead to a decrease in the price offered for such labor. Such market mechanisms surely have had a profound effect on the Soviet economy despite the political controls over the labor force.

LABOR FORCE CHANGES DURING THE SOVIET PERIOD

Each of the demographic factors discussed above—the low population growth rate, the disproportionate loss of males, the changes in family structure, the movement of population from the countryside to the cities—

---

[12]*Itogi 1959 g.*, p. 11; *Itogi 1970 g., tom 1*, p. 7; USSR, Tsentral'noe Statisticheskoe Upravlenie, *Narodnoe khoziaistvo SSSR v 1975 g.* (M, 1975), p. 11.

[13]*Itogi 1959 g.*, pp. 39, 280, 290; *Itogi 1970 g., tom 1*, p. 77. The 1926 figures exclude the number of workers in forestry and on private plots of land. I am uncertain of the definition of agricultural workers used in the 1926 census, as collectivization did not seriously begin until 1929.

influenced labor force supply and demand during the Soviet period. In the first decade following the 1917 Revolution—a period of extreme economic disruption—there was considerable social experimentation aimed at eliminating the patriarchal nature of the family. Great emphasis was placed on improving the status of women through widening their participation in the labor force: "Lenin saw in the liberation of women, the weaker sex, a symbol of the general liberation, though he placed more stress on the psychological factor of participation in social production as a source of personality development, which would then serve to put women on equal footing with men."[14] Increased participation of women would have required both a substantial investment in facilities to relieve them of constraining family responsibilities and a rapid expansion of the economy to provide opportunities for them outside agriculture. An asset to those seeking to bring about reform was the lack of strong resistance to employing women in industry or having them engage in heavy labor—something they had been accustomed to in the countryside. As already noted, prior to the Revolution, and especially during the First World War, substantial numbers of women had been employed in diverse industrial occupations.

The early efforts of the Soviet government were frustrated by the Civil War and the slow recovery and growth of the economy during most of the 1920's. Some inroads were made during this period, in large part through direct government efforts to force employers to hire established quotas of women; but what Geiger has called the "extensive" communal dining facilities, children's institutions, and laundries developed during War Communism "could not be continued for financial reasons, and owners and managers of private enterprises during the NEP period were reluctant to invest in such uneconomic ventures as crèches and restaurants."[15] It was not until the late 1920's and early 1930's that the government could again begin to put substantial investments into these facilities. The Second World War brought an abrupt end to such investments, and only decades later was it possible to return to the construction of facilities sufficient to accommodate a substantial proportion of the population.[16]

As Professor Farnsworth's discussion of the 1926 marriage law debate clearly shows, in the depressed economy of the mid-1920's women were the first to suffer. The construction industry illustrates both the inroads and the problems of females during these years. As elsewhere in the economy, women were finally making an entrance into the construction industry, which before the Revolution had employed only male migrant workers. The number of women involved was small, though—in urban areas of European Russia reaching 1.55 percent of all construction workers in 1926. Yet

[14]H. Kent Geiger, *The Family in Soviet Russia* (Cambridge, Mass., 1968), p. 45.
[15]*Ibid.*, pp. 57–58.
[16]Dodge, pp. 78–87.

women constituted 6.4 percent of the unemployed in the field.[17] There was reason for considerable concern that, without work, women recently liberated from the constraints of the prerevolutionary social system might turn to prostitution. The authors of the First Five-Year Plan also feared that the projected expansion of heavy industry would further reduce employment opportunities for women.[18]

The 1920's had begun with the fervor and idealism of the Revolution. Women were to gain new freedom from changed relations between the sexes supported by law, by a network of institutions designed to eliminate oppressive domestic chores, and by greatly expanded occupational opportunities. The occupations were to provide women with an income and thus with an independence from their fathers and husbands totally absent in tsarist times. But the lack of resources of the young Soviet government, the disruption of the economy, the extreme conservatism of the population, and perhaps a general naïveté about the process of social change all contributed to serious shortcomings in the realization of these goals. Conditions began to change in the late 1920's with the onset of rapid industrialization and urbanization. The demand for labor started to outstrip the supply, and women were drawn into the labor force in massive numbers. By 1930 increased female employment was planned for all areas of production. The minimum quotas for females in vocational schools, training classes, and in certain professions and trades had become completely unnecessary by the end of the 1930's. Also, the small cohort born during the First World War meant that there would be an especially insufficient number of young workers to meet the needs of industry during the 1930's. (A comparable phenomenon occurred in the mid-1960's as a consequence of the few births during the Second World War.) In the USSR as a whole, women constituted 82 percent of the 4,047,000 workers who entered the labor force between 1932 and 1937.

The entrance of women into the labor force during this period was thus fostered by a "general rise in the demand for labor that could have been met by either male or female labor," as opposed to a rise in "demand for female labor in particular."[19] In this respect the situation of the USSR differs very markedly from that of the United States, where increased female labor-force participation was prompted primarily by the rapid development of the service sector. As Table 1 indicates, a rapid growth in the proportion of women among Soviet workers took place in virtually every branch of the economy during the 1930's.[20] This growth was particularly marked in con-

[17] M. T. Gol'tsman, "Sostav stroitel'nykh rabochikh SSSR v gody pervoi piatiletki," in D. A. Baevskii, ed., *Izmeneniia v chislennosti i sostave sovetskogo rabochego klassa* (M, 1961), pp. 168–69), 171–72.

[18] Dodge, p. 165.

[19] Valerie K. Oppenheimer, "Demographic Influence on Female Employment and the Status of Women," *American Journal of Sociology*, 78 (Jan. 1973), p. 949.

[20] The 1926 census has detailed data on labor-force participation that remain to be analyzed.

TABLE 1

Percentages and Frequency Distribution of Women in Branches of the Soviet Economy, 1929, 1933, and 1940

Branch of the economy	Percent female			Frequency distribution		
	1929	1933	1940	1929	1933	1940
Industry	28%	31%	41%	.36	.36	.38
Construction	7	16	23	.02	.04	.03
State farms and subsidiary agricultural enterprises	28	26	34	.13	.09	.05
Machine and tractor service stations	–	7	11	–	.00	.00
Transportation	9	14	21	.04	.04	.06
Communication	28	38	48	.01	.01	.02
Trade, public dining, procurement, material-technical supply	19	41	44	.04	.13	.12
Public health	65	71	76	.09	.07	.10
Education, science, and scientific services	54	56	58	.14	.13	.15
Government and social institutions, credit, and insurance	19	29	35	.08	.07	.06
Other branches	31	14	18	.09	.04	.04
TOTAL	27%	30%	38%	1.00	1.00	1.01

SOURCE: Norton T. Dodge, *Women in the Soviet Economy* (Baltimore, Md., 1966), pp. 178–79.

struction and transportation, and once again it is instructive to consider the construction industry. Between 1928 and 1932, 340,000 females entered this industry. In late 1932, a labor union census showed that outside Central Asia women constituted 15.9 percent of those engaged in industrial and residential construction and 17.3 percent of those in railroad construction.[21] Yet Table 1 shows clearly that despite women's progress in construction and transportation, and a small increase in the proportion of females working in industry, by the mid-1930's the shift of women into the areas of trade, health, science, and education was unmistakable.

Excluding agricultural occupations, a necessarily crude calculation of the distribution of females compared to males in the labor force in the 1930's indicates that during this period of extreme demand for labor and rapid growth in the number of female nonagricultural workers the degree of occupational segregation declined somewhat.[22] As will be shown below, this was not the case after 1939.

[21] Gol'tsman, pp. 174–75.

[22] The Index of dissimilarity shows the difference between the distribution of females and males within occupations. For the methodology, see Dudley L. Poston, Jr., and Gordon C. Johnson, "Industrialization and Professional Differentiation by Sex in the Metropolitan Southwest," *Social Science Quarterly* (Sept. 1973), pp. 331–48; and Edward Gross, "Plus ça change . . . ? The Sexual Structure of Occupations Over Time," *Social Problems*, 16 (Fall 1968), pp. 198–208.

The labor-force participation rate of Russian women has always been very high. This is especially true when agricultural work done in the private sector—a category usually excluded from Soviet statistics—is classified as employment. City living forced women to alter the ways they previously had contributed to the household economy. There is no reason to believe that increases in the earnings of males in the early postrevolutionary decades reduced the traditional family dependence on female productivity. In fact, the already unbalanced sex ratio probably enhanced this dependency. As Geiger points out, many women may have prepared for or sought employment to allay the uncertainties brought about in part by the purges of the latter half of the 1930's. Geiger asserts that "in the atmosphere of sudden disappearance and secret trials, husbands and wives were concerned with the problem of the family's economic survival if the husband were arrested."[23] Surely, though, the traumas experienced during this period were surpassed by those of the Second World War.

The devastation and population losses during the war kept demand for female labor high, while at the same time preempting resources for child-care centers, public dining facilities, modern housing, domestic appliances, and so on. Between 1940 and 1960, though the number of women in the Soviet labor force rose by more than 30 million, the number of places in children's institutions (insufficient to begin with) increased by only 7 million.[24] With increasing industrialization, the proportion of the labor force in agriculture contracted.

To analyze the shifts in the nonagricultural labor force, I have divided occupations into two categories employed in the Soviet census: (1) non-professional or manual occupations, and (2) professional and semiprofessional occupations (i.e., those "requiring primarily mental exertion"). The percentage of women among the workers in the total labor force (including private subsidiary agriculture and the military) increased from 49.1 to 54.0 between 1939 and 1959. Among professional and semiprofessional personnel, though, the increase was four times as great. The number of women in these occupations increased by over 3.5 million, whereas the number of males actually declined by 300,000. The rising level of educational attainment of women and the highly unbalanced sex ratio partially account for this disproportionate increase in the number of women in professional and semiprofessional occupations. In addition, as the opportunity arose, women were probably opting to enter occupations that were physically less demanding and culturally defined as more appropriate for females. Despite the very extensive labor-force participation of women, the labeling of occupations as male and female clearly persisted. Also, the higher wages paid in heavy industry must have motivated males to seek jobs in this area and may

[23] Geiger, p. 40.
[24] P. P. Litviakov, *Demograficheskie problemy zaniatosti* (M, 1969), p. 111; V. B. Mikhailiuk, *Ispol'zovanie zhenskogo truda v narodnom khoziaistve* (M, 1970), p. 26.

TABLE 2

Percentage of Women Employed in Three Soviet Census Categories,
1939, 1959, and 1970

Year	Census category			
	Professional and semi-professional	Nonprofessional	Agriculture and forestry	Total
Using categories from the 1959 census				
1939	34.0%	33.8%	57.4%	44.0%
1959	54.3	41.8	57.5	48.1
Using categories from the 1970 census				
1959	54.2	42.0	57.6	48.7
1970	60.7	44.7	51.8	50.3

SOURCES: *Itogi 1959 g.*, pp. 228–58; *Itogi 1970 g.*, *tom* 4, pp. 24–33, 170–74.
NOTE: This table excludes workers in private subsidiary agriculture and the military; hence the totals are lower than those on p. 196.

have made men considerably less inclined to resist women's growing dominance in even the prestigious professional and semiprofessional occupations.[25]

The proportion of women among nonprofessional workers also grew significantly. Between 1939 and 1959 the number of nonprofessional workers increased by 7.9 million, with women accounting for 64 percent of this figure. The percentage of females among nonprofessional workers had been 33.2 percent in 1939; in 1959 it was 40.5 percent. Thus as the tertiary sector (i.e., the service sector, encompassing a substantial proportion of professional and semiprofessional workers) continued to expand, the difference between the patterns of male and female labor-force participation increased. A growing proportion of males were in nonprofessional occupations, whereas the female labor force was shifting into professional and semiprofessional occupations (see Table 2).

In sum, during the period of recovery from the Second World War the continued priority on rapid economic growth meant that the demand for female labor remained very high. The acute deficit of males increased the necessity for women to be able to support themselves in a society that was becoming more and more urban. Education was the key to the expanding professional and semiprofessional occupations, and women were taking advantage of it; however, women were also drawn into nonprofessional occupations in even greater numbers. Despite the evening-out of the sex ratio in the past decades, the very low birthrates during the 1930's and 1940's, plus

[25]N. Tatarinova, "Nauchno-tekhnicheskii progress i trud zhenshchin," *Voprosy ekonomiki*, 11 (1973), p. 59; *Itogi 1959 g.*, pp. 244–51, 255–58, 282–91.

the absence of any significant baby boom in the late 1940's and early 1950's such as that found in the United States and Western Europe, means that the demand for female labor will be sustained in the decades to come despite the increasingly equal numbers of males and females in the population. Indeed, because of the very low birthrates during the 1960's, by the 1980's a net decrease can be expected in the size of the working-age population of the RSFSR. Feshbach and Rapawy predict a critical shortage of labor supply in the USSR as a whole by the 1980's.[26]

Beginning at least in the late 1950's there were signs that rising prosperity was leading to increased production of consumer goods, somewhat better housing, and an increase in various types of everyday services. This may have made it easier for housewives or women working solely in private agriculture to combine family responsibilities with a full-time job. The growth of the service sector and light industry also provided employment opportunities for women who had limited skills or found other work too demanding physically. Soviet planners surely were hoping that the participation rate of this group of women would rise, for this constituted a potentially very large pool of much-needed labor. Among those aged sixteen to 54 in the RSFSR in 1959, there were 2.6 million women in private subsidiary agriculture and an additional 3.7 million women who were neither in school nor in the socialized sector of the labor force. Of the latter, 59 percent had children under the age of fourteen.[27]

Table 3 shows that between 1959 and 1970 there was a substantial rise in the participation rates of women in the groups over age twenty. The increases in the minimum salary and in pension benefits appear to have constituted an important incentive. Many older women returned to work to be able to qualify for a pension.[28]

The continued development of the service sector and of light industry was probably particularly important for tapping the labor of women in the generally small and medium-sized cities that developed around a monolithic industrial base. Given the sexual division of labor and the inadequate occupational diversification of such urban areas, the work force there consisted primarily either of males or of females. In cities where heavy industry has predominated, women have frequently complained that their having to devote themselves solely to housework was a consequence of their not being able to find suitable employment.[29] In the late 1960's, a major drive was initiated to provide part-time work and promote cottage industry. This

[26] Murray Feshbach and Stephen Rapawy, "Soviet Population and Manpower Trends and Policy" (U.S. Congress, Joint Economic Committee, 1976).

[27] *Itogi 1959 g.*, pp. 158–59.

[28] The decline in participation rates in the under-20 age groups is explained by the increase in school attendance; see Gail W. Lapidus, "USSR Women at Work: Changing Patterns," *Industrial Relations*, 14, no. 2 (May 1975), p. 182. On pensions, see Litviakov, pp. 106–7.

[29] M. Ia. Sonin, *Aktual'nye problemy ispol'zovaniia rabochei sily v SSSR* (M, 1965), p. 204; Mikhailiuk, pp. 34–35.

TABLE 3

Percentage of Women in the Labor Force by Age Group,
1926, 1959, and 1970

Age group	1926 (USSR)	1959 (USSR)	1959 (RSFSR)	1970 (USSR)
10 to 14	53%	—	—	
15 to 19	80	63%	62%	48%[a]
20 to 24	93	81	83	86
25 to 29	75	80	81	
30 to 34	75	78	79	93
35 to 39	77	77	78	
40 to 44	77	76	76	91
45 to 49	77	75	73	
50 to 54	72	69	68	77
55 to 59	68	55	47	44
60 to 64	55	48	39	25
65 to 69	47	35	30	

SOURCES: Dodge, pp. 36, 37, 262; Feshbach and Rapawy, "Soviet Population and Manpower Trends and Policy," p. 152.

NOTE: Women in private subsidiary agriculture are included.

[a] This is the rate for those aged 16 to 19.

apparently was designed to further increase the labor-force participation of housewives and the elderly: "By October 1969, the RSFSR Ministry of Light Industry was employing about 7,000 persons at home, and it was expected to expand that number shortly thereafter. By 1972 there were some 100,000 part-time active workers in the RSFSR."[30]

Between 1959 and 1970, the number of professional and semiprofessional personnel grew by about 6.8 million, with women accounting for 72 percent of this figure. However, women constituted only a slight majority (55 percent) of the 7.5 million more nonprofessional workers (excluding agriculture) in 1970 as compared to 1959. Tables 4 and 5 show the percentages of women employed in different nonprofessional occupations in the RSFSR in 1939, 1959, and 1970. Though women constituted 44.7 percent of nonprofessional workers in 1970, that figure is not nearly so impressive as those Norton Dodge cites for semiprofessional and professional women in 1965 and 1974 (58 percent of both categories in the former year, 59 percent in the latter—see Table 1 in Dodge's paper in this volume, p. 206).

Moreover, between 1959 and 1970 the movement of women out of agriculture finally outstripped that of men, resulting in a decline of 6 points in the percentage of females among these workers. This is particularly significant, for the change in women's position in agriculture has been inordinately slow relative to that in other sectors. (See the paper by Ethel Dunn

[30] Murray Feshbach and Stephen Rapawy, "Labor Constraints in the Five-Year Plan," in U.S. Congress, *Soviet Economic Prospects for the Seventies* (Washington, D.C., 1973), p. 494.

TABLE 4
The Nonprofessional Labor Force of the RSFSR, by Occupation and Sex, 1939 and 1959

Occupation	1939				1959			
	Percent female	Frequency distribution			Percent female	Frequency distribution		
		Female	Male	Difference		Female	Male	Difference
Employed at power installations and working with hoisting-transport machines	22.5%	.0117	.0206	.0089	33.8%	.0319	.0448	.0129
Metallurgical and metalworkers	13.9	.0519	.1876	.1285	17.9	.0942	.3101	.2159
Chemical workers	48.7	.0109	.0059	.0050	61.0	.0142	.0065	.0077
Employed in production of construction materials, glass, and chinaware	44.9	.0099	.0062	.0037	59.3	.0161	.0080	.0081
Woodworkers	18.1	.0177	.0408	.0231	21.4	.0159	.0420	.0261
Paper workers	57.1	.0014	.0005	.0009	66.4	.0014	.0005	.0009
Printing workers	59.6	.0096	.0033	.0063	73.7	.0085	.0022	.0063
Textile workers	76.4	.0945	.0149	.0796	85.4	.0568	.0070	.0498
Garment workers	77.1	.0526	.0080	.0446	92.6	.0596	.0034	.0562
Leather workers	32.4	.0068	.0073	.0005	52.8	.0042	.0027	.0015
Shoe workers	21.2	.0096	.0182	.0086	46.3	.0078	.0065	.0013
Food workers	42.9	.0267	.0181	.0086	71.9	.0282	.0079	.0203
Construction workers	5.2	.0123	.1144	.1021	19.9	.0512	.1481	.0929
Fishing and fishbreeding workers	19.1	.0035	.0076	.0041	15.6	.0010	.0039	.0029
Railroad workers	21.4	.0189	.0353	.0164	35.1	.0313	.0416	.0103
Water transport workers	8.5	.0015	.0081	.0066	18.2	.0027	.0088	.0061
Automotive transport and urban electrical transport workers	9.7	.0071	.0339	.0268	6.5	.0105	.1091	.0986
Postal workers, letter carriers	49.9	.0842	.0178	.0664	80.5	.0907	.0064	.0843
Public dining workers^a	70.7	.0087	.0045	.0042	91.0	.0098	.0017	.0081
Communal and household service personnel	52.7	.2306	.1056	.1250	72.3	.1853	.0511	.1342
Orderlies, nurses, nursemaids	96.1	.0391	.0080	.0383	97.7	.0435	.0007	.0428
Other nonprofessional workers^b	29.9	.2837	.3406	.0569	47.4	.2352	.1870	.0428
TOTAL	33.8%	1.0000	1.0000	.7782	41.8%	1.0000	1.0000	.9394

SOURCE: *Itogi 1959 g.,* pp. 228–43, 252–54, 278–81, 285–88.

NOTE: Reclassification of occupations in the 1970 census resulted in the slightly different figures for 1959 in this table and Table 5.

^{a}This category has been changed to conform with the 1970 reclassification of some subcategories.

^{b}This is a residual category.

elsewhere in this volume.) In 1939, 54 out of every 100 employed females worked in agriculture, and only thirteen out of every 100 had a professional or semi-professional occupation. By 1970, only fifteen out of every 100 remained in agriculture whereas 35 occupied professional or semiprofessional positions.[31]

OCCUPATIONAL SEGREGATION BY SEX

These growing differences in the distribution of males and females within the labor force give only part of the picture. In fact, what is revealed by measuring occupational segregation by sex using the *detailed* listing of nonagrarian occupations contrasts very markedly with these findings.

The analysis of the major shifts in the occupations of men and women is complicated by the difference in the classification of occupations used in the 1970 census as compared to that used in the 1959 census. Fortunately, data from the 1959 census were again presented in 1970 using the new classification. However, comparisons between 1939 and 1970 often can be made only indirectly by first analyzing change between 1939 and 1959 (according to the 1959 census) and then comparing 1959 and 1970 (from the data in the 1970 census).

Columns 1 and 5 of Table 4 and Table 5 show the percent female within each of the nonprofessional occupational categories for 1939, 1959, and 1970. From this it can be seen that the representation of women within these occupations had varied substantially, but increased most dramatically between 1939 and 1959. Again, note particularly the change in the construction industry. Columns 4 and 8 show the difference in the way males and females are distributed in occupations. The unstandardized index of dissimilarity is a summary measure of these differences and permits comparison over time.[32] An examination of the change in the size of the difference between Columns 4 and 8 shows which occupations produced the greatest change in overall occupational segregation. The largest differences were in two areas: automotive and electrical urban transportation, and machine construction and metalwork.[33]

Detailed analysis of the full list of occupational categories in the Soviet census confirmed these findings.[34] What this showed, for example, was that the difference between males and females in automotive and electrical

[31]*Itogi 1970 g., tom 6*, pp. 24–33, 170–74.
[32]This is calculated by summing the differences and dividing by two. The unstandardized measure of dissimilarity "may be interpreted as the percentage of females (or males) who have to change occupations in order that the distribution of sexes in occupations should be the same" (Poston and Johnson, pp. 337–38). The influence of an occupation on this summary measure is determined by the proportion of the labor force in that occupation. The standardized measure gives equal weight to each occupation and is thus unaffected by changes in the distribution of the labor force.
[33]This finding was based on the analysis of data in *Itogi 1959 g.*, pp. 228–58, 278–88.
[34]In the 1959 census, including residuals, there were 57 professional and semiprofessional categories and 53 nonprofessional categories. In 1970, the figures were 64 and 51, respectively.

TABLE 5
The Nonprofessional Labor Force of the RSFSR, by Occupation and Sex, 1959 and 1970

Occupation	1959 Percent female	1959 Frequency distribution Female	1959 Frequency distribution Male	1959 Frequency distribution Difference	1970 Percent female	1970 Frequency distribution Female	1970 Frequency distribution Male	1970 Frequency distribution Difference
Employed in the production of construction materials, glass, and chinaware	59.3%	.0160	.0080	.0080	59.5%	.0119	.0065	.0054
Woodworkers	21.4	.0158	.0421	.0263	25.4	.0134	.0318	.0184
Textile workers	85.4	.0564	.0070	.0494	84.8	.0377	.0055	.0322
Garment workers	92.6	.0593	.0034	.0559	94.6	.0600	.0028	.0572
Leather workers	52.8	.0041	.0027	.0014	69.1	.0029	.0011	.0018
Shoe workers	46.3	.0077	.0065	.0012	59.2	.0065	.0036	.0029
Food workers	71.9	.0280	.0079	.0201	82.4	.0254	.0044	.0210
Construction workers	19.9	.0508	.1483	.0975	29.0	.0560	.1104	.0544
Railroad workers	35.1	.0311	.0417	.0106	37.7	.0198	.0264	.0066
Automotive transport and urban electrical transport workers	6.5	.0104	.1093	.0989	4.6	.0097	.1611	.1514
Postal workers, letter carriers	80.5	.0097	.0017	.0080	89.8	.0110	.0010	.0100
Public dining workers	91.0	.0901	.0064	.0837	94.6	.1209	.0056	.1153
Orderlies, nurses, nursemaids	97.7	.0432	.0007	.0425	98.1	.0574	.0009	.0565
Machine-construction and metal workers[a]	17.1	.0849	.2983	.2134	17.3	.1027	.3972	.2945
Chemical workers	61.6	.0139	.0063	.0076	60.2	.0171	.0090	.0080
Paper and cardboard workers	68.5	.0026	.0009	.0017	67.2	.0025	.0010	.0015
Printing workers	74.2	.0072	.0018	.0054	74.6	.0060	.0016	.0044
Communal, household, and everyday service personnel	73.2	.2007	.0532	.1475	82.6	.1623	.0276	.1347
Laboratory assistants (workers)	92.4	.0038	.0002	.0036	90.7	.0122	.0010	.0112
Inspectors and sorters	83.5	.0265	.0038	.0227	89.1	.0322	.0032	.0290
Warehouse workers, weighers, receivers, and distributors	65.3	.0323	.0124	.0199	80.2	.0385	.0077	.0308
Other nonprofessional workers[b]	38.5	.2052	.2374	.0322	45.1	.1940	.1907	.0033
TOTAL	42.0%	1.0000	1.0000	.9575	44.7%	1.0000	1.0000	1.0505

SOURCE: *Itogi 1970 g.*, tom 4, pp. 24–30, 170–71.

[a] This occupation and several others in the table differ from those listed in Table 4.

[b] This is a residual category.

TABLE 6

*Unstandardized and Standardized Measures of Occupational
Segregation, 1939–70*

Year	Professional and semi-professional		Non-professional	
	Unstd.	Std.	Unstd.	Std.
Using detailed categories from the 1959 census				
1939	49.5	55.3	40.2	56.3
1959	53.1	51.8	50.2	56.3
Using detailed categories from the 1970 census				
1959	53.1	48.7	51.7	51.9
1970	50.9	49.8	53.2	56.6

SOURCES: *Itogi 1959 g.*, pp. 228–58, 278–88; *Itogi 1972 g., tom 6*, pp. 24–33, 170–74.
NOTE: The nonprofessional category excludes workers in agriculture and forestry.

urban transportation was primarily the result of female exclusion from one particular subcategory: chauffeurs or taxi drivers. In 1939, 97 percent of all such workers were men; this percentage was little changed by 1970. However, whereas in 1939 only three in every 100 nonprofessional males were in this line of work, by 1970 the figure had grown to 16 in every 100. Thus, an occupation with an extreme underrepresentation of women grew at a very rapid rate relative to other occupations. This was also true of several occupations in the area of metalwork.[35]

Despite considerable changes in the distribution of both men and women in professional and semiprofessional occupations, I found that this did not result in any appreciable change in the unstandardized measure of occupational segregation.[36] The complete pattern of change in the measures of segregation is shown in Table 6. What this reveals is a distinct continuity over time in both occupational groupings. The comparison of the standardized and unstandardized figures reveals that the slight decrease in segregation in the nonprofessional occupations was, as suggested above, solely the result of the shift in the distribution of the entire labor force and not the result of greater equality of representation of women in the occupations.

Women in the RSFSR may have had increasingly diverse occupations at least through the Second World War. The extreme conditions of those years broke down barriers to female employment in a vast number of areas. But as the sex ratio has become more balanced, and as prosperity has grown and the service sector expanded, the cultural biases regarding women's work

[35] Between 1959 and 1970 alone, the proportion of males in metalwork and machine construction rose from .298 to .397, but the percentage of females among the workers in this area remained about 17.
[36] For further discussion, see Sacks, pp. 79–87.

have returned. Though the rate of female labor-force participation in the nonagricultural sector has continued to rise, though the educational level of the population has increased markedly, and though the network of service enterprises, the production of household appliances, and the number of adequate housing units have all grown, yet differences between the work of men and women have remained. Nonetheless, this should not be interpreted as a lack of change in the status of women. The movement of women into professional and semiprofessional occupations is certainly an impressive development, as is their shift out of agriculture. Finally, women's potential for engaging in collective action may have been increased by the growth in the numbers of well-educated women segregated in professional occupations. Their segregation at work and higher education may provide the contact and consciousness needed for concerted action.

Norton T. Dodge

Women in the Professions

A PPROXIMATELY TWO-THIRDS of the Soviet women who are employed in the public sector are engaged in what the census terms "physical" occupations. Their work is seldom inspiring and is often hard and tedious. Those in the remaining more fortunate third are engaged in primarily "mental" occupations, which include those "specialist" occupations characterized as semiprofessional and professional. The importance of women in these more rewarding occupations has grown markedly over the past half century. Unfortunately, however, most Soviet women still bear a heavy, dual burden of work on the job and in the home. And because success in semiprofessional and professional occupations demands a fuller commitment than in most others, women working in these occupations often experience greater conflicts with their roles as wives, mothers, and housekeepers. Though some progress has been made in reducing women's burdens in the home, Lenin's call to liberate women from the "tyranny of husbands and the home" has had few strong advocates within top Party circles. As a result, equality in the home for Soviet women continues to be far less evident than equality in the workplace. And practical needs continue to outweigh altruistic principles in governing economic and social policies affecting women.

In this paper we shall examine current trends in the participation of women in semiprofessional and professional specialties. We shall then identify some of the factors that have encouraged women to enter and advance in certain professions and that have discouraged them from entering others. Following this general survey, we shall focus on women in several specific professions—engineering, education, scientific research, and medicine—in order to look behind the official pronouncements and

TABLE 1

Semiprofessional and Professional Women, 1928, 1941, 1955, 1965, and 1974

(Thousands)

Year	Number			Percent		
	Semi-professional	Professional	Total	Semi-professional	Professional	Total
1928	86	65	151	30%	28%	29%
1941	552	312	864	37	34	36
1955	1,960	1,155	3,115	67	53	61
1965	4,423	2,518	6,941	62	52	58
1974	8,000	4,600	12,600	63	52	59

SOURCES: 1928, 1941, and 1955 figures, Norton T. Dodge, *Women in the Soviet Economy* (Baltimore, Md., 1966), p. 185; 1965 figures, *Narodnoe khoziaistvo SSSR v 1965 g.* (M, 1966), pp. 574, 580; 1974 figures, *Narodnoe khoziaistvo SSSR v 1974 g.* (M, 1975), p. 565.

statistics to determine whether prejudice (rather than objective circumstances) has kept women from realizing their full potentials in these professions.

WOMEN'S GROWING ROLE IN SEMIPROFESSIONAL AND
PROFESSIONAL OCCUPATIONS

The occupations classed as semiprofessional and professional are distinguished chiefly by the amount and kind of educational background they require. Semiprofessional occupations are those that require specialized secondary education, although appropriate experience may suffice in some instances; professional ones are those that require higher (e.g., university-level) education. Table 1 shows the dramatic increase in the number of women in both kinds of occupation between 1928 and 1974 (from 151,000 to 12,600,000).[1] Moreover, whereas women were only 29 percent of all semiprofessionals and professionals in the labor force in 1928, by 1955 they were 61 percent. And they have remained close to 60 percent ever since. In the broader census category of primarily "mental" occupations, the percentage of women also had continued to increase—from 52 percent in 1959 to 59 percent in 1970. Since the participation of women in the Soviet economy as a whole increased from 48 to 50 percent during the 1959–70 period, the net gain for women in the primarily "mental" occupations was five percentage points beyond the average increase for women in all occupations, which suggests a continuing qualitative improvement in female employment.

The horizontal distribution of women in the professions. Of particular interest are the changing numbers and proportions of semiprofessional and professional women in the various fields shown for the thirteen-year period

[1] For a comprehensive review of earlier patterns, see Norton T. Dodge, *Women in the Soviet Economy* (Baltimore, Md., 1966).

1955–68 in Table 2. Among semiprofessionals, there was a 374 percent increase in the number of women technicians, and a 327 percent increase in women statisticians, planners, and commodity specialists. In the professional category, the most noteworthy increases in the numbers of women were among engineers (283 percent) and economists, economist-statisticians, and commodity specialists (321 percent). The percentages of semiprofessional women in the Soviet economy are higher than those in any Western economy, although the profile is roughly similar to that of the major industrial powers. It is worth noting, too, how little change occurred between 1955 and 1968 in the percentages of women versus men in most semiprofessional occupations. The only major change was in the category

TABLE 2

Semiprofessional and Professional Women, by Jobs, 1955 and 1968

(*Thousands*)

Job	Number		Pct. change	Percent	
	1955	1968		1955	1968
Semiprofessional					
1. Technicians	309	1,459	374%	38%	38%
2. Agronomists, zootechnicians, veterinarians, foresters	116	263"	126	46	48"
3. Statisticians, planners, commodity specialists	144	614[b]	327	77	78[b]
4. Legal personnel	7	n.a.	n.a.	30	n.a.
5. Medical personnel (including dentists)	668	1,575	136	91	93
6. Teachers, librarians, and cultural personnel	639	1,200	88	78	85
TOTAL	1,960	5,597	186	67	63
Professional					
1. Engineers (including geologists)	168	644	283	28	31
2. Agronomists, zootechnicians, veterinarians, foresters	65	143	120	41	40
3. Economists, economist-statisticians, commodity specialists	62	261[c]	321	54	64[c]
4. Legal personnel	15	n.a.	n.a.	32	n.a.
5. Physicians (excluding dentists)	228	399	75	76	72
6. Teachers and university graduates,[d] librarians, and cultural personnel	606	1,503	148	67	69
TOTAL	1,155	3,122	170	53	52

SOURCES: Norton T. Dodge, *Women in the Soviet Economy* (Baltimore, Md., 1966), pp. 189, 194; *Vestnik statistiki*, 1970, No. 1, p. 91.

[a] Excludes foresters.
[b] Excludes commodity specialists.
[c] Excludes commodity specialists and economist-statisticians.
[d] Excludes geologists, legal personnel, physicians, economists.

TABLE 3

Semiprofessional or Professional Occupations Completely or
Largely Dominated by Women, 1970

Occupation[a]	Number of women (thousands)	Percent of women
Completely dominated (over 90 percent women)		
1. Nurses	1,275	99%
2. Kindergarten heads and teachers in boarding schools	825	98
3. Cashiers	668	94
4. Secretaries and other office workers	580	95
5. Heads of libraries and librarians	310	95
6. Typists and stenographers	243	99
Largely dominated (70 to 90 percent women)		
1. Teachers in primary, eight-year, and all secondary schools and programs; heads of primary schools; teachers and foremen in industrial education	2,176	72
2. Bookkeepers and tally clerks	2,021	85
3. Laboratory workers (except nontechnical workers)	618	85
4. Economists and planners	565	82
5. Communications workers	498	83
6. Physicians	417	74
7. *Fel'dshers* and midwives	362	83
8. Data processors (except administrators)	263	77

SOURCE: *Itogi vsesoiuznoi perepisi naseleniia 1970 goda, tom VI* (M, 1973), pp. 165–69.
[a] Only those occupations employing more than 200,000 women are listed.

teachers, librarians, and cultural personnel, where the share of women increased seven percentage points.

Although the 52 percent of professionals who were women in 1968 is a figure well below the 63 percent of semiprofessionals who were women in that year, the percentage of women in these two categories represents an impressive achievement by any standard. Especially in such fields as medicine, agronomy, and engineering, the proportion of Soviet women in professional roles is high in comparison to what it is in the United States and other Western countries.

Data from the 1970 census show that the trend toward large numbers and high proportions of women physicians, engineers, technical foremen, laboratory workers, and technicians is continuing.[2] Table 3 breaks down the 1970 census data to show semiprofessional and professional occupations that are completely or largely dominated by women. What is striking about this table is that though the occupations completely dominated by women are those one would expect from experience elsewhere, the occupations largely dominated by women are quite different. Soviet women are

[2] *Itogi vsesoiuznoi perepisi naseleniia 1970 goda, tom VI* (M, 1973), pp. 165–69, translated in Norton T. Dodge, "The Role of Women in the Soviet Economy" in NATO Directorate of Economic Affairs, comp., *Economic Aspects of Life in the USSR* (Brussels, 1975), pp. 189–93.

TABLE 4

*Professional Occupations with Relatively High Numbers
and/or Percentages of Women, 1970*

Occupation	Number of women (thousands)	Percent of women
Planning and record-keeping personnel		
1. Economists and planners	565	82%
2. Inspectors, controllers, checkers	385	68
Medical personnel		
1. Physicians	417	74
2. Dentists	48	77
3. Chief physicians and other heads of public health institutions	32	53
Engineering and technical personnel		
1. Engineers	1,121	40
2. Designers and draftsmen	349	57
3. Technical personnel in railways	46	43
Scientific personnel, teachers, and training personnel		
1. Heads of scientific research institutes and organizations; scientific personnel (except teachers in higher educational institutions)	182	40
2. Teachers in higher educational institutions	130	43

SOURCE: See source for Table 3.

highly represented in a number of professions where their share is much smaller in Europe or in the United States. For example, 82 percent of Soviet economists and planners, 83 percent of communications workers, and 74 percent of physicians are women. Table 4 shows some additional professions that have unusually high proportions of women in the Soviet Union. Apart from the high proportion of women among physicians (74 percent), dentists (77 percent), and medical administrators (53 percent), of special interest are the high percentages of women among designers and draftsmen (57 percent), engineers (40 percent), teachers in higher education (43 percent), and scientific research personnel (40 percent).

By contrast, in the United States only 7 percent of physicians and fewer than 2 percent of dentists are women. In France, Great Britain, Italy, and Germany, the proportion of women physicians is larger than in the United States (ranging between 13 and 20 percent), but the proportion of women dentists remains low. An exception to this pattern is Finland, where more than three-quarters of the dentists are women. In none of these countries does the proportion of women teaching in higher education exceed 21 percent; and in all instances the percentage of women engineers is negligible.[3]

[3] Marjory Galenson, *Women and Work: An International Comparison* (Ithaca, N.Y., 1973), pp. 24–27.

TABLE 5
Semiprofessional and Professional Occupations Showing
Major Changes in the Proportion of Women Employed
Between 1959 and 1970

Occupation	Number of women		Percent of women		1970 as a percentage of 1959
	1959	1970	1959	1970	
Upward changes					
1. Engineers (including chief specialists)	268	1,121	32%	40%	125%
2. Technicians (except in agricultural and veterinary work)	230	586	45	59	131
3. Data processors (except administrators)	269	263	61	77	126
4. Directors, heads of stores and trade organizations	166	241	49	64	131
5. Heads of procurement and supply organizations	105	214	26	48	185
6. Sales personnel	58	194	47	69	147
7. Dispatchers (except in railway, water, or air transport)	69	193	51	65	127
8. Normsetters	100	169	61	76	125
9. Heads of organizations of government administration; heads of Party, Komsomol, trade union, and other social organizations and their structural subdivisions	100	128	26	32	123
10. Radio operators, telegraphers	82	119	62	74	119
11. Agents and expediters	54	91	37	54	146
12. Heads of public dining facilities (except buffets)	30	59	53	69	130
13. Heads of schools and programs (except heads of primary schools)	26	57	23	32	139
14. Writers, journalists, editors	26	47	35	45	129
15. Technical workers in railway transport (excluding those included elsewhere)	28	46	28	43	154
16. Veterinary technicians and veterinary fel'dshers	26	43	23	36	157
17. Heads of collective-farm fermy	22	18	16	22	138
Downward changes					
1. Physicians	265	417	79	74	94
2. Agronomists	67	70	40	35	88
3. Dentists	26	48	83	77	93
4. Physical culture and sports personnel	29	33	27	24	89

SOURCE: See source for Table 3.

The proportion of women did not decrease significantly in any major Soviet profession between 1959 and 1970, although slight declines occurred among physicians (79 to 74 percent), dentists (83 to 77 percent), and agronomists (40 to 35 percent). In the first two instances, deliberate efforts were reportedly made to increase the proportion of men. In many professions, by contrast, the proportion of women increased significantly either in relative or in absolute terms (see Table 5). Indeed, the proportion of women has been rising in many of the more attractive occupations, such as heads of retail stores or trade organizations and heads of supply organizations. However, the proportion of women has not increased significantly in many of the most attractive professions, such as enterprise directors, scientific research workers, or teachers in higher education.

Women earning advanced degrees. From educational statistics, particularly those relating to advanced degrees, we can gain some insights into the likelihood of changes in the proportions of women entering various professions. From name endings, we can estimate the percent of women receiving candidate and doctoral degrees by field. Tables 6 and 7 show the numbers and distributions of candidate and doctoral degrees, respectively, awarded by field for selected years from the 1930's to the 1970's. Though we cannot assume a direct relationship between the number of degrees awarded to women in a professional field and the number of women entering that profession, a change in the one is likely to be a harbinger of a change in the other.

One of the first things we should note about Table 6 is the great increase in the total numbers of degrees awarded women between 1936–37 and 1971–73. There was a first tremendous increase in candidate degrees awarded between 1936–37 (a two-year period, to be sure), and 1956–58, and a second increase between 1962–64 and 1971–73. It is significant that the percentages of women receiving candidate degrees were greatest (32.8 percent) in the two periods that saw the greatest absolute increases in degrees awarded. A similar phenomenon can be seen in Table 7 for doctoral degrees.

Looking at the most recent period (1971–73) in both tables, we can see that the percent of women obtaining the candidate degree in the sciences was not as large as that in the social sciences and humanities (31.8 percent versus 37.8 percent); for the doctoral degree, however, the relationship was reversed (21.4 percent versus 18.5 percent). Within the basic sciences, women were best represented in biology and chemistry at both degree levels; within the applied sciences, medicine showed high proportions of women at both levels; and within the social sciences and humanities, literature and linguistics showed high proportions of women at both levels. However, among doctoral-degree recipients there were anomalously high proportions of women in technology and economics (especially as compared with the figures for 1962–64). A fuller investigation of some of these degree

TABLE 6

Number and Distribution of Candidate Degrees Awarded, and Estimated Percentage of Women Receiving Degrees, by Field, Selected Years

Field	1936–37			1956–58			1962–64			1971–73		
	Total degrees awarded	Percentage distribution	Pct. of women awarded degrees	Total degrees awarded	Percentage distribution	Pct. of women awarded degrees	Total degrees awarded	Percentage distribution	Pct. of women awarded degrees	Total degrees awarded	Percentage distribution	Pct. of women awarded degrees
Natural science	836	26.3%	23.8%	2,585	19.9%	38.3%	3,571	24.9%	25.5%	9,369	23.6%	41.5%
Physics and mathematics	247	7.8	6.1	632	4.9	23.1	779	5.4	16.8	1,165	2.9	21.2
Chemistry	221	6.9	25.9	566	4.4	52.6	496	3.5	38.2	2,942	7.5	54.3
Biology	308	9.7	36.8	433	3.3	66.5	427	3.0	53.2	3,823	9.6	57.6
Geology	60	1.9	22.7	333	2.6	27.0	479	3.3	26.9	1,439	3.6	25.8
Applied science	2,077	65.3%	19.0%	6,492	49.9%	31.4%	7,723	53.9%	30.1%	22,802	57.6%	26.7%
Technology	568	17.9	4.4	3,176	24.4	18.5	2,962	20.7	12.4	12,977	32.8	16.0
Agriculture, veterinary medicine	461	14.5	19.5	1,908	14.7	36.3	1,529	10.7	28.6	3,445	8.7	28.3
Medicine	1,048	32.9	28.6	1,408	10.8	54.4	3,232	22.5	47.0	6,380	16.1	46.9
SUBTOTAL: Natural and applied science	2,913	91.5%	20.4%	9,077	69.8%	33.4%	11,294	70.8%	28.7%	32,171	81.2%	31.8%
Social sciences and humanities	269	8.5%	21.0%	3,924	30.2%	31.5%	3,044	21.2%	25.3%	7,432	18.8%	37.8%
Economics	49	1.5	10.7	878	6.8	22.0	863	6.0	15.9	3,413	8.7	32.2
History	46	1.4	17.2	917	7.1	27.2	630	4.4	20.4	1,587	4.0	33.3
Literature and linguistics	67	2.1	27.0	908	7.0	45.9	599	4.2	44.2	1,360	3.5	49.7
Pedagogy	56	1.8	28.6	256	6.0	41.3	243	1.7	35.5	1,072	2.6	43.6
TOTAL	3,182	100.0%	20.5%	13,001	100.0%	32.8%	14,338	100.0%	27.9%	39,603	100.0%	32.8%

SOURCES: Norton T. Dodge, *Women in the Soviet Economy* (Baltimore, Md., 1966), p. 279, and estimates from 1971 to 1974 issues of *Knizhnaia letopis': dopolnitel'nyi vypusk*.
NOTE: Some components do not add up to totals because some categories have been omitted.

TABLE 7

Number and Distribution of Doctoral Degrees Awarded, and Estimated Percentage
of Women Receiving Degrees, by Field, Selected Years

Field	1936–37			1956–58			1962–64			1971–73		
	Total degrees awarded	Percentage distribution	Pct. of women awarded degrees	Total degrees awarded	Percentage distribution	Pct. of women awarded degrees	Total degrees awarded	Percentage distribution	Pct. of women awarded degrees	Total degrees awarded	Percentage distribution	Pct. of women awarded degrees
Natural science	93	18.3%	15.1%	162	26.7%	8.3%	291	21.4%	16.8%	1,168	25.4%	16.7%
Physics and mathematics	28	5.4	7.7	45	7.4	0.0	58	4.3	7.7	401	8.7	5.5
Chemistry	12	2.4	12.5	23	3.8	17.6	24	1.8	40.0	216	4.7	23.0
Biology	38	7.5	23.8	21	3.5	28.6	42	3.1	30.8	392	8.5	27.4
Geology	15	3.0	9.1	28	4.6	10.5	63	4.6	23.1	159	3.5	12.6
Applied science	399	78.4%	8.4%	316	52.1%	15.5%	757	55.8%	26.3%	2,358	51.3%	23.8%
Technology	59	11.6	0.0	157	25.9	3.6	196	14.4	28.6	752	16.4	51.2
Agriculture, veterinary medicine	15	3.0	0.0	93	15.3	12.5	132	9.7	13.0	312	6.7	12.1
Medicine	325	63.8	10.7	66	10.9	51.2	429	31.6	42.3	1,294	28.1	46.9
SUBTOTAL: Natural and applied science	492	96.7%	9.6%	478	78.9%	13.1%	1,048	77.2%	23.7%	3,526	76.7%	21.4%
Social sciences and humanities	17	3.3%	8.3%	128	21.1%	19.8%	309	22.8%	11.3%	1,073	23.3%	18.5%
Economics	3	0.6	50.0	27	4.5	11.8	70	5.2	11.9	262	5.7	73.9
History	6	1.2	0.0	17	2.8	10.0	89	6.6	9.3	542	11.8	20.7
Literature and linguistics	5	1.0	0.0	39	6.4	37.5	50	3.7	14.3	204	4.4	25.9
Pedagogy	1	0.2	0.0	8	1.3	40.0	19	1.4	20.0	65	1.4	21.1
TOTAL	509	100.0%	9.6%	606	100.0%	14.8%	1,357	100.0%	21.2%	4,599	100.0%	20.7%

SOURCE: See sources for Table 6.
NOTE: Some components do not add up to totals because some categories have been omitted.

preferences and the changes in them would be desirable, particularly if more reliable data become available.

WOMEN IN THE VERTICAL STRUCTURE OF OCCUPATIONS

Examination of the distribution of women among the various semiprofessional and professional occupations has already revealed something about the place of women within the vertical structure of each economic sector or branch (such as education or health). If we examine the extent to which women have been able to progress from relatively unskilled, low-paid jobs within each sector to high-paid jobs requiring professional skills and executive capabilities, we find that the prospects for advancement to the top of any profession remain much more restricted for women than for men— despite the fact that the prospects for a Soviet woman entering a professional career and succeeding in it are much more favorable than for an American or European woman. The proportion of Soviet women in administrative and professional jobs—although much higher now than before the Second World War—decreases with each successive increase in rank whatever the economic branch, occupational group, or profession. Even in such fields as education and health, where women predominate, men dominate the upper ranks. This pattern is even more accentuated in the domain of science and technology, where fewer women are found at the beginning lower levels.[4] Thus female specialists in all professional occupations are found concentrated in the lower and middle echelons, and the role of women in managerial and administrative positions remains limited in virtually every economic sector.

WOMEN IN MANAGEMENT AND ADMINISTRATION

If we begin with agriculture, the sector that employs the largest number of women, we find a most unfavorable vertical structure of employment. Although women are 56 percent of the workers engaged in "physical" occupations in agriculture (excluding workers engaged primarily in private subsidiary agriculture, where women make up 90 percent of the total), they are scarcely represented at all among collective farm chairmen (only about 2 percent) or other top management. In most parts of the Soviet Union women are poorly represented in the lower managerial ranks of agriculture as well.[5] Only in recent years have census data suggested that women are gaining ground in some levels of agricultural administration. The proportion of women heading *fermy* (subfarms of collective farms), for example, increased from 16 percent in 1959 to 22 percent in 1970.[6]

---

[4] See Dodge, *Women in the Soviet Economy*, chap. 12.
[5] See Robert C. Stuart, "Structural Change and the Quality of Soviet Collective Farm Management, 1952–1966," in James Millar, ed., *The Soviet Rural Community* (Urbana, Ill., 1971), pp. 129–30; and Norton T. Dodge and Murray Feshbach, "The Role of Women in Soviet Agriculture" in Jerzy F. Karcz, ed., *Soviet and East European Agriculture* (Berkeley, Calif., 1967), pp. 265–305.
[6] *Itogi vsesoiuznoi . . . tom VI*, p. 167.

TABLE 8

*Percent of Women in Responsible Positions in Industry,
1963 and 1973*

	Percent of Women	
Position	1963	1973
Enterprise directors	7%	9%
Chief engineers	16	–
Shop chiefs and their deputies	12	16"
Chiefs of shifts, factory bays, sectors, shop labs, and their deputies	22	
Chiefs of sections, offices, groups of plant services, workshops, labs, and their deputies	20	26"
Engineers (except engineer-economists and engineer ratesetters)	38	49
Technicians (except technician-ratesetters)	65	78
Foremen	20	24
Chief and senior bookkeepers	36	53
Engineer-economists, economists, planners, and statisticians	70	86
TOTAL	34%	–

SOURCES: *Zhenshchiny i deti v SSSR* (M, 1969), p. 102 and *Zhenshchiny v SSSR* (M, 1975), p. 80.
" A close but not exact approximation to the 1963 categories.

Women administrators are found more often in industry than in tradition-bound agriculture; but even in industry, where substantial improvement has occurred, the vertical structure of female employment suggests continuing underrepresentation of women in the top positions (see Table 8). In 1973, the latest year for which data are available, only 9 percent of the enterprise directors were women. At lower administrative levels, however, the percentages of women in various administrative positions varied from 16 to 26 percent.

The distribution of women and their importance as administrators vary greatly among the various industrial branches. Although no specific statistics are available, enrollment figures by engineering field indicate that men dominate the administration of the natural-resource industries, the transportation industry, and heavy industry, whereas women play a larger but still relatively small role in the food-products, consumer-goods, and related light industries. We should not forget, however, that the role of women as administrators in Soviet industry is far greater than it is in any of the leading Western countries.

In construction enterprises, the proportion of women among administrators and specialists increased sharply between 1940 and 1956 from 9 to 22 percent. However, little improvement seems to have occurred since 1956, when women were 10 percent of the category "heads of construction enterprises, chief engineers, and other leading specialists and their deputies."[7] At the next lower administrative level women were only 14 percent.

[7] Calculated from *Zhenshchina v SSSR* (M, 1960), p. 48. Fuller figures are given in Dodge, *Women in the Soviet Economy*, Table 120, p. 204.

Only as chief accountants and head bookkeepers, and as laboratory heads, were the percentages of women substantial (41 and 60 percent, respectively).

The proportion of women administrators is much larger in the trade, procurement and supply, food services, and communications sectors than in construction, transportation, and heavy industry. The census data for 1970 (see Table 9) show that in retail trade women made up almost two-thirds of the top leadership, and in food service almost three-quarters. If data about administrators in cultural fields were not combined with data on other occupations, another area with an important proportion of female administrators would undoubtedly be revealed. In these service sectors of the economy women seem to have taken the lead as administrators.

The role of women in the administration of government and Party activities is also substantial. In 1959, women made up 26 percent of the heads of organs of government administration; of Party, Komsomol, trade union, and other social organizations; and of their subdivisions. By 1970 the proportion had increased by almost a quarter to 32 percent, indicating substantial gains for women.[8] As the papers by Moses and Hough elsewhere in this volume indicate, women in government and Party administration are largely confined to the lower administrative levels; the upper reaches of administration are almost exclusively a male domain. Nevertheless, compared with women's roles in government in other countries, that of Soviet women is impressive. In 1966, for example, women made up 40 percent of the directors of sectors and divisions and deputy directors of divisions, and 25 percent of the chairmen, secretaries, and deputies of the executive committee, of a Leningrad District Soviet.[9] In 1970, nine women were chairwomen or deputy chairwomen of the fifteen republic councils of ministers, and five of them were in Transcaucasia and Central Asia. Of the 21 women among the 538 members, thirteen were from these republics.[10] It would appear from these statistics that a deliberate effort has been made to bring women into prominent positions in public life in these largely Moslem or non-Slavic republics, where women were particularly repressed before the Revolution.

The proportion of women in the Party has increased from less than 10 percent in the early 1920's to 23 percent at present, yet the percentage of women in the higher Party circles is very small. Women have never been more than 4 percent of the Central Committee membership, and it was only under Khrushchev that the first woman was admitted to the Party Presidium (Ekaterina Furtseva). Nonetheless, in spite of these recent gains, women continue to play an extremely limited role in the top Party ranks.[11]

---

[8] *Itogi vsesoiuznoi . . . tom VI*, pp. 165–69.
[9] V. G. Lebin and M. N. Perfil'ev, *Kadry apparata upravleniia v SSSR* (L, 1970), p. 176.
[10] *Women in the Soviet Union: Statistical Returns* (M, 1970), p. 16.
[11] For a full discussion see Gail Lapidus, "Political Mobilization, Participation, and Leadership: Women in Soviet Politics," *Comparative Politics*, 8, no. 1 (Oct. 1975).

TABLE 9

Percent of Women Administrators in the Areas of Retail Trade,
Procurement and Supply, and Food Service, 1959 and 1970

Occupation	Percent of Women	
	1959	1970
Directors and heads of stores and trade organizations	49%	64%
Heads of departments and divisions of stores	85	83
Heads of procurement and supply organizations	26	48
Heads of public dining facilities (except buffets)	66	73

SOURCE: See Norton T. Dodge, "The Role of Women in the Soviet Economy," *Economic Aspects of Life in the USSR* (Brussels, 1975), Appendix Table, p. 192.

WOMEN IN FOUR SELECTED PROFESSIONS

Women in engineering. In the Soviet Union a woman engineer is no longer an oddity. Major successes were achieved in changing the attitude of women toward entering technical and engineering fields, as evidenced by the fourfold increase in the proportion of women enrolled in engineering courses between 1926 and 1939. With the exception of the war years and the period immediately following, when the enrollment of women reached 60 percent, the proportion of women taking engineering courses has fluctuated between 26 and 28 percent until the last five years, when it rose to its present level of 40 percent.[12]

The interests of women within engineering vary considerably. In the 1956–57 academic year, for example, when women made up 36 percent of engineering students, the percentages of women in specialized engineering fields ranged from a low of 16.6 percent in mining engineering to a high of 74.5 percent in food-products technology. Other specialties in which women predominated were consumer-goods-industry technology (74 percent), hydrology and meteorology (63 percent), and chemical engineering (60 percent). The generally less onerous working conditions in these particular fields—in contrast to the heavy, more demanding work, often in remote areas, in the fields of mining, transportation, and machine building—encouraged the participation of women in them.

What has attracted Soviet women to engineering? A number of factors: the encouragement of teachers, success in school, and in recent years encouragement at home. Also, engineering has been depicted as a field through which a vital contribution to industrial growth can be made. Such favorable publicity in the media undoubtedly has had a positive effect. We might also expect the high pay of successful engineers to be a source of attraction, but nothing in the literature suggests that financial rewards are an overt factor in the choice of engineering as a career.[13]

[12] *Narodnoe khoziaistvo SSSR v 1974 g.* (M, 1975), p. 699.
[13] S. A. Kugel' and O. M. Nikandrov, *Molodye inzhenery* (M, 1971), pp. 88–99.

TABLE 10
*Percent of Women Employed in Primary and Secondary Education
in 1960–61 and 1974–75*

	Percent of women	
Position	1960–61	1974–75
Directors of secondary schools	20%	28%
Directors of eight-year schools	23	31
Deputy directors of secondary schools	53	65
Deputy directors of eight-year schools	54	61
Directors of primary schools	69	81
Teachers (except teacher-administrators)		
grades 5 to 11	– ⎫	81
grades 1 to 4	87 ⎭	
TOTAL: Teachers and Administrators	70%	71%

SOURCES: *Zhenshchiny i deti v SSSR* (M, 1963), p. 127; *Zhenshchiny i deti v SSSR* (M, 1969), p. 105; *Vestnik statistiki*, 1976, no. 1, p. 88.

As in other fields, the proportion of women among engineering adminis-trators and specialists declines with each increase in rank and responsibil-ity. For example, in planning and design organizations, where more than half the professional employees are engineers, although the proportion of women among all professionals was 41 percent, the proportion at the top level was much smaller—only some 8 percent in 1956. The probability that a woman would eventually be employed in the highest echelon was only one-eighth the probability that a man would be.[14]

Women in education. Women play a very important role in Soviet educa-tion, where they make up a large majority of the profession. Nonetheless, education illustrates the pattern, still characteristic in the Soviet Union and elsewhere, of a declining proportion of women as one ascends the profes-sional ladder. This is immediately evident when one looks at the proportion of women among teachers in primary and secondary schools and in higher education.

As in the United States, men in the Soviet Union tend to shun teaching at the primary level because of its low pay and low prestige. As a result, the lower teaching ranks are filled with women. But only a surprisingly small proportion of women occupy top-level administrative positions in the schools. Though over 70 percent of all primary and secondary education personnel and over 90 percent of the teachers of grades 1 to 11 were women in 1974–75, women constituted only 31 percent of the directors of eight-year schools and 28 percent of the directors of secondary schools. We can see from Table 10, however, that these figures represent a significant im-provement over the situation in 1960–61.

When we turn to examine the role of women in higher education, we find

[14]Dodge, *Women in the Soviet Economy*, p. 212.

that they play a substantial and increasing one—particularly when compared to the one they play in the United States and other Western countries (see Table 11). The proportion of women with the highest academic rank in the sciences (academicians, corresponding members, and full professors), although small, has roughly doubled since 1950. The percentage of women among associate professors of science has also grown over this period, increasing from 14.7 to 22.1 percent. Moreover, the ratio of the percentage of top-rank women academics to the percentage of women associate professors has increased from .38 to .46 (5.6/14.7 versus 10.2/22.1). Yet despite these improvements, men continue to dominate the upper ranks.

Women's importance in higher education differs substantially from field to field, corresponding closely to the proportion of women that have received advanced degrees in each field (compare Tables 6 and 7). Women faculty predominated in only one field—philology (67.7 percent).[15] In four other fields they made up almost half the academic personnel—medicine (48 percent), biology (47.8 percent), chemistry (45.3 percent), and pedagogy (40 percent). The smallest proportions of women faculty were in technology (10.5 percent), law (12.7 percent), economics (16.3 percent), and the combined field of physics and mathematics (21.1 percent).

Women in research. Women play an important role in scientific research at research institutes, institutions of higher learning, and elsewhere in the economy. Again one finds a decreasing proportion of women as one ascends the career ladder. However, there has been improvement in recent years. Between 1950 and 1973 the proportion of female research workers holding doctorates (including those in higher education) increased from 7.2 to 13.4 percent (see Table 11). Improvement can also be seen by the increase in the ratio of the percentage of women doctors of science to the percentage of women candidates of science between 1950 and 1973—from .29 to .49 (7.2/25.0 versus 13.4/27.6)—reflecting the substantially larger proportion of women who now continue on to complete the doctorate.

Despite such improvements in the qualifications of female scientific workers, males continue to dominate the upper ranks of all the scientific disciplines, just as they dominate the top leadership and administrative posts in most other branches of the economy. No women at all are to be found in the upper reaches of the USSR Academy of Sciences, and very few are to be found among the full and corresponding members of the all-union, republic, and specialized academies. Furthermore, few women are employed in the top administrative positions of the hundreds of academy research institutes.

The share of women among all specialists working in research institutes was an impressive 52 percent in 1956. (Two categories of institutes are involved here: institutes under the auspices of the Soviet academies of

---

[15] A. Ia. Sinetskii, *Professorsko-prepodavatel'skie kadry vysshei shkoly SSSR* (M, 1950), pp. 138–39. Although the present average is higher, the distribution appears to be similar.

TABLE 11

Number and Percent of Women Research Workers in Research Establishments, in Higher Educational Institutions, and in Other Areas of the Economy, by Degree and Rank, 1950–74

Degree or rank	1950		1960		1965		1970		1974	
	Number	Percent	Number	Percent	Number	Percent	Number	Percent	Number	Percent
Number having higher degrees:										
Doctor of science	600	7.2%	1,100	10.1%	1,400	9.5%	3,100	13.1%	4,400	13.9%
Candidate of science	11,400	25.0	28,800	30.7	34,800	29.9	60,700	27.0	83,700	27.0
Number having scholarly rank:										
Academician, corresponding member, professor	500	5.6	700	7.1	1,100	8.8	1,800	9.9	2,300	10.2
Associate professor	3,200	14.7	6,200	17.1	9,500	19.6	14,400	24.5	18,800	22.3
Senior research worker	3,500	30.7	5,800	28.6	8,300	28.9	9,800	21.3	12,100	23.7
Junior research worker and assistant	9,400	48.0	13,600	50.9	25,000	51.1	24,300	49.8	23,900	49.4
TOTAL	59,000	36.3%	128,700	36.3%	254,800	38.8%	359,900	38.8%	464,600	39.7%

SOURCE: Narodnoe khoziaistvo SSSR v 1972 g. (M. 1973), p. 129; and Narodnoe khoziaistvo SSSR v 1974 g. (M. 1975), pp. 143–44.

science, conducting both theoretical and applied research; and institutes sponsored by state committees or ministries, dealing mainly with technological design research and the testing of products and processing.) The share of women at the lower level—among laboratory technicians and technicians without administrative responsibilities—was substantially higher (78 and 64 percent, respectively), as might be expected, whereas their share among scientific research personnel was a smaller 50 percent. The percentage of research engineers who are women was lower (40 percent), but was still well above the average for all engineers employed in the economy (29 percent), indicating women's greater preference for the kind of engineering done in research institutes over that done in industrial enterprises and construction. In the top echelons of research institutes the percentage of women shrinks, although not so drastically as in a number of other professional activities.

Other indicators reveal something of women's capacity for research or research productivity. Few female scientific workers have won prizes such as the Lenin prize; those who have were usually members of a team headed by a man. Women do better as contributors of papers and articles to scholarly journals, but their contributions are approximately half what would be expected given their proportion among professionals in the various fields. We must conclude, therefore, that the scholarly achievement and productivity of women are lower than those of men, for reasons to be examined later.[16] This lower professional capacity is, of course, of great practical significance and concern for those responsible for the effective development and utilization of manpower resources.

Women in medicine. Although there was a tradition of women studying and working in medicine under the tsars, the major gains for women in the medical profession have come under the Soviet regime.[17] Women physicians increased from 10 percent of the total in 1913 to 77 percent in 1950—a proportion unequaled anywhere else in the world. Among the qualified middle-level medical personnel, the overwhelming majority are women—all but a few of the nurses and more than 85 percent of the *fel'dshers*. Women also outnumber men in pharmacology.

The proportion of women physicians has been declining since 1950, and now stands at 70 percent. A further decline is likely because female enrollment in medical institutes has now stabilized at approximately 54 percent of total enrollment. There are a number of reasons for this decline. Medicine has become more attractive to men. In recent years it has become more technologically and scientifically oriented, and the pay of physicians has improved relative to other professions. In addition, the government has sought to increase the proportion of men among physicians for at least two reasons: first, there are assignment problems with women (e.g., men are

---

[16] Dodge, *Women in the Soviet Economy*, chap. 12, discusses the achievements of women in science and technology and gives the publication record of women in a broad range of fields.
[17] *Ibid.*, chaps. 7 and 11.

needed as military physicians and in remote, hardship posts); and second, men carry a greater work load than women. Male physicians reportedly work an average of 270 days per year, whereas women physicians work 155, or 42 percent fewer.[18]

A recent study in the RSFSR, where more than 50 percent of all Soviet physicians work, indicates that the most popular specialty among women is internal medicine—30 percent of all women physicians listed it as their specialty. Also popular is pediatrics, where 18 percent of the RSFSR's women physicians are employed. Obstetrics, with 9 percent, and stomatology, with 6 percent, come next, followed by surgery, with almost 6 percent. (The figure for women surgeons is only slightly higher than the U.S. figure of 5.1 percent.) The percentage of women in the other dozen specialties trails off gradually. The ratio of women to men within these specialties differs greatly, however. The 18 percent of women specializing in pediatrics account for 93.3 percent of all pediatricians in the RSFSR. Pediatrics is, therefore, almost exclusively a specialty of women. The lowest proportion of women is in neurosurgery (24.9 percent), a proportion which is not negligible but indicative of men's dominance in surgery.

The proportion of women among medical administrators is smaller than their share among medical specialists. Among the heads of divisions in medical establishments and the heads of offices and laboratory chiefs, the share of women was a substantial 73 percent; but among heads of medical establishments, deputy chiefs, and head physicians it was 57 percent.

In 1974, 51 percent of the research workers and teaching staff at medical institutes were women. Of this number, there were 20 academicians and corresponding members of the Academy of Medical Sciences (10 percent of the total membership); 42 directors of research institutes; 1,028 full professors (26 percent of all full professors); 1,946 with doctorates in medical science (31 percent of the total); 12,714 associate professors (40 percent of the total); and 18,382 with candidate degrees in medical science (50 percent of the total). These are percentages above those of other professions but well below the proportionate share of women in the medical professions as a whole.[19]

Even in the favorable circumstances of the Soviet Union a woman physician faces more obstacles than does a man in the climb up the career ladder. A woman often is not able to concentrate as fully on her career as a man. Some of the obstacles are of a woman's own choosing or, more accurately, are forced upon her by the many demands of a husband, children, household chores, and so on. Mark Field points out resemblances between

[18] Cited by George Rosch, "Situation, évolution et perspectives effectoire de médecins en France et dans les pays d'Europe et aux Etats Unis," *Association Médicale Mondiale* (Mar. 24, 1969), p. 9, n. 7.
[19] M. D. Piradova, "The Role of Women in the Public Health Care System in the USSR," paper presented at the International Conference on Women in Health, Washington, D.C., June 16–18, 1975 (mimeo.), p. 13.

the situations of Soviet women physicians and American elementary-school teachers: both have important functions but receive relatively low salaries, little prestige, and few prerogatives; and the women in these occupations view them not so much as "careers" as ways of earning a living.[20]

Yet despite Field's comparison, we should note that hundreds of women hold leading posts in the ministries of health of the USSR and of the individual republics. For many years Mariia Kovrigina was Minister of Health of the USSR; twelve women are currently vice-ministers in the health ministries of the USSR and union republics; three women are ministers of health in autonomous republics; and 48 women head departments at health ministries. Moreover, women head regional, city, and district health-care departments; they administer large hospitals, epidemiological stations, dispensaries, ambulance stations, health resorts, and medical units at industrial enterprises.[21] It is clear, then, that for a capable woman with sufficient drive and commitment all doors have been opened.

WOMEN'S DOUBLE BURDEN AND PROFESSIONAL PRODUCTIVITY

The diminishing proportions of women we have noted in the higher ranks of professional occupations reflect primarily the negative impact on women's productivity of their home responsibilities. Beyond noting women's special responsibilities as wives and mothers, we must also include the negative effects of both career interruptions owing to childbirth and special job assignment problems. The problem of continued Soviet male chauvinism should not be overlooked either.

The extent of Soviet women's double burden is shown by the substantial number of extra hours women spend each week on housework, child care, food purchases, and self-care in comparison with men. To redistribute this burden more equally between men and women, radically different attitudes about household responsibilities must be developed in Soviet men, and more and better child-care facilities, labor-saving household aids, and shopping arrangements must be provided.

Some of the adverse factors inhibiting the effectiveness of professional women will not be eradicated or even substantially reduced in the near future. Nonetheless, great progress has been made in altering the image of women's role in Soviet society. The intellectual, career-oriented young woman with high aspirations finds much more support and social approbation today than her counterpart did a few decades ago. Over the years the professional productivity of women undoubtedly will increase, and a higher proportion of women should appear in the upper echelons of the professions. In the meantime, men will continue to fill most of these higher, more demanding posts.

[20] Mark G. Field, *Doctor and Patient in Soviet Russia* (Cambridge, Mass., 1957), p. 193.
[21] Piradova, p. 15.

Although the Soviet regime continues to cherish the revolutionary goal of equality of the sexes, the projected date for the full achievement of this goal (like that for so many others) seems to have receded. Although the Soviet leadership claims to be pursuing the goal of equality, it does so only up to a point—the point at which the drive for equality comes into conflict with higher-priority goals for achieving economic growth and military strength. Until women achieve real influence in the political sphere, or until change comes from other causes, there seems little doubt that the growth-oriented goals of the regime will prevail over altruistic concerns for attaining revolutionary ideals and improving the status of women.

These comments should not detract from the fact that the numbers and proportions of Soviet women in interesting and challenging semiprofessional and professional occupations exceed by far the numbers and proportions of women in such occupations in any nonsocialist society. The Soviet regime has opened many new doors to women. Women's options have greatly increased, and women have responded impressively to the new opportunities to enter the major professions. Although early progress was particularly rapid, the role of women in the professions continued to grow. Further improvements will occur as women's double burden is gradually reduced and as male attitudes are transformed for the better.

Janet G. Chapman

Equal Pay for Equal Work?

THE PRINCIPLES of equal pay for equal work and of equal rights for women and men in all spheres of life are embodied in the Soviet Constitution (Articles 118 and 122). Yet in the USSR, as in other countries, women earn on average less than men. Soviet economists and sociologists acknowledge this, though separate statistics on men's and women's earnings are not published (or even collected, so far as I know). Some evidence about the extent of male-female differentiation in earnings is provided by summary data on the regular Soviet family budget studies, and some can be found in occasional surveys. For example, recent studies of the family budgets of Soviet wage earners and salaried workers indicate that, as a rule, the earnings of the second earner—usually the wife—are about two-thirds the earnings of the first earner—usually the husband.[1] A Leningrad survey of the mid-1960's showed women's earnings to be 69.3 percent of men's,[2] and a survey of one industrial area in the late 1960's showed women's earnings to be about 64 percent of men's.[3] A 1970 survey of workers under 30 in the machinery industry in Leningrad showed women's earnings to be lower

[1] I. E. Kunel'skii, *Sotsial'no-ekonomicheskie problemy zarabotnoi platy* (M, 1972), pp. 63–64. A 1966 survey of women workers in a confectionery factory in Moscow, in a watch factory in Penza, and in housing administration in Leningrad showed very few families where the wife's earnings exceeded the husband's; in most cases the wife's earnings were equal to the husband's or lower by 20 to 25 rubles. Average per capita monthly income of those surveyed was 60 rubles in Moscow, 70 rubles in Penza, and 50–80 rubles in Leningrad. G. V. Osipov and Jan Szczepański, eds., *Sotsial'nye problemy truda i proizvodstva* (M, 1969), pp. 427, 431.

[2] E. Z. Danilova, *Sotsial'nye problemy truda zhenshchiny-rabotnitsy* (M, 1968), p. 23.

[3] L. A. Gordon and E. V. Klopov, "Some Problems of the Social Structure of the Soviet Working Class," in Murray Yanowitch and Wesley A. Fisher, eds., *Social Stratification and Mobility in the USSR* (White Plains, N.Y., 1973), p. 41.

than men's by an unspecified amount.[4] These scattered data confirm that an earnings differential exists in the USSR. However, it is probably narrower there than it is in the United States. As the statistics of the U.S. Census Bureau show, in 1973, among U.S. families where both husbands and wives had earnings, the wife's earnings were 37 percent of the husband's in white families and 52 percent of the husband's in black families. In the same year, the average earnings of women working full-time all year were 55 percent of those of men.[5]

There are a number of factors that might account for the lower earnings of Soviet women vis-à-vis men. Male-female differences in rates of pay, in occupational structure, in level of education and skill, in experience, in productivity, and in hours worked are the principal ones. The purpose of this paper, however, is not to account for differences in average earnings in the USSR but to determine whether men and women are paid the same for identical or equivalent work. There are two main issues here. First, are rates of pay the same for women and men performing identical or equivalent work? Second, do women have equal access to jobs for which they are qualified?

Insofar as the first question is concerned, there is no evidence—and little reason to believe—that different rates of pay exist for men and women in the same occupation. The Soviet citizens with whom I discussed this issue (including professional women) appeared to be convinced that there is no discrimination in pay rates within the same job and occupational or skill rank. In the case of piecework, for instance, earnings may differ but the basic rates and rules concerning extra pay for extra output are the same for both sexes.

However, as the paper in this volume by Norton Dodge demonstrates, there exists a substantial male-female imbalance in the vertical structure of many, if not most, Soviet occupations. Despite the fact that Soviet women are found in large numbers in occupations generally considered "male" ones in the United States, they are concentrated in the lower levels of those occupations. But it is the implications of imbalance in the horizontal plane, not in the vertical one, that I want to explore in this paper, for certain branches of industry and sectors of the economy are dominated by women workers, just as certain others are dominated by men. In general, the branches of industry and the sectors of the economy where women workers predominate are the ones where earnings are lower.[6] In view of this tendency for men and women to be concentrated in different occupations, the

---

[4] E. K. Vasil'eva, *Sotsial'no-professional'nyi uroven' gorodskoi molodezhi* (L, 1973), p. 115.

[5] U.S. Bureau of the Census, *Current Population Reports*, Series P-60, No. 97, "Money Incomes in 1973 of Families and Persons in the United States" (Washington, D.C., 1975), pp. 133–34, 161.

[6] Taking 1966 average earnings by branch of industry and sector of the economy and by broad skill groups, and weighting the earnings by the proportions of men and women in each category, William Moskoff found that women's earnings averaged 87.7 percent of men's. This

important question is whether rates of pay for men and women differ across industries or sectors of the economy when men and women perform the same or "equivalent" work. The justification for this emphasis is twofold: there are hard data on rates of pay, and the pay structure is centrally determined and reflects official policy.

We will make two sets of comparisons between rates of pay in predominantly male and predominantly female occupations and sectors. First, we will examine the basic wage rates for manual workers in industry, comparing the rates in industries where women predominate with those in industries where men predominate. Second, we will take the starting salary rates for a few of the major semiprofessional and professional occupations dominated by men and compare them with those for similar occupations dominated by women.

INDUSTRIAL WAGE RATES

Women predominate in the food industry and in the so-called light industries—the textile, garment, shoe, and leather industries. Of the total wage earners employed in the food industry, 55 percent are women; but if we exclude the predominantly male (and high-paying) fishing industry, the proportion of women is higher still—70 to 72 percent in bread-baking and confectionery, for example. In the light industries, women account for 64 to 84 percent of the wage earners. And though women make up about 40 percent of the wage earners in the large machinery industry, men predominate in the coal and other extraction industries, in the metallurgical and chemical industries, and in other heavy industries.[7]

It is in the food and light industries—precisely where women predominate—that the basic wage rates are lowest. This may be seen by comparing the grade 1 basic wage rates in the different industries in Table 1. Since the wage reform of 1956–60, the starting rates in the food and light industries have been at or near the minimum wage, whereas the starting rates in the predominately male industries have been above it.

In principle, every job grade requires the same level of education and skill in every industry. In practice, however, there are many difficulties in comparing and grading jobs in different industries as requiring "equivalent" qualifications and "equivalent work." Nonetheless, Soviet economists and others concerned with wage rates have devoted much effort toward achieving the goal of complete standardization of job classifications, and it is my impression that though they fall short (by their own admission), they make a sincere effort to evaluate different jobs as objectively and rationally as

---

still underestimates the male-female earnings gap since available data are inadequate to take into account the relative preponderance of men in the higher-skilled and higher-level-administrative jobs. William Moskoff, "An Estimate of the Soviet Male-Female Income Gap," *The ACES Bulletin*, 16, no. 2 (Fall 1974), pp. 21–31.

[7] These are 1967 figures from USSR, Tsentral'noe Statisticheskoe Upravlenie, *Trud v SSSR* (M, 1968), p. 120.

TABLE 1

Basic Wage Scales, Selected Soviet Industries, 1960

(*Rubles per month*)

Industry and no. of grades	Grade 1 wage rate	Multiplier for top rate
Food and light industries (all with 6 grades)		
Grain and milk processing, rural	40	1.80
Food (main branches)	45	1.80
Garments	48–51	1.80
Textiles	51–54	1.80
Shoes, leather goods	48–52	1.80
Heavy industries		
Oil refining (6 grades)	52	2.00
Machinery (6 grades)	53–56	2.00
Chemicals (7 grades)	46	2.30
Cement (7 grades)	53	2.40
Nonferrous metallurgy (7 grades)	58	2.60
Ferrous metallurgy (10 grades)	51	3.20
Underground extraction		
Coal (8 grades)	61	3.75
Iron ore (8 grades)	55	3.20
Nonferrous ores (7 grades)	62	2.86
Gas and oil (6 grades)	66	2.42

SOURCE: Janet G. Chapman, *Wage Variation in Soviet Industry: The Impact of the 1956–60 Wage Reform* (Santa Monica, Calif., 1970), p. 26 and Appendix B.

NOTE: The grade 1 rate is for work under normal conditions; where industries have different rates for piecework and timework, I have given the rate for pieceworkers (the rate for timeworkers is somewhat lower). Rates for work in hot and dangerous conditions are higher than those shown. The minimum wage was 40 rubles per month in 1960.

possible.[8] (I refer to the job descriptions; it is possible that there are errors and/or cases of discrimination in assigning individual workers to job grades.) Note, however, that even if we assume perfect equivalency among jobs of the same grade in different industries, the range of basic rates (reflecting skill differentials) is narrower in the food and light industries than in the heavy industries with the same number of grades (see Table 1). Thus in 1960, the top basic monthly rate (grade 6) in rural milk and grain processing was 72 rubles (1.8×40 rubles), whereas in oil refining and the machinery industry it was 104 to 112 rubles (2.0×52 rubles to 2.0×56 rubles). Top rates in industries with more than six grades were even higher (the highest was 230 rubles in underground coal mining), but these reflected the additional skills needed beyond the grade 6 level as well as the larger percentage increases between grades.

Furthermore, various supplements to the basic wage rates have generally favored the heavy industries. Maximum bonuses established in the 1956–

[8] See Leonard Kirsch, *Soviet Wages: Changes in Structure and Administration Since 1956* (Cambridge, Mass., 1972), chaps. 4 and 5.

6o reform were 30 percent of the wage in light industry and 40 percent in heavy industry. The supplements to basic wage rates for working conditions have generally been smaller in the food and light industries than in other industries, and regional increments to the basic wage have been more generous in heavy than in light industries for many years.[9] Some of these discriminatory aspects of wage formation have been modified: with the revised management and incentive system, limits on bonuses for wage earners have been abolished; and the Far North and Siberian regional supplements have been extended to all industries.[10] The 1971–75 reform envisaged a substantial increase in the percentage increment for arduous working conditions in the light industries. A premium for night-shift work of 50 percent of the basic rate has been established for the bread-baking and textile industries in view of the three-shift regime prevailing in them and in view of the large proportion of women they employ. The night-shift premium in other industries is 20 percent.[11]

PROFESSIONAL AND SEMIPROFESSIONAL SALARY RATES

To compare relative pay levels in the primarily female and primarily male semiprofessional and professional occupations, we focus on starting salary rates for selected occupations requiring specialized secondary or higher education. Here I take length of education as a proxy for "equivalency" in work; this is adequate for starting rates, though it is less precise than the job classifications for manual industrial occupations.

For occupations requiring higher education, we will compare starting salary rates for the predominantly female occupations of teacher (with higher education), physician, and pharmacist with the starting salary rates for engineers. Engineering is primarily a male occupation, though by 1970 some 40 percent of engineers were women. It might be noted that the engineer salary rates apply also to economists, and that the majority of economists (82 percent in 1970) are women.[12] For occupations requiring a specialized secondary education, we will compare the starting salary rates for the predominantly female occupations of teacher (with specialized secondary education), dentist, *fel'dsher* (assistant physician), and nurse with the starting rates for technicians. Our last comparison will be between the technician's salary and that of the accountant (*bukhgalter*). The accountant is representative of a number of clerical occupations requiring specialized secondary education. Accountants' salaries are in the next to highest of the five groups into which clerical workers are classified. Clerical

---

[9] Janet G. Chapman, *Wage Variation in Soviet Industry: The Impact of the 1956–60 Wage Reform* (Santa Monica, Calif., 1970), pp. 36–40.

[10] Janet G. Chapman, "Labor Mobility and Labor Allocation in the USSR," in Association for Comparative Economics, *Proceedings of Annual Meetings, Labor Mobility* (mimeo., July 1971), p. 13.

[11] A. P. Volkov, ed,, *Trud i zarabotnaia plata v SSSR* (M, 1974), p. 399.

[12] See Table 3 in Norton Dodge's paper in this volume, p. 208.

TABLE 2

Starting Salary Rates for Engineers, Technicians,
and Accountants, Selected Years, 1956–72

(*Rubles per month*)

Year rates established	Branch	Engineers	Technicians	Accountants
1956–60	Heavy industries (most)	90–100	70–75	65–70
	Food and light industries	80	70	60
	Construction	100	85	70
1964–65	Trade	80	70	55–60
	Higher education	90	–	–
1969–71	Construction materials	110	90	*a*
	Food and light industries	80	70	65.7
	Construction	123	104	–
	Trade	80	70	62.5
	Railroad transport	120	105	–
Planned 1972–75	Machinery industry	115	86–92	*b*
	Heavy industries (other)	112–25	90	*b*
	Food and light industries	96–100	84–88	*b*

SOURCES: V. V. Kazakin and M. V. Dremin, *Novye usloviia oplaty truda v stroitel'stve* (M, 1961), pp. 24–25; S. J. Cerniglia, *Wages in the USSR, 1950–1966: Construction* (Washington, D.C., 1967), p. 19; A. Dolgopolova and A. Shakhmagon, *Oplata truda na predpriiatiiakh pishchevoi i rybnoi promyshlennosti* (M, 1963), pp. 149, 192; L. Kostin, *Wages in the USSR* (M, 1960), pp. 60–61, 83; A. G. Aganbegian and V. F. Maier, *Zarabotnaia plata v SSSR* (M, 1959), pp. 142, 145; George Hoffberg, *Wages in the USSR, 1950–1967: Education* (Washington, D.C., 1969), p. 40; S. Rapawy, *Wages in the USSR, 1950–1958: Trade* (Washington, D.C., 1970), pp. 30, 32, 36; *CDSP*, 21, no. 1, p. 28; *Sotsialisticheskii trud*, 1968, no. 1, p. 86, and 1973, no. 10, pp. 36–37; L. E. Kunel'skii, *Sotsial'no-ekonomischeskie problemy zarabotnoi platy* (M, 1972), pp. 67, 192; A. P. Volkov, ed., *Trud i zarabotnaia plata v SSSR* (M, 1974), p. 398.

a The minimum office worker salary in this branch was 75 rubles, so the accountant salary must have been considerably above that (see Kunel'skii, p. 67).

b Presumably well above 70 rubles, the new minimum wage.

workers at all levels are predominantly women. The starting salary rates for the occupations mentioned above are shown in Tables 2, 3, and 4.

Starting rates seem reasonably appropriate for determining whether there are sex biases in semiprofessional and professional rates of pay. It is difficult, in any case, to make comparisons of higher rates, particularly since the paths up the salary scale differ. Teachers' and doctors' salaries rise by steps with the length of employment. For teachers with higher education, for instance, the current basic salary ranges from 100 rubles for those employed less than five years to 145 rubles for those with over 25 years' service.[13] There are also, of course, various administrative positions with higher salary rates. In contrast, a range of rates is set for ordinary engineers, and advances within this range are based on the director's evaluation of performance and qualifications. The range for engineers in ferrous metallurgy established in 1956–60 was 90 to 120 rubles in large enterprises and 90 to 110 rubles in smaller enterprises.[14] Beyond this range there are

[13]*Trud*, Sept. 7, 1972; translated in *CDSP*, 25, no. 2, p. 16.

[14]Leonid Kostin, *Wages in the USSR* (M, 1960), pp. 60–61.

TABLE 3

Starting Salary Rates for Urban Teachers in
General-Education Schools, 1946–72

(Rubles per month)

Years	Teachers with higher education	Teachers with specialized secondary education	Teachers with general secondary education
1946–48	53–61.5	50–57.5	45–50
1948–64	57–71	57.5–66	52–57.5
1964–72	80	67–72[a]	60[a]
Sept. 1972	100	85	–

SOURCES: For 1946–48, Murray Yanowitch, "Changes in the Soviet Money Wage Level since 1940," *American Slavic and East European Review*, 14, no. 2 (April 1955), 201; for 1964, *Pravda* and *Izvestiia*, July 14, 1964 (*CDSP*, 16, no. 9, pp. 14–15), and George Hoffberg, *Wages in the USSR, 1950–1967: Education*, p. 35; for 1972, *Trud*, Sept. 7, 1972 (*CDSP*, 25, no. 2, p. 16).

[a] These rates were probably increased somewhat in 1968.

various higher-level positions, such as senior engineer, special engineer, and chief engineer. Many enterprise directors started as engineers.

For engineers, technicians, and accountants, starting salary rates differ according to the industry and the branch of the economy, with rates higher in heavy industry than in the food and light industries and the service branches (Table 2). Teachers' starting salary rates (Table 3) differed until 1964 according to the grade taught, with the highest salaries going to teachers of grades 8 to 10 and the lowest going to teachers of grades 1 to 4. Also, until 1964 teachers' salaries were lower in rural areas than in urban ones.

We turn first to the comparison of salaries for occupations requiring a higher education. A course of higher education runs for four to five years following the ten-year general education; for physicians, though, the course is six years plus a one-year internship.[15] Comparing the salaries for teachers with higher education with those for engineers (Tables 2 and 3), it is clear that teachers' salaries have been well below those of engineers for many years. In late 1964, the monthly starting rate for teachers with higher education was raised to the starting rate set in the late 1950's for engineers in the food and light industries (80 rubles). In September 1972, the teachers' starting rate was raised to approximately the level that was to be established for engineers in the food and light industries during the 1972–75 period. The comparison between starting salaries of physicians and engineers (Tables 2 and 4) gives a similar picture. However, physicians did receive an increase in salary shortly before the wage reform in industry of 1956–60, whereas the rates set for teachers in 1948 remained in effect until 1964. Pharmacists' salaries appear to move along with physicians' salaries, but at a consistently lower level; presumably the occupation of pharmacist

[15] *USSR Education* (M, 1973), p. 81.

TABLE 4

Starting Salary Rates for Semiprofessional and Professional
Medical Personnel, Selected Years, 1942–72

(Rubles per month)

| | With higher education | | | | With specialized secondary education | |
Years	Urban physicians	Rural physicians	Pharmacists	Dentists	Urban fel'dshers	Urban nurses
1942–52	50	55	–	–	–	–
1952–55	60	64	–	–	–	32.5
1955–64	72.5	75	65	55	50	45
Nov. 1964	90	100–105	80	72	65	70
Sept. 1972	100–110	110–38	–	–	–	–

SOURCES: Mark Field, Doctor and Patient in Soviet Russia (Cambridge, Mass., 1957), pp. 90, 104; V. A. Shavrin, Gosudarstvennyi biudzhet SSSR (M, 1951), pp. 84–85; N. DeWitt, Education and Professional Employment in the USSR (Washington, D.C., 1961), p. 812; Mark Field, Soviet Socialized Medicine (New York, 1967), pp. 129–30; Pravda and Izvestiia, July 14, 1964 (CDSP, 16, no. 9, pp. 14–15); Sotsialisticheskii trud, 1964, no. 8, pp. 19–22, and 1965, no. 1, pp. 7–12; A. P. Volkov, ed., Trud i zarabotnaia plata v SSSR (M, 1974); Pravda, Aug. 19 and 22, 1972 (CDSP, 24, no. 34, p. 8).

is considered less responsible than that of physician. Both are predominantly women's occupations.

To turn now to semiprofessional occupations, Dodge reports that since the mid-1950's women have been over 60 percent of all those employed who have a specialized secondary education. The occupation of technician represents the bottom of the salaried group of engineering and technical workers. It is taken here as the typical male semiprofessional occupation. This was true only in the past, however, for during the 1960's women came to constitute almost 60 percent of technicians.[16] Most of the accountants and others in the office jobs in the same salary class requiring a specialized secondary education are women. These include goods managers (tovaroved), translators, managers of warehouses, and chiefs of archives. Women are about 84 percent of those in education and culture with a specialized secondary education and 93 percent of the medical personnel with specialized secondary education.[17]

It is clear from Table 2 that accountants are paid less than technicians. Also, salaries of teachers and medical personnel with specialized secondary education (Tables 3 and 4) were well below technicians' salaries. In late 1964, the starting salary rates for teachers with specialized secondary education and for dentists and nurses were brought up to the starting rate established for technicians in the food and light industries during the

[16] The census data presented in Dodge's paper indicate that women were 45 percent of technicians in 1959 and 59 percent of technicians in 1970 (see his Table 5). The proportion of women among employed persons who were educated as technicians remained close to 38 percent from 1957 through 1966. Trud v SSSR, pp. 286, 294.

[17] These are 1966 figures from Trud v SSSR, p. 294.

1956–60 wage reform. In September 1972, salaries of teachers with specialized secondary education were raised to the level planned to be introduced for technicians in the food and light industries during 1972–75. Salaries of middle medical personnel were increased somewhat in 1968 in connection with the establishment of the 60-ruble minimum monthly wage and were scheduled for a further increase in late 1975.

Various features of the payment system beyond the basic salary rates should be mentioned here. For engineers and technicians, bonuses are an integral part of the pay system and may amount to a substantial addition to the base salary. Clerical personnel are not generally entitled to bonuses. Teachers are routinely paid a supplement for correcting written work (5 to 10 rubles a month under the 1964 legislation), and this should probably be considered part of the base pay. There are various additional duties, such as acting as head of a study room or laboratory, or taking on various administrative tasks in the smaller schools, for which teachers are paid extra. Teachers with a higher degree (candidate or doctor of sciences) and those with the title "honored teacher" receive an extra 10 rubles a month. Medical personnel with a higher degree receive monthly supplements of 10 to 20 rubles. Physicians and pharmacists may receive an additional 10 to 30 rubles monthly, and middle medical personnel an additional 8 rubles monthly, if they are certified as especially qualified. Teachers and doctors may also supplement their incomes by taking on additional jobs; for instance, physicians often do private consulting, which has been made feasible by the adoption of a shorter standard workweek. As a general rule, the bonus provisions for engineers undoubtedly mean a larger supplement to their basic salary than most teachers can earn; but doctors' earnings, including income from private practice, are often very high.

Provisions are made for increments in pay for dangerous conditions and for night work, primarily in industry and in the medical profession. Regional coefficients for remote regions and for regions with difficult living conditions are applicable to all the occupations we are discussing, though before 1964 they were less widely and less generously applied to the teaching and medical professions than to heavy industry. Rural teachers and physicians, and some rural *fel'dshers*, midwives, and nurses, are entitled to a free apartment and utilities,[18] a very valuable fringe benefit given Soviet rural housing conditions.

The workweek for teachers and physicians is shorter—nominally, at least—than that for engineers, technicians, and clerical workers. The standard workweek for teachers is 24 hours in the elementary grades and

---

[18]These various supplements, as provided in the 1964 legislation, are summarized in more detail by George Hoffman in U.S. Bureau of the Census, International Population Reports, Series P-95, no. 64, *Wages in the USSR, 1950–1966: Health Services* (Washington, D.C., 1969), pp. 15–18, 33–34; and International Population Reports, Series P-95, no. 66, *Wages in the USSR, 1950–1967: Education* (Washington, D.C., 1969), pp. 14–18, 29–31.

eighteen hours in the fourth or fifth grades and up. The standard workday for physicians is five and a half hours in out-patient clinics and dispensaries and six and a half hours in regular hospitals; the workday is also six and a half hours for all middle medical personnel.[19] These figures compare with the standard Soviet workweeks of 48 hours (before 1956), 46 hours (1956–65), and 41 hours (since 1965). For hours of classroom teaching above the standard number, teachers are paid proportionately more. It is not clear whether a similar system is in effect for physicians.

The shorter hours are said to be one of the attractions of the fields of medicine and education for women.[20] If the work is actually completed within the specified shorter workweek, there would be some grounds for paying lower salaries to teachers and doctors than to engineers on the full workweek. Sociological surveys indicate that the teacher's real workweek, including home preparation, is considerably longer than the statutory eighteen to 24 hours.[21] Nevertheless, there is an advantage in being able to leave the school or hospital early in order to pick up children, buy groceries, and prepare dinner for the family.

THE QUESTION OF "EQUAL" WORK

As Dodge points out, though Soviet women now fill over half of all semi-professional and professional jobs, their proportion falls as the level of responsibility and salary rises. It appears to be the case, too, that women industrial wage earners are predominantly in the lower grades. In a majority of 50 enterprises in different industries and areas surveyed in 1965, there were no women in the top grades (5 and 6). A Leningrad survey in the 1960's indicated that there were twice as many women as men among the unskilled workers and half as many women as men among the skilled workers. Also, women are more likely to be in manual jobs (for which the pay is often lower) than in mechanized ones.[22] Thus there are clearly vertical and horizontal sex imbalances in the Soviet work structure.

To some extent this sex differentiation reflects women's work preferences. There is considerable evidence from sociological studies of how secondary-school students rate various occupations that sex differences exist in occupational preferences.[23] Other papers in this volume touch on the reasons for these preferences, but we should simply note here that there seem to be no limits to access to education that would hinder a woman from

[19] V. A. Shavrin, *Gosudarstvennyi biudzhet SSSR* (M, 1951), pp. 57, 85.

[20] Marjorie Galenson, *Women at Work: An International Comparison* (Ithaca, N.Y., 1973), p. 88.

[21] A May 1967 study showed the average teacher's week was 50.4 to 57.4 hours in Novosibirsk and 51 hours in Sverdlovsk. L. S. Bliakhman and O. I. Shkaratan, *NTR, rabochii klass, intelligentsiia* (M, 1973), p. 300. Unfortunately, it is not clear whether this includes paid-for classroom hours in addition to the standard teacher's week.

[22] V. B. Mikhailiuk, *Izpol'zovanie zhenskogo truda v narodnom khoziaistve* (M, 1970), pp. 72–74; Danilova, pp. 19–24.

[23] See, e.g., the articles by V. V. Vodzinskaia and L. F. Liss in Yanowitch and Fisher.

training for the occupation of her preference. The level of education now attained is approximately equal among young men and women, although this was less true in the past. Thus many older women must be less qualified than their male cohorts.

Of principal concern here are restrictions on a woman's freedom to take the kind of work she prefers and to advance as fast or as far as men do. Such restrictions, according to Soviet writers both male and female, stem primarily from the nature of the nuclear family and the role of woman as childbearer, child-raiser, and housewife, as well as worker. The married woman feels her first responsibility is to her family and home, and accordingly her career objectives are usually more limited than a man's. She may be less willing to take on demanding work or heavy administrative responsibilities. Moreover, the husband's job usually determines her place of residence, so that she is less mobile than a man. Given also the scarcity of housing, a woman may find it easier to take an inferior job near her home than to find an apartment near a more desirable job. Child-care and housework are considerably more burdensome for Soviet than for American working women, and Soviet men rarely share this burden.[24] Soviet working women grumble about the "second shift." Although child-care facilities are much more extensive in the USSR than in the U.S., the supply apparently still does not meet the demand. The availability and quality of most other services, and especially of household machinery, though improved in recent years, still fall far short of what American women are accustomed to. Shopping is extremely time-consuming because of frequent shortages, the inefficiency of Soviet retailing, and the absence of refrigerators in half of Soviet homes.[25] The married woman thus has much less time and energy than either the unmarried woman or the man to devote to upgrading her skills, participating in other forms of activity, and taking on the additional responsibilities at work or after work that lead to promotions.[26] Even at work she may find her concentration divided between her job and her home and children.[27] Interruptions of work for childbirth and child care also mean that the working mother's experience on the job is often less than the man's. Though a recent Soviet law guarantees that a woman who takes up to a year's leave to care for a newborn child may return to her job, there are often practical difficulties in returning to the same or equivalent work.

[24] Time budget studies, which have been carried out frequently, show that Soviet women spend much time and men little in housework and child care. A personal experience in 1974 suggests that though men are seen in shops, they shop infrequently; in a brief visit to the self-service grocery store in Novosibirsk, I was twice asked by men where to find products only one of which I had in my cart.

[25] USSR, Tsentral'noe Statisticheskoe Upravlenie, *Narodnoe khoziaistvo SSSR v 1973 g.* (M, 1974), p. 631.

[26] The survey of young workers in the Leningrad machinery industry indicated that the women started work with a somewhat higher level of education than the men but that fewer women than men pursued further education while at work. Vasil'eva, pp. 102–3.

[27] Osipov and Szczepański, p. 442.

All of these pressures and restrictions are real. No doubt it is also true that there is some unofficial discrimination and that these problems may be used as rationalizations by employers to give preference to men over women with equal qualifications in hiring and promotion. Soviet scholars, in informal conversation, acknowledge that this may happen. There is, however, no way to quantify the extent of discrimination.

Certain jobs are specifically forbidden to women. These restrictions appear to be legitimately related to the protection of the woman's health, and similar restrictions apply to young people of both sexes. There are, however, complaints that the list of prohibited jobs, initiated in 1932, has not kept up with technological change, so that some well-paid skilled jobs that are no longer dangerous are still closed to women and some new jobs that are dangerous are not yet on the prohibited list.[28] Beyond this, I see no evidence of any official policy—whether to encourage women to enter certain occupations or to restrict them from entering others—that might be said to be intended to create or perpetuate the substantial sex differentiation in the Soviet occupational structure. In fact, as Dodge points out, there have been recent efforts to reduce the preponderance of women in medicine. But generally, there seems to have been no systematic planning of the use of women workers.[29]

In recent years there has been increased concern with the specific problems of women workers, and there have been efforts to improve their opportunities and their working conditions. This concern appears to stem from the increasing shortage of labor, the approach to the limits of women's participation in the labor force, and the lessened financial pressure for wives to work as real wage levels have increased. The special provisions intended to protect women workers, particularly in their role as childbearers and mothers, have always been a feature of Soviet labor policy but have been substantially improved in recent years. Such provisions may create a preference on the part of employers for male employees. I have not seen any complaints on this subject by Soviet women;[30] on the contrary, they appear to take a positive attitude toward such provisions.

CONCLUSIONS

This survey indicates that the rate of pay for men and women in the same job is the same; but in sectors where women predominate, both earnings and basic wage and salary rates are lower than they are in sectors where men predominate. The relative levels of pay in the different sectors appear to reflect the priority the Soviet leaders have placed on heavy industry since

---

[28] Mikhailiuk, pp. 69–71; A. G. Kharchev and S. I. Golod, *Professional'naia rabota zhenshchin i sem'ia* (L, 1971), p. 164.

[29] The only plan that included a balance of female labor for industry was the First Five-Year Plan, according to Mikhailiuk (p. 58).

[30] There have been complaints that employers sometimes refuse to hire young workers assigned them since young workers work a short day for a full day's pay.

the late 1920's, for, according to official statements, the starting wage rates in different industries take into account the relative national importance of the industry. The official policy (though not always practice) on pay of educational and health workers is that salaries of physicians and teachers with higher education should equal those of engineers in light industry, and that salaries of educational and health personnel with specialized secondary education should equal those of technicians in light industry. Some statements also mention the relative importance of sectors and the leading role of the material-production sectors.[31]

The same priorities are reflected also in the timing of wage and salary increases. The wage reform begun in 1956 and further outlined in 1958 in the Seven-Year Plan for 1959–65 provided for the establishment of a minimum wage of 40 rubles per month and for the completion of the reform in all sectors of the economy by the end of 1962. The wage reform and the 40-ruble minimum wage were introduced first in the heavy industries and then in other material-production branches and in scientific work. However, extension of the reform to the service branches was delayed until late 1964 and 1965.[32] This is because when difficulties arise or when plans are overambitious (recall that Khrushchev's Seven-Year Plan had to be abandoned), it is the lower-priority industries or sectors that lose out.

The timing of the current wage reform, as outlined in the Ninth Five-Year Plan for 1971–75, made something of an exception to the general rule in that salaries of doctors and teachers were planned to be among the first raised. This was to be done in September 1972. With a few exceptions, raises for workers in the material-production branches were to begin in 1972 only for those in the Far North, the Far East, Siberia, and the Urals; those in other regions were scheduled for increases in 1973 and 1974. However, other workers in education and health were to wait for their raises until 1975. The doctors' and teachers' raises were implemented on schedule, but there has apparently been some delay in the implementation of the rest of the wage reform.[33]

It has been amply demonstrated in earlier work that differential wages have been the prime tool in the Soviet regime's efforts to attract workers to the occupations, sectors, and regions where they are needed and to change the distribution of the labor force as required by changing priorities and supply conditions in the labor market. Allocative efficiency may be inconsistent with the principle of "equal pay for equal work." It is more consistent

---

[31]A. G. Aganbegian and V. F. Maier, *Zarabotnaia plata v SSSR* (M, 1959), pp. 180–81; V. F. Maier, *Zarabotnaia plata v period perekhoda k kommunizmu* (M, 1968), p. 188; *Sotsialisticheskii trud*, no. 8 (1964), p. 12; *Voprosy ekonomiki*, no. 10 (1964), pp. 5–8; I. N. Popov-Cherkasov, *Zarabotnaia plata rabotnikov sfery obsluzhivaniia* (M, 1967), p. 9; and Volkov, pp. 224, 524.

[32]Chapman, *Wage Variation*, pp. 18–23.

[33]"Ninth Five-Year Plan for 1971–75," *CDSP*, 25, no. 2, p. 10. See also *Pravda*, Dec. 19, 1974; translated in *CDSP*, 26, no. 51, pp. 11, 14.

with the alternative (also officially promulgated) principle of wage determination under socialism as "payment according to contribution." This latter method permits evaluation of the results of work according to the prevailing preferences of the system's leaders rather than simply by quantity and quality.

The priorities of the Soviet leaders, and their heavy reliance on a differential wage system to achieve the desired allocation of labor, have generally been accepted as the explanation for the differential rates of pay between industries and sectors. This has clearly resulted in a dual wage structure—one for the high-priority producer goods industries and one for the consumer goods and services sectors. When we look at the occupational structure of the labor force by sex, we can see that it largely reflects the dual wage structure. Clearly, something of a dual labor market divided along sex lines has developed. Although there are numerous and complex factors behind this development, it is important to ask whether this duality is being perpetuated and institutionalized. We have seen that salaries of engineers and clerical workers are lower in the consumer goods than in the producer goods industries, and that the salaries of doctors and teachers (the leading women's professions) are pegged at rates equivalent to those of engineers in the light industries (where engineers are predominately female). Are we to interpret these facts as reflecting a policy of establishing an appropriate—but separate—wage and salary scale within the female labor market? [34]

If this is the case, it is still not clear that it reflects discrimination along sex lines. For one thing, the policy of favoring the producer goods industries has probably resulted in productivity increases there that were more rapid and greater than those in the consumer goods industries and the service sector; this would provide an economic justification for higher pay in these more productive industries.

Probably more important, though, are demand-supply conditions, mentioned also in Sacks's paper. Given the predominance of women in the consumer goods industries, in clerical work, in education, and in health and other services, it is not hard to understand why wages in these sectors are relatively low. One has first to consider the great increase in the number of women in the total labor force, and to realize that this has meant a considerably faster growth in the female labor force than in the male one. Further, the rate of increase in educational level has been faster for women than for men. [35] If in addition women have tended, for whatever reasons, to take jobs

[34] Or could it be that the recent rise in salaries of teachers and doctors is intended to attract more men to these positions? It is notoriously difficult to get women doctors to stay in rural areas; the dim prospect of finding a suitable husband there is usually given as a prime reason. It was pointed out by a woman teacher that the September 1972 increase in teachers' pay not only would improve the standard of living for teachers but would attract better teachers and also men. And this, she said, would solve one problem of contemporary education—the psychological necessity for men as well as women to participate in the raising and education of children. Bliakhman and Shkaratan, p. 301.

[35] Women made up about one-quarter of the wage earners and salaried workers in 1928 and have been around half the labor force in the 1960's and 1970's. USSR, Tsentral'noe Statis-

in a limited number of sectors, this may have led to "crowding" and a situation of excess supply in those sectors.

The factors inhibiting the rise of women along the skill scale seem to be connected mainly with the working woman's role as mother and housewife. Relative "overcrowding" of some of the primarily female employment sectors may be a further factor. There is some evidence that in the food and light industries there are more workers able to perform the top-grade jobs than there are jobs available, whereas in at least some industries where men predominate there are shortages of workers qualified for top-grade jobs.[36]

A number of current trends may lead toward improved relative earnings and greater opportunities for advancement for Soviet women. As auxiliary work, which is now performed manually and very frequently by women, becomes increasingly mechanized, its arduousness will be lightened and the pay for it will be increased. The recent modification of priorities by the Soviet leadership toward a greater stress on consumer goods and services will increase the demand for workers in these sectors and should lead, and to some extent already has led, to some decrease in differentiation between rates of pay in these and in the predominantly male sectors.[37] As the educational level becomes more equal at all age levels, and as the married woman's burden of child care and housework is lightened by improved services and increased help from her husband, the upward mobility of women will be enhanced.

---

ticheskoe Upravlenie, *Narodnoe khoziaistvo SSSR v 1972 g.* (M, 1973), p. 512. Of all those employed with a specialized secondary education or higher education, 29 percent were women in 1928; the figure for women has been around 59 percent since 1960. *Vestnik statistiki*, no. 1 (1975), p. 88.

[36] Kirsch, p. 108.

[37] See L. A. Kostin, *Organizatsiia oplaty truda* (M, 1973), pp. 14–16; Volkov, p. 266; Iu. Pak in *Sotsialisticheskii trud*, no. 9 (1973), p. 16.

PART THREE

Women, Society, and Politics

Peter H. Juviler

Women and Sex in Soviet Law

S OVIET POLICYMAKERS have been perennially divided over the meaning of their goal of the liberation of women and over the methods of
attaining it. Issues of method have touched above all on intervention
through law to regulate women's public and private lives. As other papers in
this volume indicate, the issues of regulating women's *public* role so as to
reconcile their duties as workers and mothers remain largely unresolved.

On the other hand, the issues of regulating women's *private* lives have
been largely resolved. It is this aspect of women's liberation in Soviet policy
that forms the subject of the present chapter. My purpose is to explore how
far the family law reforms of 1955–68, in conjunction with existing criminal law, have gone to assure women's freedom of choice and equality in
their private roles as sex partners, childbearers, and spouses. I have tried
also to contribute to our understanding of how the Soviet regime uses law to
reshape and regulate society.

My main sources are three bodies of Soviet law: the Fundamental Principles of Law on Marriage and the Family of the USSR and Union Republics
of 1968 (hereafter referred to as Principles of Family Law); the Russian
Republic Code of Marriage and the Family of 1970 (hereafter RFC), which
is a detailed elaboration of the Principles of Family Law; and the Russian
Republic Criminal Code of 1960 (hereafter RCC).[1] The reader should not

[1] Principles of Family Law, "Osnovy zakonodatel'stva Soiuza SSR i soiuznykh respublik o
brake i sem'e," and its enabling act, specifying effective date of Oct. 1, 1968, and retroactive
and nonretroactive provisions of the Principles of Family Law as well as the fact that children
born out of wedlock have the same rights and obligations vis-à-vis their registered parents and
the relatives of these parents as children born in wedlock do, "Ob utverzhdenii Osnov
zakonodatel'stva Soiuza SSSR i soiuznykh respublik o brake i sem'e," both acts published as
the law of June 27, 1968, *Vedomosti Verkhovnogo Soveta SSSR*, 27 (1968), item 241; RFC
appeared as a law of Nov. 1, 1969, *Kodeks o brake i sem'e RSFSR* (M, 1969) and in the same

assume that Russian law is in effect law for the entire Soviet Union. True, the RSFSR is the primus inter pares of the republics, and Russian codes have often served as models for the non-Russian ones. But significant departures from Russian codes do crop up. I have noted such departures in some significant cases. Sometimes the departures reflect a special local need to combat Moslem traditions; sometimes there is no apparent reason for the discrepancies. But systematic speculation about the possible reasons behind them would require a fuller treatment than is possible here.

WOMEN AS SEX PARTNERS

Formal protection of women's right to free choice about when to engage in or refrain from sexual relations was seen as only a passing necessity on the eve of the Bolshevik Revolution. Lenin and other Bolsheviks believed, as Marxists, that the socialist revolution would bring on very quickly a new kind of society free from exploitation, class conflict, and crime. Keeping social order and protecting women would come to be a matter of simple public intervention without elaborate laws and enforcement as capitalism receded into the past. Lenin argued in *State and Revolution*: "We are not Utopians and in no way deny that *individual persons* may commit excesses or that such excesses must be suppressed. But, in the first place, no special machinery, no special apparatus of coercion is needed for this: it will be accomplished by the armed people itself, as simply and readily as any crowd of civilized people in modern society intervenes to stop a fight or to prevent a woman from being molested."[2]

Yet it soon became necessary to employ "a special apparatus of coercion" to preserve public order and protect women from violation. Gradually an elaborate system of courts reappeared to replace the tsarist courts which, though reformed by the Provisional Government during its short rule in 1917, had been initially abolished by the Bolsheviks. Judges in the new Bolshevik courts were admonished at first to apply the criminal laws of the overthrown regimes where they did not contradict decrees of the Workers' and Peasants' Government or the judges' "revolutionary legal consciousness." Guiding Principles of Criminal Law appeared in 1919, and the first detailed criminal code in 1922. That code contained several rules specifically protecting women. Those rules, and their later elaboration in various decrees and in the reforms of 1958–61, are the subject of this section.[3]

---

text, only updated as of 1975 with subsequent enactments and court guiding explanations, *Kodeks o brake i sem'e RSFSR: s prilozheniem postateino-sistematizirovannykh materialov po sostoianiiu na 20 fevralia 1975 goda* (M, 1975); RCC appeared most recently as *Ugolovnyi kodeks RSFSR s izmeneniiami i dopolneniiami na 1 ianvaria 1975 goda* . . . (M, 1975), as revised from the original code passed Oct. 27, 1960, *Vedomosti Verkhovnogo Soveta RSFSR*, 40 (1960), item 591.

[2]V. I. Lenin. "Gosudarstvo i pravo" (Aug.–Sept. 1917), *Polnoe sobranie sochinenii* (M, 1958–65), vol. 33, pp. 89–91.

[3]*Sbornik dokumentov*, hereinafter the abbreviation for *Sbornik dokumentov po istorii ugolovnogo zakonodatel'stva SSSR i RSFSR 1917–1952* (M, 1953); John N. Hazard, *Settling*

Some of these code provisions try to protect women from sexual relations they do not want or that may be injurious to them, or try to preserve women's freedom of choice as sex partners; others are intended to prevent women from engaging in relations the regime deems socially dangerous, that is, to restrict women's freedom of choice as well as to protect it.

During the economic reconstruction of the NEP period, women resumed their steady exodus from full-time housework into jobs outside the home. Many other women, bereft of family owing to past fighting and famine, depended on the largesse of not always scrupulous men whose households they joined. To protect women thus subordinated to men in private or public life, the regime added to the understanding of rape the new crime of taking advantage of a woman's dependent position at home or at work to compel her to have sexual relations—a crime punishable, like rape, by no less than three years' confinement.[4] Current criminal law—as, for example, Article 118 of the RCC—separates this offense from rape and provides for up to three years' confinement. The criminal codes of the Kazakh, Latvian, and Estonian republics offer no such protection, however—an "unfounded omission" according to a Soviet legal expert.[5]

Convictions under RCC Article 118 are relatively few; rapes account for 90 to 95 percent of all sex-crime convictions.[6] In what follows I want to discuss the definition of rape, the rules of evidence in rape cases, and the weight given to the victim's conduct. Article 117 of the RCC replaces Article 169 of the 1922 code. It defines ordinary rape as "sexual intercourse by use of force or threats or by taking advantage of the helpless state of the victim."[7] The sentence for rape of this sort is three to seven years' imprisonment. But there are two more serious classifications listed in Article 117: aggravated rape, "rape accompanied by threat of murder or by serious injury, or committed by a person with a record of a previous rape conviction," for which the penalty is five to ten years; and especially aggravated rape, which was made a capital offense (along with many other crimes) by the edict of February 15, 1962. That edict added the italicized phrases to this definition: "rape *accomplished by a group of persons or* by an especially

---

Disputes in Soviet Society: The Formative Years of Soviet Legal Institutions (New York, 1960); Peter H. Juviler, *Revolutionary Law and Order: Politics and Social Change in the USSR* (New York, 1976), chap. 4; John Gorgone, "Soviet Jurists in the Legislative Arena: The Reform of Criminal Procedure, 1956–1958," *Soviet Union*, 3, part 1 (1976), pp. 1–35.

[4] Decree of July 10, 1923, RCC (1922) Article 169a, *Sbornik dokumentov*, p. 165.

[5] Most other non-Russian criminal codes are more severe than the RCC. They make mere dependence sufficient to prosecute upon complaint. Georgia and Moldavia, however, require that the accused specifically used the complainant's dependence by threatening to deprive her of her job, bonuses, housing, etc. V. N. Ivanov, *Ugolovnoe zakonodatel'stvo Soiuza SSR i soiuznykh respublik: Edinstvo i osobennosti* (M, 1973), p. 100.

[6] A. A. Gertsenzon, V. K. Zvirbul', et al., *Kriminologiia* (M, 1968) (hereinafter *Kriminologiia*), p. 418.

[7] Sodomy is counted as rape. Homosexuality, a crime since the decree of December 17, 1933, is only a male offense under RCC Article 121; nothing is said about lesbianism. The penalties for aggravated homosexual offenses are considerably lower than those for comparable heterosexual offenses.

dangerous recidivist or entailing especially grave consequences, and also rape of a minor, is punished by deprivation of freedom for a period of from eight to fifteen years, with or without exile for two to five years, *or by the death penalty.*"[8] The fact that a third of rape convictions are for group rapes may explain its addition to the code as an especially aggravated offense. Women face prosecution for rape only if they help in a group rape.

The courts distinguish rape, a criminal offense, from seduction and breach of promise, for which criminal law provides no remedy. In a land-mark decision, the USSR Supreme Court overturned a lower court's rape conviction in the following case. A woman consented to have sexual rela-tions with her suitor after he took out a marriage application. When she became pregnant, though, he left her, whereupon she brought a charge of rape against him. The lower court convicted him of rape, but the Supreme Court held that immoral conduct like the suitor's was a proper subject for social censure, not criminal sanction.[9] Her consent appears to have been the deciding factor here, for other decisions indicate that marrying the rape victim after the fact mitigates but does not deflect all punishment.[10] And indeed, a husband may be convicted of rape for forcing his wife to have sexual relations with him.[11]

Soviet courts do not follow specially legislated rules of evidence in rape

[8]The edict of February 15, 1962, also raised minimum confinement from seven to eight years and added a two-year minimum for the optional exile sentence. The original and post-edict texts of the rape Article 117 may be compared in M. D. Shargorodskii and N. A. Beliaev, eds., *Kommentarii k ugolovnomu kodeksu RSFSR 1960 g.* (L, 1962), p. 233. The penalty under RCC (1922) was much less: no less than three years for rape and five years for aggravated rape (defined more narrowly as rape leading to suicide), *Sbornik dokumentov*, p. 136.

Malyi case. Directive of the USSR Supreme Court, Mar. 28, 1964, in G. Z. Anashkin, ed., *Sbornik postanovlenii plenuma i opredelenii kollegii Verkhovnogo Suda SSSR po ugolovnym delam 1959–1971* (M, 1973), pp. 241–43 and G. Z. Anashkin, I. I. Karpets, and B. S. Nikiforov, eds., *Kommentarii k ugolovnomu kodeksu RSFSR* (M, 1971) (hereinafter cited as *Kommentarii*), pp. 283–84. For a dissenting view, see A. F. Gorkin, V. V. Kulikov, N. V. Radutnaia, and I. D. Perlov, eds., *Nastol'naia kniga sud'i* (M, 1972), p. 586.

On homosexuality, see *Sbornik dokumentov*, pp. 340–41, and John N. Hazard, *Communists and Their Law: A Search for the Common Core of the Legal Systems of the Marxian Socialist States* (Chicago, 1969), p. 457. On one use of the homosexuality statute, see the case of Sergei Paradzhanov, film director, sentenced to six years' hard labor, *Bulletin of the College of Communications and Fine Arts* (Southern Illinois University, Carbondale), 14 (1974), p. 2. Three republics do not treat sodomy as rape. *Ugolovnoe zakonodatel'stvo Soiuza SSR i soiuznykh respublik* (2 vols.; M, 1963).

Kriminologiia, p. 420, reports rapist and victim acquainted in 40 percent of a sample of cases. I found them acquainted in over half of a much smaller sample of cases where the USSR Supreme Court left in force conviction for rape in some degree from ordinary to aggra-vated, as reported in the court Bulletins: Anashkin, ed., *Sbornik*, pp. 241–53; *Biulleten' Verkhovnogo Suda SSSR* (hereinafter *Biulleten'*) 1 (1973), pp. 22–25; 2 (1973), pp. 18–20; 3 (1972), pp. 21–23, 25–26; 6 (1972), pp. 30–32; 4 (1971), pp. 24–25, 36–37. On other circum-stances associated with rape, see "Zadachi sudov v bor'be protiv p'ianstva i alkogolizma," *Sovetskaia iustitsiia* (hereinafter cited as *SIu*), 17 (1972), p. 5; "Usilim bor'bu protiv p'ianstva i alkogolizma," *Sotsialisticheskaia zakonnost'*, 9 (1971), p. 9.

[9]*SIu*, 8 (1959), pp. 93–94.

[10]Decision No. 3 of the USSR Supreme Court in the case of G. A. Mosiniian, *Biulleten'*, 4 (1971), pp. 36–37.

[11]*Kommentarii*, p. 280; Gorkin et al., *Nastol'naia kniga sud'i*, pp. 583–84.

cases—for example, requiring corroboration in rape cases but not in cases involving other crimes.[12] Still, rape cases involve some special procedures and instructions to the lower courts. Unless the victim is legally incapacitated, it is she and nobody else who must bring the complaint in ordinary rape cases and she who must request criminal prosecution. This provision is designed to protect her privacy from being violated against her will, says the handbook for judges. This handbook also advises jurists that sometimes a woman who has consented to sexual relations with the defendant "will make a complaint of alleged rape when she is found out, because she is ashamed or is influenced by friends or parents or is pursuing certain purposes of her own. Juveniles are subjected to especially heavy pressure by people around them."[13]

The physicians called in to inspect the scene of the alleged rape and to examine and question the alleged victim and suspect receive similar warnings from the Soviet text on forensic medicine: they are told to exercise great tact and care in probing intimate relations, "since sometimes rape is simulated or the suspect slandered for motives of personal gain." The medical examiners must weigh the evidence about whether and how the rape took place. Was the alleged victim deflowered? Had she led a previous sex life? What was the sequence of events in a group rape? Was the rape normal or by sodomy? Did grave consequences ensue, i.e., were there serious injuries, pregnancy (especially of a minor), infection with venereal disease, or death from such causes as heart attack, injuries to sex organs, or suicide? If death was not a consequence of the sex act itself, was there rape accompanied by murder—an aggravated form of homicide and a capital offense under Article 102 of the RCC? Was death caused by a sadistic act after willing intercourse? Or did the murderer have intercourse with his victim's corpse (a crime of "desecrating the corpse" in the Estonian criminal code)?[14]

After the government stepped up its attack on rape and other violent crime in 1962, the USSR Supreme Court in 1964 admonished lower courts to "ascertain carefully how things occurred and what relations were between defendant and victim."[15] Its *Bulletin* is sprinkled with reports of reversals of rape convictions because of conflicting testimony by the victims, and with reports of lowered penalties because the rapist did not know, and could not have known, that his victim was under eighteen (making the rape a capital offense). For example, the Supreme Court reclassified the conviction of two males, aged eighteen and fifteen, who had raped a thirteen-year-old girl in a wheat field they were harvesting on the grounds that her

---

[12] Karen DeCrow, *Sexist Justice* (New York, 1975), pp. 231–39.
[13] Gorkin et al., *Nastol'naia kniga sud'i*, pp. 578–79.
[14] O. Kh. Porksheian and V. V. Pomilin, eds., *Sudebnaia medetsina* (M, 1974), pp. 224–32.
[15] Directive of the USSR Supreme Court Plenum, Mar. 25, 1964, section 3, in *Sbornik postanovlenii plenuma Verkhovnogo Suda SSSR, 1924–1973* (M, 1974), p. 483.

testimony to investigators and to the medical examiners lacked consistency. It indicated fear of parental censure and gave signs that she went willingly with the boys deep into the standing wheat. The Supreme Court found the eighteen-year-old guilty not of rape but of the lesser offense of intercourse with a person under sixteen; since the fifteen-year-old could not be punished for that crime, he went free.[16] In another case, a man met a seventeen-year-old girl at an outdoor dance. They drank together in the street, and then he invited her to a friend's apartment, where they drank some more. He raped the girl there. To escape, she jumped from the second-floor balcony, injuring herself. The USSR Supreme Court requalified the rape from especially aggravated (rape of a minor) to ordinary because the man did not know his victim's age and had reason to believe she was over eighteen (he knew she was married and had recently had an abortion, and she looked mature beyond her years).[17]

Law enforcement officials and criminologists, on the watch for false rape charges or indiscretions among rape complainants, tend to be suspicious about how rape victims got into their difficulties in the first place.[18] Studies indicate that roughly half of all rapes occur among acquaintances (often of short standing, and often after drinking). Many of the victims had even gone home with the assailants. A study of rape victims by the criminologist V. S. Minskaia claims to show that often "the behavior of the victim contributes to" her rape. She says the USSR Supreme Court had this in mind when it issued the 1964 directive to lower courts to look with special care into the relations between rapist and victim. She suggests that "if the victim's behavior before the rape or information about her reputation influenced the guilty party to seek to rape her, these may be considered mitigating factors." Minskaia will not accept that such policy may infringe on women's protection against sexual violation. "Not to look into the victim's reputation and behavior," she asserts, "does not contribute to public morality." According to Minskaia, 71 percent of the victims in her sample of

---

[16]Decision of the USSR Supreme Court Criminal Bench in the case of A. S. Danilov and V. A. Leongardt, *Biulleten'* 6 (1973), pp. 26–28. Youths may be punished for that crime only when they are 16 or older.

[17]Decree of the Plenum of the USSR Supreme Court in the case of V. N. Starchak, *Biulleten'*, 2 (1972), pp. 11–12.

[18]See, e.g., the impressions of a prosecutor's pretrial investigator. Approving of the closed-door hearings in rape trials to respect the modesty and dignity of the victims, he then raises the question of how modest they really are. Rape victims, he says, are usually women twenty years old or younger. A majority of rape cases involve youths or adolescents. In a rape case he had just investigated he found that "all of those involved without exception, both the young men and the girls, had an utterly obtuse idea of honor, manly dignity, maidenly modesty, and the equality of the sexes: they all had a utilitarian view of intimate relations. . . ." Aleksandr Shpeier, "Notes of an Investigator: A Difficult Subject," *Literaturnaia gazeta*, July 2, 1966; transl. in *CDSP*, XVIII: 28. See also the complaint of NOW's president on behalf of rape victims in the U.S., who encounter what she believes to be discriminatory attitudes of law enforcement people asking the complainant whether she was being provocative, and who face cross-examination about their previous sex experiences even though a man's previous rape convictions in some states are not admitted in evidence (DeCrow, *Sexist Justice*, pp. 236–38).

rape cases were chance pickups just hours or days before the rape, 55 percent were drunk before the rape, 30 percent drank with the assailant beforehand, 27.5 percent went to the rapist's home, 27 percent were previously inclined to drinking or sexual promiscuity, and 15 percent had been raped before. Many victims had allowed themselves to be kissed and caressed in a "risky" situation.

The establishment of the fact that a rape victim had had prior sexual relations mitigates the crime for Minskaia: "One of the indices of the moral outlook of juvenile and young victims (up to the age of 23) is whether or not they had had sexual relations with men before the crime was committed." Minskaia agrees with the Supreme Court's finding of mitigating circumstances in the following case. A young woman is sitting on the grass in the town square drinking with a man, barely an acquaintance, who she knows is much older than she and married with children. Minskaia considers her indiscretion to be a mitigating factor in what followed. Seeing that she is very drunk, two young men summon three friends, and the five of them drag her off into the bushes and rape her. All the while she knows what is happening to her but cannot put up an effective resistance because of her intoxication.[19]

The list of mitigating circumstances proposed or implied by Minskaia seems to involve almost any case in which victim and assaulter knew one another before the crime and in which the victim was not a virgin. Judges seem to agree with her—at least where the victim can be shown to have acted provocatively. (The RCC, though, does not list victims' provocative behavior as a mitigating factor.) When men were convicted of especially aggravated rape, Minskaia reports, the defendants received sentences of less than the legal minimum of eight years in 55 percent of the cases, eight to twelve in 40 percent, and thirteen to fifteen years (the maximum) in only 5 percent. Judges seldom apply the death penalty, even in the worst cases. The relative leniency shown by the judges in this most severe rape classification is even more justified, she asserts, in cases of aggravated and ordinary rape.

The Soviet equivalent of statutory rape involves intercourse with very young members of the opposite sex—"very young" being variously defined in republic criminal codes as persons who have not reached puberty,[20] persons under sixteen,[21] persons either under sixteen or who have not reached puberty,[22] or persons who have not reached marital age.[23] Penalties range from three years to a maximum of six. The RCC, moreover, lists an aggra-

[19]V. S. Minskaia, "Opyt viktimologicheskogo izucheniia iznasilovaniia," *Voprosy bor'by s prestupnost'iu*, 17 (1972), pp. 24–31.
[20]The Russian, Uzbek, Ukrainian, Belorussian, and Lithuanian codes.
[21]The codes of the Kazakh, Azerbaidzhanian, Moldavian, Latvian, Kirgiz, Tadzhik, Turkmen, and Estonian republics.
[22]The Armenian code.
[23]The Azerbaidzhanian code.

vated form of this offense covering perversions committed with very young persons of the same or opposite sex.[24]

It remains to discuss briefly the laws governing those legally proscribed areas of sexual activity that women may engage in by choice rather than by force. Curiously, prostitution per se has never been listed as a crime in the Soviet Union. There are undoubtedly ideological reasons for this, since prostitution was considered by Marxist theorists to be a phenomenon associated with the exploitation of women under capitalism. When antiparasite laws began to operate in the union republics between 1957 and 1961, prostitutes were among the social deviants (gamblers, petty speculators, all those living wholly or partly off "unearned income" and not punished under criminal law, political dissenters, and so on) sent off to administrative exile for up to five years. When parasitism became a crime USSR-wide in 1970, prostitutes faced the possibility of up to one year's confinement (two for repeaters).[25] Allegedly promiscuous mothers, including those working as prostitutes part- or full-time, face also the possible civil penalty of being deprived of parental rights.[26] So in a roundabout way prostitution may bring on legal sanctions against the women practicing it. Legal sanctions against pimps and those compelling or inducing women to engage in prostitution are more direct: they have been in the law since the first, 1922 criminal code.[27] Article 210 of the RCC is meant in part to serve as a deterrent to prostitution, since it threatens up to five years' confinement for persons "who draw juveniles into criminal activity, drunkenness, beggary, prostitution, gambling, or the use of narcotics," and for persons who use juveniles "to help sustain a parasitic existence." But four out of five cases brought under this article involve inducing juveniles to drink.[28]

A further risk of engaging in prostitution involves the possibility of falling afoul of the laws on spreading venereal disease. Like the laws on rape, laws on spreading venereal disease appeared in the 1922 criminal code and entailed increasingly severe penalties as time went by. The 1922 code set a penalty of up to three years' confinement for *knowingly* infecting a person with venereal disease. A decree of 1923 changed the crime to one of simply

[24]*Kommentarii*, pp. 285–89; RCC Article 119-2; Ivanov, *Ugolovnoe zakonodatel'stvo*, pp. 102–3.

[25]RCC Article 209-1; *Kommentarii*, p. 447; Interview with Soviet jurist, 1959; Juviler, *Revolutionary Law and Order*, pp. 76–78, 92; *Vedomosti Verkhovnogo Soveta RSFSR*, 33 (1975), items 688–99.

[26]Under the Principles of Family Law this punishment is possible for parents "who have a harmful influence on their children with their immoral, antisocial behavior, [or who] are chronic alcoholics or drug addicts," or who abuse or deliberately neglect their children (Article 19). In eleven republics other than the RSFSR, deprivation of parental rights is possible also in criminal actions of the sort in question here without separate civil action. Ivanov, *Ugolovnoe zakonodatel'stvo*, pp. 34–37; A. M. Beliakova and E. M. Vorozheikin, *Sovetskoe semeinoe pravo* (M, 1974), pp. 217–18.

[27]RCC (1922) Articles 170–71, *Sbornik dokumentov*, p. 136; RCC Article 226.

[28]A. N. Ignatov, *Ugolovnyi zakon okhraniaet prava nesovershennoletnikh* (M, 1971), pp. 60, 67, 68.

"infecting a person with venereal disease," whether knowingly or not.[29] The present code adds a penalty of up to five years' confinement for a second offense, for infecting a minor, or for infecting two or more persons—the last provision being another sanction against prostitutes and loose women. Government concern with the health problem posed by venereal disease resulted in the USSR edict of October 20, 1971, which set a penalty of two years' confinement or a fine of 100 rubles (nearly a month's average industrial wage) for offenders who place others in danger of infection by having sexual relations or engaging in other sexual acts when they know they are suffering from venereal disease. In 1973 the Supreme Court interpreted the 1971 edict as covering even cases where the party exposed to possible infection knew of the offender's venereal disease but decided despite this knowledge to have sexual relations with the offender.[30]

This brief history has shown that present provisions protecting women's freedom of choice as sex partners date back to the earliest Soviet practice and the first Soviet criminal code. If anything, the "special apparatus of coercion" applying those provisions has struck harder than ever to enforce legal protection in recent years. Law impinges on men's homosexual relations but not on women's. Convicted sexual violators of women face more punishment than do sexual violators of other men. But penalties aimed against prostitution and the spread of venereal disease reach out farther and harder now against women's practice of prostitution than they did in the early years.

WOMEN AS CHILDBEARERS

How the state should intervene in the personal lives and relationships of women as childbearers remained until the Brezhnev administration a complex and controversial issue of Soviet legal policy. Successive codes had taken different stances on this issue as social priorities of the regime changed.

The legislative task for the Bolsheviks during the stormy revolutionary period of War Communism, 1917–21, was relatively simple. During those years social priorities and women's liberation fitted well, even reinforced one another. The top social priority was to eradicate inequality and the basis of traditional privilege and potentially counterrevolutionary social power— church influence, the landowning class, capitalists, and family patriarchalism.[31] Through family law the Bolsheviks tried to help speed Russia's social transformation by breaking the hold of the church over the family and the hold over women of the male heads of family, whose authority most

---

[29] RCC (1922) Article 155, *Sbornik dokumentov*, p. 134; Decree of July 10, 1923, *ibid.*, p. 164.

[30] RCC Articles 115, 115-1. For its interpretation see *Kommentarii*, pp. 277–78. "On Court Practice in Cases of Spreading Venereal Disease," Directive of the Plenum of the USSR Supreme Court, Oct. 8, 1973, in *Biulleten'*, 6 (1973), p. 17.

[31] Beliakova and Vorozheikin, *Sovetskoe semeinoe pravo*, pp. 62–63.

churches supported. The Bolsheviks had before them the guidelines of Friedrich Engels's *Origin of the Family, Private Property, and the State*, which pointed to the family and its subjection of women as a symptom and support of the exploitative social order and a means for preserving private property and passing it on from male to male. Yet the guidelines of Engels and other socialists hardly went beyond the vaguest allusions about how in fact the socialist community would accomplish the collectivist upbringing of children after the revolution and relieve women of their special burdens as wives and mothers. Time and again, Soviet ideologues and experts have suggested that children be raised communally and that the family become solely a love match and a distant point of support for children in state or community nurseries and schools. Yet ever since Strumilin's plans for communist communities were rejected in 1961 and Khrushchev's plans for mass boarding schools fell through in 1963–64, the law has reflected a tendency toward emphasizing rather than deemphasizing family ties.[32] But again, how to emphasize them has been the issue—one now resolved for the time being as far as family law is concerned.

At first seeking social transformation with urgent speed, the Bolsheviks rewrote family law within weeks of their takeover. Their decrees of December 18 and 19, 1917, established the following founding priciples of Soviet family law pertaining directly or indirectly to women's emancipation: (1) civil marriage, duly registered with ZAGS (as the civil registry office is commonly called, after its Russian initials), alone having the force of law; (2) monogamy; (3) freedom of registered marriage, without barriers of race or creed, as a voluntary union based on mutual consent; (4) the equality of women with men in all aspects of family life; (5) freedom of divorce; (6) the protection of motherhood; (7) the legal equality of extramarital children with children born in registered wedlock. These principles entered the first Russian family code of 1918.[33]

The legislation of 1917 and 1918 gave unmarried (*odinokie*, or "single") mothers some chance of protection. All men proven to have had sexual relations, however casual, with an unmarried mother around the time of conception could be ordered in court to share the status and responsibility

[32] Frederick Engels, *The Origin of the Family, Private Property and the State: In the Light of the Researches of Lewis H. Morgan* (1884) (New York, 1941), p. 67; Excerpts from A. M. Kollontai and A. M. Sabsovich in Rudolf Schlesinger, ed., *Changing Attitudes in Soviet Russia: The Family in the U.S.S.R.: Documents and Readings* (London, 1949), pp. 59–69, 159–71; V. I. Kufaev, *Iunye pravonarushiteli* (2d ed.; M, 1925), pp. 27–28; Peter Juviler, "Soviet Families," *Survey*, 60 (1966), pp. 51–61.

[33] "On Civil Marriage, On Children and On Keeping Civil Registry Books," decree of Dec. 18, 1917, *Sobranie Uzakonenii i Rasporiazhenii Rabochego i Krest'ianskogo Pravitel'stva RSFSR*, 11 (1917), item 160; "On Divorce," decree published Dec. 19, 1917, *Ibid.*, 10 (1917), item 152; "On the Separation of Church and State," decree of Jan. 23, 1918, *Ibid.*, 18 (1918), item 263; *I-u kodeks zakonov RSFSR ob aktakh grazhdanskogo sostoianiia, brachnom, semeinom i opekunskom prave*, and the Introduction of A. G. Goikhbarg, "Pervyi kodeks zakonov RSFSR," (M, 1918), this 1918 family code first published in *Sobranie uzakonenii*, 76-77(1918), item 88; G. M. Sverdlov, *Sovetskoe semeinoe pravo* (M, 1958), pp. 59–70.

of the father of her child. A butt of ridicule, this collective paternity was eliminated from the next major family legislation, the 1926 family code of the RSFSR (which was imitated in similar, if not identical, codes in the other union republics). Henceforth the court was required to single out one man as legal father.

The effort to protect women through family law reached its high-water mark in the 1926 family code through the recognition of de facto marriage and, to a lesser extent, through the introduction of community property. (For a comprehensive discussion of the background to the adoption of the 1926 family code, see the paper by Professor Farnsworth in this volume.) Proof of de facto marriage, according to this widely unpopular provision, was "the fact of cohabitation, the maintenance during the cohabitation of a common household, and the spouses' declaration of their conjugal relations to third persons in letters and other documents and also, depending on the circumstances, mutual material support, joint upbringing of children, etc."[34]

One problem with the 1926 provision was that as it attempted to increase the protection for women in unregistered marriages, it reduced protection for women in registered marriages. For along with registered divorce there now existed de facto divorce. De facto marriage automatically superseded a prior registered marriage. De facto bigamy crept in this way, too. And registered divorce became a casual thing. It could be obtained through the mere unilateral registration of the break and a postcard from ZAGS sent to the last known address of the divorced spouse.[35]

Stalin at first retained the family legislation of the NEP period of the 1920's during his "revolution from above." But as that upheaval of collectivization and rapid industrialization subsided by 1934, Stalin began to turn to social consolidation and replenishment. After the tolls of war, civil war, famine, deportations, and hardships from 1914 through the First Five-Year Plan, Stalin moved to change the status of the family from that of a barely tolerated "survival of the past" to that of an indispensable primary cell in Soviet society. With the support of many who had opposed the 1926 family code, Stalin's legislators in 1935 passed a ban on abortions of first pregnancies. Then the decree of June 27, 1936, banned all nontherapeutic abortions, increased penalties for support-payment defaulters, eliminated postcard divorces by requiring the presence of both spouses to register divorce, and introduced a scale of progressively higher fees for successive divorces. Since women were increasingly being compelled by circumstances to go out to work, it was women who, barred from legal abortions, carried the burden of Stalin's quest for a fertile "Soviet family of a new type," and for more numerous and better disciplined cohorts of children. This turnabout

[34]*Kodeks zakonov o brake, sem'e i opeke* (1926) (M, 1931), Articles 10, 12.
[35]*Ibid.*, Articles 17–19, 138, Commentary 8; John N. Hazard, *Law and Social Change in the U.S.S.R.* (Toronto, 1953), pp. 247–48.

in 1935 and 1936 has been viewed, with good reason, as the first step in Stalin's pronatalist policy.

The second step came after the mass purges and Nazi invasion had again decimated the Soviet populace. Responding to these calamities, the Soviet regime again turned to the law. Its edict of July 8, 1944, reiterated the goal of "strengthening the family." Increasing the birthrate was the top priority. The edict responded to a special and poignant aspect of the demographic crisis, the huge surplus of women over men (roughly three women for every two men). The strategy of the 1944 edict was to encourage unmarried women to have children by retaining the ban on nontherapeutic abortions and by giving unmarried mothers the choice of a moderate state allowance for every child or of placing the child free of charge in a state home. The edict simultaneously strengthened the legal bonds of the registered family to maximize its stability and fertility by making divorce an expensive and complicated procedure that required approval in two courts. Moreover, it acted to preserve the registered family by insulating it from the consequences of the extramarital liaisons of the husband, such as paternity suits and the accompanying scandals and strains. The unwed mothers lost all possibility of suing to establish paternity, and fathers could not even voluntarily acknowledge paternity. Only registered marriage created the full legal rights and obligations of fatherhood (or adoption, legal again since 1926, but requiring the permission of one's spouse). The 1944 edict also set up various administrative measures to encourage women to be childbearers: orders and medals for mothers of large families; family allowances for mothers with three or more children (instead of seven or more, as was previously the case); expanded child-care facilities; and greater labor law protection for pregnant women.[36] Here, as Professor Farnsworth says in her chapter, was some of the substance of Aleksandra Kollontai's General Insurance Fund for relieving women as childbearers from dependence on their men and for getting women out of the house. But the social purposes and the profamily slant of the edict were far from being in the spirit of either Kollontai's proposals or the founding principles of Bolshevik family law. In 1947, even the substance of the edict was gutted when the state reduced allowances to unwed mothers.

Support for Stalin's various family measures from 1935 through 1944 must have been far from unanimous among his followers, for they countenanced a series of piecemeal changes after his death that moved law and

[36] Decrees of 1936 and 1944 and discussion appear in Schlesinger, *Changing Attitudes*, pp. 169–87, 251–390. On the Marxist ideological justification for this, see Aleksander W. Rudzinski, "Is there a Specific Socialist Marriage Law?" *Polish Civilization: Selected Papers Presented at the First Congress of the Polish Institute of Arts and Sciences in America, Nov. 25, 26, 27, 1968, in New York*, ed. by Damian S. Wandycz (New York, 1969), pp. 1–8; an example of his point is in Sverdlov, *Sovetskoe semeinoe pravo*, p. 133. See also Helen Desfosses, "Women and Pro-Natalism in the USSR," paper prepared for the Stanford University Conference on Women in Russia, May 29–June 1, 1975.

policy away from compelling motherhood toward encouraging it. Maternity became less a matter of social responsibility and more a matter of free choice as the government legalized abortions in 1955, lengthened maternity leaves in 1956, and progressively lightened birth-stimulation income taxes during the 1950's.[37] Court practice was allowed to move in the direction of liberalizing the application of divorce law and finding loopholes to enforce child support by unmarried fathers in some cases where they had been responsible in fact for the upbringing of their children.[38] Moreover, clearly undecided about what to keep and what to scrap of the residue of the 1944 edict, the Soviet regime allowed a vigorous and highly critical reform attack on the edict, in a debate that dragged out over fourteen years.[39] This long debate, together with efforts to recodify family law and to move toward freer choice and greater equality for women, culminated in the 1968 Principles of Family Law, some of whose provisions we shall examine shortly. But when I deal with the Principles of Family Law or any other laws regulating women's conduct and personal relations, I do not mean to imply that these are the only determinants of their conduct and the only way the state tries to regulate it. Elsewhere in this volume one encounters information about social policies that must influence women's choices as childbearers: the prudery about sex education; the continued shortage of modern means of contraception and counseling; the improvements in social welfare policies, such as those Professor Madison has described; women's double burden as workers and housewives; and the loss of esteem, and even patience, for mothers of many children among some segments of the population.[40]

Here, I want to focus on two areas that bear on the current legal status of women as childbearers: the first is the question of the dividing line between legal and illegal abortions; the second concerns the legal rights and obligations of unwed mothers and their children under the 1968 Principles of Family Law.

Rules governing abortions are of paramount importance to women in

[37] Unless otherwise stated, this summary of the reform episode of 1954–64 is based on Peter H. Juviler, "Family Reforms on the Road to Communism," in Peter H. Juviler and Henry W. Morton, eds., *Soviet Policy-Making: Studies of Communism in Transition* (New York, 1967), pp. 29–60.

[38] Peter H. Juviler, "Marriage and Divorce," *Survey*, 48 (1963), pp. 114–16.

[39] *Ibid.*, pp. 104–5, 112–14; see also Juviler, "Family Reforms."

[40] See the paper by Bernice Madison elsewhere in this volume; see also George St. George, *Our Soviet Sister* (New York, 1973), pp. 105, 157–76; William M. Mandel, *Soviet Women* (Garden City, N.Y., 1975), pp. 237–39, 262–64, 267–68; E. Ryzikova and R. Edel'shtein, "Sotsial'no-pravovaia pomoshch' zhenshchine materi," *Slu*, (1974), pp. 5–6; S. Lapteva, "Adolescent Mothers—Reflections on Confidential Letters," *Komsomol'skaia pravda*, Feb. 16, 1975 (condensed in *CDSP*, 27, no. 8) (on faulty sex education and its consequences). On socially discouraging attitudes toward large families and their mothers, see V. Kuchina, "Mnogodetnaia sem'ia: predmet udivleniia ili primer dlia podrazhaniia?" *Literaturnaia gazeta*, Nov. 20, 1974; V. Kuchina, "Eshcho raz o moei gordosti i obide," *Literaturnaia gazeta*, Feb. 26, 1975.

societies, or segments of society, where knowledge about or availability of means of contraception are limited—especially in Soviet society, where women are highly motivated to limit the number of children they have. Abortions cost a modest five rubles and qualify patients for up to ten days of unpaid leave without loss of seniority. Fees and loss of pay are waived for women with incomes of less than 60 rubles a month, for women who miscarry, or for women whose fetuses are aborted on doctor's orders.[41]

Soviet health law permits women to have abortions without special permission only through the third month of pregnancy. After the third month, abortion is not an absolute right but a concession on the part of hospital authorities to the extreme youth of the pregnant applicant or to her unsuitability for motherhood.[42]

Abortions become criminal offenses only when they are performed (1) outside clinics (a misdemeanor entailing up to one year's confinement or correctional tasks); (2) by persons without medical training (a felony entailing up to two years' confinement); or (3) as a business. In the latter case, and when an abortion performed outside a clinic or by a person without medical training has grave consequences, the offense is classed as an aggravated felony entailing up to eight years' confinement.[43]

When it comes to distinguishing abortion from murder, the dividing line is "the emergence of the fetus." Abortion is "intrauterine destruction of the fetus"; murder is destruction of the fetus as it leaves the mother.[44] The moment delimiting abortion from murder, Soviet commentary holds, "is taken to be the beginning of childbirth, that is the emergence of the head of the fetus. If the child is dealt a fatal injury before fully leaving his mother's body or is strangled deliberately with its umbilical cord, these acts are considered to be murder."[45]

Thus Soviet women face different legal definitions than American women do. Under the U.S. Supreme Court ruling of 1973 the test of life in the U.S. is the viability of the fetus, not its emergence from the mother in childbirth; the time limit for unqualified right to abortion for all the U.S. is not three months but six months.

A mother, it is said, should feel neither material need nor shame when bearing her child in Soviet society.[46] Nevertheless, the prospect of motherhood is a shock or depressant for some women. A woman's trauma may be so severe, her male friend or husband may be so alienated by her pregnancy, or she may be subjected to such parental anger or social stigma that she may be driven to abandon, strangle, or expose her child. The example is

---

[41] K. Batygin, M. Lirtsman, and I. Trefilov, *Posobie po gosudarstvennomu sotsial'nomu strakhovaniiu* (M, 1972), pp. 191–92; St. George, *Our Soviet Sister*, p. 106.
[42] Mandel, *Soviet Women*, p. 116.
[43] RCC Article 116, and *Kommentarii*, pp. 278–79.
[44] *Kommentarii*, p. 257.
[45] Ignatov, *Ugolovnyi zakon okhraniaet*, p. 12.
[46] *Ibid.*, p. 9.

cited of one woman, who "kept the fact of her pregnancy hidden from her parents and decided after her lover left her to get rid of the child so that nobody would know about it. She went outdoors at the last moment, had the child in the snowy street, waited for it to freeze to death, and then threw it into an ice hole in a nearby pond."[47] Under the RCC, such an act may be qualified all the way from manslaughter (up to three years' confinement) to aggravated murder (eight to fifteen years' confinement, or death). That the mother herself killed the child is neither aggravation nor mitigation.[48] Neither the RCC nor the Belorussian, Georgian, Armenian, or Kazakh criminal code recognizes in the mother's act a special crime of "infanticide." The ten other union republics do however; they treat "infanticide" as manslaughter or murder under mitigating circumstances.[49] Yet in such cases infanticide becomes murder if the mother has fed the child or cared for it in any way before killing it. And if anyone other than the mother kills the child (even during or right after birth), he or she is liable to punishment for murder, not infanticide.[50]

Have Soviet legislators endeavored to protect childbearing women in ways other than through regulating abortion procedures? The answer is yes—but again, unevenly from republic to republic. For example, the RSFSR alone excuses pregnant women or mothers of children under eight from sentence of exile; a women sentenced to exile who becomes pregnant after sentencing may have her exile delayed until the child is one.[51] Pregnancy is one of nine mitigating factors listed by RCC Article 38. Article 102-g makes the murder of a pregnant woman a capital offense. Capital punishment must be replaced with another sentence if a woman was pregnant (1) when the crime was committed, (2) at sentencing, or (3) at the time of the scheduled execution.[52]

Soviet labor law states that pregnant women and mothers nursing or with children up to one year old may not be refused work, be dismissed, or suffer a reduction of pay. The antidiscrimination rules get punitive teeth in the republic criminal codes, with the inexplicable exceptions of Estonia and, partially, Latvia.[53] Like many other modern states, the Soviet Union recog-

---

[47]*Ibid.*, p. 10.

[48]*Kommentarii*, p. 457.

[49]Five republics punish infanticide with up to three-year sentences (the Ukraine, Moldavia, Uzbekistan, Azerbaidzhan, and Kirgizia), one with up to four years (Estonia), and four with up to five years (Latvia, Lithuania, Tadzhikistan, and Turkmenia). Ignatov, *Ugolovnyi zakon okhraniaet*, pp. 8–10; *Ugolovnoe zakonodatel'stvo*, I, p. 36 (Article 106 of the Lithuanian Code, not listed by Ignatov).

[50]Ignatov, *Ugolovnyi zakon okhraniaet*, pp. 12–13.

[51]RCC Articles 25, 26; *Russian Republic Code of Criminal Procedure*, Article 361.

[52]*Kommentarii*, p. 62.

[53]N. Sheptulina, "Povyshenie garantii trudovykh prav zhenshchin v usloviiakh razvitogo sotsialisticheskogo obshchestva," *SIu*, 5 (1974), pp. 3–4; RCC Articles 138, 139, *Kommentarii*, p. 302; Ivanov, *Ugolovnoe zakonodatel'stvo*, p. 119.

A pregnant women, or nursing mother, or mother of children up to a year old may not be asked to work overtime, to work on holidays, or to go on work trips. If she has a child one to

nizes the importance of special protections for pregnant women; but like many other modern states, too, the Soviet Union encounters difficulties in enforcing those protections.[54]

Recognizing a woman's right to decide on motherhood left unresolved an urgent issue of policy about the claims of unwed mothers against the fathers of their children. Critics of the 1944 edict wanted to return to the status quo ante under the 1926 family code, which recognized children's rights and mothers' claims on the bases of blood descent. They attacked the 1944 edict as a violation of those founding principles of family legislation supported by Lenin in 1917–18. Opponents of change argued that the legislation annulled by the 1944 edict had enabled unscrupulous women to victimize men and had encouraged women's promiscuity. The reformers retorted by asking about the promiscuity of completely irresponsible men. A very pronatalist Khrushchev heeded the conservatives' argument and held up publication of a draft Principles of Family Law in 1964. Reform efforts resumed after Khrushchev's fall, and ended in the legislative compromise represented by the 1968 Principles of Family Law and the republic family codes.[55]

The reform completely eliminated two discriminatory provisions of the 1944 edict that had upset and humiliated unwed mothers and extramarital children: (1) the old form of birth certificate, with its crossed out blank space under the entry for "father's name"; and (2) the bar to a father's voluntarily acknowledging his paternity.[56] It partially eliminated a third discriminatory provision that had protected men from paternity suits. A mother may now sue to establish paternity, but she must do more than merely show that the respondent in her civil suit is the child's biological father (this provision of the laws of 1917–44 has not been restored). The court will recognize a respondent's paternal obligations only on certain carefully specified grounds, one of which is that a de facto marriage must have existed, for however short a time, before the child's birth and certainly at the time it was conceived. The court will establish paternity only if "the mother of the child and the respondent lived together and maintained a common household, or jointly supported or brought up the child, or if there is irrefutable proof that the respondent acknowledged his paternity" (Article

---

eight years old, a trip assignment or overtime must have her agreement, and refusal is not a labor infraction.

[54] The subject of the need for more protection of women's working conditions and health came up at a meeting of the Commissions of Health and Social Welfare of the Council of the Union and the Council of Nationalities of the USSR Supreme Soviet, *Vedomosti Verkhovnogo Soveta SSSR*, 36 (1974), p. 609. See also below on laws protecting pregnant wives and wives with children up to one year old in provisions on support and divorce.

[55] On the debates and the delay, see my "Family Reforms," pp. 51–52, 60; on passage of the 1968 reform, see my "Whom the State Has Joined: Family Ties in Soviet Law," in Donald Barry, George Ginsburgs, and Peter Maggs, eds., *The Individual and the State in Soviet Law* (forthcoming).

[56] See Principles of Family Law, Articles 16, 17, and its enabling act (see note 1), Article 3.

16). Such a proof may be a statement in court or a document, such as a signed photo or (as in one case) a lottery ticket signed "to my dear daughter Svetlana from her Papa."[57] The narrowness of the grounds means that in practice only a few percent of extramarital births involve court-established paternity, whereas somewhere near half involve voluntary acknowledgment of paternity.[58] The mothers of many scores of thousands of extramarital children must rely for extra support beyond regular state allowances on the very small monthly state allowances to unwed mothers (a maximum total of 10 rubles for three or more children monthly). Whereas child support awarded by the courts continues until the child reaches eighteen, state grants to unwed mothers continue only until the child reaches twelve. This leaves many unwed mothers disadvantaged as childbearers when compared with married mothers.[59] But the Soviet regime is no longer a revolutionary one. It should not surprise us, then, that on a highly controversial issue it endorsed a compromise between conservatives and reformers.

If a mother is not one of those free spirits deliberately having children outside marriage,[60] and if she wishes to avoid the possibility of discrimination against her child, she might do better to have an abortion—a more dismal but surer way to equal status and equal burdens with males.

WOMEN AS SPOUSES

Soviet law has always decreed the equality and freedom of women in marriage by giving them the right to choose their surnames and their place of residence and by ruling against the taking of child brides. A minimum marriage age of eighteen has stood on the books in the RSFSR since 1926, and was written into the 1968 Principles of Family Law. But as a concession to established law in some republics, the 1968 Principles allow the republics to provide for lowering the marriage age up to two years in exceptional cases.[61] Exceptional cases mean in practice the pregnancy or motherhood of the prospective bride or the fact that the husband is being taken away by the military draft. But republic codes show no consistency in their formal provisions about how far the marriage age may be lowered.

The Uzbek and Ukrainian family codes contravene the Principles of Family law by setting the minimum marriage age at 17, instead of 18, for females. Uzbekistan has no other provisions for age lowering. The other republic codes allow age lowering of only up to one year—in six cases for females only, another departure from all-Union law and equality. But custom, practice, and local need stretch the law. Though the Russian Republic

[57] M. V. Materova, *Sudebnoe rassmotrenie del ob ustanovlenii otsovstva* (M, 1972), p. 94.
[58] *Ibid.*, p. 73–74, 76.
[59] Jan Gorecki, "Communist Family Patterns: Law as an Implement of Change," *University of Illinois Law Forum* (1972), pp. 134–35; Decree of the USSR government of August 12, 1970, No. 659, reprinted in RFC, pp. 55–57.
[60] For an example, see St. George, *Our Soviet Sister*, pp. 73–78.
[61] Principles of Family Law, Article 10. On local soviet permission, see RFC, Article 15.

allows the greatest reduction of marriage age—two years—there are higher proportions of females sixteen and seventeen years old among married women in all but four of the non-Russian republics. Among the other republics there is a huge spread in the proportion of married women under eighteen—a spread reflecting something other than family codes. In Lithuania eight married women out of a thousand are sixteen or seventeen years old. In Armenia there are nine times as many, or 72 per thousand—84 per thousand in the villages.[62]

The law of the Russian empire obliged a wife "to follow her husband as head of the family, to love and respect him, to submit to him in every respect."[63] A Soviet wife's full legal equality, long enshrined in the law, is asserted now in the Principles of Family Law, Article 3: "Women and men enjoy equal personal and property rights in family relations." A wife may indeed refuse "to follow her husband." If he tries to force sexual relations on her, she may lodge a criminal complaint of rape against him. The law lists support obligations to spouse and children, as well as general rules for property division, without regard to sex. But the law in fact recognizes that women still have an unequal position in Soviet society. That inequality has to do with women's double burden and with other factors touched on elsewhere in this book. The Principles of Family Law stipulate that even when not earning outside income a spouse has equal rights to the ownership and control of community property, as wives often had in practice in court cases before the 1968 reform wrote practice into law. Community property is all the accumulated property earned by either spouse during marriage. This provision protects the wife who devoted much of her married life to caring for her family.[64] For the same reason, the law provides that a spouse is entitled to support from the other spouse if disabled and without pension, even if the disability sets in up to one year after divorce, or up to five years after divorce if the spouse seeking support is disabled and reaches retirement age during that time. Support stops when the disablement does or when the recipient remarries. A wife is entitled to support from her husband when pregnant or up to a year after her child's birth.[65] There is no alimony for able-bodied spouses after divorce other than child support payments for minor children left with the other spouse, or for

---

[62] On republic-age rules, see Beliakova and Vorozheikin, *Sovetskoe semeinoe pravo*, p. 94; V. A. Riasentsev, *Semeinoe pravo* (M, 1971), pp. 73–74; S. Palastina and A. Pergament, "Sovetskoe semeinoe zakonodatel'stvo o pravakh zhenshchin," *Slu*, 5 (1974), p. 8. On marital states, see *Itogi vsesoiuznoi perepisi naseleniia 1970 goda*, 1972, pp. 263–68.

[63] Quoted in Gorecki, "Communist Family Patterns," p. 131.

[64] Principles of Family Law, Article 12. Community property may be divided in unequal shares in the interests of minor children or the special interests of one spouse.

[65] Principles of Family Law, Article 13. On the earlier situation and prior RSFSR reforms, as well as on procedural improvements for the USSR, see edict of Feb. 12, 1968, "O vnesenii izmenenii i dopolnenii v kodeks zakonov o brake, sem'e i opeke RSFSR i grazhdanskii protsessual'nyi kodeks RSFSR," *Slu*, 7 (1968), pp. 24–25; A. Pergament, "Novoe v semeinom zakonodatel'stve," *Slu*, 8 (1968), pp. 12–14; edict of July 21, 1967, "Ob uluchshenii poriadka uplaty i vzyskaniia alimentov na soderzhanie detei," *Slu*, 17 (1967), p. 26.

needy, disabled adult children. These are payments large enough (up to half income for three or more children) to squeeze howls of protest from men. Men do most of the paying.[66]

A woman may not be sued for divorce during pregnancy or up to one year afterward without her consent—a restriction also new in 1968. As a prelude to reform, divorce court practice eased after Stalin. This sent divorce rates per 1,000 population from 0.4 in 1950 (67,400 divorces) to 1.6 (354,500 divorces) in 1965. The latter year's divorce revision simplified procedure by making divorce obtainable in a single court and eliminated the expensive, embarrassing, and delaying publication of notice. The revision went into effect on January 1, 1966. As a result, the divorce rate nearly doubled that year to 2.8 per 1,000 (646,000) divorces. The rate has stayed at about that level since, despite substantial divorce fees.[67] The 1965 divorce revision procedures were carried over into the 1968 reform, so that there remain (1) a possibility of court-decreed reconciliation delays, (2) the same grounds (family breakup), and (3) the same tariff of registration fees allotted by the court (50–200 rubles) and paid to ZAGS when the divorce is registered in order for it to go into force. But the 1968 reform added the possibility of divorce without court suit by registration with ZAGS (only when divorce is by mutual consent, and only under the following restrictive conditions: payment of a 50-ruble fee, a three-month waiting period for cooling off, and the absence of minor children by the marriage).[68]

ZAGS officials with whom I spoke in 1968 expected the new high divorce rates to subside after the backlog of divorces delayed by the 1944 edict had disappeared. But the dissolution of marriages continued at the average rate of about 650,000 divorces annually between 1966 and 1973; the figure for 1973 was 678,000, or 2.7 per 1,000 inhabitants,[69] for 1974, 731,000, or 2.9 per 1,000, and for 1975, 789,000, or 3.1 per 1,000.[70] In Latvia the 1973 divorce rate was 4.8—one divorce for every two marriages.[71] The rate was about 6.0 in Moscow and 6.3 in Riga in the early 1970's.[72]

Actual divorce rates are higher yet. A divorce enters statistics as formally concluded only "from the moment the divorce is registered in the book of registration of acts of civil status" at the ZAGS registry office. Since this

[66] St. George, *Our Soviet Sister*, pp. 89–90; Principles of Family Law, Article 22. See also Bernice Madison's paper elsewhere in this volume.

[67] Viktor Perevedentsev, "Marriage and the Family," *Soviet Law and Government*, 13, no. 2 (1974), p. 95.

[68] S. N. Bratus and P. E. Orlovskii, eds., *Kommentarii k kodeksu o brake i sem'e RSFSR* (M, 1971), p. 58; RFC, Article 37. On grounds for dissolution on unilateral petition, such as missing spouse or spouse sentenced to confinement of more than three years, see Principles of Family Law, Article 14; on invalidation of marriage, including the new provision on invalidation of fictitious marriages, see Article 15.

[69] Larisa Kuznetsova, "Zhenikhi—smelee!" *Literaturnaia gazeta*, Jan. 1, 1975, her total confirmed by rate of 2.7 in *Narodnoe khoziaistvo SSSR v 1973 godu* (M, 1974), p. 48.

[70] *Narodnoe khoziaistvo SSSR v 1975 godu* (M, 1976), pp. 7, 44.

[71] *Latvijas PSR: Tautas Simnieciba 1973 Godā. Narodnoe Khoziaistvo Latviiskoi SSR v 1973 godu* (Riga, 1974), p. 26.

[72] St. George, *Our Soviet Sister*, p. 142.

entails paying the divorce fee, spouses tend to put off registration until it is absolutely necessary for steps like remarriage and changes in housing and property rights.[73]

A Soviet woman dealing with state agencies or appearing in court on a family matter such as divorce, custody, paternity, support, division of property and housing, inheritance, or deprivation of parental rights is relatively unlikely to feel a "male club atmosphere." In the RSFSR, 60 percent of all those employed in dispensing justice are said to be women.[74] Hence it is probable that most of the legal personnel a woman may encounter—from the lawyer helping her file suit or defend against it to the court office staff, the judge, the court secretary, and the bailiff—will be women.

Criminal law protection of Soviet spouses in traditionally Moslem areas has entailed a protracted legal, political, even physical battle to secure for women realization of constitutional and legal protection.[75] Criminal codes of the Turkmen, Tadzhik, Uzbek, and Kirgiz republics make it a capital offense of first-degree murder (up to fifteen years or death) to kill a woman in the name of the *adat*, Moslem family law, or, as the codes put it, on the basis of "survivals of the past," "survivals of tribal life," or "survivals of the old way of life."[76]

The RCC, in Articles 232–36, aims at such "survivals" as polygamy. But these articles apply only to persons living in regions where the antisocial acts they punish "constitute survivals of local custom."[77] Under RCC Article 235, bigamists and polygamists face deprivation of freedom or correctional tasks for up to one year. Registry clerks aiding or abetting them face felony charges of malfeasance in office.[78] There is no crime of bigamy or polygamy in the criminal codes of the Ukrainian, Belorussian, Lithuanian, Latvian, Estonian, and Moldavian republics.[79]

RCC Article 233 prescribes deprivation of freedom for up to two years for all persons involved in compelling a woman to enter into marriage or to continue in marriage against her will, for all involved in trying to prevent a woman from marrying, and for all involved in abducting a woman for the purpose of having her marry (this not to mean ritual abduction). In various versions, the criminal codes of Uzbekistan, Kirgizia, Kazakhstan, Tadzhikistan, Armenia, and Turkmenia also penalize abduction and compulsion.[80]

---

[73] Perevedentsev, "Marriage and the Family," p. 95; and Bratus and Orlovskii, pp. 70–71; Article 40 of the RSFSR Famly Code.

[74] See DeCrow, *Sexist Justice*, p. 206, on the "male club atmosphere"; the 60 percent figure is from "Den' solidarnosti zhenshchin vsego mira," *SIu*, 5 (1974), p. 1.

[75] Schlesinger, *Changing Attitudes*, pp. 188–223; Gregory Massell, *The Surrogate Proletariat: Moslem Women and Revolutionary Strategies in Soviet Central Asia 1919–1929* (Princeton, N.J., 1974).

[76] Ivanov, *Ugolovnoe zakonodatel'stvo*, p. 84.

[77] *Kommentarii*, p. 485.

[78] RCC Article 173; *Kommentarii*, p. 485.

[79] Ivanov, *Ugolovnoe zakonodatel'stvo*, p. 204.

[80] The Azerbaidzhan criminal code omits the offense of compelling to continue in marriage. The Azerbaidzhan and Tadzhikstan criminal codes qualify compulsion as meaning "accom-

Concluding a marriage agreement according to local custom with a person under marital age is punishable by up to two years' confinement or one year of correctional tasks, but only in the Russian and Tadzhik republics.[81]

Article 232 of the RCC threatens the parents, kin, or relatives by marriage of a bride who accept a bride-price for her of money, cattle, or other valuables with a year's confinement or correctional tasks, plus confiscation of the payment. The groom, parents, kin, and relatives by marriage who pay the bride-price face correctional labor of up to one year or "social censure." Criminal codes of the Kirgiz, Tadzhik, Armenian, and Turkmen republics contain similar but not identical penalties for the custom of *kalym*, buying and selling the bride. The Armenian Republic adds the point that payment in personal labor may also be counted as criminal *kalym*.[82]

Bride-buying goes on under cover of "Komsomol weddings," and with the connivance of village officialdom. *Kalym* running up to 15,000 rubles in money, valuables, and livestock is taken to be a measure of family wealth and the bride's desirability. The more educated the bride the lower the *kalym*, however, because "everybody knows that the more educated a girl is, the harder it is to make a prisoner out of her and keep her submissive to parents and husband." A furor shook the Turkmen Party from top to bottom following revelations of such activities, and the result was a republicwide campaign down to the village level "to intensify the struggle against the feudal *bey* treatment of women" and to enforce existing and new criminal penalties for *kalym* and for *kaitarma*—the custom of taking back and holding a bride and her property until the balance of the bride-price is paid.

RCC Article 134 makes it a crime punishable by up to two years' confinement to obstruct a woman's participation in state, community, or cultural activities by use or threat of force. Criminal codes of six other republics, including Turkmenia, carry similar penalties, some more broadly applied. It appears harder to enforce such laws than to write them. Hence the bursts of social activism and mass agitation, and the periodic reminders to law enforcers about the rules they are to enforce.[83]

---

panied by the use or threat of violence." The Kazakhstan criminal code does not specify that abduction be with the purpose of having the woman marry. On the other hand, the Turkmenia criminal code details another purpose—for the sake of having the women enter into unregistered marital relations. The Azerbaidzhan criminal code has an aggravated form of coercion—abducting a woman not of marital age. The Kirgizia criminal code has one of abducting a woman who has not reached the age of sixteen in order to enter into unregistered marital relations (with a sentence of two to seven years). On all these provisions, see Ivanov, *Ugolovnoe zakonodatel'stvo*, pp. 204–5.

[81]*Ibid.*, p. 204.

[82]*Ibid.*

[83]Toushan Esenova, "Nenavistnyi kalym," *Literaturnaia gazeta*, May 22, 1974. "Rezonans: 'Nenavistnyi kalym; Redaktsiia 'Literaturnoi gazety' poluchila pis'mo pervogo sekretaria TsK KP Turkmenistana M.G. Gapurova," *ibid.*, July 24, 1974. Toushan Esenova, "Protiv perezhitkov proshlovo: Vsem mirom," *ibid.*, May 28, 1975. The Uzbek code (Article 134) for example covers "other acts violating women's equality." The Kazakh code (Article 120) has a clause covering "other acts violating women's equality if they entail force or threat of force," plus "use of financial and other dependency" of the woman—a substantial difference. Ivanov, *Ugolovnoe zakonodatel'stvo*, p. 116.

CONCLUSIONS

Long gone are the days when Soviet law tried to force idealized prescriptions for women's liberation upon a recalcitrant population, as in 1917–18 and 1926, or tried to force the replacement of the ideals of emancipation with those of fecund familyhood, as in 1936 and 1944. Since the reforms of the 1950's and 1960's, law touching women as females has moved closer to some compromise between the ideal and the practical, closer to a reflection of trends in public attitudes (insofar as they can be ascertained and generalized from the debates over reform). The law is now less internally consistent and reflects some of the contradictory aspects of the contemporary Soviet scene—notably in such areas as abortion, paternity, and divorce. Untrammeled by religious imperatives, Soviet law touching women's roles as females seems, for all its contradictions, to be relatively far along in doing what the law can, with its limited reach, to give women an equality and freedom of choice consistent with the social ideals of 1917. Contradictions, and flashes of sex-role stereotyping, remain, as in all accreted and much-changed bodies of law. Women as sex partners are more strongly protected than men are against violation—involuntary sexual relations and harm therefrom—to the extent that criminal law and its sanctions can offer protection. Also they have greater freedom of choice, since only male homosexuality is punishable by law. The articles against premature and premature-perverted relations in fact protect mainly women, judging from the text on forensic medicine and legal commentary.

Insofar as law touches women as sex partners, it implicitly casts them as either modest and chaste or corrupting and tempting. Men are cast as the sexual aggressors and perverts, especially in the articles on men's taking advantage of women's dependent position and on rape and homosexuality. Sex-role images implied in the law become explicit in learned commentary and reports of social attitudes. The Soviet victimology of rape is redolent with warnings against scheming women or pressures by horrified parents to turn a lark leading to pregnancy into rape. It also exudes a double standard. A man's past sex life, except for unexpunged rape, enters not at all into the legal commentary; but signs of a past sex life by a woman under 23 should raise the warning signal in rape cases, according to the commentator. Judges seem to agree that somehow rape cases must not appear to condone women's immorality, and that the way to do this is to deny them the full remedy and deterrence of stiff criminal law by extensive mitigation of sentences even in cases of aggravated rape. By its silence on prostitution per se, the criminal law treats prostitutes as victims. But through antiparasite administrative work and exile penalties (and since 1970 criminal penalties), as well as through stiffened penalties for spreading venereal diease, the law treats prostitutes as offenders also.

When it comes to freedom of childbearing the limited reach of the law shows up doubly—in how far it yet has to go to legislate emancipation (despite impressive social welfare provisions), and in how far beyond the law social change must go to complete this emancipation. Even if women had total control over policy and law in this area, would one clear, profeminist policy emerge? Given the signs of disagreement among women, probably not. Unwed mothers have fared better since 1968. But the safeguards of the 1968 reforms against women's victimizing men with entrapment or unfounded paternity suits still left unwed mothers and their children unequal before the law; though their position was improved, they still face greater legal inequality than they did in pre-Stalinist family law.

From entering marriage to dissolving it, Soviet wives enjoy equality save in those areas beyond the reach of the law. Secularizers and feminists may find Soviet law on marriage and property, if not women's social positions, to be advanced and enlightened. They may see restrictions on divorce that were not present under the first Bolshevik marriage and family codes of 1917–18, and they may note that this reflects an abandonment of the goal of dispensing eventually with the educational role of the family and the economic dependence of women. They may also note that the law cuts both ways on support, though it reserves some areas of extra protection for divorced spouses, the meaning of which only court practice will tell.

Thus the final impressions that Soviet law and legal practice leave about the liberation of women in their roles as sex partners, childbearers, and spouses remain problematic. One may well emphasize, in concluding, either how far Soviet women have come toward liberation, toward freedom of choice and equality in their personal lives, or how far they have yet to go. It may be said that relative both to their past situation and to the situation of women in many other industrialized countries, they have come a long way toward liberation.[84] But any overall generalization is likely to leave a misleading impression in this highly charged and universally unresolved question.

[84] For an introductory comparison of family policies, see Bernard I. Murstein, *Love, Sex and Marriage Through the Ages* (New York, 1974).

Richard B. Dobson

Educational Policies and Attainment

S OON AFTER coming to power, the Soviet leaders stressed in their policy pronouncements the importance of raising the people's cultural level and of equalizing the position of men and women in education, as in other areas. Though progress had been made in the last decade of the tsarist regime, Russian women were still educationally disadvantaged in comparison to men. Just before the First World War, more than twice as many women as men were illiterate; girls accounted for only about one-third of all pupils in primary and secondary schools, and young women for less than one-fifth of the enrollment in higher educational institutions.[1] In the eyes of the new leaders, education was an essential means of liberating women from ignorance and superstition, of preparing them for active working lives, and of reducing inequality between the sexes.

As a step toward achieving the last of these objectives, coeducation was established at all levels in 1918. In the 1920's and 1930's, the government vigorously pressed its campaign to abolish illiteracy, and enrollments in educational institutions expanded rapidly.[2] Female enrollment rose markedly in both absolute and relative terms. The proportion of girls among secondary-school pupils edged upward to 40 percent during the 1920's and approached 50 percent in the 1930's. In 1927, women were nearly 40 per-

I wish to thank Natalie Rogoff Ramsøy and Michael P. Sacks for their comments on an earlier draft of this article.

[1] Nicholas Hans, *History of Russian Educational Policy (1701–1917)* (New York, 1964), p. 200; Norton T. Dodge, *Women in the Soviet Economy: Their Role in Economic, Scientific, and Technical Development* (Baltimore, Md., 1966), p. 106.

[2] The extreme disparity in the literacy rates of the two sexes shown in the 1897 census had been greatly reduced by 1939 and altogether eliminated by the time of the 1970 census. USSR, Tsentral'noe Statisticheskoe Upravlenie (hereafter TsSU), *Narodnoe obrazovanie, nauka i kul'tura v SSSR: statisticheskii sbornik* (M, 1971), pp. 21, 78, 151.

cent of those enrolled in specialized secondary institutions; by 1940 they were more than half. In higher educational institutions, women increased their share in enrollments from less than a third in the late 1920's to 43 percent in 1940. Behind these increases lay the government's commitment to equality of educational opportunity. In some cases, this policy took the form of specific measures on women's behalf, such as a 1929 decree establishing a minimum quota for women in the entering classes of institutions of higher learning.[3]

During the war years, as young men were drawn into the armed forces and suffered heavy losses in the fighting, women's representation in specialized secondary schools and higher educational institutions rose to its highest point. In 1945, women accounted for 69 percent of all day and evening students in specialized secondary schools and an even higher share (77 percent) of those in universities and institutes. In the postwar period, when war veterans and those with work experience were given preference in admissions, the proportion of women declined. Yet in 1959, when women's share among students in specialized secondary schools reached its low point (46 percent), the absolute number of women enrolled still exceeded that of the war years. The same situation could be found in the area of higher education: though women's share among the students declined to 42 percent in 1961, the absolute number of women in higher educational institutions was almost twice as large as it had been in 1945.[4] Moreover, as Table 1 shows, in the course of the 1960's not only did women's enrollment rise again in relative terms, but their numbers more than doubled. By 1974, they constituted 53 percent of the students in Soviet specialized secondary schools and 50 percent of the students in higher educational institutions.[5]

The resulting rise in women's educational level is reflected in census data from the RSFSR, shown in Table 2. Though women in the general population have made impressive gains in moving beyond the elementary level, they have lagged behind men at each point. It is noteworthy, however, that in the employed population by 1959 a higher proportion of women than men had at least an incomplete secondary education. In the area of higher education, employed men had only a slight edge over working women in 1959 and 1970.[6]

[3] Dodge, especially Tables 53 and 57, pp. 110, 112. Since women made up nearly 30 percent of the total enrollment in higher education in 1929, it was presumably in the industrial, agricultural, and socioeconomic fields that the new quotas had their effect. (*Ibid.*, pp. 111–12.) The regulation may also have reflected concern that women's enrollment might decline as higher education was expanded and as an increasing share of the students came from the workers' faculties (*rabfaki*).

[4] *Ibid.*, pp. 110, 112.

[5] The increase in female representation in the 1960's appears to be linked with a change of admission policy—a renewed stress on academic performance for the selection of students.

[6] Through 1961, an "incomplete secondary education" denoted the completion of seven years of schooling in the general-education school; since then, eight years of schooling have been counted as "incomplete secondary." The differences in educational attainment between

TABLE 1

Women's Enrollment in Institutions of Higher Learning and Specialized
Secondary Schools in the USSR and the RSFSR, Selected Years

Year	Institutions of higher learning		Specialized secondary schools	
	Number of women enrolled	Percentage of total enrollment	Number of women enrolled	Percentage of total enrollment
USSR				
1950	661,100	53%	700,700	54%
1960	1,030,300	43	968,000	47
1970	2,244,500	49	2,369,500	54
1974	2,376,600	50	2,373,200	53
RSFSR				
1960	668,700	45	622,300	49
1965	1,065,100	45	1,169,400	52
1970	1,355,100	51	1,460,900	56
1974	1,447,800	52	1,496,100	56

SOURCES: USSR, Tsentral'noe Statisticheskoe Upravlenie, *Narodnoe obrazovanie, nauka i kul'tura: statisticheskii sbornik* (M, 1971), pp. 151, 186; USSR, TsSU, *Narodnoe khoziaistvo SSSR v 1974 godu* (M, 1975), pp. 690, 699; RSFSR, TsSU, *Narodnoe khoziaistvo RSFSR v 1965 godu* (M, 1966), p. 478; RSFSR, TsSU, *Narodnoe khoziaistvo RSFSR v 1974 godu* (M, 1975), p. 487.

NOTE: The figures pertain to women enrolled in all programs (day, evening, and correspondence) in these institutions at the beginning of the academic year.

Owing to this rapid growth of education, women of successive age cohorts differ appreciably in their educational attainment. In the RSFSR at the time of the 1970 census, women with at least an incomplete secondary education were 15 percent of women in their late fifties, better than 50 percent of women in their forties, and more than 90 percent of women in their twenties. Only one woman in 50 in the late-fifties group had completed a higher education, compared with one in 20 among those in their forties and nearly one in 10 between 30 and 39.[7]

The educational system in which Russian women study today was largely shaped by policies adopted in the early 1930's. The 1920's had been a period of experimentation: traditional subjects such as Latin had been dropped from the curriculum, and schools were organized along polytechnic lines with the aim of combining work and study. Learning according to the "project method," students worked together on projects cutting across traditional academic disciplines. In a volte-face signaled by a series of decrees

---

rural and urban women have been much greater than the differences between the sexes. In 1939, for each 1,000 women (age ten or over) living in towns in the RSFSR, 199 had obtained at least an incomplete secondary education. In rural areas, the comparable figure was only 36. By the same standard, thirteen of the urban women had completed a higher education, against only one in the countryside. These differences are still pronounced. Thus in 1970, of every 1,000 women living in the RSFSR (at least ten years of age), 564 of the urban women but only 290 of the rural women had received at least an incomplete secondary education; and whereas 55 of the urban women were graduates of institutions of higher learning, only twelve of their rural sisters were. USSR, TsSU, *Itogi vsesoiuznoi perepisi naseleniia 1970 goda* (M, 1972), vol. 3, pp. 364–65.

[7]*Ibid.*, pp. 8–9.

TABLE 2
Educational Attainment in the RSFSR, by Sex, 1939, 1959, and 1970

Educational level	Per 1,000 population aged 10 or over		Per 1,000 of the employed population	
	Males	Females	Males	Females
1939				
Complete higher education	12	5	16	10
Incomplete secondary to incomplete higher education	114	88	119	99
Total attaining at least incomplete secondary education	126	93	135	109
1959				
Complete higher education	29	22	36	35
Incomplete secondary to incomplete higher education	355	323	392	417
Total attaining at least incomplete secondary education	384	345	428	452
1970				
Complete higher education	49	39	68	65
Incomplete secondary to incomplete higher education	472	424	578	602
Total attaining at least incomplete secondary education	521	463	646	667

SOURCE: USSR, Tsentral'noe Statisticheskoe Upravlenie, *Itogi vsesoiuznoi perepisi naseleniia 1970 goda* (M, 1972), vol. 3, pp. 364–65, 559.
NOTE: Since 1961 new additions to the "incomplete secondary education" category in the censuses must have completed eight years of schooling. The standard until then was seven years, and those who met it are so counted in the 1970 census.

in the early 1930's, there was a return to more traditional methods of instruction. The Soviet school assumed an academic cast more like that of the prerevolutionary *gimnaziia* than that of the labor school of the 1920's. The teacher's classroom authority was reaffirmed, discipline stressed, and grades restored. Once again uniforms were required for boys and girls.

Today all children—except those who are physically handicapped or who pose serious disciplinary problems—are obliged to complete eight years of schooling within the general-education school. As a rule, a child enters the first grade at the age of seven, after having spent one or more years in a preschool. The eight years are broken down into three years of elementary schooling followed by five years that form the first cycle of secondary education. The kind of departmentalized instruction that usually begins in the seventh grade in American schools begins in the fourth grade in most Soviet schools. The general-education school is coeducational, and, with minor exceptions, boys and girls are exposed to a common curriculum in which mathematics and science occupy a prominent place.[8]

[8]"Osnovy zakonodatel'stva Soiuza SSR i soiuznykh respublik o narodnom obrazovanii," in A. A. Abakumov, N. P. Kuzin, F. I. Puzyrev, and L. F. Litvinov, comps., *Narodnoe ob-*

TABLE 3

Percentages of Youths, Ages 16 to 19, with Less Than Eight Years of Schooling, RSFSR, 1970

Sex	Urban	Rural	All
Males	13.6%	21.9%	16.3%
Females	5.0	13.0	7.3
Both	9.3%	17.9%	11.9%

SOURCE: USSR, TsSU, *Itogi vsesoiuznoi perepisi naseleniia 1970 goda*, vol. 3, pp. 6–9, 30–33, 54–57.

Since young people begin school at age of seven, it is expected that they will have completed eight years of schooling (that is, "an incomplete secondary education") by the time they are sixteen. As of 1970, as Table 3 shows, 12 percent of the adolescents between the ages of 16 and 19 in the RSFSR had failed to graduate from the eighth grade. Both sex and place of residence clearly have a bearing on the rate of achievement. More than twice as many males as females had not completed the eighth grade, and about twice as many rural as urban children had fallen behind. The sharpest contrast is that between boys in rural areas and girls in towns: one out of five of the former had not reached the mandatory level, as against one out of twenty of the latter.

The majority of pupils who graduate from the eighth grade enter the ninth grade of the general-education school, and a large share of the remainder continue their studies in other types of educational institutions. Whereas the general-education school provides pupils with basic knowledge and skills, the other institutions are designed to prepare young people for specific kinds of work. Pupils who leave the general-education school after the eighth grade may choose to complete their secondary education in evening school while working, to enroll in vocational-technical schools offering one- to three-year courses for various skilled workers' occupations, or to compete for admission to specialized secondary institutions. The last-named—most of which are called *tekhnikums*—offer three- to four-year courses for "semiprofessional" occupations (e.g., technicians, nurses, librarians, accountants). In short, there are a number of alternatives, and a youngster may receive a "complete secondary education" in a variety of ways—either by graduating from the tenth grade of the general-education school, by completing the course of general study in an evening school, or by graduating from a *tekhnikum*. In addition, a growing number of the

razovanie v SSSR: Obshcheobrazovatel'naia shkola: Sbornik dokumentov, 1917–1973 gg. (M, 1974), pp. 92–104. On preschool facilities, see Bernice Madison's paper elsewhere in this volume and Kitty D. Weaver, *Lenin's Grandchildren: Preschool Education in the Soviet Union* (New York, 1971); see also Susan Jacoby, *Inside Soviet Schools* (New York, 1974).

vocational-technical schools are adopting a curriculum that combines vocational training with secondary education.[9]

All young people who have completed their secondary education through one of these programs are eligible to compete for admission to higher educational institutions (abbreviated *vuzy*, or in the singular *vuz*), but most *vuz* entrants are selected from among the recent graduates of the academically oriented general-education school. Those who gain admission embark upon a course of study, usually lasting five years, that leads to a college degree, or *diplom*, in a given specialty (e.g., chemistry, philology, engineering). Secondary-school graduates who do not enter *vuzy* have an array of options similar to the eighth-grade graduates'. That is, some may enter vocational-technical schools or apply to *tekhnikums* designed for pupils who have already completed their secondary education. Others may go to work or combine work with part-time study at a *vuz* or *tekhnikum*.[10]

The Soviet system of higher education differs from the American system in a number of important respects. For one thing, all of the institutions are state-owned and managed, being administered by the USSR Ministry of Higher and Specialized Secondary Education. The number of students accepted in various subjects is determined in consultation with the state planning agencies so as to achieve a distribution of graduates that corresponds to the economy's expected manpower needs. As a result, there are many more openings in technical specialties like engineering and in the natural sciences than in the social sciences or humanities. Moreover, most Soviet students are enrolled in technical institutes, rather than universities, and pursue a course of study typically much more specialized from the outset than that of their American counterparts. There are no liberal-arts colleges. In contrast to the great majority of American students, who engage in full-time study, about half of Soviet students work full-time while studying in evening or correspondence courses. Finally, no fees are charged for tuition in Soviet higher educational institutions (or for study in any of the other schools), and three-quarters of the full-time *vuz* students receive living stipends from the state.

[9] USSR, TsSU, *Itogi 1970*, vol. 3, pp. 8–9, 32–33, 56–57. In accord with government efforts to achieve universal secondary education, the proportion of eighth-grade graduates continuing on in their schooling has been growing. In 1973 fully 95 percent of the 5,000,000 graduates moved into further studies of some kind: 58 percent went on to the ninth grade of the general-education school, 10 percent enrolled in specialized secondary schools, 6 percent entered vocational-technical schools, and 21 percent continued their study in evening school while working. M. Sonin and E. Zhil'tsov, "Povyshat' uroven' podgotovki molodezhi k trudu," *Kommunist*, 14 (1974) pp. 37–49; see trans. in *CDSP*, 27, no. 2, p. 3.

[10] On educational policy and the structure of the educational system, see Nicholas DeWitt, *Education and Professional Employment in the U.S.S.R.* (Washington, D.C., 1961); George Z. F. Bereday, William W. Brickman, and Gerald H. Read, eds., *The Changing Soviet School* (Cambridge, Mass., 1960); Nigel Grant, *Soviet Education*, rev. ed. (Harmondsworth, Eng., 1970); Seymour M. Rosen, *Education and Modernization in the USSR* (Reading, Mass., 1971); and Tamara Revenko, *L'Enseignement supérieur en l'Union soviétique: Analyse structurelle et statistique* (Paris, 1973). For pertinent major decrees and laws, see Abakumov et al.

Despite the measures the government has taken to make education accessible to citizens of both sexes and of varying social origins, the education that a woman receives, as we shall see, is largely determined by her academic performance and aspirations; and these, in turn, are conditioned by her sex and social origins. In the rest of this paper I examine how this conditioning operates, with particular attention to the effect of changing educational policies and to the ways in which girls and boys differ in their performance, aspirations, and vocational orientations.

GIRLS' PERFORMANCE IN SCHOOL

Studies of schoolchildren conducted in the RSFSR show consistently that girls achieve higher levels of academic performance than boys. According to a study carried out in Leningrad in the latter half of the 1960's, 27 percent of the girls received high marks in the humanities, and 14 percent got high grades in the exact sciences. Only half as many boys made as good a showing in the two fields.[11] Similarly, a 1970 survey of pupils in grades 7–10 in the town of Ufa showed that girls were twice as likely as boys to receive only "good" and "excellent" grades (4 and 5 points). Boys made up just 28 percent of the pupils with these high grades, but 75 percent of the failing students.[12] Generally, boys account for some three-fourths of the pupils who repeat grades and almost all of those who drop out of school before finishing the eighth grade.[13]

Notwithstanding the generally uniform curriculum, there are some significant differences in boys' and girls' activities in school. At the seventh-grade level, for example, pupils are required to devote two hours each week to the study of "labor."

By this age [writes Susan Jacoby] "labor" means metal-working for boys and home economics for girls. At the first Soviet school I visited I said I found it strange that

[11] E. K. Vasil'eva, *Sotsial'no-professional'nyi uroven' gorodskoi molodezhi (Po materialam vyborochnogo obsledovaniia shkol'nikov i molodezhi Leningrada)* (L, 1973), p. 16. See in English translation, E. K. Vasil'eva, *The Young People of Leningrad: School and Work Options and Attitudes,* with an introduction by Richard B. Dobson (White Plains, N.Y., 1976). These figures (and the ones that follow) are for pupils with consistently high grades. It may be that, as in the United States, there is greater variance in boys' grades than in girls'. Those boys who get high marks in some subjects but low marks in others would not be included here.
[12] L. G. Zemtsov, "Sotsial'nye problemy obshcheobrazovatel'noi shkoly v SSSR na sovremennom etape," unpublished dissertation for the degree of Candidate of Sciences (Ufa, 1971), p. 165. See also V. D. Popov, "Nekotorye sotsiologo-pedagogicheskie problemy vtorogodnichestva i otseva," in R. G. Gurova, ed., *Sotsiologicheskie problemy obrazovaniia i vospitaniia* (M, 1973), p. 35.
[13] In 1965, the Minister of Education of the RSFSR reported that about 70 percent of the grade repeaters in elementary and secondary schools were boys. In the first two grades, there were no appreciable differences between boys and girls in this respect. But thereafter the proportion of boys among those forced to repeat increased markedly, to reach a peak in grades 5 and 6. In the upper grades (9–11), the differences between boys and girls became much smaller. M. Kashin, "The Problem of Grade Repeating," in Fred Ablin, ed., *Contemporary Soviet Education* (White Plains, N.Y., 1969), p. 168. See also Popov, "Nekotorye sotsiologo-pedagogicheskie problemy," p. 35; and by the same author, "Papa, mama, i syn-vtorogodnik," *Zhurnalist,* 5 (1973), p. 19.

girls and boys should be pigeonholed into these sex-stereotyped subjects when nearly all Soviet women worked (many of them with metal in factories). The principal replied, "Yes, yes, but the woman still has the responsibility for the home. She needs to learn something about cooking and sewing and caring for her family. The boys certainly wouldn't like to take these classes.[14]

Similarly, in the upper grades, when all pupils study military training for two hours each week, boys are given combat training, whereas girls are taught basic first aid techniques. In extracurricular activities, boys are more likely to participate in athletic and technical sections and clubs, and girls in amateur talent clubs devoted to music, dance, and singing.[15]

It is clear that boys are also much more prone to get into trouble. V. D. Popov reports that "among boys there are twice as many violations of the norms of behavior [in school] and absences from class as among girls. Moreover, among boys violations such as smoking, use of alcoholic beverages, hooliganism, stealing, and premature entrance into sexual life are nearly seven times higher than among girls."[16] The over-age boys who have had to repeat grades are often a disruptive element. "The character-molding potential of these adolescents' influence on the younger students is very great," one teacher points out. "First in horror, then with secret envy, their younger classmates watch them cutting classes, playing cards, smoking, and using profane language."[17]

The Leningrad sociologist E. K. Vasil'eva finds that girls are twice as likely as boys to be class monitors or student leaders, and that boys are twice as likely to take on no "civic assignment" in school whatsoever. This appears to be a general pattern, as suggested by a special letter of the Ministry of Education of the RSFSR calling attention to the fact that girls were twice as numerous as boys in the Young Pioneer and Komsomol *aktiv*, and usually had the most important assignments. Empirical research by Urie Bronfenbrenner further confirms that "it is Soviet girls in particular who support the society's values, and—both as individuals and in their collectives—exert pressure on others to conform to standards of good behavior." The girls' "dominance" in the school perhaps intensifies the boys' striving for independence and involvement in the less structured, more spontaneous setting of the peer-group outside school. Another social scientist, even as he

---

[14] Jacoby, p. 103.

[15] *Ibid.*, p. 104; Iu. K. Babansky, "Optimalization of the Teaching Process (Preventing Failing Grades Among Schoolchildren)," *Soviet Education*, 15, no. 12 (Oct. 1973), p. 52; F. N. Rekunov and N. A. Shlapak, "The Career Plans of Graduates of Rural Schools," in M. N. Rutkevich, ed., *The Career Plans of Youth*, trans. and ed. Murray Yanowitch (White Plains, N.Y., 1969), p. 108.

[16] "Nekotorye sotsiologo-pedagogicheskie problemy," p. 36. Many of these boys are failing pupils. According to N. Shchelokov, the USSR Minister of Internal Affairs, 48 percent of all the "difficult" children who show up in detention rooms and 90 percent of the youth who commit crimes are grade-repeaters. Popov, "Papa, mama, i syn-vtorogodnik," p. 19.

[17] L. Zakharova, "Uroki bez peremenok," *Izvestiia*, Sept. 5, 1972, p. 5 (see trans. in *CDSP*, 24, no. 36, p. 29).

stresses the need for more research on sex differences (especially problems related to boys' performance in school), voices some concern about the "ever more noticeable predominance of girls in organs of self-administration."[18]

The behavior of girls in school provides some obvious contrasts with their position as women later in life. Though girls tend to get better grades than boys, they are much less likely than men to become "high achievers" who distinguish themselves by their academic productivity and originality. And despite their relative "dominance" in the school, they are much less likely than men to become members of the Communist Party or to rise to positions of authority.

In seeking to explain why girls outshine boys at this early stage, Soviet social scientists single out three main factors: differences in socialization according to traditional sex types, the earlier maturation of girls, and the feminization of the teaching profession. As Iu. K. Babanskii observes: "Traditional upbringing in the family is oriented toward training the girls for the role of a future mother, housewife, and rearer of children and toward training her for less arduous production activity. All this is reflected in the nature of girls' games (playing with dolls and utensils, games in which girls play the role of mother, childrearer, etc.)." Boys, he notes, are encouraged to develop the qualities of strength, independence, forthrightness, and audacity, whereas girls are inculcated with "the qualities of maidenly honor, dignity, moderation, restraint, and balance, and the ability to raise children, which forms stricter norms of self-regulation in their behavior": "Thus, while the pugnacity of boys is not congenital (even though they are unquestionably more active biologically), the nature of the previous upbringing, the style of folk pedagogy, and reliance on it in the school predetermine greater mobility, greater independence in behavior, and less strict self-control and self-appraisal among boys than among girls."[19] The qualities instilled in girls obviously work for good performance in school: girls will obey the teacher and dutifully (and neatly) complete their homework assignments. On the other hand, the traits developed in boys (boldness, independence, mobility) may tend to be of advantage to them in their later careers, when enterprise and independence are called for. It is precisely at this later stage, moreover, that girls will be directly confronted with the dilemma of career versus family, though they have been prepared for the role of mother from the earliest age. Indeed, in helping to enforce the rules of good behavior in the school, girls are performing tasks analogous to those that they will later carry out in raising their own children. That is, they are learning to conduct *vospitanie*, "upbringing."

---

[18] Vasil'eva, p. 16; Babansky, pp. 53–54; Urie Bronfenbrenner, *Two Worlds of Childhood: U.S. and U.S.S.R.* (New York, 1973), p. 83; V. I. Zhuravlev, "Samovoznikaiushchie gruppy podrostkov i molodezhi po mestu zhitel'stva," in Gurova, p. 80.
[19] Babansky, pp. 50–51, 52.

Many Soviet social scientists attribute some of the observed differences to the fact that girls mature earlier than boys. And others ascribe them at least in part to the fact that four out of five teachers are women, contending that women teachers provide appropriate models for the girls and have difficulty instilling discipline in the boys.[20] Two American researchers who have recently looked into the question of dominance and compliance among children conclude: "Boys are more dominant than girls, in the sense that they more frequently attempt to dominate others, but their dominance attempts are *primarily directed toward one another*. Girls are more compliant, but *primarily toward adults*. It is possible that girls form a coalition with the more dominant adults as a means of coping with the greater aggressiveness of boys, whose dominance they do not accept."[21] A similar portrait emerges from Soviet materials. "Thus," one Soviet teacher writes, "by their maturity and their closeness to the majority of their mentors, girls turn out to be the 'masters' in the school. Well, and if in the Druzhina council or the Komsomol committee there are two or three boys for every ten girls, what are the majority going to vote for—military study or dances?"[22]

After the eighth grade, boys are somewhat more likely than girls to leave the general-education school in order to enroll in a *tekhnikum* or vocational-technical school or to start working. Consequently, girls outnumber boys in the upper grades.[23] Boys and girls continue to follow a basically common curriculum in the ninth and tenth grades. However, since the mid-1960's more and more schools have begun to offer elective courses (*fakul'tativy*) in the upper grades, and increasing numbers of "specialized" (*profilirovannye*) general-education schools designed for children with an aptitude for mathematics, physics, chemistry, foreign languages, and other disciplines have been established. Admission in some of these schools is gained through competitions (so-called olympiads); in others, admission depends primarily on the parents' decision and the school administration's willingness to accept the children. Impressionistic data suggest that girls are more likely to excel in the humanities, and boys in various scientific specialities, especially physics and mathematics. And, indeed, certain statistics tend to support that view: in the 1964–65 school year, for instance, girls made up only 11 percent of the 357 pupils receiving intensified training in physics and mathematics at the special boarding school attached to Moscow State University.[24]

[20] USSR, TsSU, *Narodnoe obrazovanie*, p. 120; Popov, "Nekotorye sotsiologo-pedagogicheskie problemy," p. 36.
[21] Eleanor Emmons Maccoby and Carol Nagy Jacklin, *Psychology of Sex Differences* (Stanford, Calif., 1974), p. 273.
[22] V. Bezdenezhenykh, "V zashchitu mal'chishek," *Sem'ia i shkola*, 2 (1972), p. 28; Bronfenbrenner, pp. 69–72, 77–78.
[23] In 1970, girls were 49 percent of the pupils in grades 5–8 in the RSFSR, but 58 percent of those in grades 9–10. USSR, TsSU, *Narodnoe obrazovanie*, p. 91.
[24] In the first connection, see, for example, Iu. V. Sharov, "Tipy sovremennykh starsheklassnikov," in V. T. Lisovskii, comp., *Molodezh' i obrazovanie* (M, 1972), p. 61. The enrollment

GIRLS' VOCATIONAL ASPIRATIONS

Girls' occupational preferences are important for an understanding not only of the kind of training they seek, but of the processes by which traditional sex distinctions in the occupational sphere are maintained (or modified) from one generation to another. In a survey, conducted in the mid-1960's, tenth-graders in the Leningrad area were asked which occupations they considered most attractive. Out of a list of 40 possibilities, both rural and urban girls placed the following among the ten most attractive occupations: worker in literature and art, pilot, mathematician, medical scientist, physician, philologist, and geologist. The urban girls also put three academic jobs in the top ten (physicist, university teacher, and philosopher), whereas the rural girls showed a preference for three technical specialties (chemical, radio, and mechanical engineer).[25] These findings are suggestive of the high aspirations of girls graduating from Soviet secondary schools and of the diversity of occupations that they feel are accessible to them.

There is considerable agreement among boys and girls on the most attractive and least attractive jobs: both rate work in agriculture and in services as least desirable and the professions requiring a specialized secondary or higher education (e.g., doctor, scientist, engineer) as most desirable. However, boys and girls diverge markedly in their evaluations of the relative attractiveness of various types of occupations. Boys tend to rank workers' occupations higher than girls do, favoring, for example, such jobs as locksmith, mechanic, tractor or combine operator, steel founder, and mechanical engineer. Girls, on the other hand, clearly favor nonmanual (*sluzhashchie*) work. "Feminine" preferences include positions in the fields of literature, art, culture, education and medicine. Among secondary-school students aspiring to professional positions, boys tend to be most strongly drawn to technical fields, to put work in the natural sciences in second place, and to regard the humanities as least desirable. In contrast, girls find the humanities most attractive, place the natural sciences in second place, and consider technical work least attractive.[26]

In evaluating occupations, Soviet school children appear to give considerable attention to what they perceive to be the "opportunities for creativity"

figures are from A. V. Zosimovskii, "An Interesting Experiment (Experience in Instruction in a Specialized School)," in Ablin, p. 127. For an excellent general discussion of these schools, see John Dunstan, "An Educational Experiment: Soviet Mathematics and Physics Boarding Schools," *Soviet Studies*, 27 (Oct. 1975), pp. 545–73.

[25] V. V. Vodzinskaia, "Orientations Toward Occupations," in Murray Yanowitch and Wesley A. Fisher, eds. and trans., *Social Stratification and Mobility in the USSR* (White Plains, N.Y., 1973), p. 172, Table 7.

[26] See Murray Yanowitch and Norton T. Dodge, "The Social Evaluation of Occupations in the Soviet Union," *Slavic Review*, 28 (Dec. 1969), pp. 619–43; M. N. Rutkevich and F. R. Filippov, *Sotsial'nye peremeshcheniia* (M, 1970), pp. 113–14; Vodzinskaia, p. 171, Table 6; and V. N. Shubkin, *Sotsiologicheskie opyty* (M, 1970), pp. 174–75, 185–86.

in a given type of work. In this regard, too, boys and girls differ. Girls, for instance, think that work as a kindergarten teacher, in culture and education, in philology, and even in nonmechanized agricultural jobs afford greater opportunity for creativity than boys do. Conversely, they tend to downgrade technical vocations that boys regard as more creative, such as automatic equipment setter, repair mechanic, radio technician, and radio engineer. Significantly, all the occupations that the boys consider relatively creative are linked with mechanical operations. These differences, says the sociologist V. V. Vodzinskaia, "testify to the presence of definite stereotypes in the perception of 'masculine' and 'feminine' work."[27]

As a rule, rural girls have more modest aspirations than their urban counterparts; they are much more likely to want to become a primary- or secondary-school teacher, for example, than a physicist or some other type of scientist. For a great many of these girls, vocational aspirations are closely bound up with the desire not only to rise in social status, but to move to town. Moreover, recent surveys of young villagers conducted in four provinces of the RSFSR show that girls far surpass boys in their aspirations, and in fact were twice as likely to respond that they wished to graduate from a *tekhnikum* or *vuz* (higher educational institution) and then work either in town or in the countryside in a nonagricultural specialty. Boys, on the other hand, much more often expressed the desire to work in agriculture or to become urban workers.[28]

In the past decade, Soviet sociologists and planners have become aware of the discrepancy between young people's vocational aspirations and the economy's manpower needs. Many of the jobs that the young see as unattractive are precisely in the sectors deemed likely to be in greatest need of new workers, notably agriculture, industry, and services. Hence, the ambitions of growing numbers of young people to rise to higher positions or to leave the farm are a matter of some concern, invoking the specter of future labor shortages or high turnovers in critical branches of the economy. At the same time, many girls are frustrated in their desire to enter a *tekhnikum* or an institute, and not nearly as many village girls succeed in moving to town as would like to. As Tarasov and his colleagues found, employed rural women were much more likely than working men to say that they chose their work "by chance" rather than "according to a calling."[29] But then a great many urban women, too, must settle for work that they find "uncreative" and unsatisfying.

Another problem is that the desire for education—especially higher

---

[27] Vodzinskaia, pp. 175, 178 (Table 8).

[28] A. F. Tarasov, V. A. Tikhonov, M. M. Marusin, V. G. Ignatov, V. N. Ovchinnikov, O. Iu. Mamedov, A. D. Gladkii, *Professional'naia orientatsiia sel'skoi molodezhi* (M, 1973), pp. 12–42. It is the better-educated youth, in particular, who are most likely to want to move to town. Iu. V. Arutiunian, *Sotsial'naia struktura sel'skogo naseleniia SSSR* (M, 1971), pp. 159, 171, 283.

[29] Tarasov et al., p. 66.

education—is often dictated by social considerations unrelated to the choice of a particular specialty. The possession of a diploma is associated with high social standing and respectability.

"I might have stayed on that job," Ira [a young woman in Iaroslavl] said with some emotion, "but there was no incentive to do so—no future in it. There will be new competitive exams in Moscow. My goal is to better myself. The trouble is that in our country people don't judge others by up-to-date standards but by stereotypes. A master barber's customers are not accustomed to considering him as someone with a good reputation. A doctor is trusted—but a hairdresser, not a bit. It is perhaps because the hairdresser has no diploma?"[30]

In striving to get an advanced education, girls may choose a school simply because the standards are relatively low and the competition less intense, regardless of whether they feel particularly suited for that school's specialty.[31] As a girl student at a technological institute put it: "If only you knew how bored, how sick of it I am. . . . But what can we do, really? We girls look at it this way: If we can't get into the medical institute or the pedagogical institute, what's left? Only the technological institute!"[32]

The problem of high aspirations and "unrealistic" plans is not a new one, though it became especially acute in the 1960's as more and more young people finished secondary school. The school reforms enacted under Khrushchev in 1958 were designed to train young people for needed occupations and to overcome their evident disdain for manual labor. Vocational training was incorporated within the general-educational school; every school in effect became a "polytechnic" in which pupils learned a trade. But this system was rejected as unpractical in the mid-1960's: too few of the pupils ended up using the skills they had learned; parents, children, and pedagogues alike felt that work training diverted the pupils from the "serious" task of study; and in terms of the benefits derived, the program was considered too costly.

Since then, some schools have introduced vocational guidance programs to reduce the discrepancy between aspirations and possibilities. Pupils now learn about various trades, and those who leave school are referred to employment agencies. Concurrently, the government has embarked on a policy of expanding and upgrading the vocational-technical schools, with an emphasis on training workers in the specific trades needed by the economy. An increasing number of eighth-grade graduates are expected to go to these schools, whose total enrollment increased 88 percent to 1.4 million between 1966 and 1975.[33]

---

[30] I. Ovchinnikova and I. Preslovskaia, "Kem khochesh' byt'?," *Izvestiia*, Feb. 6, 1973, p. 5 (see trans. in *CDSP*, 25, no. 6, p. 12).

[31] Rutkevich and Filippov, p. 244; V. T. Lisovskii and A. V. Dmitriev, *Lichnost' studenta* (L, 1974), pp. 43–44.

[32] Ovchinnikova and Preslovskaia, p. 12.

[33] F. R. Filippov, *Obrazovanie v usloviiakh razvitogo sotsializma* (M, 1976), p. 33. Though

THE IMPACT OF SOCIAL ORIGINS ON PERFORMANCE
AND ASPIRATIONS

The kind of family and the community in which a girl grows up exert a marked influence on her academic achievement and educational plans. Generally speaking, the material and cultural advantages enjoyed by girls from better-educated, more well-to-do families are reflected early on in their school years. They not only get better grades than their less privileged age-mates, but have higher aspirations and receive more support from their families in pursuing their education.[34]

Rural girls are particularly disadvantaged. For a start, they are more likely than their urban sisters to come from low-income families or to have parents with low educational levels. But beyond this they are more likely to attend small, understaffed schools whose teachers have low qualifications. In addition to these handicaps, the graduates of rural schools are "in an unequal position compared with the youth from large towns, where there is a broad range of possibilities for acquiring knowledge (olympiads, special schools, lecture courses, television broadcasts, the system of tutoring, etc.)."[35] Still, the great majority of rural girls now complete at least eight years of schooling, and the gap between town and country has been reduced as the average level of schooling of rural youth has risen. However, girls from the villages still lag well behind urban girls beyond the secondary-school level. In many cases this may be because they have little confidence in their ability to pass entrance examinations and are reluctant to risk failure. In some cases, certainly, there are psychological and material impediments to their migrating to town and living away from their parents.[36]

---

these schools have had low prestige in the past, their standing is expected to rise as more are converted into "secondary vocational-technical schools" whose curriculum more nearly approaches that of the regular secondary schools. In some cities, such as Leningrad, the number of eighth-grade graduates taken into the upper grades of the regular school is being cut back substantially in order to direct pupils into the trade schools. See Richard B. Dobson, "Education, Equality, and the Economy: Problems of Leningrad Youth," introduction to Vasil'eva, *The Young People of Leningrad*, pp. vii–xxxi.

[34] For a more complete discussion of the influence of social background on educational attainment, see Richard B. Dobson, "Social Status and Inequality of Access to Higher Education in the Soviet Union," in J. Karabel and A. H. Halsey, eds., *Power and Ideology in Education* (New York, 1977), pp. 254–75, and by the same author, "Mobility and Stratification in the Soviet Union," *Annual Review of Sociology*, vol. 3 (1977), pp. 36–68.

[35] Lisovskii and Dmitriev, p. 44.

[36] S. N. Ikonnikova, *Molodezh': Sotsiologicheskii i sotsial'no-psikhologicheskii analiz* (L, 1974), p. 79. In 1970, 71 of every 1,000 women between the ages of 20 and 29 living in urban areas of the RSFSR had completed a higher education; in rural areas, the comparable figure was 40. USSR, TsSU, *Itogi 1970*, vol. 3, pp. 32–33, 56–57. This disparity in large measure reflects differences in educational opportunity between rural and urban women. But it is also true that rural girls who succeed in getting a higher education may find it possible (and certainly desirable) to continue living in town, a fact that would inflate the urban figures. On the other hand, the fact that a considerable proportion of the women *vuz* graduates are sent to work in the countryside on obligatory three-year assignments would raise the rural figures.

How important the social-occupational status of parents is to the educational attainment of their children is clearly reflected in a study by A. P. Avrov. Working with 1959 census returns for Sverdlovsk Province, Avrov found that the proportion of girls between the ages of 14 and 34 who had left school with no more than seven years of schooling increased markedly as the social-occupational status of the head of the household declined. The proportion of daughters who had gone no further than the seventh grade increased from 6 percent among professionals to 14 percent among semiprofessionals, 22 percent among skilled workers, and 41 percent among semiskilled and unskilled manual and nonmanual workers. On the other hand, girls from higher-status families were much more likely to receive a higher education: in this same broad age group, 40 percent of the girls from the households of professionals and 20 percent from those of semiprofessionals had gone to college, compared with only 8 percent and 5 percent for skilled and low-skilled workers, respectively.[37]

The majority of secondary-school graduates, girls as well as boys, hope to continue their education in a specialized secondary or higher educational institution. Four-fifths of the tenth graders polled in the city of Sverdlovsk in 1970 expressed that objective.[38] Though a slightly greater proportion of boys aspired to a higher education, the variations in educational aspirations according to the pupils' sex were very small compared with the differences related to the parents' social-occupational status. Three-quarters of the sons and daughters of professionals and semiprofessionals planned to enroll in a *vuz* following graduation, whereas just 13 percent were thinking of studying in a *tekhnikum* or vocational school, and still fewer were planning to go to work. Among working-class youth, three students out of ten were planning to go to college, a comparable number intended to enroll in a *tekhnikum* or vocational school, and nearly four out of ten said that they were planning to go to work.[39]

Not only are the daughters of well-educated parents more likely to aspire to higher education; they are more likely to pass the entrance examinations than other girls. Among applicants to Novosibirsk State University in 1968, for example, 55 percent of the women from families in which at least one parent had received a specialized secondary or higher education passed the examinations. This compares with a success rate of only 37 percent for girls

[37] *Rol' sem'i v vybore professii i formirovanii obrazovatel'nogo urovnia molodezhi (statistiko-ekonomicheskoe issledovanie)*, the author's abstract (*avtoreferat*) of an unpublished dissertation for the degree of Candidate of Sciences (L, 1970), p. 7.

[38] V. V. Ksenofontova, "Zhiznennye plany shkol'noi molodezhi i ikh realizatsiia," unpublished dissertation for the degree of Candidate of Sciences (Sverdlovsk, 1972), p. 229. Though high, this figure is consistent with what sociologists have found in other major towns. See, for example, Zev Katz, "Sociology in the Soviet Union," *Problems of Communism*, 20, no. 3 (May–June 1971), p. 35; and M. Kh. Titma, *Vybor professii kak sotsial'naia problema* (M, 1975), pp. 111–16.

[39] Ksenofontova, pp. 94, 229.

whose parents had gone no further than secondary school.[40] According to the 1970 Sverdlovsk study, three-fifths of the tenth-grade graduates who had succeeded in gaining admission to a *vuz* following graduation were from intelligentsia families, and many of the others were children of white-collar workers. Only a quarter were of working-class background.[41] Thus, because of their superior academic performance, higher aspirations, and motivation, children from better-educated, higher-status families were much more numerous among students in higher educational institutions, whereas working-class youth predominated in the *tekhnikums* and vocational-technical schools.

A girl's social origins not only affect her chances of advancing to the higher levels of the educational system, but also determine to some degree the type of education she is likely to receive. As a rule, the more "prestigious" a specialty, the higher the standards for admission to the institutions providing training in that discipline, and the higher the social status of the girls enrolled. Many surveys have shown that girls typically would rather be physicians than secondary-school teachers and would rather teach in a secondary school than in a primary school. That girls of higher social status are more successful than those of humbler origins in satisfying these preferences is clear from the composition of the student bodies of the corresponding educational institutions. In 1969, for example, 77 percent of the students enrolled in the lower-level teacher-training schools (*peduchilishcha*) and 52 percent of those in pedagogical institutes in the RSFSR were classified as workers or peasants or their children, against only 37 percent of that background in the medical schools.[42]

GIRLS IN VOCATIONAL SCHOOLS

The number of girls enrolled in vocational-technical schools (*professional'no-tekhnicheskie uchilishcha*) has grown rapidly, in both absolute

---

[40] L. F. Liss, "Sotsial'nye faktory, vliiaiushchie na protsess vybora profesii (Opyt konkretno-sotsiologicheskikh issledovanii)," unpublished dissertation for the degree of Candidate of Sciences (Novosibirsk, 1969), p. 398. Analyzing the results on the entrance examinations, Liss found that men had an appreciably higher success rate than women and noted: "The more difficult the requirements [in a given specialty], the greater is the gap between boys and girls in the results." For instance, among those applying in 1967 and 1968, three to five times as many boys as girls got excellent grades on the written mathematics exams (p. 241). He also found that the parents' educational and occupational level appeared to exert a stronger influence on the girls' chances of success than on the boys' (p. 254).

[41] Ksenofontova, p. 196.

[42] According to bookkeeping procedures of the Central Statistical Administration, students are classified either by their social origins or by their achieved social position. That is, students who had worked for two years (or perhaps less) are identified as "workers," "collective farmers," or "white-collar workers" according to their position in the work force. The others are classified according to the status of the head of the family household, usually the father. B. M. Cheknev, V. S. Nekhoroshev, L. A. Blinov, "Pervye itogi raboty podgotovitel'nykh otdelenii meditsinskikh institutov Rossiiskoi federatsii," *Sovetskoe zdravookhranenie*, 10 (1971), p. 42; A. K. Iurenko, "K voprosu ob izmenenii sotsial'nogo sostava sovetskogo studenchestva (na materialakh pedagogicheskikh institutov RSFSR)," in V. G. Generalov, ed., *Voprosy nauchnogo kommunizma: sbornik statei* (M, 1971), pp. 80–81.

and relative terms. Whereas in 1950 just 30,000 girls entered these schools, by 1960 the number had jumped to 135,000, and by 1970, to 476,000. Concurrently, the proportion of girls in the entering classes rose from 8 percent to 26 percent.[43]

The principal reason for the continued predominance of boys in these schools is their heavy focus on "masculine" occupations (e.g., miners, metallurgical workers, farm machine operators). This is particularly true of the agricultural schools, where boys account for 90 percent of the enrollment.[44]

A study of the sex composition of vocational schools in Odessa in the early 1960's revealed that girls tend to be heavily concentrated in the schools that provided training in "feminine" specialties. All of those schools in which there were no girls at all, or in which girls made up an insignificant fraction of the pupils (10–15 percent), taught "masculine," largely mechanical, trades. The girls, in contrast, gravitated toward the crafts, making up 80–95 percent of the pupils in the schools devoted to such skills as carpentry and cabinetmaking, sewing and design, and plastering and housepainting. In short, what emerged from the study was a distinct pattern of separate "feminine" and "masculine" occupations in which the overwhelming majority of girls are drawn into certain kinds of work and away from others.[45]

Nor is this pattern purely a matter of choice. Women's opportunities are evidently limited by both administrative barriers and employers' discriminatory practices. Though in 1967 restrictions on the enrollment of women in certain specialties were lifted, there continue to be limitations on their opportunities for training in a number of occupations, such as repairman. In addition, women are hampered by what the economist V. B. Mikhailiuk deplores as the doubtful practice of determining the sex composition of the entering classes of vocational schools on the basis of employers' orders. Employers may request only boys for jobs at which girls may be equally well suited. "As a result," she states, "girls study mainly those occupations in which simply by tradition female labor is widely employed."[46]

WOMEN IN SPECIALIZED SECONDARY, HIGHER, AND POSTGRADUATE EDUCATION

In selecting a specialty for advanced study, young women show decidedly different preferences than men. In 1968, for example, only 40 percent of the women applicants to five Leningrad *vuzy* wanted to specialize in a technical field, compared with 70 percent of the men. Within the univer-

---

[43] USSR, TsSU, *Narodnoe obrazovanie*, p. 222.
[44] N. I. Sidorov and M. T. Makhan'kova, *Effektivnoe ispol'zovanie truda molodezhi* (M, 1974), p. 41; Tarasov et al., p. 47.
[45] V. B. Mikhailiuk, *Ispol'zovanie zhenskogo truda v narodnom khoziaistve* (M, 1970), pp. 80–81.
[46] *Ibid.*, pp. 79–80.

sities, where women predominate, there is a similar differentiation between "masculine" and "feminine" specialties. For example, at Novosibirsk State University women constituted a clear and sometimes overwhelming majority of the applicants to certain faculties between 1962 and 1970, notably language study (89–94 percent), chemistry (71–76 percent, 1962–65; 59–62 percent, 1967–70), biology (66–74 percent), and history (62–66 percent). At the same time other faculties plainly held few attractions for women, among them applied mathematics (31–33 percent), geology (28–33 percent), and physics (10–14 percent).[47]

These preferences are also clearly reflected in the enrollment figures presented in Table 4. Both in the RSFSR and in the country as a whole, women have largely predominated over the years in the fields of education and the arts, economics and law, and health, physical culture, and sports, whereas men have predominated in agriculture and in the more technical fields linked with industry, construction, transportation, and communications. Within each field of study, women have been relatively more numerous in the specialized secondary schools. Indeed, as the table shows, in 1973 they accounted for more than 80 percent of the enrollment in the specialized secondary schools in the "primarily female" category.

In hard figures, the 50 percent of women among the students in higher educational institutions in 1974 translates to some 2.38 million; and the 53 percent in the specialized secondary schools to roughly 2.37 million. In the RSFSR, as the table indicates, the women's share was still higher, though only by a percentage point or two. In the Soviet Union as a whole in 1970, Russian women accounted for 63 percent of all female *vuz* students and 65 percent of all female students in the specialized secondary schools, thus considerably exceeding their representation in the general population.[48]

Notwithstanding the great number of women in higher and specialized secondary institutions, studies conducted in Leningrad, Novosibirsk, and elsewhere indicate that young women succeed far less often than men in their attempts to pursue a full-time education after secondary school. For example, though twice as many women as men applied for admission to five major *vuzy* in 1968, the entering class was roughly divided half and half: only one out of five of the women applicants, compared with one out of two

[47] D. A. Andreeva, G. A. Zhuravleva, T. G. Pospelova, "Obshcheobrazovatel'naia podgotovka abiturientov k postupleniiu v vuz," in L. N. Kell' and Iu. M. Misnik, eds., *Organizatsiia priëma v vuzy i tekhnikumy (iz opyta raboty leningradskikh vuzov i tekhnikumov)* (L, 1970), p. 97; L. F. Liss, "The Social Conditioning of Occupational Choice," in Yanowitch and Fisher, p. 282.

[48] Russian women's chances for a specialized secondary or higher education continue to exceed those of women from the traditionally Moslem communities, where despite the government's earnest efforts to "liberate" women, patriarchal traditions continue to make themselves felt. For all the undoubtedly impressive gains that women of Uzbek, Kazakh, Tadzhik, Turkmen, Azerbaidzhani, or Kirgiz nationality have made in the past 40 years, they continue to be seriously underrepresented in these two branches of the educational system. In 1970, for example, only a third of the students of Uzbek or Azerbaidzhani nationality at these levels and less than a quarter of the students of Tadzhik or Turkmen nationality were women. USSR, TsSU, *Narodnoe obrazovanie*, pp. 197–211.

TABLE 4

*Women as a Percentage of Students in Institutions of Higher Learning
and Specialized Secondary Schools in the USSR and the RSFSR,
by Field of Study, Selected Years*

Field of study and type of institution	USSR				RSFSR			
	1950	1960	1970	1974	1960	1965	1970	1974
Education, art, and cinematography								
Institutions of higher learning	71%	63%	66%	68%	69%	70%	71%	71%
Specialized secondary schools	77	76	81	81	83	86	85	84
Health and physical education								
Institutions of higher learning	65	56	56	57	60	58	60	60
Specialized secondary schools	85	84	87	88	87	90	90	91
Economics and law								
Institutions of higher learning	57	49	60	62	49	53	61	62
Specialized secondary schools	73	75	83	84	80	84	88	89
Industry, construction, transportation, and communications								
Institutions of higher learning	30	30	38	40	31	32	40	41
Specialized secondary schools	35	33	40	40	35	37	43	42
Agriculture								
Institutions of higher learning	39	27	30	32	30	27	34	36
Specialized secondary schools	41	38	37	37	42	38	41	41
Percentage of total enrollment								
Institutions of higher learning	53%	43%	49%	50%	45%	45%	51%	52%
Specialized secondary schools	54%	47%	54%	53%	49%	52%	56%	56%

SOURCES: Same as for Table 1.
NOTE: The data cover women enrolled in all programs (day, evening, and correspondence) at the beginning of the academic year.

of the men, gained admission.[49] That same year half of the boys but less than a third of the girls who graduated from secondary schools in Leningrad became full-time students in higher educational institutions in the fall. Conversely, half of the girls but just over a third of the boys went to work, a

[49] Andreeva et al., p. 97. Much the same pattern was found among applicants to Moscow *vuzy* in 1966. See V. S. Nemchenko, G. I. Shinakova, L. S. Belkina, R. P. Kolosova, and G. M. Kochetov, *Professional'naia adaptatsiia molodezhi* (M, 1969), p. 46.

distribution that is particularly anomalous considering that fewer girls—
and an insignificant 0.6 percent at that—expressed a desire to work full-
time after graduation. When these boys and girls were asked why they
had gone to work, the boys more often spoke of a lack of desire to continue
their studies and of a wish to be independent. More of the girls failed to pass
the entrance examinations for a *vuz*, though their grades were on the average higher than the boys'. Comments the sociologist E. K. Vasil'eva, who
collected these data: "It is conventional to consider women's being burdened with housework and their concern for children as the basic reasons
for the continuing inequality in their position. But certainly among tenth-
grade graduates few of the girls are married and still fewer have children. It
would be incorrect to explain the existing position [of women] by [imputing]
less of a desire among girls to continue their study."[50]

Evidently, one of the reasons that women are not as successful in realizing their plans for higher education is that they are so strongly oriented
toward the fields of medicine, teaching, and the humanities, where the
openings are more limited than in many of the technical disciplines, and
have been increasing at a much slower rate. Accordingly the competition
for entry into these fields is especially fierce; the result, as Vasil'eva notes, is
that "even though a woman in a large town realizes her equal right to education, she achieves it through additional personal effort as compared with a
man."[51] Which is to say that more of the women may find it necessary to
combine study with part-time work or to sit for the entrance examinations
over and over in their attempts to gain admission.

Moreover, high marks in the examinations do not necessarily assure enrollment. In some cases, a quota system or preferential admissions policy
for men is used to reduce the percentage of women admitted. Norton Dodge
was told by a medical official that "once the cut-off score on the entrance
examination had been determined, all men with this score were accepted
before the remaining vacancies were filled by women." This practice,
Dodge goes on to explain, arises out of the Soviet planners' concern with
economic rationality, or more bluntly, with maximizing the return on the
heavy costs of training.[52] That such considerations dictate admissions practice is occasionally referred to in the Soviet press. Vasil'eva cites, in this
connection, an article in *Komsomol'skaia pravda* by a professor of pediatric
surgery, S. Doletskii, who freely admitted the practice of holding women to
more rigorous standards than men on the entrance examinations for medical school but who defended the practice on economic grounds:

Boys, and this must not be concealed, are accepted by a medical institute with lower
passing grades than girls. . . . However sad this may be, there are more difficulties

[50]Vasil'eva, *Sotsial'no-professional'nyi uroven'*, pp. 36, 46.
[51]*Ibid.*, p. 58. See also Iu. N. Kozyrev, "Potrebnost' naseleniia v vysshem obrazovanii i otbor
molodezhi v vuzy," in Lisovskii, p. 175.
[52]Dodge, pp. 113, 116–17.

with girls than boys in medicine. [Problems arise from women's] married life, [from their] inability to move at will when it comes to assignments after graduation [and their] leaving work temporarily and permanently when the family's interests are placed above professional ones, especially in those cases where material conditions permit. Boys may not always have more profound knowledge, they do not always know how to apply it, but so far as the future is concerned, they are, as a rule, turned into workers on whom one can more readily depend.[53]

Little information has been published on the use of sex quotas in *vuz* admissions. Consequently, it is impossible to assess the overall impact of such practices, but as Vasil'eva points out, they plainly "restrict women's social mobility."

Though women make up a high percentage of the *vuz* students, they are less likely than men to go on for graduate study. In 1950 women accounted for 39 percent of all graduate students in the USSR, but their share has since declined, to stand at 23 percent in 1960 and only 28 percent in 1974. No doubt the difficulties of combining advanced study with family responsibilities weigh heavily on women at this level.[54] Whether overt or more subtle forms of discrimination also play some part in this is difficult to establish.

Women are relatively more numerous among those earning the degree of Candidate of Sciences (the approximate equivalent of the American Ph.D.) than among those receiving the more selective degree of Doctor of Sciences.[55] As Norton Dodge has estimated elsewhere in this volume, women accounted for about a third of the candidate degrees and about a fifth of the doctorates awarded between 1971 and 1973. Among all holders of the candidate degree, the proportion of women increased from 25 percent in 1950 to 29 percent in 1960 and then declined to 27 percent in 1974. And though their proportion among doctors of science doubled over that period, rising from 7 percent in 1950 to 14 percent in 1974, they are still clearly far behind men in this respect.[56]

As in the case of advanced degree holders, there are far fewer women than men employed in teaching and research at the higher levels of responsibility. In 1974, for example, women accounted for half of the junior researchers and "assistants" but just 22 percent of the docents ("associate

---

[53] S. Doletskii, "Dva balla vysshe mechty," *Komsomol'skaia pravda*, Dec. 22, 1970, cited in Vasil'eva, *Sotsial'no-professional'nyi uroven'*, p. 60.

[54] USSR, TsSU, *Narodnoe obrazovanie*, pp. 272, 278. On the problem of the woman graduate student with a child, see Elena Tsugulieva, "A vinovat malysh," *Izvestiia*, Dec. 17, 1971, p. 3 (trans. in *CDSP*, 23, no. 50, pp. 26–27).

[55] As at the undergraduate level, women are unevenly distributed among specialites. In the pure sciences, women Candidates of Science have been strongly represented in chemistry and biology, but relatively weakly represented in physics and mathematics. In the applied fields, they have made up a sizable share of those in medicine, but only a small fraction in technology. In the humanities and social sciences, their representation has been strongest in literature and linguistics and in pedagogy. See Dodge, pp. 135–37.

[56] USSR, TsSU, *Narodnoe obrazovanie*, pp. 246, 271. USSR, TsSU, *Narodnoe khoziaistvo SSSR v 1974 g.* (M, 1975), pp. 143–44.

professors") and a mere 10 percent of the academicians and full professors. Yet low as these figures are, they nevertheless show some improvement since 1960, when the proportion of women in the last two categories was 17 percent and 7 percent, respectively.[57]

CONSEQUENCES AND CORRELATES OF EDUCATIONAL ATTAINMENT

It is certainly true that education is important for women's careers. Their ability to gain desirable positions—occupations that enjoy a certain prestige, afford self-expression, are interesting and "creative," and fetch good pay—depends in large measure on their educational preparation. Nonetheless, as V. B. Mikhailiuk points out, the implications of education are not the same for women as for men:

Because of their being burdened with housework and child-raising, women are often compelled to choose work, not according to their aptitude or even according to the specialty they acquired in the course of study, but according to "the force of circumstances." The proximity of the enterprise to the place of residence is most often indicated [as a limiting factor]. This is a not-insignificant reason for the fact that the range of occupational specialization is significantly wider among men than among women.[58]

Though the educational level of women approximates that of men, they tend to earn less and to contribute less to the family budget. They are much less likely to participate in "rationalization" and "innovation" at work than men of comparable educational attainment, and increased education does not appear to result in greater participation in such activities, as it does with men.[59] Women are also much less likely to study part-time while working; as a result, men are more successful in raising their educational level and occupational qualifications. In most professional fields, men are more "productive" and are more likely to be promoted to important administrative positions.[60] In short, women continue to lag behind their male counterparts in earned income and in chances for advancement. This lag is largely attributable to their family responsibilities and the heavy obligations these entail—the "double burden" of a full workday, plus long hours of housework.

Yet the education a woman has received appears to have a significant impact on her everyday life. It is likely that in the course of schooling, Soviet women become more aware of the possibilities open to them, broaden their interests, acquire new cultural standards, and develop a greater desire for self-fulfillment outside of the family. Certainly the inverse relationship be-

[57] *Ibid.*   [58] Mikhailiuk, p. 72.
[59] *Ibid.*, p. 115; L. A. Gordon and E. V. Klopov, *Chelovek posle raboty: Sotsial'nye problemy byta i vnerabochego vremeni* (M, 1972), p. 205.
[60] Mikhailiuk, pp. 74–76, 112–13, 146. See also Sidorov and Makhan'kova, p. 41; and Dodge, *Women in the Soviet Economy.*

tween educational level and fertility has not gone unnoticed: surveys have shown that better-educated women consider the "ideal" family to be smaller, expect to bear fewer children, and actually give birth to fewer children than their less-educated sisters. V. A. Belova explains, in terms familiar to Western demographers, that women with a low educational level do not necessarily value children more than the more highly-educated, but rather put a lower "cost" on what is required for their upbringing:

Parents, as a rule, strive to give their children an education that is no lower than their own. Therefore, as the parents' educational level rises, their standards for the minimum needed in the upbringing of each child rises, too. Not only is there an increase in material expenditures; there is also an increase in the expenditure of time, which is no less important for a woman with considerable professional interest in her work. Thus, the "cost" of raising each child grows.[61]

Better-educated women are far less inclined than the more poorly educated to believe that endless hours of housework are simply the "woman's lot," and many devote much less time to housework each week. In the view of the Soviet sociologists L. A. Gordon and E. V. Klopov, the educated woman is more apt to acquire various labor-saving devices like a vacuum cleaner and a washing machine, not simply because she typically earns more money than the average woman, but because having higher cultural standards and more diverse interests, she "de-emphasizes" housework.[62]

These differences in values are reflected in the way in which women with different educational attainments spend their leisure time or establish social relationships. Better-educated women are quite "active" in their cultural pursuits. They spend less time watching television and more time reading newspapers and books then their less-educated sisters. They also go to the theater and ballet more often and devote more time to independent study. And because they typically establish many of their friendships on the basis of these interests, they are not inclined to depend as heavily on neighbors and relatives for their social contacts as the less-educated woman is wont to do.[63]

The fact that better-educated women (like Soviet women in general) tend

---

[61] V. A. Belova, *Chislo detei v sem'e* (M, 1975), p. 142. Belova also refers to a survey showing that in general the more highly educated a woman becomes, the less she expects to have the number of children she characterizes as "ideal" (p. 140). Of course, many factors other than educational level affect fertility rates. Urbanization, for example, is associated with a decrease in fertility rates and with a narrowing of the differences in birthrates among women of different educational levels. See R. I. Sifman, *Dinamika rozhdaemosti v SSSR* (M, 1974), pp. 135–36.

[62] *Chelovek posle raboty*, pp. 280, 285–87. Gordon and Klopov find the correlation between the level of education and the ownership of household appliances "all the more curious, since in the workers' milieu a high degree of education is by no means always connected with substantial differences in family well-being" (p. 111). See also A. G. Kharchev and S. I. Golod, *Professional'naia rabota zhenshchin i sem'ia* (L, 1971), p. 79.

[63] Gordon and Klopov, pp. 167, 170–72, 174–76. See also Tables 27, 28, 30–34, 54–55 in the *Prilozhenie* to *Chelovek*; and Kharchev and Golod, pp. 101–3, 108–9.

to marry men of approximately the same educational attainment has a direct bearing not only on the family's standard of living, but also on its cultural standards and style of life. It is commonly believed that the relationship between more highly educated couples is likely to be relatively "egalitarian" compared with the clearly patriarchial pattern of the traditional Russian household. To the extent that this is true, it appears to be due not so much to the husband's assuming some of the tasks that have conventionally been defined as women's work as to the wife's freeing herself from housework and pursuing broader interests and activities. Do better-educated women succeed in gaining more help from their husbands in looking after the children? Not according to Kharchev and Golod. In fact, their survey of working women in Leningrad and Kostroma indicates that the reverse is true: only 46 percent of the women who had special technical training reported that their husbands helped with the children, compared with 66 percent of those in low-skill occupations. This finding came as a surprise to the researchers, who comment: "With an improvement of the methodology, this result might change, since in all likelihood it is affected by the fact that as women's level of skill and education rises, their demands on other members of the family and, consequently, the standards by which they measure the degree of help also rise." [64] Educated women, that is, are probably more demanding of their spouses than other wives. [65]

CONCLUSION

In a broad historical perspective, there is no question that the Soviet Union's educational policies have contributed to greater equality between the sexes and to women's social advancement. Not only has the state bent itself to give all women the rudiments of education; it has actively encouraged them to pursue more advanced training. And the successes of its policies cannot be denied: today young women in the USSR have reached a higher educational level, on the average, than men; and in the work force, women outnumber men among professional and semiprofessional workers. Moreover, by international standards, the country has a very high representation of women in such fields as engineering and science, thanks in part, no doubt, to the fact that girls had been exposed from early schooldays to a curriculum heavily weighted toward mathematics and technical subjects.

However, more recent modifications of the curriculum, which allow pupils in the upper grades of the general-education school somewhat more latitude in the choice of subjects, may result in a sharper division between

[64] *Profesional'naia rabota zhenshchin*, pp. 90–91. Compare Arutiunian, p. 216.

[65] This may be true, but the notion that better-educated or higher status couples are more egalitarian than the average man and wife in the USSR is certainly put in doubt by Michael Sacks' analysis of Soviet time-budget research. Sacks finds that the degree of inequality (as measured by the amount of time men spend on housework divided by the amount women spend) does not decrease in families where the spouses are more highly educated, and indeed may even increase. See Michael P. Sacks, *Women's Work in Soviet Russia* (New York, 1976).

girls and boys. When given a choice, the Russian schoolgirl would probably take an "elective" in language study, for instance, rather than radio electronics, whereas a boy would be inclined to do the opposite. Aside from this, there are still certain differences in the standard curriculum which reinforce traditional conceptions of sex roles. Thus girls, but not boys, are taught sewing and cooking in preparation for their later role as homemakers.

The deeply entrenched sex distinctions in society at large continue to be mirrored, too, in boys' and girls' evaluations of occupations, which determine in some measure their actual distribution in the educational system and in the work force. The resulting occupational distribution is viewed as far from ideal. As we noted, some educators regard the feminization of the teaching profession as undesirable because women teachers seem less successful in providing appropriate models for boys and in instilling discipline in them, and other authorities express the view that the predominance of women among doctors is economically unsound. In order to increase the number of men entering these specialties, admissions committees may give preference to men over women applicants who are no less well qualified.

As in other countries, a woman's social origins continue to bear heavily upon the amount or type of education she receives. By the late 1960's, indeed, the issue of inequality of opportunity among social groups had come to be recognized as a serious social problem. In response, the government has made a renewed effort to improve the quality of rural schools and their teaching staffs and has affirmed that rural youth should be given preference in admission to certain specialties needed in the countryside. If properly implemented, these measures should help reduce the gap in opportunities between children who grow up in towns and in villages.[66]

Addressing itself to the problem, the government also took steps in 1969 to establish preparatory divisions at higher educational institutions that would provide remedial training for various categories of "disadvantaged" youth—those who have been working, who have grown up on collective farms, or who have served in the armed forces. Since then, the number of programs has proliferated, and a growing share of the college students have passed through them. The programs' overall effectiveness, however, continues to be a matter of dispute, for a large number of the graduates do not measure up to the regular academic standards and drop out before completing their degree. Furthermore, it is far from clear that the programs are serving mainly those young people who are disadvantaged because of their social origins, as opposed to those who went to work simply because they failed entrance examinations the first time around. Even more difficult to

[66] Statement of the CC CPSU and Council of Ministers of the USSR, "O merakh po dal'neishemu uluchsheniiu usloviikh raboty sel'skoi obshcheobrazovatel'noi shkoly," in Abakumov et al., pp. 243–46, and Rutkevich and Filippov, pp. 145–47.

assess is the impact on women's opportunities, owing to the lack of published information on the number of women in such programs.[67]

In the view of some educators, recent changes in entrance standards may improve women's chances for admission to higher educational institutions. In 1972, it was decided that an applicant's secondary-school grades should be given equal weight along with grades on entrance examinations and that the Russian-language composition should be deemed as important as any other examination. The net result, some judge, is to increase women applicants' chances, since they tend to get higher grades in secondary school and to express themselves better in written work.[68] It seems unlikely, however, that this will lead to a marked increase in women's representation in the student body, which for several years has been close to 50 percent. For one thing, the preparatory programs, for which demobilized servicemen are eligible, may draw in a larger share of males, and the preferential treatment given to male applicants in such fields as medicine and teaching would also work to the men's advantage.

To assure all Soviet women equal access to advanced education, it remains necessary to reduce differences in opportunity for women from various social groups, as well as the still pronounced disparity between Russian women and women of other nationalities, especially those belonging to Central Asian ethnic groups. Beyond this, there is clearly room to give women more opportunities for postgraduate training and for promotion at work. Until, however, role conceptions themselves are fundamentally changed, the responsibilities of home and family will still fall mainly upon the woman, and she will have by no means as much time or energy to devote to further study or to professional advancement as will a man with comparable training. Given the persistence of traditional conceptions of women's roles and the current discussion about the importance of women as mothers, it is unlikely that abrupt changes will occur.

[67] Rutkevich and Filippov, pp. 145–47; Lisovskii and Dmitriev, pp. 46–47; Dobson, "Social Status"; Dobson, "Education, Equality, and the Economy."

[68] "School Grades to Figure in Admissions: New Rules for Admission to Higher Educational Institutions," *Pravda*, March 15, 1972, p. 6; partial trans. in *CDSP*, 24, no. 11, p. 29. See also "The Grade Average," *Izvestiia*, May 25, 1974, p. 5; partial trans. in CDSP, 26, no. 21, p. 10.

Mollie Schwartz Rosenhan

Images of Male and Female in Children's Readers

I love grandmother's hands. . . .
Oh, how many wonders do these hands create?
Now they are ripping, now sewing, now sweeping,
Now making something.
How tastily they toast the bread!
How thickly they sprinkle the poppy seeds!
How roughly they scrub the steps!
And so tenderly they caress—

Grandfather knows many true stories and fables:
About the moon and sun, about wild beasts and birds.
I ask him different questions:
Where? What for? Soon? How many? Why?
My grandfather can answer any question. . . .

IS EVERYBODY'S grandmother a paragon of domestic virtue, whose most remarkable attributes radiate from her hands—that is, from her excellence at household tasks? And what of the universal grandfather? Is he truly omniscient, the ultimate fount of knowledge and the implicit source of validation?

And what does it matter? These are, after all, simplistic little stories taken from the opening pages of a first-year reading book.[1] These are innocuous little entertainments, designed to provide an insignificant vehicle for the really important task: a lesson in syntax, in consonant blends, in rhyme or some other critical aspect of language.

This paper argues that it does indeed matter, that the insignificant vehicle itself has some pedagogical function, even though it may initially appear extraneous and petty. Whether or not the individual child's grandmother or grandfather is like the grandmother described is secondary (as is the question of whether or not a child even has grandparents). What is primary is that a normative grandfather and grandmother are being defined. And the normative definition is simultaneously a description of sex-appropriate traits. Grandmother and grandfather are distinct and different. Grandmother's place is associated with home and hearth. She excels in women's tasks. Her skillful and caressing hands provide the physical and

---

[1] L. Kvetko, "Babushkiny ruki," and R. Gamzatov, "Moi dedushka," two sequential poems in M. S. Vasil'eva, L. A. Gorbushina, E. I. Nikitina, and M. I. Omorokova, *Rodnaia rech'* (M, 1972), pp. 17–18.

emotional nurturance that have long been identified with the female. The grandfather's place is in the world. He knows of "moon and sun . . . beasts and birds." His rationality and knowledge are both traits commonly defined as male. However subtly, appropriate models of male and female have been presented to the child.

The awareness that childhood education is a potent tool in creating particular kinds of adults is not new. In the Soviet case, Lenin early indicated his sensitivity to the role of education in creating "the new Soviet citizen." Addressing the First Congress of Teachers in 1918, he declared: 'The victory of the Revolution can only be consolidated by the school—the training of future generations will anchor everything won by the Revolution." [2] Krupskaia, who had been concerned with the nature and role of education in social democracy even before the Bolshevik seizure of power,[3] devoted a great part of her subsequent work to educational theory. In a speech to the Young Communist League she stated: "Our kindergartens and schools should serve as models of how children should be brought up as a new people, as builders of socialism."[4] This consciousness of the function of education is a continuous motif in the history of Soviet educational theory, manifesting itself not only in official rhetoric but also in the most practical and basic ways. For example, it is transformed into detailed, programmatic instructions in the teachers' manuals in daily use in Soviet schools.[5] Each game, each song, each dance, each little administrative ritual is designed to teach a socially desirable value and/or behavior (e.g., caring for the next younger age cohort, restraining aggression, subordination to the collective). Almost all Western investigators are impressed with the facts that classroom decorum, materials employed, and methods of discipline all are geared to be in harmony with explicit official objectives.[6]

Education in the Soviet Union is an integral part of the total *vospitanie* (upbringing) of the individual. Though specific teaching methods and plans of school organization have fallen in and out of vogue, there has been a continuous desire to blur the boundaries between home and school, to unify learning and labor, and to join formal knowledge with experience. This paper is concerned with one aspect of *vospitanie*: the socialization of children into appropriate sex-role behaviors, with particular emphasis on this process as it relates to the present and projected status of women. Recent American scholarship on sex-role differentiation has tended to focus

[2] Lenin, quoted in Manya Gordon, *Workers Before and After Lenin* (New York, 1941), p. 433.

[3] See, e.g., Krupskaia's essay "Public Education and Democracy" (1915).

[4] N. K. Krupskaia, "About Youth," in her *On Education* (M, 1940), p. 181.

[5] See, e.g., Henry Chauncey, ed., *Soviet Pre-School Education, Vol. 2, Teacher's Commentary* (New York, 1969). For the program intended for school-age children, see *Programma vospitatel'noi raboty shkoly* (M, 1960).

[6] See Urie Bronfenbrenner, *Two Worlds of Childhood* (New York, 1972); Susan Jacoby, *Inside Soviet Schools* (New York, 1974); and Kitty Weaver, *Lenin's Grandchildren: Preschool Education in the Soviet Union* (New York, 1971).

on consciousness and socialization techniques, rather than simply on economic and political conditions. Though sex-role socialization occurs in many ways, one of the strongest is observational learning—in this case, modeling. The kinds of stories children read, for example, tacitly teach children not only about language arts, but about the kinds of roles boys and girls are expected to assume. The central and ancillary characters in the story—the roles they act, the social functions they fulfill, and the rewards they obtain—communicate to each child a template of expected behaviors. They channel a child's aspirations, directing fantasy and covert rehearsal in directions that will obtain social approval.

In this study I examine the content of four children's readers used in Soviet Russian schools during the primary years in order to explore, first, the nature of Soviet sex-role stereotypes and, second, the relationship between these stereotypes and the realities of the position of contemporary Soviet women. Some of the behavioral categories developed by earlier American researchers have been incorporated in this study in the hope that some meaningful comparisons might be made. I have also added categories of behavior that seem more important in Soviet than in American society. The readers examined here include a primer, two first-year books, and one second-year book, all published in 1971 or 1972, and all selected at random from ten or so books in use in Russian schools during the 1973–74 academic year.[7] All the texts were taken from different series. A total of 213 stories were analyzed, only those stories having human actors being rated.[8] All of these human characters were counted and recorded—no matter how brief their appearance—and every discrete behavior by each was listed. Information about whether the character was a parent was also noted, as were the environments of the stories. Finally, the occupations given for males and females were listed (see Table 1).[9]

Assessing the nature of a behavior proved difficult because of the virtual impossibility of creating ironclad definitions and mutually exclusive categories. For example, should feeding birds in winter be considered "nurturant" behavior? Is aiding a child with a homework problem that should be

---

[7] The four readers are the primer *Bukvar'* (M, 1972); the first-year book *Rodnaia rech'* (referred to as *Native Speech* in the text); another first-year book by M. S. Vasil'eva, V. M. Fedosenko, M. I. Omorokova, et al. entitled *Zvëzdochka* (M, 1971) (cited as *Little Star* in the text); and the second-year book edited by E. I. Nikitina and entitled *Rodnoe slovo* (4th ed., M, 1972) (referred to as *Native Word* in the text).

[8] Stories about nature, technology, and agriculture were excluded from the sample, as were stories in which the main character was of unspecified sex (first person narrative and poems), adaptations of folk tales and classical writings from prerevolutionary Russia, and lyric poetry. Although an argument might be made for the inclusion of tales about anthropomorphized animals and elements of nature (such as "Grandfather Frost"), there are complications of gender and traditional expression in the Russian language that might distort the findings. The figure of 213 represents some 40 percent of the total number of stories in the four books.

[9] My research design has been influenced by a number of recent studies on sex-role stereotyping, though unfortunately there is no consensus on the significant variables to be examined. The pioneer study, which included data on sex differences, was Irwin Child, Elmer

TABLE 1
Occupations Mentioned in the 213 Stories Analyzed, by Sex

Male		Female
Bus driver	Factory worker*	Factory worker*
Gardener	Policeman	Teacher
Militiaman	Gatekeeper	Tractor driver
Soldier	Test pilot	Construction engineer
Frontier guard	Hunter	Doctor*
Draftsman	Messenger	Postal worker
Doctor*	Shopkeeper	Operator of thresher
Worker	Metalworker	Dishwasher
Combine driver	Submarine instructor	Dressmaker
Ship captain	Party leader	Secretary
Sailor	Poet	Milkmaid
Machine gunner	Steel foundry worker	Worker in chicken house
Military officer		
Typesetter		
	TOTAL: 26	TOTAL: 12

NOTE: Occupations followed by an asterisk were mentioned for both males and females.

done alone "altruistic"? Table 2 lists the behavioral categories I developed and the definitions I used for them.

Male characters appeared more frequently than females in these stories, so that there was a proportionately greater likelihood of a given behavior being associated with a male than with a female. Consequently, the incidence of each behavior for females was multiplied by the ratio of male to female characters (this was done separately for the child and adult categories). Next, a binomial test was computed for each behavior, with the a priori probability of each behavior being associated with either gender set at .5. Table 3 lists the results, with behaviors grouped according to whether they were primarily associated with females, males, or neither sex. The findings are dramatic: the stories present a view of adult males as sources of directive and instructive behavior, altruistic, and politically involved. The male has a favorable self-image and is concerned with his advancement. He has potential for leadership. Though male children are sometimes selfish and antisocial, this is not true of male adults. A boy rarely engages in nurturant behavior and only infrequently participates in household tasks. The

Potter, and Estelle Levine, "Children's Textbooks and Personality Development: An Explanation in the Social Psychology of Education," *Psychological Monographs*, 60, no. 3 (1946), pp. 1–54. For more recent studies, see Marjorie Uren, "The Image of Women in Textbooks," in Vivian Gornick and Barbara Moran, eds., *Women in Sexist Society: Studies in Power and Powerlessness* (New York, 1972), pp. 318–28; Lenore J. Weitzman and Diane Rizzo, *Images of Males and Females in Elementary School Textbooks* (New York, 1974); Lenore J. Weitzman, Deborah Eifler, Elizabeth Hokada, and Catherine Ross, "Sex Role Socialization in Picture Books for Pre-School Children," *American Journal of Sociology*, 77, no. 6 (May 1972); Women on Words and Images, *Dick and Jane as Victims* (Princeton, N.J., 1972); Carol Nagy Jacklin and Carl K. Tittle, "Sex Role Stereotyping in the Public Schools," *Harvard Educational Review*, 43, no. 3 (August 1973).

adult female, on the other hand, is heavily involved in traditional household tasks and nurturance in these stories. Women tend to be presented as emotionally expressive and supportive of the advancement of others, though relatively unconcerned with their own self-advancement. They tend to be careless. They also engage in more passive activities (reading, sitting, watching) than men do. Not only are they uninvolved politically, they are actually politically naive.

The difference in political sophistication and involvement of males and females is sufficiently startling to deserve further discussion. The nature of political models and activities in the stories was somewhat unexpected, in that I did not find a single story explicitly describing the activities of the Communist Party and its members today. The stories emphasized group solidarity, rather than individuating children for specific praiseworthy behavior.

TABLE 2

Behavioral Categories and Their Definitions,
with Examples

Nurturant: Caring for others (e.g., nursing, feeding, comforting)

Aggressive: Engaging in physical acts only (e.g., being destructive, hitting, pushing, shoving, breaking, as well as offensive military action)

Constructive/Productive: Making useful things (e.g., a snow hill for sledding)

Physically Exertive: Engaging in sports, hiking, farming, running, jumping, scrubbing; also heavy labor in general

Directive/Instructive: Showing someone how to do something, teaching, demonstrating

Problem-solving: Providing a solution to a specific, stated problem

Imaginative: Engaging in fantasy

Altruistic: Doing good for another individual or a group (e.g., sharing lunch, lending gloves)

Expressive of Emotion: Manifesting fear, joy, sorrow, etc.

Repressive of Emotion: Acting in the face of fear, restraining appropriate laughter and expression of pleasure, forcing back tears

Selfish/Antisocial: Being unwilling to share possessions, participate in group projects, do one's share of necessary labor

Validative: Praising an activity or skill, confirming the legitimacy of an idea or proposed activity

Leading: Initiating and being followed in an action

Conforming: Following the lead of others

Self-defining: Making statements, both positive and negative, about oneself

Politically Involved: Participating in political activities or organizations, attending demonstrations or parades, knowing the implications and political significance of actions

Politically Naive: Not participating in political activities when possible, being unaware of the political implications or significance of actions

Careless: Being unconcerned with the consequences of behavior

Planning: Showing forethought and a concern with the consequences of behavior

Household: Cooking, ironing, sewing, cleaning, washing, polishing

Child Care: General tending, i.e., custodial as distinguished from educational child-adult interactions

---

TABLE 3

Incidence of Component Behaviors for Male, Female, and Nonstereotyped
Children and Adults in the 213 Stories Analyzed

| | Incidence of behaviors | | | | P < | |
| | Children | | Adults | | | |
Type of behaviors	Female	Male	Female	Male	Children	Adults
Behaviors primarily						
associated with females						
Nurturant	18	13	58	13	—	.0001
Expressive of emotion	24	25	44	21	—	.003
Conformist	3	11	9	2	.03	.03
Self-defining, negative	4	0	2.3	0	.02	—
Politically naive	16	4	7	1	—	.04
Careless	14	15	5	0	—	.05
Household	45	7	57	1	.0007	.00003
Child care	13	5	78	6	—	.00003
Reading	9	6	9	1	—	.001
Listening	9	11	16	3	—	.002
Watching	9	11	19	6	—	.02
Supportive of others'						
advancement	0	3	23	13	—	.07
Behaviors primarily						
associated with males						
Physically assertive	25	54	30	36	.0008	—
Directive/instructive	6	15	28	68	.04	.0005
Altruistic	16	18	19	33	—	.05
Selfish/antisocial	4	20	2	7	.001	—
Leading	3	12	2	19	.02	.001
Self-defining, positive	3	6	2.3	8	—	.06
Politically involved	8	14	5	64	.06	.0001
Self-advancing	1	7	2	8	.04	.06
Behaviors not clearly						
associated with either gender						
Aggressive	4	10	9	12		
Constructive/productive	35	46	49	42		
Fantasy	13	12	2	1		
Problem-solving	25	21	16	21		
Repressive of emotion	4	6	12	5		
Validative	0	0	9	11		
Careful	10	10	19	16		
Sitting	7	5	7	2		

NOTE: The figures have been corrected for the disproportionate number of males to females in the stories by multiplying the absolute incidence of behaviors for females by the ratio of male to female characters.

Stories that presented specific models for imitation were of three kinds: those concerned with the revolutionary activity of Russian workers and of the Bolsheviks before 1917; those focused on "class-conscious" workers in contemporary capitalist states; and those centered on Soviet citizens engaged in such activities as visiting the Lenin Museum, attending a May Day Parade, or explaining some significant historical event to a child. This last category of stories, ostensibly intended to illustrate proper political consciousness, might as easily be seen as intended to instill in children a sense of patriotism.

There were 40 stories I considered political; 24 of these were rooted in the past, and only one, "Tania, the Revolutionary," had a female as its central character. In this story, Tania, a little girl, hides the type her father has used to print an illegal pamphlet in a pitcher of milk during a search by the tsarist police. Her quick thinking and action save her father from arrest. Yet Tania's mother is in no way involved with her husband's underground activities, is ignorant of the plans for an armed uprising, and is so thoroughly frightened of his participation that he reprimands her: "You are chattering nonsense! Are you not the wife of a Bolshevik? You dare to be a coward!"[10]

Tania's mother's behavior is not atypical. In *Little Star* there is a similar story, "Maiovka." In this tale, a male worker is also involved in the preparation of illegal pamphlets to be distributed at a May Day demonstration and is also visited by the police. This time the quick thinking of a male child saves the pamphlets and the father. The sole female to appear in the story is the worker's wife, who is the boy's mother. She does three things in the story: she "silently prepares dinner," she lies to the detective who comes to confiscate the leaflets; and she cries after the detective departs.[11]

All the stories about Lenin (fourteen) that are not about his family portray him as interacting with other males. In "Red Berries," which was printed in both *Native Speech* and *Little Star*,[12] Lenin is hiding with a Finnish worker in the countryside. His identity is known to the worker, but not to the worker's wife, who had not been asked in the first place about the stranger's joining the family. All the wife does in the story is cook and serve. The husband comes home late at night, having attended meetings of revolutionary workers. Two male workers come to move Lenin to another hiding place. For several days in October of 1917 the husband disappears to participate in the Revolution. Even those stories that emphasize Lenin's great love for children recall Lenin with male children.

In all four books, there was only one story about Krupskaia, and it was not among the stories commemorating the October Revolution, Lenin's Birthday, or May Day. Instead it was included in a section on International Women's Day. The story describes Krupskaia in exile and is concerned with her contribution as secretary of the newspaper *Iskra*—specifically, with her abilities to answer all the mail and to decipher codes.

The substantial participation of women in contemporary Soviet economic and political life makes the absence of women in significant roles in these children's stories all the more astounding. Beyond the implications of the behaviors presented in these books, there is the simple fact that male characters predominate. There were 118 child female characters but 167 child males. The gap widens in the presentation of adults: only 73 adult

[10] E. Vereiskaia, "Tania revoliutsionerka," in *Rodnoe slovo*, p. 73.
[11] M. Roomos, "Maiovka," in *Zvëzdochka*, pp. 170–75.
[12] A. Kononov, "Krasnye iagody," in *Rodnaia rech'*, pp. 146–48.

females appear, as opposed to 170 adult males. Indeed, the disparity grows with the sophistication of the reading materials. In the primer, males and females received fairly equal exposure: there were 57 girls and 49 boys, 12 adult females and 10 adult males. In *Little Star*, one of the first-year texts, there were 18 female and 33 male children, and 14 female and 43 male adults. In the second-year book, *Native Word*, the gap widens: there were 18 female to 47 male children; and only 23 female to 74 male adults.

The disparity in the incidence of male and female characters seems highly correlated with the complexity of the stories. In the primer, the stories are extremely simple. The child's limited vocabulary puts constraints on the development of a story line. Moreover, the child's introduction to printed words occurs most easily through stories that are readily identifiable as parts of his or her experience—going to the park, playing doctor, helping a younger child, and doing minimal chores around the house. In the first- and second-year readers, however, the stories grow longer and more complicated, and there is some character development. And it is here that males come to be an ever more dominant presence. Of course, there is no inherent reason for women to play diminishing roles as story line and plot thicken, but that is overwhelmingly the case.

After behaviors and numbers, there is the matter of environments. Though there are no significant differences in the settings where we find children in the stories, there are notable differences among adults. Women are found more often than men at home or at work; men are found more often than women in the out-of-doors and in political settings. And at work, men tend to have more varied and adventuresome occupations than women have.

Women were overwhelmingly identified in the stories as mothers and grandmothers, whereas men were less commonly identified as fathers or grandfathers. For example, 71 percent of the women were identified as the primary parent, whereas only 18 percent of the males were so identified. In total, 41 percent of all actions described for females involved fulfilling role obligations traditionally associated with women: child care, 18 percent; household tasks, 13 percent; and nurturance, 10 percent. The percentages for men performing these same three roles were 1 percent, 2 percent, and 3 percent, respectively.

Though the women in these texts are not exclusively mothers, they are without question primarily mothers. The stories often mention that the woman has a job outside the home, but they usually elaborate on her mothering role, not on her work role. In those few stories that do seek to transmit to the child knowledge of a woman's activities as a worker outside the home, the woman is generally described as a mother who is also a worker. One example is a poem called "Mama—The Tractor Driver."[13]

[13] A. Brodskii, "Mama—traktoristka," in *Rodnaia rech'*, p. 78.

Significantly, this poem does not appear with other stories having to do with agricultural labor but is included in a unit on International Woman's Day. Soviet men, on the other hand, are described in a broad spectrum of activities, almost all of which take place outside the home. Indeed, even when a man is pictured in a parental role it often involves taking his child to a parade or playing a game with the child.

The hierarchy of involvement as it emerges from these stories is clear. Women are mothers first and "something else" second. Very little richness of description or detail is assigned to women's jobs, whereas their mothering roles are elaborated. The lesson is possibly not lost on young Soviet readers: women have jobs, men have careers.

Two historical features of the Russian (and Soviet) consciousness should be noted in explaining the importance of the mothering role in the children's literature. The first is the cult of motherhood; the second is the unofficial policy of pronatalism.

The adoration of motherhood has been and continues to be a powerful theme in Russian literature. For Tolstoi, as an example, motherhood redeemed and even transformed woman's evil eroticism.[14] Even in contemporary Soviet literature the chaste, sacrificing, sheltering mother figure remains prominent. In Vera Dunham's words, "Without maternal worship, in whatever form, Russian lyricism would be unrecognizable."[15] We need not stop with literature. Krupskaia, the selfless and childless revolutionary, wrote that "Woman is either a mother or a prospective one. Maternal instincts are strong in her. These instincts are a great power and they bring joy to the mother, [who] is a born educator."[16] A contemporary sociologist has claimed that "the female, in general, is emotionally subtler and more sensitive than the male. From these [qualities] come the specifics of the maternal role."[17]

The matter of pronatalism is more complex. Other papers in this volume have pointed up the conflicts and contradictions that have arisen during the Soviet period as the theoretical commitment to women's liberation and control over their own bodies (as exemplified in early laws permitting abortions, for example) has come up against harsh demographic realities. Thus far the Soviet government has refrained from banning or limiting abortions and other birth-control measures, despite concern for the falling birthrate, and has adopted only positive inducements to increase family size. For example, there is a system of monetary incentives for "mother heroines" who produce large families.

Between the cult of motherhood and pronatalism, it is not surprising that,

[14]For an interesting exposition of this thesis, see Ruth Crego Benson, *Women in Tolstoy: The Ideal and the Erotic* (Urbana, Ill., 1973)

[15]Vera S. Dunham, "The Changing Image of Women in Soviet Literature," in Donald Brown, ed., *The Role and Status of Women in the Soviet Union* (New York, 1968), p. 65.

[16]Krupskaia, "About Youth," p. 150.

[17]I. S. Kon, "Zachem nuzhny otsy?" *Literaturnaia gazeta*, Feb. 28, 1973, p. 11.

in the children's readers, International Women's Day is metamorphosed into a sentimental Soviet version of Mother's Day. All the readers (except the primer) include a unit to celebrate March 8. Of the 23 separate stories and poems in these units, only four were concerned with women who were not identified as mothers; the story about Krupskaia (already described); one poem designed to impart the moral lesson that all old women should be treated as though they were one's own grandmother;[18] and two stories about Vera Vasil'evna, a physician who overcame her fear of heights when called upon to treat a sick child in a village so remote that she not only had to fly there but had to parachute out of the plane as well.[19] All of the remaining nineteen were specifically concerned with mothers. Only one focuses on a woman whose status as a mother is totally irrelevant to the theme of the story: this story, entitled "Galia's Mother," describes how during the Second World War Galia's mother (who is not identified in her own right), though wounded, inched her way across miles of frozen snow, through the fascist lines, to deliver a package to the Red Army.[20] The others are eulogies to Mother. The following excerpt, though especially sentimental, is not atypical.

Mama!

The most beautiful word on earth is "Mama." It is the first word a person utters and it rings in all languages with equal tenderness.

A mother has the kindest and most affectionate hands; they know how to do everything. A mother has the most loyal and sensitive heart; the love in it will never be extinguished, and it remains indifferent to nothing.

And no matter how old you are—five or fifty—you always need a mother—her affection—her opinion. And the greater your love for your mother, the happier and brighter your life.[21]

Another poem, actually called "Mother's Day," describes how a good child should treat his or her mother on her special day.[22]

The idealization of mothers, the strong sentiments of pronatalism, and the existence of a holiday celebrating women leads to an interesting and unfortunate distortion. Surely Krupskaia was not the only woman who had a role in the Revolution? Surely Galia's mother was not the only female hero of the resistance to fascism? Surely there are women who are major scientists, inventors, and engineers, and women with responsible roles in government?

What can the facts that most of the "celebration of women" is essentially a eulogizing of motherhood and that female heroes are, in large measure, absent from other sections mean? One is led to suspect that the failure to

[18] V. Oseeva, "Prosto starushka," in *Rodnaia rech'*, p. 79.

[19] E. Trukhin, "Chelovek zabolel," in *Rodnaia rech'*, pp. 80–82, and *Rodnoe slovo*, pp. 199–203.

[20] "Galina mama," in *Rodnaia rech'*, pp. 83–85.

[21] Z. Voskresenskaia, "Mama," in *Rodnoe slovo*, p. 193.

[22] "Mamin den'," in *Rodnaia rech'*, p. 76.

honor female heroes and to elaborate their autonomous, nonfamilial roles is not an oversight but a deliberate policy. Do the Soviet authorities fear that such honor and elaboration might undermine a significant feature of Soviet social organization?

The socialization of women as reflected in these samples of children's literature is consistent with, and sheds interesting light on, two apparent anomalies that others have noted regarding women in the Soviet work force. First, nearly 85 percent of Soviet women are estimated to work outside the home at present. Yet they are heavily concentrated in certain specific areas of the economy (such as health care, credit and insurance, and public services), and underrepresented in construction, industry, and transportation.[23] Although the specific pattern of sex-role stereotyping in the labor force is markedly different from that in the United States (women are well represented in certain branches of engineering, for example), such stereotyping does occur. Second, regardless of the sector in which they are found, women appear to cluster at the bottom of the occupational pyramid. This is not to say that some women are not found in positions of authority, leadership, and responsibility; but women tend to be underrepresented in higher echelons in relation to their numbers in the labor force.

With regard to the high concentration of women in the service sector, it has been suggested that women enter fields in which they feel most comfortable, and that service industries represent fields in which paid employment has psychological and substantive continuity with roles performed by the traditional homemaker.[24] To the extent that the data presented here speak to matters of socialization—and especially to covert rehearsal of sex-typed roles—this view finds support. Women are described in these stories as more concerned than men with the care of children, with cooking and food preparation, and with household tasks. Hence we should not be surprised to find that if women consider their families their primary responsibility and source of personal gratification, they will select those jobs that are most compatible with marriage and motherhood and avoid those jobs and promotions that would interfere with their first priority.[25]

Almost all Western observers consider the second anomaly mentioned above to stem in part from the extremely heavy burden placed on Soviet women as both full-time workers and wives and mothers. In the readers analyzed these dual roles showed up sharply. Both men and women were identified as workers, but only one adult male was described as engaging in household chores (seven male children were so described).[26] "The emanci-

[23] See Gail W. Lapidus, "USSR Women at Work: Changing Patterns," *Industrial Relations*, 14, no. 2 (May 1975); see also her paper in this volume.

[24] William Mandel, "Soviet Women in the Work Force and Professions," *American Behavioral Scientist*, 14 (Nov.–Dec. 1971), pp. 255–80.

[25] For a fuller discussion of the relationship between job and personal satisfaction, see the paper by Bernice Madison in this volume.

[26] One must be cautious in evaluating the greater incidence of male children engaging in household tasks, as compared with male adults. On the one hand, it might point to an in-

pation of women," in terms of labor, has freed women to assume male roles and responsibilities, but neither in theory nor in fact has the emancipation of women meant the assumption by men of traditional female roles and responsibilities. This "double burden" has broad implications. In studies of time budgets, women have been reported to have less time available for professional self-advancement than men.[27] Although only one story in my sample had self-advancement as its central theme, it had to do with how mother and children were quietly doing their chores (housework and homework) so as not to disturb Papa, who was studying for an examination.[28] In a survey made in 1960, women were found to have one hour less of free time each day than men, and also to have to make do with an hour less sleep.[29] There is little reason to believe that the relative pattern of time allocations has changed in the past fifteen years. And there can be little question about the basic thesis that the dual role of women, being both physically and psychologically depleting, accounts heavily both for their occupational choices and for their relative lack of upward mobility within the labor hierarchy. Precisely because women have dual roles (where men have mainly one), and precisely because their primary role is mother and their secondary role is "something else," women are less likely than men to be motivated to ascend to the top; rather, as our data suggest, their role is to support the advancement of others, which is consistent with the nurturance the cult of motherhood requires.

Performing household tasks, taking primary responsibility for child-rearing, and meeting the requirements of a full-time job have come to be viewed as an unjustly heavy burden on women by some within Soviet society itself. Natalia Baranskaia's novella *A Week Like Any Other*, published in 1969 in *Novyi Mir*, probably provides the most accurate portrayal of the frustration and frenzy experienced by that stratum of well educated, professionally involved Soviet women who take their maternal obligations very seriously and try to attain excellence in all their roles. The heroine, Olga, fears that she has failed both as a mother and as a professional, and her anguish is acknowledged as one that many Soviet women identify with. The anguish experienced by many women in the face of this double burden is considered an important component in both the rising divorce rate and the falling birthrate.[30]

---

creased awareness of the need to involve males in these tasks in a society where women work. On the other hand, children have always been expected to do chores in the home, with notions of the child as servant going back to medieval times. Most important, though the child recognizes himself as a child, his aspiration is to be an adult. And the adult male plays no role in the running of the household. It is reasonable to assume that the male child projects himself into an adulthood that will not include household tasks.

[27]G. V. Osipov and S. F. Frolov, "Vnerabochee vremia i ego ispol'zovanie," *Sotsiologiia v SSSR*, 2 (M, 1966), p. 238.

[28]A. Barto, "U papy ekzamen," in *Rodnaia rech'*, p. 16.

[29]Norton T. Dodge, *Women in the Soviet Economy* (Baltimore, Md., 1966), p. 93.

[30]See the paper by Bernice Madison elsewhere in this volume; see also Maia Ganina and Viktor Perevedentsev, "Neizbezhnost' garmonii," in *Literaturnaia gazeta*, Mar. 5, 1975, p. 10;

The solutions that have been proposed to improve the situation of Soviet women include suggestions to increase the number of child-care centers (and to design them to provide care for children at any time, not only while the mother is working), to expand public dining facilities, to inaugurate a convenience food industry, and to make available labor-saving appliances in greater numbers. Other proposals would alter female employment patterns by making more part-time work available, by shortening the work day, or by providing work that could be done at home.[31] Yet it is significant that all these solutions focus entirely on women and envision no expansion in the involvement of men in household and child-care tasks. Though they concede that women have rights to dignity and leisure, these proposed solutions are predicated on a view that the relationship between the sexes is based on complementary harmony, with separate spheres of activity. These spheres contain essentially the same types of behaviors we found in the reading texts for young children. This suggests strongly that the stereotyping in the texts reflects current reality and current attitudes. And to the extent that children are influenced by these models, we can expect the basic stereotypes to remain unchanged for a long time.

Women's problems continue to be defined as the specific problems of women, rather than as human problems that implicate and affect men and women equally. The specifically Soviet version of equality of the sexes assumes immutable differences that dictate differences in roles and social policy: males and females are accepted as having different natures, different psychologies, different strengths. Notions of basic sameness are alien and apparently repugnant to Soviet thought.

The ideological position on the relationship of the sexes, the tenacity of traditional roles that receive social support, and the continuation of pronatalist policies make it unlikely that androgyny—which has become a central goal for many Western feminists[32]—will be seriously considered in the Soviet Union as a possible avenue to "genuine emancipation" in the foreseeable future.

Vera Kuchina, "Odin rebenok v sem'e," *Literaturnaia gazeta*, Feb. 26, 1975, p. 12; Helen Desfosses, "Population Policy in the USSR," *Problems of Communism*, 22, no. 4 (July–Aug. 1973); and Helen Desfosses, "Demography, Ideology, and Politics in the USSR," *Soviet Studies*, 26, no. 4 (April 1976).

[31] Kon, "Zachem nuzhny otsy?"

[32] Androgyny refers to a unity of feminine and masculine characteristics within a single individual. Implying the broadest range of behaviors, attitudes, and goals, it has been a concept of great attraction to many feminists until very recently. In the last several years it has come to be questioned by some as insufficiently "radical," since it is based on the acceptance of masculine and feminine as separate, distinct traits. Some writers have substituted the term "sex role transcendence" for it. For a broader sense of the debate, see *Women's Studies*, 2 (1974) and *Women: A Journal of Liberation* (Spring 1975).

Bernice Madison

Social Services for Women: Problems and Priorities

THE MAJOR purpose of Soviet social service programs for women is to ensure that no woman is felt behind as the country develops, and that each is helped to realize her potential. The social services for women that I shall cover in this paper are broadly of two types: programs centered on income maintenance (such as social insurance), and personal services centered on developmental, rehabilitative, and access needs (such as adoption and marital counseling).[1]

For the sake of clearer analysis, I discuss these services in four sets based on the different roles women play: as wives, mothers, parents, workers. In practice, of course, some programs and the problems they address are interrelated and overlap; and provisions for women frequently determine what is provided for children and vice versa.

What I am interested in primarily is the services that are currently available in the USSR, and especially in the problems that arise when policy is implemented in practice and their import for the future. But to set the stage for this discussion, we may usefully begin with a few words about the historical development of social services for women and children under the Soviet system.

FROM THE REVOLUTION TO THE PRESENT

The years 1917–25 saw the passage of many laws to secularize marriage, liberalize divorce, and emancipate women and children. Women were given employment rights equal to those of men; pregnant women, nursing

---

[1] There are other, allied programs, primarily curative and educational, that might well have been included because of their influence on the character and the delivery of the services I discuss. Unfortunately, the constraints of space do not permit me to deal with them here.

mothers, and mothers with many children were granted special privileges; distinctions between legitimate and illegitimate children were erased; and child labor was abolished. But the resources provided for social services were so meager and the responsible administrative bodies in such a state of chaos that social welfare agencies could neither enforce the new laws nor effectively assist the large number of women and children who fell victims to the general social disorganization that engulfed the country during this period and continued into the 1930's.

In 1935 the government set out to restore family stability and to return the responsibility for the support of children to parents. To this end, it made modest family allowances available to mothers of large families; expanded the network of socio-legal bureaus established in 1933 to assist mothers to deal with social problems; greatly increased the number of preschools; strengthened the services for delinquent and handicapped children; improved institutional care; and initiated guardianship, adoption, and foster-care programs on a limited scale.

The Second World War not only interrupted these programs but reintroduced many of the problems they had helped to solve. The government's reaction, as reflected in the 1944 Code of Family Law, was to put even greater emphasis on the importance of the marriage bond and the "Communist" family unit. The status of unmarried mothers and illegitimate children was considerably impaired, and divorce was made difficult. The early postwar years saw a concerted effort to assist couples in fulfilling their parental duties, albeit as partners of the state. Family allowances were liberalized; the number of nurseries, kindergartens, summer playgrounds, and camps was increased; and child labor laws, inoperative during the war, were revived and strengthened.

In 1956 women benefited equally with men from the wide-ranging revamping of social insurance provisions, and they likewise shared equally with men in the reforms for industrial and white-collar workers that followed, which transformed a restricted, harsh, and clumsily administered program of meager benefits into a system of social security that compares favorably with the systems of other advanced nations. But because most of the burden of family responsibilities falls to the wife in the USSR, women could not qualify themselves for better-paid jobs as readily as men or remain in jobs as long as men—factors that in some cases made them ineligible for social-insurance benefits and in other cases resulted in comparatively low benefits. On the other hand, in their roles as mothers, women workers have been treated generously by social insurance. This generosity was only belatedly extended to the women who work on collective farms. Collective farm workers, men and women alike, were excluded from social insurance until 1965, and they have consistently lagged behind other workers since, with harsher eligibility requirements and lower benefits.

At least partly in response to widely felt social inequities, the 1968 Family

Code eased divorce procedures and made the lot of unmarried mothers less humiliating.[2] It remains to be seen to what extent this code will generate social services to assist women to respond to the new demands made on them with the country's rapid technological development.

CURRENT SOCIAL SERVICES FOR WOMEN AS WIVES

Most Soviet women appear to be eager to marry and to stay married. Most seem to attach much greater importance to their families than to their jobs. Thus the things women like or dislike about their jobs may often merely reflect the extent to which the job demands mesh with or complicate the family situation. Women, especially those of 30 years or more, are more grieved than men by the lack of a satisfying personal life, by the falling apart or the absence of a family.[3] This helps explain why, although nationality is an important consideration to prospective spouses (in 1959 only 102 out of every 1,000 marriages were ethnically mixed), Russian women enter into mixed marriages more often than Russian men.[4]

Soviet studies show that women seek through marriage to satisfy their personal and emotional needs, to find intellectual stimulation, to improve their standard of living, and to escape loneliness—as well as to raise successfully one or two children, with the help of their husbands. It is not surprising that of the avalanche of letters responding to an article on computer matchmaking, the majority came from single women who favored it because of personal concerns (as opposed to a concern about others). It is clear from outpourings like this that Soviet women are not man-haters; rather they are searching "for a male who might truly be a great man."[5]

Yet not only is it difficult for Soviet women to find a "great man"; it is often impossible for them to find a man at all. One important reason for the drop in marriages between 1960 and 1970—from 12.1 to 9.7 per 1,000 population—appears to be the fact that men of marriageable age are becoming less interested in establishing families; in 1970 there were 9.4 million unmarried males in the 20 to 40 age group. Men typically marry later than women, and the gap widens with age. Those who marry at 30 (and later) take brides who are roughly ten years younger; and middle-aged men frequently marry young women. This means that a woman's chances of get-

[2] Bernice Madison, "Social Services for Families and Children in the Soviet Union Since 1967," *Slavic Review*, 31 (Dec. 1972), pp. 831–53.

[3] V. Sokolov, "Chelovek i delo," *Literaturnaia gazeta*, Dec. 2, 1970, p. 12; Iu. Solopanov and V. Kvashis, "Retsidiv i retsidivisty," *Sovetskaia iustitsiia*, 7 (Apr. 1972), pp. 9–10.

[4] Iu. V. Arutiunian, "A Concrete Sociological Study of Ethnic Relations," *Soviet Sociology*, 11, no. 3–4 (1972–73), p. 279; E. K. Vasil'eva, "An Ethnodemographic Characterization of Family Structure in Kazan' in 1967," *Soviet Sociology*, 10, no. 1 (1971), p. 85.

[5] D. Valentei, "Problemy sotsial'noi zhizni: o demograficheskom povedenii," *Pravda*, Aug. 16, 1972 (see trans. in *CDSP*, 24, no. 33, p. 14); V. Shliapontokh, "Acquaintanceships and Weddings: A Sociological Analysis of the Data of a Discussion," *Soviet Sociology*, 10, no. 2 (1971), pp. 191–202; Iu. Tomashevskii, "Povest' o zhenshchine," *Literaturnaia gazeta*, June 24, 1974 (see trans. in *CDSP*, 26, no. 44, p. 17).

ting married drop sharply after age 25, are negligible after 30 (only one in nine women in the 30–35 age group got married in 1970), and are infinitesimal after 35. In contrast, a man of 30 is an eligible prospect. Especially lonely are unmarried women 44 and older—64.8 percent of that age group in 1970.[6]

When the probability of finding a husband is small, "would-be brides are not too discriminating," nor do they always insist on a registered marriage. In 1970, some 1,345,000 women reported themselves as married, while their so-called husbands said they were not. Nor is the "egotistic" preference of bachelors for temporary liaisons likely to diminish, for sex outside marriage is becoming more and more the accepted thing, though vestiges of the double standard remain.[7] In addition to the growing distaste of men for marriage, there are certain features of the economy that tend to lessen women's chances for marriage, and create problems for them. An important one of these is the concentration of light industry, whose work force is on the average three-quarters female, in cities with demographically unbalanced populations—with disproportionately high illegitimacy, divorce, and juvenile delinquency rates as a result. In 1972, the prominent Soviet demographer Viktor Perevedentsev urged that the government discontinue creating such "cities of brides" and "cities of bridegrooms," noting that though this problem had been under discussion for years, nothing had changed.[8]

But for many women marriage brings its own problems, not least because family conflicts tend to be exacerbated by the demands of daily life in Soviet society. Numerous studies in fact show that few married women in the USSR have sufficient free time for personal development, for an enjoyable rearing of children, and for the rest needed to renew expended energy. For those with jobs the additional time used up in travel, shopping, housework, and other home duties—the "second shift"—results in a thirteen-to-fifteen-hour day. Preschools and extended-day schools are usually available to them only during their working hours; after work the children must be brought home. Many women who do not hold jobs put in similarly long hours, perhaps ten to twelve a day, because they are charged with the care of young children or aged relatives. Husbands are likely to have twice as much free time as their wives, and to be much less tired at the end of each day and at the beginning of vacations.[9]

Soviet women offer two reasons for this state of affairs, according to a

[6]V. Perevedentsev, "Speshit' li zamuzh?," *Liternaturnaia gazeta*, Aug. 30, 1972 (see trans. in *CDSP*, 24, no. 37, pp. 1–3); S. I. Bruk, "Ethnographic Processes in the USSR (On Materials from the 1970 Census)," *Soviet Review*, 13, no. 3 (1972), p. 212.

[7]V. Perevedentsev, "Marriage and the Family," *Soviet Law and Government*, 13, no. 2 (1974), p. 91; S. I. Golod, "Sociological Problems of Sexual Morality," *Soviet Review*, 11, no. 2 (1970), p. 137.

[8]"Speshit' li zamuzh?"

[9]N. Sheptulina, "Tekhnicheskii progress i voprosy pravovogo regulirovaniia truda zhenshchin," *Sovetskaia iustitsiia*, 20 (Nov. 1971), pp. 5–6.

recent symposium: "the current level of mechanization of daily life" enters the home with such "timidity" that "it offers no possibility for a radical solution," and "the family . . . is very slow about adapting itself to new conditions."[10] Households are notoriously lacking in modern conveniences and aids, and those that are available tend to be of outmoded construction and poor quality, requiring frequent repairs and servicing. But such services, which have developed at a slower pace than planned, are often unavailable or at best slow and inefficient. The daily shopping struggle for food and for such essential items as handkerchiefs, socks, toothpaste, and soap powder is often commented on. As for the family "adapting itself to new conditions," the traditional male disdain for household work is a deep-rooted attitude, and many husbands still consider it beneath their dignity to help their overburdened wives. Nor is that load lightened by the fact that though food preparation is one of the most time-consuming and demanding of the daily household tasks, the overwhelming majority of families prefer home cooking as both better and cheaper.[11]

Many women cannot afford to work at less than a full-time job. But there are many others who would like to work only part-time under suitable conditions. However, the drive to meet this need, begun in 1966 and the subject of subsequent legislation, has not gained momentum, and finding a part-time job often turns into an "agonizing problem."[12]

At least as agonizing for many is the problem of separation or divorce. Though divorce is universally deplored in the USSR as injurious to the society, to the family, and to the individual, official statistics show that it has been skyrocketing: from 3.2 per 100 marriages in 1950 to 10.4 in 1960 and 27 in 1973.[13] The lowest rates are reported in areas where the traditional family structure has been least affected by modernization, notably in farming villages and among the Central Asian nationalities; the highest are found in cities of more than 500,000 population and among intellectuals.

Some Soviet writers differentiate between divorces that result from "thoughtless" marriages and those that are initiated by women "to regain their self-respect." Among the "thoughtless" type of marriages they class those of the very young, of people who do not know each other very well, and of couples who marry simply because it is the thing to do. These "fragile" unions easily succumb to the pressures created by low income, by the housing shortages that force many newlyweds to live with parents, and by the simple lack of psychological preparation for marriage.

As for the divorces initiated by women who find married life demeaning,

---

[10] M. Pavlova, "Zhenshchina doma i na rabote," *Literaturnaia gazeta*, May 27, 1970, p. 12.

[11] A. G. Kharchev, ["Today's Family and Its Problems"], *Zhurnalist*, Nov. 1972 (see trans. in *CDSP*, 25, no. 8, pp. 18–19).

[12] V. Glazyrin, "Voprosy sovetskogo prava: nepolnyi rabochii den'," *Izvestiia*, Apr. 13, 1972 (see trans. in *CDSP*, 24, no. 15, p. 19).

[13] Perevedentsev, ["Statistics: Almost All About Women"], *Zhurnalist*, Mar. 1975 (see trans. in *CDSP*, 27, no. 23, p. 10). See also Peter H. Juviler's paper in this volume.

a majority involve unions of more than five years' duration, and in half the cases there are minor children. A common complaint is the alcoholism of the husband; indeed this is the reason given in 20 to 40 percent of *all* divorces.[14] That alcoholic men not only heap bodily injuries and humiliations on both their wives and children, but also contribute heavily to the crime rate is widely reported. In the Bashkir Autonomous Republic, for example, fully half of the "hooligan" acts and crimes against individuals are ascribed to domestic and "everyday" conflicts. The aggressors in the overwhelming majority of these cases are men; 55 percent of the time their victims are their wives, and 11 percent of the time, some other family member. The wife's refusal to give her husband money for more drink or her demand that he stop drinking often sparks these crimes.[15] Though alcoholism among women is becoming "a new item on the agenda,"[16] female alcoholics are still decidedly in the minority. But their numbers are rising, as are the numbers of male alcoholics, despite the government's strenuous efforts to contain the problem. The treatment of alcoholics, moreover, is not making appreciable progress, in good part because fewer than a quarter of the confirmed alcoholics agree to treatment. This resistance, combined with shortcomings in the delivery of services, has led physicians to conclude that "the possibilities of the treatment and preventive-care clinics are very limited."[17]

Infidelity and the absence of a sense of family duty on the part of husbands also contribute to making married life intolerable for some women. In addition, the lack of contact on the intellectual level, which destroys the "mutual satisfaction [that] exists when marriage is the companionship of two personalities who intellectually enrich each other," is increasingly offered as an explanation for family breakups. This trend may reflect the growing educational attainments of women, who are now outpacing men in education at every level, except the postgraduate, in all but four Central Asian republics; this is especially true of women in the 20-to-30 age group in urban areas.[18]

The Soviet jurist V. Chekalin claims that "about one-half of the divorces could be averted."[19] Several services are now available to assist in this direction, notably sex-education programs, marital counseling, and reconcili-

[14] A. Gorkin, "Concern for the Soviet Family," *Soviet Review*, 10, no. 3 (1969), p. 49; V. Chekalin, "The Family and Family Relationships Under Socialism," *Soviet Law and Government*, 12, no. 4 (1974), p. 80; Robert G. Kaiser, "Love Marriage . . . Divorce," *Washington Post*, June 19, 1974, section A, p. 10.

[15] F. Giliazev, "Izuchenie prestuplenii, sovershaemykh na pochve semeinobytovykh konfliktov," *Sotsialisticheskaia zakonnost'*, Jan. 1973; trans. in *CDSP*, 25, no. 18.

[16] A. Sergeev, ["A Crucial Topic: On the Trail of a Great Killer"], *Literaturnaia Rossiia*, Feb. 8, 1974; trans. in *CDSP*, 26, no. 6.

[17] N. M. Khodakov, "P'ianitsa glazami vracha," *Literaturnaia gazeta*, July 10, 1974 (see trans. in *CDSP*, 26, no. 29, pp. 8–9).

[18] Chekalin, p. 86; V. Perevedentsev, "Dogoniaite zhenshchin!," *Literaturnaia gazeta*, Mar. 7, 1973 (see trans. in *CDSP*, 25, no. 30, p. 32).

[19] "The Family," p. 87.

ation courts. Some, however, are at best rudimentary. This is particularly so in the case of sex education. Yet in the opinion of increasing numbers of Soviet observers, many family problems result from the simple lack of elementary knowledge about sex. This failing, they propose, could be remedied by making the "specific aspects of sexual upbringing" an important part of the overall program of education. So far, however, this has not come to pass; these "specific aspects" are still largely neglected in the schools. In part this is the result of a shortage of qualified personnel and teaching materials. But it is also the result of a widespread continuing antagonism toward sex education on the part of the public at large and indeed on the part of many teachers. Teachers and parents are said to surround the topic of sex with a "conspiracy of silence," and as a result many young people are still forced to learn about sex "on the streets."[20]

In the circumstances, it is no surprise to find a psychiatrist reporting that there is a "crying need" for marriage counseling for young couples. Noting that physicians especially trained in this branch of medicine are now working in "only a minute portion of our vast country," he argues that the problem calls for the establishment of a broad network of agencies across the land. In response to pressure by the Leningrad Young Communist League, a marriage counseling service for young couples—for a fee—was initiated in 1972. Despite the cost, in that year alone more than 3,000 persons were "advised," some having made special trips from other cities for the purpose. Moreover, letters of inquiry were received from all over the country. It seems fair to conclude, as did those who kept track of this project, that Soviet citizens are ready to use, and to pay for, this kind of service.[21]

Many Soviet writers have observed that the *kollektiv* can do much to help smooth out marital difficulties. As one puts it, "an attitude of goodwill and tact on the part of those close to the couple and of comrades at work who enjoy moral authority can ... be an active force in effecting a reconciliation."[22] One such group of "comrades at work" is the Comrades' Court, whose major responsibility is to maintain labor discipline, but which on occasion tries to save "parents for children" and to work with "problem families." Though some of these groups may do "good work," many admittedly operate in a desultory manner, or not at all. I have found no data that would indicate what specific steps these courts might take to help women deal with family problems or how successful they are, but there is some evidence that women who plead for assistance are often ignored. Whether

---

[20] V. Viona, "Razvodov ne budet," *Literaturnaia gazeta*, June 3, 1970, p. 13; A. G. Khripkova, "Voprosy polovogo vospitaniia," *Sovetskaia pedagogika*, 3 (Mar. 1970), p. 95; Henry P. David, *Family Planning and Abortion in the Socialist Countries of Central and Eastern Europe: A Compendium of Observations and Readings* (New York, 1970), p. 54.

[21] P. B. Posvianskii, ["Two People Make a Family—Things Young Married Couples Must Know"], *Iunost'*, July 1973 (see trans. in *CDSP*, 25, no. 45, pp. 18–19); A. Danilov, "Khotite byt' shchastlivymi?," *Komsomol'skaia pravda*, Nov. 29, 1972 (see trans. in *CDSP*, 25, no. 8, p. 18).

[22] Chekalin, p. 87.

this is valid or not, that "problem" families are ignored, and even despised, by other kinds of *kollektivy* is quite amply documented.[23]

Comrades' Courts have no legal obligation to attempt reconciliation. But the courts of the state are bound by law to try to prevent the dissolution of a marriage. They can postpone divorce cases and set a period of up to six months for a possible reconciliation. Despite the claim that these waiting periods can prevent 25 to 33 percent of divorces, a recent investigation indicates that judges rarely postpone cases—even when the respondent objects to the dissolution. Since the Soviet laws do not spell out the grounds for divorce, in order to establish that a couple cannot continue to live together, the court must make a comprehensive examination of the relationship between them and of the circumstances that led to the request for divorce. Many courts fail to do this, and frequently dissolve marriages because of temporary fallings-out and conflicts triggered by some flash cause. Often a divorce trial is limited to a brief questioning of the spouses to probe their willingness to reconcile.[24]

The problem of child support and alimony payments also falls to the courts. Relevant laws permit either parent to make voluntary child-support payments through a payroll deduction at his or her place of work, but in practice it is almost always the man who is the liable parent. Few men choose this course, however; by far the most payments issue from court orders. Typical is the situation in Pskov, where in 1973 only 12 of 1,210 child-support payments withheld from employees in 40 establishments were made voluntarily. Since 1967 collections have been facilitated by garnisheeing, but even so, in 1970 the number of complaints by women about the failure of their children's fathers to carry out court orders was reported to be "impressive." The situation is exacerbated by half-hearted or inefficient administration (or both) on the part of employers, courts, and police. Many women find it difficult and humiliating to collect support but are forced to persist because their own salaries are inadequate and because in divorce cases the wife's portion of the couple's total property cannot be increased in the interests of children.[25] In the courts of Krasnoiarsk *oblast*, for example, more than one-third of all civil cases are related to child support.[26]

---

[23]"Tovarishcheskie sudy i ukreplenie trudovoi distsipliny," *Sovetskaia iustitsiia*, 4 (Feb. 1973), pp. 1–2; Iu. Lubashev, "Vyiavlenie sudom obstoiatel'stv, sposobstvovavshikh soversheniiu nasil' stvennykh prestuplenii," *Sovetskaia iustitsiia*, 14 (July 1972), p. 9; M. Odinets, "Tut malo sochuvstviia," *Pravda*, Nov. 26, 1974.

[24]B. Stolbov, "Applying the Legislation on Marriage and the Family," *Soviet Law and Government*, 12, no. 1 (1973), pp. 81–82.

[25]Stolbov, p. 84; A. Lugovskaia, "Ispolnenie sudebnykh reshenii o vzyskanii alimentov," *Sovetskaia iustitsiia*, 23 (1970), pp. 10–11; N. Ershova, "Razdel imushchestva suprugov," *Sovetskaia iustitsiia*, 18 (Sep. 1973), p. 18.

[26]I. Gorokhov, "Kak uskorit' rassmotrenie del o vzyskanii alimentov," *Sovetskaia iustitsiia*, 5 (Mar. 1973), p. 28. Support payments are exacted from a parent as follows: for one child, one-fourth of the responsible party's wage or income; for two children, one-third; for three or more children, one-half. These amounts may be reduced by a court. This occurs (1) if the

The obligation, under Soviet law, of spouses to support each other is construed to extend to alimony payments to a former wife in certain instances. A divorced woman who is pregnant is entitled to alimony through her pregnancy and until the child reaches age one; and since 1971 alimony rights have also been conferred on women who become invalids within a year of their divorce or who reach pension age five years after the divorce—provided that they are needy and unable to work, and that their former husbands possess sufficient means. Neither "need" nor "sufficient" is legally defined. The law stipulates merely that in examining a spouse's resources, the court must take into account income, savings, and property other than items of "basic necessity,"[27] but this does not exclude the judge from using his or her discretion in assessing a woman's need or a man's ability to pay.

CURRENT SOCIAL SERVICES FOR WOMEN AS MOTHERS

During the Soviet era, the government has been firm and increasingly generous in its services to mothers. But what was once the simple encouragement of motherhood has turned into pressure, owing to the fear that the post–World War II decline in the birthrate and the rise in the average age of the population will lead to shortages of essential manpower in the future. Increasingly, women are urged to bear the "ideal" three children. Those who are conducting the "struggle against one-child families" warn parents that an only child is likely to have trouble relating to the *kollektiv*, to be lonely, to develop into an egotistical "family despot," and to be prone to delinquency; that depriving children of siblings is a high price to pay for giving one child special advantages; and that one-child families are less stable and encourage a "consumer attitude toward life."[28]

From the available data, this is a point on which men and women largely disagree. A survey of 26,000 requests for abortions—20,000 in urban and 6,000 in rural areas—was conducted in 1958–59 in the Russian Republic. Few of the women involved were single. The most frequent reason the women gave for wishing to terminate a pregnancy, stated by more than 40 percent of the rural women and more than 30 percent of the urban women, was "unwilling to have child." But their partners, in sharp contrast, pro-

---

person has other minor children who would be less well provided for than those receiving the support payments; (2) if the person is a Group I or Group II invalid; (3) if the children are working and have an adequate income; or (4) if the children are being fully maintained by the state or by a civil organization. But this last does not apply to children placed in institutions. In that case a parent, usually the father, is obliged to devote the same percentage of his income to their support as he would to a child in the custody of his spouse. See A. Gorkin, "Concern for the Soviet Family," *Soviet Review*, 10, no. 3 (1969), p. 51.

[27] N. Shishigina, "Vzyskanie sredstv na soderzhanie supruga," *Sovetskaia iustitsiia*, 16 (May 1973), pp. 14–15.

[28] Valentei, p. 3; B. Urlanis, "Otets, mat', troe detei," *Literaturnaia gazeta*, Sep. 27, 1972, p. 13 (see trans. in *CDSP*, 24, no. 48, p. 8); M. Alemaskin, ["The Trouble with an Only Child: Family Despot"], *Literaturnaia gazeta*, Feb. 14, 1973, p. 11; A. G. Kharchev, ["Today's Family and Its Problems"], *Zhurnalist*, Nov. 1972, p. 59.

nounced themselves "unwilling" fathers in only 2.9 percent of the urban cases and only 3.1 percent of the rural cases. Another survey, in 1972, found that 58 percent of the married couples studied held identical views on the further growth of their families. It also found that the highest point of agreement was reached when both wished to have two children. When it came to the question of additional children, the rate of agreement declined, with a measurably higher proportion of husbands than wives favoring the "ideal" number of three.[29]

Yet even Boris Urlanis, a major advocate of the "ideal" three, recognizes that "raising three children in Soviet society is admittedly not an easy matter, given today's urban living conditions and the fact that most women work." Many women point out that these "conditions" tend especially to work against large families as the cultural level of women rises and they begin to demand a better home life and material comforts for their children. Others, however, hint at a "selfish frame of mind"—in themselves and in others. One way such "selfish" women handle their guilt feelings is to agree ostensibly with the official position, while in fact opposing it. A "representative" survey of more than 33,000 women showed that on the average they considered 2.9 children desirable—almost the "ideal" three. That figure, however, was two to two-and-a-half times higher than the number of children the respondents actually had. Similarly, a 1970 Moscow survey of 5,093 married women between the ages of 18 and 40 found that they typically favored 2.5 children when on average they had just 1.04.[30]

Still, despite the very real concern over the falling birthrates, no one of standing in the USSR advocates making abortion illegal again. It would plainly be both an unpopular and an unrealistic measure in view of the estimated seven to ten million abortions that are performed annually. Rather, suggested solutions have included liberalizing the eligibility for pregnancy and maternity leave and increasing the benefits; modifying family allowances to cover more children and to equalize children's economic circumstances; giving priority to large famlies in allocating housing; providing an income supplement for poor families; and paying women to stay home with their children for three to five years after birth.

The last proposal, based on a measure introduced in Hungary in 1966, aroused a storm of debate when it was first advanced some few years later.[31] Proponents argued that because the state must provide nurseries and preschools for the children of working women, society gains financially by

[29]See David M. Heer, ed., *Readings on Population* (Englewood Cliffs, N.J., 1968), p. 210; and V. A. Belova, "Family Size and Public Opinion," *Soviet Sociology*, 11, no. 2 (1972), pp. 126–45.
[30]Urlanis, p. 8; G. Kiseleva, "Odin? Dva? Tri?," *Literaturnaia gazeta*, July 4, 1973 (see trans. in *CDSP*, 25, no. 41, pp. 14, 32).
[31]See, e.g., *Literaturnaia gazeta*, Jan. 22, 1969, p. 11; Mar. 19, 1969, p. 11; Apr. 16, 1969, p. 11; Aug. 13, 1969, p. 12. For details of the Hungarian program, see Alice Hermann (with Sandor Komlosi), *Early Child Care in Hungary* (New York, 1972), p. 36.

allowing a mother to stay home;[32] that the birthrate among dependent housewives is higher than among working women; that if mothers were paid for child-rearing, they would earn decent pensions; and that in a society with rising living standards, bringing up children is more complex, and requires, among other things, that children get the full attention of their mothers during certain stages. Opponents argued that in staying home to raise three children, a woman would use up fifteen to eighteen of the most creative years of her life and be reduced to a perennial dependent; that society would experience a large economic and social loss; that higher education for women would lose its meaning; that women would again become merely domestic servants; that even a three-year interruption in work would make it impossible for women to become and to remain qualified specialists; and that the kind of women who would presumably most wish to stay home—those equipped only for unskilled, dull, and monotonous jobs—would not raise their children as well as preschools would. The opponents prevailed.

Though, as I have said, the Soviet government does not contemplate making abortions illegal, as the major means of controlling births in the USSR, they are strongly discouraged. The official policy is to persuade as many women as possible to see each pregnancy through to full term. The usual practice is for a gynecologist to discuss with each woman her reasons for seeking abortion and to warn her of possible adverse consequences. If nothing will deter her from that course, her application must be approved. But if the request is motivated by some difficult social situation susceptible to solution, the gynecologist may refer the woman to a socio-legal bureau staffed by lawyers and nurses. These bureaus, located in medical facilities, have been in existence since 1933. Their functions have multiplied over the years but are still centered on serving women as mothers. Bureau lawyers assist mothers with their problems at home and at work; help them in establishing paternity, registering births, and exacting support from their husbands for themselves and their children; and arrange for nursery care, or if need be, for the institutionalization or adoption of their children. If a woman is judged to be not a "good parent," a bureau lawyer will assist the appropriate officials in depriving her of her parental rights.[33]

From all accounts, however, these bureaus have little success in dissuading their clients from having abortions. A survey of Moscow working women found that even when there were no children in the family, 78

---

[32] See K. Vermishev, "Stimulirovanie rosta naseleniia," *Planovoe khoziaistvo*, 12 (Dec. 1972), pp. 102–7. Vermishev is concerned mainly with weighing the costs of maintaining state nurseries for children between the ages of two and six, along with various other provisions for working mothers, against the costs of paying a standard yearly allowance to a mother who would leave work to take care of two or three children until they reach school age. Working mothers, he finds, cost the government 1.8–3.4 times what the non-working mothers cost, even when the consequent reduction in the work force is considered.

[33] E. Ryzikova and R. Edel'shtein, "Sotsial'no-pravovaia pomoshch' zhenshchine—materi," *Sovetskaia iustitsiia*, 5 (Mar. 1974), p. 5.

percent of the undesired pregnancies were aborted; when there was one child, the figure rose to 97 percent; and when there were two or more children, to fully 100 percent.[34] Furthermore, the socio-legal bureaus are largely confined to the large cities. They are not mandated by law but are founded simply at the initiative of medical personnel.

Another way in which the state encourages motherhood is by granting all pregnant working women a generous amount of maternity leave. Maternity leave provisions have been available since 1922 and have been modified several times since then. The current benefits date back to the immediate post–World War II period. Women who work in industry or at white-collar jobs are now entitled to 112 days paid leave, 56 days before confinement and 56 days after. For twins or an abnormal birth, the period after birth is extended to 70 days. Women who adopt newborn infants also are granted 56 and 70 days' leave when they adopt one child or twins, respectively. Before 1973, the amount of pay involved in such leaves depended on the length of employment and on trade union membership. The law as then amended removed these two conditions and granted women full pay for the entire period. For women collective farm workers, such benefits have been slower to come. Leaves of similar duration but conditioned on longer employment did not become available until 1965. In 1969, the benefits for women who were chairpersons of farms, agricultural specialists, and farm-machinery operators were raised to match those of the city women; the 1973 law brought all women collective farm workers into parity.

Since 1970, working women have been permitted to take additional unpaid maternity leave, up to one year, without prejudice to their job ratings. This period is counted into their total, uninterrupted work record.

Yet it is clear from the frequent complaints voiced in various sources, by women and authorities alike, that the administration of maternity leave does not always adhere to legal requirements. We hear, for example, of regulations governing vacations and pay raises for pregnant women being ignored, and of those who ask for easier jobs, to which they are entitled, being fired. And other features of the law are evidently violated as well.

As for adoptive mothers, though adoption enjoys official approval, only the most rudimentary services are available to a woman who wishes to adopt a child—if indeed she gets any at all. Prospective parents must find a child to adopt on their own, and even then, where an abandoned child looks to be a likely candidate, they would be blocked in their plans if the mother cannot be found to relinquish her claim to the child. Nor does Soviet adoption practice assure proper protection for all concerned. In some instances the district and city soviets approve an adoption without the written agreement of the institution in which the child was found, as required by law. Annulment is justified if the child's interests so require, or if the adoption

[34] A. K., "A Demographic Problem: Female Employment and the Birthrate," *Soviet Review*, 11 no. 1 (1970), p. 78.

was completed contrary to law (as, for example, when the adoptee proves to be mentally retarded). When the court grants an annulment, it must also decide what to do with the child. One alternative is to return him to his natural parents. If they are able-bodied, have not been stripped of their parental rights, and are not themselves plaintiffs in the case, they are obliged to look after and support the child. This alternative appears to nullify the very concept of adoption. The downgrading of adoption is implied also by not counting adopted children as one of the five that entitle a woman to retire at 50 instead of the usual 55. In any case, considering that the two principal reasons for the requests for annulment are divorce and poor personal relations between the adopted child and the parents, one has to question the care with which the adoption study and the placement follow-up— if any—are conducted.[35]

However minimal the services offered the adoptive mother, in theory at least, she has recourse to some. There exist no specialized services at all for the unwed mother—or for her illegitimate child. And this despite estimates suggesting that there have been a sizable number of illegitimate children all through the Soviet period. These estimates are borne out by some recent statistics. One study shows, for example, that in 1970 one of every ten live births was out of wedlock; translated into round figures this means 400,000 illegitimate babies. Though there is some evidence that this rate represented a substantial drop from the 1950's, a 1973 report for Belorussia, which is said to reflect "a trend in many parts of the country," points to a decided increase in the following decade: "In 1959 there were 2.7 illegitimate births per 1,000 unmarried women between the ages of 15 and 19; in 1970 there were 7.1. For ages 20 to 24 the figures were 16.3 in 1959 and 73.9 in 1970; for ages 25 to 29, there were 36.8 and 98.1; for ages 30 to 34, there were 39.1 and 87.2; for ages 35 to 39, there were 27.1 and 47.4." The report divides unwed mothers into two types: "the forlorn and pitiable young girls for whom bearing a child is a humiliating, frightening misfortune; [and] the lonely women whose chances for marriage decrease with each year after about 30—since men of their age usually want to marry younger women—and who actively desire to have a family." From the thumbnail sketches of the lives of these women and children provided therein, the report's conclusion seems well justified: "One cannot conceal the fact that the unmarried mother often becomes the target of humiliating abuse—and stones of malice are tossed at her child as well. One need not speak of the children who have never known their fathers—it is a sad, tragic theme."[36]

The only provisions that make it somewhat easier for an unwed mother to

[35] K. Cherviakov, "Voprosy usynovleniia v sudebnoi praktike," *Sovetskaia iustitsiia*, 4 (Feb. 1973), p. 4.
[36] L. Kuznetsova, "Obeshchal zhenit'sia, ..." *Literaturnaia gazeta*, Apr. 14, 1973 (see trans. in *CDSP*, 25, no. 35, p. 15).

raise her child—the choice the state wants her to make—are aimed at easing her financial burden. She gets benefits from the family allowance system for a longer period than other women and she pays less for nursery care. On the other hand, she and her child are ineligible for dependents' supplements or survivors' pensions from social insurance and social security. Nevertheless, the majority of "lone" mothers are said to keep and raise their children, and to use institutional care for only short periods, even though they are not required to pay for it. Few, it is claimed, put their children up for adoption, even by relatives.

CURRENT SOCIAL SERVICES FOR WOMEN AS PARENTS

Soviet mothers play the primary role in child-rearing and in making decisions that affect children. Studies show that children tend to feel closer to their mothers than their fathers, and to take more note of their mothers' advice and demands. In short, writes Igor Kon, "researchers with one voice state that the role of the father in the upbringing of children cannot be compared with the mother's role." He and other social scientists, increasingly concerned about this "matriarchy," are pressing for a greater involvement of fathers in child-rearing.[37]

The Soviet government makes several types of income maintenance programs available to families (or to mothers who are heads of households) for the care of children living at home. A woman "in need" receives a lump-sum payment for the support of a new infant for the first nine months of its life. How much she gets is pegged to the number of children she has. In 1974, these payments started at twelve rubles for a layette and eighteen rubles for the newborn's food for the first and second child, then rose progressively up to a maximum of 250 rubles for food for the eleventh child.[38]

The state also pays family allowances to families with four or more children, and to unmarried mothers starting with the first child. For the fourth child and all subsequent children the married mother receives monthly payments starting at the child's first birthday and continuing until he reaches age five. For unmarried mothers payments start from the child's birth and continue until he reaches the age of twelve. But these allowances have failed to keep pace with the rising wage levels over the years, to the point where they now contribute an insignificant amount to the family budget. Moreover, since most couples have only one or two children, decreasing numbers of families benefit from the allowance program. In 1966, only 558,000 families or 1 percent of all families in the country received

---

[37] T. Gerasimova and I. Prelovskaia, "V krugu sem'i: domashnii ochag," *Izvestiia*, Apr. 29, 1973 (see trans. in *CDSP*, 25, no. 17, p. 19); I. Kon, "Zachem nuzhny otsy?," *Literaturnaia gazeta*, Feb. 28, 1973, p. 11. The matriarchal pattern is continued in the schools. In 1970 women constituted 87 percent of all teachers in grades 1–4 of day-session general education schools and 75 percent of those in grades 5–11. Preschools are almost universally staffed by women.

[38] *Sotsial'noe obespechenie*, 10 (Oct. 1974), p. 59.

such allowances; by 1973 the number of all mothers, married and unmarried, to whom allowances were paid dropped to 2.8 million.[39] In addition to illegitimate children, the chief beneficiaries today are in the rural areas and in Central Asian communities, where families are still fairly large, but there is no evidence that these payments have contributed much to raising the standard of living among the poor children on whose behalf they are made.

In 1965, the government set as the poverty line for Soviet families 206 rubles a month for a family of four, or 51.5 rubles per person. Considering that in 1971 the minimum wage for industrial and white-collar workers was set at 70 rubles a month, and that as late as 1974 their average gross earnings were still only 139.5 (the monthly gross average for collective farmers was expected to rise to 98 rubles by 1975), and recalling also that many women with three or more children do not work ouside the home or do so only sporadically, it is obvious that millions of families have long been living below the poverty line.[40]

The fact has not escaped the government, which in 1971 announced a family income supplement program. It did not begin operating until November 1, 1974, though how badly it was needed can be gauged from the fact that it was budgeted at 1.8 billion rubles per year, compared with the 438 million spent in 1969 on family allowances. Under this program a mother is paid a supplement of twelve rubles a month at her place of work or study (or a father, if the mother is not working or studying) for each child under age eight in families in which the average total income per family member does not exceed 50 rubles a month. Wages, salaries, bonuses, pay for work in the communal sector of collective farms, allowances, and stipends, as well as income from personal plots of land, are all counted in computing the family's total income. The supplement is not in addition to cash benefits already being received. Some 12.5 million children are expected to benefit from this program, but many are sure to remain in poverty, specifically, those whose families' per capita income is below 38–40 rubles per month and those whose age excludes their families from help. Furthermore, not only is the poverty level itself too low to encourage women to stop working, but the horizontal redistribution of income the program achieves, from childless families to those with children, promises to have little impact on the nonegalitarian structure of Soviet wages.

Since 1968, allowances for support have also been made available to women (and men) who wish to take children without adequate means of their own into their homes. This change was made in the hope of recruiting a larger number of suitable persons as foster parents and guardians.

Finally, in the way of cash benefits, one can count the paid leave granted to working mothers for the care of sick children. Under liberalized regula-

---

[39]*Vestnik statistiki*, 1 (1975), p. 92 (Table 21); R. Kallistratova, "Rozhdaemost' i pravo," *Sovetskaia iustitsiia*, 2 (Jan. 1971), p. 15.
[40]A. K., "A Demographic Problem," p. 80.

tions issued in 1973, a married mother is permitted to stay home to care for a sick child under age fourteen for seven calendar days per illness, and an unmarried mother is given ten days' leave. If the sick child is under two, the mother is given a certificate of leave even if there is another adult family member who can care for the child.

As for the personal social services available to women as parents, the most important by far—certainly to working mothers—are the facilities for the care of young children. By 1970, there were 9.3 million youngsters in permanent preschools and 5 million in seasonal ones.[41] There is no doubt that these numbers reflect impressive and steady gains. But at the same time they mean that only some 50 percent of urban and 30 percent of rural children of preschool age were then being cared for in these centers. Those levels are considerably below the 65 percent of all eligible children predicted for the end of the decade. As of 1972 no republic had yet fulfilled its plan for the construction of preschools; neither had any of the industries that employ large numbers of women.[42] And yet in January 1972 one million children were said to be on the list of "pending applications." That shortages are especially severe for rural families is suggested by the fact that of the children served by permanent preschools in 1973, 8.2 million lived in urban communities, and only 2.3 million in rural areas. As a matter of fact, eight million of these children lived in only two republics, the RSFSR and the Ukraine, meaning that only 2.5 million attended preschools in the other thirteen republics.[43] To an important extent, these shortages explain why most women take additional unpaid maternity leave despite the loss of earnings and job opportunities involved.

In any case, because of the poor quality of the care in some preschools, many mothers are hesitant to use the available facilities, especially for very young children. Parents are especially dissatisfied with what they see as a stress on the preschools' custodial rather than developmental function and with the lack of attention to individual differences among children. Rural families are the most disadvantaged in this regard as well, and expressions of parental dissatisfaction are frequent.

Working mothers likewise have access to facilities for the care of children in primary grades in the form of extended-day schools. These schools, established in 1956, are designed to supervise children in off-school hours when no family supervision is available and to care for those who are not making normal progress in school. By 1973, six million children were enrolled in these schools—an impressive development but far from what the advocates of extended-day education had predicted in the 1960's, when these schools were promoted as the "prevalent mass-type school" of the future. One important deterrent to their growth has been their relatively high cost: a per

[41]*Vestnik statistiki*, 1 (1975), p. 93 (Table 25).
[42]*Uchitel'skaia gazeta*, Feb. 24, 1973.
[43]*Vestnik statistiki*, 1 (1975), pp. 93, 94 (Tables 25 and 26).

capita annual expenditure of 150 rubles, compared with 80–90 rubles for regular primary and secondary schools. To some extent this reflects the expense of the two daily meals provided in these schools, which is shouldered in whole or in part by the state in many cases. But beyond this, the generally low public esteem in which these schools are held has helped impede their development. In many places they have shown themselves to be a blind alley for the child, and for that reason parents are often unwilling to avail themselves of this service.

In regard to the services available for parents with educable "defective" children, no statistics on the schooling and care of such children are at hand. The official claim is that all are accommodated. Many of these children apparently live at home and attend special schools until age eighteen; some are institutionalized and go home only on weekends and holidays. Teachers assist their parents, through individual conferences and group discussions, by explaining the meaning of retardation, the limits that it may impose on a child's ability to participate in "normal" activities, and more especially, the potential and strength the child possesses for developing his particular mental and physical capacities to the full.

Parents with severely defective children, who represent approximately 11.5 percent of all the physically and medically handicapped, are by official policy supposed to institutionalize their children and to pay for their support if income permits. According to estimates, however, at least 16 to 20 percent of these children were not accommodated in 1970 and probably remained with their families.[44]

A popular service available to parents—because it relieves them of child care for a time and at the same time provides wholesome recreation for their children—is vacations for youngsters in camps and playgrounds. In 1973 more than 14,000,000 children enjoyed vacations of varying duration in such facilities—an impressive number. But because eligibility is determined by the children's membership in Young Pioneers or their parents' membership in trade unions, or both—as well as by the availability of facilities—many are excluded. To what extent their parents can provide vacations out of their own resources, it is not possible to determine. It is known, however, that resorts that cater to families are a recent development and as yet are not always successful in providing recreation for the children.

That juvenile delinquency in the USSR is on the increase is strongly suggested by information from a variety of Soviet sources. It is also clear that the parents of pre-delinquents and delinquents are unable to supervise them properly or to arrange adequate care for them because of illness, difficult work schedules, disorganized family life, and family breakups.

---

[44] This percentage is suggested by the figure of 4,000 children awaiting placement in March 1968 in the RSFSR, where in 1969 21,000 children were already institutionalized. Plans called for the construction of fourteen new homes with a capacity of 2,355 places by the end of 1970. See *Sotsial'noe obespechenie*, 3 (Mar. 1968), pp. 40–41.

These parents, apparently beset by serious social problems themselves, especially need services when their youngsters are placed on probation or released on parole so that they either continue to live with their parents or not far away, in their home communities. Yet preventive work is either absent or ineffective in many jurisdictions, and recidivism among probationers and parolees is high. The reasons for this state of affairs are said to include the failure of Commissions of Juvenile Affairs—the major responsible official body—to reach all of the youngsters involved or to serve them adequately when they are reached; the insufficient number of paid probation officers; and the lack of training among these officers as well as among unpaid "social upbringers" who volunteer their services. Similarly, in many localities the militia—another responsible organ—fails to register all juvenile offenders, as it is supposed to do, and confines its preventive and reforming efforts to infrequent and ineffective talks at the militia station.

CURRENT SOCIAL SERVICES FOR WOMEN AS WORKERS

More than four-fifths of Soviet women of working age hold jobs. Most have no choice but to work, either because their husband's salary is not enough to make ends meet or because they themselves are family heads. This last is no rare occurrence: in 1959, 28.6 percent of all families were headed by women; and in 1970 the number of such families was described as "impressive."[45] Moreover, government policy strives to increase women's participation in the labor force, and social forces now in evidence are not likely to diminish it in the near future.

Like men, women are entitled either to social security or to social insurance benefits, as *kolkhoz* members to the former and as urban workers and employees to the latter, provided they are eligible. Under both systems, women can receive old-age, disability, and survivors' pensions, and cash sickness benefits (for temporary disability). The liberalizations that have been introduced since 1956 have increased coverage, improved benefits, and brought the two systems closer together. But in all respects the benefits for collective farm members continue to be more limited. For example, when Group III disability coverage (for least serious injuries and diseases) was extended to collective farm workers in 1968, only job-connected disabilities were covered; injuries and diseases from general causes were specifically excluded, though these are covered for industrial and white-collar workers.

The principal difference in eligibility conditions for men and women concerns retirement. Men normally retire with a pension at age 60 with 25 years of work; women can draw a full pension at 55 with 20 years' employ-

---

[45] Murray Feshbach, *Manpower Trends in the USSR: 1950 to 1980* (U.S. Department of Commerce, Bureau of the Census, Foreign Demographic Analysis Division, May 1971), pp. 8, 9; V. S. Tadevosian, "Okhrana prav odinokoi materi i eë rebenka," *Sovetskoe gosudarstvo i pravo*, 11 (1971), p. 27.

ment. In certain types of work—underground, under harmful or onerous conditions, in hot shops—the age and work requirements are reduced for both sexes, with the five years' difference retained. The retirement age is lowered for blind men to 50, for blind women to 40. Women who bear and rear five or more children to age eight (excluding, as we have seen, adopted ones) are permitted to retire at 50.

Despite improvements, most pensions are pitifully low. Indeed, if the average pension were to be spent wholly on food, it would not suffice to purchase more than 30 percent of the "scientifically determined norms of nourishment." At least one-half of all pensioners exist on a per capita income of less than 50 rubles a month, that is, below the official poverty line. The claim that old-age pensions average 70 percent of the beneficiary's previous earnings may be correct, though I think this is questionable. But in any case this does not mean they are adequate for current expenses. Furthermore, inadequate pensions are not supplemented on a regular basis: all that is provided is the "one-time" grant, which is given sparingly and only in "emergencies."

Inadequate pensions are especially hard on women—not only for those who "give many years of their lives to the family, bringing up children and carrying out household duties, as a result of which they do not acquire the work record needed to be eligible for pensions,"[46] but also for those who work long and hard and do acquire the necessary work record. In the first instance, if the woman is a dependent of a pensioner, he will receive a supplement of only 10 percent of his pension for her; for two or more dependents, only an additional 15 percent is granted. If a homemaker is the sole survivor—*and* is 55 or an invalid—her pension will amount to from 23 to 60 rubles per month; for herself and one child under sixteen (or if in school, under eighteen) the range is 45 to 120 rubles; and for herself and two or more dependents (brothers, sisters, and grandchildren can be counted) she will get 70 to 120 rubles. These higher amounts were introduced in December 1974. A reduction of 15 percent is possible if a pensioner has access to a private plot of land—a regulation that is hard on many rural women. From examples in the available literature explaining how pensions for survivors are figured, it is clear that these benefits cannot lift many widows and their dependents above the official poverty line.[47] Yet among those who are forced to make do on survivors' benefits the number of women is disproportionately high—in part because the woman's life expectancy is greater than the man's and in part because widows are far less likely to marry for a second time than widowers.

Women who are entitled to pensions on their own work record typically

---

[46]S. Palastina and A. Pergament, "Sovetskoe semeinoe zakonodatel'stvo o pravakh zhenshchin," *Sovetskaia iustitsiia*, 5 (Mar. 1974), p. 8.

[47]See, notably, *Sotsial'noe obespechenie*, 2 (Feb. 1972), pp. 62–63; and 10 (Oct. 1972), pp. 54–55.

draw lower pensions than men because the level of benefits depends on prior earnings—as well as the type, length, and continuity of employment. Since women are more likely to be employed in unskilled occupations than men, and are largely excluded from the hazardous or onerous occupations that pay relatively higher wages, their average wages are perforce lower; this disparity is especially pronounced in farmwork.

In order to encourage the elderly to continue working, a 1964 amendment granted a flat 50 percent of pension in additional income to men and women of retirement age who would take employment in various industries and occupations, a 75 percent supplement to those who returned to work in the Urals, Siberia, and the Far East, and full pensions to those who were still capable of working in hazardous occupations. As a result, 800,000 pensioners returned to the labor force. At the end of 1969 coverage was expanded and the program was extended through 1975. A 1973 investigation in Kiev found that from 60 to 70 percent of those eligible decided to continue working, and that the bulk of those who chose not to return to work were women. For most of these women, family and living circumstances counted heavily in the decision. Four times as often as men, women cited as their reason for remaining in retirement such things as helping with grandchildren or taking care of the housework so younger members of the family would have more time to study, work, and relax. Some simply coud not continue to work because of poor health (as was true of men also); others stayed on for only a short time. Some would have accepted part-time jobs, but as we have seen, these are not widely available.[48]

As the average age of the population has increased, the proportion of those of retirement age or older has grown, to reach 15 percent in 1970. The pensioners among them then numbered 36.2 million, almost 75 percent of whom were women. This huge imbalance is due not only to the lower age of retirement for women, but also to their greater life expectancy, which was ten years or so longer than men's at that time. In 1970, there were only 477 men over 60 for every 1,000 women in that age group. The percentage of persons 60 or over is especially high in the rural areas, with the result that there are vast numbers of elderly women in those areas who are even worse off than their urban sisters, thanks to the leaner social security provisions for collective farm workers.[49] Nor is the possibility of living in poverty during their retirement years lessened by the last line of defense against want—public assistance.

Public assistance grants, which differ from republic to republic, in fact do

---

[48] Bernice Madison, "Soviet Income Maintenance Policy for the 1970s," *Journal of Social Policy*, 2, no. 2 (Apr. 1973), pp. 97–117; G. M. Moskalets and N. N. Sachuk, "Nekotorye sotsial'no-gigienicheskie i sotsiologicheskie aspekty struktury svobodnogo vremeni pensionerov," *Sovetskoe zdravookhranenie*, 10 (1973), pp. 15–20.

[49] A. Kvasha, "Pokolenie 2000 goda," *Literaturnaia gazeta*, Mar. 22, 1972 (see trans. in CDSP, XXIV:II, pp. 13–14); Perevedentsev, "Dogoniaite zhenshchin"; Bruk, p. 215.

little to lift recipients out of dire poverty. Persons who are ineligible for social insurance or social security are supposed to be helped by "responsible relatives," whose payments can be exacted by civil suit and are set at levels commensurate with their incomes. If a person has no close relatives to fall back on, is destitute, and is totally or almost totally disabled, he or she is entitled to a grant of from ten to twenty rubles a month, depending on the place of residence.

Needy aged and disabled persons who have no families and who cannot get along without a caretaker can enter an institution and receive full support—if there is room for them. The fact is, institutional care is by no means available to all who need and want it. In 1968, for example, though at least 605,000 persons required such care, only some 250,000 could be accommodated. For years, plans calling for increases in institutional facilities have been underfulfilled. Moreover, personnel in the existing facilities are only minimally educated when hired, and few have been known to raise their level of competence during employment.[50]

Not surprisingly, the collective farm member is in the worst position of all in this respect. The farm may render assistance out of its own moneys or share in supporting an institution for the aged and disabled of several farms. But neither practice is undertaken on a significant scale, and the shortages of facilities are compounded by the disproportionately large number of aged in the rural population—a majority of them women.

For those aged and disabled industrial and white-collar workers no longer in the labor force who request service, each republic's Ministry of Social Welfare provides "material-household assistance," that is, friendly visiting by an employee of the ministry, who may at times lend a hand in doing the laundry, shopping, or housework, or make sure the pensioner gets his or her special diet, or help out in some other way. But these services are limited in scope, and the ministry workers, mostly women, have no special training and often possess only minimal education. They are sometimes assisted by volunteers, themselves pensioners.

For elderly or ailing persons who are still in the labor force, work-related personal social services are rendered by elected, unpaid trade union activists—"social insurance delegates." They concentrate on friendly visiting and help with "daily living" for the temporarily ill; on facilitating and overseeing job placement for the disabled and for those who are soon to retire and wish to continue working; and on assisting with applications for pensions or other benefits and for admittance to sanatoriums and health, recreational, and educational facilities. What is done for a particular person depends on the trade union's perception of that person's needs and on the degree of concern and commitment of the individual delegate. In 1975, these delegates were said to number 2,000,000, of whom half were women.

[50] M. M. Kravchenko, "Uspekh piatiletki reshaiut kadry," *Sotsial'noe obespechenie*, 2 (Feb. 1972), p. 5.

None had any training for the helping function as it relates to emotionally based needs.

For the deaf and the blind, in and out of the labor force, similar services are provided by volunteers from the All-Union societies. Though the efforts to reach as many of these people as possible appear to be genuine, these services reach relatively few of the inhabitants of the rural communities. As for collective farm workers, friendly visiting and other such personal services are nonexistent.[51]

An array of vocational rehabilitation services is provided in all of the country's republics, though only to a limited degree in rural communities. They include medical care and surgical procedures, prosthetic devices, vocational training, and job placement. For the majority of the persons in this program positions are found in state enterprises, among non-handicapped workers. Others are placed in state enterprises that have special sections for workers with certain types of handicapping conditions; in enterprises run by the Deaf and Blind societies; and in sheltered workshops administered by welfare agencies. Some are trained in jobs that can be done at home. Placement in special sections in industry is being extended to include those affected with cardio-vascular, nervous, mental, pulmonary, and other disorders. In 1970, more than 4,000,000 disabled persons were working, 88 percent of them in the Russian republic. It is fair to assume that many of the 4,000,000 were women.

In that same year, the physically disabled were provided training in 37 occupations free of charge. But there is no evidence that these rehabilitation efforts were accompanied by any routine psychologically oriented counseling. That such counseling may be badly needed by some, especially women, is suggested by the poignant findings of Drs. Sh. Gvasaliia and K. Listov in their study of how men and women workers adjusted to the loss of an extremity. Men, they found, invariably made excellent adjustments: retrained for better jobs, they earned good money; those who were single got married; all participated extensively and without embarrassment in social life. In contrast, the women almost invariably experienced the disability as a pervasive tragedy: retrained for other occupations, they also continued to work, but this in no way made up for their sense of uselessness in the home—the traditional female outlet for excellence and satisfaction. The single ones remained single; several of the married women were abandoned by their husbands. In the end the two doctors (both men) "lined up on the side of the women": "A woman desires to be beautiful, elegant, always attractive to men—and this is understandable. For this reason, in our view, it is not fair to equate a woman who loses an extremity with a man who suf-

---

[51] Under Soviet law, children are obligated to attend to the needs of parents who are unable to work but are secure materially. But the law does not contain sanctions for failure to carry out this responsibility: pressure is expected to come from a collective, such as a Comrades' Court or a medical or social organization. See G. Ekaterinoslavskaia, "Alimentnye obiazatel'-stva detei," *Sovetskaia iustitsiia*, 10 (May 1972), pp. 12–13.

fers the same trauma. In such a case, it seems to us, it is necessary to evaluate the woman's remaining work ability somewhat differently in determining the degree of her disability. This is the only approach that is humane and ethical."[52]

CONCLUSIONS

There has been a pronounced expansion of social services for women during the Soviet period, and services have become more generous, more diversified, and more accessible. But as is true elsewhere, enormous gaps continue to exist between blueprint and reality. Recall, for example, the waiting lists for preschools and the largely custodial function that many of them perform; the paucity of personal social services and their rudimentary and unskilled nature; the uneven distribution of services between urban and rural communities; and the failure of income maintenance programs to lift many eligible individuals and families out of poverty.

Soviet authorities attribute most of the quantitative shortcomings of their social service programs to the disparities between social needs and economic possibilities, to the "contradictions of progress" that are both real and ideologically acknowledged. Such shortcomings will be largely overcome, they contend, as increasing quantities of facilities and goods become available in the future: more nurseries, more refrigerators, more extended-day schools. That increases in the volume of goods and services are needed, and that to an important extent they depend on economic resources, is obvious. But the allocation of an increased share of resources to this sphere presupposes a reordering of priorities that places a higher value than is now the case on the fulfillment of the needs and aspirations of people, above all women and children, as humans rather than merely as actual or potential productive units.

Less easy for the authorities to explain—and to ameliorate—are the qualitative weaknesses that often turn good blueprints into welfare disservices, especially in the efforts to deal with the kinds of destructive interpersonal relationships and antisocial behavior that require professional help. Social services have been notably ineffective in helping to create the "new Soviet man," an individual who presumably would not need those services. Officially, these inadequacies too are attributed to "progress," but in this context progress is identified as a process that itself creates new and more complicated problems, difficult to solve because "consciousness"— thoughts, values, feelings—changes more slowly than social and economic conditions. Increasingly, more effective help with these problems points to the need for competent personnel, especially in view of the negligible contributions of the *kollektivy* in this realm and their lack of success in changing the behavior of their members to any significant degree. Though "concrete" measures harking back to the days of Kollontai are still regularly

[52]"Vstanem na storonu zhenshchin," *Sotsial'noe obespechenie*, 12 (Dec. 1970), pp. 42–43.

proposed at official conferences,[53] more and more they are recognized as too simplistic to be measurably effective standing alone. Competence spells the professionalization of social services, an undertaking that would require a major increase in or redistribution of resources (or both). In addition to providing training—to impart knowledge, instill values, and teach skills—professionalization would demand that personnel be thoroughly grounded in theory and in their precise functions, and that they be granted an appropriate status in society. All this, in turn, would call for an underpinning of respectable research, including not only an experimentation that is based on sophisticated methodology but an evaluation of results that is fearless and honest. As the leading women from socialist countries concluded at a 1970 Moscow symposium, unless proposals for innovations are scientifically based and responsive to modern conditions, the "cursed woman question" will persist.[54] And so will the cursed social services question.

Yet in seeking scientifically based data, especially of an evaluative nature, Soviet scholars and practitioners today are not much farther along than their tsarist predecessors. Significant evaluative research in social services simply does not exist—to say nothing of the huge gaps in published statistical information. Take social insurance and social security, for example. Not a single investigation has been published that addresses such questions as the adequacy of benefits, the living standards and living arrangements of the beneficiaries, or any of the host of other questions that would shed light on the actual life styles of pensioners. Though the current system of family allowances dates back to 1944, not a single study concerning its significance in family life has appeared. Especially disturbing is the total silence surrounding public assistance, whose recipients are possibly the most disadvantaged group in the country. Nor are there any studies about institutional care for the aged and disabled as a way of life, with all its psychological, emotional, and physiological implications. And yet the Kiev Institute of Gerontology, founded in 1968 and the only one of its kind in the Soviet Union, regards the expansion of institutional care for these groups as the most feasible solution to their problems—ignoring completely the fact that most of the aged could remain in their own homes if supportive services were made available. Not a single study has been devoted to friendly visiting.

The literature is completely silent about children who have been adopted or placed with guardians and trustees. The same is true of the problems facing illegitimate children and their mothers. What discussions there are of institutional care for normal children are hearsay accounts, far removed

[53] A. G. Kharchev and S. I. Golod, "Recommendations of the Symposium on Women's Employment and the Family, Minsk, June 21–24, 1969," *Soviet Sociology*, 12 no. 2 (1973), pp. 84–95. See also Barbara Evans Clements, "Emancipation Through Communism: The Ideology of A. M. Kollontai," *Slavic Review*, 32, no. 2 (June 1973), p. 331.

[54] Pavlova, "Zhenshchina doma."

indeed from a scientific assessment of its impact on the social, emotional, and intellectual development of these children. Not a single research effort is devoted to following up these children after they leave. Likewise with "defective" children; the research concerning such children offers no clue to the mental health aspects of their lives, or those of their parents. The same holds for the research on the vocational rehabilitation of adults.

Nor has anything been written about the administrative appellate process within social service bureaucracies—if, indeed, such a process exists. No cases of judicial appeal are on record. Yet there is no doubt that the number of dissatisfied recipients is considerable, especially in the income maintenance programs. The conclusion is inescapable that the achievement of social justice through safe and dignified channels is not an overriding consideration.

The unwillingness of Soviet policy-makers to allow for maladjustment and deviance in their society—if for no other reason, as indicators for the direction of change in social policy—introduces ambivalence and uncertainty into the practice in social services. It is reflected most clearly in the failure to provide specialized social services, for instance, for unmarried mothers and their children. These women and children are supposed to be happy and productive simply because they live in a socialist state—though data to the contrary are abundant. The same attitude is implied in regard to adoptive applicants. The purpose of the specialized services that do exist is sometimes defeated by "standard" procedures: "giant" institutions; preschools for children ranging in age all the way from three months to seven years; an inflexible separation of the "defective" children from the "normal," though the majority of those who are categorized as defective are expected on reaching adulthood to become integrated productively into "normal" environments; the exclusion from adoption of all but "perfect" children, a backward and unrealistic practice. Writes one educator: "We speak of the role of the family in child-rearing in general, on a large scale, in global terms, substituting mass undertakings for the painstaking work with individual parents. But difficult children, as a rule, come from families that have fallen apart, in which parents do not engage in child-rearing."[55] A less rigid view would recognize that the very progress the society has made produces increasing demands for alternative services, for more flexibility, for more genuine individualization—in short, for an approach that can, when necessary, move beyond a mass base of minimum, standard provision.

Soviet women may be expected to support policies that increase the scope and adequacy of the universal social services now available to them and their children; to favor an ongoing evaluation of the impact of services in the light of changing conditions; and to press for more effective implemen-

[55] E. Knokhinov, "Prichiny nashikh poter'," *Pravda*, June 4, 1974, p. 3.

tation, especially at the local level where the drama of daily life is played out. They will surely become more concerned with the need to create better specialized services, and to staff all services with competent professionals interested in helping each woman enhance the quality of her life. In this way, social services can contribute importantly to a more pluralistic social fabric that would offer Soviet women more options in coping with problems they experience as *persons* who must play many sorts of roles.

Joel C. Moses

Women in Political Roles

IN RECENT YEARS, Western scholars have demonstrated an increasing interest in the political status of women in the Soviet Union. In some part, to be sure, their studies have been prompted by the women's liberation movement in the West, the emergence of women as a major academic focus and concern, and the search for alternative models of women in a society that claims to have made great strides toward the complete equality of the sexes. But it would be wrong to dismiss the entire development as merely a Western academic fad. Sex discrimination in the USSR is a problem that is at least obliquely recognized even by Soviet demographers, economists, and sociologists; and Western scholarship but mirrors an increasing concern with the effects of that discrimination (if not its roots) within the Soviet Union itself.

That concern has surfaced most conspicuously with the debate over solutions to a number of serious and otherwise unrelated socioeconomic problems, notably the declining birthrate among Slavic ethnic groups, labor shortages and falling productivity in key industrial sectors, consumer and worker dissatisfaction with the inadequate level of goods and services, and the increasing incidence of divorces, sexual promiscuity, and juvenile delinquency in major Soviet urban centers.[1] As Western scholars and even some specialists in the Soviet Union have at least implied, all these prob-

This paper is adapted from Joel C. Moses, "Indoctrination as a Female Political Role in the Soviet Union," *Comparative Politics*, 8, no. 4 (July 1976), © 1976 by the City University of New York, and appears by permission of *Comparative Politics*.

[1] On the nexus of labor and population problems, see Helen Desfosses Cohn, "Population Policy in the USSR," *Problems of Communism*, 12, no. 4 (1973), pp. 41–55; V. B. Mikhailiuk, *Ispol'zovanie zhenskogo truda v narodnom khoziaistve* (M, 1970); A. G. Kharchev and S. I. Golod, *Professional'naia rabota zhenshchin i sem'ia* (L, 1971); N. A. Sakharova, *Optimal'nye vozmozhnosti ispol'zovaniia zhenskogo truda v sfere obshchestvennogo proizvodstva* (Kiev,

lems directly or indirectly reflect the frustrations of Soviet women as a group; and all these problems to some extent derive from the persistent inability of Soviet women as a latent interest group to have their distinct views and alternatives adequately articulated. Because of the almost complete exclusion of women from the major policy-making centers, problems have continued to be defined and solutions offered from the perspective, and indeed biases, of a male-dominated leadership.

That women have been virtually denied access into the Soviet political elite and a significant voice in policy, despite a long-standing tenet of official doctrine to the contrary, is clear from the separate studies of Barbara Jancar and Gail Lapidus.[2] Basing their findings primarily on the aggregate statistics of membership in the republic and All-Union Central Committees and state Councils of Ministers, both have ably demonstrated how women have traditionally been underrepresented in these key policy-making organs. Like the recent chairman of the All-Union Council of Nationalities in the Supreme Soviet, Ia. S. Nasriddinova, whose only apparent function during her brief tenure was the organization of receptions for visiting delegations from the Third World, some women have been conspicuously placed in important-sounding positions for external propaganda purposes. Influential female professional politicians, however, have been relatively few in the Soviet system, for women are typically thwarted in their political ambitions early in their political careers by being diverted into secondary "female" positions. Consider, for example, that whereas a high proportion of women are consistently to be found among the deputies elected to the local urban and district soviets (comparable to city and village councils in the United States), a review of Party cadre policy in 1974 revealed that less than 4 percent of the urban and district Party first secretaries in the USSR were women, and that in a number of *oblasti*, *krais*, and even whole republics, not one woman was to be found as the chairman of an urban district executive committee (comparable to the mayor of a city in the United States) in the state apparatus.[3]

What this review does not reveal, however, and what even Jancar and Lapidus fail to provide, are conclusive explanations for the lack of political

---

1973); and A. E. Kotliar and S. Ia. Turchaninova, *Zaniatost' zhenshchin v proizvodstve (Statistiko-sotsiologicheskii ocherk)* (M, 1975). For works reflecting the growing concern with juvenile delinquency and sexual promiscuity, see A. G. Kharchev, *Trudnyi put' k zrelosti* (M, 1975); "Soviet Deplores a Sexual Adventurism Among Youth," *The New York Times*, Nov. 24, 1973, p. 8; and V. Perevedentsev, "Sem'ia: vchera, segodnia, zavtra . . . (zametki sotsiologa)," *Nash sovremennik*, 6 (June 1975), pp. 118–31. See also Bernice Madison's paper in this volume.

[2] Barbara W. Jancar, "Women and Soviet Politics," in Henry W. Morton and Rudolf L. Tökés, eds., *Soviet Politics and Society in the 1970's* (New York, 1974); Gail W. Lapidus, "Political Mobilization, Participation and Leadership: Women in Soviet Politics," *Comparative Politics*, 8, no. 1 (Oct. 1976), pp. 90–118.

[3] *Voprosy vnutripartiinoi zhizni i rukovodiashchei deiatel'nosti KPSS na sovremennom etape* (M, 1974), pp. 192–93. This volume was written under the auspices of the Department of Party Building in the Central Committee Academy of Social Sciences.

power among Soviet women. For example, both contend that the recruit-ment policies of the Party and the socialization process incline women to accept early political sex roles or functions from which they have little op-portunity for career advancement or mobility into higher levels of the politi-cal system. But except for isolated examples of early female career types and speculative evidence, neither they nor anyone else that I know of has systematically identified the kinds of political career roles into which women are steered and why these particular career roles have proved so counterproductive to political mobility. Let us see if we can do both.

DATA AND ANALYSIS

In order to identify the source of political sex discrimination in the Soviet Union, we shall examine the range of elected and administrative political positions held by women in 25 regions of the Russian and Ukrainian repub-lics of the USSR. The comparative universe of female political careers in the regions will include all women elected to the regional committee (*obkom*) bureaus from 1955 through 1973 of a total known 810 bureau members during this period,[4] and a more exact profile of all known women holding political office and identifiable by references in the 25 regional newspapers over a ten-month period of 1970. The 25 regions represent the very diverse cross-section of highly urban industrial to rural agricultural population centers found in both republics, and they are located in 11 of the 13 major historic-economic Regional Areas (see Table 1).[5]

We shall study with particular interest the number of women assigned to varying regional positions, what the general functional responsibilities of these positions appear to denote, and the career prospects linked with specific regional positions and functional specializations. This approach will allow us to (1) isolate the patterns by which women are recruited for leadership positions at this still early period of their careers in a region; (2) trace the specific career dimensions for a defined universe of female politi-cal leaders (*obkom* bureau members) over time; and (3) compare the

[4] Culled data for the 810 officials from the standard Soviet and Western published biograph-ical directories, from lists of delegates in stenographic reports of All-Union and Ukrainian Party congresses from 1956 through 1971, from the actual regional newspapers for 1970 and limited parts of 1966–67 and 1973, and from numerous career-biographical references found in the principal All-Union and republic newspapers and periodicals for 1948 through 1973 (including *Pravda, Izvestiia, Partiinaia zhizn', Sovetskaia Rossiia, Pravda Ukrainy,* and *Komsomol'skaia pravda*). For a fuller study of the regional elites in the 25 regions, see Joel C. Moses, *Regional Party Leadership and Policy-Making in the USSR* (New York, 1974), pp. 159–246.

[5] As an indication of the diversity of the regions, here are some of their demographic charac-teristics in 1970: by urbanization, they ranged from 30 percent to 82 percent (median: 53 percent); by the number of students in higher educational institutions, from 41 to 576 stu-dents per 10,000 (median: 150); by the number of specialists in the work force who had com-pleted their higher education, from 177 to 442 per 10,000 (median: 261); and by the absolute number of engineers and technicians with higher and middle education in the work force, from 13,000 to 149,000 (median: 57,400).

TABLE 1

*The 11 Regional Areas and 25 Component Regions of the Russian
and Ukrainian Republics Under Study*

Regional Areas	Regions (*oblasts*)
Northwest	Kaliningrad, Vologda
Central	Briansk, Kaluga, Iaroslavl', Orel, Smolensk
Central Black Earth	Belgorod, Kursk, Tambov
Volga-Viatka	Kirov
Volga	Volgograd, Saratov
North Caucasus	Rostov
Urals	Perm'
Western Siberia	Kemerovo, Novosibirsk, Tomsk
Southeast Ukraine	Dnepropetrovsk, Kharkov, Zaporozhe
South Ukraine	Crimea, Odessa
Southwest Ukraine	Lvov, Transcarpathia

NOTE: The Regional Areas of Eastern Siberia and the Far East in the RSFSR were not surveyed.

female recruitment patterns in diverse regions of two separate republics.

In the Soviet Union, the elite at the regional level of the power structure could be roughly equated with the composition of the *obkom* bureau and those 13–15 comparable regional leadership positions that have conferred simultaneous membership as a full or candidate member of the *obkom* bureaus from 1955 through 1973.[6] If women are discouraged from seeking political influence early in their careers, we would expect to find both that very few women are elected to the regional elite, and that most of those who are elected have conformed to the narrowly prescribed female career options.

Both expectations appear to be borne out in Table 2. As we see, women were elected to the bureaus in only 16 of the regions between 1955 and 1973; and even if one counts O. K. Sazonova twice, for separate terms in two bureaus, the number of women elected represents but 3.2 percent of all the bureau members identified during this 19-year period. In half of these regions no more than one woman was ever elected, and in only five did two or more women serve simultaneously on a bureau.

[6] That is to say, I have assumed that individuals elected to any of 13 to 15 different leadership positions at the regional level have by that fact also simultaneously been elected full or candidate members of the *obkom* bureaus since 1955, constituting regional political "cabinets" within the Soviet Communist Party. The positions that I have assumed confer simultaneous membership within these regional political "cabinets" are the five *obkom* secretaries; the head of the *obkom* organizational-Party work department; the first secretary of the capital *gorkom*; the chairman and first deputy chairman of the regional executive committee (*oblispolkom*); the leaders of the three "mass" organizations (Komsomol, trade-unions council, and people's control commission); the editor of the regional newspaper; the chairman of the regional *sovnarkhoz* (1957–64); and the first secretaries of specific urban-district Party organizations within individual regions. Though also an *obkom* bureau member, the head of the regional KGB (security police) was excluded. For an analysis of these positions, see Moses, pp. 159–246.

Even in this small sample, the female bureau members differ significantly from their male counterparts in their origins, their career potential, and their tenure on the bureau. For example, the typical male member during this period was recruited to the bureau for the first time from a position outside the region and, once assigned to the regional elite, was freely rotated about, to hold several positions with different responsibilities on the same bureau.[7] In contrast, almost all of the women were "locals," recruited directly from lower positions within the region; and all but one held only one position during their tenure on the *obkom* bureau. If a highly mobile "generalist," tested frequently in several different leadership positions and locales, is preferred in reassignments to the central organs, then even the female elite in these 25 regions would be seriously disqualified for consideration for further promotion by the parochialism of their political associations and by the limited geographical context in which they have been able to prove their leadership capabilities.

Not unrelatedly, perhaps, only two of the female bureau members were appointed to higher political office in the central organs; and one was a non-local woman who had actually been recruited to the bureau for the first time from outside the region. In both cases, the office was the same: the RSFSR Minister of Social Security, a post apparently reserved since Stalin as the female position in the Russian Republic Council of Ministers.[8] For the other female bureau members, we see a distinctly different recruitment pattern, which finds most either retained in the same bureau position almost permanently or elected to a bureau position for a very brief period (almost as a token gesture to female representation in the regional leadership) before being demoted to lower-ranking positions in the regional hierarchy. Thus, in 27 percent of the cases (seven of twenty-six), the woman had held the same position on the *obkom* bureau for over a decade (compared with less than 3 percent of all male bureau members). On the other hand, even discounting two female bureau members whose abrupt dismissal from the regional elite followed specific charges of political malfeasance,[9] simple tokenism still appears to be a more prevalent consideration in selecting women to *obkom* bureaus. This pattern of tokenism is reflected in the fact that 14 women had remained on the *obkom* bureaus less than four years (through the end of 1973).

[7] Moses, pp. 163–65, 213–35. Although since 1965 a significant new trend has seen an increasing percentage of bureau members recruited from lower positions within the same region.

[8] D. P. Komarova, the current RSFSR Minister of Social Security (Dec. 1967–), was both first secretary of the Briansk district (1960–64) and chairman of the Briansk *oblispolkom* (1960–66). L. P. Lykova, her predecessor in the ministry and now Deputy Chairman of the RSFSR Council of Ministers for Cultural Affairs, was an *obkom* second secretary in the Ivanovo region (1952–55) and then in Smolensk (1958–61). Lykova followed N. A. Murav'iova in that office (1952–61), meaning that a woman has held the position for at least the last 25 years.

[9] L. V. Gladkaia, *obkom* ideology secretary of the Odessa region (1963–70), was removed from the regional elite in late 1970 or early 1971. Her removal at this time coincided with the

TABLE 2
Female Obkom Bureau Members, 1955–73

	Number of positions			Type of position						
Regions	1955–64	1965–73[a]	Total 1955–73[a]	Second secretary	Industry secretary	Ideology secretary	Chairman, regional executive committee	Chairman, control commission	Chairman, trade-unions council	First secretary Komsomol
Briansk	1	1	1			1				
Dnepropetrovsk	1		1			1				
Iaroslavl	1	1(1)	2(1)		1(1)	1				
Kaliningrad		1(1)	1(1)					1(1)		
Kaluga	2	2(1)	3(1)				1			2(1)[b]
Kemerovo	1	1	1			1				
Kharkov	1		1		1					
Kirov	1		1							1
Kursk	3	1	3			2[c]				1[c]
Odessa	1	2(1)	2(1)		1(1)				1	
Perm	2	1	2		1	1				
Saratov		1(1)	1(1)		1(1)					
Smolensk	1	1(1)	2(1)	1		1(1)				
Tambov	1	2(1)	2(1)			1[b]				1(1)
Volgograd	1		1			1				
Zaporozhe	2		2		1	1				
TOTAL	19	14(7)	26(7)	1	6(3)	11(1)	1	1(1)	1	5(2)

SOURCES: Compiled from various All-Union and republic periodicals and newspapers (1948–73); newspapers of the 25 regions (1966–67, 1970, 1973); Deputaty Verkhovnogo Soveta SSSR (M., 1958, 1962, 1966, 1970); Ezhegodniki Bol'shoi Sovetskoi Entsiklopedii (M., 1958–73); Biographic Directory of Soviet Officials (Washington, D.C., 1957, 1960, 1963, 1966); and lists of delegates in stenographic reports of All-Union and Ukrainian Party Congresses (M., Kiev, 1956–71).

[a] Bureau members elected for the first time in 1965–73 are indicated in parentheses.

[b] O. K. Sazonova, regional Komsomol first secretary of Kaluga (1957–60), obkom ideology secretary of Tambov (1963–74).

[c] I. A. Vlasova, both regional Komsomol first secretary (1957–1959) and industrial obkom ideology secretary (1963–64) of Kursk.

The data in Table 2 also refute any contention that the central leadership in recent years has undertaken a concerted effort to attract more women into the regional elite: as we see, there were only seven new women promoted to the bureaus after 1964. Actually, most of the women were first elected bureau members in the period between 1958 and 1964, a time when Khrushchev had unsuccessfully attempted to alter the general composition of the local Party leadership and, in what could be interpreted as a related tactic, had openly criticized sex discrimination and the low proportion of women in Party leadership positions.[10] In recent years, a similar renewed emphasis on the necessity of recruiting more women to political leadership positions has appeared in Party journals and in reviews of cadre policy organized within the Central Committee.[11] Yet because of a general reduction in bureau turnover and recruitment since 1965,[12] the real opportunities for women to advance into regional bureau positions have been still further reduced; and by 1973, at least, the renewed commitment to political equality had obviously not been implemented in such a manner as to threaten the male dominance of the elite in the 25 regions. On the contrary, a clearer indication is that four of the women elected bureau members under Khrushchev were demoted to lower regional offices immediately after his overthrow and the reconsolidation of bifurcated regional bureaus in late 1964.[13]

Partial information on four of the seven women elected for the first time after 1964 suggests a more overriding concern for "safe" women with established political records and status-quo orientations. Both Z. M. Bubnova, the *obkom* industry secretary of Saratov, and T. N. Iarovaia, the *obkom* ideology secretary of Smolensk, were in their late forties when they first became bureau members.[14] Similarly, A. P. Sochneva, the industry secre-

---

extensive replacement of the Odessa Party leadership, which was apparently implicated in wide-scale local corruption. See Moses, pp. 48–53; and *Voprosy vnutripartiinoi zhizni*, p. 202. M. Ia. Koshkareva, the Perm' *obkom* ideology secretary (1955–57), was removed following criticism of both her and the *obkom* agricultural secretary for "formalistic-bureaucratic" leadership of agricultural and indoctrination policies in the rural villages of the region. See *Pravda*, Oct. 10, 1956; and *Sovetskaia Rossiia*, Apr. 16, 1957, and Feb. 28, 1958.

[10] I. A. Kurganov, *Zhenshchiny i kommunizm* (New York, 1968), pp. 34–36.

[11] For example, P. Leonov, "Razvitie XXIV s"ezdom KPSS leninskikh printsipov raboty s kadrami," *Kommunist*, 18 (Dec. 1971), p. 52; N. Tartyshev, "Partiinaia zabota o kadrakh," *Kommunist*, 4 (Mar. 1974), p. 30; and most recently, the 1974 review of cadre policy in the Central Committee's Academy of Social Sciences, *Voprosy vnutripartiinoi zhizni*, pp. 192–93.

[12] Moses, pp. 173–93.

[13] In Volgograd, Z. V. Dubrovina, the *obkom* ideology secretary of the industrial secretariat (1963–64), became the ideology secretary of the capital *gorkom* (1965–73); in Dnepropetrovsk, S. P. Khvostenko, the *obkom* ideology secretary (1955–64), became the deputy chairman of the *oblispolkom* for cultural-educational problems (1965–71); in Kursk, I. A. Vlasova, the *obkom* ideology secretary of the industrial secretariat (1963–64), became the ideology secretary of the capital *gorkom* (1965–71); and in Kharkov, N. A. Pernach, the *obkom* industry secretary (1960–64), became the deputy chairman of the *oblispolkom* for local industry (1965–69).

[14] *Vedomosti Verkhovnogo Soveta SSSR*, Dec. 26, 1968, and Oct. 2, 1969. Though little biographical information is available for either official, prior to their elections to the *obkom*

tary of the Iaroslavl capital in 1970, was promoted to perform the same duties at the regional level as the *obkom* industry secretary in 1972, when she was 46. Z. P. Nazarenko, for several years the deputy chairman of the Odessa regional government responsible for retail trade and consumer services, was elected to the Odessa bureau as an *obkom* secretary in 1972. Though her background as a consumer affairs specialist no doubt counted heavily in her elevation to this post, she probably owed her promotion as much to the scandal that brought down most of the former regional elite as to the sudden priority given to consumer problems at the local level in the USSR since 1971 and the 24th Party Congress.[15] Importantly, by their ages and extended prior administrative roles, it would be difficult to assume that Bubnova, Iarovaia, Sochneva, and Nazarenko were recruited to provide dynamic new feminine initiatives in the policy areas under their aegis.

If few women have been elected to the *obkom* bureaus in the 25 regions and even fewer have later been promoted to the central organs, a significant reason may be found in the limited range of positions that the female bureau members have held. Eleven of the women in ten regions were elected to the bureaus as the *obkom* ideology secretary, a position supervising the cultural-academic institutions and the broad range of activities commonly referred to as "propaganda-agitation" (*agitprop*) in a region. If we include the very similar position of Komsomol first secretary, held by four women in Kaluga, Kirov, and Tambov, a total of 15 of the 26 female bureau members would be characterized by their elected positions as "indoctrination" specialists. Even though most of the leadership positions in this functional area, like all others, have been filled by men, the functional area of indoctrination thus appears to be a sex-typed profession reserved for women and the principal career option by default available to a woman who aspires to any form of regional political elite status.

The validity of this proposition is supported on a broader scale when we analyze the distribution of women by their specialized political functions. These are identifiable throughout the regional hierarchy in the 25 regions over a 10-month period of 1970, as shown in Table 3. Like those few women elevated to the *obkom* bureaus over the 19-year period, over 50 percent of the women at all levels of the regional hierarchy (61 of 119) held an official position or fulfilled responsibilities that classified them as indoctri-

---

bureaus in 1965–66, Bubnova held an unknown lower-ranking position in Saratov (see list of delegates from Saratov in the stenographic report of the 21st All-Union Party Congress in 1959); and Iarovaia had been first secretary of the Pochinok district in Smolensk (see list of delegates from Smolensk in the stenographic report of the 22nd All-Union Party Congress in 1962).

[15] On Sochneva, see *Severnyi rabochii* (Iaroslavl), Jan. 24, July 17, and Sept. 30, 1970; May 26, 1973. On Nazarenko's earlier career, see *Izvestiia*, Sept. 18, 1954, and June 16, 1967. Suggestive that Nazarenko's experience was a major consideration in her election, the very *obkom* plenum at which she was elected secretary reviewed as its main topic the progress of regional retail trade and public works organizations. See *Pravda Ukrainy*, Feb. 16, 1972. Nazarenko's election also may have been intended to fill the token female position in the bureau, left vacant since early 1971 by the removal of the ideology secretary Gladkaia.

TABLE 3

Functional Specialization of Women Officeholders in the 25 Surveyed Regions of the Ukrainian and Russian Republics, 1970

Specialization[a]	Number of women[b]	Types of position included[c]
Indoctrination	61	*Obkom* ideology secretary; ideology secretaries of urban-district Party organizations; heads of *obkom agitprop* and science-education institutions departments; heads of urban-district *agitprop* departments; regional and urban-district Komsomol secretaries; deputy chairmen of *oblispolkom* for cultural-education problems; heads of regional and urban-district public education departments; editors of urban-district newspapers; directors of homes of political education and popular creativity; directors of regional *Znanie* (Knowledge) society
Cadres	16	*Obkom* and urban-district cadres secretaries; *obkom* and urban-district heads of organizational–Party work departments; chairmen of regional and urban-district trade-union councils and people's control commissions; secretary of *oblispolkom*; head of organizational-instruction departments of *oblispolkom*
Social welfare	11	*Oblispolkom* deputy chairmen for consumer problems (light industry and trade); heads of *obkom* and urban-district industry-food and finance-commercial establishments departments; directors of state urban planning and everyday services departments
Agriculture	10	*Oblispolkom* chairman or deputy chairman in charge of agricultural affairs; directors of state regional and *obkom* departments of agriculture; agricultural secretaries of urban-district Party organizations; directors of regional administrations or departments for state farms and rural construction
Industry	6	*Obkom* industry secretary; industry secretaries of urban-district Party organizations; directors of state regional and *obkom* departments for matters related to industry, construction, and transportation
Judicial	1	Procurator; chairman of the regional college of advocates; head of the regional Ministry of Internal Affairs; head of the regional Committee for State Security
Other	14	Urban-district Party secretaries with unknown responsibilities

SOURCE: Regional newspapers, Jan.–Oct. 1970.

[a] My classification is based on two criteria: official responsibilities normally associated with a position and the context of an official's participation in such activities as local Party plenums and conferences.

[b] I have included only those women holding an administrative or elective political office. Female collective farm chairmen, state farm directors, enterprise directors, and secretaries of primary Party organizations have been deliberately excluded. In cases where a person's sex was not specified, I made a determination on the basis of surname and verb endings.

None of these lists is complete. I simply list here, for illustration, some of the titles I culled in my newspaper survey.

nation specialists. In 16 of the regions in 1970, women figured prominently in the formation of indoctrination policy by holding at least one of the six major indoctrination offices in the region: *obkom* ideology secretary; heads of the *obkom agitprop* and science-educational institutions departments; ideology secretary of the regional capital urban committee (*gorkom*); director of the state cultural administration; and deputy chairman of the regional executive committee (*oblispolkom*) responsible for cultural-educational problems. In eight of the regions (Kemerovo, Kursk, Orel, Saratov, Smolensk, Tambov, Vologda, and Zaporozhe), women held at least two of the six major indoctrination offices and together accounted for 35 percent of the indoctrination policy elite.[16] A much less systematic examination of All-Union, republic, and regional newspapers both before and after 1970 also suggests that the recruiting of women for indoctrination work has been a fairly standard pattern in the 25 regions since 1955.[17]

The disproportionate number of indoctrination specialists both among female bureau members and among women at all levels of the regional hierarchy is particularly noteworthy because, as several Western scholars have emphasized, indoctrination officials have traditionally held a rather low status within the Party elite, and ideology tends to rank well down on the priority list of regional Party leaders.[18] When officials responsible for indoctrination affairs in a region are not deliberately shunted aside by Party leaders, then all too often their training in a university or pedagogical institute and their humanistic backgrounds prove incompatible with the specialized economic training and production-oriented concerns of many regional Party leaders.

The antagonism between indoctrination officials and Party leaders in the Soviet Union has been compared to the traditional role conflict in bureaucracies between the "man of words" and the "man of deeds." Unless ideolog-

---

[16]Vologda in fact had seven women in important indoctrination positions during 1970, the most of any region. The head of the *obkom agitprop* department and an instructor in that department were women, as were the directors of the regional home of political education, the regional cultural administration, and the regional home of popular creativity, the deputy director of the regional *Znanie* (Knowledge) society, and the deputy chairman of the regional planning commission (responsible for schools).

[17]Here are a few examples among many. A. A. Krylova, deputy chairman of the *oblispolkom* for cultural-educational problems of Odessa (1959–61), cited in *Pravda Ukrainy*, Aug. 20, 1959, and May 17, 1961. A. Timofeeva, deputy head of the L'vov *obkom agitprop* department (1955), cited in *Literaturnaia gazeta*, Sept. 13, 1955. M. I. Kursheva, graduate of the Novocherkassk Teachers Institute in 1952, head of the *agitprop* department of the Kagal'nitskii district of Rostov (1952–60) and ideology secretary of that region's Zernogradskii district (1960–66), cited in *Molot* (Rostov), Oct. 20, 1966. A. N. Golubeva, head of the Vologda regional state cultural administration (1970–73), cited in *Krasnyi sever* (Vologda), Jan. 10, 1970, and May 25, 1973.

[18]Notably, John A. Armstrong, *The Soviet Bureaucratic Elite: A Case Study of the Ukrainian Apparatus* (New York, 1959) pp. 95–101; Philip D. Stewart, *Political Power in the Soviet Union: A Study of Decision-Making in Stalingrad* (New York, 1968), pp. 75–78; Jerry F. Hough, *The Soviet Prefects: The Local Party Organs in Industrial Decision-Making* (Cambridge, Mass., 1969), pp. 144–48; and Frederick J. Fleron, "System Attributes and Career Attributes: The Soviet Political Leadership System, 1952 to 1965," in Carl Beck et al., *Comparative Communist Political Leadership* (New York, 1973), pp. 69–77.

ical discontent were to reach the stage of local riots or other forms of open political defiance, ideology as a distinct policy area is unlikely to be considered significant enough to merit more than a pro forma rhetorical emphasis on the part of regional leaders. Most leaders can only look on ideological problems as annoying diversions on their limited time, which might be better spent in meeting agricultural or industrial quotas. It is indicative of this general lack of concern that few *obkom* plenums are devoted entirely to a separate review of ideological policy or the performance of indoctrination officials, even though ideological factors may be considered indirectly during the course of assessing general economic problems at plenary meetings.[19] Ideology and indoctrination specialists may be viewed with even greater disdain in regions populated by ethnic minorities, where the blatant Russian-inspired content of the ideology is resented by local ethnic leaders with their own distinct nationalistic beliefs and values.[20]

Extending the analysis on the basis of our findings for the 25 regions, we would speculate that the sex bias in the regional Party may contribute significantly to this functional antagonism and may even help reinforce the group identity among female indoctrination specialists themselves. From the perspective of male Party leaders, though men actually account for the majority of indoctrination specialists, the largest segment of politically active women at the regional level is conspicuously identified with indoctrination policy. Seeking self-justification for their own priorities, Party leaders may rationalize their devaluation of indoctrination not merely as an annoying intrusion on their time, but as a functional conflict that seemingly has been transformed into a struggle between themselves as pragmatic "men of deeds" and indoctrination specialists as impractical "women of words." In turn, from the perspective of female indoctrination specialists, career frustrations and their perceived sexual caste in the Party may harden their resolve that indoctrination should be granted a higher priority by leaders who are biased as much against their sex as against the nature of their work. Thus, the rigid political orthodoxy that characterizes some locales may parallel the number of influential women among regional indoctrination specialists and may well be perpetuated by the perverse need of these women to rationalize their own marginal status in the Soviet political system.[21]

---

[19] Moses, pp. 91–99.

[20] Teresa Rakowska-Harmstone, *Russia and Nationalism in Central Asia: The Case of Tadzhikistan* (Baltimore, 1970), pp. 193–205. A recent exception that may prove the rule is the large number of *obkom* plenums specifically convened to consider ideological problems in the Ukraine since 1973 (and since the removal of the Ukrainian Party First Secretary, P. E. Shelest, for encouraging nationalistic "deviations"). That the suddenly high priority assigned to ideological problems at the regional level represents a departure from normal routines is obvious. In 1970, for example, only on *obkom* plenum in the seven Ukrainian regions under study was convened specifically to discuss such problems.

[21] A major policy conflict within the Soviet indoctrination *apparatus* itself some years ago found at least two women—T. I. Arkhipova, the virtually permanent ideology secretary of the Kursk *obkom*, and Z. M. Kruglova, the ideology secretary of Leningrad—vigorously defending

Trained and skilled in this one, narrow specialization, the female indoctrination official who commits herself to a political career probably has less of an opportunity for advancement within or beyond the regional hierarchy than officials who have specialized in agricultural or industrial problems at the regional level. As a Komsomol first secretary, a young woman with political ambitions is unlikely to find herself in the bureau leadership for more than a brief period, since in several regions this office almost routinely changes hands every two or three years.[22] In most cases, the former occupant is then reassigned to a lower regional position. But even if she were to become the *obkom* ideological secretary, her career prospects would be dim. Indoctrination is rarely a road to leadership positions at the republic or national level, where technical administrators or generalist Party *apparatchiki* have the clear edge.[23] Elevation to the *obkom* bureau may well represent the highest elite status to which she could reasonably aspire. Indeed, only one woman from our 25 regions, M. T. Poberei, moved up to become a full member of the All-Union Central Committee in the period under study—and her election, in 1971, could be credited more to a desire for a certain conspicuous percentage of women or agricultural specialists on the Central Committee than to her service in the lowly position of first secretary of an agricultural district in Volgograd.[24]

As pertinent examples of the career limitations confronting female indoctrination specialists, let us review the typical careers of three *obkom* ideology secretaries—Z. V. Kuz'mina, of Kemerovo; T. I. Arkhipova, of Kursk; and O. K. Sazonova, of Tambov. Kuz'mina had been identified with indoctrination responsibilities as the ideology secretary of either the capital *gorkom* or *obkom* over the entire period of my study, which is to say at least 19 consecutive years, beginning in January 1954. Similarly, Arkhipova, before her apparent retirement in 1971–72, had occupied the same position in the Kursk bureau ever since her appointment in 1954. More clear-cut even than these cases is that of Sazonova, for whom potentially higher political

---

the more orthodox *agitprop* personnel and methods against a proposed uniform upgrading and professionalization of indoctrination specialists in the Soviet Union. See Aryeh L. Unger, "Politinformator or Agitator: A Decision Blocked," *Problems of Communism*, 19, no. 5 (1970), pp. 35, 36–37.

[22] Between 1965 and 1975, this post turned over from three to five times in 12 of our regions: Dnepropetrovsk, Kemerovo, Kharkov, Kursk, Lvov, Novosibirsk, Orel, Saratov, Tambov, Volgograd, Vologda, and Zaporozhe. Examples of former Komsomol first secretaries reassigned to lower-ranking positions are Iu. P. Kochetkov, who after holding that post in Saratov in 1966 went on to become secretary of the Saratov Aviation Plant Committee in 1970, and V. V. Durdinets, the Komsomol first secretary of Lvov in 1965–66, later (in 1970) head of the *obkom* administrative organs department.

[23] In the 20 years between 1954 and 1974, 185 officials from our 25 regions were transferred to other areas or to positions in the central organs of Kiev and Moscow. Significantly, only 25 of them were *obkom* ideology secretaries or regional Komsomol first secretaries immediately prior to their transfer. Only three of the 185 were women; and the exception that may prove the rule for female indoctrination specialists is that the only two women transferred to the center, Lykova and Komarova, were both very definitely not indoctrination specialists in their regional career origins (see footnote 8).

[24] See her biography in *Ezhegodnik Bol'shoi Sovetskoi Entsiklopedii* (M, 1972).

office could have been anticipated. Only 40 years old at the time of her election as the Tambov *obkom* ideology secretary in 1964, and with a candidate degree in economics (equivalent to an American doctorate), Sazonova had also been the Komsomol first secretary of the Kaluga region (in 1957–60) and could thus not be accused of the limited career parochialism so typical of the "local" female bureau members recruited from within their regions since 1955. Yet Sazonova was still the Tambov *obkom* secretary as late as 1974; and in both her Kaluga and Tambov tenures, though her title changed, she had the identical assignment of supervising political agitation among rural youth.[25]

Even within this "female" specialty, women appear to represent a distinctly marginal subgroup in strictly geographical terms. Thus, we find that 11 male regional indoctrination officials who got their start in the regions of Kharkov, Lvov, and Novosibirsk were promoted to important indoctrination offices in central organs between 1954 and 1974.[26] That the ability to advance in what is generally conceded to be a low-potential career field should coincide with service in three of the major academic and cultural centers of the Soviet Union certainly suggests variations in the political status of indoctrination positions according to different locales. In regions like these, where the presence of great numbers of intellectuals dictates a very high political priority and concern, the supervision of local indoctrination policy almost certainly carries a correspondingly higher status and career potential.[27] With greater initial visibility and presumably a more demanding practical-administrative background in their policy area, indoctrination officials from such cultural centers may therefore be given first priority in considerations for promotion to higher political office.

In contrast, not one woman was even elected to the position of *obkom* ideology secretary in these three regions in our period. For that matter, as our cross-sectional analysis of women in political positions in 1970 indicates, female indoctrination specialists tend to be predominate in just the opposite kinds of regional locales—rural, agricultural regions with few cultural-academic institutions, little probable visibility or political status associated with indoctrination policy, and little potential in career mobility for other than agricultural specialists. In that year, as we saw, the regions

---

[25] On Kuz'mina's career: *Trud*, Jan. 10, 1954; *Pravda*, Feb. 8, 1963, Feb. 10, 1972; and *Kuzbass* (Kemerovo), Aug. 13, 1970, May 27, 1973. On Arkhipova: *Izvestiia*, Mar. 18, 1954; *Narodnoe obrazovanie*, 2 (Feb. 1956), p. 75; *Pravda*, Jan. 23, 1963, Oct. 18, 1966; and *Kurskaia pravda* (Kursk), Mar. 31 and July 16–18, 1970. On Sazonova: *Sel'skoe khoziaistvo*, Sept. 26, 1957; *Komsomol'skaia pravda*, Feb. 19, 1958; *Izvestiia*, Jan. 7, 1964, Apr. 17, 1974; *Sovetskaia Rossiia*, Apr. 20, 1966; and *Tambovskaia pravda* (Tambov), July 5, Aug. 14, and Aug. 23, 1970, May 28, 1973.

[26] V. G. Furov and V. I. Koval' (Novosibirsk); R. V. Babiichuk, B. D. Kotik, V. V. Kulik, V. E. Malanchuk, V. N. Mazur, and B. V. Okpysh (Lvov); Iu. Iu. Kondufor, A. D. Skaba, and Iu. A. Skliarov (Kharkov). Interestingly, and somewhat ironically, in 1975 Skliarov, as deputy head of the All-Union Central Committee Department of Propaganda, was assigned responsibility for the domestic mass media coverage of events surrounding the International Women's Year. See *Izvestiia*, Apr. 10, 1975, p. 4.

[27] Moses, pp. 92–93, 98–99.

where women held at least two of the six major indoctrination offices were primarily rural: Kursk, Orel, Smolensk, Tambov, and Vologda. Meanwhile, Kharkov, Lvov, and Novosibirsk between them had only one important female indoctrination specialist, the deputy chairman of the Lvov regional government responsible for cultural-educational problems. Even when female indoctrination specialists like Arkhipova and Sazonova have been recruited to regional elite positions, it has been primarily in agricultural regions; and as for the prestigious regional indoctrination positions outside Moscow and Leningrad in the major cultural-academic centers, they have clearly remained a male preserve.

Though my own data apply only to the opportunity structure for women in 25 regions of the Russian and Ukrainian republics, examples of female professional politicians in other places and at higher administrative levels of the USSR tend to confirm that there exists a farily uniform cadre policy, implemented throughout the political system, that sets women into a distinct political role. The bulk of the most prominent female Party and state officials, particularly among the non-Slavic nationalities, can likewise be found assigned to indoctrination tasks. In 1948, for example, three of the four women in the Party *apparatus* of the Stalinabad *gorkom* of Tadzhikistan were the *gorkom* propaganda secretary and the heads of the *gorkom* departments of propaganda-agitation and work among women. And 25 years later, we see this pattern apparently sustained in that republic, for I. R. Rakhimova, the only woman among 72 republic secretaries elected in the Soviet Union in 1972–73, was the Tadzhik republic ideology secretary and had held that position continuously since 1966.[28] Kuluipa Konduchalova, cited as the most successful female politician in a 1967 survey of the Kirgiz republic, was the Kirgiz Minister of Culture at the time. Along with the female head of the Kirgiz Party Department of Culture (D. Nusupova) and the female Deputy Chairman of the Kirgiz Council of Ministers for Cultural Affairs (S. Begmatova), Konduchalova would be best characterized as an indoctrination *apparatchik* by the nature of her career assignments over her 30-year career. She had been more or less directly involved with the problems of propaganda-agitation and work among women ever since her graduation from the Frunze Pedagogical Institute. Finally, to judge by surnames, the current head of the Turkmen Party Department of Culture and the last three Deputy Chairmen of the Turkmen Council of Ministers for Cultural Affairs have been women.[29]

[28] Rakowska-Harmstone, p. 109; Hedwig Kraus, "The Present Composition of the Secretaries of the Union Republic CP Central Committees," *Radio Liberty Research Bulletin*, Feb. 5, 1973, p. 1. Moreover, in the decade after 1961, M. Karimova, the only woman identifiable by surname in a major position in the state republic *apparatus*, was Deputy Chairman of the Tadzhik Council of Ministers for Cultural Affairs. See Grey Hodnett and Val Ogareff, *Leaders of the Soviet Republics, 1955–1972* (Canberra, 1973), pp. 294, 301.

[29] On Konduchalova, see Z. S. Tatybekova, *Zhenshchiny Sovetskogo Kirgizstana v bor'be za sotsializm i kommunizm* (Frunze, 1967), p. 204; and *Bol'shaia Sovetskaia Entsiklopediia* (M, 1953), vol. 51, p. 158. On Nusupova, Begmatova, and the Turkmen officeholders, see Hodnett and Ogareff, pp. 188, 192, 324, 328.

At the regional and district level, a 1973 ethnographic study of female emancipation in the Gorno-Altai autonomous region of Western Siberia singled out several female propagandists and agitators as models of politically successful women. M. Sarueva, who we may infer was the *obkom* ideology secretary, was reported to have held the same position for a "long time," a longevity exemplifying the similar limited career opportunities that kept Arkhipova in Kursk and Kuz'mina in Kemerova as virtually the permanent *obkom* ideology secretaries of their regions.[30] Significantly, as a purported model for all Soviet women, Kh. Ia. Iakubdzhanova, the Uzbek second secretary of the October borough in Tashkent, was the only contemporary female Party leader portrayed in a 1969 volume of journalistic essays on female Soviet Communists. Like many of the indoctrination specialists, a graduate of a pedagogical institute, Iakubdzhanova first taught at a secondary school in her native October borough before assuming responsibility for educational problems in the borough's Komsomol and Party organizations. Though officially elevated to the position of Party second secretary, her principal function continued to be the political oversight of schools in the October borough, as suggested by the vignettes of her daily activities presented in the essay.[31]

At the All-Union level, the key political centers of Moscow and Leningrad have traditionally proved to be the most reliable stepping-stones to the political elite for women in the Soviet Union. From the Twentieth Party Congress (1956) through the Twenty-fourth (1971), 21 women career politicians were elected to the All-Union Central Committee and Central Auditing Commission. Sixteen of the 21 had begun their careers and worked long in the two centers, and 13 had graduated from one of their higher educational institutions.[32] What is particularly noteworthy is that a majority of these women had achieved their high political status by avoiding the training that would have portended indoctrination careers. Fifteen of the 21 had graduated from an industrial, agricultural, or economic institute and had served in a broad array of administrative, political, agricultural, and industrial assignments, particularly in management positions in light industry and textiles. The most striking example is Ekaterina Furtseva, the only woman ever to have been elected to the Party's All-Union Politburo (1957–61). Though she was All-Union Minister of Culture till her death in 1974, Furtseva defies the single classification of an indoctrination specialist, for she was a graduate of the Moscow Lomonosov Institute of

[30]Ye. M. Toshchakova, *Zhenshchina v obshchestve i sem'e u sovremennykh altaitsev* (Novosibirsk, 1973), pp. 54–55. See also the discussion of the most prominent early female Party worker in the region, the propagandist Katiuk Tordokova, pp. 20–22.

[31]"Sekretar' raikoma," in *Skvoz' gody i buri (o zhenshchinakh kommunistkakh)* (M, 1969), pp. 21–36.

[32]A list of all women elected to the Central Committee and the Central Auditing Commission through the early 1970's is included in Jancar, "Women in Politics," pp. 155–60. From that list, I excluded all but professional political women. Biographies on the 21 remaining women are from the *Ezhegodniki Bol'shoi Sovetskoi Entsiklopedii; Deputaty Verkhovnogo Soveta SSSR*; and the last two editions of the *Bol'shaia Sovetskaia Entsiklopediia*.

Chemical Technology (and later the Higher Party School) and rose through the Moscow *apparatus* to hold the positions of second and first Party secretary of the Moscow city committee for eight years. On the other hand, even in the Moscow and Leningrad Party organizations an important share of the women in leadership positions have been indoctrination specialists,[33] and as a Soviet journal has frankly conceded, in an article directed to its Western audience, many female Party functionaries have been deliberately recruited from among former lower-school and college teachers in order to apply their specific educational skills in Party work.[34]

CONCLUSION

In this study, we have examined the backgrounds and positions of a limited sample of professional political women in the Soviet Union. We have also identified one political role into which the largest number of these women have been recruited at the regional level. This does not mean, to be sure, that women are recruited only into indoctrination functional responsibilities in the Soviet political system. Even among the group we have studied, a certain minority of the women would be definitely classified as agricultural, industrial, cadre, or judicial career specialists. Moreover, an important stratum of professional political women can also be found in a second major female role among those local officials with direct policy responsibility for consumer welfare services and institutions (like the previously cited Nazarenko, elected to the Odessa bureau in 1972).[35] Nevertheless, the limited political career potential of most Soviet women and their

[33]Two recent and successful examples are A. P. Shaposhnikova, the Soviet Deputy Minister of Higher and Middle Specialized Education, and Z. M. Kruglova, the Soviet Deputy Minister of Culture. Before her appointment to this post in 1972, Shaposhnikova was deputy head of the Zhdanov district *agitprop* department in Moscow (1960), district ideology secretary of Zhdanov (1961–65), and ideology secretary of the Moscow *gorkom* (1965–71). Kruglova had served as ideology secretary of the Leningrad *gorkom* and later *obkom* for 12 years prior to being elevated to the Ministry in early 1975. On Shaposhnikova, see *Pravda*, Sept. 5, 1961, May 6, 1966, July 31, 1967, Dec. 30, 1970; *Sovetskaia kul'tura*, Feb. 18, 1967; and *Sovetskaia Rossiia*, Jan. 22, 1960, May 28, 1963, Dec. 30, 1965. On Kruglova, see *Ezhegodnik*, 1971; Unger, pp. 36–37; and *Izvestiia*, Oct. 17, 1974, Feb. 13, 1975.

[34]See *Soviet Life*, 3 (Mar. 1974), p. 11. This article is devoted to T. N. Nikolaeva, one of the six indoctrination specialists among the 21 women elected to the Central Committee or Auditing Commission. Nikolaeva perhaps had the unique advantage of beginning her career in Ivanovo, a major center of textile industry, for as a female Party official in a region with a very high percentage of women employed in the work force, she was bound to draw the special attention of Party leaders. Nikolaeva graduated from the Ivanovo Pedagogical Institute, taught in primary schools for several years, served as the head of the *agitprop* departments of the Ivanovo capital *gorkom* and *obkom*, and, finally, in 1959, was elected the *obkom* first Party secretary. She stayed in that post only briefly (January-March) before being named Secretary of the All-Union Trade-Unions Council. She has held the position ever since and is currently responsible for union cultural facilities and amateur art groups.

[35]A question of overlapping functional responsibilities could also be raised in respect to the position of the ideology secretary in the regional network. As Jerry F. Hough has pointed out to me, in recent years the *obkom* ideology secretary has also been invested with the regional responsibility for all social welfare and health policies. Yet for all this, it is important to note that nine of 61 female indoctrination specialists in our 1970 sample held positions as heads of

general exclusion from central policy-making later on can be ascribed in good part to the career stigma arising from their early diversion into certain marginal political roles, and especially indoctrination.

From a cross-cultural perspective, Soviet women who have accepted this "housekeeping" function of indoctrination appear conditioned to a role not unlike that characteristic of Western female political activists. Significantly, in a recent attitudinal study, differences in the career styles and motivations of male and female American politicians were shown to parallel sex-role differences learned in the family. The male politician is drawn initially into politics because of self-serving career considerations, and, like the husband within the family, tends to specialize in the "instrumental" functions of the system (whether party or family), preoccupying himself with external task responsibilities. The female politician, on the other hand, is much less ambitious and career-oriented, and is inclined to play the same supportive role in politics as she plays in the family. That is, like the wife, a female political activist tends to specialize in the "expressive functions of those concerned with the *internal affairs of the system, the maintenance of integrative relations between its members.*"[36] The analogy is even more apt in the Soviet case, where "husband" and "wife" roles have clearly been carried over and institutionalized in the political system: the ambitious male Party careerists, the "men of deeds," with their primary "instrumental" functions of industrial and agricultural production, and the female indoctrination specialists, the "women of words," with their primary "expressive" functions performed in sustaining mass commitment to the belief system and the Party (family). As in the United States, these differences in career styles and motivations inevitably lead to the male dominance of major public and Party offices.[37]

Female professional politicians may also be constrained in their career options by the same set of circumstances that have limited the range of

---

the more doctrinaire *agitprop* departments at the regional or urban-district level, that a significant percentage of the others held positions as directors of political education networks or related indoctrination institutions, and that the persons who are selected as ideology secretaries still appear to be valued primarily for their career experience in and knowledge of propaganda-agitation.

[36] Edmond Constantini and Kenneth Craik, "Women as Politicians: The Social Background, Personality, and Political Careers of Female Party Leaders," *Journal of Social Issues,* 28, no. 2 (1972), p. 235. Italics in the original, citing Talcott Parsons and Robert Bales, *Family Socialization and Interaction Process* (New York, 1955), p. 347.

[37] We could also speculate that the Soviet political bureaucracy may gain certain hidden benefits from the late entry of women into professional political roles and their low expectations of any career advancement. Less driven by personal ambition and thus less likely to fall into the more typically male bureaucratic pathology of "careerism," women may evince more dedication and pragmatism in the actual execution of their daily political responsibilities. Suggestive in this connection is a recent study on American women in politics, in which a significant majority of American female state legislators are shown to have begun their political careers fairly late in life and to have few career goals outside their own legislative districts, but to have unique "problem-solving" capabilities. See Jeane Kirkpatrick, *Political Woman* (New York, 1974).

specializations available to women in the Soviet economy. As others in this volume have pointed out, the Soviet working woman is unduly handicapped in comparison to her male counterpart because she must bear by herself the full burden of the family responsibility. Soviet husbands refuse to share the responsibilities of the household and the children, so the professional woman must divert an inordinate amount of her time away from her career. Since she cannot suspend these family obligations to return to school in another region or to improvise her daily work schedule, a woman is unable to compete for the more highly skilled industrial-engineering positions, which require constant retraining and many additional hours outside the normal work period spent every day at an industrial enterprise. The unpredictable interruptions of the home further increase the likelihood of periodic leaves of absence among professional women and reduce their continuous accumulated seniority in an industrial enterprise. Consequently, a woman has less opportunity to expand her professional skills on the job and, because of loss of seniority, will be bypassed in favor of her male counterpart in promotion to a higher position. In addition, even before she is married, a woman tends to specialize only in the lower-salaried skilled trades, in which female labor has been applied extensively in the past, because of her exclusion from certain kinds of traditionally male-dominated vocational-technical schools and higher institutes. A professional woman in the Soviet Union generally experiences low mobility, is often forced to select a specialization well below the level of her educational training and real potential, and is frequently assigned to those specialized positions that are the simplest, least interesting, and lowest paying, and that offer the least future career prospects.

It may well be that a position as an indoctrination specialist at the regional level for quite similar reasons represents the most feasible vocational goal for the politically ambitious married woman with children. Unlike Party industrial and agricultural professionals, an indoctrination specialist will not be required constantly to upgrade her technical qualifications or to attend retraining courses for two years at the Higher Party School in Moscow; periodic retraining seminars in her line are offered during the year within each region. In addition, her work routine, keyed to the regular school year, elections, and specifically timed propaganda campaigns, is likely to be fairly predictable and standardized, at least compared with the uncertainties and incessant pressures that would confront her as a Party specialist in agricultural and industrial affairs. As a result, she will be better able to adapt her professional Party career to her daily family responsibilities. Not least, given societal norms that obligate even a female professional politician to sacrifice her career in order to stay with her husband and care for her family, the lower salary and career potential associated with indoctrination may simply be calculated liabilities that she is ready to assume. Otherwise, if she accepted a functional responsibility with a high probability of transfer in the Party *apparatus* outside a region and that came to pass, she would have to contend with the wounded male ego of her husband and the need to find him a new position in her reassigned locale. Few professional political women are likely to be blessed with such an understanding husband as the one recently cited as "typical," who remained at home to care for his wife's two younger children during the two years that she was reassigned to Leningrad.[38] Because of her primary family obligations, a woman may be unable to involve herself actively in a professional political career until a much later stage of life than a man. The ages of women holding political office in our 25 regions during 1970 tend to support this conclusion: 15 of the 18 women for whom birth dates could be determined were at least 45 years old. Nine of the 11 women who were still bureau members in 1973 averaged 52 years (they ranged from 47 to 57 years of age, with only the two Komsomol first secretaries in Tambov and Kaluga in their mid-30's).

Finally, if the relevant success models of women are mainly indoctrination specialists who graduated from a pedagogical institute, then a young Party member will be cued to obtain her educational degree and adopt that same political career specialization. This tendency is reinforced by the fact that Soviet girls from their earliest schooldays play an important role in inducing conformity to societal values in classroom collectives, so that in a sense the indoctrination specialist's role becomes a very natural adult extension of an early female political role learned during childhood.[39] Thus, a successful female indoctrination specialist like M. Ia. Karklin, the Latvian Republic Minister of Education, may be very typical in perceiving the early motivation for her political career in her childhood school involvement as a Young Pioneer leader (the Young Pioneers is the mass political organization for children between 9 and 15 years old).[40]

It is of some significance that an increasing number of Soviet sociologists and economists have become concerned with the unique problems of women in the Soviet labor force, and that their studies have been published at all during the past seven years. Along with other signs of an ongoing debate that surfaces more frequently in Soviet periodicals (particularly, in such professional journals as *Sotsiologicheskie issledovaniia*, *Voprosy ekonomiki*, and *Voprosy filosofii*), their publication suggests a growing awareness in major policy circles that a problem of sexual inequality does in fact exist in the Soviet Union. This tentative admission may only have been compelled by the immediacy of the pressing socioeconomic problems cited

---

[38] V. S. Belova, *Reshenie zhenskogo voprosa v SSSR* (M, 1975), pp. 45–46.

[39] On the importance of role models for the profession selected by a Soviet woman, see Cynthia Fuchs Epstein, *Women's Place: Options and Limits in Professional Careers* (Berkeley, Calif., 1971), p. 159. On girls and Soviet schools, see Urie Bronfenbrenner, *Two Worlds of Childhood: U.S.A. and U.S.S.R.* (New York, 1970), p. 80; and Richard Dobson's paper elsewhere in this volume.

[40] L. Iashunina, ed., *100 interv'iu s sovetskimi zhenshchinami* (M, 1975), pp. 167–68.

at the beginning of this paper; but some Soviet women have even raised nagging doubts about the alleged political opportunities for women in the Soviet Union. In 1973, a Latvian woman concluded in her published candidate dissertation on women in socialism that, though "the very highest posts in all areas of activity are accessible to women in socialism, at the same time we cannot ignore the factual situation by which in contemporary society men primarily direct state and social affairs and have greater possibilities of displaying their mental, organizational, and creative capabilities." The obstacles to leadership advancement for women continue to be male prejudices against women, primary family obligations, and the low positive self-image among women themselves.[41] According to L. Iu. Diržinskaite, the female Deputy Chairman of the Lithuanian Republic Council of Ministers, the underrepresentation of women in leadership roles in Lithuania can be directly attributed to male prejudices about the inability of women to cope with major leadership responsibilities.[42]

On the other hand, it would be premature to expect that the debate will be allowed to broaden so far as to probe the real sources of sex discrimination. For such a basic examination would eventually question the very nature of the power structure in the Soviet Union and the values and positions of those who have perpetuated sex discrimination. Thus, even V. B. Mikhailiuk, one economist who has studied the problems of women in the labor force, concludes her book with only a mild reproach to the "subjective miscalculations" of plant directors who have allowed sex inequities, and suggests an improvement in consumer services to relieve the working housewife.[43] She never asks where these "subjective miscalculations" are made—or why. Questions can be asked and remedies offered only as they carefully proceed from the ideological tenet that Soviet women have achieved complete political and social equality.

Boris Ponomarev, a veteran Bolshevik and candidate member of the All-Union Party Politburo, reaffirmed this fundamental tenet in 1974, during an award ceremony honoring the Committee of Soviet Women. He asserted that all forms of sex discrimination have been eliminated in the Soviet Union and proposed that the model of Soviet women should receive even greater publicity and worldwide recognition to commemorate the United Nations' declaration of 1975 as International Women's Year.[44] As the highest ranking official in the Central Committee *apparatus* identified with International Women's Year, Ponomarev was able to carry out his proposal: the model of Soviet women was a featured propaganda theme in the USSR throughout 1975.

[41] A. K. Iurtsinia, "Razvitie lichnosti zhenshchiny pri sotsializme," unpublished candidate dissertation precis (Riga, 1973), pp. 19–21. The dissertation was published under the title *Zhenshchina—lichnost' (pri sotsializme)* in Riga in 1975.

[42] *Sovetskaia Litva*, Dec. 29, 1975.

[43] *Ispol'zovanie zhenskogo truda*, pp. 148–50.

[44] Vysokoe priznanie," *Izvestiia*, Feb. 16, 1974.

Interestingly enough, the propaganda campaign produced the barest admission of a continuing "psychological barrier" to the promotion of women at the regional political level (but on whose part was not made clear: either some leaders were afraid to entrust a responsible post to a woman, it was supposed, or else women themselves doubted their own abilities and for "various pretexts" refused assignments to leadership work).[45] Yet the greatest irony of the propaganda campaign was surely lost on Ponomarev and the campaign's organizers: that those primarily responsible for promulgating the theme of complete female equality during 1975 were the very female indoctrination specialists whose own position perhaps most clearly testifies to the actual inequality of Soviet women.

[45]See "Povyshat' politicheskuiu i proizvodstvennuiu aktivnost' zhenshchin—s plenuma Ivanovskogo obkoma KPSS," *Partiinaia zhizn'*, 16 (Aug. 1975), pp. 39–45. Still, too much should not be read into passing references to problems still encountered by women in the Soviet Union at formal Party plenums. It is standard form for leaders to present both the positive achievements and the remaining difficulties when policies are reviewed at Party meetings.

Jerry F. Hough

Women and Women's Issues in Soviet Policy Debates

WESTERN STUDENTS of the situation of women in the Soviet Union have concluded, first, that Soviet women occupy an inferior economic and political position vis-à-vis Soviet men and, second (with some surprise), that Soviet women have a weak sense of this inequality, particularly in comparison with American feminists. When asked about this matter, Soviet man and women agree that "American-like" feminist attitudes are not very widespread in the Soviet Union; but they often seem to see no reason why such attitudes should have developed and even seem perplexed at the charge of sex discrimination (except as a private, intrafamily phenomenon). One scholar at the Institute of State and Law in Moscoe expressed this attitude succinctly when I told him I was writing an article on the "woman question" in the Soviet Union: "It will be a short article," he responded quickly.

There is a great temptation to treat the absence of a strong feminist movement in the Soviet Union as a manifestation of the backwardness of Soviet women's "consciousness" and to focus on possible explanations for this "backwardness" (such as Soviet censorship and restrictions on issue-oriented group activity). But such an approach would be of dubious methodological soundness, implying as it would that the current feminist consciousness is the only "true" one. Hence this paper will deal with women's issues essentially as Soviet women see them. Though I will conclude with some speculations about the possible evolution of Soviet women's views in the future, I will examine primarily the current pattern of women's participation in policy debates, the issues women raise, and the evidence (highly tentative) about whether women's participation may have an impact on the course of events.

PATTERNS OF PARTICIPATION

There are many types of policy discussions in the Soviet Union, and they take place in many settings. At one extreme are the sensitive and secret debates within the Party Politburo; at the other are the published letters and articles in Soviet newspapers and journals. In between are the myriad committee and council discussions on issues such as local school policy, for example, which might be debated in the district soviet, the teachers' council at the school, or even the school's parent committee.

Women's participation is very limited in the policy debates at the highest levels—around the table at the Politburo, the Secretariat, or the Council of Ministers; in the collegia of the ministries; or in the Party bureaus at the republic and regional levels. With the exception of Ekaterina Furtseva, no woman has ever been named to the Politburo; and since the early 1920's women have never been more than 4.2 percent of the members of the Central Committee.[1] In the postwar period, Furtseva and Mariia Kovrigina (the Minister of Health in the mid-1950's) have been the only women ministers, and Furtseva the only Central Committee secretary; therefore, they have been the only women with the right to take part in the debates in the Council of Ministers and the Secretariat. At present there is no woman among the heads of the Central Committee departments (otdels), and so far as I know there has not been one in the entire postwar period. Moreover, I have been able to identify only two women among the approximately 200 deputy department heads and heads of sections (sektors) of the Central Committee.[2] In 1975, the number of women among the 550 to 560 deputy ministers and deputy chairmen of the ministries and state committees of the USSR Council of Ministers was a mere seven.[3] This suggests that there can be little female participation in committee meetings attended by officials who rank just below the top level.

[1] Women were only 2.5 percent of the voting members and 5.2 percent of the candidate members elected to the Central Committee at the 24th Party Congress in 1971. See Gail Warshofsky Lapidus, *Women in Soviet Society* (Berkeley, Calif., 1977), and her paper elsewhere in the present volume.

[2] Identification of deputy department heads and section heads within the Central Committee apparatus must be made through the press, but the given total of some 200 should be fairly accurate. The unidentified officials are primarily in the areas of heavy industry and defenses and are unlikely to include women. The one woman identified is Z. P. Tumanova, first deputy head of the culture department.

[3] I calculated the number of deputy ministers and deputy chairmen from announcements of appointments and removals in *Postanovleniia Soveta Ministrov SSSR* (unfortunately, not available in the West) and from death notices in the press. The seven women deputy ministers as of April 1975 were Z. M. Kruglova (Culture), A. T. Lavrent'eva (Light Industry), Ia. S. Nasridinnova (Building Materials Industry), E. Ch. Novikova (Health—she is deputy minister for women's and children's care), M. L. Riabova (Finance—she is apparently the deputy minister for education-culture-health financing), A. P. Shaposhnikova (Higher and Specialized-Secondary Education), and M. I. Zhuravleva (Education).

The participation rates for women in the top republic and regional collegial bodies are not much higher than those at the All-Union level. In 1972, 2.2 percent of the members of the republic Party bureaus were women, a figure little different from the roughly 3 percent of women Joel Moses found acting as officials at the *obkom* bureau level in the RSFSR and the Ukraine.[4] In 1973, the proportion of women chairmen and deputy chairmen of the executive committees of the *oblast* soviets in the RSFSR was not much higher—5.5 percent. In the executive committees as a whole, however, women were 11 percent of the members.[5]

Yet these figures should not lead us to think that women do not participate in any Soviet decision-making or in any political-policy discussions. The rate of female participation in the large policy bodies with formal authority is much higher than it is in the inner bureaus; and women are better represented at lower territorial levels than at higher ones. Thus in 1975 women were 31 percent of the USSR Supreme Soviet deputies, 35 percent of the deputies at the union republic level, 39 percent of the deputies at the autonomous republic level, 46 percent of the deputies at the *oblast* level, and 48 percent of the deputies in the cities, *raions*, and villages.[6] Even within the Party the percentage of women among committee members seems to rise sharply below the All-Union level. In early 1976, 22.9 percent were members and candidate members of the republic central committees and *obkoms* and their auditing commissions, and 28.9 percent were members of the *gorkoms* and *raikoms*.[7]

Among speakers at sessions of the large, formally supreme bodies, the proportion of women is fairly low at the higher Party levels but more substantial within the soviets. Only 2 percent of the speakers at the sessions of the All-Union Party Central Committee from 1965 to 1974 were women; this contrasts with the 8 percent of women speakers at fifteen sessions of republic central committees in mid-1975, and with the 10 percent of women speakers in 24 plenary sessions of regional Party committees in early 1975.[8] Women were better represented as speakers before government bodies than before Party ones: in the 1966–73 period they were 10.5

[4]The figure of 2.2 percent was calculated from Grey Hodnett and Val Ogareff, *Leaders of the Soviet Republics, 1955–1972* (Canberra, Australia, 1973); for the percentage from Joel C. Moses, see his paper elsewhere in this volume.
[5]The figure on deputy chairmen is based on a count of 60 of the 71 *oblasts*, *krais*, and autonomous republics in the RSFSR. The chairman and deputy chairmen of an executive committee, together with its secretary (on whom I unfortunately did not collect information), constitute an inner bureau that meets more frequently than the full committee. The figure for women on executive committees as a whole is based on a sample of 25 of these 71 regions.
[6]*Deputaty Verkhovnogo Soveta SSSR, Deviatyi sozyv* (M, 1974), p. 3; *Izvestiia*, June 21, 1975, pp. 1–2.
[7]*Partiinaia zhizn'*, no. 10 (May 1976), p. 20.
[8]These figures are based on a count of participants in the debates, but do not include the official reporters and co-reporters. Here, as elsewhere, those speakers whose sex could not be determined by their name or accompanying verb endings were excluded from the calculation.

percent of the speakers at sessions of the All-Union Supreme Soviet; in eight republic supreme soviet sessions in mid-1975 they were 20 percent of the speakers; and in the soviet sessions of the RSFSR *oblasts, krais,* and autonomous republics from 1967 to 1975 they were 24 percent.[9] The rate of female participation in the Supreme Soviet debates shows no change in pattern over time, but that in the regions rose from 20 percent in 1967–69 to 22 percent in 1969–71, 24 percent in 1971–73, and 30 percent in 1973–75. An incomplete examination of the regional press in early 1975 found that women provided 27 percent of the speakers at nine sessions of city soviets in the RSFSR.[10]

Women's participation in the collective organs of trade unions is also comparatively high: in 1975, women were 34.5 percent of the members of the All-Union Central Council of Trade Unions (VTsSPS), and 46.1 percent of the members of the republic, *krai,* and *oblast* councils and auditing commissions. By my own count, 15 percent of the speakers at the 1973–75 plenary sessions of the VTsSPS were women, as were 35 percent of the speakers at 14 *oblast* trade union conferences early in 1975. In addition, the Presidium of the VTsSPS has a commission for work among women, and it in turn has counterparts in the enterprises and farms.[11]

This type of participation could, of course, be dismissed as ritualistic or ceremonial, but such an interpretation would overlook the nature of the audience at the sessions in question. These Party, soviet, and even trade union meetings are attended not only by the nonelite deputies and delegates but also—and invariably—by the top decision-makers and administrators in the area; thus, whatever the likelihood that an argument made by a speaker will affect the law or resolution adopted at the session, at least that argument unquestionably does reach those who make subsequent decisions. Even judging by truncated and censored press reports, it is also unquestionably true that speeches in the *oblast* soviets and other conferences (just like published articles) do not merely reflect a set "Party line" but generally contain concrete suggestions on matters within the competence of local officials. There is no reason to doubt the autonomy of the suggestions being made; there is every reason to assume that they represent a serious attempt to influence Party and government decisions.

Female participation also varies with the type of policy area, as I show in Tables 1 and 2, and it can become quite substantial in some areas—notably health, education, and welfare.[12] Thus, though only 10.5 percent of the

[9]The RSFSR figures are based on 60 of 71 *oblasts, krais,* and autonomous republics.

[10]This figure is suspect not only because of the size of the sample but also because of the disparity within it. Female participation was in the 30–35 percent range in seven sessions, and close to 10 percent in the other two; it is difficult to know how aberrant the latter two were.

[11]*Politicheskoe samoobrazovanie,* no. 7 (1975), p. 26.

[12]I use the label "health, education, and welfare" in preference to "indoctrination" for several reasons. First, indoctrination is not a word normally used in discussions of policy areas in the West, and consequently its use may not contribute to the development of empirical comparative analysis. Second, there are fewer women in posts that clearly seem to involve "pro-

TABLE 1

Women Speakers in Soviet Sessions Devoted to Different Policy Subjects:
RSFSR Oblasts, Krais, and Autonomous Republics, 1967–75

Subject of the soviet session	Total number of speakers[a]	Percentage of women speakers
Health	507	37.7%
Socialist obligations taken before holidays	958	35.6
Culture	291	33.3
Education and youth questions	1,261	28.9
Trade, services, housing, utilities	1,714	26.7
Next year's plan and budget	5,039	24.9
Report of the executive committee	1,646	24.4
Industry and consumer goods production	810	23.8
Conservation	291	21.5
Agriculture	2,083	19.6
Miscellaneous	536	18.5
Law enforcement and the courts	453	18.1
Construction	1,542	13.7

SOURCES: Regional newspaper clippings on soviet sessions in 60 of the 71 RSFSR *oblasts, krais,* and autonomous republics.

[a] This represents the total number whose sex was determined. The wide variations in numbers in this column reflect differences in the number of sessions devoted to each topic.

All-Union Supreme Soviet speakers from 1966 to 1973 were women, the proportion of women participants in the discussions on health, education, and family matters was 31 percent. In the regional soviets the proportion of women speakers in sessions devoted to health, education, or culture was 32 percent (compared with 23 percent in sessions devoted to other subjects). Indeed, in the area of health, education, welfare, and culture a significant number of women participate even in debates within the inner committees on which top officials sit. Table 2 indicates the proportion of women in top policy positions in this area in the republics in 1975, and the pattern shown there is also found within the RSFSR regions.

Women constituted 11 percent of 113 "ideological secretaries" of the RSFSR regional Party committees (this is the secretary in charge of health, education, and welfare questions, as well as of propaganda and agitation) identified in the 1966–75 period; 11 percent of 115 RSFSR regional education departments; 27 percent of 99 heads of the regional social security

paganda" or "indoctrination" than in those dealing more purely with health, education, and welfare. As Table 2 indicates, there was not a single woman in a key republic "media" or "indoctrination" post in 1975; and from 1955 to 1975 only 3 percent of the heads of the agitation-propaganda (*agitprop*) departments of the republic central committees, 4 percent of the chairmen of the state committees for television and radio, and 4 percent of the chairmen of the state publishing committees (two, one, and one persons, respectively) have been women. In the RSFSR *oblasts, krais,* and autonomous republics, women were 8 percent of the identifiable heads of *agitprop* departments of the regional Party committees (72 women), 7 percent of chairmen of the regional TV-radio committees (54 women), and 1 percent of the regional newspaper editors (108 women).

TABLE 2

Percentage of Women Among Top Republic Officials
by Area of Specialty, Summer 1975

Type of institution	Number of officials identified[a]	Percentage of women officials
Control instruments[b]	99	0.0%
Heavy industry, construction, transportation[c]	156	0.6
Agriculture[d]	89	1.1
Light industry, trade, consumer services[e]	146	8.9
Health, education, culture[f]	115	13.0
Social security[g]	15	60.0
The mass media[h]	86	0.0

SOURCES: Russian-language republic newspapers, particularly the issues of June 19, 1975, which contained lists of newly elected deputies to the republic supreme soviets, and the issues devoted to the subsequent sessions of the supreme soviets.

[a] A few positions were not occupied in the summer of 1975, and a few of the occupants were not identified.

[b] The officials included here are the organizational secretary of the Party Central Committee, the head of the organizational-Party work and administrative organs departments of the Central Committee, the Chairman of the KGB, the Minister of Internal Affairs, the *Prokuror*, and the Chairman of the People's Control Committee. There also are no women among the Ministers of Finance and the Chairmen of Gosplan, who might also be included in this category.

[c] The officials included here are the deputy chairman (or chairmen) of the Council of Ministers supervising these branches, the heads of the industrial-transportation, construction-urban economy, and any specialized heavy industry departments of the Party Central Committee, the various construction ministers, the Chairman of Gosstroi, the Minister of Automobile Transportation, the Minister of Timber and Woodworking Industry, and occasional additional heavy industry ministers named in different republics.

[d] The officials included here are the agricultural secretary of the Party Central Committee, the deputy chairman (or deputy chairmen) of the Council of Ministers supervising agriculture, the head of the agricultural department of the Central Committee, the Minister of Agriculture, the Minister of Reclamation and Water Resources, the Minister of Procurements, and (in one case) the Minister of State Farms.

[e] The officials included here are the deputy chairman (or deputy chairmen) of the Council of Ministers supervising these branches, the head of the light industry-food industry department of the Party Central Committee, the head of the trade-services department or of the trade-planning-financial organs department of the Central Committee (whichever existed in the republic), the Minister of Consumer Services, the Minister of Communal Economy, the Minister of the Food Industry, the Minister of Light Industry, the Minister of Local Industry, the Minister of the Meat and Dairy Industry, the Minister of Trade, and several scattered light industry ministers which exist in individual republics.

[f] The officials included here are the deputy chairman of the Council of Ministers supervising these branches, the heads of the science-education and culture departments of the Party Central Committee, the Minister of Culture, the Minister of Education, the Minister of Health, the Minister of Higher and Specialized Secondary Education, and the Chairman of the State Committee for Vocational-Technical Education. If the last two types of official (which include no women) are excluded, the percentage of women in the category rises to 16.9 percent.

[g] The official included in this category is the Minister of Social Security. If this official is included with the health-education-culture officials in a general health-education-welfare category, the percentage of women in it would be 18.4 percent—23.1 percent if the higher education and vocational education heads are excluded.

[h] The officials included in this category are the head of the propaganda-agitation department of the Party Central Committee, the Chairman of the State Committee for Television and Radio, the Chairman of the State Committee for Publishing, the Chairman of the State Committee for Movies, and the editors of the leading Russian-language and native-language newspaper respectively.

departments; 20 percent of 117 deputy chairmen in charge of education, health, and culture questions on the executive committees of the regional soviets; and 35 percent of the heads of the science-education departments of the regional Party committees.[13] At the city level, the proportion of women among these officials was considerably higher: for example, 38 percent among heads of 50 city education departments in the RSFSR, and 42 percent of 52 "ideological secretaries" of the city Party committees. In this area women clearly are in a position to make their voices heard.

It is important to note that participation in policy debates is not limited to those who sit in legislative bodies or hold high administrative posts. If the rates of participation of American women in policy discussions were judged by the percentage of women in Congress or in the cabinets of the federal or state governments, the conclusions would be little more accurate than those we might be tempted to draw about the Soviet Union based on the material set out above. As Peter Juviler and Norton Dodge have rightly emphasized in their papers in this volume, women are extremely well represented among Soviet professionals normally involved in policy advocacy and analysis as part of their vocation. For example, in 1970 women constituted 43 percent of *vuz* (college) teachers, 40 percent of Soviet scientists, 45 percent of Soviet journalists and writers, and 82 percent of Soviet economists and planners. Moreover, they were 32 percent of the "leaders of organs of state administration, Party, Komsomol, trade union, and other public organizations, and their structural subdivisions."[14] Even in the Central Committee apparatus, more than 18 percent of those responsible staff officials below the level of section head seem to be women—at least among those staff officials who stay in the apparatus until the age of 50.[15]

Women also have the opportunity to participate in voluntary "public" organizations and in the discussions within them, but the scale of this par-

[13] These figures were calculated from a number of central and regional sources. Judging by the deputy heads of regional social security departments of the RSFSR identified in *Sotsial'noe obespechenie* in the last few years (33 percent of the 55 officials identified were women), the proportion of women may well be higher among the top deputies of these officials.

[14] TsSU, *Itogi vsesoiuznoi perepisi naseleniia 1970 goda* (M, 1973), vol. 6, pp. 167–69.

[15] *Vedomosti Verkhovnogo Soveta RSFSR* regularly publishes lists of certain categories of officials who receive an award on their 50th and 60th birthdays. Lower officials of the Central Committee apparatus are one of the categories, and it seems that every official in that category who reaches the appropriate age receives an award. From 1970 to mid-1975, 18 percent of the "responsible officials" and "instructors" receiving awards were women. The percentage was higher among nonresponsible employees and associates, presumably often clerical personnel. From other evidence it is clear that most of the "responsible officials" are also "instructors," but a few are heads of sections (particularly in sensitive departments such as the international department). Hence the number of women among instructors aged 50 and 60 should be above 18 percent. However, this figure is probably too high for the Central Committee apparatus, for the majority of instructors are below the age of 50, and many move back to the state apparatus after a short period of work in the Central Committee. Those of the latter group on whom we have data are predominantly men, and hence the true figure for the apparatus as a whole is probably in the 10–15 percent range.

ticipation is difficult to determine because of the lack of data. Nevertheless, it is clear that girls and young women are often as politically active as their male counterparts—probably more so in school, where 52.4 percent of all Komsomol members are women, and 57.1 percent of all secretaries of primary Komsomol organizations.[16] However the overall level of female participation declines precipitously with marriage and particularly with the birth of a child. Even in the Komsomol, only 40 percent of the members are women;[17] the comparable figure for Party members is only 23 percent. A mere 5 percent of all women between ages of 31 and 60 are party members, compared with some 22 percent of all men in that age group.[18] Though statistics about female involvement in other "public" organizations are seldom published, Soviet scholars privately report a tendency toward sex segregation in patterns of participation. Some public organizations are said to be overwhelmingly male (e.g., the auxiliary police, or *druzhinniki*), whereas others are said to be overwhelmingly female (e.g., councils in clubs and libraries, and parents' committees in the schools).[19]

Finally, women can also communicate directly with the political authorities or the newspapers, either to register a complaint or to make a policy suggestion. Again, no information on the sex of letter writers is available, but I found that about 20 percent of the articles and letters with suggestions for change or criticisms published in *Pravda* and *Izvestiia* in early 1975 were written by women; in *Sovetskaia kul'tura*—an organ of the Party Central Committee that deals with "culture" in both the literary-artistic and the anthropological senses of the word—I found that 44 percent of articles and letters were by women.

THE ISSUES RAISED BY WOMEN

Despite shortcomings in the published statistics, it is not difficult to gain a rough sense of the degree of women's participation in Soviet policy debates. But does this participation have any particularly feminine content— that is, does it raise issues of special importance to women? And does it matter whether or not women do participate? These important questions are as difficult to answer as they are interesting.

In principle, it should be relatively easy to compare the contents of wom-

---

[16] *VLKSM, Nagliadnoe posobie* (M, 1975), pp. 26, 86.

[17] I. M. Slepenkov and B. V. Kniazov, *Molodezh' sela segodnia* (M, 1972), p. 115; *Pravda*, Sept. 5, 1972, p. 2.

[18] See Jerry F. Hough, "Party Saturation in the Soviet Union," in Paul Cocks, R. V. Daniels, and Nancy Heer, eds., *Essays in Soviet Politics* (Cambridge, Mass., 1976).

[19] In some areas there are overtly female public organizations. For example, Volgograd *oblast* has a commission for work among women (*Volgogradskaia pravda*, Mar. 8, 1975, p. 1), and Voronezh has a city women's council (*Kommuna*, Mar. 8, 1975, p. 1). Moscow, on the other hand, seems devoid of such organizations. Most are concentrated in the Central Asian and Transcaucasian republics and in the autonomous republics. For a discussion of women's councils in Tashkent *oblast* and in Turkmenia, see *Politicheskoe samoobrazovanie*, 1966, no. 3, p. 106, and 1968, no. 3, p. 114.

en's and men's contributions to Soviet policy debates—at least if one assumes that the published record is fairly representative of the positions taken in committee sessions. One could compare women's articles in different forums—perhaps distinguishing among the policy positions taken by women of differing backgrounds—with those written by men of various backgrounds. Such a study would be very illuminating—all the more so because no one has ever analyzed the scope of Soviet published debates and the patterns within them in any comprehensive way, even aside from the question of distinctions between male and female participation.

Within the confines of one section of one paper I can do little more than advance several impressionistic hypotheses based on a fairly narrow reading of Soviet sources (chiefly a careful examination of a few months of *Pravda, Izvestiia,* and *Sovetskaia kul'tura* in late 1974 and early 1975). Nevertheless, even this brief immersion in the press does leave clear impressions of the themes or subjects that are raised frequently in articles and letters written by women.

One of the types of women's communication found most often in the media is the defense of professional or occupational interests, which generally takes the form of an appeal either for better working conditions or for a policy change to allot more funds for the function women perform or the clients they serve. In this respect, women's articles and letters are little different from men's, but the fact that there is considerable sex segregation within the economy means that men and women often are defending the interests and perspectives of different occupations and professions. Appeals for expenditures in the realm of health, education, and culture are more likely to be written by women (and to benefit women employed in these areas) than are appeals for support of heavy industry.

A second type of frequent communication by women to the newspapers is stimulated by their child-raising and shopping responsibilities. Again and again, one reads complaints about the quality of some consumer goods, appeals to provide music education to average children, demands for changes in bus schedules or routes, or complaints on behalf of a child (e.g., about the quality of the New Year's tree in the classroom). Many men also write about the quality of goods sold in stores, but the public defense of children's interests seems predominantly an activity of women.

A third focus for women writers, as their greater participation in *Sovetskaia kul'tura* than in *Pravda* and *Izvestiia* suggests, is the realm of culture broadly defined. Certainly women letter writers often evince interest in questions involving literature or the movies: for example, a suggestion for care of a poet's grave is apt to emanate from a woman, and a debate on the "star system" in Soviet entertainment is likely to be a woman's debate in large part.[20] But women also seem disproportionately to be the

---

[20] For the "star system" debate, see *Sovetskaia kul'tura*, Dec. 17, 1974, Jan. 7, 1975, and Jan. 14, 1975.

source of demands for *kulturnost'* in behavior (the offenders usually are said to be men) or in entertainment (the offenders seem to be those who cater to teenagers' tastes).

But what about the type of article that reveals the "consciousness" of a Western feminist—sensitivity about sex-role differences and dissatisfaction with them; a sense of grievance about men's attitudes toward women in general; a belief that there is a pattern of discrimination against women (e.g., that wages in jobs largely staffed by women are low primarily because they *are* staffed by women); a feeling that government and employers (and in the Soviet Union they are essentially the same) practice and/or sanction discrimination because their top officials are men, and that women need power to correct the situation? To what extent are such ideas expressed?

Certainly the Soviet press reveals a sense that the behavior and roles of men and women are different in many respects. One reads statements to the effect that girls are more conscientious than boys in school and therefore receive higher grades.[21] One finds references to men's belief that "woman's work lowers a man," and to the resulting inequality in the division of labor between husband and wife in household duties.[22] An article in *Pravda* notes that marriage usually produces a major decline in the level of political activity of young female Party members.[23] Such statements and articles have appeared frequently in the press, along with an occasional complaint by a woman of unfair treatment at work. One woman foreman reported, for example, that her fuel-apparatus plant had a "woman's shop" in which women performed basically the same jobs as men in the other shops but were given the smaller parts to make because their hands were smaller and more agile. Since small parts sell for less than large ones but take no less time to assemble, and since wages are based on a piecework formula that takes product value into account, the women's wages were in practice lower than those of men doing the same work.[24]

What seems to be absent from the published Soviet discussion of the position of women is the view that all differences in treatment are wrong and/or that women are subject to systematic discrimination. Newspaper articles and works of fiction do suggest that the problems involved in combining a job with housework and child-raising make women's lot a difficult one in the Soviet Union if they have children and a husband with traditional attitudes toward housework. These problems were perhaps best expressed in Natal'ia Baranskaia's novella "Nedelia kak nedelia" ("A Week Like Any Other"), which appeared in 1969 in *Novyi mir*.[25] Though suggestions for policy changes are sometimes made in such articles and stories (e.g., that labor-saving appliances should be produced in greater quantity to ease the

[21] Gail Warshofsky Lapidus, *Women in Soviet Society* (Berkeley, Calif., 1977).
[22] *Sovetskaia zhenshchina*, 1975, no. 2, p. 35.
[23] *Pravda*, Sept. 5, 1975, p. 2.
[24] *Ibid.*, Jan. 31, 1975, p. 3.
[25] *Novyi mir*, 1969, no. 11 (Nov.), pp. 23–55.

burdens of housework, that more efficient procedures should be introduced in the stores to reduce the time required for shopping, that part-time jobs should be created for women), the dominant motif is generally that husbands' attitudes have to be changed.[26] It is because women's problems are seen as "cultural" ones (in the anthropological sense) and not as political ones that so many of the articles on women appear in *Sovetskaia kul'tura* rather than in *Pravda* and *Izvestiia*.

The degree to which a universalized sense of grievance has failed to develop seems to be best illustrated by a type of article that appears very frequently—one that complains about the low level of pay and the poor working conditions in some occupation or line of work. The article traditionally refers to the difficulties of attracting and keeping qualified personnel in the occupation, and demands an improvement in wages and working conditions in order to correct the situation. In practice, low-paying jobs usually contain large percentages of women, and complaints about them thus really represent appeals for an improvement in the situation of a group of women. In December 1974 alone, *Pravda* and *Sovetskaia kul'tura* carried articles of this type about livestock workers, bookkeepers, sales clerks, waitresses, seamstresses, and graduates of library schools.[27] Yet not one of these articles mentioned that the occupation was staffed primarily by women, let alone suggested that part of the problem might be a tendency —unconscious or otherwise—for "women's jobs" to be paid too little. The articles written by women were no different in this respect from those written by men.

It could be argued, of course, that Soviet censorship prevents the expression of a sense of discrimination that is in fact deeply felt. This is a real possibility, for though there must be at least a few ardent feminists in the Soviet Union, no frontal attack on the way women are treated has ever been published. However, before we conclude that censorship is creating a totally distorted view of the opinions of Soviet women, we should consider two facts.

First, there are policy areas in which actors do manage to make their real sense of being discriminated against get through the censor's filter into the Soviet press. (One thinks here of the issue of policy toward the countryside.) Certainly the "woman question" is not so sensitive that a real sense of grievance—if felt—would not similarly filter through into the press. However, since no such sense emerges from the press, except on the aforementioned issue of husbands' assistance (or nonassistance) in household chores, I think we can conclude that it does not exist.

Second, leading women intellectuals in the Soviet Union often made statements in conversation that they surely would not have made if they

---

[26] For one of the best such articles on the learning of sex roles in the early socialization process, see *Sovetskaia kul'tura*, Feb. 4, 1975.

[27] *Ibid.*, Dec. 5, 1974, and Dec. 17, 1974; *Pravda*, Dec. 12, 1974, and Dec. 26, 1974.

had often been exposed to Western-style feminist arguments in private and
knew the connotations that might be drawn from their words. For example,
despite the large number of female heads of household in the Soviet Union,
one woman casually explained the low wages of doctors by asserting that
doctors are predominantly women, that their salaries usually are the second
salaries in the family, and that the question of higher wages is of secondary
importance (*na vtoroi plan*) for them. Another spoke of the superfeminist
of the "women's department type" (*zhenotdelskogo tipa*) as a phenomenon
of the past, and fortunately so. Several spoke of lower rates of political participation of women as the result of a natural (and not particularly worri-
some) division of labor between men and women: both men and women
have regular jobs, and the man combines his with political activities (really
duties) and the woman hers with household responsibilities.

Few Soviet women with whom I have spoken would have any quarrel
with the female vice-president of the Academy of Pedagogical Sciences and
member of the Presidium of the Committee of Soviet Women who asserted
in a published interview that "woman by her biological essence is a
mother—a teacher-trainer [*vospitatel'nitsa*]" and that she has "an inborn
ability to deal with small children, an instinctive pedagogical approach."
This scholar stated that girls rightfully cannot enter 135 of 1,110 professions taught in *tekhnikums* because of the need to consider their "motherly
mission," and she defended the preference given to boys in admission to
pedagogical institutes (apparently almost any boy who applies is admitted)
on the grounds that men teachers are needed in the upper grades so that
boys can receive "uncompromising male conversation" (*beskompromisnye
muzhskie razgovory*).[28]

I would like to emphasize once more the tentativeness of my analysis and
conclusions in this section. We lack reliable data on women's attitudes, and
even conclusions about the content of women's published contributions are
not supported by a sound statistical analysis of a large number of Soviet
articles. Nevertheless, my analysis does rest on a considerable reading of
the press, and is not likely to be totally incorrect. Clearly there is reliable
evidence on the uneven distribution of women among various professions,
as there is widespread testimony that women bear a disproportionate share
of the responsibility for household work. It would not be surprising to find
that women's participation in policy debates stems primarily from the activities to which they devote much of their time, but for the moment we cannot
substantiate this hypothesis.

THE IMPACT OF WOMEN'S PARTICIPATION

If women's contributions to the policy debates in the Soviet Union do
differ from men's, does this really matter? Do the expression of policy

---

[28] This interview was distributed by Novosti for publication by any editor who thought it
worthwhile. One place of publication was *Leninskaia pravda* (Karela), Apr. 18, 1975.

suggestions and the public defense of interests in the Soviet Union—whether by women or men—have any impact upon policy outcomes?

Unfortunately, the degree to which a given group does or does not have influence or power in the policy arena, the degree to which any participation has an impact, is perhaps the most difficult question in political science,[29] and almost no effort has been made to study it seriously in the Soviet setting. Obviously we cannot observe the impact of women's participation in the Soviet Union directly (if, indeed, that would be the proper methodology in any case); but it may perhaps be worthwhile to examine one piece of indirect evidence that has tantalizing implications.

As we begin to explore the patterns of influence in the Soviet Union in general, one of the most striking facts to emerge is the enormous regional variation on almost any social welfare or political indicator imaginable. Despite our expectations based on an image of a highly centralized system—and contrary to my own expectations of a few years ago—such indicators as the number of hospital beds per capita, the number of square meters of housing per capita, the proportion of preschool children in day-care centers, and the retail-trade turnover (and thus surely wages) per capita all differ widely from region to region, both in absolute terms and in terms of the speed with which the services are being developed. Presumably something must explain these variations, and presumably that something is related to the power or influence of the different groups involved.

Among the indicators on which there turns out to be great regional variation is the percentage of women speaking at soviet sessions in the *oblasts*, *krais*, and autonomous republics of the RSFSR. In the 1967–71 period, for example, women made up 21.6 percent of the speakers in the Russian republic as whole; but they were only 9 percent of the speakers in the Tuva Autonomous Republic and 12 percent in both Briansk and Voronezh *oblasts*, whereas they were 33 percent in both Novgorod *oblast* and the Chechen-Ingush Autonomous Republic and 37 percent in Kaliningrad *oblast*. What this variation reflects is far from clear, but it is not a random phenomenon: if the variation were random, there would be no correlation between the percentage of women speaking at the 1967–71 sessions and the percentage speaking at the 1971–75 sessions; but in fact there is a .53 correlation, indicating substantial continuity over time.[30] Women's participation in *oblast* soviets tended to be slightly greater in more urbanized areas, but this explanation only accounts for a small part of the variation, most of which must be related to such factors as local traditions or political culture, the values of the local elite, the preferences of top regional officials, the degree to which women seek to speak, and so forth.

[29] See Jerry F. Hough, "The Soviet Experience and the Measurement of Power," *Journal of Politics*, 37, no. 3 (Aug. 1975), pp. 685–710.
[30] The correlation does not reflect any overlap in the 1971 data: the 1967–71 figures include only sessions held prior to June 1971, whereas the 1971–75 figures include only sessions held in June or later.

In trying to determine whether this variation in women's participation was associated—for whatever reason—with variations in policy outcomes, I was drawn to the indicator of availability of preschool day-care as one that seemed particularly closely related to women's concerns (both in the Soviet Union and in the United States).[31] This policy area has shown considerable activity during the Khrushchev and Brezhnev periods, and there was a major increase in the proportion of preschool children enrolled in day-care institutions during these years. In 1959, approximately 12 percent of the children under 7 in the RSFSR were in nursery school or kindergarten; that figure increased to approximately 39 percent in 1970.[32] But on this indicator, as on others, there was great diversity within the RSFSR: the proportion of children enrolled in day-care institutions in 1970 ranged from 10 percent in the Dagestan Autonomous Republic, at one extreme, to 70 percent in Magadan *oblast* and the Komi Autonomous Republic, at the other.

Unfortunately, I have no information on the level of women's participation in the regions during those years in which the 1959–70 rates of growth were really determined, but it does turn out that those regions with the highest female participation rates in the regional soviets from 1967 to 1971 also had the most complete day-care facilities in 1970 (correlation = .19). As Table 3 indicates, those regions with a high rate of female participation were particularly unlikely to have a very poor record in providing day-care facilities, whereas those with a low rate were particularly unlikely to have an excellent record.

A good deal of the statistical association between women's participation in regional soviets and the level of day-care being provided seems related to differences in levels of urbanization from region to region. However, if one first uses regression analysis to calculate the relationship between the level of urbanization and the proportion of children in day-care institutions across regions and then compares each region's actual record with that which the regression equation predicted for its level of urbanization, women's participation again seems related to deviations from the norm, particularly in those cases in which the participation was especially low. In the twenty *oblasts* and autonomous republics in which women constituted less than 19 percent of the speakers, only six had a higher percentage of children in day-care centers than was predicted for their level of urbanization, whereas fourteen had a lower percentage than predicted (27 of the other oblasts and autonomous republics had a record that was better than expected, 18 a record worse than expected).

[31] For example, when the Ivanovo *obkom* devoted a session to the situation of women in the *oblast* in 1975, the availability of day-care for preschoolers was an issue prominently mentioned.

[32] The data on the number of children under 7 in the regions was extrapolated from *Itogi vsesoiuznoi perepisi naseleniia 1970 goda*, vol. 2, pp. 76–162. The data on the number of children in day-care institutions comes from *Narodnoe khoziaistvo RSFSR v 1958 g.* (M, 1959), and *Narodnoe khoziaistvo RSFSR v 1969 g.* (M, 1970), pp. 384–87.

TABLE 3

Women Speakers at Soviet Sessions by Percent of Children in Day-Care Centers[a]:
RSFSR Oblasts and Autonomous Republics

Women speakers at soviet sessions, 1967–71[b]	Children in day-care centers, 1970[c]		
	Over 41 percent	25–41 percent	Under 25 percent
Over 22 percent	52% (N = 14)[d]	41% (N = 11)	7% (N = 2)
19–22 percent	39% (N = 7)	28% (N = 5)	33% (N = 6)
Under 19 percent	20% (N = 2)	65% (N = 13)	25% (N = 5)

[a] The term day-care centers includes both nursery schools (*iasli*) and kindergartens (*detskie sady*).
[b] Expressed as a percentage of total speakers.
[c] Expressed as a percentage of all children in a given area.
[d] "N" indicates the number of RSFSR *oblasts* and autonomous republics for which data are included.

A more meaningful indicator of the possible impact of participation would be the relationship between the percentage of women speakers and the record established by the region after the participation had taken place. Though data on the number of children aged six and under at the *oblast* level are only available for census years,[33] the annual statistical handbooks of the RSFSR do reveal the number of children in preschool institutions in each region; from this source it is possible (1) to determine the percent increase in the number of children six and under in day-care centers from the beginning of 1970 to the beginning of 1974, and (2) to compare the results with the data on women's participation in 1967–71.

In practice, it turned out that the regions with the smallest percent increase in the number of children enrolled in preschool institutions between 1970 and 1974 tended to be those that already had the highest proportion of children enrolled in 1970. (The correlation was −.41.) Given the relationship noted above between level of day-care and level of women's participation in regional soviets in 1970, it follows that the day-care systems of many of the regions with a high percentage of women speakers inevitably grew slowly between 1970 and 1974. If the systems were already excellent, they usually had little room (or reason) for especially rapid improvement; if the systems were poor, they often showed above-average percent increases simply because of the small size of the original base. The consequence of these two factors was a negative correlation (−.15) between the 1970–74 growth in number of children in day-care institutions and the 1967–71 levels of female participation.

Yet, there were regions that provided a middle level of day-care in 1970, and in these cases the picture was quite different from what the overall correlation suggests. If we look at the 25 *oblasts* and autonomous republics that had from 25 to 40 percent of children in day-care institutions in 1970,

[33] Apparently these data have been published in a Soviet statistical handbook, *Naselenie SSSR*, which was not available to me when this paper was being written.

we find a fairly strong relationship between women's participation in the 1967–71 soviets and the 1970–74 percentage rate of growth in the number of children enrolled in day-care institutions. Of those twelve regions in which at least 22 percent of the speakers were women, ten experienced a 15 percent or higher increase in the number of children enrolled, whereas two had a lower growth rate; of those eighteen regions with less than 22 percent female speakers, five showed at least a 15 percent increase in the number of children enrolled, whereas thirteen experienced an increase of less than 15 percent.

One can, of course, make what one wants of these data. The strength of the statistical relationships is not extremely great—and no one should expect it to be. Certainly it would be desirable to have a longer run of data on women's participation to judge whether the relationships are consistent. Certainly it could be argued that the presence of day-care centers permits participation, rather than that participation leads to greater attention to women's concerns. (However, women elected to the regional soviets are hardly likely to have trouble finding places in day-care centers for their own children.) And certainly it is quite possible that participation in the *oblast* soviet is more of a surrogate statistic for participation in other institutions and settings where women's real impact is felt.

Nonetheless, we do remain with the facts that there is tremendous variation in the percentage of women speaking in soviet sessions from one region to another (a surprising finding in itself), and that—for whatever reason—this variation was correlated with the relative performance of the region in providing day-care facilities. At a minimum, this correlation suggests that we need to explore more fully the possibility that local participation—even in institutions that we have tended to dismiss (probably incorrectly) as purely ceremonial in character—may be related to differences in outcomes. If such a relationship is proved to exist, as I think it can be, then there is no reason to believe that variations in women's participation have less significance than variations in men's.

THE FUTURE

A specialist on the Soviet Union may be interested primarily in the patterns of female participation in that country and in the possible impact that that participation may have on the policy processes; but a Western feminist is certain to be more curious about the significance of the set of attitudes held by Soviet women. Women in the Soviet Union have achieved a number of goals of American feminists—e.g., equal entry into almost all professions and equal pay for identical jobs—but they generally have failed to attain representation in proportion to their numbers in the highest political-administrative positions and in the highest-paying mass occupations. Moreover, they have not achieved a redistribution of the household duties in the direction of greater equality in sharing the burden between husbands and wives. Though disadvantaged groups often become increasingly militant as their positions improve, Soviet women do not seem to have reacted in this manner to the halfway situation in which they find themselves.

From certain perspectives, it is surprising that feminism has not developed more rapidly than it has in the Soviet Union. No longer is there an Iron Curtain isolating the Soviet Union from contact with worldwide intellectual currents, and with the Soviet press reporting some of the activities of Western feminists and the types of discrimination they are fighting, one might well have expected some Soviet women to make "improper" analogies and to begin to speak out against such conditions in their own country. Indeed, given the tendency for a segment of Soviet youth to search out and adopt the newest Western fashions in clothes and music, one would expect some Soviet young women to become Western-style feminists just to be faddish.

If the Western feminist movement does continue to grow in strength, it seems almost certain that increasing echoes of it will be heard in the Soviet Union. But the question, of course, is whether the relative failure of the feminist movement to find resonance in the Soviet Union thus far (in comparison, say, with the environmentalist movement) means that it may be as ephemeral as the worldwide "youth revolution" of the late 1960's, which likewise had little Soviet counterpart.

As one who sees many reasons for the continuing growth of the feminist movement in the United States, I hardly would predict that developments to date in the Soviet Union preclude such a growth in the United States. One can say, however, that Soviet debates which relate peripherally to the women's issue, as well as Soviet explanations for the attitudes of Soviet women made in private conversations do indicate the existence of anti-feminist interests and values that (except to a limited extent in the recent ERA battles) have not been fully expressed in American debates of recent years—interests and values that may partially explain the failure of Soviet women to adopt a Western feminist position, interests and values that Western feminists surely will have to confront in their own countries before they even approach final victory.

When the possibility of Soviet women's following the Western model is raised in private conversation in the Soviet Union, one discovers that some Soviet women do yearn for a Western model—but it is the model of a part-time housewife with part-time employment, or even of a full-time housewife. Basically, this yearning stems from a belief that a 40-hour-a-week job, combined with even 50 percent of the child-raising and household responsibilities, is simply too time-consuming to permit a proper amount of leisure—especially when the number of children rises above one. If equality with men (including entry into top-level professional-administrative jobs that require much more than 40 hours of work a week) has this cost, some Soviet women are doubtful about the level of dignity and pleasure that is provided either the husband or the wife in such equal partnerships. To some Soviet women, the division of labor within the traditional Western middle-class family appears, rightly or wrongly, to be a luxury they hope a rising standard of living ultimately will afford them. Within the present Soviet context, such women prefer a narrowly defined, 40-hour-a-week job to the kind of commitment to career—let alone the political activity associated with Party membership—that usually is necessary for administrative promotion.

Full-time employment in the Soviet Union has had a very visible consequence that has become the subject of considerable public concern and debate—the failure of many couples to have more than one child. Some of the concern over this development has nationalist overtones (involving the fear either that the country will have insufficient population in face of the "Chinese danger," or, more usually, that the relatively rural non-Russian peoples with high birthrates will come to outnumber ethnic Russians within the Soviet Union); some of it has an economic base (involving a fear that low levels of reproduction by the most skilled and educated elements of the population are undesirable from the point of view of future economic growth). But much of the concern also flows from the family-oriented values of many women themselves. Polls reveal that most urban women would prefer to have more than one child (even when they actually have only one), and published letters and articles by women indicate that many believe that children without brothers and sisters tend to become spoiled and egotistical. The argument that women should become more career-oriented and should struggle to enter more time-consuming administrative and political positions faces the counterargument that such a development would worsen an already serious family problem unless husbands were willing to abandon their career orientation.

A number of Soviet women (unlike Western feminists) look upon political participation less as a privilege and an opportunity than as an onerous obligation. Many seem relieved that housework provides an acceptable excuse for avoiding political activity, and may even interpret their husbands' involvement in such activities as an equitable counterpart to their own household duties. (It may be reflective of this attitude that many of the complaints about female political passivity come from men—and men who are political officials at that.)

Such a set of opinions about political participation might be dismissed as a justifiable reaction to the peculiar nature of participation in the Soviet Union—specifically, to the inability of Soviet citizens to have an impact on decision-making through their participation. However, such a view of political participation in the Soviet Union is almost surely wrong, for it ignores the basic insights about collective action developed by theorists such as Mancur Olson.[34] Olson argues that though participation by members of a

---

[34] See Jerry F. Hough, "Political Participation in the Soviet Union," *Soviet Studies*, 28, no. 1 (Jan. 1976), pp. 3–20; and Mancur Olson, *The Logic of Collective Action* (Cambridge, Mass., 1965).

group may be vital in increasing the power of the group as a whole and in permitting it to achieve its goals, such participation is often not in the individual self-interest of particular members of the group. As a consequence, even in the West participation often must be stimulated either by compulsion or by concrete side payments.

From this perspective, though it may be unfortunate from the point of view of Soviet women as a whole that they are not pressured to participate as much as Soviet men, the attitude individual women display is hardly irrational. In fact, it is actually an extremely widespread attitude in the West. Moreover, since the value of time can be a key element in an Olsonian equation, it is far from paradoxical that Soviet scholars report the most active women in community group activities—and, therefore, those best placed to promote women's interests in this sphere—to be the relatively small number of "unliberated" full-time housewives.

The impact of these counterpressures to the acceptance of a full-fledged feminist ideology by Soviet women is difficult to judge. Nevertheless, in trying to explain the absence of a strong feminist movement in the Soviet Union, we should consider the possibility that limitations on free discussion in the Soviet press have been a much less significant factor than Soviet women's greater exposure to discussions of the difficulties produced by full integration of both husbands and wives into the job market and their personal experience in this respect. The relative political quiescence of Soviet women conceivably could signify the existence of almost insuperable obstacles to the realization of the full "feminist" program unless there are much more radical divisions of labor between husband and wife than either Soviet or Western society has even begun to face, let alone accept. This is hardly a hypothesis on which it is possible to adduce any convincing evidence in either direction, but the future development of women's attitudes in the Soviet Union may reveal much about the limits or opportunities that greater occupational equality will create.

Colette Shulman

The Individual and the Collective

T HE TWO SYMBOLIC values—"individual" and "collective"—and the
tension between them are at the heart of the situation of women in
Russia, and indeed of Soviet society generally.

In reflecting on this theme, I began by looking into the word *lichnost'*—
how it is understood and used at different levels of society. Russian-English
dictionaries translate *lichnost'* as "personality," "person," or "identity," and
its adjective as "personal" or "private." But none of these equivalents begins
to convey the meanings and associations that *lichnost'* acquired in the culture of the prerevolutionary Russian intelligentsia, where it meant something like "spiritual distinctiveness"—a quality that was valued much more
highly than *individual'nost'*. To express the difference somewhat bluntly,
everyone has a certain *individual'nost'* that stems from his or her personal
traits and preoccupations. But when a person creates or does something of
significance to the whole society, this becomes an expression of *lichnost'*,
conveying a spirit that is broader than that of the individual alone.[1]

[1] The stress in this concept fell on the larger entity—the community, the society, the nation.
In effect, the people were the real *lichnost'* in the minds of many Russian thinkers. Even
Konstantin Kavelin, a Westerner at heart and a moderate liberal, wrote in a letter to Dos-
toyevsky in 1880 that Russians had had no chance to develop a *samostoiatel'nuiu
natsional'nuiu lichnost'* (an independent distinctive national personality). With the accent
not on the development of the individual, it was an easy slide to the prevailing Soviet view that
a person can attain *lichnost'* only within the society and in total harmony with it.

There were, as we know, some who did not lose sight of the individual, and their sense of
isolation from their own culture was nowhere more powerfully expressed than by Alexander
Herzen in his introduction to *From the Other Shore*, where he gave his reason for not returning to Russia from Western Europe. "The liberty of the individual is the greatest thing of all,"
wrote Herzen. "In our country the individual has always been crushed," and he applauded
"the protest of the independent individual [*protest nezavisimoi lichnosti*]."

For the millions of Russians who in the past four decades have come out of the peasantry
into the working class and up into the technical-scientific intelligentsia and the political

I do not detect at the official level in the Soviet Union any serious tendency toward an understanding of true *lichnost'*. A move in this direction
would run up against the widespread and deeply ingrained attitude that is
reflected in the following vignette. When a Soviet official was told by one of
his compatriots that the *Communist Manifesto* states "the free development of each is the condition for the free development of all," the official
replied that he was absolutely sure that Marx had put it the other way
around.

Yet beneath the surface of official life, I sensed in many of the Russians
whom I met in Moscow—and they tended to be among the intelligentsia
—a growing desire for individuality and creativity and for ways of expressing these qualities more openly. My purpose in this paper is to explore
this theme in regard to women.

In my observation virtually all Russian girls looking into their futures see
themselves in two major roles: as married women with one or two children,
and as working women holding down lifelong jobs. Marriage is central to
young Russian women for life without a husband seems senseless; everyone wants to get married, even those girls from families of the intelligentsia
whom I have sometimes heard say, more as a gesture of independence
than a reflection of true intent, "I want to have children but not to get

---

elite—those who make up the bulk of today's urban population—the word *lichnost'* has everyday specific meanings that are neutral or even uncomplimentary to a person. The Soviet
militia uses the term *ustanovit' lichnost'* (to establish someone's identity). It is commonly
used to describe someone of sharply delineated personality: on/ona ochen' sil'naia lichnost'
(he/she is a very strong personality). Sometimes a person is called a *svetlaia* or *sviataia
lichnost'*—a radiant or saintly person, but a more commonly heard idiom is *podozritel'naia* or
tiomnaia lichnost', a suspicious or shady character. You occasionally even hear young schoolchildren using the phrase, "nu ty i lichnost'" to scold a playmate who is being uncooperative
in the sense of selfish behavior not in the interests of the group.

The phrase *vsestoronnee razvitie lichnosti* (the all-around development of the individual
and his or her personality) came into lively discussion among Party ideologists, scholars, and
educators in the late 1950's and early 1960's, partly through the revived interest in the young
Marx, and was incorporated into the Party program of 1961. As used at this official level,
lichnost' is a vague disembodied word that conveys very little to the broad Soviet public or even
to the present-day Soviet intelligentsia. Its older and complex meaning of the inner qualities of
a person make for his or her spiritual distinctiveness is not widely understood.

What a mass circulation newspaper like *Komsomol'skaia Pravda* means when it writes
about developing *lichnost'* is that everyone should seek to develop positive traits of character,
and it would then enumerate for its young readers such traits as love of work, responsiveness,
and honesty, all of which are of unquestionable benefit to the collective rather than reflections
of an individual distinctiveness that might at times conflict with the collective.

Moreover, when *lichnost'* occurs in the Soviet press it often carries a negative connotation:
eto evo lichnye ustremleniia (those are his personal aspirations) or *on stavit svoiu lichnost'
vysshe vsekh* (he puts his own interests above those of the group). The outstanding example of
such behavior was *kul't lichnosti* (the cult of the individual), the official term of condemnation
for the latter-day Stalin and his policies. Not only was this a monstrous distortion of the true
concept of *lichnost'*, but it also sharpened an existing dilemma.

On the one hand, *kul't lichnosti* is presented as a terrible sin against Soviet society, while
on the other hand people are repeatedly urged to develop their *lichnost'*. How to do so without
letting it get out of hand and rise above the interests of the group? This is all very puzzling to a
thoughtful person trying to make sense out of the variety and confusion about personality in
Russia, especially in the present climate in which words and phrases have become degraded
through mindless overuse. The average Russian gives this subject no thought whatsoever.

married—I don't think I'll ever find the ideal man." Most girls do not take it for granted that they will even find a decent husband, much less an ideal one. They have absorbed from their mothers and grandmothers the prevailing truth that men have long been a problem for Russian women—in times of war because there were not enough of them to go around, but in peacetime and every other time, too, because widespread heavy drinking inflicts a burden on Russian family life ("if my husband didn't beat me, how would I know that he loves me," goes the old proverb). The prevailing stereotype is still that of the dominant matriarch holding the family together without much help, and indeed nowadays one often hears women in the cities complain that men are becoming emasculated. All this makes for considerable anxiety, especially in a girl whose only goal is to find a husband, but I see no sign that young women at any level of the society are even considering the idea of remaining single as an acceptable alternative to marriage.

At the same time, it never occurs to a Russian girl that after graduation she might take a job only long enough to see herself into marriage. Her mother works, her older sister works—a Russian woman works throughout her lifetime because it is the accepted thing to do, and financially necessary. A writer friend of mine reflected, "It is my opinion that there is a sort of inferiority complex on the part of those few women who do not work: not external social pressure so much as something they feel inside; they feel unlike everyone else."

In the minds of most girls of the intelligentsia and some from the urban working class, the guidelines for what to do after high school are fairly uniform and loosely formulated: get admitted to study in an institute and then get a job that is interesting and not too hard. Many girls commit themselves to an occupation early, at seventeen, whereas most boys have the additional two years of military service in which to mature (and which deflect some from ever resuming their full-time formal education). There are no school guidance counselors or psychologists to encourage girls (or indeed young people of either sex) to look within themselves and ask, "Who am I in the process of becoming, what am I best suited to do in life, and given my strengths and weaknesses, where can I find fulfillment in my work?" Indeed the very asking of such questions assumes that a range of educational and occupational alternatives are acutally accessible to young women when the time comes to pick a course to follow. In practive, their range of choice has been extremely limited, partly by the huge excess of institute applicants over available places and partly by the mobilizational campaigns of the Komsomol and the pressure to "go where the country needs you."

Erik Erikson's views, to the extent that they are borne out by the experience of American youth, have made us aware that identity problems sharpen at that time in puberty when the adolescent's images of his or her future roles become inescapable. Does this hold true for at least some teenage girls in Russia? I have asked myself, less in anticipation of finding much similarity with American adolescents than in the hope of gaining insight through contrast, whether Russian girls at certain levels of society undergo a personal identity crisis in anything like the sense in which Erikson defined it—as a developmental process, sometimes full of conflict, that is both psychological and social, involving a search for oneself and for one's communality. The question is relevant to the theme of *lichnost' i kollektiv* (the individual and the collective).

In the social part of identity, says Erikson, "youth depends on the ideological coherence of the world it is meant to take over, and therefore is sensitively aware of whether the system is strong enough in its traditional form to 'confirm' and to be confirmed by the identity process or so rigid or brittle as to suggest renovation, reformation, or revolution."[2] It is my impression that for most Russian girls the identity process is not particularly aggravated by their images of their future roles. There is such a high degree of correspondence and compatibility between the values and views transmitted by parents in most social groups and those transmitted by the schools and the official media that young people overwhelmingly do tend to the prevailing Soviet value system. I think this is especially true of women. Exempt from the harsh school of military service and for the most part from the pressures of political infighting for promotion to high jobs, with their lives rooted in caring for home, husband, and children, Soviet women retain a wholeness of spirit and a capacity for belief that make them less vulnerable than men to disillusionment and cynicism. I sense that in spite of their double burden of work, women by and large accept the Soviet government's claim to have vastly improved the lot of women and opened to them the doors of professional life.

But for all that, there are some young women in the intelligentsia, especially among those with interests in the humanities, who have a clear image of the work they would like to do and who encounter such obstacles in reaching for their goal as to feel intense frustration. I have in mind one particular young woman who was twice rejected by Moscow University and once by an institute of literature, even though her school grades were high and she showed a real talent for writing. Her first reaction was an offhand, "Well, I don't need a diploma—those places don't give you an education anyway—and I can study on my own at home." After several years of trying to do this, while working part-time at a routine job, she began to have second thoughts, to feel that perhaps after all she did need a diploma to make a professional place for herself. For most girls in this situation, and boys too, for that matter, deepening frustration eventually leads them to accept whatever occupation is most readily available through whatever institute will take them in. In some cases it can lead to a degree of alienation that is even more intense than in Western societies—to what Erikson calls "the

[2] Erik H. Erikson, *Life History and the Historical Moment* (New York, 1975), p. 20.

specific rage" that can come when identity development "loses the promise of an assured wholeness."[3]

Some Soviet young people—and the "democratic movement" has given us insight into them—perceive the officially proclaimed values of the society as false ones. Isolated, rebuffed by the authorities in their efforts to open a dialogue, they become radicalized, and as a result their search for a personal identity manifests itself not in a positive and constructive form, but in a struggle against anything around them. They come to feel that this is the only way they can achieve and defend their own *lichnost'*.

One of the interesting aspects of the "democratic movement" was that there were substantially fewer women than men taking a formative and visible role in it. Women who were distantly sympathetic tended to get drawn into activism through the participation of their husbands and in response to repressions against one in their midst. This brought out their ordinary desire to help someone in trouble whom they knew and admired, to plead with the authorities for leniency, and to send packages of food and clothing to prisoners in the labor camps and support their families back home. In a way, for some though by no means all of these women, their sense of identity was no more than a reflection of the groups to which they belonged. This was brought to my attention by the comment of a young woman who emigrated recently. "You know," she said, "all these years I have existed through my friends, rather than on my own, and now that I am here, I realize that I don't know who I am."

Erikson may be right when he says that the American experience highlights identity problems, that such problems tend to "become urgent wherever Americanization spreads." Because women in Russia, for the most part, do not give the impression that they have gone through an identity crisis, does this mean that they are alienated from their own deepest identities? Russian women do have identities associated with their multiple roles—family, professional, and volunteer social activist—but the concept of a personal identity apart from the collective is one that so far belongs only to the Russian counterculture. Perhaps it is slowly, very slowly, gaining ground, for nowadays in Moscow and Leningrad some members of the intelligentsia talk more about *nakhozhdenie sebia* (finding oneself) and about how to live so as *ne lomat' sebia* (not to break oneself).

Reflecting on the kinds of satisfactions that Russian women draw from their jobs and their work-collectives, I find that even with individual and group variations there are certain common themes. Leaving home in the mornings is an escape from house chores at the psychological level only, and even then a very limited one. The chores lie in wait, the drudgery of evenings and weekends, and there is no doubt in my mind that many urban women would now prefer to work half-days or the equivalent so as to get a better hold on the home situation. (As it is, those with young children end

[3]*Life History and the Historical Moment*, p. 20.

up working only half- to two-thirds time, but without the predictability of knowing when they will be at home so that they can plan ahead.)

The additional family income is a satisfaction as well as a necessity. Together with the accumulated experience of holding a job, it gives women a feeling of independence and the confidence that if their husbands were to die or leave them, they would somehow manage on their own. In Natal'ia Baranskaia's "Nedelia kak nedelia" ("A Week Like Any Other"), a story that rings true not only for women of the intelligentsia, 26-year-old Olga, a wife and mother of two and an institute graduate working in a laboratory, speaks for many when she says emphatically, "I value my independence." It is a feeling that in my view is one of the great inner strengths of Russian women. If such women got the kinds of effective support they need from the Soviet government, we would not sometimes hear them exclaim in despair that they are *over*-independent and *over*-liberated. Even today many of the most ordinary tasks of everyday life, such as shopping, are unnecessarily time-consuming and difficult, a drudgery that could long ago have been lightened by a political leadership truly concerned to ease the burdens of its women.

There are many women at the middle and upper ranges of the intelligentsia who find the work they do at their jobs interesting and satisfying, even with all the frustrations (shortages of supplies and equipment, and that feeling of always working well below your potential because of constant exhaustion, not to speak of the powerful official and social deterrents to initiative and creativity). And there are large numbers of women, perhaps especially in provincial cities and small towns and in the countryside, who find fulfillment in social "activism," working as trade union, Party, and Komsomol organizers, as propagandists and lecturers and volunteers of all kinds.

If I had to select the one satisfaction most widely felt by the working woman at all levels of society, I would say that it is the work-collective as a source of community and communication and of mutual support in coping with the daily problems of life. And here I mean not the official formal collectives, but the intangible organic ones that women themselves create, with their own leaders and norms of conduct and laws of friendship. Russian women still have a primarily oral tradition of communication, even those with a higher education, if only because their work load leaves little time for professional and recreational reading and letter-writing. The bulk of their day is spent in the office or the factory, and quite naturally it is there that they unburden themselves to one another. The working environment is conducive to this unburdening—several or many people together in one room, with time on their hands because of the inefficient rhythms of work in most places (it is sometimes said that a woman "wants a job in order to get some rest"). The result is a lot of *babii razgovor* (women's talk). To be sure, some of this is gossip of a sort that thoughtful women shy away from, but intermingled with it is a generous sharing of moods and feelings, of joys and frustrations, that is somehow more central to Russian life than it is to our own culture.

Russian women would sink if all they got from one another was an on-the-run, "Hi, how are you?" . . . "I'm fine." At the core of a good *babii raz-govor* is the genuine interest of two women in each other's personality, an interest that in effect says, "You, with all your thoughts and preoccupations, are really necessary to me; I count on you for support." As one woman put it, comparing our two countries, "In America you run to psychiatrists be-cause, as far as I can gather, you do not have the *institut druzhby* [the tra-dition of close everyday friendship] that we have in Russia. We are very much tied to our milieu, and there we share everything with one another—hiding nothing or very little. We like to share our sorrows; we love to feel sorry for and to help one another."

As I think about what this woman said, two episodes come to mind from literature and life. One is the scene in "Nedelia kak nedelia" when Olga and two friends, who regularly take turns doing the marketing for one another, have all joined forces during the Friday lunch-break to help carry back the heavy load for three households for the weekend. As they are returning to work, Olga thinks to herself, "I am happy because there are three of us, because I am not alone." The other episode is the story I heard many years ago about an American woman who had given birth in a Moscow hospital room where several Russian women were also delivering. When she related this experience to some other Americans, their shocked reaction was, "What, no privacy!" To which a Russian woman listener responded, "Pri-vacy? Why who would want to be alone at a time like that?" There are Russian proverbs about the importance of being together at the critical moments of life, like the one that tells us *na miru i smert' krasna* (even death is good when you are in the mir).

Privatnost' (privacy) is a seldom used noun. There is the more common expression *zhelanie uedineniia* (a desire for seclusion), with the group as the starting point, so that privacy takes on the meaning of retiring or seclud-ing oneself from the collective. There is also the expression *byt' samim soboi na edine* (to be alone with oneself, especially in the sense of taking stock and being honest with oneself). Girls, and boys too, grow up in envi-ronments of such close company that they seldom have occasion to be on their own in this way. A young Moscow woman whose parents had gone away for some months, leaving her alone in the apartment, said in a letter to a friend that the experience "was a joy, because to live alone with myself is an old dream of mine." She was discovering at the age of 23 what it is to have extended undisturbed time for reflecting and collecting one's thoughts.

Much has been written by students of Russia about the roots in prerevo-lutionary life of the traditional feeling of community. Wright Miller, who

observed Russians in the cities before, during, and after the Second World
War, concluded that the old village sense of community had simply transplanted itself, somewhat weakened, into industrial surroundings: the Russians, in his view, still believed in the importance of the common sharing of
an experience; they still reflected "the unspoken requirement of society in
general that people should not feel or behave as though they were separate
from each other."[4] Even today there are scenes of urban life that recall the
village, such as the older women who sit on benches and exchange remarks
about everyone and everything around them. But comparisons at this level
can now be misleading. The uprooting of millions, the disruption of family
ties, the terror and its aftermath, the ideological conditioning in the schools
and through the media, the changes in living patterns with industrialization
—all have had effects so profound as to cut most of the urban population
loose from the old village traditions and feelings of natural community. For
40 years Russians have lived in an enforced close collectivity more intense
than anything they ever experienced in the village.

Now many of them have had too much of it, and they seek relief, both
physical and psychological. As a Soviet sociologist writes, they "are so fed
up with the relations between neighbors in crowded apartments, in communal kitchens (the kitchen psychoses), that on receiving their own separate apartments, they avoid all everyday contacts for quite some time. They
find it terrible even to recall their past experience. They say, 'I don't want
my neighbor to see how I eat and drink and relax and live.' "[5] Communal
living contributes to a very real *peregruzka nervnoi sistemy* (strain of the
nervous system). It is something that one finds among many women of the
intelligentsia; some say that they feel in a mood of almost continuous irrita-
tion because everything in daily life is so hard to accomplish.

Soviet power draws heavily on the dynamism and social activeness of
women. Reflect back for just a moment to the 1940's and early 1950's when
much of the country's adult male population was enlisted in one of four
armies: the army of the dead, the army of the imprisoned, the regular army
and security forces, and the army of bureaucrats who administer things. It
was women's energy that flowed in to fill the huge gaps in the economy and
family life, indeed and in the society as a whole. The women of that time
became accustomed to doing everything themselves; they had no one to
depend on; they really were independent, by necessity rather than choice.

Even today, though young urban women are visibly more focused on
themselves, on their appearance and private lives, most women continue to
center their energies and activities around the collective. But their willingness to endure, which was a strength in time of war and terror, is increasingly becoming a weakness in the sense that exhaustion contributes to a

[4] Wright Miller, *Russians As People* (New York, 1961), p. 112.
[5] N. Solov'ev, "Sosedskie otnosheniia i printsip kollektivizma v bytu," in *Sotsial'nye
issledovaniia*, vol. 7 (M, 1971), pp. 98–99.

passive outlook about their own situation. Symbolic of this is the scene in "Nedelia kak nedelia" where the women laughingly speculate about the purpose of a questionnaire that they have been asked to fill out. They agree that the sociologists must be wondering why women do not have more children, and are about to come up with a new plan—at least two babies per couple. "All joking aside," says one woman, "I think, girls, that this questionnaire is not for nothing. They're going to give us mothers some benefits. Right? They'll shorten our working day, maybe they'll even start to pay us for more than just three days of absence from work when our kids are home sick. You wait and see; if they're studying the situation, it means they're going to do something about it." [6]

This psychology of resigned reliance on the paternalism of higher authority—a kind of simple folk hopefulness—is of course characteristic of the whole society, and in fairness to women it should be said that on the whole they show more initiative and determination than men in putting pressure on local officials to get things done.

To the extent that the hope of women everywhere is in participation, in being communal as well as individual, Russian women have an advantage. By the traditions of their culture they grow naturally into a communality of friendship, of sharing their deepest feelings and supporting one another in daily life. This communality has no organizational form; it is a spirit that is to be found within some formal collectives and not others, but it is usually strongest in the informal circles of like-thinking friends that are independent of all official collectives. Whether this spirit will survive into an era of higher living standards and fewer of the physical and psychological burdens that tended to encourage the sharing process remains to be seen.

Upward mobility has led large numbers of Russian women to establish themselves in professional roles. A few of them have now come into a phase of growth in which they are no longer content with an identity based solely on their participation in the collective—they are discovering the meaning of that part of *lichnost'* which is the development of the individual. For women in Western culture, self-realization tends to be defined almost wholly in individual terms because Western culture begins with the individual at the center of its concerns. *Lichnost'* in its fullest sense signifies finding one's identity and fulfillment in the context of a feeling of solidarity with the group. What I sense in some of these Russian women is that in developing their individuality, they seek to bring it into harmony with the cultural tradition of self-realization through the community. But the important point of departure for them is the voluntary nature of belonging to a group. For they believe that the full realization of *lichnost'* can mature only under conditions where association is voluntary and not directed from the political center.

---

[6] Natal'ia Baranskaia, "Nedelia kak nedelia," *Novyi mir*, 1969, no. 11, p. 27.

I think of the Russian woman as standing precariously in the middle of one of those wide Moscow boulevards with cars rushing by on either side. The Bolshevik Revolution brought her part of the way across. To get to the other side she still has to undergo a spiritual revolution that is one of the goals of women's liberation everywhere.

And of men's, too, for that matter.

Alexander Dallin

Conclusion

THE PAPERS IN this volume cover such a wide range of subjects and offer such a variety of insights that these concluding reflections can touch on only a few particularly salient points. Though many of the findings are relatively straightforward and many of the comparisons that spring to mind are self-evident, the evaluation of so much diverse material is bound to raise difficulties.

To Soviet commentators and to writers friendly to the Soviet Union, the status of women has understandably been a subject of particular pride.[1] Compared to the continuing problems in such areas as housing, agriculture, civil rights, and living standards, the "solution of the woman question" does indeed offer grounds for pride and satisfaction. In literacy, education, legal rights, access to employment and professions, and "equal pay for equal work," the advances made by women since the Revolution of 1917 have been substantial. If we think of prerevolutionary history as a record of prejudice and superstition, then the Soviet era has indeed helped strip away many inequities and injustices, distortions and discriminations.

Today nearly 90 percent of all Soviet women of working age are either employed or studying. Women now make up about half the Soviet labor force in industry, about half of all Soviet students, and over two-thirds of all Soviet teachers and doctors. There are more women engineers in the USSR than in all other countries combined. Not surprisingly, then, the official message to Soviet women in International Women's Year was, in substance, "You never had it so good."[2]

[1] Cosmonaut Valentina Nikolaeva-Tereshkova, for instance, chairwoman of the Soviet Women's Committee, exclaimed that "The new way of life of women in the USSR and their new role in society are one of the most convincing arguments in favor of socialism." (*Pravda*, March 4, 1975).

[2] See *The New York Times*, March 8, 1975; see also USSR, Tsentral'noe Statisticheskoe Upravlenie (TsSU), *Zhenshchiny v SSSR* (M, 1975).

And yet, there is no question that in the Soviet Union the status of women remains in many ways inferior to that of men. This is perhaps the most appropriate comparison to make; transnational ones suffer from various difficulties of data, methodology, and imperfect indicators. Yet even the differences between the Soviet Union and, say, the United States or Sweden are frequently differences of degree, not of kind. Such a finding would indeed fit into a conceptual framework that sees the Soviet experience as an alternative path of development—a functional equivalent of, rather than an advance beyond (as Marxists had anticipated), Western capitalism. The regime has succeeded in making the USSR into a modernized superpower—at least as measured by economic indicators and military capabilities. Here it has done what some noncommunist systems have accomplished, too. But it has failed precisely in those areas where its founders had made particular, utopian claims: the areas of uniquely communist expectations and promises. This has been as true of the status of women as of many other aspects of the Leninist vision.

The experience of Soviet women may thus be seen as illustrative of, and congruent with, the general development of Soviet society and the Soviet polity. On the "woman question," as on other aspects of communist public policy, the Bolsheviks had no blueprint before the Revolution of how to proceed once they came to power. The Leninists shared the conviction that socialism would automatically and inevitably "solve" the "woman question," just as it would "solve" the problems of crime, nationalism, and racism. All social problems, they believed, were by-products of the inequities of the capitalist order and were bound to disappear in the benign environment of proletarian socialism. Originally, the family was expected to wither, along with other bourgeois institutions, including the army and the state itself. It was natural that the first decade of Soviet rule—and in particular, the years of the so-called New Economic Policy—should have witnessed considerable debate on and experimentation with all aspects of cultural and economic life, above all with respect to the family, sex, and the role of women.

If there ensued a dramatic departure from the naïve, chic, and romantic idealism of the early days, this reversal paralleled the whole shift in atmosphere and advocacy from John Reed's *Ten Days That Shook the World* to Solzhenitsyn's *One Day in the Life of Ivan Denisovich*.[3] The dissolution of the Women's Section of the Party at the end of the 1920's fitted the emergent Stalinist pattern of eliminating all secondary associations and allegiances throughout Soviet life, coincided with the destruction of the Party's Jewish Sections, and anticipated the ban on the organization of "Old Bolsheviks" and later of veterans and partisans of the Second World War.

[3]On the abandonment of illusions, see Alexander Dallin, "Retreat From Optimism," in Severyn Bialer et al., eds., *Radicalism in the Contemporary Age*, III (Boulder, Col., 1977).

Claiming a monopoly on loyalties, the Stalinist model made state and society coterminous.

All of Soviet society experienced, under Stalin, the impact of a single set of overriding priorities to whose attainment everything else had to be subordinated. The fate of women was scarcely among the topmost priorities. The mobilization approach to economic development meant a universal obligation to labor, a shift from (limited) permissiveness to discipline and control, and the neglect of parts of the economy (such as the service and consumer-goods sectors). Even as they were finding both opportunity and necessity to work and study, women suffered from the lag in these sectors.

If women were found in fewer and fewer numbers as one ascended to higher levels of the political pyramid, this was no less true of peasants and manual workers. Like other groups in Soviet society, women benefited from the "thaw" that followed Stalin's death, from the changes in welfare and family legislation, from slowly improving housing conditions and rising standards of living, and from greater flexibility and candor. The status of women today is only one of many facets of Soviet life marked by profound ambiguities; it has also been one of the numerous areas paradoxically affected by "unintended consequences" of communist development.[4]

Just as has been true of other parts of Soviet life, there has been a gradual and growing awareness of the residual effects—and the recrudescence—of prerevolutionary Russian culture and attitudes (and their equivalents among other nationalities of the USSR), and of the various constraints under which even a seemingly omnipotent regime labors. Some observers might even speculate whether the debate now beginning on the status of women inside the Soviet Union may not be seen as one more facet of the concealed contest among latent interest groups in the Soviet political arena.[5]

As has often been the case in other matters, Eastern Europe has proven again to be more open in voicing grievances and alternatives in regard to sex roles, protective legislation, and working conditions.[6] And just as the arrival of "full" communism in the USSR has been indefinitely postponed, so also has the "full" liberation of Soviet women.

A review of the Soviet experience suggests, perhaps a bit unexpectedly, that despite the distinctiveness of Soviet ideology and the Soviet system there are striking similarities in the general trends manifested in modern societies. Everywhere—the Soviet Union included—women still have to deal with families, pregnancies, housework, and careers. The role conflicts and the tensions between private and public roles, as well as the hypocrisy

[4] For a discussion of this concept, see Chalmers Johnson, ed., *Change in Communist Systems* (Stanford, Calif., 1970).

[5] On the "group" approach to Soviet politics, see, for instance, H. Gordon Skilling and Franklyn Griffiths, eds., *Interest Groups in Soviet Politics* (Princeton, N.J., 1971).

[6] See, e.g., Helen Scott, *Does Socialism Liberate Women?* (Boston, 1974).

on sexual questions, are all familiar and well-nigh universal features of modern life.

Thus the Soviet experience has not really given rise to fundamentally new patterns of family relations. After the early years of experimentation, the Party reverted to a conservative policy of "strengthening" the family. As elsewhere, the trend has been toward a nuclear family (though in the USSR, as in some other countries, there is probably more significant intergenerational contact than in the U.S.).[7] In essence, the Soviet Union has provided no new answers to the strains between "biology" and "equality." The increased employment of women has been characteristic of all modern and modernizing societies, for economic growth generates new jobs everywhere. Technology is bound to make female employment outside the home more manageable by easing domestic work and by providing such by-products as specialized education, urbanization, and transportation.

In regard to the effects of modernization on sex roles, then, the Soviet Union differs from other industrialized societies largely in degree. Everywhere technology tends to reduce the "rational" basis for sex differentiation by providing a vast array of new tools, from contraceptives to washing machines. Hence the demographic and physiological aspects of sex differentiation tend to be of decreasing importance.[8]

Virtually everywhere in the civilized world the trend has been toward equal rights for women, and at least in law those rights have been increasingly achieved (albeit not everywhere and not in all regards). That Soviet women can choose their marital partners according to their own free choice is a relatively recent development in Russia as much as in the West. The Soviet Union has shared in the dramatic changes, in this century, in the reduction of mortality rates and in the lengthening of life expectancy, just as it has shared in the many public-health and medical accomplishments of the Western world. Childbirth has become remarkably safer, and so— relatively speaking—has abortion. And, though recognizing the particular vigor with which such advances have been pursued in the Soviet Union (as well as the differential rates of change among different countries), one must conclude that the basic institutional and political solutions advanced there have been essentially no different from those explored and practiced in other countries: social-welfare legislation, day-care centers, birth control, labor-saving devices, legal provision for equal pay, a growing percentage of women working and educated, and so on.

The Soviet Union is also sharing in certain organic, ubiquitous social tendencies. For instance, there as elsewhere there is an inverse correlation between the ratio of men to women and the percentage of women in the labor force. There as elsewhere there is a correlation between participation rates in the labor force and a declining birthrate, especially among urban

---

[7] Cf. Urie Bronfenbrenner, *Two Worlds of Childhood* (New York, 1970).

[8] See Evelyne Sullerot, *Woman, Society and Change* (New York, 1974), p. 13.

and educated women. In fact, we can echo the conclusion that "everywhere we find that women are excluded from certain crucial economic or political activities, that their roles as wives and mothers are associated with fewer powers and prerogatives than are the roles of men. It seems fair to say, then, that all contemporary societies are to some extent male-dominated, and although the degree and expression of female subordination vary greatly, sexual asymmetry is presently a universal fact of human social life."[9]

There are of course lessons here that cut both ways. On the one hand, the experience of some European countries suggests that the implementation of social-welfare provisions and "equal pay for equal work" do not at all require an authoritarian framework of the Soviet type. On the other hand, it is instructive that the higher participation rate of women in the Soviet Union apparently has not made Soviet males feel any less "virile" as a consequence.

In some other regards, we still lack adequate information to make firm comparisons. Thus we have no firm basis for judging whether in the USSR women tend to be politically more conservative than men—as is often alleged to be true elsewhere. Nor is it clear whether the official pronatalist policy and propaganda of the Soviet authorities have succeeded in making the USSR an exception to the general tendency in virtually all advanced societies that makes the maternal role, in the female's self-perception, less central and defining for women.

Still, the distinguishing features of the Soviet experience need to be recognized, too. They can be subsumed under the rubrics of heredity and environment. Soviet society inherited the accumulated backwardness and underdevelopment that characterized tsarist Russia—the bulk of its women unschooled and unskilled—as well as the pervasive and multifarious manifestations of what these days is labeled male chauvinism.[10] It is axiomatic in social history that however revolutionary this or that regime, and however radical the changes it introduces in policy or ideology, it still must deal with the same people and take as its point of departure the existing popular attitudes and norms of behavior. The Olga of our first chapter remains part of the cultural universe of the modern Olga described in the last. Today's Soviet Union is only a few years removed from a peasant society—not completely removed, at that—and inevitably (albeit awkwardly and ambiguously) many of the traditional values and habits, from proverbs to public baths, still survive.

Before the Revolution, the resigned acceptance of authority had extended to Russian women, too. True, this had begun to change well before 1917,

---

[9] Michelle Z. Rosaldo and Louise Lamphere, eds., *Woman, Culture, and Society* (Stanford, Calif., 1974), p. 3. See also Scott, p. 201.

[10] For one interpretation of the effects of these features on the evolution of the Soviet state see Roger Pethybridge, *The Social Prelude to Stalinism* (New York, 1974).

and not only for the *intelligentka*-activist or the new urban working-class woman.[11] In fact, a good case can be made that, in terms of personal initiative and commitment, women were more profoundly and originally involved in Russian revolutionary politics before the 1917 Revolution and in the period immediately following it than in later years, when Soviet women who attempted to assume a public role found themselves locked into the new hierarchy, the new discipline, the new law and order—all of which turned out to promote and train and mobilize women for production and reproduction. It might be unkind but not incorrect to suggest that Soviet officialdom, obsessed with output statistics and conformity, located women on their mental map somewhere between generators and milk cows. In practice, women were debarred from the top decision-making levels of the political elite.

The Leninists' "derivative" view of women's emancipation was bound to shape their priorities. So did Stalinist totalism, which made work by women well-nigh a must—as a political and moral as well as an economic necessity for the Soviet family. What Soviet women were given, by way of opportunities and institutions (such as day-care centers and kindergartens) was not conferred as a matter of generosity or "liberation" but was essentially shaped by the Stalinist perception of *raison d'état*. More than one Soviet generation has been conditioned by the authoritative choice to place state interests above private concerns.

The Stalin years also isolated the country from the outside world and thus made it impossible for the population to benefit by learning from the best thinking and research in many fields of social policy, whether child-rearing or small-group sociology, birth control or the psychological effects of institutional care. In the same vein, the Stalin era left the USSR obliged to observe all manner of dogmatic "orthodoxies" (such as Lysenkoite pseudoenvironmentalism, anti-Malthusianism, and denial of psychological variables), with obvious costs for the problems here under review.

Many (but not all) of these barriers and curtains have since been lifted. A somewhat more pragmatic and realistic approach now prevails, but serious problems remain, beginning with the persistent official denial that a serious "woman question" even exists in the Soviet Union today.

The continuing ban on the formation of voluntary associations is also bound to have an effect on Soviet women's activity, although the recent experience of other groups suggests that there are peculiar techniques by which Soviet institutions and citizens can gain access to policy-makers, can articulate their views (within obvious limits), and can seek to influence decisions relevant to their own concerns. To be sure, this is likely to make less for dramatic new departures than for a more realistic but at best creeping gradualism.

[11] See, e.g., Vera S. Dunham, "The Strong-Woman Motif," in Cyril E. Black, ed., *The Transformation of Russian Society* (Cambridge, Mass., 1960).

As yet one can only speculate about the cumulative, long-range impact of "collective" institutional rearing of new generations, as compared to the nurturing by traditional family units.

It would be pointless to try to restate here the many distinctive aspects of the conditions in which Soviet women find themselves: the papers in this volume amply address this question. But, if the preceding remarks have focused on particular tensions and liabilities, mention must also be made of some distinctive attainments. An oversimplified but tenable view sees women in capitalist societies as a quasi proletariat. Historical studies do support the view that, at least in its early phases, capitalism has tended to increase the gap between male and female. Collective systems (however erratic and distorted their practice), on the other hand, typically seek to reduce inequalities, and this extends to inequalities between the sexes as well. And in fact, in spite of the important wage differentials brought out in this volume, the gap between male and female compensation is not so great in the Soviet Union as it is in Western Europe or the United States. Moreover, opportunities for education, including higher and technical education, (though not for part-time work) are no doubt more readily and cheaply available to Soviet women than to their sisters abroad.

Granted the strains of combining motherhood with career, Soviet women normally do not experience the long discontinuity—with all its attendant problems of job security and loss of professional skill—that mothers who interrupt their employment typically face in the West. We may also hazard the supposition that Soviet women generally do not have the perception of an ostensible inferiority, the guilt feelings, and the conflicts over being social transvestites—"traitors to their sex"—that mark many other "modern" women. Some observers would also stress, by contrast with contemporary American society, the absence in the Soviet Union of an overwhelming preoccupation with the erotic.

But of course Soviet life is full of ambiguities and ironies. One is women's attitude toward work. It seems certain that the overwhelming majority of Soviet women are effectively socialized to consider working outside the home a normal and natural thing to do. Though economic necessity—the need for a "second income" to make ends meet—is in most cases the foremost motivation, recent Soviet studies suggest that even in the absence of such a compelling incentive many women would still want to work. The place of work—the "collective"—is often the locus of "significant others" for the Soviet woman; moreover, the place of work or study frequently supersedes the dreary, cramped, unexciting home in which there is scant opportunity for fulfillment. Whereas abroad the feminist quest has encompassed the right to work, in the Soviet Union some women would nonetheless press instead for the right and the ability *not* to work. Elsewhere this has characteristically been a middle-class demand; and perhaps, as the functional equivalent of a middle class develops ever more clearly in the USSR, this demand (assuming it can be afforded) will be more loudly and widely voiced.

It does of course, run head-on into the state's priorities. To permit more women not to work (actually there are already several million "housewives" without outside employment) or, as has at times been suggested in gingerly fashion, to let mothers of young children work part-time, would mean reducing the "social utility" of female labor in the economy—and this at a time when the Soviet Union faces a severe shortage of labor reserves. It would mean permitting individual choice to subvert planned goals. There is a notable ambivalence in Soviet discussions on the present and future status of women, and there are obvious inconsistencies in present practice. After all, a state that forcefully promotes a pronatalist policy, if only to counteract the declining birthrate, does allow abortion on demand during the first months of pregnancy. And a state that vigorously supports the traditional family has acceded to pressures for easier and cheaper divorce, with the result that the divorce rate has been skyrocketing over the last twenty years.[12]

Such phenomena illustrate the limits of what public policy can do and exemplify the constraints under which Soviet policy-makers must labor. As economic growth and social change slow down, and as the great political transformations recede into the past, options and opportunities within the system decline, fluidity and "give" begin to vanish, and attitudes freeze in established molds. Policy-makers must then deal with interlocking pieces of a giant puzzle in which every decision involves a trade-off, and every gain involves cost.

Thus questions about Soviet reality defy simple yes-or-no answers. Human problems, as is so often the case, prove to be more recalcitrant than the self-appointed engineers of the human soul—or their enemies— imagined. Results, it turns out, are not uniformly benign or malignant, and the picture neither white nor black. Ultimately, what we see depends on where we stand.

It is important to be aware of the diversity and controversy—albeit muted and often abortive—that have been virtual constants in this domain, as they have been in many other aspects of Soviet public life. As the papers in this volume show, the years after the Revolution witnessed vigorous debate over the relationship of feminism and socialism, and over the ambitious visions of socializing housework and instituting massive public catering. The mid-1920's saw the climax of an interesting argument over marriage and family. Even under Stalin, the mid-1930's brought truncated arguments

[12]Viktor Perevedentsev, in "Pochti vsio o zhenshchinakh," *Zhurnalist*, March 1975; trans. in CDSP, XXVII:23, p. 10, gives the following official figures for divorces per 1,000 marriages in selected years: 1950, 32; 1960, 104; 1965, 179; 1966, 309; 1970, 269; 1973, 270. See also the chapter by Bernice Madison above.

over a new abortion law. The Second World War, with its untold suffering and trauma, created new and unforeseen challenges and opportunities for Soviet women. After 1945 women faced new dilemmas about whether to stay in their newly gained roles or, in effect, to return home.[13] In the post-Stalin years, many controversial issues relating to women, home, and work have at last been seriously studied and are beginning to be candidly discussed.

Though it may be too soon to say, there are indications that in the last several years—despite the slowing of social change—something has again begun to change. The quality of information and of the issues raised has risen markedly. The heightened concern with women's status and "women's liberation" abroad seems to be seeping through—as are numerous other concerns, from environmental pollution to the uses of mathematics in the social sciences—and helping to shape the invisible agenda of policy problems confronting Soviet society. What are some of these issues?

Uppermost seems to be the tension between work and home, the problem of the "double shift" or the "double burden" borne by Soviet women. The strains inherent in combining employment with family obligations are common to all modern societies, but they appear to be especially severe in the Soviet case. As was mentioned earlier, most Soviet women have no choice: they cannot afford not to work. Moreover, a social stigma attaches to being "only" a homemaker. Much to the authorities' chagrin, one effect of the "double burden" has been to exacerbate the drop in the Soviet (and especially the urban) birthrate. Yet substantially the same problem surfaces even where no children, or no small children, add to the woman's responsibilities at home. As we have seen, even without economic pressures many women would want to get out of the home: recent Soviet studies identify elements of status, escape from home, and personal development as widespread motives here. Baranskaia's short story, referred to by several of the authors in this volume, and the considerable discussion it provoked, support the same point.[14] It is no longer the case that marriage provides women's only route to social advancement. On the contrary, now that education and outside employment have opened up new tracks, marriage and family care can become roadblocks to upward mobility. Even official Soviet publications explicitly recognize the unfairness of the "double burden" and the various shortages of goods and services that compound it.[15] Indeed, Soviet sociological research has amply documented one crucial aspect of the prob-

---

[13] See Vera S. Dunham, *In Stalin's Time* (New York, 1976), chap. 13.

[14] See also Georgie Anne Geyer, *The Young Russians* (Homewood, Ill., 1975), pp. 194–96.

[15] See Gail Lapidus' discussion in her paper in this volume. Quasi-official recognition has been accorded these questions by publication of an article in the Communist Party's "theoretical" journal. See L. Gordon, E. Klopov, and L. Onikov, "Sotsial'nye problemy byta," *Kommunist*, 17 (1974), 49–60.

lem—the differential use of "leisure" time for domestic work. In the words of an authoritative Soviet account,

the enormous importance of the social problems engendered by time-consuming housework is due in part to the inequality of women and men in the daily routine. . . . Working women devote from 2 to 2.5 times more of their time to housework than do the men; therefore they have less opportunity for rest, raising their professional skills, and cultural level—in general, less opportunity for their development.
. . .
This gap is approximately twelve hours a week among unmarried youth and young childless families, but reaches 18–20 hours a week in families with minor children. Although, as the family expands and the volume of housework increases, men must take care of a growing amount of household activities, their share is even smaller. . . . Obviously, waiting on the husband is an important part of the domestic obligations of married working women.[16]

The same study goes on to argue cogently that "these patterns—and consequently the inequality of women in the daily routine—are reinforced when and if women share the conviction that housework is 'women's work,' that the predominance of the woman's role in household chores is not only natural but even satisfactory." Though such notions may no longer be so widespread as before, "nevertheless, that the ideas of the exceptional role of women in running the household still dominate is shown in the excessive importance that many women attribute to their prestige as a good housewife."[17]

By comparison with, say, American conditions, the strain is substantially aggravated by the shortage or absence of services and appliances; and though there has recently been an effort to increase their availability, the Soviet press continues to recount numerous complaints about poor quality, shortages, and lags in production.[18]

To put it differently, the severity of the problem is due to the fact that in the Soviet Union the quality of life is not propitious to equality in life. In part, of course, this is the result of political choices made over the past half

[16] L. Gordon and E. Klopov, *Man After Work* (M, 1975), pp. 72–73.

[17] *Ibid.*, pp. 74–75. See also pp. 176–82 and Appendix. The basic time expenditure of workers, in hours and minutes per week, included the following telling figures (p. 263):

	Women	*Men*
Housework	27 hrs., 20 min.	11 hrs., 40 min.
Daily cultural activities	11 hrs., 50 min.	19 hrs., 50 min.
Sleeping, eating, idle time	60 hrs., 30 min.	66 hrs., 30 min.

The four most frequent "daily activities" listed for women are cooking, housecleaning, shopping, and caring for clothes (in that order); for men they are watching television, shopping, reading newspapers, and being idle. Women's problem is further complicated by the decline of the *babushka*—the grandmother—as an institution widely used to assist with domestic chores and child care. See also Charlotte Saikowski, "The Cry is For 'Liberation' from Household Toil," *The Christian Science Monitor*, June 10, 1971.

[18] See, e.g., *Pravda*, Feb. 13, 1975; V. I. Starodub, *Zhenshchina i obshchestvennyi trud* (L, 1975), pp. 81–83; Evgenii Vorozheikin, *Molodym suprugam o brake i sem'e* (M, 1975), pp. 25ff., a curious booklet of advice to newlyweds. Official Soviet statistics (TsSU, *Zhenshchiny v*

century, e.g., regarding priorities in resource allocation; in part, it is a function of values and attitudes in the population itself.[19]

Whereas all sorts of technical and organizational "solutions" to these problems are discussed, the central issue underlying the widespread demand for a new "division of labor" between male and female in the home and in child-rearing, is the attitude of the Soviet man. This, and not communist doctrine, is the real problem of ideology that confronts Soviet women. As elsewhere, there are abundant indications and illustrations of all manner of subtle discrimination, "put down," and scorn. Women still do most of the dirty work.[20] Sex-role stereotypes abound; the analysis of Soviet primers in one of the papers in this volume provides telling examples of this phenomenon, which almost certainly has been unintended and unperceived by Soviet authors and authorities. (The attitude problem extends to women themselves. For instance, most Soviet mothers still want to have a boy rather than a girl—and not only because there are fewer males in the society.)

Some women have become aware of the double standard. As one Soviet acquaintance complained to an American correspondent, "A man can fool around with other women, drink, even be lackadaisical toward his job, and this is generally forgiven. But if a woman does the same things, she is criticized for taking a light-hearted attitude toward her marriage and her work."[21] It probably remains true that female identity roles are defined largely by males.

This, then, is the other side of the "dialectics of backwardness."[22] It has

---

SSSR, p. 118) claim an increased stress on services, as measured in millions of rubles, as follows:

	1965	1970	1975
Shoe repair	189	370	466
Clothing repair and sewing	576	1,018	1,249
Repair of TVs, radios, machinery, automobiles, etc.	169	436	818
Dry cleaning and dyeing	42	94	142
Beauty parlors and barbershops	255	398	496

[19] Under "quality of life," passing mention should be made of the rapidly rising divorce rate and alcoholism (which has been cited in at least 40 percent of Soviet divorces as a cause—and is bound to be a source of strain in innumerable other marriages). Indirectly, the pressure of domestic duties is cited in some Soviet studies as one reason why some women do not seek to advance to more responsible positions: both the threshold of tolerable pressures and the lack of time for additional studies or time-consuming executive positions help account for the self-imposed reluctance of some women to seek further "upward mobility."

[20] Cf. also the general assumption that work "inside" is deemed inferior to work "outside" the house (Sullerot, p. 23).

[21] Hedrick Smith, *The Russians* (New York, 1976), p. 135. Most visitors to the Soviet Union will be able to relate anecdotes illustrating unintended manifestations of male chauvinism. Thus when a child is sick, the nursery will call the mother, not the father, home from work. In entertaining visiting foreign delegations, Soviet (male) hosts accompany them to the opera's orchestra and their wives sit in the balcony. Though statistics are lacking, the number of men with driver's licenses seems to be far greater than the number of women with them.

[22] For a discussion of the concept inherent in Lenin's argument that Russia could outstrip the more developed Western democracies, see Alfred G. Meyer, *Leninism* (Cambridge, Mass., 1957), chap. 12.

proven far simpler to build steel mills and jets than to produce a real "cultural revolution" altering deep-seated, age-old habits and attitudes. So much for facile nonsense about "brainwashing." Had the Soviet state been born in—or had it achieved—relative affluence, it would have been easier for males and females to redistribute the burden (and, paradoxically, would have made it less imperative to do so insofar as the strain—but not equity—was concerned).

Another major cluster of issues that are finally being discussed somewhat more openly concerns the neglect of sex and sex education. Not only erotica but virtually all references to sexuality in print or public discussion (other than in specialized publications) are still taboo. Sexual (like all other) "deviance" is proscribed and persecuted. One may well speak of a "hung up" generation of Soviet citizens, where a variety of traditional and situational variables have combined to engender pervasive hypocrisy and concealment.

Perhaps there were elements of "backwardness" in the Leninist approach as well. Alongside his commitment to undo social wrongs—be they to women, to the proletariat, or to ethnic minorities—Lenin's attitude toward sex and marriage was typical of the ascetic, single-minded revolutionary. It mirrored pre-Freudian assumptions of spurious rationality; Marxism was, after all, the last creed of "bourgeois" enlightenment.

One need not belabor the extent and variety of the ways in which these inhibitions have been harmful to efforts of Soviet citizens aimed at self-knowledge and at recognition and study of the affective aspects of personality, and have been detrimental even to elementary knowledge of birth control and the physiology of sex. Typical of a spate of recent Soviet articles was one headlined "Girl's Ignorance Leads to Pregnancy."[23]

This, too, is part of the price being paid for the blinders that follow from the "derivative" approach to "women's liberation." "The liberation of female sexuality," writes Sheila Rowbotham, "is such an important part of the politics of women's liberation that this neglect of the mechanisms of sexual and personal transformation had serious consequences in allowing a great narrowing in the definition of what constitutes liberation."[24]

Though there are still ringing affirmations of the old line (to the point of suggesting, in terms familiar to the American reader, that "propaganda in favor of 'sexual freedom' " is being conducted by alien forces seeking to subvert the system by "shaking the moral convictions of the youth"[25]), a significant change in attitudes and behavior, especially of urban youth, appears to be taking place.

[23] For a selection, see CDSP, XXV:45, XXVI:42, and XXVII:8. See also James F. Clarity, "Soviet Letters on Sex Get No Replies," The New York Times, Feb. 23, 1975; and Mark Gayn, "Soviet Sex and Seduction," San Francisco Examiner and Chronicle, June 17, 1973.
[24] Sheila Rowbotham, Women, Resistance and Revolution (New York, 1974), p. 152.
[25] Sovetskaia kul'tura, June 21, 1974.

The new morality—or perhaps amorality—once again bears a striking resemblance to its analogue in the West (even though it is difficult to evaluate). Surely the statistics and survey data on premarital and extramarital sex, promiscuity, abortion, and "illegitimate" children leave little doubt that, in the words of a leading Soviet demographer, "the trend toward equality of the sexes in production is clear, but the changes occurring in family and everyday life are considerably more complex and contradictory."[26] Though these trends require further study, even anecdotal accounts fully tally with these impressions, which in one's most optimistic reading may be seen to herald a decline of sham Victorianism in the USSR.[27]

This sketch cannot be concluded without reiterating that Soviet women themselves are a part of the problem. Many of them appear preoccupied with the symbols and paraphernalia of traditional femininity, with comforts and conveniences, a desire for consumerism and cosmetics, and a belief in the perpetuation of privileged and protective practices and legislation. At least in these respects they have gained some ground, as is shown by the fact that fashions and "beauty" are now accepted as desirable and no longer proscribed as hopelessly bourgeois. But this, of course, is scarcely the road to "liberation."

Clearly, the educational and career successes of Soviet women are remarkable and unique. Just as clearly, Soviet women do not share political power in any significant degree. They remain discriminated against in a wide variety of subtle and often no doubt unwitting ways.

What has become clear is that there is more—much more—to emancipation than the removal of obstacles to participation in the economy, or than a change in the ownership of the "means of production." Soviet society abounds in unsolved problems that had not been foreseen, including problems of the relationship between individual and community, family and career. Ambiguities are created by the tension between choices in the most private areas of personal life and the controls pervading public life. What seemed like answers—for instance, day-care centers—have generated new questions. Friedrich Engels remarked in his *Origin of the Family* that "every step forward is also relatively a step backward." He had not anticipated that the dialectic would continue to operate under "socialist" conditions.

Leninism lacked—and its followers still lack—a dedication to the spontaneity of human relationships. Indeed, the suspicion of—and hostility

---

[26] Perevedentsev, p. 9. One of his most substantial surveys documenting the high incidence of premarital sex and adultery appeared in the June 1975 issue of *Nash sovremennik*. See also the frank surveys by Iuri Riurikov in *Molodoi kommunist*, 10–11 (1975) (trans. in *CDSP*, XXVIII:15).

[27] See among recent accounts Geyer, chaps. 14–15; George Feifer, *Our Motherland* (New York, 1973), chap. 5; Smith, chap. 5; and Susan Jacoby, *Moscow Conversations* (New York, 1972), chap. 9. Less reliable are Yuri Brokhin, *Hustling on Gorky Street* (New York, 1975), and Yuri Kuper, *Holy Fools in Moscow* (New York, 1974).

to—spontaneity remains one of the more massive obstacles to true "liberation from above" in the Communist world. But this applies as much to Soviet men as it does to Soviet women. No less important, as external observers we must beware of imposing our own values and preferences on Soviet reality. Perhaps the fairest and most telling test of successes and failures would be a gauge of individual fulfillment—how much satisfaction do women achieve in Soviet life, and at what price? But this we are unable to measure and assess.

Index

Index